edited by
Ralph M. Kramer
University of California at Berkeley
Harry Specht
University of California at Berkeley

Third Edition

READINGS IN

COMMUNITY ORGANIZATION PRACTICE

Prentice-Hall, Inc., Engelwood Cliffs, New Jersey 07632

Library of Congress Cataloging in Publication Data
Main entry under title:

READINGS IN COMMUNITY ORGANIZATION PRACTICE.

   Includes bibliographical references.
   1. Community organization—Addresses, essays,
lectures.   2. Community development—Addresses,
essays, lectures.   I. Kramer, Ralph M.
II. Specht, Harry.
HV41.R387   1983.   304′.3   82-10166
ISBN 0-13-755751-5

Editorial production supervision
   and interior design by *Edith Riker*
Cover design by *Ray Lundgren*
Manufacturing buyer *John Hall*

© 1983, 1975, 1969 by Prentice-Hall, Inc., Englewood Cliffs, NJ 07632

All rights reserved. No part of this book
may be reproduced in any form or
by any means without permission in writing
from the publisher.

Printed in the United States of America

10   9   8   7   6   5   4   3   2   1

ISBN 0-13-755751-5

Prentice-Hall International, Inc., *London*
Prentice-Hall of Australia Pty. Limited, *Sydney*
Editora Prentice-Hall do Brasil, Ltda, Rio de Janeiro
Prentice-Hall Canada Inc., *Toronto*
Prentice-Hall of India Private Limited, *New Delhi*
Prentice-Hall of Japan, Inc., *Tokyo*
Prentice-Hall of Southeast Asia Pte. Ltd., *Singapore*
Whitehall Books Limited, *Wellington, New Zealand*

CONTENTS

INTRODUCTION

Give me a lever long enough and a prop strong enough, I can move the world. . . .

Archimedes

The third edition of this book comes forth at a time in which social welfare, social services, and social work are under siege in many countries. The first edition appeared in the 1960s, when community organization practice achieved a prominent and a significant place as a recognized method of social work. The great expansion in interest, scholarship, and jobs in community organization was, of course, a reflection of the general ebullience, expansiveness, and turbulence of that decade. In the second edition, which was published in the 1970s, we noted that there was some degree of disillusionment and disappointment about the uses and the potential of community action. We noted, too, that the profession had become more subdued, and we suggested that there would be in the next decade a demand for a higher degree of technical knowledge in community organization practice.

The 1980s look to be a decade in which many Western democracies will retreat from the commitment to the welfare state made at midcentury. It may be that current trends indicate only that these commitments are being refined or redefined; but there is a high degree of similarity in current policies toward social welfare in such countries as the United States, the United Kingdom, the Federal Republic of Germany, the Netherlands, and Australia, and the similar intent of these policies seems to be to dismantle rather than to reorganize social welfare systems. Thus monetarism in the United Kingdom and the Reagan administration's "slim-line" budgeting policies in Washington, D.C., are based on similar assumptions which can be summarized as follows: Our society has become overregulated by government, which intervenes excessively in the market and in the private lives of individuals. The economic limits of public taxation have been reached; high levels of taxation encourage unrealistically high wages and high levels of public borrowing which fuel inflation, discourage investment, and lower industrial productivity. Following these assumptions, monetarism prescribes that inflation must be "squeezed" out of the economy by cutting public expenditures and taxes and by allowing unemployment to rise and consumer demand to fall. The social and the political assumptions of conservative government can be summarized in the aphorism "That government is best which governs least." The prescriptions that flow from these assumptions add up to *deregulation*. The Reagan administration has abandoned the belief that the federal government bears a primary responsibility for assuring citizens a minimal level of living in respect to the environment, social welfare, and civil rights.

These policies affect most severely the lives of the poorest members of our society. For many these policies will result in a life of grinding poverty instead of mere poverty; for others, such as the working poor, the result will be the loss of hope. Whether monetarism and slim-line budgeting will, in fact, reduce inflation and increase productivity remains to be seen. Experience in the United Kingdom from 1979 to 1982 was not reassuring. In that period unemployment soared. The effects of these policies on productivity and inflation were not encouraging; and programs of income supports and social services were retrenched. Thus the social welfare context of the 1980s is considerably different from those of preceding decades.

The introductory remarks will be presented in five parts. First, we will describe briefly the historical development of community organization practice. In the second section we will outline the present social and organizational context of community organization practice. Third, we will offer a definition of current community organization practice. In the fourth section we will discuss the use of theory in community organization practice. In the last section we will discuss our reasons for selecting the papers included in this volume and provide the reader with an outline of the book.

HISTORICAL DEVELOPMENT OF COMMUNITY ORGANIZATION

The practice of community organization developed from a conglomeration of practical programmatic efforts. Many disparate threads have been woven into this colorful and oddly textured fabric.

Organizing Charities: A New Order in Voluntarism

In the United States the term *community organization* was first used shortly before World War I by sociologists and adult educators. Only since the 1940s has community organization been taught as a professional practice, primarily in schools of social work. Only in 1962 was community organization recognized as a field of specialization for graduate study in social work by the Council of Social Work Education.

In the early part of the twentieth century, private philanthropy bore the major burden for community welfare and the relief of poverty and dependency in the United States. The Charity Organization Society movement, which began in the 1880s, was among the first efforts undertaken to achieve some degree of rational order in the field of social welfare and was the immediate predecessor of efforts at community organization. The economic depression of 1873, the rapid advance of industrialization, increases in immigration, and the movement of rural populations to urban areas were the problems to which these first efforts were addressed. Patterned on the London Society for Organizing Charitable Relief and Repressing Mendicancy, the Charity Organization Society was believed to offer a solution to such alleged evils of benevolent charity as indiscriminate giving, fraud, and duplication. In the spirit of the times, it was expected that the eventual assimilation of the poor would occur through moral uplift and education.

Councils of Social Agencies were first organized in 1908. Continuing in the vein begun by the Charity Organization Society movement, Councils of Social Agencies pressed for efficiency, centralization, and specialization within the voluntary social welfare field and for effective leadership in joint planning and the development of standards for services. These goals still persist in community councils. During World War I, community services designed to meet the problems of servicemen and dislocated families proliferated. In the field of social welfare, "Community War Chests" were developed. These centralized fund-raising agencies were organized to achieve efficiency and the coordinated use of funds. These organizations were the beginnings of what was to become the Community Chests and Councils of Social Agencies movement, the first large-scale attempt at overall community planning and the control of charitable funds.

The settlement houses, a second important social movement of the early part of the century, based many of their programs on social action to promote social legislation. Whereas the Charity Organization movement represented the community's attempt to help individuals adjust to social situations by the use of scientific helping processes, the settlement movement represented the community's desire to change society to meet people's needs. The reformers of the settlements, namely, Jane Addams, Lillian Wald, and Florence Kelly, developed techniques for promoting social legislation and political action to achieve change. Workmen's compensation laws, the White House Conference on Children, child labor laws, the establishment of the Children's Bureau, and some of the social experiments of the New Deal can be attributed in part to the actions and the spirit of the settlement movement.

These early developments in community organization reflected such changes taking place in American society as the growth of giant corporations and the search for techniques to rationalize industrial management. Big givers and businessmen supported the development of more rational controls, budgeting, and the systematic organization of philanthropic enterprise. Voluntary associations supported by individual philanthropists (the "humanitarian industrialists") became the cornerstone of social action. Thus community organization, born as a function rather than a cause, was dedicated to achieving a higher degree of control and order in a field that had grown out of the combined desires of giving charity and creating social change. It was dominated by and applied to philanthropic agencies primarily to enhance their efficiency.[1]

The reform tradition of social work was submerged in the twenties, thirties, and forties by the preeminence accorded to social casework practice, which had become markedly influenced by psychoanalytic concepts. In the 1930s major responsibility for providing income supports for the poor shifted from voluntary agencies to the newly established public welfare bureaucracies and from local to state and federal governments. These shifts resulted in the reorientation of community organization away from concern with programs serving the masses of urban poor and minority groups. Consequently, for the next two decades community organization efforts, along with the efforts of private philanthropy, were focused on community problems left to voluntary action, those concerned with counseling and guidance, health, recreation and group services, and adult education. The composition and the structure of community organization agencies reflected these concerns by drawing their leadership from local elites, philanthropists, and professionals in voluntary social agencies.

Process versus Program: Social Movements versus Professionalism

In the early part of this century there were several large-scale attempts to organize masses of citizens for community improvement and social change. In 1917 the short-lived Cincinnati Social Unit Project, a relatively unknown ancestor of the War on Poverty, demonstrated that residents of neighborhoods could be organized to plan and operate their own social service programs and serve as a political force for change.[2]

The Chicago Area Project, begun in 1934 by the State of Illinois, was an innovative program aimed at helping residents of slum areas to organize in order to prevent juvenile delinquency.[3] The American labor movement provided a rich source of practical organizing experience throughout the 1920s and 1930s. Because the labor movement, like the civil rights movement of the 1960s, was concerned primarily with solving the practical problems of building strength as a movement, its intellectual leadership did not develop a theoretical literature.[4]

The organization of the Back of the Yards movement in Chicago by Saul Alinsky in the early 1940s, which is reported in his book *Reveille for Radicals*,[5] was another landmark in community organization practice. Alinsky's ideas about the development of conflict-oriented "People's Organizations" did not achieve popular recognition for twenty-five years. The ideology of social class conflict on which Alinsky's community organization efforts were based was not popular at the time as a result of social upheavals caused by World War II.

The war gave impetus to the largest attempts at community organization to that date. Through the United States Office of Civilian Defense, established in 1941, thousands of community councils, block committees, and neighborhood associations were organized to support the war effort.

The spirit of cooperation created by total mobilization and the submergence of intergroup conflict provided a great thrust to planning, technical assistance, and administrative organization in community work. These methods were adopted in mobilizing community resources to achieve common goals related to the war effort. Citizen participation and interagency coordination were stressed. But with the end of the war, the incentives for collaboration diminished. This experience left little residue in most communities.

Before the war the Lane Report to the National Conference of Social

Work (1939) identified community organization as a method of social work practice. According to this report, community organization is concerned with

> (a) the discovery and definition of needs; (b) the elimination and prevention of social needs and disabilities, so far as possible; and (c) the articulation of resources and needs, and the constant readjustment of resources in order to better meet changing needs.[6]

The resources/needs conception of the Lane report has remained a central feature of community organization practice to date. The report placed major emphasis on social welfare programs and agencies rather than on the community as the major instrument to deal with need. Finally, the report conceived of community organization as both a field *and* a process or method. The field was considered highly restrictive in conception in that the major instruments of community action were perceived to be social welfare agencies with the council of social agencies as the central organizing system.

Both Pray[7] and Newstetter,[8] in 1948, defined community organization as a social work *process* primarily concerned with problems of relationships and not with societal change because the latter appeared to be too broad an objective with which to deal. The central objective of community organization practice in their view was to facilitate the *process* of social adjustment; it was not concerned with achieving any particular product or form of adjustment. Community organizers were warned to "guard themselves against . . . insidious temptation to choose for the community a plan which the organizer . . . carries through."[9] Research, planning, administration, and interpretation were not considered community organization when dissociated from the process of helping to build interrelationships.

The issues dealt with in these formulations continue to concern practitioners today. Several of the readings deal with the varied roles of the community organizer: the "enabler," the "expert," the "manipulator," and the "technician." They describe how such roles are utilized within a framework of professional values. The knowledge and the skill required for these different roles were described by Murray Ross.[10] Writing in 1955, Ross made extensive use of social science materials. He defined community organization as a process in which planning is used as a *tool* to achieve cooperative and collaborative attitudes and practices in work with community groups. Because it was based on an assessment of the elements of both task and process goals, Ross's definition of community organization was not restricted to the welfare field.

Social Revolution

The civil rights movement of the late 1950s and early 1960s, along with major federal programs in housing and urban renewal, and the War on Poverty, resulted in a dramatic broadening of community organizations practice.[11] In that period many people concerned with community welfare came to the view that the programs of the New Deal had failed to cope effectively with the social problems of poverty, dependency, ghettoes, racism, and unemployment. Evidence began to mount that redevelopment and urban renewal programs, which began in the late forties, had produced the same kinds of social problems as those produced by the institutionalized systems of welfare, education, and corrections, which had created almost as many problems as they had been designed to solve.

New means were sought for enlisting the support of the community in carrying out change. The 1954 amendments to the *Housing Act of 1949*, for example, required citizen participation in the preparation of "workable programs." At the time, this innovation appeared to planners to be a major stumbling block to the attainment of their objectives. Until then city planning had been concerned primarily with short-run locational decisions regarding land use and industrial interests and with the long-range formulation of a comprehensive master plan. Efforts to eliminate slums and urban blight centered interest on traffic patterns, zoning, and the design of the city as an economic enterprise. Frequently plans for redevelopment and urban renewal were made without sufficient consideration of the social consequences of planning and of planning as a social process. Human relations personnel—intergroup relations workers, social workers, psychologists—were frequently brought in to deal with the "social components" of planning as an ineffective afterthought.

Even worse, human relations personnel were often brought in to planning to find ways to sell the program to the opposition. Thus the "social" goals of planning were frequently dictated by economic and political interests, and the function of the social planner was perceived to be that of making goals more palatable to an increasingly resistant community. As a result, civil rights groups, neighborhood associations, and many politically liberal and radical organizations believed increasingly that community organization and social planning were essentially "establishment-oriented" practices with interests opposed to those who bore the hardships of the relocation process.

Several new models of community organization emerged in those years including the comprehensive planning models encouraged and supported by the President's Committee on Juvenile Delinquency, the "gray areas" project of the Ford Foundation, the Community Action Programs of the Office of Economic Opportunity, and grass roots and self-help programs. In many of these newer attempts at community organization, city planners, community organizers, and the personnel of social welfare agencies were brought together to undertake joint planning. Increased attention was given to the importance of developing and supporting the participation of citizens, especially the poor, in planning. Title II of the *Demonstration Cities and Metropolitan Redevelopment Act of 1966*, which established the Model Cities Program, extended some of the newer ideas about citizen participation in planning and the coordination of services to model neighborhoods and entire metropolitan areas.

Community work, neighborhood work, the organization of tenants, and block organization in low-income areas developed at an exceedingly rapid pace in the late sixties and early seventies. Frequently these kinds of groups and organizations were fostered and aided both with funds and with technical expertise by national policies and programs described in the preceding paragraphs. Single organizations and coalitions of organizations realized some successes in changing and redirecting the services and programs of established agencies and institutions. By the 1980s the fervor and the enthusiasm of these movements were considerably diminished. However, scholarly and professional debate about the meaning, utility, and methods used in locality-based organizing continues.

Citizen Participation and Institutional Reorganization

CITIZEN PARTICIPATION: The concentration on community action and citizen participation at a time when government and nation were growing ever larger and more complex is somewhat paradoxical. It is explained in part by the growth of awareness in the 1960s of the linkage between social class and ethnic characteristics and in part by the traditional community organization concern with creating a better match between social problems and social needs. These linkages constituted the essential ideology of the civil rights movement of that time. However, the emphasis of the movement was put on race and ethnicity rather than on social class. In response to the civil rights movement (which had become a congeries of movements in the seventies), government, foundations, voluntary organizations, and a variety of professional associations invested resources in "grass roots" organizing, including efforts to organize neighborhoods, tenements, welfare clients, social services consumers, the "unaffiliated," and a variety of other populations.[12]

Citizen participation developed considerably between 1964 and 1980, and in part it developed in ways that were not entirely anticipated. In the late 1960s and the early 1970s there was a shift in the focus of attention in programs of community organization and social planning. The Community Action Programs of the War on Poverty had put major emphasis on participation as a value. The policy of "maximum feasible participation" in the *Economic Opportunity Act of 1964* gave impetus to grass roots organizing efforts. The legislation supported this impetus because it provided that Community Action Programs could be constituted by a variety of public or private groups. The 1966 legislation establishing the Model Cities Program called for a rapprochement between the grass roots and established political leadership by requiring that the local governing body of the city or county be the vehicle for implementation. Although the Model Cities Program had been conceived in the spirit of the Community Action Programs, a different legislative intent was imputed in the years during which the Model Cities Program was in operation. In 1970 the Department of Housing and Urban Development introduced programs known as Planned Variations and Annual Arrangements, the net effect of which was to shift major authority and resources for planning to the chief executives of the cities and away from neighborhoods and organizations of residents. As the precursor of federal revenue sharing and block grants, the Model Cities Program was the first attempt at dispersing power from the federal to the local level and concentrating power at the local level.[13]

The emphasis on self-help and citizen participation in the decades of the sixties and the seventies was fed by several streams of thought. Organization theory and theories of community power influenced community organization practice significantly. As a result of the work of Floyd Hunter and other researchers, it was recognized that power in community life is not as simple as classical democratic theory suggested; Hunter described community power as a force manipulated by an identifiable elite.[14] Other research indicates that community power is sometimes pluralist, frequently informal, often hidden and disguised, and otherwise difficult to identify. It varies from situation to situation, depending on leadership, the degree of consensus, the extent of organization, the mechanisms of government, and the kinds of problems dealt with.[15]

The recognition of racial and social class differences as a reality of American life was made inescapable by the civil rights movement and other movements for change that followed it. Conceptions of power and social change formulated by Hunter and others led community organizers to reconsider the heavy reliance in community organization practice on educational and collaborative methods. Social conflict came to be perceived as an important tool in urban community organizing. The style and tactics of Saul Alinsky, anathema to social welfare for over twenty years, were discovered by civil rights organizers, war on poverty workers, and others in community work. These techniques were found to be useful in engaging the interests and the energies of masses of alienated and unorganized ghetto dwellers and other low-income people.[16]

Community development practiced in underdeveloped countries and rural areas of the United States provided another source of wisdom because it gives primary emphasis to citizen participation. After World War II, a vast number of community-based efforts were undertaken in the newly developing countries, many of which had been under colonial rule, to overcome apathy and improve living conditions through self-help. In the United States community development practice draws heavily on the methods developed in adult education programs, reflecting in part their origins in university extension programs. This form of practice is utilized in urban areas to develop community solidarity and build mechanisms to encourage citizen self-help.[17]

In recent years these different varieties of self-help have achieved a great degree of authenticity through the development of "new careers" programs. Whether referred to as programs for "subprofessionals," "indigenous workers," or "new careerists," the basic idea is that the acquisition of credentials through formal educational institutions is not the only means by which workers can achieve professional competence as providers of human services. Job experience and life experience (especially experience in coping with problems that are the concern of social change programs designed to eliminate poverty and racism) are recognized by many as significant bases from which to develop practice knowledge and skill.[18]

Both Saul Alinsky and the community development professionals operate primarily on the basis of principles and value considerations which they induce from practice. In addition, Alinsky provides clear operational instructions. In both cases theory is neither explicit nor at high levels of generalization. Alinsky's mode of practice is based on a kind of Utopian-humanistic ideology that says something like this: "All groups are moved by self-interest, the poor and nonpoor alike; as soon as the poor understand this, they'll be able to get power and control their destiny." An equally doctrinaire view of community development relies more heavily on educational techniques and is supported by a neopopulist view of democracy that can be paraphrased as follows: "Most people are good and will cooperate to help change society; if that goodness can be released, the community will be able to deal with its problems." However, adequate empirical evidence for the effectiveness of either approach to organizing and planning is lacking. Systematic evaluation of these practice principles is still required.

There are many issues and problems associated with the various programmatic forms of citizen participation. This subject will be discussed in Chapter 2 of this book. Among the many questions that are salient to this subject are the following: *Who* should participate? *How* should participants be selected? What *authority* should participants have? What kinds of *compensation* should they receive? What should be the *objectives* of citizen participation?

INSTITUTIONAL REORGANIZATION. Along with citizen participation, the federal government's interest in community action in recent years has been related to the less popular and dramatic concerns about coordination and the integration of social services. This concern is intimately tied to changes that have taken place in the relationships between the federal and the state governments over the last fifty years. In the United States, state governments have primary responsibility and authority for the delivery of social services. However, since the 1930s the federal government has had a prominent role in financing social services and until recently played a large role in program planning and in the development of the social services.

For most of this century until the 1960s, it appeared that the states would not survive as significant, viable units of government. In 1933 Luther Gulick, an eminent scholar on government, wrote as follows on the decline of state government:

> Is the state the appropriate instrumentality for the discharge of . . . [important] functions? The answer is not a matter of conjecture or delicate appraisal. It is a matter of brutal record. The American state is finished. I do not predict that the states will go, but affirm that they have gone.[19]

The Great Depression found the states unprepared to deal with the enormous economic and social problems left in its wake. The states, primarily rurally oriented, did not have the financial, the administrative, and the policymaking powers required to deal with the effects of the depression, which fell most heavily on urban areas. The centralization of power in the federal government that occurred under Roosevelt's New Deal program was a significant change in American politics. The balance of governmental power shifted from the state capitals to Washington, D.C. As Leuchtenberg observed,

> The White House, not the State House, became the focus of all government— the fountainhead of ideas, the initiator of action, the representative of the national interest.[20]

The trend toward centralization in American government was strengthened during World War II as increased authority for policymaking and decision making was vested in Washington, D.C. for the mobilization of resources to prosecute the war. Following World War II, state and local services, especially in the areas of health and education, were at an extremely low ebb. Many services had been curtailed during the war, and improvements in government and facilities had been all but suspended. Personnel losses associated with the war effort were severe.

The system of categorical grants to state governments was the primary means developed by the federal government to use its resources to exercise initiative in public policy and program development at the local level. With federal planning and financing and state administration, many program services developed as intergovernmental ventures. Examples are the *Housing Act of 1949* and the *Elementary and Secondary Education Act of 1965.*

Leach cites the growth of the categorical grant system as one of the major factors associated with the emergence of the states as significant instruments for dealing with the needs of American communities in the latter part of the century.[21] The federal resources offered through these programs were major incentives to the states to undertake new service programs directly and through their local instrumentalities. In addition, the federal government had frequently demonstrated by the 1960s the limits of its own effectiveness in promoting and developing policy for locally delivered services.

These are some of the factors that have brought about what Daniel Elazar refers to as a quiet revolution in state government. Elazar says that these developments "transformed state government . . . to a solid instrument for meeting needs of American society today." According to him, the states are viable units of government. Since World War II and especially since Vietnam they have "been carrying the brunt of domestic governmental processes in the United States."[22]

Generally speaking, the basic thrust leading to the reorganization of the human services in the states has been in the direction of achieving higher degrees of integration, coordination, and comprehensiveness. Among human services agencies, the term *services integration* is used to refer to a variety of objectives, ranging from macrolevel concerns with integrated and comprehensive planning among several levels and agencies of government to microlevel concerns with case management and the collocation of services. Services integration includes such specific objectives as coordinating systems for budgeting and allocating resources; consolidation of administration, purchasing, information, and record keeping systems; and grants management.[23]

The need for reorganization in the human services systems of the states had been evident in the social services since the end of the 19th century. However, the role of the states in service provision was preempted by the federal government from the depression years through the post-World War II period. Awareness of the need for state reorganization began to grow in the 1950s and 1960s with the ever-more voluminous number of federal-state categorical programs addressed to social problems, which resulted in the development of hundreds of categorical grant programs utilizing different sets of procedures for application, funding, budgeting, reporting, and auditing.

A number of integrative efforts were made by the federal government in the 1960s to foster higher degrees of integration of human services. The *Economic Opportunities Act,* the *Model Cities Program,* and the *Neighborhood Service Programs (1966)* are examples of such efforts. In 1970 the work of the DHEW task force on services integration resulted in the creation of an interagency services demonstration program, referred to as SITO (Services Integration Targets of Opportunity), to develop models for integrating different levels of government. The DHEW-supported *Allied Services Act of 1970* (which was not passed by Congress) was another such effort.

General revenue sharing and the specialized revenue-sharing programs of the federal departments (for example, the *Housing and Community Development Act of 1974* and *Title XX, 1974*) were, in large part, responses to the lack of success of federal initiatives in generating program integration and planning efforts at the state and local levels.

Complementary to these federal efforts at decentralization, the states were undertaking the reorganization of their systems for the provision of human services on a grand scale. The need for integrative mechanisms was especially sharp at the state and local levels of government because state-administered structures were frequently unable to manage, much less plan for, hundreds of federal categorical programs initiated in the 1950s and 1960s. In many states these programs were administered by scores of state and local agencies, boards, and commissions. Concern about the escalating costs of human services and fragmentation, duplication, and lack of accountability in their administration resulted in a variety of efforts to reorganize state human services programs.

Since 1965 over half the states have reorganized human services programs.[24] Generally human services refers to the following eight areas of service (1) public assistance/social services; (2) health; (3) mental health; (4) mental retardation; (5) corrections; (6) youth services; (7) vocational rehabilitation; (8) employment services. The objective of reorganization efforts is to bring about changes in administrative relationships between two or more of these eight functional service areas and to group them into an "umbrella" agency. There is, of course, no high degree of consensus about the best mix of functions to place in one agency. By 1980 only two states (Arizona and California) had brought all eight together into one "superagency." At the moment administrative parlance suggests that a "comprehensive human resources agency" (CHRA) is one in which four or more of these functions are lodged in one administrative unit.[25] However, this figure seems arbitrary in light of the current dearth of operational experience with and knowledge about the many different combinations that are possible. As the authors of the most systematic study of CHRAs carried out to date have commented, "No state can be said to have an integrated system (of human services) in operation."[26]

THE CONTEXT OF PRACTICE IN THE 1980s

By the middle of the 1970s there was a noticeable diminution in the amount of public and professional attention devoted to social action and community organization at the grass roots. Certainly, with the end of the Vietnam War and the abatement of student protest, populist activism diminished considerably. But a good part of grass roots participation did not disappear; it only moved to another arena—from the fringes of social institutions into the center of things. Put briefly, between the early 1960s movement for civil rights and the revenue-sharing programs of the 1970s, agencies of government became the major sponsors and supporters of grass roots and consumer participation in community planning and in agency decision making for programs. This development was manifest in various pieces of social legislation that set legal requirements for citizen participation in the planning and the implementation of *the Title XX amendments to the Social Security Act, 1975, the Comprehensive Employment and Training Act of 1973*, and *the amendments to the Older Americans Act, 1973*.

This does not necessarily mean that government did the job well or that what was done by government was for the greatest good. That remains to be seen. Reservations about these developments are merited on the basis of experience, which instructs us that the institutionalization of social reform movements leads inexorably to their bureaucratization and stultification.[27] If government had deliberately planned a means by which to take spontaneity and vigor out of the grass roots movements of the 1960s, none better than the system which seemingly evolved by itself over those years, with the urging and the support of many grass roots organizations, could have been devised.

The statutory programs of the 1970s were created in an institutional context that gave primacy to the values of citizen participation and program coordination in such areas as services for the aged, community mental health, education, housing, and medical care. In this institutional context three characteristics of community organization practice became important (1) a functional area focus (for example, aging); (2) concern with relationships among units of government; (3) emphasis on the technical aspects of practice. The functional area focus became important because legislation—particularly special revenue-sharing programs—focused on certain population groups. Concern with relationships among units of government increased in that context because of the legal and the political complexities of interactions among the many governmental and voluntary agencies involved in program planning and implementation. The technical aspects of practice became prominent because the social services programs created were quite large from the point of view of the amounts of money, the size of the organizations, and the numbers of personnel and clients involved.[28]

The future of social planning and community organization from the perspective of the 1980s is unclear. Generally, the Reagan administration abandoned interest in giving direction to the states in the planning and the development of social services programs. Many programs were combined into block grants to the states. Alone with these block grants was a large cutback in federal financial support for social services. Federal legislation for these grants explicitly eschewed state-federal sharing of costs, discussion of program content, and concern with standards of practice. In truth, the Reagan administration is the embodiment of the conservative belief in "governing least."

THE NEED TO COUNTERBALANCE THE TECHNOCRATIC IMPULSE.[29] There is much to commend the increased demand for technical expertise in practice that has developed in recent decades. The profession's emerging response to this demand is evident. Recent texts on community organization and social planning feature instruction on a variety of analytic techniques, including the use of input-output analysis, PERT, the use of Delphi technique, the development of social indicators, the preparation of financial statements, and needs-assessment procedures.[30] Graduate programs in social work are placing increased emphasis on the uses of computer technology in research.

We believe that the expansion of the components of technical knowledge in training for organizing and planning is a positive and a welcome development—a development that will result in arming professionals with useful tools to aid in rational planning and decision making. However, it is also a seductive development that merits careful attention. Most of the well-established professions (for example, medicine, engineering, architecture) have had long standing romances with esoteric technology. In the practice of community organization, this involvement with technology is just beginning to find expression in professional training curricula. However, it is important that the technocratic impulse in these curricula not be allowed to obscure the sociopolitical components of professional training that deal with the management of social relations, negotiations, and coordination with people, groups, and organizations. The traditional emphasis on sociopolitical skills has served as a major distinction between social work planners and planners in other fields.[31]

The continued significance of the sociopolitical components of professional education is underlined by the findings of recent studies of social planning. In their analysis of the Title XX program, for example, Gilbert and Specht studied the relationship between the planning strategies of the Area Agencies on Aging (AAA) and the extent to which they received Title XX resource allocations. Of various planning strategies they found that the AAA mobilization of strong political support showed the highest correlation with positive outcomes of Title XX resource allocations for the aged.[32]

Further evidence of the importance of sociopolitical skills is revealed in an in-depth study by Hemmens, Bergman, and Moroney of fifty-two social policy planners who were graduates of schools of public policy and city planning. The findings are informative because education for social planning in schools of public policy and city planning has traditionally placed greater emphasis on the technical knowledge component of planning than has education for social work. In this study it was found that in general the practitioners interviewed "do not use high-level analytic skills on the job. Mathematical skills used are limited primarily to arithmetic and percentage calculations; reasoning skills to common sense."[33] The study reports that when practitioners were asked for suggestions on changes in professional education,

> The greatest felt need is for communication skills. . . . Process skills were the second most common felt need among practitioners. It was apparent in all the sessions that what was meant by process skills are the tasks of agency operations. Specifically, the participants are concerned with organizing and running technical meetings, with setting agendas, and getting groups to follow them, and with management of daily work to meet organization schedules . . . . Comparatively few participants saw the need for additional training in analytic techniques.[34]

Because education for community organization practice continues to embrace an increasing amount of technical knowledge, the findings noted in the studies are worth pondering.

COMMUNITY ORGANIZATION PRACTICE:
A DEFINITION

An exhaustive definition of community organization practice will not be attempted here. Several recent publications provide detailed descriptions of the various strands and threads in this effort, as well as the difficulties of producing a satisfactory definition. For the purposes of discussion and to introduce the sections of the reader, however, we shall define community organization practice as follows:

> Community organization refers to various methods of intervention whereby a professional change agent helps a community action system composed of individuals, groups, or organizations engage in planned collective action in order to deal with social problems within a democratic system of values. It is concerned with programs aimed at social change with primary reference to environmental conditions and social institutions. It involves two major interrelated concerns (a) the *interactional processes* of working with an action system, which include identifying, recruiting, and working with the members, and developing organizational and interpersonal relationships among them which facilitate their efforts; (b) the *technical tasks* involved in identifying problem areas, analyzing causes, formulating plans, developing strategies, mobilizing the resources necessary to effect action, and assessing the outcomes of programs.

The phrase *methods of intervention* connotes conscious behavior on the part of a "professional" change agent who uses the processes of organizing and planning. By "professional" we mean someone who is able to utilize and evaluate a body of knowledge, principles, and values in his or her work. "Community" refers to a wide range of collectivities—neighborhoods, population subgroups (ethnic, racial, social, political), cities, regions, or the nation as a whole.

Essentially then we are discussing the methods by which a professional person deliberately intervenes in the process of change and attempts to help organize the efforts of action systems to influence some community condition or policy. The process of change goes on continuously in communities; our interest, however, is focused on the practice of *purposive* change directed by a *professional* person.

Goals: Process versus Task

The knowledge requirements of practice are functions of both the goals and the values of a profession. The identification of goals is itself one of the important tasks of the practitioner. One set of goals in community organization practice grows out of the practitioner's activities in identifying the specific and tangible outcomes sought by action systems and helping to actualize these goals. These might be called "task," "analytic," or "programmatic" goals. They involve the identification of specific objectives and the development of means and resources to implement them. A second set of goals relates to the worker's perceptions of, hopes for, and relationships with the people who constitute the action system. These are called "process," "interactional," or "relationship" goals; they refer to the enhancement and the strengthening of the civic, social, and political competence of participants. The selection of goals usually involves an attempt to strike a balance between task and process.

Goals for action on social problems frequently compete with and contradict one another. An example is the contradiction between working to achieve the integration of schools (and thereby enable residents to move beyond ghetto walls) versus working to build strength and solidarity in ghetto institutions and among residents of the ghetto. In addition, other goals of the profession and of organizations, some manifest and some latent, intrude upon practice. Because community resources are finite and because the goals of social action often impinge on one another, goals must be ordered by the worker to give some direction to these efforts.

Goals for community action are usually determined in interactions among the sponsor, the action system, and the practitioner. Our purpose here is not to identify the goals and the values of community organization but rather to urge the reader to take note of the different ways in which the authors included in this volume deal with these kinds of questions.

Types of Community Organization

It will become apparent that the readings apply to many different kinds of community action, ranging from neighborhood organizations to national social planning, and that different techniques, styles, and methods of organizing are used. In this discussion we use the term *community organization* to encompass this wide range of efforts.

The question of whether there are several methods or one underlying method that uses different models for action is discussed by some of the authors in this volume. Various typologies of community organization have been based on the following combinations of elements: (1) the *character of the action system* (for example, grass roots organizations, "elitist" planning councils); (2) the *locality* (for example, neighborhood, region); (3) the *substantive nature of problems dealt with* (for example, housing, education); (4) the *character of the issues* (for example, conflict-generating issues, consensus-producing issues); (5) the *character of the "target" system* (that is, the system to be changed, for example, public assistance agency, board of education); (6) the *organizational structures developed* (for example, mass movements, planning committees of professionals representing agencies); (7) the *role of the professional worker* (for example, activist, enabler); (8) the *sponsor of the project* (for example, voluntary association, public agency).

In some models of community organization there is a clustering of goals, activities, and techniques that characterizes specific types.[35] For example, models describing work with low-income, disadvantaged groups are frequently associated with activist workers who build grass roots organizations in local communities and attempt to generate conflict to encourage and enlarge the participation of residents in dealing with welfare bureaucracies and other governmental agencies.

To illustrate the range of social collectivities among which community organizers practice, we will describe two hypothetical models of community organizing based on the character of the action system. We present these models in a somewhat oversimplified form. The two models are (a) community development and (b) social planning. The action system in community development is composed of individuals who are directly affected by the problem of concern; in social planning it is composed mainly of representatives of organizations.

COMMUNITY DEVELOPMENT refers to efforts to mobilize the people who are directly affected by a community condition (that is, the "victims," the unaffiliated, the unorganized, and the nonparticipating) into groups and organizations to enable them to take action on the social problems and issues that concern them. A typical feature of these efforts is the concern with building new organizations among people who have not been previously organized to take social action on a problem.

SOCIAL PLANNING refers to efforts to integrate and coordinate the work of agencies and organizations of the community as well as extracommunity action systems; it also involves efforts aimed at bringing about changes in the attitudes, structures, functions, resources, decision-making patterns, policies, and practices of voluntary and public agencies. Although the task undertaken may have reference to a local community (for example, implementing a plan for housing development) or to extracommunity systems (for example, lobbying for a national program in Washington, D.C.), a major feature of this model is that the action system is composed of people who are legally and structurally tied to community agencies and organizations, and their behavior in the action system is regulated and guided by these commitments.

The differences in the knowledge and the skill requirements of these two models of practice are more of degree and priority than of kind. For example, the process goals for each model of community organization are similar.

Process Goals

COMMUNITY DEVELOPMENT	*SOCIAL PLANNING*
1. strengthen social bonds among residents;	1. develop intraorganizational and interorganizational communication and planning systems;
2. enable individuals to assume leadership roles;	2. encourage the utilization of administrative and political leadership;
3. increase communication with other systems.	3. develop mechanisms for citizen participation and the interagency coordination of effort.

Although there are stylistic differences that may be related to the social class, ethnic, and organizational capabilities of the actors involved, the tasks that flow from these goals are similar. The knowledge that the two workers will utilize (for example, organizational structures, small groups, and group dynamics) comes from the same sources. For example, with regard to the second of each of these sets of goals, the community organizer wants to help and encourage people to gain competence in participating in the planning of change. In community development this might mean teaching the leaders of a newly formed neighborhood organization how to use Robert's *Rules of Order*, and in social planning it might involve helping the executive of a large organization design a planning structure to support efforts for organizational change.

There are several reasons to support the view that the knowledge requirements for community organization of all types are similar. First, action systems may change continually; if not in their manifest structure, then in their goals or in their interactions with other systems. The local grass roots organization may merge or work with other grass roots organizations, promoting the ascendancy of integrative rather than community-building goals; or a social planning action system may utilize or work with community development types of systems. Conceivably, a goal assigned to one model may be adopted by another. For example, a social planner dealing with a large agency may have the goal of "increasing utilization and demands for service"; a similar goal could be adopted by a grass roots organization. *All practitioners, regardless of the particular model of practice they use, help people identify problems, develop organizations, plan and carry out programs, and assess their efforts.*

Second, different models of practice sometimes refer to action systems at different stages of development. It might seem *prima facie* that each model requires a different kind of practitioner. It might appear that a community developer helping tenants organize to protest unfair practices and punitive measures of a housing authority behaves in ways different from a social planner helping the Department of Housing and Urban Development (HUD) develop a five-year program plan. A community developer requires a style of personal behavior that gives him or her access to organizations of the poor, the capacity to work many hours and long nights, the ability to devise quick tactical maneuvers, and the talent to participate in carrying out confrontational or dramatic events in public. A planner, on the other hand, must be able to speak authoritatively with elected and appointed officials and handle figures and budgets easily. In addition, she or he must have a knowledge of the laws, regulations, and administrative organization of HUD. A planner must present himself or herself as a "solid citizen." Notwithstanding these differences each practitioner requires the same kinds of knowledge to carry out the tasks involved in his or her work.

Nevertheless, each faces distinctive dilemmas. Practitioners who are primarily concerned with the community-building aspects of the work are faced with dilemmas involving the limitations of local action, the insufficiency of power to affect vertical decision making, and the tendency to retreat to the rhetoric of sociotherapy or disruptive strategies. Those concerned with social planning confront the fragmentation of power and the lack of moral commitment to structural change. Both are confronted with the loss of confidence in gradualism, the exceedingly great powers of government and bureaucracies, and the limited knowledge base and technology of the human service professions.

THE USES OF THEORY

The selections in this volume are from both social scientists and community organization practitioners. It will be evident that there are some wide gaps in the theory used by community organizers and social planners. One of our objectives, which will be accomplished in the introductory commentary for each set of readings, is to identify these gaps in the hope that students and colleagues will be encouraged to fill them in.

The response of some practitioners to the theoretical selections may be, "but it's so much more complicated in real life than they say," or "they don't tell you what to do." Believing that the point of theory is not just to understand the world, but to change it, these practitioners may demand more from theory than it can provide.

Ideologically oriented writers may evoke a more enthusiastic response from practitioners because these writers describe their own successful experiences. These experiences are frequently dramatic and moving, and practitioners can recognize some of their own problems in them. Although the identification of the pace and the complexity of community organization work is important in the development of practice theory, most case histories describe only the writers' personal styles of working, and working style is often the unique product of an individual's artistic capacity to integrate his or her personal sensibilities in a given set of sociopolitical circumstances, an important aspect of community work but not a substitute for knowledge. The personal style that a professional uses in practice is something that is developed on an individual basis over several years. We caution aspiring professionals to avoid taking on someone else's way of behaving and to take the time needed to develop their own styles. *Ex post facto* accounts of personal experiences can be described with confidence and given meaning. However, these accounts cannot be verified or replicated. That is, in theoretical terms, anecdotal accounts of practice do not provide systematically tested generalizations and propositions about the factors involved in practice which enable others to anticipate the consequences of intervention. Morris Raphael Cohen, the eminent American philosopher, once described this strain between the concrete and the abstract as

> . . . efforts of the human intellect [which] may be viewed as a tension between two poles, one to do justice to the fullness of the concrete case before us, the other to grasp an underlying abstract universal principle that controls more than the one case before us.

Theories are generalizations. For that reason practice theory may only illuminate *choices:* It rarely provides specific instructions. Take, for example, the following proposition from Charles Levine's paper, "Organizational Decline and Cutback Management."

> To maintain order and capacity when undergoing decline, organizations need mechanisms like long-term contracts with clauses that make pensions non-portable if broken at the employee's discretion.

This proposition indicates to practitioners that there are particular features of an organization to which they ought to attend under certain circumstances. Levine defines such terms as *decline, order,* and *capacity*. He also describes some of the other variables that will bear on the kinds of choices that are made. But the article does not tell a practitioner what to do. We believe that knowledge that increases the range of choice enhances a practitioner's ability to practice. However, the elucidation of choices increases complexity.

Simple and clear instructions for practitioners are available, although they may not be very helpful. Consider the following assertion.

> The potential power of a poor people's organization is measured in numbers; it is broadly based rather than concentrated, decentralized rather than centralized.[36]

There are no complexities or qualifications to deal with here. A practitioner need not be bothered with choices regarding types of poor people, types of organizations, or the conditions under which concentration or decentralization might be most useful.

Theory, then, provides practitioners with a coherent way to organize the variables that have a bearing on their work. As Kurt Lewin noted several decades ago, there is nothing so practical as a good theory.

At this time, however, theory for practice is still in a fairly primitive stage of development. Theoreticians are only beginning to define and test basic concepts such as organization, power, and "participation." There are few, if any, social science theories about community work in the sense of logically, interrelated propositions that enable prediction. There are mainly a host of discrete findings, often superficial and contradictory. Relatively few of them pertain to the nature of planned change. There are numerous typologies, taxonomies, hypotheses, metaphors, conceptual frameworks, and other substitutes for theory. As practitioners read different accounts of studies of organizational change and community power structures, they often confront different hypotheses, tested with different research methods, based on different modes of organizational and community change, making it difficult to compare experiences and measure them against a common standard that would permit them to make predictions in their work.

On the other hand, as practitioners and researchers struggle to codify practice wisdom, an applied social science will develop that will be useful for practice. Gradually the salient variables of practice are being defined and tested, and systematic principles are being derived about their relationships to one another, enabling practitioners to draw hypotheses to test in practice. Specious relationships are eliminated because this kind of self-correcting system helps practitioners to validate the outcomes of practice. Theory built on factual investigation is simply a means of codifying, testing, and evaluating what we know so that it can be communicated and built upon. As Hans Zetterberg has noted, "The defining characteristic of a scientifically competent practitioner is . . . his use of scientific knowledge in solving problems repeatedly encountered in his occupation."[37] In selecting papers for this book we have favored work that moves in the direction of developing theory.

Theory is developed in two analytically distinct ways: *inductively,* as a process whereby principles are derived from the real world of practice and action, that is, as an abstraction of experiences that can be applied to a large number of similar cases. *Deductively* theory is developed by testing propositions derived from social science. Both inductive and deductive theorizing make systematic use of scientific methods; under such conditions they frequently find mutual interests in applied research. The tension between the two frequently occurs because of the differing goals of practitioners and theoreticians; practitioners tend to be concerned with finding answers and solutions to the immediate and real problems they encounter, whereas theoreticians tend to be committed to enlarging their field of knowledge.

Sabatier and Mazmanian's paper, "The Conditions of Effective Implementation: A Guide to Accomplishing Policy Objectives," is an example of inductive theorizing. Moving from a review of empirical studies of actual programs, they develop some propositions about practice for implementing programs in general.

Examples of deductive theorizing are provided by Roland Warren's paper, "A Community Model" and Litwak and others' "Community Participation in Bureaucratic Organizations: Principles and Strategies." Warren *starts* with a theoretical framework drawn from social systems theory which utilizes such concepts as socialization and social control. From this framework he deduces specific propositions about community analysis. Litwak and others utilize several sociological theories about communities and organizations to derive principles of practice with community groups.

Readers will note that most of the papers included in this volume are closer to the inductive type of theorizing, which is, of course, indicative of the fact that theory for community organization practice is still in an early stage of development.

The difficulty with much inductive work is that propositions are not formulated to provide sufficient generalizability and clarity that would be useful to practitioners who work under a variety of conditions; frequently this kind of work does not contribute to the building of knowledge in a consistent and rigorous fashion. This kind of work often consists of a series of anecdotes and intuitions that sometimes work because they contain some wisdom but just as often fail because of a lack of wisdom or because the knowledge has not been identified. Deductive work, on the other hand, is frequently too abstract and not sufficiently related to the problems and issues that practitioners encounter in their day-to-day work.

Although practice theory of either a deductive or an inductive variety is developed through the same methods and procedures as any other theory, it involves two sets of purposes: One set of purposes is represented by what might be called "know-why" propositions. These propositions constitute foundation knowledge about the structure and the function of social systems and processes. They include descriptions, explanations, and predictions about how social systems operate under various conditions. These propositions pertain to such ideas as the properties, the etiology, the behavior, and the life cycle of social phenomena and can help in analyzing a problematic state of affairs. The papers in Part I, "Context," are examples of this kind of work. The second set of purposes of practice theory is represented by what can be called "know-how" propositions, which are prescriptions about how to *change* systems and conditions. This kind of knowledge should include methodological principles that specify goals, incorporate values, and give directions for action in an "if you do x, then y will be the result" form, telling the practitioner what type of intervention is the most effective under specific conditions. The papers in Chapter 3, "Professional Change Agents and Their Strategies," contain such propositions.

SELECTED READINGS

Our selection of readings on the practice of community organization was guided by our experiences in selecting materials for students in a school of social welfare as well as by the many practitioners that we have met in the broad array of programs and services that use community organization methods.

In this third edition of the reader we have modified our criteria of selection to some extent. In the first edition we selected journal articles, unpublished fugitive pieces, and original papers that introduced students to the varieties of community organization practice. In compiling the second edition we emphasized selections from several significant textbooks on community organization and social planning that appeared between 1965 and 1975. Our intent was to introduce students to new material which we believed represented a previously unavailable level of in-depth analysis of practice. For the third edition we have chosen to emphasize those elements in community organizing which we think will be of increasing importance for practitioners in the 1980s and 1990s: participation, program planning, and policy analysis. These three elements constitute major areas of knowledge that will be increasingly significant in the current context of practice.

The material included in earlier editions is, of course, of utility. Our intention has always been to provide the student with material that represents *current* thinking in the field. The previous significant works that are the intellectual building blocks of professional practice are cited frequently in our introductory sections and by many of the authors included in this volume. Students who are planning to become professional community organizers and social planners will want to read these works.

We have not selected salient materials readily available in paperbacks, and because our interest is in current practice, we have not used works of historical interest in the development of community organization. There are many other sources of knowledge from which we have not included selections, such as literature in the form of policy and institutional analysis about the many substantive issues of public social policy with which community action systems deal, namely, housing, welfare, education, civil rights, criminal justice, and aging. Other important areas related to community organization that are not covered are small group theory, professional education, administration, and supervision. Obviously, a volume of introductory readings cannot deal with all the cognate subject matter of the field. We have selected several papers that illustrate the ways in which social planners-community organizers use these ideas in general and in such specific areas as community mental health and urban planning.

The selections are organized in five parts based on major inductive categories. There is an introductory statement to each part in which selections are placed in the context of the current state of knowledge of the subject. Chapter 1 deals with the contexts of practice, which includes communities and organizations. All the papers in Chapter 2 deal with the subject of participation in community organization and social planning. Chapters 3 and 4 deal with major aspects of practice, program development, and planning design. Finally, Chapter 5 covers various aspects of social policy. Policy analysis is the intellectual substance of community organization and planning. The policy choices that are available to community action and social planning groups constitute a subject matter that has not been sufficiently integrated in the methodological concerns of practice.

The selections included in this reader have contributed significantly to the growing body of knowledge about how professional change agents do their work. By increasing their knowledge about communities, organizations, processes, and methods through which to bring about social change, practitioners' choices are considerably enlarged and their practice achieves greater depth. It is important that these ideas be developed. If the practice of community organization is left to the choice of the sponsoring agency, as is frequently the case, or to the personal ideological predisposition of the worker, then planners and organizers will utilize approaches to community problem solving that are limited either to the wishes of their employers or to their own individual hopes and dreams. Organizational goals and personal ideology are important variables in social action. However, practice that is based on a body of knowledge that is no wider than that found in an agency manual or a worker's life experience will be narrow and shallow. It is not likely that either organizational dicta or personal ideologies will constitute a contribution from planners and community developers that will be sufficient to merit society's recognition of them as professionals.

Moreover, it appears that the last decades of the century may be a time of antiwelfare governments. Organizations that provide social services, and the professionals associated with them, may face difficult times in which they will have to defend their programs, justify their use of resources, and struggle to survive. We do not believe that professional knowledge will be the only element needed to survive in that struggle. The skillful use of political and social relationships can be extremely useful. However, professional practice based on knowledge can enable communities to make more efficient use of resources and can help in winning the respect and the support of the community. Knowledge is a resource that will be more important than ever in community organization and in planning and developing policies and programs.

NOTES

1. Roy Lubove, *The Professional Altruist: The Emergence of Social Work as a Career* (Cambridge, Mass.: Harvard University Press, 1965).
2. Sidney Dillick, *Community Organization for Neighborhood Development: Past and Present* (William Morrow & Co., Inc., 1953).
3. Solomon Kobrin, "The Chicago Area Project—A 25-Year Assessment," *The Annals of the American Academy of Political and Social Science,* 233 (March 1959): 19–29.
4. Harold L. Wilensky, *Intellectuals in Labor Unions: Organizational Pressures on Professional Roles* (New York: The Free Press, 1956).
5. Saul Alinsky, *Reveille for Radicals* (Chicago: University of Chicago Press, 1946).
6. Robert P. Lane, "The Field of Community Organization," *Proceedings, National Conference of Social Work, 1939* (New York: Columbia University Press, 1948), pp. 205–17.
7. Kenneth L. M. Pray, "When Is Community Organization Social Work Practice?" *Proceedings, National Conference of Social Work, 1947* (New York: Columbia University Press, 1948), pp. 194–204.
8. Wilber I. Newstetter, "The Social Intergroup Work Process," *Proceedings, National Conference of Social Work, 1947* (New York: Columbia University Press, 1948), pp. 205–17.
9. Pray, op. cit., p. 202.
10. Murray G. Ross, *Community Organization: Theory and Principles* (New York: Harper & Row, Publishers, 1955).
11. For various accounts of this period, see Peter Marris and Martin Rein, *Dilemmas of Social Reform* (New York: Lieber-Atherton, Inc., 1967), and Bernard J. Frieden and Marshall Kaplan, *The Politics of Neglect: Urban Aid from Model Cities to Revenue Sharing* (Cambridge, Mass.: MIT Press, 1975).
12. For example, see Ad Hoc Committee on Advocacy, "The Social Worker as Advocate: Champion of Social Victims," *Social Work,* 14:2 (April 1969): 16–22; George Brager, "Advocacy and Political Behavior," *Social Work,* 13:2 (April 1968): 5–15; George Brager, "Organizing the Unaffiliated in a Low-Income Area," *Social Work,* 8:2 (April 1963): 34–40; George Brager and Harry Specht, *Community Organizing* (New York: Columbia University Press, 1973); John Erlich, "The Turned-on Generation: New Antiestablishment Action Roles," *Social Work,* 16:4 (October 1971): 22–27; Charles Grosser, "Neighborhood Development Projects Serving the Urban

Poor," in *Community Action Against Poverty: Readings from the Mobilization for Youth Experience,* eds. George Brager and Francis Purcell (New Haven: College and University Press, 1967); John Turner, *Neighborhood Organization for Community Action* (New York: National Association of Social Workers, 1968).

13. Neil Gilbert, Armin Rosenkranz, and Harry Specht, "Dialectics of Social Planning," *Social Work,* 18:2 (March 1976): 278–86.

14. Floyd Hunter, *Community Power Structure* (Chapel Hill, N.C.: University of North Carolina Press, 1952).

15. For example, see Terry N. Clark, ed., *Community Structure and Decision Making: Comparative Analysis* (San Francisco: Chandler Publishing Co., 1968).

16. Alinsky, op. cit.

17. William W. Biddle with Loureide J. Biddle, *The Community Development Process: The Rediscovery of Local Initiative* (New York: Holt, Rinehart and Winston, Inc., 1965).

18. For example, see Charles Grosser, William Henry, and James G. Kelly, eds., *Non-Professionals in the Human Services* (San Francisco: Jossey-Bass, Inc., 1969); Alan Gartner and Frank Riessman, "New Training for New Services," *Social Work,* 17:6 (November 1972): 55–63.

19. Luther H. Gulick, "Reorganization of the State," *Civil Engineering* (August 1933): 420, quoted in *The Book of the States, 1976–77,* vol. 21 (Lexington, Ky.: The Council of State Governments, 1976), p. 21.

20. William E. Leuchtenberg, *Franklin D. Roosevelt and the New Deal* (New York, 1962), as quoted in *The Book of the States,* op. cit., p. 24.

21. Richard H. Leach, "A Quiet Revolution: 1933–76," *The Book of the States, 1976–77,* vol. 21 (Lexington, Ky.: The Council of State Governments, 1976), pp. 21–24.

22. Daniel J. Elazar, "The New Federalism: Can the States Be Trusted?" *The Public Interest,* 38 (Spring 1974): 381.

23. The Council of State Governments, *Human Services Integration: State Functions in Implementation* (Lexington, Ky., 1974).

24. R. Douglas Roederer, "State Public Assistance Programs," *The Book of the States, 1976–77,* vol. 21 (Lexington, Ky.: The Council of State Governments, 1976), p. 381.

25. Council of State Governments, op. cit.

26. Ibid., p. 1.

27. C. Wendell King, *Social Movements in the United States* (New York: Random House, Inc., 1956).

28. Harry Specht, "The Grass Roots and Government in Social Planning and Community Organization," *Administration in Social Work,* 2:3 (Fall 1978): 319–334.

29. The remaining paragraphs in Part II of the Introduction are paraphrased from a paper by Neil Gilbert and Harry Specht, "The Integration of Sociopolitical and Technical Knowledge Components in Education for Indirect-Service Practice," *Annual Program Meeting of the Council of Social Work Education* (Boston, Mass., March 1979).

30. Neil Gilbert and Harry Specht, eds. *Planning for Social Welfare: Issues, Models, and Tasks* (Englewood Cliffs, N.J.: Prentice-Hall, Inc., 1977).

31. Richard Bolan, "The Social Relations of the Planner," *Journal of the American Institute of Planners,* 37 (November 1971): 287–396.

32. Neil Gilbert and Harry Specht, "Title XX Planning by Area Agencies on Aging: Effects, Outcomes and Policy Implications," *The Gerontologist,* 19:3 (1979): 264–74.

33. G. Hemmans, E. Bergman, and R. Moroney, "The Practitioners' View of Social Planning," *Journal of the American Institute of Planners,* 44 (April 1978): 181–92.

34. Ibid., p. 183.

35. Jack Rothman, "Three Models of Community Organization Practice," *Social Work Practice, 1968* (New York: Columbia University Press, 1968), pp. 16–47.

36. Si Kahn, *How People Get Power* (New York: McGraw-Hill Book Company, 1970), p. 18.

37. Hans L. Zetterberg, *On Theory and Verification in Sociology* (Totowa, N.J.: The Bedminster Press, 1963), p. 18.

1

CONTEXTS

Community and Organization

The professional practice of community organization and social planning takes place in the two interrelated contexts of community and organization. Both can be conceived as the *sources* of problem conditions to be ameliorated, the *targets* of citizen action, and the *structural vehicles* for planned change. Organizations are also the *sponsors* of efforts to improve community conditions. Community and organization constitute the environment, which contains the major elements that influence practice decisions, such as decisions regarding the definition of the problem condition to be changed, the choice of strategies, the relevant actors and action systems to be involved, and the resources for influence which can be used. Thus the concepts of community and organization help establish the boundaries of collective action, shaping its limits as well as its possibilities. Each of the five articles in this section contributes to a theory-based practice by illustrating different ways of conceptualizing the primary contextual variables of community and organization. Warren and Panzetta offer two examples of community models, and Gummer and Levine focus on organizational behavior. The article by Likwak and his associates is a rare example of a theory-based linkage between community and bureaucratic organizations.

COMMUNITY

Regardless of how the community is conceived, there is agreement that knowledge about "it" is a prerequisite to the practice of community organization, planning, and the administration of human service agencies. But what does it mean to "know your community"? If community refers to the pattern of relationships among groups of people who share some common values, fate, or function in a locality, then the parameters of this knowledge as well as its specific content are not easy to establish partly because the salient pattern of relationships among actors in a community varies with each problem selected for attention. The community with which one works in trying to prevent neighborhood juvenile delinquency is not the same as the constellation of agencies, organizations, and groups involved in developing service programs for the elderly. In the case of community mental health, two types of community are involved. According to Panzetta, these types are often confused in community mental health: the functional community to be worked with and the catchment area.

As an organizing principle, the concept of community helps the professional focus on the most important attributes and relationships as well as exclude others by establishing boundaries for the analysis, that is, certain organizations, groups, roles, and power relationships, not others, are selected for attention. Although an analytic view of the community may appear to distort and oversimplify the fluid intricacies of reality, it does provide one way of thinking about these relationships. The concept suggests a means of managing the complex and interdependent character of systems in which "everything appears to depend on everything else."

What kinds of knowledge about the structure and the function of the community do professionals need? Of primary importance are the character, the role, and the influence of the major population groups and institutions that constitute the geographic community and the distribution of influence in decision-making structures. Professionals also need to have a developmental perspective on the community, a sense of the dominant trends, pace, and patterns of significant change. They also need an orientation in which to view the perceived demands and interests of relevant groups against the actual and the potential resources of various institutional systems and their capacities for change. Finally, this contextual orientation should be supported by specific information about the physical, ecological, political, and economic characteristics of the community.

Whether professionals work in a geographic community such as a neighborhood with a high proportion of ethnic minorities or in traditional, functional communities such as the aged or the disabled or in newer ones such as sexually oriented minorities as well as women, they must ask themselves a series of initial and continuing questions regarding the nature of the community to be worked with. The kinds of questions asked and the kinds of information needed to answer them are shaped by the nature of the mandate of the sponsoring organizations, the professionals' values and goals, and the character of the action systems to be worked with. To help the action system formulate feasible goals and appropriate strategies, professionals must know about the structure and the function of relevant community population groups, formal organizations, voluntary associations, and social institutions.

Ideally, organizers-planners should have a theory that enables them to order the vast array of data about the community. At best, however, there are only orientations and frameworks that suggest the critical nature of certain factors affecting the behavior of various community systems. It is generally acknowledged that there is no "theory of community" in the sense of a series of interrelated propositions that explains and predicts community behavior. Innumerable community case studies and surveys offer various substitutes or facsimiles for theory, such as typologies, ideologies, metaphors, and hypotheses. Most of the descriptive studies have focused on the demographic character of the community, its institutions and values, and its power structures. Although the findings do not yield a coherent picture of community life, they do suggest sensitizing concepts and analytic categories that direct attention to the horizontal (local) and the vertical (extracommunity) axes of a community, reference groups, monolithic and pluralistic decision-making structures, community influentials, social stratification, status, norms, values, and so on.

A frequently used framework applied to both communities and organizations is that of a social system which is illustrated in "A Community Model" by Roland L. Warren. Warren defines community in terms of five major activities that have locality relevance. He also identifies the major dimensions along which American communities differ. (It has been estimated that there are over ninety definitions of community in the literature on the subject.) These conceptions are part of a working vocabulary which is adapted to the interrelated nature of community structures and processes. Although systems concepts are helpful for describing macrophenomena and useful for thinking about the interdependence of community subsystems, they are less capable of generating explanations or predictions in a form that can be applied to planned change.

Reflecting experience in the field of community mental health, Anthony Panzetta provides another view of community in "The Concept of the Community: The Short Circuit of the Mental Health Movement." Some of the multiple referents of the term *community* and its identification with place and process are analyzed against the background of such political-ethnic issues as community control and consumer involvement. Also useful to the practitioner is Panzetta's discussion of the practical and strategic consequences of the different theoretical approaches to the community, such as the frequent confusion of a catchment area with the concept of *gemeinschaft*.

ORGANIZATION

As an integral part of the formal structure of a community, organizations are the principal modes of providing human services that are intended to have an impact on social problems. Efforts to change the policies and practices of social agencies or the composition of their governing bodies are among the recurrent tasks in community organization. Whether initiated as part of a process of community development or of social planning, the goals are similar although the methods may vary. Changes are usually sought in organizational behavior to obtain greater access for clientele, to ensure more accountability and more appropriate services for them, and to bring about greater coherence, continuity, and coordinated effort in service delivery systems or a greater measure of effectiveness, efficiency, and equity.

Effective professional attention to these processes of organizational change, whether externally or internally induced, requires an understanding of the structure and the function of the professional's sponsoring agency and the organizations to be changed. This kind of understanding should include information about the history and the philosophy of the agency and policymaking and operating systems, including linkages to other organizations and institutions. These kinds of data are essential prerequisites to the formulation of change strategies that take into consideration such elements as access to the organization, points of leverage, inducements to change, and appropriate resources for influence.

Organization theory, which draws heavily on sociology and political science, provides a rich vocabulary to describe the character and the role of bureaucracies and agencies and offers considerable empirical data, typologies, and hypotheses to help explain the behavior of participants. These materials draw attention to the rational and formal aspects of the organization, as well as to its nonrational and informal dimensions. This literature includes studies of the social structure of policymaking and case studies of schools, hospitals, prisons, welfare departments, and other governmental and voluntary agencies. These studies reveal the complexity and the difficulty of attempting to change organizations.

Most formal organizations appear to function as quasi-political systems, balancing the needs and the interests of policymakers, constituencies, functionaries, and clientele. In striving to maintain the conditions necessary for institutional stability and structural and functional integrity, most bureaucracies tend to resist change. Hence it is of critical importance that there be an accurate appraisal of the potential change capability of the organization that the action system seeks to change. By identifying which groups make what kinds of decisions and estimating their probable responses based on past performance and current status to proposed changes, a professional can assess the forces opposed to, in favor of, or unconcerned with the change objectives. Information about the distribution of power in the operating system, possible role conflicts, and the nature of communication networks may then suggest what forms of education, persuasion, and pressure may be effective with particular elements in the organization concerned with a specific issue.

There are many models of organizational behavior that can be employed in analyzing practice, but most of them can be grouped in two main classes: natural systems and rational systems. In "A Power-Politics Approach to Social Welfare Organizations," Burton Gummer concludes that neither of these models is appropriate in analyzing human service organizations, most of which have ambiguous and indeterminant goals and technologies. In addition, these kinds of organizations tend to place great reliance on the relationships of professionals and clients, and they lack valid and reliable means for determining effectiveness. Gummer proposes a political economy model. This model directs attention to self-interest and competition for control of resources as the major determinants of organizational goals. This power-politics approach aids in understanding organizational change, and it can be useful to practitioners who are concerned with influencing the policies and the programs of human service organizations.

Moving from the theoretical and analytical, "Organizational Decline and Cutback Management" by Charles Levine utilizes organization and administration theory in describing the development of strategic responses to reductions in agency income. There is widespread agreement that the decade of the 1980s will be dominated by the slowed growth of the welfare state. A scarcity of resources will result in the cutback of funds for most human service organizations. In the past organization theory and administration theory have been rooted in assumptions of growth. Levine reappraises the sources of organizational decline in describing some principles for the design and management of public organizations in a future that may be characterized by diminished income. Whether rooted in internal or external political, economic, and technical conditions, analyses of the causes of organizational decline can be useful in deciding whether to resist or facilitate the change and in selecting the most appropriate tactics of cutback management.

From the perspective of declining organizations that confront major changes in their fiscal environment, we move to consideration of the interrelationships between an organization and its community. This is the focus of "Community Participation in Bureaucratic Organizations: Principles and Strategies" by Eugene Litwak and his associates. Under what conditions can community groups influence bureaucracies? Hypotheses deduced from balance theory suggest that under certain conditions, bureaucracies should be approached by experts hired by community groups and under other conditions, by indigenous workers. They also suggest when conflict tactics might be more effective. A wide range of relationships between bureaucracies and community groups is evaluated under typical situations encountered in practice.

Roland L. Warren
A Community Model

It is the inescapable fact that people's clustering together in space has important influences on their daily activities that perhaps gives us our best clue to a definition of the community as a social entity. We shall consider a community to be *that combination of social units and systems that perform the major social functions having locality relevance.* In other words, by *community* we mean the organization of social activities to afford people daily local access to those broad areas of activity that are necessary in day-to-day living. [W]e shall organize our description and analysis of such activities around five major functions that have such locality relevance. These functions are:

1. Production-distribution-consumption
2. Socialization
3. Social control
4. Social participation
5. Mutual support

The Community In America, 3rd edition by Roland L. Warren. Copyright © 1978 by Houghton Mifflin Company. Used by permission.

While all have locality relevance, they are not necessarily functions over which the community exercises exclusive responsibility or over which it has complete control. On the contrary, the organization of society to perform these functions at the community level involves a strong tie between locally based units such as businesses, schools, governments, and voluntary associations and social systems extending far beyond the confines of the community. Rather than being extraneous to the present consideration of the community, these relationships to extracommunity systems will be an important focus of attention. . . . Nor, as we shall see, does it mean that these functions are not performed by other types of social systems such as informal groups, formal associations, and whole societies. The community, however, is especially characterized by the organization of these functions on a locality basis.

The function of *production-distribution-consumption* relates to local participation in the process of producing, distributing, and consuming those goods and services that are a part of daily living and access to which is desirable in the immediate locality. While it is customary to consider economic entrepreneurs, most typically the modern business corporation, as the principal providers of such goods and services, all community institutions, whether industrial, business, professional, religious, educational, governmental, or whatever, provide such goods and services. Indeed, the conditions under which one such unit or another provides the particular goods or services are an important consideration, and the switch in their provision from one type of auspices to another has important implications. . . .

The function of *socialization* involves a process by which society or one of its constituent social units transmits prevailing knowledge, social values, and behavior patterns to its individual members. Through this process the individual comes to take on the way of living of his or her society rather than that of some other. The process is particularly important and noticeable in the early years of the individual, but it extends throughout one's life. In American communities the formal school system is ordinarily considered the principal community institution discharging this function, although it is recognized that individual families have an important role to play, particularly in the early years, and that many other groups are also active in the process.

The function of *social control* involves the process through which a group influences the behavior of its members toward conformity with its norms. Here, too, several different social units perform this function on the community level. Customarily, formal government is considered particularly pertinent, since by definition government has ultimate coercive power over the individual through the enforcement of universally applicable laws. The

police and the courts are especially relevant in the performance of the social-control function by local government, but, as we shall see, many other social units, including the family, the school, the church, and the social agency, also play a large part.

An important community function is that of providing local access to *social participation*. Perhaps the most widely prevalent unit for providing this participation is the religious organization—church or synagogue—and we shall consider these organizations in the context of their great importance in performing this function. Ordinarily, one thinks of voluntary organizations of various sorts as the community's most important units for channeling social participation. Nevertheless, many different types of social unit, including businesses, government offices, and voluntary and public health and welfare agencies, provide, through their formal activity, important avenues of social participation to their employees or volunteer workers in the course of the performance of their occupational tasks. Likewise, family and kinship groups, friendship groups, and other less formal groupings provide important channels of social participation.

A final major community function is that of providing *mutual support* on the local level. Traditionally, such mutual support, whether in the form of care in time of sickness, exchange of labor, or helping a local family in economic distress, has been performed locally very largely under such primary-group auspices as family and relatives, neighborhood groups, friendship groups, and local religious groups. Specialization of function, along with other social changes, . . . has led to a gradual change in auspices for many of these mutual-support functions: to public welfare departments, to private health and welfare agencies, to governmental and commercial insurance companies, and so on. Perhaps the present archetype of the community-based mutual-support unit might be the voluntary agency in the field of health and welfare, but the distribution of this function, like others, through a wide range of social auspices is an important aspect of the current situation in American communities. . . .

As the above implies, the definition of the community in terms of the systems that perform the major social functions having locality relevance leads to an emphasis on community functions rather than on community institutions. A conventional way of describing the related community phenomena is to consider the various institutional areas of the community: its economic institutions, its government, its educational institutions, its religious institutions, and perhaps its health and welfare, recreational, communicational, or other institutions. As noted, however, these institutional areas correspond only very loosely to the major locality-relevant functions. As already indicated, most of these functions are performed by a great variety of institutional auspices. The present period is characterized by important shifts in the performance of these functions from one set of community auspices to another. Hence, a functional rather than an institutional approach seems to have the greatest potential for bringing out this cross-institutional distribution of important community functions.

A problem facing any student of American communities is how to make general statements that apply widely despite the many gradations in size and other characteristics that differentiate one community from another. One possible approach is to consider numerous different "ideal types" of communities and to make general statements only about each type. Another alternative is to confine one's statements to relationships that are so general that they apply to all communities, regardless of the important differences existing among them. Another possible approach is to consider some of the important dimensions along which communities differ from each other, relate these dimensions to general statements applicable to all communities, and then "locate" any particular community or type of community under discussion at a particular point along each such dimension. Thus, one can set up a dimensional field that is broad enough to encompass all communities and make meaningful statements about them on an appropriately abstract level; at the same time the dimensional field can provide a means for describing the difference between one community and another with respect to location within the multidimensional field. Statements about specific communities can thus have general relevance as long as the location of the community within the field is known. Stein has made an attempt to apply this procedure to the analysis of American communities, employing his three main analytical concepts—urbanization, industrialization, and bureaucratization—as the dimensions of his field.[1] For our present consideration, a somewhat different set of dimensions will be employed. Their relevance and importance will become apparent in subsequent chapters, so they will receive only brief treatment here.

The first of the ways in which American communities differ from each other in their structure and function relates to *the dimension of autonomy.* Our postulate is that American communities differ along this dimension and that this difference is relevant to an approach defining the community in terms of its functions. In considering any community, we shall be interested in the extent to which it is dependent on or independent of extracommunity units in the performance of its five functions.

The second type of difference is in *the extent to which the service areas of local units (stores, churches, schools, and so on) coincide or fail to coincide.* At the one extreme, the service areas coincide and hence everyone within the community service area boundary is served by institutions from the same community. At the other extreme, there is relatively little coincidence of service areas, and people may find themselves living within the school district of a locality to the east, going to church in a locality to the south, trading at a trade center to the north, and so on, without any common geographic center of community activities and without a common geographic area of service.

A somewhat different type of variation concerns the extent of *psychological identification with a common locality*. In some communities a strong sense of local identification is apparent; that is, the local inhabitants consider the community as an important reference group. At the other extreme are communities whose inhabitants have little sense of relationship to one another, little sense of the community as a significant social group, and little sense of "belonging" to the community.

A final dimension will be the extent to which the community's *horizontal pattern* is strong or weak. The horizontal pattern is the structural and functional relation of the various local units (individuals and social systems) to each other. . . . In some communities the sentiments, behavior patterns, and social systemic interconnections of the horizontal pattern may be strong, in others weak.

In considering community differences, specific instances can be contained within a more generalized frame of reference by using these four dimensions. Putting this graphically, we can say that communities differ on all four of the following dimensions, and we can meaningfully locate each community at some point on each of the lines going from one extreme to another (see Figure 1).

THE COMMUNITY '"PROBLEM"

So far we have discussed some changes that have taken place in American communities, some theoretical difficulties involved in community studies, and the functional conception of the community that we shall use in this book. Let us turn now to a somewhat different type of problem, perhaps much more meaningful to nonsociologists. In their eyes, the problem lends urgency to the study of communities, giving it an importance that mere theoretical interest would not afford. For through their newspapers and television and through their own experience, discerning Americans have come to the uneasy realization that all is not right with their community living, that undesirable situations appear with growing frequency or intensity and that these are not the adventitious difficulty of one community or another so much as the parts of a general pattern of community living. "Something is wrong

Figure 1 Four dimensions on which American communities differ.

		0	1	2	3	4	
1. Local autonomy:	Independent						Dependent
2. Coincidence of service areas:	Coincide						Differ
3. Psychological identification with locality:	Strong						Weak
4. Horizontal pattern:	Strong						Weak

with the system"; there is a *community problem.*

It is apparent that certain types of "problems" are broadly characteristic of contemporary American communities. While most noticeable in the metropolitan areas, most of them are apparent in smaller communities as well. They appear in such forms as the increasing indebtedness of central cities, the spread of urban blight and slums, the lack of affordable, adequate housing, the economic dependence of large numbers of people in the population, poorly financed and staffed schools, high delinquency and crime rates, institutional racism, inadequate provisions for the mentally ill, the problem of the aged, the need for industrial development, the conflict of local and national agencies for the free donor's dollar, the pollution of air and water, the problem of affording rapid transit for commuters at a reasonable price and at a reasonable profit, and the problem of downtown traffic congestion. The list is almost endless, and each of the problems mentioned could be subdivided into numerous problematical aspects.

On this level, one can continue naming specific problems almost indefinitely. Are such problems simply a host of disparate plagues with which the modern community, Job-like, is made to suffer? Or are they in some sense interrelated? If so, how? This book is not problem-oriented in the sense of being an analysis of community problems and what might be done about them. Yet no systematic treatise on the community can overlook their existence or neglect to explore their interrelations with each other and with other aspects of community living.

Perhaps we can shed some light by examining community behavior as it has developed and changed in recent decades. A closer look at some of the underlying processes taking place within the community may afford a backdrop against which the community conditions that we interpret as "problems" can be understood as part and parcel of the system of community living that has developed in America. The alternative approach is to take each problem out of its situational context and treat it in relative isolation from the basic community conditions that produced it. To do so is to operate on a superficial and often ineffectual level, as many concerned citizens who have attempted to cope with these problems can attest. . . .

Meanwhile, it is well to distinguish between the existence of a problem and the existence of the ability to take effective action to resolve it. Looked at another way, if no social system is "perfect," then each system will produce certain "problems." They are, in a sense, the price paid for whatever advantages that particular system of community living entails. We can thus inquire what sorts of problems are generated in American communities and also how effectively they are dealt with.

One sees not only specific problems of one type or another, but also the general problem of inability of the community to organize its forces effectively to cope with its specific problems. Let us consider this last for a moment. The question now becomes: What are the conditions of American community living that make it difficult for people to muster their resources on the community level to cope with their problems?

Certainly, one part of the answer is the fact that many of the problems that are confronted on the community level simply are not solvable on that level, but are *problems of the larger society of which the community is a part.* Any single community's effort is as little or nothing as against the forces of the larger society. Much important behavior that takes place at the community level takes place within units, groups, companies, and other entities that themselves are integral parts of larger state or national systems. It is a thesis of this book that such units often are more closely related to these larger systems than to other components of the local community. Thus, problems of the larger society are not something that are adventitiously imported into the local community like a germ carried by some visitor, but rather they are conditions inhering in the systems of which the community's various units are a part, and the community's units share these conditions as a basic part of their very existence.

Thus, for example, problems of unemployment or of inflation are not amenable to solution community by community, although some palliative action on the community level may attentuate the former. On a somewhat different plane, certain problems are more closely related to the interaction that takes place within the community itself. These problems include those arising from marital and family conflict, from the vicious fund-raising controversy between national and local health and welfare organizations, and difficulties in the central city that are attendant upon the flight to the suburbs of upper- and middle-income groups along with the retail stores that serve them. Nevertheless, such difficulties are a part of the larger cultural patterns of living, which communities share by being a part of American society.

As an example, the problem of family breakdown in the local community is partly, at least, a result of forces in the wider culture, such as conflicting role expectations in marriage, discontinuity in the socialization process, emphasis on hedonistic romantic irresponsibility in the courtship process, decline in opportunities for useful functions performed by children, and separation of the economic sustenance function from the home. Just as communities are not islands isolated from the major social systems of American society, so they are not cultural islands separated from the broad forces of cultural development and change that characterize the major institutions of American society. In sum, many problems that communities face are simply beyond resolving through the effective mustering of resources at the community level alone.

A closely related barrier to effective community action is the *loss of community autonomy* over specific institutions or organizations located within it and closely intermeshed with its welfare. The decision of the absentee-owned company to discontinue its branch plant and the decision of the state highway department to build the new road on the east side of the river rather than on the west represent decisions by community-based units over which the community exercises little control.

To ineffectiveness of possible action at the community level and loss of community autonomy can be added a third barrier to effective community action, one that seems on the surface, at least, to be more nearly under the potential control of community people. This barrier consists of a number of related phenomena that may best be characterized as *lack of identification with the community.*

Perhaps the most widely recognized aspect of such lack of identification of the individual with the community is the much deplored *apathy* of citizens regarding community affairs. People who plunge into community problems with a concern for community improvement often complain with despair that "you can't get anybody interested" in whatever the problem happens to be. So many problems seem to depend for their effective confrontation on sustaining the interest and activity of a large number of people over a sufficient period of time to bring about the remedies thought to be desirable that the alleged apathy of citizens seems to be a paramount stumbling block. The point is often distorted by unrealistic comparisons with overidealized depictions of New England town meetings or by invidious comparisons with some community where "people got together and really did something about it."

Yet there is a valid point here. The increasing association of people on the basis of common occupational or other interests, rather than on the basis of locality alone (as among neighbors), is no doubt a contributing factor. The union man, the banker, and the school administrator often have strong vocational ties to their own groups, and they have less in common vocationally than, say, three farmers living in the same rural neighborhood. Even in recreational and civic activity, association is often on the basis of specialized interest. Thus, the apathy is not complete, for interests often run high in specialized concerns. It consists, instead, of a lack of interest in community-wide concerns that cut across the various specialized interests and thus become "nobody's business."

Over the years, communities have grown larger and larger. The problem of direct as against representative participation arises in large social bodies, not only in government but in various community affairs. Attempts to solve this problem have been no freer of defects in other aspects of community participation than they have in political representation. Community councils, for example, represent an attempt to involve both individuals and organizations in processes of community-wide betterment. They have been extremely sporadic, and even at their best they seldom attain active participation from more than a small minority of the citizenry. Participation in community activities thus usually takes place through participation in some specialized interest group such as a health association, a chamber of commerce, or a better government league, each having its own sphere of interests and activities and its loyal supporters who can generally be relied upon to rally to a cause within their sphere of interests, but not necessarily outside it.

One might ask what else might reasonably be expected, for time does not permit each individual citizen to participate actively in all the concerns that have broad community import. Thus, what is often interpreted as apathy, as "nobody cares," is merely an instance of the hard fact that the number of legitimate community concerns is so great that individual citizens could not actively concern themselves with all of them even if they wanted to and of course many do not.

The increasing transiency of residents of the suburbs has already been mentioned. The constant moving back and forth across the country in search of the better job, as a result of the company's planned policy of personnel rotation, or for whatever reason, puts a premium on the tree that can survive with shallow roots, a point that William H. Whyte has made with great effectiveness in his study of *The Organization Man*.[2] The knowledge that one will probably not remain for many years in the community where one is now living seems unlikely to favor civic participation, and the really remarkable thing is that participation does run so high precisely in the suburbs that show such a great degree of transiency.

Failure to identify with the community takes still another form, which might be called *alienation*.[3] An example is the extent to which useful participation roles are increasingly unavailable to the aged in American communities. Numerous studies of the "problems of the aged" document the point that as people grow older, their roles in family, religious organization, occupation, and voluntary civic endeavor become less meaningful and less active. Compulsory retirement, the friction caused by having older inlaws living with the nuclear family, the fast pace that turns to youthful leadership and new ideas rather than to the wisdom accumulated from another day by older people—all these tend to estrange the elderly from normal avenues of community participation and force them into a state of dependency that is caused less by their inability to function effectively than by the community's inability to make vital use of them. The fact that this estrangement occurs at the very time when shortages in vital community jobs are experienced, particularly in the professions, and when the need for volunteer services in health and welfare agencies is greater than ever, makes the situation particularly ironic.

Groups of people who hold values different from those dominant in the community represent another type of estrangement, which may even constitute a deliberate rebellion against the community's values. These small groups take various forms: splinter sects, practitioners of various cults, members of the "counterculture," revolutionaries, and so on. Many such groups perform a useful function in challenging the validity of the prevailing values, as gadflies to the conscience of society. Delinquency, vice, and mental illness, on the other hand, represent an order of deviance whose usefulness to the community is far less apparent. They all have in common, though, the estrangement of the individual from the usual values, behavior systems, and satisfactions of the community. There is considerable evidence that such estrangement is widely characteristic of people in the lowest socioeconomic status, the so-called lower-lower class as described by Warner, Hollingshead, and others.[4] So basically different is their whole pattern of living that they might well constitute a completely different culture.[5]

Estrangement from commonly held values has, since Durkheim, come to be described by the term *anomie*, or normlessness,[6] a situation in which there is little sharing of commonly accepted values and social control over behavior becomes ineffectual. In analyzing the disintegration of a New England community, Homans observes:

> If the good opinion of his neighbors is a reward to a man, then a loss of their good opinion will hurt him, but if this loss does not follow a breach of a norm, where is the punishment? And how can it follow, when the norms themselves are not well defined?[7]

The society-wide character of many problems, lack of community autonomy, and lack of identification with the community are three barriers to the efficient mustering of forces to comfort community problems. As a final [comment], it might be well to relate these characteristics to the rise of a process that has come to be called "community development." For one way of describing community development is to say that it is a process of helping community people to analyze their problems, to exercise as large a measure of autonomy as possible and feasible, and to promote a greater identification of the individual citizen and the individual organization with the community as a whole. Through such a process, communities may be helped to confront their problems as effectively as possible.

The deliberate attempt by community people to work together to guide the future of their communities and the development of a corresponding set of techniques for assisting community people in such a process constitute important advances in the current changes occurring in American communities. . . .

NOTES

1. Maurice R. Stein, *The Eclipse of Community: An Interpretation of American Studies* (Princeton: Princeton University Press, 1960).

2. *The Organization Man* (Garden City: Doubleday Anchor, 1957).

3. For an analysis of the various meanings applied to this term in the sociological literature, see Melvin Seeman, "On the Meaning of Alienation," *American Sociological Review,* vol. 24, no. 6 (December 1959).

4. See, for example, W. Lloyd Warner and Paul S.

Lunt, *The Social Life of a Modern Community* (New Haven, Conn.: Yale University Press, 1941), especially chap. 22; see also August B. Hollingshead and Frederick C. Redlich, *Social Class and Mental Illness: A Community Study* (New York: John Wiley & Sons, 1958).

5. Different class-based subcultures have given rise to the theme of a "culture of poverty," which has become highly controverted in recent years—not so much over the existence of different lifestyles associated with social stratification as over the relationship of lifestyles to poverty. If the lifestyle of the culture of poverty is presumed to "cause" poverty, presumably the problem should be faced through changing the behavior patterns of poor people through various means of resocialization: psychotherapy, social casework, counseling, and so on. The culture of poverty approach is thus seen by many as an intellectual basis for neglecting deficiencies in the American social structure that are believed by many to be the prime factors.

For an overview of the issues, see Charles A. Valentine, *Culture and Poverty: Critique and Counter Proposals* (Chicago: University of Chicago Press, 1968).

6. Emile Durkheim, *Suicide*, trans. John A. Spaulding and George Simpson (Glencoe, Ill.: Free Press, 1951).

7. George C. Homans, *The Human Group* (New York: Harcourt, Brace, 1950), p. 366.

Anthony F. Panzetta

The Concept of Community: The Short Circuit of the Mental Health Movement

Certain words have a way of taking on meanings never intended. Words of a high level of abstraction are like that. Because they touch so many diverse phenomena, these abstract terms are both practical and impractical at the same time. "Community" is an example of such a word. It can be applied in a variety of situations and so is versatile as a one-word concept. But it also is prone to multiple connotative meanings and so can be easily misunderstood.[1]

In today's mental health vocabulary, "community" has taken a prominent position. To some, it rings a public health note; to others, it has a sociopolitical connotation. It may suggest a neighborhood, a district, or an ethnic grouping. It may generate a mood of warmth and togetherness, or one of pragmatic association. It has a current mystique, however, which transcends any of the usual denotative or connotative

Reprinted with permission of author and publisher from *Community Mental Health: Myth and Reality* (Philadelphia, Pennsylvania: Lea & Febiger, 1972), Chapter 1, pp. 1–22.

meanings. This is a mystique of value, an inherent sense of goodness attached to the various concepts of community. To be pro-community is to be virtuous; to be anti-community is to be evil. Both assessments precede any attempt to clarify what is meant by "community."

GEMEINSCHAFT AND GESELLSCHAFT

Sociologists have grappled with the concept of community since Comte and, before him, philosophers since Plato. It is unlikely that we shall settle on the ultimate choice here. There is a useful distinction for our purposes, however, that was elaborated by Tönnies in his use of the terms *gemeinschaft* and *gesellschaft*.[2] A *gemeinschaft* community is characterized by an implicit bond which relates person to person. Like the extended family, such a community is held together by common values, affection, mutual dependence, respect, and a sense of status hierarchy. There are no formal rules of relationship and the roles of the members of that community are set by the traditions and cultural expectations of the group. This type of community is becoming increasingly rare and depends for its existence on a rural or feudal type of social organization.

Today's dominant type of community is *gesellschaft* in nature.[2] Here the bonds are formal and explicit. People relate to one another through formulated guidelines or even through rules and regulations. Affection and dependence on one another for survival is rarely operative. In the *gesellschaft* community, people come together through formal institutions, like their place of employment, their church, professional or civic organization, etc. Very often, great blocks of time are spent in these vertical groupings (in institutions usually away from the area of their home), in contrast to the lesser blocks of time spent in horizontal groupings (in their home neighborhood).

It is the reality of the *gesellschaft* and the longing for the *gemeinschaft* which often leads to a misorientation of "community-minded" psychiatrists. While it is true that there are territorial commitments which all persons make to their "home," and while it is true that these commitments are apt to carry with them affective and durable qualities,[3] it is anachronistic to program for a form of social organization that no longer exists (*gemeinschaft*). It would seem much more reasonable to program for the dominant form, i.e., the *gesellschaft*. If there are existent *gemeinschaft* forms in the population, then these can be taken into account, but not to the exclusion of the more prevalent *gesellschaft* forms.

The visible manifestation of the *gemeinschaft* approach to community mental health planning is the "catchment area." Here, a geographic area is designated as target area and all those who live within the specific boundaries are members of the mythical *gemeinschaft*. This horizontal approach to community makes sense from a limited public health point of view because it allows for the assignment of responsibility. But this goal, i.e., the fixing of responsibility, is an operational accomplishment and does not speak to the issue of community.

There is a further paradox implicit in this approach. One of the ways a *gemeinschaft* group is maintained is by a radical provincialism. Remnants of such groups remain in some of the ethnic communities of Chicago and they have been able to maintain this old world coherence by inbreeding and careful exclusion of cultural values of the pluralistic community around them. They have resisted acculturation to an extent (although this is disappearing rapidly) and so are set apart. The Amish settlements of Pennsylvania and Indiana are better examples of the *gemeinschaft* community. But again, in all of these examples, the *gemeinschaft* is preserved by a nonintegrative approach to the larger surround. The paradox in this rests with the black neighborhoods which, to some extent, have also maintained a *gemeinschaft* way of life but by enforced exclusion from the larger community. Since many, if not most, of the community mental health centers are in black areas, they are forced to program their services in such a way so as to reinforce the separatist ethos of that area. Although this may fit into the plans of the militant black activist, it should be recognized as what it is, a closed market.

A visible remaining example of *gemeinschaft* living which persists throughout modern society (although under great pressure) is the family. It makes great sense to program for family-oriented services since this social form is naturally occurring and durable. But it is possible to program for family-oriented services without paying a great deal of attention to the horizontal community orientation.

This perspective, which differentiates the vertical (institutional) community from the horizontal (geographic) community and which separates the *gesellschaft* (formal) relationship from the *gemeinschaft* (mutual dependent) relationship, can and should clarify some of the inherent difficulties as mental health centers program for their assigned "community" (catchment area).

The resolution of this seeming dilemma lies in the careful application of logical definition. If the overriding consideration is the need for a system which fixes medical and paramedical responsibility, then the catchment area concept may indeed be optimum. But to go further and equate catchment area with "community" is a nonsequitur. If the primary goal is to develop programs which fit the idiosyncrasies of a discrete community, then the catchment area concept is meaningless unless the boundaries of the catchment area coincide with the boundaries of an existing *gemeinschaft* community and if such a community is identified, then we must realize that our efforts may very well serve to reinforce the separatist and exclusionary character of the *gemeinschaft* community.

WHERE: COMMUNITY AS CATCHMENT AREA

In a clear way, the catchment area community is a "where" community. Its definition is dependent on street names, buildings, and general demography. It can be isolated on a wall map which then becomes an impressive addition to one's office, particularly if there is a war games disposition. Colored pins can point out the structural parts of this community and a sense of "my turf" is quickly established. The basic orienting grid to one's thinking becomes "those people living between Susquehanna and Diamond streets." The great temptation is to assume that "those people" are alike one another in their sense of community, i.e., they share common beliefs, common problems, and common aspirations. What in fact is the reality?

There is a commonality which presents itself in the "where" community if that community is sufficiently oppressed. The social indicators of such a community are familiar in language today, i.e., high death rates, high infant mortality, dilapidated housing, high crime rates, and so on. And so the common factors extracted from such a community become logical targets for intervention. These are the "symptoms" of the "where" community and hence the illusory logical target for the community psychiatrist. But the roots of these "symptoms" are not "where" in their vulnerability. A geographic approach may give topographic clues to what is between these boundaries, but it also fixes you to the outfield when the real action is in the infield. The dilapidated house on Diamond Street is a complex phenomena derived from City Hall, the money market, the suburban ethos, as well as from events and people within the catchment area. If we choose to define our mental health goals in this grand dimension, then we had better not assume a catchment area orientation in our programming.

The analysis of a "where" community is usually written in the language of demography and epidemiology. This defined population approach gives valuable information about the target population, but it is important to realize the type of information that is supplied. The information on incidence and prevalence, for example, is only as good as those criteria used for the identification of a "case." The more abstract these criteria, the more unreliable are the results. Because of the availability of rather discrete criteria for the identification of schizophrenia, this has become a favorite object of epidemiologic study,[4] and the results of such studies have a higher degree of reliability than studies of more diffusely defined conditions, e.g., the *Mid-Town Manhattan Study*.[5]

The point of all this should be clarified here. If a community is defined in "where" terms, its analysis, i.e., the dissection of its "problems," is biased in the direction of measurable and gross phenomena. What emerges is a picture of the social disorder of that area as reflected in incidence and prevalence rates of the high-visibility problems. Programming for the "where" community will therefore inevitably tend toward these high-visibility problems. This may or may not correspond with planning objectives derived from other considerations. It is reasonable to proceed from this point of view, providing one realizes what is happening. And again, what happens is that the high-visibility problems surface and become the crying targets for a "where" oriented community program.

In my experience in a mental health center with a catchment area "where" approach, the above proved quite accurate. Although we initially programmed for general psychiatric disorders, we felt the pull towards the high-visibility problems of juvenile crime, unemployment, alcoholism, and addiction, geriatrics, and mental retardation, quite soon after we were operational. It led some to wish we had planned originally for these high-visibility problems and it led others to frustration, since few of these visibility problems are "attractive" or "responsive" to the psychiatric and parapsychiatric professions. So despite an earlier general orientation, the consequence of a "where" approach may shift the focus of attention elsewhere.

A collateral effect of this horizontal concept of community is to place a pseudo-sociologic aura around one's efforts. This may be an exciting prospect initially, as one becomes imbued with the sense of innovation and the illusion of being an instrument of social change. However, illusion it is because entrance to the social institutions which create and devour the social condition require skills, power, and time beyond the resources of the mental health center as

a collective force or the psychiatrist as a well-meaning individual. The problem is that an aura does exist and it takes time before this aura is recognized for what it is. During the interim, staff and program may very easily be pulled down the road to its inevitable disillusioning dead end.

WHEN: COMMUNITY AS EPIPHENOMENON

One of the alternate ways to consider the concept of community is to place it into a dimension of time. We have all been aware, at one time or another, of a sense of community which comes and then goes. People commonly band together to accomplish certain discrete goals and then disband. Organizations often prove to be "when" communities as they bring people together in common pursuit over a period of time. If we wished to look back, with a reverent historical purview, to the feudal *gemeinschaft* communities, we would still note the dissolution of that communal form over time.

Time, of course, changes all things or, more correctly, all things change in time. The great leveler of human grandiosity, history, has been able to chronicle, with predictable certainty, the demise of all sorts of social organizations. Civilizations and families alike are modified or terminated. But too great a preoccupation with the dimension of time becomes distressing and discouraging. After all, we must acknowledge our own temporal finiteness and the even greater temporal finiteness of our work. To feel that one's work must endure forever or to fear that one's work will be washed away immediately is to be equally absurd at either pole.

The hard-core reality of the temporal dilemma is that it is very difficult to correctly estimate (*a*) if the phenomena we are observing is an artifact of the time or a durable reality and (*b*) if our response to the phenomena is appropriate to its duration. Is it a short-range solution to a long-range problem or, conversely, a long-range solution to a short-range problem? The dilemma is more often than not worked out in retrospect.

When time is applied to concepts of community, it brings to them an element of uncertainty which should humble the community expert. Most so-called communities are so time-bound that they come and go like evanescent clouds. The conditions which create a community are themselves so fragile that community itself is more correctly an epiphenomenon than a primary reality in its own right. This concept of community as epiphenomenon is exceedingly important for anyone who is working in "community-oriented" work. An epiphenomenon is a phenomenon which occurs as a result of preexisting phenomena or set of conditions. An epiphenomenon is nothing unless the preexisting events occur. And likewise, a community, in its "when" sense, does not exist unless certain conditions exist. Epiphenomenon, simply defined, is a secondary phenomenon accompanying another and caused by it. There is, for example, a theory of mind called epiphenomenalism which states that mental processes are epiphenomena of brain processes.

These necessary conditions would seem quite important to be aware of, yet it is extraordinary to witness the degree to which they are ignored by "community-oriented" workers. There is probably no greater cohesive force by which people come together into an epiphenomenon community than that of oppression. The history of the Jews and now the black experience in this country are graphic documentation of this. To take away the oppression is to take away much of the binding power of the community. To take away the oppression is to dissolve the epiphenomenon.

Working classes after the Industrial Revolution learned the lesson well, and the organized labor movement in this country was the epiphenomenon of that capitalistic oppression. Even today, unions are maintained as organizations only as well as management is able to play the role of potential oppressors, or be placed in that role by union leaders.

Oppression is only one of two necessary conditions for the epiphenomenal community. The second is leadership. That sense of shared values, common goals, and kinship which is community must be articulated and transmitted to those persons who are to comprise the community. An oppressed people remain fragmented and isolated as long as no one stands to call them together, point out their common plight, articulate their frustration, and present a plan for joint effort. Community implies unity, and unity implies the condensation of many voices to one or few. Given the two necessary conditions, oppression and leadership, a community is born; take either of them away and the epiphenomenon vanishes.

A predictable objection arises here. Is it not so that there are examples of communities which persist without these two preconditions? Is not the family such a community? Again we must return to the distinction made earlier between *gemeinschaft* and *gesellschaft* communities. The *gemeinschaft* community exists only in rare instances outside family life. The traditions and way of life which nourished and sustained the *gemeinschaft* community are gone. And so we see as the prevalent form the *gesellschaft* community. It is my contention that there are episodic variations in the usual *gesellschaft* model which tend to take on the characteristics of the *gemeinschaft* community, and that these variations occur as a result of two major conditions coming together. The resulting "sense" of community lasts only as long as these conditions and so the *gemeinschaft* community is not a durable *gemeinschaft* at all—but rather a fragile state which we can term an epiphenomenon.

There are several implications of this perspective for community psychiatry. Those community mental health programs which have developed in suburban or affluent areas are characteristically oriented towards the provision of services to individuals or families. Their community orientation is primarily geographic and a function of fixing responsibility for various services. They have inadvertently, but accurately, perceived the lack of *gemeinschaft*. Those community mental health programs that have developed in urban centers, with a predominantly black and oppressed constituency, have noted a sense of community and have tried in myriad ways to relate to that sense of community. It is here that the confusion is generated.

If a mental health center assumes that the community is bound together in an historical and romantic way and makes overtures for joint responsibilities, it will soon enough discover that the community will act and respond "as community" only in those issues directly related to oppression or related to the roles and prerogatives of their leaders. It will not receive a sustained community input on those more pedestrian issues that have to do with the delivery of psychiatric services. If the psychiatric services can somehow be brought into the oppression equation, then interest may exist, but it will be short-lived. Again, I must clarify this statement. Community interest—that is, the *representative* sentiment of a large group of persons expressed by responsible leadership—can be sustained only in those areas directly related to their binding power as a community, i.e., the binding power of oppression and leadership. The interest in a mental health program can be generated in isolated "community" individuals who, for one reason or another, are interested in mental health matters, but do *not* assume that these interested individuals can represent a community in matters other than those related to their oppression. Even in the latter area representative views are difficult to identify.

The confusion is brought into stark relief when the community mental health center seeks to "find" its community. Who speaks for the community? is the plaintive cry. The answer, of course, is that there is no community out there, as there is no community out in the suburbs unless you are interested in getting to the epiphenomenal community, which is there for reasons already noted. In that case, their response is a relatively predictable one—and it is inexorably linked to issues of great social import. That community voice will speak to the mental health center about oppression and demand that the center take a role in their struggle. Many centers have and will attempt to get into that struggle. They are then epiphenomenal centers which will ultimately depend for their existence on the maintenance of an oppressed community.

If a center "turns its back to the community" and selects out those residents of the area interested in the center's conception of mental health services, then it runs the high risk of being identified as not truly a "community" mental health center.

HOW: COMMUNITY AS INSTRUMENT

If the foregoing concept of epiphenomenal community is plausible, then what remains to be discussed is the functional role of that tentative community. If there are urban communities, marked by oppression and secondary communal "togetherness," then *how* do they operate in their common goals? What is the basis of their instrumental effectiveness? Although there are many ways to address these questions, I shall select the following approach because it captures the reality of today's urban life.

The ultimate instrumental force with which a "community" may attempt to impose its collective will is that of confrontation. After all, there would be no "community" had there not first been a condition of oppression and, hence, a state of imminent conflict. The very creative force responsible for the emergence of community is itself a real or imagined threat and so the counterforce is its putative equal, counterthreat.

The point of this is to identify the fundamental force which, on the one hand, serves as the community's power and, on the other, serves as a reinforcement of its sense of being an oppressed victim and, hence, a reinforcement of its sense of community. This force of confrontation must be analyzed into its various forms and a would-be provider of "community mental health services" must accurately perceive its proper relation vis-à-vis these forms of confrontation.

A community has at least four levels of confrontation that it can mobilize: (1) as physical force; (2) as antiparticipant; (3) as franchiser; (4) as consumer.

Physical Force

This leaves little to the imagination and essentially is a call to violent opposition. It has become a common device in today's urban brinkmanship and is characterized by a burst from threat to action. It should be clear that the relationship of a mental health center to its "community" cannot be fashioned after this type of functional community role. The "takeover" approach, wherein "community" members literally force institutional personnel out of offices etc., and then proceed to effectively close down the operation of the institution, is an example of the physical force approach. As a technique for a community to impose its collective will upon an institu-

tion, it is the most dramatic. When applied to a fragile institution, like a community mental health center, it promotes confusion and dismemberment.

Antiparticipant

A community may view an institution as sufficiently contrary to its needs so as to take a vocal stand in opposition to its existence. One can imagine the mental health center whose real or imagined program is thought to be a further instrument of societal oppression. With that provocation, a community could urge that no one participate as patient or employee or in support of the center. Again, this hostile relationship can hardly serve as a model for center-community interaction. It is a fact, however, that many centers are being described as instruments of social oppression and militant opposition has developed in many instances. But again let me draw out the important distinction. Although there may be articulate and militant opponents to a program, it is a non sequitur to ascribe this opposition to the ubiquitous "community." Truly antiparticipant reaction from "the community," i.e., a broad level, grass roots opposition, could develop only if a center could (a) capture the attention of the entire community, (b) behave in a blatantly oppressive fashion so as to generate their cohesive opposition, and/or (c) through distorted charges of great magnitude, be incorrectly perceived as oppressor. These are extremely unlikely conditions and so also is a truly antiparticipatory response from the community.

Franchiser

A community takes on a special relationship with a center if it is in the position of franchiser. This suggests ultimate sponsorship by the community, with consequent control (or "power" in today's vocabulary) of program, personnel, and funds. On the face of it, this would seem an ideal way for a community to "confront" an institution which attempts to provide it service.[6] However, the magic of the word covers the underlying absurdity. A community, in its true sense, does not organize itself in such a way as to provide an authoritative control over an institution. It will not yield a "representative" body with the abiding interest and competence to "control" so idiosyncratic an institution as a mental health center. To be sure, isolated individuals from here and there, for this reason or that, will rise "on behalf of the community," but there is little reason to expect in them the mandate or wisdom of the people for whom they wish to speak. It very quickly becomes an argument based on the viscera . . . a little community is better than none at all, isn't it?

Let us assume, however, that a community has developed its own internal system of representative voice and action. There are communities of this type. Here, I am not referring to the usual governmental structures which in their own way are "representative," but rather refer to area organizations (such as in the Woodlawn area of Chicago).[7] Such organizations have a way of maintaining their identity for functions far removed from their original intent. An organization formed to deal with housing or education could conceivably provide the sponsorship of a mental health center, but to suppose that it is a "community" vehicle for control, support, and responsibility, may or may not follow. If the level of communication and mutual trust between the people of the community and the representative organization is consistent and durable, then it may well be an ideal franchiser of mental health services. It would be naive, however, to hope to create a new community organization concurrently with a new mental health center. Both require enormous inputs of dedication, sophistication, and organizational skill. To have two mutually dependent institutions go through their separate and idiosyncratic processes together is to invite their mutual dissolution.

Consumer

The ultimate power of a community is the power inherent in those persons who, by common need, accept or reject the role of service consumer. If the goal of an institution, like a mental health center, is to provide a service, then there can be no greater control than that which operates in the decision of a consumer to use or not use the service. To be able to extend this "power" to "the community" necessitates a relatively free market atmosphere. It means the provision of alternative services and the right of patients to choose that service which more closely meets *their* idiosyncratic need. To close the options by creating catchment area boundaries is to imprison the people of that area and to insure their dependence on what could be an arbitrary mental health program, whether by professional design or by design of those "professional" community representatives who speak with neither mandate nor clear vision.

The dilemma becomes clearer, however, when we fully appreciate the impasse. Given a catchment area exclusivity, we find a community voice impossible or improbable in each of the four functional strategies open to it. This leaves us with a peculiar conclusion: A community mental health center is neither of the community, by the community, or for the community.

Given the reality of today's catchment area approach, with the consequent closed market for the consumer, the only viable functional role left for "the community" is as franchiser. As already noted, however, this will only be possible in rare instances. Again, at the risk of being overly redundant, let me restate that the concept of community in the foregoing refers to the evanescent *gemeinschaft* still to be found in oppressed populations. It refers to their collective, and therefore representative, needs and demands and *not* the interpreted needs and demands of a pseudocommunity as articulated by self-appointed "representatives."

COMMUNITY CONTROL: GRASSROOTS AND WEEDS

Community mental health centers face the same dilemma in relating to community as do all other service oriented institutions. They are considerably more at risk because of connotations of terms like mental illness and mental health. Having been born into times of accelerated change, they can hardly succeed in forging a self-identity. People are now "seeing" irrelevance in all or most institutions and so the wish or demand for institutional change runs rampant. "If they can't make their institution more relevant we will!" So goes the cry from the people . . . or at least some of the people. "They" are usually thought of as alien, hostile, and malevolent, while "we" are dedicated, altruistic, and intrinsically instrumental. In today's heightened atmosphere of confrontation, the way to resolve a problem is to "confront" it, and so it is pure logic to confront the caretakers.

The balance to the above is that many institutions are, in fact, unable to meet increased demands. The demands are now quantitatively and qualitatively more complex. The charge of irrelevance becomes an issue and a fact as long as the "demands" are not carefully defined and as long as priorities within institutions are not set. An institution that says to a community, "we shall attack mental illness" or "we shall promote mental health" is simply setting itself up for the rejoinder "you are irrelevant."

And so the issue of community influence, whether as the franchiser or as consumer, is integrally linked to the issue of program goals. Someone has to decide what these goals shall be. A community will never succeed in imposing its goals on a center that is unwilling to accept them and a center will never succeed in imposing its goals on a community if there are no consumers. The commonplace "battle for control" is an exercise in futility for both combatants.

A starting point is imperative. Let us start at the community end. If the foregoing has any merit, we can anticipate two relevant community roles: (1) as franchiser and (2) as consumer. Either of these roles are possible, but their possibility depends on the extant nature of the particular community in question. As I have indicated, a franchising community necessitates an existing "representative" body. The "incorporation" of interested community persons is an exercise in illusion. The incorporated body is as much a *special interest group* as any institution. Their special interest will emerge from their own narrow perspectives. To be willing to relate to such a franchising group is no different than relating to any institutional franchiser. To relate to a true community franchiser is desirable but difficult to attain.

What seems a rational premise is that the search for the "community" be abandoned. A search for the Grail would be as rewarding. What then should a mental health center set about to do vis-à-vis its "community"? Contrary to the romantic readiness to do the community will, a mental health center must know, in advance, what it is it can do and wishes to do. Armed with this sense of identity and purpose, it can turn to "its community" and identify itself. As part of its process of deciding what it is and what it can and wishes to do, it must also decide to what degree it wishes to balance its internal decision making processes by the inclusion of persons *identifiable* as (*a*) area residents; (*b*) vitally interested in the work of the center; (*c*) with the ability to conceptualize the types of problems and types of solutions involved; (*d*) with a willingness to participate and an ability to disagree as well as agree. This is "organizational sensitization," i.e., the conscious internal process of keeping an organization open to the life style and "needs" of its potential consumers. This is a process that should be initiated from within the center. It cannot easily be imposed from without because that breeds organizational coercion and not sensitization. If a center's leadership does not choose to support and welcome the voices of its potential consumers, then it simply will not have a sensitized organization. One may wish it to be otherwise, but the difference between rhetoric and performance lies within those who must perform. This is nowhere more true than in the highly personalized and complex task of intervening into human behavior. As long as an organization can maintain an internal system of self-regulation, so as to constantly focus and refocus on its task, it will remain viable. This internal system of self-regulation will not work well unless it is truly internalized, i.e., unless there are multilevel consumer-oriented inputs. No consumer-oriented institution can survive unless it pays attention to its market. The market research department, within consumer-oriented industry, is a fundamental system which keeps organizational goals relevant to consumer needs. An analogic system within community mental health centers is critical. The dependence on external inputs, such as with the common use of an advisory board structure, quickly degenerates into a pro forma relationship if there is no internal system of consumer influence.

Some centers have been able to maintain organizational sensitization by carefully seeing to it that area residents with the aforementioned criteria are hired for "meaningful" jobs within the center. The indigenous worker trend may be more important because of its influence as an agent of organizational sensitization than for its more explicit manpower resource role. If this is working well, then good balance can come from an advisory board structure, providing the advisors and the internal staff have open communication with each other.

The point to all of this is to demythologize the term community and refocus the issue around organizational sensitization. Simply stated, this means the awareness of an organization of the multiple problems, some subtle and some not, related to doing its task. It implies neither a predetermined task nor a task arrived at by representative election. Presumably, there are some tasks for which persons in the mental health professions are particularly suited, and some for which they are not. Once those tasks are made clear and decided on as organizational goals, then, and only then, should an organization turn to its potential consumer for help in maintaining its awareness to the problems in reaching its goals. If those goals are not the ultimate goals for a "community" (presuming those could be discovered), then it will simply become a service institution for a population group, with a priority (or "relevance") less than ultimate. It means being willing to see oneself as less than the savior institution and being willing to say to "community" voices, that the mental health center is not the grand instrument of social renovation.

ISSUE OF BLACK AND WHITE

This dilemma about community must be placed into perspective, especially in regards to its racial implications. The popularization of the concept of community is a corollary to the entire social awareness reaction of the last decade. One of the fundamental catalysts of this social consciousness has been, and continues to be, the Negro struggle for equality. The tragic dimensions of this social revolution dwarf other processes involved in institutional renovation. Nearly every institution is caught up in its own attempt at renewal, but the contagion and drama of the Negro plight has attached itself to these various institutions. Their own future course now becomes enmeshed in the working out of the black identity process.

It is conceivable that because community psychiatry has come into vogue in the wake of the black revolution, its own identity and working through will be confounded by the vagaries of the more historically profound movement. There is a double-edge sword here. On the one hand, the moral impetus of the black revolution has imbued the community psychiatry movement with an aura of moral righteousness and therefore its personnel has been enthusiastic and committed. On the other hand, it has created a whole series of illusory goals, abstractly related to sacred concepts of mental health, and therefore may have sealed its own ultimate frustration. Highly committed persons in an inevitably frustrating task . . . therein lies the potential tragic element.

The movements are distinct and separate. One, the black revolution, is profound and touches the total fabric of our social structure. The other, the community psychiatry movement, is a moment in time, a transition stage between a narrow view of care to the mentally ill and a broader view with yet uncertain borders. Each has its own goals and processes. To begin to apply the jargon of mental health, developed to understand the individual, to institutions, communities and value systems, is to invite the collective wrath of those whose expectations will have been raised beyond our capacity.

There are so many red herrings with racial implications in the community psychiatry movement that it is common to see the staff of a large urban mental health center devour itself as it seeks some new guilt reducing strategy. The amount of effort turned towards a therapeutic community approach becomes enormous. The irony, however, is that the object of this therapeutic preoccupation is the center staff *itself* and not those persons for whom, presumably, the center exists. To ignore the reality of racial bias and its effects on the personnel of a center would be naive, but preoccupation with organizational cleansing is a trap as self-limiting as any.

SELECTED REFERENCES

1. ARENSBERG, C. M., KIMBALL, S. T. *Culture and Community.* New York, Harcourt Brace & World Inc., 1965.
2. NISBET, R. A. *The Sociological Tradition.* New York, Basic Books, Inc., Publishers, 1966.
3. ARDREY, R. *The Territorial Imperative.* New York, Atheneum Publishers, 1966.
4. PASAMANICK, B., SCARPITTI, F. R., DINITZ, S. *Schizophrenics in the Community.* New York, Appleton-Century-Crofts, 1967.
5. SROLE, L., LANGER, T. S., MICHAEL, S. T., ET AL. *Mental Health in the Metropolis.* New York, McGraw-Hill Book Co., Inc., 1962.
6. SMITH, M. B., HOBBS, N. *The Community and the Community Mental Health Center.* Washington, D.C., American Psychological Association, 1966.
7. KELLAM, S. G., SCHIFF, S. K. The Woodlawn mental health center. *Soc. Sci. Rev.* 10:255, 1966.

Burton Gummer

A Power-Politics Approach to Social Welfare Organizations

The past decade has seen a steadily growing involvement of social workers in the planning and administration of the social services. This development in social work practice has been paralleled by the increased attention social work scholars have given to understanding the nature of the social welfare agency as a particular type of formal organization.[1] The knowledge generated by these studies has served, to a significant extent, as the theoretical infrastructure for the practice of planning and administration. Most of these studies, however, have had to rely on models for organizational analysis which are directed toward the economic organization. As understanding of the special characteristics of the social welfare enterprise has increased, it has become apparent that the standard paradigms for organizational analysis have serious limitations when applied to human-service organizations and that new models have to be constructed if we are to portray accurately the functioning of these kinds of organizations.

The purpose of this article is to relate a recent development in the field of organizational analysis, the application of political concepts to organizational behavior, to the social welfare organization, as a first step in constructing a framework for analysis that will be responsive to the special nature of the human-service agency. This article will proceed by first showing the limitations of some of the existing models

Reprinted from *Social Service Review* 52:3 (September 1978), pp. 349–61, with permission of the author and the University of Chicago Press. Copyright 1978 by the University of Chicago. All rights reserved.

for organizational analysis for the study of the social agency and then presenting the outlines of a "power-politics" approach which can overcome these limitations.

TWO THEMES IN THE STUDY OF ORGANIZATIONS

Of the many attempts to categorize the theories about formal organizations that have emerged in this century, one that stands out is Gouldner's seminal discussion of the organization as either a "rational" or a "natural-system" model.[2] In the first model, the organization ". . . is conceived as an 'instrument'—that is, as a rationally conceived means to the realization of expressly advanced group goals. Its structures are understood as tools deliberately established for the efficient realization of these group purposes."[3] This model is predicated on the assumption that the *raison d'être* of any organization is that it is the best (i.e., the most efficient) means for achieving a goal. Means and goals are the key variables within this model. The rational analysis of organizational behavior involves the identification, in specific and operational terms, of a goal or set of goals that an organization wishes to pursue and the selection of the best way (in terms of the most efficient use of organizational resources) for achieving them. The structure of an organization is seen as the most rational arrangement of its parts into a mechanism for efficient goal attainment.

In the natural-system model, the organization is seen as ". . . a 'natural whole,' or system. The realization of the goals of the system as a whole is but one of several important needs to which the organization is oriented. . . . The organization . . . strives to survive and to maintain its equilibrium, and this striving may persist even after its explicitly held goals have been successfully attained. . . . The natural-system model is typically based upon an underlying 'organismic' model which stresses the interdependence of the component parts."[4] The organizational system is viewed as consisting of subsystems, each of which performs a function needed for the system's continued operation. Katz and Kahn, for example, identify the major subsystems of an organization as those units responsible for the production of goods or services, procurement of resources, maintenance of internal patterns of behavior, adaptation to changes in the organization's environment, and management or the integration of all subsystems.[5] The system model stresses the integration of these interdependent parts in a way that will promote both the effective functioning of the system and its maintenance (i.e., preservation) as an autonomous unit.[6]

As with any theoretical framework, these models make certain initial assumptions about the phenomena they are directed to, and their usefulness is contingent upon the validity of these assumptions. The rational model, for example, makes assumptions about the nature of the organization's goals and its means (i.e., technologies) for pursuing those goals. In order to apply this model, an organization must have objectives that are clearly and concretely specified; there must be widespread support for these among key organizational members; the means for pursuing them must be developed to the point where one alternative can be clearly distinguished from another; and there must be some way of predicting the potential effectiveness and the costs involved in an alternative for meeting the objectives.

Because of the nature of these assumptions, this model has been, and continues

to be, used most often for the analysis of the economic organization; even there, several analysts question whether these assumptions are, in fact, valid.[7] Without getting into the debate of whether this model is appropriate for analyzing any organization, a strong case can be made that it is not appropriate for looking at the social welfare organization because the conditions upon which the model is predicated are absent in most of these organizations. Social welfare organizations are notorious for having goal statements that are so general and abstract that their usefulness in guiding decision making within the organization is practically nil. A major reason for this is that these organizations generally pursue objectives over which there is considerable disagreement in the larger society. This general lack of consensus about the purposes of social welfare has its counterpart within the profession itself, where there are major ideological differences about the goals of social services.[8] As Donnison has pointed out, all social welfare activities ultimately deal with some notion of the "social health" of the society. Moreover, he continues, "there is no generally understood state of 'social health' toward which all people strive; our disagreements on this question form the subject matter of politics the world over."[9] The result of this is that the societal mandate to the social welfare organization is usually vague and inchoate, a situation further compounded by dissension among the members of the organization itself.[10] Goal statements that come out of this milieu are most appropriately seen as political rhetoric, the function of which, as Kenneth Burke has shrewdly observed, is "to sharpen up the pointless and blunt the too sharply pointed."[11] While these kinds of amorphous statements serve an important purpose in enabling contending interests to develop a structure for dealing with their differences, they are not to be mistaken for specific and tangible statements of objectives that are necessary for rational decision making to occur.[12]

Besides clearly and concretely stated goals, the rational model assumes that the decision maker will be able to choose among competing means for achieving these goals. In order to do this, an organization's technologies must be advanced to the point that one method can be clearly distinguished from another and some estimate can be made of the potential effectiveness and costs of a particular one. This is certainly not the case in social work. The nature of casework as a technology, for instance, remains vague and diffuse, so that it is hard to specify exactly what activities are entailed, let alone assess their effectiveness in goal attainment or the costs involved.[13] The absence of the conditions necessary for rational decision making in most social welfare organizations means that these, rather than being arenas for rational action, conform more to what Cohen and his colleagues have referred to as "organized anarchies."[14]

The assumptions behind the natural-system model are no less problematic for the social welfare organization. Critical is the concept of homeostasis, which Thompson defines as a process of "self-stabilization, which spontaneously, or naturally, governs the necessary relationships among parts and activities and thereby keeps the system viable in the face of disturbances stemming from the environment."[15] This concept, moreover, proceeds from a further assumption of the existence in any given system of a high degree of interdependence among its subunits. That is, for homeostasis to be an operable concept, a system's subunits must be dependent upon each other to the extent that the system as a whole cannot function unless these units are properly integrated. The degree of system interdependence, however, is an empirical question and cannot be assumed. Gouldner sheds considerable light on the ways in which interdependence can vary in social systems through his concept of the "functional autonomy" of the parts of a system. Functional autonomy is defined as

". . . the degree to which any one part is dependent on others for the satisfaction of its needs. Systems in which parts have 'high' functional autonomy may be regarded as having a 'low' degree of system interdependence; conversely, systems in which parts have 'low' functional autonomy have a 'high' degree of system interdependence. The concept of functional autonomy directs attention to the fact that *some* parts may survive separation from others, that parts vary in their dependence upon one another, and that their interdependence is not necessarily symmetrical."[16]

An organization can be viewed in systemic terms and analyzed as such to the extent that it can be shown that the various units comprising it must rely on each other in order to get their work done. When this is not the case in a particular organization, the units are operating in a parallel rather than interdependent way, and it would be misleading to treat them as part of an integrated system of activities. While there is little empirical evidence regarding the extent of functional interdependence in social work agencies, the undifferentiated nature of the technology (e.g., casework) and the relatively limited division of labor in these organizations seem to show a low degree of interdependence among the units comprising them.

The concept of homeostasis is inextricably linked to another assumption within the natural-system model, namely, the existence of an unequivocal way to assess overall system functioning. That is, the model assumes that there is a criterion against which the performance of a given system can be measured and judged to be a success or a failure. The elusiveness of such a standard has plagued social system theorists since the introduction of this model into social science thinking.[17] When can one say that a system is not functioning? Any system that continues to exist as an autonomous unit can, in one sense, be said to be functioning. But sheer survival is only one way of looking at functioning. Function can also refer to the benefits that the system provides for another system, that is, its products or outputs; it is in this way that the term is usually used in the natural-system approach.[18] But therein lies the rub; the social welfare organization (and most nonprofit organizations) does not produce easily identifiable outputs. The central distinction between nonprofit and profit-making organizations is that the latter must relate to output markets which provide a usable standard for measuring their effectiveness in dollar terms. Downs's discussion of the impact of the absence of output markets on government bureaus is equally applicable to the social welfare organization: ". . . bureaus are economically one-faced rather than two-faced. They have input-markets where they buy the scarce resources they need to produce their outputs. But they face no economic markets whatever on the output side. Therefore, they have no direct way of evaluating their outputs in relation to the costs of the inputs used to make them. . . . The inability of bureaus to rely on markets as objective indicators of output value affects their entire operation."[19] The lack of output indicators in the nonprofit organization has led some analysts to argue that these organizations can only be evaluated in terms of their inputs, that is, their ability to attract increasing amounts of resources.[20]

The interrelationship of the three concepts of homeostasis, functional autonomy of subunits, and effective system functioning adds a new twist to the age-old dilemma of the chicken and the egg; namely, the rooster is now involved in this quandary. The lack of clear measures of system functioning (particularly in nonprofit organizations) prevents any realistic assessment of how well a system is integrated, even assuming that the parts of the system are, in fact, dependent on each other for their survival.

A POWER-POLITICS APPROACH

There is a third theme in the study of organizations that has appeared in the past decade or so; it will be referred to as the power-politics approach. This framework views the organization as essentially a political arena in which interest groups compete for the control of organizational resources. This approach seems particularly appropriate for analyzing and understanding social welfare organizations, because it does not rely on any of the assumptions contained in the frameworks discussed above. The power-politics approach, instead, proceeds from the central assumption that organizational members seek to promote their own self-interests. These interests are determined by one's place in the organization, place being a function of hierarchical position (vertical place) and functional specialty (horizontal place). One's behavior in an organization is thus assumed to be directed toward securing and enhancing one's place in the organization.[21] The interests of organizational members will be advanced through their ability to establish control over the resources coming into the organization.[22] Moreover, the processes employed by the members for this purpose are seen as essentially political.[23]

All students of organizations recognize the importance of resources, since organizations would cease to function if they were unable to secure a regular and sufficient supply to sustain their work. The students of the power-politics approach, however, draw attention to the fact that resources, aside from their importance in the organization's productive work, are also the bases for power on interpersonal, group, and organizational levels. Power has been defined as the ability of person A to control and direct the behavior of person B by means of A's control over resources needed by B.[24] Organizational power, by extension, is generated when a person or unit within the organization is able to establish more or less exclusive control over resources, thus enabling that person or unit to direct the behavior of others dependent upon those resources.[25] The power-politics approach stresses political processes as the primary way in which individuals or units are able to establish control over resources. Politics is defined by Banfield as "the activity (negotiation, argument, discussion, application of force, or persuasion) by which an issue is agitated or settled."[26] The issues to be settled in the political arena of the organization are how and by whom decisions about resource allocation are to be made. The following discussion will elaborate upon the nature of control over resources in the power-politics approach and show its applicability to the analysis of social welfare organizations.

RESOURCES. Yuchtman and Seashore define organizational resources as ". . . (more or less) generalized means, or facilities, that are potentially useable—however indirectly—in relationships between the organization and its environment."[27] Resources, then, can be considered as means for accomplishing organizational purposes that are "imported" by the organization from its environment. In the social welfare organization, for example, the principal resources are money, personnel, clients, and sanction from the community. Since the present concern is with resources as the bases for power in organizations, the two aspects of this definition that are most critical are the degrees to which resources are generalizable and controllable.

The generalizability of a resource has two dimensions: the degree to which one resource can be exchanged for another (what Yuchtman and Seashore call a resource's "liquidity"),[28] and the extent to which one resource can be used for a variety of purposes (which will be referred to here as its "transferability"). Money and credit are high in liquidity, while availabili-

ty of time and ideological commitment to a particular program are low. A psychiatrically trained social worker specializing in the problems of autistic children is an example of a highly nontransferable resource, while one with a generic background is a highly transferable resource within an agency. Organizations with resources that are high in liquidity and/or transferability can be expected to have a high level of internal political activity, due to the efforts of subunits to gain control of these resources. These kinds of resources, because of their generalizability, can be used by a variety of organizational units regardless of the unit's functional specialty.

The controllability of a resource refers to the ease with which individuals within the organization are able to establish control over its use. This, in turn, will be a function of the extent to which the resource comes into the organization unencumbered by external constraints on its use. The kinds of external constraints that can be placed on social welfare organizations regarding the use of resources range from the statutory prescriptions for public monies to client-advocacy groups' demands that clients be dealt with in ways specified by them.[29] The amount of external constraint placed on the use of an organizational resource, regardless of the generalizability of the resource itself, will affect the degree of political bargaining that can take place within the organization over the disposition of the resource. That is, resources designated for a particular use by an outside body cannot be bargained for within the organization. An example of a liquid resource that, while highly generalizable, has become less amenable to control by recipient organizations is the federal funds granted to the states in support of social services. In 1963 the federal government spent a little under $200 million in social services grants to the states; by 1972 this figure had risen to over $1.5 billion.[30]

Moreover, as Derthick points out in her astute analysis of this situation, the funds were "uncontrollable" (from the government's perspective) because the federal government attached few or no conditions to their use.[31] The lack of external constraints made these funds highly controllable by the recipient organization. Since 1972, however, the pendulum has swung in the opposite direction, with the federal government imposing stricter guidelines and accountability procedures on the use of these monies, thus reducing their controllability by recipient organizations.[32] The resource retained its liquidity—it is still money—but lost its controllability (by recipient organizations). Generalizability and controllability of resources together are the necessary and sufficient conditions for determining the absolute level of political activity within an organization.

CONTROL STRUCTURE. The control structure of an organization refers to the way that power is distributed within it. The aspect of the control or power structure that is most relevant here is the extent to which power is concentrated in the hands of a few individuals or dispersed among many throughout the organization. The first situation is usually referred to as a centralized control structure, while the second is a decentralized structure.[33]

Since power is based on control over resources, the amount of power an individual or unit is able to exercise will be directly related to the amount of resources at its disposal. In organizations where many units have access to resources, and no one unit is in a position to exercise control over the bulk of the resources coming in, we can speak of a highly diffuse power situation in which political activity among units will be high as they compete and negotiate with each other to secure and expand their share of resources. In organizations in which one unit is able to exercise total or near-total control over the bulk of the resources, there is a concentrated

power situation, and internal political activity will decrease. The latter situation can be analyzed in terms of the rational model of organizational behavior, since the dominant power group can establish its goals as the overall goals of the organization and can make rational decisions in pursuit of them since it has power to implement those decisions.

Politics and rationality can be seen in competition for determining resource distribution within an organization. In an economically oriented society such as ours there is a tendency toward rationality. That is, *ceteris paribus*, rational decisions will be preferred over nonrational ones. Rationality, however, assumes a clear statement of objectives and the ability to rank preferentially the alternatives for reaching them according to the criterion of efficiency. In the absence of these conditions another method for determining resource distribution must be found. The power-politics approach suggests that the ability to organize and agitate issues (i.e., to engage in political behavior) is a method of determining resource distribution that comes into play when the conditions for rational decision making are not present.

The proponents of the rational model argue that rationality determines the shape of the control structure; that is, those who have the most power in an organization should have that power because they are the ones most suited to direct the operations of the organization. The power-politics approach simply reverses this argument. The goals of an organization are not assumed, but evolve out of the struggle for control over resources. At any given time they are the goals of the group within the organization that has attained ascendancy (however temporary) in the competition for resources. Those who are able to gain control over resources are then able to impose their goals on the organization as a whole. Whatever rationality there is in the structure and operations of the organization is a function of the ability of one group to "seize the day," to establish its dominance over others through its control over resources.

THE POLITICS OF ORGANIZATIONAL CHANGE. Mayer Zald, one of the leading proponents of a political approach to studying organizations, argues that a central strength of this orientation is its insight into an understanding of the nature of organizational change. "The political-economy framework is not a substitute for decision-theory, the human-relations approach, or the concept of organizational rationality. For analysis of organizational change, however, it does claim to subsume these others."[34] The power-politics approach is explicitly concerned with the processes of organizational change. Flowing from its concern with resources as determinants of organizational behavior, its views change in organizations as primarily a function of the shifting patterns of resource availability. That is, as the kinds and amounts of resources available to an organization change, the internal arrangements for their control and distribution (i.e., the structure of the organization) can be expected to change in a process of organizational adaptation to its environment.

As a productive system an organization is constantly using up resources in its work. In the case of the social welfare organization, there must be a constant supply of money, clients, personnel, and community sanctions for it to function. These come from the organization's environment, which allocates resources for those things it "wants done or can be persuaded to support."[35] The organization is thus dependent upon its environment in the sense that it must adapt its internal structure and operations in order to respond to changing environmental requirements. The power-politics approach suggests that this process of adaptation can best be understood in terms of the capacities of different units in the organization to establish hegemony over others by means of their access to and control over new resources.

Within the power-politics framework the structure of an organization at any given time is seen as the product of the most recent struggle for power among organizational subunits, with the "winner" establishing the agenda for organizational action. The dominant unit is able to elevate its goals and priorities to those of the total organization. Why a particular unit is able to establish this control is a function of two factors: the degree to which the unit is organized to take action on its own behalf in negotiating for resources, and the relevance of its functional specialty to the demands placed on the organization by the environment. In a sense, the unit must be able to "sell" itself and have something to "sell." The second characteristic, moreover, will be in the long run the deciding factor in a struggle for control. A unit may have great potential for engaging in internal political struggles because of its cohesiveness, high morale, and effective and ambitious leadership, but be lacking in the functional specialization needed by the organization. It is possible that this unit may be able to establish control over resources because of its strength as a cohesive and purposive social unit. This victory, however, will be short lived unless the unit is able to acquire or develop the technical capabilities the organization needs to satisfy the expectations set by the environment.

Developments in the operation of public assistance programs over the past fifteen years offer an illustration of how this process works. Public assistance agencies generally entail three functional specializations: management, eligibility determination, and social services. The influence of social services rose steadily from 1945 to 1962.[36] Starting with the publication in 1945 of Charlotte Towle's *Common Human Needs*,[37] and ending with the passage of the 1962 amendments to the Social Security Act, the social service (i.e., casework) perspective came to dominate the entire public assistance operation. The functional specialty offered by caseworkers includes a method for individual rehabilitation and change through counseling. This unit was able to attain dominance within public assistance because of the congruence between its specialized skills and the prevailing mood of the time on financial dependency. Namely, the causes of poverty were to be found in the shortcomings and defects (usually of a psychological nature) of the poor, to be remedied by some form of psychological rehabilitation.[38] The goals of social workers became those of the overall public assistance program, and the 1962 amendments provided for the allocation of monies to expand the casework capacities of public welfare agencies.

Contrary to all expectations, the number of people receiving assistance rose dramatically in the 1960s.[39] As a result, the public agenda shifted from concern with rehabilitating the poor (assuming that that was once a real concern of the public at large and not just of social workers) to ways of dealing with the mounting costs of the public assistance program.[40] Federal and state legislatures began to redeploy public assistance funds away from service activities and placed the highest priority on the development of effective management. The influence of the caseworkers waned and the "age of the manager" arrived, with consequent changes in the internal structure of public assistance agencies.[41]

CONCLUSIONS

The power-politics approach directs attention to the critical role played by organizational resources and the impact that struggles for their control by members have on the overall structure and operations of the organization. The strongest criticism that can be leveled at any conceptual attempt to guide one's understanding of a situation is that it is irrelevant. This has been the basis of much of the criticism of both the rational and natural-system approaches to social welfare organizations. The power-politics approach starts from an assumption about organizational life that has a great deal of "face validity" and proceeds to identify variables and dynamics that are critical in shaping the actual operations of organizations. Because of this, the power-politics approach appears to have considerable potential for guiding thinking and research to produce fruitful results in our understanding of the realities of social welfare organizations.

NOTES

1. See, e.g., James R. Greenley and Stuart A. Kirk, "Organizational Characteristics and the Distribution of Services to Applicants," *Journal of Health and Social Behavior* 14, no. 1 (March 1973): 70–79; Archie Hanlan, "Casework Beyond Bureaucracy," *Social Casework* 52 (April 1971): 195–98; Dwight Harshbarger, "The Human Service Organization," in *A Handbook of Human Service Organizations,* ed. Harold W. Demone, Jr., and Dwight Harshbarger (New York: Behavioral Publications, 1974); Yeheskel Hasenfeld, "People Processing Organizations: An Exchange Approach," *American Sociological Review* 37, no. 3 (June 1972): 256–63; Ralph M. Kramer, "The Organizational Character of the Voluntary Service Agency in Israel," *Social Service Review* 49, no. 3 (September 1975): 321–43; David Street, Robert Vintner, and Charles Perrow, *Organization for Treatment: A Comparative Study of Institutions for Delinquents* (New York: Free Press, 1966); Robert D. Vintner, "Analysis of Treatment Organizations," *Social Work* 8, no. 3 (July 1963): 3–15; Mayer N. Zald, "Organizations as Polities: An Analysis of Community Organization Agencies," *Social Work* 11, no. 4 (October 1966): 56–65.
2. Alvin W. Gouldner, "Organizational Analysis," in *Sociology Today,* ed. Robert K. Merton, Leonard Bloom, and Leonard S. Cottrell (New York: Basic Books, 1959).
3. Ibid., p. 404.
4. Ibid., pp. 405–6.
5. Daniel Katz and Robert L. Kahn, *The Social Psychology of Organizations* (New York: John Wiley & Sons, 1966), pp. 39–47.
6. See Philip Selznick, "Foundations of the Theory of Organization," *American Sociological Review* 13, no. 1 (February 1948): 25–35.
7. See Petro Georgiou, "The Goal Paradigm and Notes toward a Counter Paradigm," *Administrative Science Quarterly* 18, no. 3 (September 1973): 291–310; J. Kenneth Benson, "Organizations:

A Dialectical View," *Administrative Science Quarterly* 22, no. 1 (March 1977): 1–21.

8. Clarke A. Chambers, "An Historical Perspective on Political Action vs. Individualized Treatment," in *Current Issues in Social Work Seen in Historical Perspective* (New York: Council on Social Work Education, 1962); William Schwartz, "Private Troubles and Public Issues: One Social Work Job or Two?" in *Social Welfare Forum, 1969* (New York: Columbia University Press, 1969).

9. David D. Donnison, "Observations on University Training for Social Workers in Great Britain and North America," *Social Service Review* 29 (December 1955): 341–50, quotation from pp. 349–50.

10. For an excellent analysis of the impact that vague, unspecified, or nonexistent goal formulations can have on the administration of a social welfare program see Martha Derthick, *Uncontrollable Spending for Social Services Grants* (Washington, D.C.: Brookings Institution, 1975), esp. pp. 1–14.

11. Kenneth Burke, *A Grammar of Motives* (New York: Prentice-Hall, Inc., 1945), p. 393.

12. See the discussion of the "expediency of abstraction" in Neil Gilbert and Harry Specht, *Dimensions of Social Welfare Policy* (Englewood Cliffs, N.J.: Prentice-Hall, Inc., 1974), pp. 91–95.

13. See, e.g., the discussion of the definitions of casework in Joel Fischer, "Is Casework Effective? A Review," *Social Work* 18, no. 1 (January 1973): 5–21.

14. "These are organizations—or decision situations—characterized by three properties. The first is problematic preferences. . . . The organization operates on the basis of a variety of inconsistent and ill-defined preferences. . . . The second property is unclear technology. Although the organization manages to survive and even produce, its own processes are not understood by its members. . . . The third property is fluid participation. Participants vary in the amount of time and effort they devote to different domains; involvement varies from one time to another" (Michael D. Cohen, James G. March, and Johan P. Olsen, "A Garbage Can Model of Organizational Choice," *Administrative Science Quarterly* 17, no. 1 [March 1972]: 1–25).

15. James D. Thompson, *Organizations in Action: Social Science Bases of Administrative Theory* (New York: McGraw-Hill Book Co., 1967), p. 7.

16. Gouldner (n. 2 above), p. 419, emphasis in original.

17. For discussions of this problem at the macrosocietal and the microorganizational levels, see David Lockwood, "Some Remarks on 'The Social System,'" *British Journal of Sociology* 7, no. 2 (June 1956): 134–46; and Benson (n. 7 above), pp. 1–21.

18. Parsons defines an organization as "a system which, as the attainment of its goal, 'produces' an identifiable something which can be utilized in some way by another system; that is, the output of the organization is, for some other system, an input." Talcott Parsons, "Suggestions for a Sociological Approach to the Theory of Organizations. I," *Administrative Science Quarterly* 1, no. 1 (June 1956): 64–65.

19. Anthony Downs, *Inside Bureaucracy* (Boston: Little, Brown & Co., 1967), pp. 29–30.

20. Ephraim Yuchtman and Stanley E. Seashore, "A Systems Resources Approach to Organizational Effectiveness," *American Sociological Review* 32, no. 6 (December 1967): 891–903; Downs, pp. 5–23.

21. See Andrew Pettigrew, *The Politics of Organizational Decision-Making* (London: Tavistock Publications, Ltd., 1973), pp. 17–18.

22. Paul E. White, "Resources as Determinants of Organizational Behavior," *Administrative Science Quarterly* 19, no. 3 (September 1974): 366–79; Mayer N. Zald, *Organizational Change: The Political Economy of the YMCA* (Chicago: University of Chicago Press, 1970).

23. Tom Burns, "Micro-Politics: Mechanisms of Institutional Change," *Administrative Science Quarterly* 6, no. 3 (December 1961): 257–81; Zald, *Organizational Change*, pp. 17–24, 232–40.

24. Walter Buckley, *Sociology and Modern Systems Theory* (Englewood Cliffs, N.J.: Prentice-Hall, Inc., 1967), pp. 176–85; Robert A. Dahl, "The Concept of Power," *Behavioral Science* 2 (July 1957): 201–15; Richard M. Emerson, "Power-Dependence Relations," *American Sociological Review* 27, no. 1 (February 1962): 31–41; John R. P. French, Jr., and Bertram Raven, "The Bases of Social Power," in *Group Dynamics: Research and Theory*, ed. Dorwin Cartwright and Alvin Zander, 3d ed. (New York: Harper & Row, 1968).

25. Arnold S. Tannenbaum, *Control in Organizations* (New York: McGraw-Hill Book Co., 1968), pp. 3–29.

26. Edward C. Banfield, "Note on Conceptual Scheme," in *Politics, Planning and the Public Interest*, ed. Martin Meyerson and Edward C. Banfield (Glencoe, Ill.: Free Press, 1955), p. 304.

27. Yuchtman and Seashore, p. 900.

28. Ibid.

29. See White, pp. 367–68.

30. Derthick (n. 10 above), p. 8, table 1.

31. Ibid., pp. 1–14.

32. Melvin Mogulof, "Elements of a Special-Revenue-Sharing Proposal for the Social Services: Goal Setting, Decategorization, Planning, and Evaluation," *Social Service Review* 47, no. 4 (December 1973): 593–604; Edward Newman and Jerry Turem, "The Crisis of Accountability," *So-*

cial Work 19, no. 1 (January 1974): 5–16; Bruce L. R. Smith, "Accountability and Independence in the Contract State," in *The Dilemma of Accountability in Modern Government: Independence versus Control*, ed. Bruce L. R. Smith and D. C. Hague (London: Macmillan Co., 1971).

33. Marshall W. Meyer, "The Two Authority Structures of Bureaucratic Organization," *Administrative Science Quarterly* 13, no. 2 (September 1968): 211–28.
34. Zald, *Organizational Change*, p. 241.
35. James D. Thompson and William J. McEwan, "Organizational Goals and Environment: Goal-Setting as an Interaction Process," *American Sociological Review* 23, no. 1 (February 1958): 23–31.
36. Charles E. Gilbert, "Policy-Making in Public Welfare: The 1962 Amendments," *Political Science Quarterly* 81, no. 2 (June 1966): 196–224; Alfred J. Kahn, "Social Services in Relation to

Income Security," *Social Service Review* 39 (December 1965): 381–89.
37. Charlotte Towle, *Common Human Needs*, rev. ed. (New York: National Association of Social Workers, Inc., 1965).
38. Samuel Mencher, "Perspectives on Recent Welfare Legislation, Fore and Aft," *Social Work* 8 (July 1963): 59–64; Irving F. Lukoff and Samuel Mencher, "A Critique of the Conceptual Foundation of the Community Research Associates," *Social Service Review* 36 (December 1962): 433–43.
39. John M. Lynch, "Trends in Number of AFDC Recipients: 1961–1965," *Welfare in Review* 5, no. 5 (May 1967): 7–13.
40. Edward Banfield, "Welfare: A Crisis without 'Solutions,'" *Public Interest*, no. 16 (Summer 1969), pp. 89–101.
41. Jerry S. Turem, "The Call for a Management Stance," *Social Work* 19, no. 5 (September 1974): 615–23.

Charles H. Levine

Organizational Decline and Cutback Management

Government organizations are neither immortal nor unshrinkable.[1] Like growth, organizational decline and death, by erosion or plan, is a form of organizational change; but all the problems of managing organizational change are compounded by a scarcity of slack resources.[2] This feature of declining organizations—the diminution of the cushion of spare resources necessary for coping with uncertainty, risking innovation, and rewarding loyalty and cooperation—presents for government a problem that simultaneously challenges the underlying premises and feasibility of both contemporary management systems and the institutions of pluralist liberal democracy.[3]

Reprinted with permission of the author and publisher from *Public Administration Review* 38:4 (July/August 1978), pp. 316–325. Copyright 1978 by The American Society for Public Administration, 1225 Connecticut Avenue, N.W., Washington, D.C. All rights reserved.

Growth and decline are issues of a grand scale usually tackled by only the most brave or foolhardy of macro social theorists. The division of scholarly labor between social theorists and students of management is now so complete that the link between the great questions of political economy and the more earthly problems of managing public organizations is rarely forged. This bifurcation is more understandable when one acknowledges that managers and organization analysts have for decades (at least since the Roosevelt Administration and the wide acceptance of Keynesian economics) been able to subsume their concern for societal level instability under broad assumptions of abundance and continous and unlimited economic growth.[4] Indeed, almost all of our public management strategies are predicated on assumptions of the continuing enlargement of public revenues and expenditures. These expansionist assumptions are particularly prevalent in public financial management systems that anticipate budgeting by incremental additions to a secure base.[5] Recent events and gloomy forecasts, however, have called into question the validity and generality of these assumptions and have created a need to reopen inquiry into the effects of resource scarcity on public organizations and their management systems. These events and forecasts, ranging from taxpayer revolts like California's successful Proposition 13 campaign and financial crises like the near collapse into bankruptcy of New York City's government and the agonizing retrenchment of its bureaucracy, to the foreboding predictions of the "limits of growth" modelers, also relink issues of political economy of the most monumental significance to practices of public management.[6]

We know very little about the decline of public organizations and the management of cutbacks. This may be because even though some federal agencies like the Works Progress Administration, Economic Recovery Administration, Department of Defense, National Aeronautics and Space Administration, the Office of Economic Opportunity, and many state and local agencies have expanded and then contracted,[7] or even died, the public sector as a whole has expanded enormously over the last four decades. In this period of expansion and optimism among proponents of an active government, isolated incidents of zero growth and decline have been considered anomalous; and the difficulties faced by the management of declining agencies coping with retrenchment have been regarded as outside the mainstream of public management concerns. It is a sign of our times—labeled by Kenneth Boulding as the "Era of Slowdown"—that we are now reappraising cases of public organization decline and death as exemplars and forerunners in order to provide strategies for the design and management of *mainstream* public administration in a future dominated by resource scarcity.[8]

The decline and death of government organizations is a symptom, a problem, and a contingency. It is a symptom of resource scarcity at a societal, even global, level that is creating the necessity for governments to terminate some programs, lower the activity level of others, and confront tradeoffs between new demands and old programs rather than to expand whenever a new public problem arises. It is a problem for managers who must maintain organizational capacity by devising new managerial arrangements within prevailing structures that were designed under assumptions of growth. It is a contingency for public employees and clients; employees who must sustain their morale and productivity in the face of increasing control from above and shrinking opportunities for creativity and promotion while clients must find alternative sources for the services governments may no longer be able to provide.

ORGANIZATIONAL DECLINE AND ADMINISTRATIVE THEORY

Growth is a common denominator that links contemporary management theory to its historical antecedents and management practices with public policy choices. William Scott has observed that ". . . organization growth creates organizational abundance, or surplus, which is used by management to buy off internal consensus from the potentially conflicting interest group segments that compete for resources in organizations."[9] As a common denominator, growth has provided a criterion to gauge the acceptability of government policies and has defined many of the problems to be solved by management action and organizational research. So great is our enthusiasm for growth that even when an organizational decline seems inevitable and irreversible, it is nearly impossible to get elected officials, public managers, citizens, or management theorists to confront cutback and decremental planning situations as anything more than temporary slowdowns. Nevertheless, the reality of zero growth and absolute decline, at least in some sectors, regions, communities, and organizations, means that management and public policy theory must be expanded to incorporate non-growth as an initial condition that applies in some cases. If Scott's assertions about the pervasiveness of a growth ideology in management are correct, our management and policy paradigms will have to be replaced or augmented by new frameworks to help to identify critical questions and strategies for action. Put squarely, without growth, how do we manage public organizations?

We have no ready or comprehensive answers to this question, only hunches and shards of evidence to serve as points of departure. Under conditions and assumptions of decline, the ponderables, puzzles, and paradoxes of organizational management take on new complexities. For example, organizations cannot be cut back by merely reversing the sequence of activity and resource allocation by which their parts were originally assembled. Organizations are organic social wholes with emergent qualities which allow their parts to recombine into intricately interwoven semilattices when they are brought together. In his study of NASA's growth and drawdown, Paul Schulman has observed that viable public programs must attain "capture points" of public goal and resource commitments, and these organizational thresholds or "critical masses" are characterized by their indivisibility.[10] Therefore, to attempt to disaggregate and cutback on one element of such an intricate and delicate political and organization arrangement may jeopardize the functioning and equilibrium of an entire organization.

Moreover, retrenchment compounds the choice of management strategies with paradoxes. When slack resources abound, money for the development of management planning, control, information systems, and the conduct of policy analysis is plentiful even though these systems are rel-

atively irrelevant to decision making.[11] Under conditions of abundance, habit, intuition, snap judgments and other forms of informal analysis will suffice for most decisions because the costs of making mistakes can be easily absorbed without threatening the organization's survival.[12] However, in times of austerity, when these control and analytic tools are needed to help to minimize the risk of making mistakes, the money for their development and implementation is unavailable.

Similarly, without slack resources to produce "win-win" consensus-building solutions and to provide side payments to overcome resistance to change, organizations will have difficulty innovating and maintaining flexibility. Yet, these are precisely the activities needed to maintain capacity while contracting, especially when the overriding imperative is to minimize the perturbations of adjusting to new organizational equilibriums at successively lower levels of funding and activity.[13]

Lack of growth also creates a number of serious personnel problems. For example, the need to reward managers for directing organizational contraction and termination is a problem because without growth there are few promotions and rewards available to motivate and retain successful and loyal managers—particularly when compared to job opportunities for talented managers outside the declining organization.[14] Also, without expansion, public organizations that are constrained by merit and career tenure systems are unable to attract and accommodate new young talent. Without an inflow of younger employees, the average age of employees is forced up, and the organization's skill pool becomes frozen at the very time younger, more flexible, more mobile, less expensive and (some would argue) more creative employees are needed.[15]

Decline forces us to set some of our logic for rationally structuring organizations on end and upside down. For instance, under conditions of growth and abundance, one problem for managers and organizational designers is how to set up *exclusionary* mechanisms to prevent *"free riders"* (employees and clients who share in the consumption of the organization's collective benefits without sharing the burden that produced the benefit) from taking advantage of the enriched common pool of resources. In contrast, under conditions of decline and austerity, the problem for managers and organizational designers is how to set up *inclusionary* mechanisms to prevent organizational participants from avoiding the sharing of the *"public bads"* (increased burdens) that result from the depletion of the common pool of resources.[16] In other words, to maintain order and capacity when undergoing decline, organizations need mechanisms like long-term contracts with clauses that make pensions non-portable if broken at the employee's discretion. These mechanisms need to be carefully designed to penalize and constrain *"free exiters"* and cheap exits at the convenience of the employees while still allowing managers to cut and induce into retirement marginally performing and unneeded employees.

As a final example, inflation erodes steady states so that staying even actually requires extracting more resources from the organization's environment and effectuating greater internal economies. The irony of managing decline in the public sector is particularly compelling under conditions of recession or so called "stagflation." During these periods of economic hardship and uncertainty, pressure is put on the federal government to follow Keynesian dictates and spend more through deficit financing; at the same time, critical public opinion and legal mandates require some individual agencies (and many state and local governments) to balance their budgets, and in some instances to spend less.

These characteristics of declining public organizations are like pieces of a subtle jigsaw puzzle whose parameters can only be guessed at and whose abstruseness deepens with each new attempt to fit its edges together. To overcome our tendency to regard decline in public organizations as anomalous, we need to develop a catalogue of what we already know about declining public organizations. A typology of *causes* of public organizational decline and corresponding sets of *tactics* and *decision rules* available for managing cutbacks will serve as a beginning.

THE CAUSES OF PUBLIC ORGANIZATION DECLINE

Cutting back any kind of organization is difficult, but a good deal of the problem of cutting back public organizations is compounded by their special status as authoritative, nonmarket extensions of the state.[17] Public organizations are used to deliver services that usually have no direct or easily measurable monetary value or when market arrangements fail to provide the necessary level of revenues to support the desired level or distribution of services. Since budgets depend on appropriations and not sales, the diminution or termination of public organizations and programs or conversely their maintenance and survival are political matters usually calling for the application of the most sophisticated attack or survival tactics in the arsenal of the skilled bureaucrat-politician.[18] These strategies are not universally propitious; they are conditioned by the causes for decline and the hoped-for results.

The causes of public organization decline can be categorized into a four-cell typology as shown in Figure 1. The causes are divided along two dimensions: (a) whether they are primarily the result of

Figure 1 Causes of Public Organization Decline

	INTERNAL	EXTERNAL
Political	Political Vulnerability	Problem Depletion
Economic/ Technical	Organizational Atrophy	Environmental Entropy

conditions located either internal or external to the organization, or (b) whether they are principally a product of political or economic/technical conditions.[19] This is admittedly a crude scheme for lumping instances of decline, but it does cover most cases and allows for some abstraction.

Of the four types, *problem depletion* is the most familiar. It covers government involvement in short-term crises like natural disasters such as floods and earthquakes, medium length governmental interventions like war mobilization and countercyclical employment programs, and longer-term public programs like polio research and treatment and space exploration—all of which involve development cycles. These cycles are characterized by a political definition of a problem followed by the extensive commitment of resources to attain critical masses and then contractions after the problem has been solved, alleviated, or has evolved into a less troublesome stage or politically popular issue.[20]

Problem depletion is largely a product of forces beyond the control of the affected organization. Three special forms of problem depletion involve demographic shifts, problem redefinition, and policy termination. The impact of demographic shifts has been vividly demonstrated in the closing of schools in neighborhoods where the school age population has shrunk. While the cause for most school closings is usually neighborhood aging—a factor outside the control of the school system—the decision to close a school is largely political. The effect of problem redefinition on public organizations is most easily illustrated by movements to *de*institutionalize the mentally ill. In these cases, the core bureaucracies responsible for treating these populations in institutions has shrunk as the rising per patient cost of hospitalization has combined witb pharmaceutical advances in antidepressants and tranquilizers to cause public attitudes and professional doctrine to shift.[21]

Policy termination has both theoretical import and policy significance. Theoretically, it is the final phase of a public policy intervention cycle and can be defined as ". . . the deliberate conclusion or cessation of specific government functions, programs, policies, or organizations."[22] Its policy relevance is underscored by recent experiments and proposals for sunset legislation which would require some programs to undergo extensive evaluations after a period of usually five years and be reauthorized or be terminated rather than be continued indefinitely.[23]

Environmental entropy occurs when the capacity of the environment to support the public organization at prevailing levels of activity erodes.[24] This type of decline covers the now familiar phenomena of financially troubled cities and regions with declining economic bases. Included in this category are: market and technological shifts like the decline in demand for domestic textiles and steel and its effect on the economies and quality of life in places like New England textile towns and steel cities like Gary, Indiana, Bethlehem, Pennsylvania, and Youngstown, Ohio,[25] transportation changes that have turned major railroad hubs and riverports of earlier decades into stagnating and declining economies; mineral depletion which has crippled mining communities; and intrametropolitan shifts of economic activity from central cities to their suburbs.[26] In these cases, population declines often have paralleled general economic declines which erode tax bases and force cities to cut services. One of the tragic side effects of environmental entrophy is that it most severely affects those who cannot move.[27] Caught in the declining city and region are the immobile and dependent: the old, the poor, and the unemployable. For these communities, the forced choice of cutting services to an ever more dependent and needy population is the cruel outcome of decline.[28]

Environmental entropy also has a political dimension. As Proposition 13 makes clear, the capacity of a government is as much a function of the willingness of tax-payers to be taxed as it is of the economic base of the taxing region. Since the demand for services and the supply of funds to support them are usually relatively independent in the public sector, taxpayer resistance can produce diminished revenues which force service reductions even though the demand and *need* for services remains high.

The *political vulnerability* of public organizations is an internal property indicating a high level of fragility and precariousness which limits their capacity to resist budget decrements and demands to contract from their environment. Of the factors which contribute to vulnerability, some seem to be more responsible for decline and death than others. Small size, internal conflict, and changes in leadership, for example, seem less telling than the lack of a base of expertise or the absence of a positive self-image and history of excellence. However, an organization's age may be the most accurate predictor of bureaucratic vulnerability. Contrary to biological reasoning, aged organizations are more flexible than young organizations and therefore rarely die or even shrink very much. Herbert Kaufman argues that one of the advantages of organizations over solitary individuals is that they do provide longer institutional memories than a human lifetime, and this means that older organizations ought to have a broader range of adaptive skills, more capacity for learning, more friends and allies, and be more innovative because they have less to fear from making a wrong decision than a younger organization.[29]

Organizational atrophy is a common phenomenon in all organizations but government organizations are particularly vulnerable because they usually lack market generated revenues to signal a malfunction and to pinpoint responsibility. Internal atrophy and declining performance which can lead to resource cutbacks or to a weakening of organizational capacity come from a host of system and management failures almost too numerous to identify. A partial list would include: inconsistent and perverse incentives, differentiation without integration, role confusion, decentralized authority with vague responsibility, too many inappropriate rules, weak oversight, stifled dissent and upward communication, rationalization of performance failure by "blaming the victim," lack of self-evaluating and self-correcting capacity, high turnover, continuous politicking for promotions and not for program resources, continuous reorganization, suspicion of outsiders, and obsolescence caused by routine adherence to past methods and technologies in the face of changing problems. No organization is immune from these problems and no organization is likely to be afflicted by them all at once, but a heavy dose of some of these breakdowns in combination can contribute to an organization's decline and even death.

Identifying and differentiating among these four types of decline situations provides a start toward cataloging and estimating the appropriateness of strategies for managing decline and cutbacks. This activity is useful because when undergoing decline, organizations face three decision tasks: first, management must decide whether it will adopt a strategy to resist decline or smooth it (i.e., reduce the impact of fluctuations in the environment that cause interruptions in the flow of work and poor performance); second, given this choice of maneuvering strategies it will have to decide what tactics are most appropriate,[30] and third, if necessary, it will have to make decisions about how and where cuts will occur. Of course, the cause of a decline will greatly affect these choices.

Strategic Choices

Public organizations behave in response to a mix of motives—some aimed at serving national (or state or local) purposes, some aimed at goals for the *organization as a whole*, and others directed toward the particularistic goals of organizational subunits. Under conditions of growth, requests for more resources by subunits usually can be easily concerted with the goals of the organization as a whole and its larger social purposes. Under decline, however, subunits usually respond to requests to make cuts in terms of their particular long-term survival needs (usually defended in terms of the injury which cutbacks would inflict on a program with lofty purposes or on a dependent clientele) irrespective of impacts on the performance of government or the organization as a whole.

The presence of powerful survival instincts in organizational subunits helps to explain why the political leadership of public organizations can be trying to respond to legislative or executive directives to cut back while at the same time the career and program leadership of subunits will be taking action to resist cuts.[31] It also helps to explain why growth can have the appearance of a rational administrative process complete with a hierarchy of objectives and broad consensus, while decline takes on the *appearance* of what James G. March has called a "garbage can problem"—arational, polycentric, fragmented, and dynamic.[32] Finally, it allows us to understand why the official rhetoric about cutbacks—whether it be to "cut the fat," "tighten our belts," "preserve future options," or "engage in a process of orderly and programmed termination"—is often at wide variance with the unofficial conduct of bureau chiefs who talk of "minimizing cutbacks to mitigate catastrophe," or "making token sacrifices until the heat's off."

Retrenchment politics dictate that organizations will respond to decrements with a mix of espoused and operative strategies that are not necessarily consistent.[33] When there is a wide divergence between the official pronouncements about the necessity for cuts and the actual occurrence of cuts, skepticism, cynicism, distrust, and noncompliance will dominate the retrenchment process and cutback management will be an adversarial process pitting top and middle management against one another. In most cases, however, conflict will not be rancorous, and strategies for dealing with decline will be a mixed bag of tactics intended either to *resist* or to *smooth* decline. The logic here is that no organization accedes to cuts with enthusiasm and will try to find a way to resist cuts; but resistance is risky. In addition to the possibility of being charged with nonfeasance, no responsible manager wants to be faced with the prospect of being unable to control where cuts will take place or confront quantum cuts with unpredictable consequences. Instead, managers will choose a less risky course and attempt to protect organizational capacity and procedures by smoothing decline and its effects on the organization.

An inventory of some of these cutback management tactics is presented in Figure 2. They are arrayed according to the type of decline problem which they can be employed to solve. This collection of tactics by no means exhausts the possible organizational responses to decline situations, nor are all the tactics exclusively directed toward meeting a single contingency. They are categorized in order to show that many familiar coping tactics correspond, even if only roughly, to an underlying logic. In this way a great deal of information about organizational responses to decline can be aggregated without explicating each tactic in great detail.[34]

The tactics intended to remove or alleviate the external political and economic causes of decline are reasonably straightforward means to revitalize eroded economic bases, reduce environmental uncertainty, protect niches, retain flexibility, or lessen dependence. The tactics for handling the internal causes of decline, however, tend to be more subtle means for strengthening organizations and managerial control. For instance, the management of decline *in the face of resistance* can be

Figure 2 Some Cutback Management Tactics

	TACTICS TO RESIST DECLINE	TACTICS TO SMOOTH DECLINE
External Political	(Problem Depletion) 1. Diversify programs, clients and constituents 2. Improve legislative liaison 3. Educate the public about the agency's mission 4. Mobilize dependent clients 5. Become "captured" by a powerful interest group or legislator 6. Threaten to cut vital or popular programs. 7. Cut a visible and widespread service a little to demonstrate client dependence	1. Make peace with competing agencies 2. Cut low prestige programs 3. Cut programs to politically weak clients 4. Sell and lend expertise to other agencies 5. Share problems with other agencies
Economic/ Technical	(Environmental Entropy) 1. Find a wider and richer revenue base (e.g., metropolitan reorganization) 2. Develop incentives to prevent disinvestment 3. Seek foundation support 4. Lure new public and private sector investment 5. Adopt user charges for services where possible	1. Improve targeting on problems 2. Plan with preservative objectives 3. Cut losses by distinguishing between capital investments and sunk costs 4. Yield concessions to taxpayers and employers to retain them
Internal Political	(Political Vulnerability) 1. Issue symbolic responses like forming study commissions and task forces 2. "Circle the wagons," i.e., develop a seige mentality to retain esprit de corps 3. Strengthen expertise	1. Change leadership at each stage in the decline process 2. Reorganize at each stage 3. Cut programs run by weak subunits 4. Shift programs to another agency 5. Get temporary exemption from personnel and budgetary regulations which limit discretion
Economic/ Technical	(Organizational Atrophy) 1. Increase hierarchical control 2. Improve productivity 3. Experiment with less costly service delivery systems 4. Automate 5. Stockpile and ration resources	1. Renegotiate long term contracts to regain flexibility 2. Install rational choice techniques like zero-base budgeting and evaluation research 3. Mortgage the future by deferring maintenance and downscaling personnel quality 4. Ask employees to make voluntary sacrifices like taking early retirements and deferring raises 5. Improve forecasting capacity to anticipate further cuts 6. Reassign surplus facilities to other users 7. Sell surplus property, lease back when needed 8. Exploit the exploitable

smoothed by changes in leadership. When hard unpopular decisions have to be made, new managers can be brought in to make the cuts, take the flak, and move on to another organization. By rotating managers into and out of the declining organization, interpersonal loyalties built up over the years will not interfere with the cutback process. This is especially useful in implementing a higher level decision to terminate an organization where managers will make the necessary cuts knowing that their next assignments will not depend on their support in the organization to be terminated.

The "exploit the explitable" tactic also calls for further explanation. Anyone familiar with the personnel practices of universities during the 1970's will recognize this tactic. It has been brought about by the glutted market for academic positions which has made many unlucky recent Ph.D.s vulnerable and exploitable. This buyers' market has coincided neatly with the need of universities facing steady states and declining enrollments to avoid long-term tenure commitments to expensive faculties. The result is a marked increase in part-time and non-tenure track positions which are renewed on a semester-to-semester basis. So while retrenchment is smoothed and organization flexibility increased, it is attained at considerable cost to the careers and job security of the exploited teachers.

Cutback management is a two-crucible problem: besides selecting tactics for either resisting or smoothing decline, if necessary, management must also select who will be let go and what programs will be curtailed or terminated. Deciding where to make cuts is a test of managerial intelligence and courage because each choice involves tradeoffs and opportunity costs that cannot be erased through the generation of new resources accrued through growth.

As with most issues of public management involving the distribution of costs, the choice of decision rules to allocate cuts usually involves the tradeoff between equity and efficiency.[35] In this case, "equity" is meant to mean the distribution of cuts across the organization with an equal probability of hurting all units and employees irrespective of impacts on the longterm capacity of the organization. "Efficiency" is meant to mean the sorting, sifting, and assignment of cuts to those people and units in the organization so that for a given budget decrement, cuts are allocated to minimize the long-term loss in total benefits to the organization as a whole, irrespective of their distribution.

Making cuts on the basis of equity is easier for managers because it is socially acceptable, easier to justify, and involves few decisionmaking costs. "Sharing the pain" is politically expedient because it appeals to common sense ideals of justice. Further, simple equity decision making avoids costs from sorting, selecting, and negotiating cuts.[36] In contrast, efficiency cuts involve costly triage analysis because the distribution of pain and inconvenience requires that the value of people and subunits to the organization have to be weighed in terms of their expected *future* contributions. In the public sector, of course, things are never quite this clear cut because a host of constraints like career status, veteran's preference, bumping rights, entitlements, and mandated programs limit managers from selecting optimal rules for making cuts. Nevertheless, the values of equity and efficiency are central to allocative decision making and provide useful criteria for judging the appropriateness of cutback rules. By applying these criteria to five of the most commonly used or proposed cutback methods—seniority, hiring freezes, even-percentage-cuts-across-the-board, productivity criteria, and zero base budgeting—we are able to make assessments of their efficacy as managerial tools.

Seniority is the most prevalent and most maligned of the five decision rules. Seniority guarantees have little to do with either equity or efficiency, *per se*. Instead, they are directed at another value of public administration; that is, the need to provide secure career-long employment to neutrally competent civil servants.[37] Because seniority is likely to be spread about the organization, unevenly, using seniority criteria for making cuts forces managers to implicitly surrender control over the impact of cuts on services and the capacity of subunits. Furthermore, since seniority usually dictates a "last-in-first-out" retention system, personnel cuts using this decision rule tend to inflict the greatest harm to minorities and women who are recent entrants in most public agencies.

A *hiring freeze* is a convenient short-run strategy to buy time and preserve options. In the short run it hurts no one already employed by the organization because hiring freezes rely on "natural attrition" through resignations, retirements, and death to diminish the size of an organization's work force. In the long run, however, hiring freezes are hardly the most equitable or efficient way to scale down organizational size. First, even though natural and self selection relieves the stress on managers, it also takes control over the decision of whom and where to cut away from management and thereby reduces the possibility of intelligent long range cutback planning. Second, hiring freezes are more likely to harm minorities and women who are most likely to be the next hired rather than the next retired. Third, attrition will likely occur at different rates among an organization's professional and technical specialties. Since resignations will most likely come from those employees with the most opportunities for employment elsewhere, during a long hiring freeze an organization may find itself short on some critically needed skills yet unable to hire people with these skills even though they may be available.

Even-percentage-cuts-across-the-board are expedient because they transfer decision-making costs lower in the organization, but they tend to be insensitive to the needs, production functions, and contributions of different units. The same percentage cut may call for hardly more than some mild belt tightening in some large unspecialized units but when translated into the elimination of one or two positions in a highly specialized, tightly integrated small unit, it may immobilize that unit.

Criticizing *productivity criteria* is more difficult but nevertheless appropriate, especially when the concept is applied to the practice of cutting low producing units and people based on their *marginal product* per increment of revenue. This method is insensitive to differences in clients served, unit capacity, effort, and need. A more appropriate criterion is one that cuts programs, organization units, and employees so that the *marginal utility* for a decrement of resources is equal across units, individuals, and programs thereby providing for *equal sacrifices* based on the *need* for resources. However, this criterion assumes organizations are fully rational actors, an assumption easily dismissed. More likely, cuts will be distributed by a mix of analysis and political bargaining.

Aggregating incompatible needs and preferences is a political problem and this is why *zero base budgeting* gets such high marks as a method for making decisions about resource allocation under conditions of decline. First, ZBB is future directed; instead of relying on an "inviolate-base-plus-increment" calculus, it allows for the analysis of both existing and proposed new activities. Second, ZBB allows for tradeoffs between programs or units below their present funding levels. Third, ZBB allows a ranking of decision packages by political bargaining and negotiation so that attention is concentrated on those packages or activities most likely to be affected by cuts.[38] As a result, ZBB allows both analysis and politics to enter into cutback decision making and therefore can incorporate an expression of the *intensity of need* for resources by participating managers and clients while also accommodating estimates of how cuts will affect the *activity levels* of their units. Nevertheless, ZBB is not without problems. Its analytic component is likely to be expensive—especially so under conditions of austerity—and to be subject to all the limitations and pitfalls of cost-benefit analysis, while its political component is likely to be costly in political terms as units fight with each other and with central management over rankings, tradeoffs, and the assignment of decrements.[39]

These five decision rules illustrate how strategic choices about cutback management can be made with or without expediency, analysis, courage, consideration of the organization's long-term health, or the effect of cuts on the lives of employees and clients. Unfortunately, for some employees and clients, and the public interest, the choice will usually be made by managers to "go along" quietly with across-the-board cuts and exit as soon as possible. The alternative for those who would prefer more responsible and toughminded decision making *to facilitate long run organizational survival* is to develop in managers and employees strong feelings of organizational loyalty and loyalty to clients, to provide disincentives to easy exit, and to encourage participation so that dissenting views on the location of cuts could emerge from the ranks of middle management, lower level employees, and clients.[40]

Ponderables

The world of the future is uncertain, but scarcity and tradeoffs seem inevitable. Boulding has argued, "in a stationary society roughly half the society will be experiencing decline while the other half will be experiencing growth."[41] If we are entering an era of general slowdown, this means that the balance in the distribution between expanding and contracting sectors, regions, and organizations will be tipped toward decline. It means that we will need

a governmental capacity for developing tradeoffs between growing and declining organizations and for intervening in regional and sectorial economies to avoid the potentially harmful effects of radical perturbations from unmanaged decline.

So far we have managed to get along without having to make conscious tradeoffs between sectors and regions. We have met declines on a "crisis-to-crisis" basis through emergency legislation and financial aid. This is a strategy that assumes declines are special cases of temporary disequilibrium, bounded in time and space, that are usually confined to a single organization, community, or region. A broad scale long-run *societal level* decline, however, is a problem of a different magnitude and to resolve it, patchwork solutions will not suffice.

There seem to be two possible directions in which to seek a way out of immobility. First is the authoritarian possibility; what Robert L. Heilbroner has called the rise of "iron governments" with civil liberties diminished and resources allocated throughout society from the central government without appeal.[42] This is a possibility abhorrent to the democratic tradition, but it comprises a possible future—if not for the United States in the near future, at least for some other less affluent nations. So far we have had little experience with cutting back on rights, entitlements, and prvileges; but scarcity may dictate "decoupling" dependent and less powerful clients and overcoming resistance through violent autocratic implementation methods.

The other possible future direction involves new images and assumptions about the nature of man, the state and the ecosystem. It involves changes in values away from material consumption, a gradual withdrawal from our fascination with economic growth, and more efficient use of resources—especially raw materials. For this possibility to occur, we will have to have a confrontation with our propensity for wishful thinking that denies that some declines are permanent. Also required is a widespread acceptance of egalitarian norms and of antigrowth and no growth ideologies which are now only nascent, and the development of a political movement to promote their incorporation into policymaking.[43] By backing away from our obsession with growth, we will also be able to diminish the "load" placed on central governments and allow for greater decentralization and the devolvement of functions.[44] In this way, we may be able to preserve democratic rights and processes while meeting a future of diminished resources.

However, the preferable future might not be the most probable future. This prospect should trouble us deeply.

NOTES

1. The intellectual foundations of this essay are too numerous to list. Three essays in particular sparked my thinking: Herbert Kaufman's *The Limits of Organizational Change* (University, Alabama: The University of Alabama Press, 1971) and *Are Government Organizations Immortal?* (Washington, DC: The Brookings Institution, 1976) and Herbert J. Gans, "Planning for Declining and Poor Cities," *Journal of the American Institute of Planners* (September, 1975), pp. 305–307. The concept of "cutback planning" is introduced in the Gans article. My initial interest in this subject stemmed from my work with a panel of the National Academy of Public Administration on a NASA-sponsored project that produced *Report of the Ad Hoc Panel on Attracting New Staff and Retaining Capability During a Period of Declining Manpower Ceilings.*

2. For an explication of the concept of "organizational slack" see Richard M. Cyert and James G. March, *A Behavioral Theory of the Firm* (Englewood Cliffs, N.J.: Prentice-Hall, 1963), pp. 36–38. They argue that because of market imperfections between payments and demands "there is ordinarily a disparity between the resources available to the organization and the payments required to maintain the coalition. This difference between total resources and total necessary payments is what we have called *organizational slack.* Slack consists in payments to members of the coalition in excess of what is required to maintain the organization. . . .

Many forms of slack typically exist: stockholders are paid dividends in excess of those required to keep stockholders (or banks) within the organization; prices are set lower than necessary to maintain adequate income from buyers; wages in excess of those required to maintain labor are paid; executives are provided with services and personal luxuries in excess of those required to keep them; subunits are permitted to grow without real concern for the relation between additional payments and additional revenue; public services are provided in excess of those required. . . . Slack operates to stabilize the system in two ways: (1) by absorbing excess resources, it retards upward adjustment of aspirations during relatively good times; (2) by providing a pool of emergency resources, it permits aspirations to be maintained (and achieved) during relatively bad times."

3. See William G. Scott, "The Management of Decline," *The Conference Board RECORD* (June, 1976), pp. 56–59 and "Organization Theory: A Reassessment," *Academy of Management Journal* (June, 1974) pp. 242–253; also Rufus E. Miles, Jr., *Awakening from the American Dream: The Social and Political Limits to Growth* (New York: Universal Books, 1976).

4. See Daniel M. Fox, *The Discovery of Abundance: Simon N. Patten and the Transformation of Social Theory* (Ithaca, N.Y.: Cornell University Press, 1967).

5. See Andrew Glassberg's contribution to this symposium, "Organizational Responses to Municipal Budget Decreases," and Edward H. Potthoff, Jr., "Pre-planning for Budget Reductions," *Public Management* (March, 1975), pp. 13–14.

6. See Donella H. Meadows, Dennis L. Meadows, Jorgen Randers, and William W. Behrens III, *The Limits to Growth* (New York: Universe Books, 1972); also Robert L. Heilbroner, *An Inquiry into the Human Prospect* (New York: W. W. Norton, 1975) and *Business Civilization in Decline* (New York: W. W. Norton, 1976).

7. See Advisory Commission on Intergovernmental Relations, *City Financial Emergencies: The Intergovernmental Dimension* (Washington, D.C.: U.S. Government Printing Office, 1973).

8. Kenneth E. Boulding, "The Management of Decline," *Change* (June, 1975), pp. 8–9 and 64. For extensive analyses of cutback management in the same field that Boulding addresses, university administration, see: Frank M. Bowen and Lyman A. Glenny, *State Budgeting for Higher Education: State Fiscal Stringency and Public Higher Education* (Berkeley, Calif.: Center for Research and Development in Higher Education, 1976); Adam Yarmolinsky, "Institutional Paralysis,"

Special Report on American Higher Education: Toward an Uncertain Future 2 Vol, *Daedalus* 104 (Winter 1975), pp. 61–67; Frederick E. Balderston, *Varieties of Financial Crisis*, (Berkeley, Calif.: Ford Foundation, 1972); The Carnegie Foundation for the Advancement of Teaching, *More Than Survival* (San Francisco: Jossey-Bass, 1975); Earl F. Cheit, *The New Depression in Higher Education* (New York: McGraw-Hill, 1975) and *The New Depression in Higher Education—Two Years Later* (Berkeley, Calif.: The Carnegie Commission on Higher Education, 1973); Lyman A. Glenny, "The Illusions of Steady States," *Change* 6 (December/January 1974–75), pp. 24–28; and John D. Millett, "What is Economic Health?" *Change* 8 (September 1976), p. 27.

9. Scott, "Organizational Theory: A Reassessment," pp. 245.

10. Paul R. Schulman, "Nonincremental Policy Making: Notes Toward an Alternative Paradigm," *American Political Science Review* (December 1975), pp. 1354–1370.

11. See Naomi Caiden and Aaron Wildavsky, *Planning Budgeting in Poor Countries* (New York: John Wiley & Sons, 1974).

12. See James W. Vaupel, "Muddling Through Analytically," in Willis D. Hawley and David Rogers (eds.) *Improving Urban Management* (Beverly Hills, Calif.: Sage Publications, 1976), pp. 124–146.

13. See Richard M. Cyert's contribution to this symposium, "The Management of Universities of Constant or Decreasing Size."

14. See National Academy of Public Administration *Report* and Glassberg, "Organizational Response to Municipal Budget Decreases."

15. See NAPA *Report* and *Cancelled Careers: The Impact of Reduction-In-Force Policies on Middle-Aged Federal Employees*, A Report to the Special Committee on Aging, United States Senate (Washington, D.C.: U.S. Government Printing Office, 1972).

16. See Albert O. Hirschman, *Exit, Voice and Loyalty: Responses to Decline in Firms, Organizations and States* (Cambridge, Mass.: Harvard University Press, 1970); also Mancur Olson, *The Logic of Collective Action* (Cambridge, Mass.: Harvard University Press, 1965).

17. The distinctive features of public organizations are discussed at greater length in Hal G. Rainey, Robert W. Backoff, and Charles H. Levine, "Comparing Public and Private Organization," *Public Administration Review* (March/April, 1976), pp. 223–244.

18. See Robert Behn's contribution to this symposium, "Closing a Government Facility," Barry Mitnick's "Deregulation as a Process of Organizational Reduction," and Herbert A. Simon, Donald W. Smithburg, and Victor A. Thompson, *Public Administration* (New York: Knopf,

1950) for discussions of the survival tactics of threatened bureaucrats.

19. This scheme is similar to those presented in Daniel Katz and Robert L. Kahn, *The Social Psychology of Organizations* (John Wiley & Sons, 1966), p. 166, and Gary L. Wamsley and Mayer N. Zald. *The Political Economy of Public Organizations: A Critique and Approach to the Study of Public Administration* (Lexington, Mass.: D.C. Heath, 1973), p. 20.

20. See Schulman, "Nonincremental Policy Making," and Charles O. Jones, "Speculative Augmentation in Federal Air Pollution Policy-Making," *Journal of Politics* (May, 1974), pp. 438–464.

21. See Robert Behn, "Closing the Massachusetts Public Training Schools," *Policy Sciences* (June, 1976), pp. 151–172; Valarie J. Bradley, "Policy Termination in Mental Health: The Hidden Agenda," *Policy Sciences* (June, 1976), pp. 215–224; and David J. Rothman, "Prisons, Asylums and Other Decaying Institutions," *The Public Interest* (Winter, 1972), pp. 3–17. A similar phenomena is occuring in some of the fields of regulation policy where deregulation is being made more politically feasible by a combination of technical and economic changes. See Mitnick, "Deregulation as a Process of Organizational Reduction."

22. Peter deLeon, "Public Policy Termination: An End and a Beginning," an essay prepared at the request of the Congressional Research Service as background for the Sunset Act of 1977.

23. There are many variations on the theme of Sunset. Gary Brewer's contribution to this symposium, "Termination: Hard Choices-Harder Questions" identifies a number of problems central to most sunset proposals.

24. For two treatments of this phenomena in the literature of organization theory see Barry M. Staw and Eugene Szwajkowski, "The Scarcity-Munificence Component of Organizational Environments and the Commission of Illegal Acts," *Administrative Science Quarterly* (September, 1975), pp. 345–354, and Barry Bozeman and E. Allen Slusher, "The Future of Public Organizations Under Assumptions of Environmental Stress," paper presented at the Annual Meeting of the American Society for Public Administration, Phoenix, Arizona, April 9–12, 1978.

25. See Thomas Muller, *Growing and Declining Urban Areas: A Fiscal Comparison* (Washington, DC: Ubran Institute, 1975).

26. See Richard P. Nathan and Charles Adams, "Understanding Central City Hardship," *Political Science Quarterly* (Spring, 1976), pp. 47–62; Terry Nichols Clark, Irene Sharp Rubin, Lynne C. Pettler, and Erwin Zimmerman, "How Many New Yorks? The New York Fiscal Crisis in Comparative Perspective." (Report No. 72 of Com-

parative Study of Community Decision-Making, University of Chicago, April, 1976); and David T. Stanley, "The Most Troubled Cities," a discussion draft prepared for a meeting of the National Urban Policy Roundtable, Academy for Contemporary Problems, Summer, 1976.

27. See Richard Child Hill, "Fiscal Collapse and Political Struggle in Decaying Central Cities in the United States," in William K. Tabb and Larry Sawers (eds.) *Marxism and The Metropolis* (New York: Oxford University Press, 1978); and H. Paul Friesema, "Black Control of Central Cities: The Hollow Prize," *Journal of the American Institute of Planners* (March, 1969), pp. 75–79.

28. See David T. Stanley, "The Most Troubled Cities" and "The Survival of Troubled Cities," a paper prepared for delivery at the 1977 Annual Meeting of the American Political Science Association, The Washington Hilton Hotel, Washington DC, September 1–4, 1977; and Martin Shefter, "New York City's Fiscal Crisis: The Politics of Inflation and Retrenchment," *The Public Interest* (Summer, 1977), pp. 98–127.

29. See Kaufman, *Are Government Organizations Immortal?* and "The Natural History of Human Organizations," *Administration and Society* (August, 1975), pp. 131–148; I have been working on this question for some time in collaboration with Ross Clayton. Our partially completed manuscript is entitled, "Organizational Aging: Progression or Degeneration." See also Edith Tilton Penrose, "Biological Analogies in the Theory of the Firm," *American Economic Review* (December, 1952), pp. 804–819 and Mason Haire, "Biological Models and Empirical Histories of the Growth of Organizations" in Mason Haire (ed.) *Modern Organization Theory* (New York: John Wiley & Sons, 1959), pp. 272–306.

30. For a fuller explanation of "smoothing" or "leveling," see James D. Thompson, *Organizations in Action* (New York: McGraw-Hill, 1967), pp. 19–24.

31. For recent analyses of related phenomena see Joel D. Aberbach and Bert A. Rockman, "Clashing Beliefs Within the Executive Branch: The Nixon Administration Bureaucracy," *American Political Science Review* (June, 1976), pp. 456–468 and Hugh Heclo, *A Government of Strangers: Executive Politics in Washington* (Washington, D.C.: The Brookings Institution, 1977).

32. See James G. March and Johan P. Olsen, *Ambiguity and Choice in Organizations* (Bergen, Norway: Universitetsforlaget, 1976); and Michael D. Cohen, James G. March, and Johan P. Olsen, "A Garbage Can Model of Organizational Choice," *Administrative Science Quarterly* (March, 1972), pp. 1–25.

33. See Charles Perrow, *Organizational Analysis: A Sociological View* (Belmont, Calif.: Wadsworth Publishing Company, 1970) and Chris Argyris

and Donald A. Schon, *Theory in Practice: Increasing Professional Effectiveness* (San Francisco, Calif.: Jossey-Bass, 1974) for discussions of the distinction between espoused and operative (i.e., "theory-in-use") strategies.

34. For extensive treatments of the tactics of bureaucrats, some of which are listed here, see Frances E. Rourke, *Bureaucracy, Politics, and Public Policy* (second edition, Boston: Little, Brown and Company, 1976); Aaron Wildavsky, *The Politics of the Budgetary Process* (second edition, Boston: Little, Brown and Company, 1974); Eugene Lewis, *American Politics in a Bureaucratic Age* (Cambridge, Mass.: Winthrop Publishers, 1977); and Simon, Smithburg and Thompson, *Public Administration.*

35. See Arthur M. Oken, *Equity and Efficiency: The Big Tradeoff* (Washington, D.C.: The Brookings Institution, 1975).

36. For a discussion of the costs of interactive decision making see Charles R. Adrian and Charles Press, "Decision Costs in Coalition Formation," *American Political Science Review* (June, 1968), pp. 556–563.

37. See Herbert Kaufman, "Emerging Conflicts in the Doctrine of Public Administration," *American Political Science Review* (December, 1956), pp. 1057–1073 and Frederick C. Mosher, *Democracy and the Public Service* (New York: Oxford University Press, 1968). Seniority criteria also have roots in the widespread belief that organizations ought to recognize people who invest heavily in them by protecting long time employees when layoffs become necessary.

38. See Peter A. Pyhrr, "The Zero-Base Approach to Government Budgeting," *Public Administrative Review* (January/February, 1977), pp. 1–8; Graeme M. Taylor, "Introduction to Zero-base Budgeting," *The Bureaucrat* (Spring, 1977), pp. 33–55.

39. See Brewer, "Termination: Hard Choices— Harder Questions"; Allen Schick, "Zero-base Budgeting and Sunset: Redundancy or Symbiosis?" *The Bureaucrat* (Spring, 1977), pp. 12–32 and "The Road From ZBB," *Public Administration Review* (March/April, 1978), pp. 177–180; and Aaron Wildavsky, "The Political Economy of Efficiency," *Public Administration Review* (December, 1966), pp. 292–310

40. See Hirschman, *Exit, Voice and Loyalty,* especially Ch. 7, "A Theory of Loyalty," pp. 76–105; Despite the attractiveness of "responsible and toughminded decision making" the constraints on managerial discretion in contraction decisions should not be underestimated. At the local level, for example, managers often have little influence on what federally funded programs will be cut back or terminated. They are often informed after funding cuts have been made in

Washington and they are expected to make appropriate adjustments in their local work forces. These downward adjustments often are also outside of a manager's control because in many cities with merit systems, veteran's preference, and strong unions, elaborate rules dictate who will be dismissed and the timing of dismissals.

41. Boulding, "The Management of Decline," p. 8.
42. See Heilbroner, *An Inquiry into the Human Prospect;* also Michael Harrington, *The Twilight of Capitalism* (New York: Simon & Schuster, 1976.)
43. For a discussion of anti-growth politics see Harvey Molotch, "The City as a Growth Ma-

chine," *American Journal of Sociology* (September, 1976), pp. 309–332.
44. Richard Rose has made a penetrating argument about the potential of governments to become "overloaded" in "Comment: What Can Ungovernability Mean?" *Futures* (April 1977), pp. 92–94. For a more detailed presentation, see his "On the Priorities of Government: A Developmental Analysis of Public Policies," *European Journal of Political Research* (September 1976), pp. 247–290. This theme is also developed by Rose in collaboration with B. Guy Peters in *Can Governments Go Bankrupt?* (New York: Basic Books, . . . 1978).

Eugene Litwak, Earl Shiroi, Libby Zimmerman, and Jessie Bernstein

Community Participation in Bureaucratic Organizations: Principles and Strategies

Recently there has been a great deal of controversy over the question of community participation in large-scale organizations. Much of this controversy has centered around organizations such as the school, police, and welfare departments. In the present paper we examine the theoretical basis for community participation in these organizations and suggest some optimal linkages that would take into account the contradictory structures and the complementary goals of the bureaucracy and of the primary group (i.e., any small face-to-face group that stresses positive affect, non-instrumental permanent and diffuse relations, such as a family or friend).

First we review the alternative theories on the relationship between primary groups and bureaucratic organizations, then discuss some of the variables that affect the linkage mechanisms selected by the primary group. Some generic social situations are discussed in order to illustrate the application of our framework.

Reprinted with permission of authors and publisher from *Interchange*, 1:4 (1970), pp. 44–60.

The present paper can be considered an extension and elaboration of the article, "A Balance Theory of Coordination between Bureaucratic Organizations and Community Primary Groups" (Litwak & Meyer, 1966), which concentrated on the opposite problem, that is, how bureaucratic organizations optimally intervene to change community primary groups.

TWO CURRENTLY HELD VIEWS

Traditional Point of View— The Power of the Bureaucracy

The traditional position on the role of bureaucratic organizations and community primary groups has been one that states that bureaucratic organizations will take over most of the functions of the primary group because they are more efficient. Furthermore, because the primary group and bureaucratic organizations have contradictory structures, they cannot both exist in very strong forms in the same society. Thus the stronger one becomes, the weaker the other becomes. This kind of reasoning has prompted many past writers to speak about the change from a folk to an urban mass society dominated by large organizations (Ogburn, 1953; Redfield, 1947; Simmel, 1950; Tönnies, 1940, esp. pp. 18–28; Weber, 1952; Wirth, 1957).

Underlying their analyses as to why the bureaucratic organization is more effective than the primary group is generally the theory that the bureaucratic organization can concentrate more knowledge and resources on solving any given problem than the primary group can. Thus the bureaucratic organization ensures optimal knowledge because it appoints and promotes people in terms of their ability to handle the designated tasks. By contrast the primary group member is born (or marries) into the group and is considered a member regardless of his ability to accomplish tasks.

The bureaucracy not only maximizes knowledge by its selection procedures, but it permits on-the-job training by its use of specialization. By contrast a family consists of a small number of people with many different, legitimate tasks. There is a division of labor within the family but there cannot be the degree of specialization that takes place in the work situation. In addition, the bureaucracy, because of its size, can support large-scale machinery that leads to effective production, e.g., a factory can have an assembly line, blast furnace, huge drill presses, etc.

The bureaucracy not only has a greater concentration of knowledge, but it must insure that the right knowledge is in the right place at the right time. Thus the bureaucracies stress rules to ensure that each specialized segment of the organization is doing things that are consistent with its other segments. In those situations where rules cannot be drawn up, the bureaucracy has hierarchal authority to ensure that once a decision is made it will be the same for the entire enterprise. By contrast the family, as a small unit, gains coordination through face-to-face contact.

The bureaucracy further guards against the intrusion of extraneous values or interpersonal likes and dislikes by insisting on a priori delimitation of duties and privileges and impersonal relations. By contrast primary group members are on call night and day. Furthermore, primary groups place a great value on positive affection and as a matter of principle insist that personal feelings come before all else.

Finally the bureaucracy permits change by separating policy from administrative decisions. Thus one can change policies without having to fire the entire organization and starting anew. By contrast primary groups usually have, as one of their chief goals, the internalization of cultural values. To change family policy (e.g., religious beliefs, political beliefs, socialization norms, social manners, etc.) requires a major resocialization process.

What should be clear is that bureaucracies can optimize knowledge by stressing aspects of group structure that are contradictory to that of the primary group. This is the basis for the traditional view that bureaucracies are most effective and that societies cannot tolerate strong forms of both bureaucracies and primary groups.

With this traditional framework there is only one way primary groups can intervene in the bureaucracy, and that is through appointing people to the top policy boards and working through them.[1]

A Contemporary Point of View

There is a second point of view, which is currently held by many sociologists. They accept much of the first analysis, but they raise a very important exception. They suggest that there are tasks for which economies of large scale and expert knowledge are not advantageous. They point out that such activities as early socialization of the child and adult tension management are tasks that are necessary for social survival and that the bureaucratic organizations cannot handle because they require positive affect. (Parsons & Bales, 1955)

Given the need for tension management and early socialization of the child and given the fact that bureaucratic organizations have contradictory structures to the primary groups, these authors conclude that bureaucratic organizations and primary groups must be kept relatively isolated from each other. If they become too close they will tend to destroy each other. As a consequence, this point of view would suggest that primary groups and bureaucratic organizations retain an alliance at arms distance. Thus, schools with children who are discipline problems or have emotional problems will inform parents and expect them to handle the matter. On the other hand, if the parent feels that the school is not performing its job effectively (e.g., a teacher is drunk in class) then the parent is supposed to protest via the regular bureaucratic channels provided for such occasions (i.e., letter to the principal or superintendent of schools). The actual correction of wrongdoing must be left to the bureaucracy.

To summarize, the clear implication of this approach is that bureaucratic organizations and community primary groups each have their own spheres and neither intervenes in the other. The most each does is to draw the attention of the other to the presumed defects. However, the ultimate judgment and treatment of these presumed defects are left in the hands of the respective groups.

THE BALANCE THEORY

There is yet another point of view that we develop in this paper. It is called the balance theory of coordination (Litwak & Meyer, 1966).

This point of view agrees with the first premise of both prior positions. The bureaucratic organizations provide the optimal organizational bases for the exercise of power insofar as concentration of specialized knowledge and economies of large scale are important. This viewpoint furthermore accepts the premise that the structures of the bureaucratic organizations and community primary groups tend to be antithetical. In the same way as the second position, the third rejects the assumption that economies of large scale and specialized knowledge are invariably important ingredients for solving problems. However, this position differs in two very important respects from the second one. First, it suggests that primary groups may exercise power in most areas of life (i.e., not just those of tension management and early socialization). Second, it suggests that the great interdependence in tasks between primary groups and bureaucratic organizations means that they cannot be kept isolated from each other without causing damage to the achievement of their respective goals. As a consequence, the balance theory predicts that the community and the bureaucracy will optimally achieve their respective goals if they operate at some midpoint in distance from each other. If they are too close their contradictory structures will cause friction. If they are too far they will not have the optimum in organizational resources. Since most persons understand the role of bureaucracy and trained knowledge, we indicate first the general bases for primary group power, i.e., when trained knowledge is not important.

The Bases for Primary Group Power—Non-Expert Tasks

Perhaps one of the most obvious situations where trained experts are of little use is where there is no real knowledge. Thus, there are many frontier areas where we have no specialized knowledge. The treatment of alcoholism, overeating, and drug addiction are but three areas where the current state of knowledge is not sufficiently great to justify highly specialized training or specialized machinery for immediate treatment.[2] The proof is that in these situations, volunteers with relatively modest training seem to be doing as well as highly trained specialists. Another area where specialized knowledge and resources make little difference is where the task is so simple to perform that the ordinary citizen has enough knowledge to perform it as well or almost as well as the specialist. Thus, the ordinary mother through the ordinary socialization process is almost as good as the expert (i.e., child specialist) in watching a child so that he does not go into the street, and if he does go into the street she is usually as capable as most experts in pulling him out of the way of an oncoming car.

Finally, there are times where the complexity of the situation, its unpredictability, and the need for great speed, make it difficult, if not impossible, to bring experts or large-scale machinery into play in time to do any good. For instance, in our illustration of a mother pulling a child out of the way of an oncoming car, it is not only the simplicity of the act that is at issue, but the inability to anticipate the crisis. Even if an expert were a little better trained, the probability of an expert (doctor) being at the proper place as compared to a primary group member (mother) is very low[3] and speed is more important than expertise. Sometimes the unpredictability of the event is based on the number of contingencies rather than the inability to anticipate it (e.g., everyday childrearing decision).

To summarize there are at least three instances where there are no advantages from specially trained experts or from economies of large scale: (1) where there is not sufficient knowledge to make training or designing machinery worthwhile, (2) where the tasks to be done are sufficiently simple so that the ordinary citizen with ordinary resources can do them as well as trained experts with large resources, and

(3) where the complexity and the unexpectedness of the situation prevent the special knowledge of experts or the advantages of large-scale machinery from being used. We refer to all such tasks where experts have no real advantage over nonexperts as *non-expert tasks*. What is important to stress is that these tasks constitute a major part of a person's life and cover every area of life (e.g., inside and outside of organizations).

Primary Groups and Speed and Flexibility

To point out that there are many tasks for which bureaucracies are not more effective than primary groups is only one part of our analysis. We submit that *the primary group is not only equal to the bureaucracy but is a more powerful base for handling non-expert tasks.* Our argument is that the very structure of the primary group, which makes it inefficient for developing trained expertise and large resources, makes it a speedier and more flexible decision-making unit for non-expert tasks. First, the primary group does not appoint persons on merit. However, that is no defect if expert knowledge is not a key factor in making a good decision (i.e., everybody has sufficient knowledge). Given this fact, there is a savings entailed by rejecting merit. One can drop the costly procedures that selection and promotion on merit entail. Second, the primary group does not stress detailed specialization. This factor is an advantage, since premature specialization or a specialist who does no better than the ordinary individual is a resource drain on the organization, slows down communication, and leads to inflexibility in decision-making (see, e.g., Vinter, 1967; Wilensky & Lebeaux, 1958).

The fact that the primary group is a small face-to-face group means that there is almost instantaneous feedback, a factor that becomes very important when dealing with unexpected and complex events. The bureaucracy can compensate for its long chain of command and use of rules where it can take advantage of its superior knowledge base or superior resources. However, when dealing with tasks where knowledge and resources provide no real advantage, the bureaucratic long lines of communication and rules produce inflexible and slower decision-making.

The positive emotional effect of the primary group and its stress on permanent relationships are virtues when non-expert tasks are at issue. In situations of uncertainty, there is often great anxiety (Blau, 1955). In such situations, decisions are much more likely to be implemented and communication is more likely to occur where members have trust in each other as well as long-standing relationships that permit them to understand each other's idiosyncrasies. Permitting positive affect is therefore functional where there are no dangers that emotional states will lead to appointment of the wrong person. Since this is the case for non-expert tasks and since primary groups permit positive affect and bureaucracies do not, we suggest that the primary group structure is more effective.

The reader should be quite clear what is being said at this point. The claim is made that primary groups are most effective for handling non-expert tasks and bureaucracies are most effective for handling expert tasks.

The balance theory, however, argues that most areas of life have tasks where there is no real expert knowledge; where the situation is too unexpected or too complex to bring to bear expert knowledge quickly enough; or where the ordinary citizen with ordinary socialization and resources can do as well as the trained expert.

Furthermore, there is evidence (Litwak & Figueira, 1968) for arguing that future technology will always insure this situation because technology is as likely to produce small-scale as large-scale economies; because it opens up new areas of ignorance

even as it closes down old; and because it simplifies tasks so the ordinary citizen can take over for the experts even as it complicates other tasks so that only trained experts can handle them.

The Interdependence of Primary Group and Bureaucratic Tasks

We have thus far tried to establish two components of the balance theory. We have pointed out that bureaucratic organizations and primary groups are able respectively to handle different tasks more effectively. We have also suggested that they are able to do so because they have different, in fact contradictory, structures.[4] What we now want to establish is that these two types of tasks are often intertwined so that bureaucracies and primary groups must work in close coordination. There is a certain face validity to this statement. For instance, it is clear that a doctor is helped enormously in his task of keeping people healthy if his clients do such non-expert tasks as maintaining good diets, taking proper exercise, etc. Teachers have a much easier time teaching if the child comes to school with an interest in education, properly fed and clothed. In all instances it is equally clear that primary groups can achieve their goals of health, education, etc., by use of experts. The exact degree of interdependence of community primary groups and bureaucracies can be measured by asking ourselves to what extent do expert and non-expert tasks require the same person, the same time, and the same place. For instance, in the school situation, one can think of at least a three-point scale. Toward the independent pole of the scale would be the non-expert tasks that can be performed within the confines of the family and the expert tasks that can be performed within the confines of the school. Such tasks involve different people, different places, and frequently different times. For instance, the family supervision of homework and the development of early language skills have a very important consequence for the type of teaching materials and the speed with which the teacher can transmit information in the classroom. These two activities are separated by place, by type of persons involved, and by time.

At the other extreme, we have the case where the expert tasks are so interdependent with non-expert tasks that they cannot be separated in place, time, or even people. For instance, it is difficult to separate classroom discipline and value socialization from the transmission of educational knowledge (e.g., math, geography). The first kind of task has more degrees of non-expertise than the second kind. Both types of tasks have to take place at the same time and same place and often the same person has to handle both.

In between these two extremes we have tasks that can be separated by people and frequently by time or by place. Thus, the Board of Education makes educational policy (generally involving non-expert tasks) that is implemented by the staff and that involves expert tasks. There is some separation in place and by people in that the Board generally meets in a central building that is physically isolated from the bulk of the school staff and has contact with only a limited number of staff members, e.g., the superintendent of schools. Street guards and luncheon attendants, who are indigenous to the neighborhood, are also performing basically nonuniform tasks and are separated from the professional staff by time and place.

We have now sought to establish the following points. The bureaucracies are best able to handle expert tasks, the primary groups are best able to handle non-expert tasks, the structures of the two organizations are contradictory, and the tasks are interdependent (i.e., to achieve most goals one needs to deal with both expert and non-expert tasks).

These points set the basis for the "balance theory of coordination" as well as suggesting the theoretical bases for community

intervention. The balance theory suggests two kinds of dangers. First, the fact that the community and the bureaucracy are not sufficiently linked to coordinate their activities means that the overall goal achievement of both organizations suffers because either the non-expert or the expert parts of the goals are not carried out. The second kind of danger emerges where the primary group members and the bureaucrats are brought into intimate everyday contact. Because of their conflicts in structures and norms, this contact could lead to serious friction between them. Alternatively it could lead to the introduction of contractual bureaucratic norms into the primary groups or the nepotistic, familistic norms into the bureaucracy. Any one of these alternatives would mean that the expert or non-expert aspects or tasks would not be done.[5]

Given the above analysis of danger from too close or not enough contact between organizations, the balance theory hypothesizes that optimal linkages between community primary groups and bureaucratic organizations are at some "middle point"—not so close as to cause structural friction and not so far as to cause lack of coordination.

If this theory is correct, then the community seeking to influence the bureaucracy must make one of several diagnoses: (1) Is the bureaucracy too distant, too close, or at the optimum point of balance? (2) What aspect of the bureaucracy do they want to influence—non-expert tasks or expert tasks?

PRINCIPLES OF COMMUNITY LINKAGES TO BUREAUCRATIC ORGANIZATIONS

The analysis suggested by the balance theory permits the generation of more specific principles of community linkages to bureaucratic organizations. The first basic principle derives from the argument that primary groups and bureaucratic organizations have their own spheres of effectiveness. The principle states that if a community primary group seeks to change expert-technical tasks within a bureaucracy it must have a linkage procedure that provides the community with experts. If a community primary group seeks to change nontechnical tasks of the bureaucracy, it need only have primary group members as links to the bureaucracy. Illustrative of a community using experts to link to the school would be where the community hired a lawyer to sue the schools. All linkages that have experts in them are called linkages with "bureaucratic intensity." Illustrative of the use of primary group members as linkages to the school would be marches, boycotts, and direct parental talks with teachers. Linkages that consist of primary group community members are called linkages with "primary group intensity." Thus the first principle can now be restated as follows: *When community primary groups seek to influence bureaucracies on technical matters, they should have linkages with bureaucratic intensity; when they seek to change non-expert matters within the bureaucracy, they should have linkages with primary group intensity.*

The second principle of linkages rests on the need for the community to establish a balanced relationship in order to avoid the conflicts between their structures and the bureaucracy. The second principle states that *when the bureaucracy and the community are very close, the community should use linkages that open up distance between it and the bureaucracy; when the community and the bureaucracy are too far, they should have linkages that bring them closer together.* For instance, when the school and community are in very close agreement about the need to establish a Black curriculum then the community can delegate the task of writing a Black history text to the school's experts and keep very indirect contact. However, if the school is against the introduction of a Black curriculum and the community is for it, then the community must insure very close contact with the experts—usually hiring their own experts.

If these two principles are simultaneously stated, then we have the four propositions indicated in Table 1. First one should look at whether the target of change is in a technical or nontechnical area. Thus if we are dealing with a technical area and the community and school are too close, one delegates the change to the experts in the school staff and exercises only indirect supervision (see No. 3, Table 1). If the problem is one of great distance, then one hires one's own experts and keeps close surveillance over the school staff (see No. 4, Table 1). If the problem is a non-expert task and the school and com-

Table 1 Community Linkage Hypothesis Based on the Balance Theory

	NON-EXPERT TASK: E.G., SETTING POLICY	EXPERT TASK: E.G., WRITING HISTORY TEXT
Community and Bureaucracy Close: e.g., both agree Black curriculum is good	1. Highly Centralized and Limited Contact: e.g., centralized board of education	3. Delegate Tasks to School Bureaucracy: e.g., history teachers selected by staff to design text
Community and Bureaucracy Distant: e.g., community wants Black curriculum and school staff does not	2. Decentralized and Close Contact: e.g., decentralized board of education, local community veto power of teacher hiring	4. Community Uses its own Experts: e.g., hires own historians or has power to name school staff who will design text

munity are too close, then one moves to a highly centralized contact through very few staff members, e.g., a centralized board of education (No. 1, Table 1). However, where the school and community are too far, one needs close supervision and moves to a procedure that provides closer face-to-face contact with many staff members, e.g., decentralized boards of education (No. 2, Table 1).

These same principles hold whether the expert and non-expert tasks are closely intertwined or not. For instance, we suggested that classroom socialization and discipline (non-expert tasks) are very interdependent with the exchange of technical knowledge, such as math or geography (expert task). We would argue that the community could handle the nonuniform aspects through varying degrees of contact with the staff. The most distance would be achieved by hiring a superintendent and trusting him to hire a principal and teacher who share common socializing and disciplinary values with the community. There would be less distance if the community insisted not only on hiring the superintendent, but also on having veto power over hiring the principal. These two, in turn, would hire the teachers who reflected the community's proper values. Finally, the least distance arises where the community members insist not only on all of the prior activity, but also upon a parent sitting in the classroom in order to insure that the teacher operates according to community norms. Our hypothesis would tell us that the first procedure would be very appropriate where the community and staff were very close, while the latter procedure would be most appropriate if the community and staff were very distant or hostile to each other.

Stages or Sequences of Change

The question arises about what else one must know in order to speak about the properties of linkages for closing and opening distance, as well as the capacities for dealing with expert and non-expert tasks. It has been pointed out that when bureaucracies seek to influence primary groups there are at least two blocks that they must overcome to close distance with a hostile audience. First is what has been called "selective listening" (Hyman & Sheatsley, 1947). People systematically refuse to even listen to messages that go counter to their beliefs. Thus, a Democratic candidate for governor might never reach Republican voters when he appears on television because Republican voters systematically refuse to tune in on speeches from opposing candidates. A second block in communication arises where one manages to overcome the first block. In this instance the audience "selectively interprets" or forgets that part of the message to which they are hostile so as to make it conform to prior beliefs (Hyman & Sheatsley, 1947).

The above analysis suggests that there are at least two steps that must be undertaken if one is to deal with a hostile audience: (1) to get their attention, and (2) to ensure they have absorbed the right message. Furthermore, these two steps are independent of each other. It is possible to get the audience's attention without necessarily getting them to absorb the message. In addition, it is possible that the technique for getting their attention might not be the same as the technique for change.

To make this point very clear, let us consider the two techniques we have mentioned thus far as available to the community groups. They can use linkages with primary group intensity (primary group members) when dealing with non-expert tasks and linkages with bureaucratic intensity (professional advocates) when dealing with expert tasks. Getting the bureaucratic attention may or may not be an expert's task. Similarly, the task of changing the organization may or may not involve experts. As a consequence, there are four possible sequences that might confront the community: (1) getting the attention of a bureaucracy is best handled by the community, but the problem of change involves experts; (2) getting the bureaucracy's attention and getting change involves the community; (3) getting attention and change might involve experts; (4) getting the bureaucracy's attention might involve experts, but getting change might involve the community. To illustrate, a community might utilize boycotts or strikes (primary group intensity) to get the school to set up a Black history course (which requires expertise). Or the community might institute a boycott or strike (primary group intensity) to get the school board to put local people in a position to make policy (non-expert primary group intensity). The community might hire a lawyer (expert) to sue the school system in order to get it to create a Black history course (involving experts) or the community might hire a lawyer (expert) to sue the school board in order to get it to put local people on the boards of education for making policy (primary group—non-expert).

Thus, in our analysis, we want to consider both the process of getting the bureaucracy's attention and the process of change as two distinct steps that are analogous to the problem of selective listening and selective interpretation that occurs when the bureaucracy seeks to change the primary group. However, before pursuing this analogy too much further, we speculate on how, in fact, the bureaucracy selectively listens so as to avoid community messages that it does not like and, if it is forced to hear the message, how it selectively interprets so as to prevent changes it does not like. This analysis, in turn, gives us a much more precise idea of the types of linkages one must employ.

Getting the Bureaucracy's Attention—Problem of Selective Perception

Following our prior analysis we suggest that the problem of getting the bureaucracy's attention might be either an expert or a non-expert task. First, we illustrate the cases where the task involves experts and then the cases where it involves non-experts. One of the major reasons for selective listening lies in the fact that bureaucracies involve specialization and knowledge above and beyond that available to the ordinary individual. As a consequence, the ordinary citizen does not have the knowledge to know which bureaucracy to go to or where to enter it. Therefore, his message is often never received by the right bureaucracy. A classic illustration of this point is the case of some New York tenants who found their water and heat turned off in midwinter (Purcell & Specht, 1967). There were five city agencies that dealt with water, i.e. one to turn it on, one to turn it off, one to handle faulty plumbing, one to keep it hot, one to handle water rates.

If a tenant managed to find the right organization he was not necessarily sure where best to enter the organization to get some results (e.g., who to speak to, whether to sue in court). If one understands that the ordinary citizen has a myriad of such organizations that he must deal with in his everyday life and that each has specialized rules and regulations, it becomes clear that in principle he would not have the kind of knowledge necessary to deal with his organizational environment.

A second factor that leads to distortion of community messages is that the bureaucrat assumes that anything offered by an "amateur" is suspect. He assumes that only bureaucracies deal with expert tasks and as a consequence experts are the only ones who can diagnose problems, etc. A third factor that often leads to distortion of messages is that any bureaucrat who is unsympathetic to the community can confuse the community by giving them wrong information. Thus, a principal in a school might tell parents that he cannot introduce a new curriculum because state law forbids it. He might not tell them that the law also has a clause that permits new curriculum in schools for experimental purposes. As a consequence, the community's desires never get beyond the principal's office. Finally, it can be argued that the community's message never gets through to bureaucracies because the community primary groups do not have the resources to wait until the message winds its way through bureaucratic channels. Thus in the case where the families were without water and heat in the winter, they needed a decision within a few days and the bureaucracy took much longer to even acknowledge the message.

If the reader considers all of these reasons for message distortion, he will find that they all involve a lack of expertise on the part of the community. This situation leads us to one of our balance theory principles. *In order to avoid selective listening on the part of the bureaucracy on issues that have to do with technical matters, the community should have an expert advocate.* Kahn, Grossman, Bandler, Clark, Galkin, and Greenwalt (1966) make this a central point in their advocation of local community information centers. It is the basic principle of the ombudsman concept as well.

However, we would also suggest that sometimes communities can get bureaucratic attention without having to appeal to expert advocates. The optimal circumstance for doing so is where communication success can be evaluated by the non-expert and where the bureaucracy is highly dependent on or vulnerable to the primary group. Thus, in our illustration we suggested that the principal could fool the community because it lacked technical knowledge of the law. In such a case, the community could not properly assess the success of the communication. However, there are many instances where it is a simple matter to assess whether the communication has been received or not, e.g., whether the board of education puts on its agenda an item on Black curriculum. In

addition, we think that bureaucracies have differential dependence on primary groups. Thus a retail merchant tends to be more vulnerable to primary group pressure than is a wholesale merchant; a political party right before an election is more vulnerable than right after; business concerns are more dependent on their workers than welfare agencies are on their clients, etc. We would argue that where the bureaucracy is vulnerable and the assessment of communication simple, the community can get bureaucratic attention by use of linkages with primary group intensity—strikes, boycotts, petitions, etc.

Thus based on our balance theory approach we would argue that the communities can overcome problems of selective listening and get bureaucracies' attention if they use linkages with bureaucratic intensity for handling the expert problems, and linkages with primary group intensity for handling the non-expert problems.

Getting the Bureaucracy to Change—Selective Interpretation

We would make the same logical analysis for change as we would for insuring the bureaucracy's attentiveness. Thus we would say that some change problems involve experts and some involve non-expert tasks and the community should use linkages that permit the use of experts and primary group members for each as necessary. To make this point clear, one can enumerate the number of ways in which organizations can change—personnel can be fired, new people hired, people can be retrained, rules and machinery can be changed, administrative styles of the organization can be changed. We would argue that all of these processes have both expert and non-expert aspects to them. Thus the assessment of a teacher might involve an assessment of his mathematical abilities (something only an expert mathematician can determine) as well as an assessment of whether he has basic values that are similar to the parents or not (something the parents can best determine). Some people take the position that teachers have no expertise at all and as a consequence the parents can do the entire job of teaching (Rogers, 1969). There are teachers who feel that parents have no role in the change process of school. We do not adopt either of these extreme positions. We think that the making up of curriculum does involve expertise (e.g., people who know history) and must take into account the community (e.g., to assess if the teacher shares common values). If the primary group seeks to make up its own curriculum and to judge the technical expertise of the teacher, then the quality of education will drop. On the other hand, we think that the teachers who seek to make judgments as to what is good for the community and what the community values should be without consulting the community directly will also succeed in lowering the educational quality of the school.

We would further suggest that the bureaucracy can resist the community on changes in areas of expertise in the same way they selectively screen out messages in technical areas—the community lacks enough information to know what has to be changed, to know whether change has taken place or not, or to have the time for change to take place. Therefore we would suggest that to handle change in expert areas the community must have expert advocates. Following the same logic we would argue that to have change in non-expert areas one could have direct intervention on the part of the community.

Variable Social Distance, Selective Perception, and Change

The analysis thus far speaks about the need to have the community use experts when dealing with technical tasks—be they ones of selective listening or selective interpretation. Similarly, when dealing with nontechnical tasks our analysis suggests that the community use linkages that contain primary group members. To this analysis we would now add our second principle—*the primary groups and the bureaucracies should be kept at a balance point.* Thus, if the task is to insure that the teacher has the proper values and the school and community are quite friendly, then the community can use a linkage that minimizes the amount of face-to-face contact between community and teachers. The community, through a large centralized board of education, hires a superintendent, who in turn hires everyone else. If there were bitter enmity between staff and community, the community would have to sit in the classroom to insure that its values were preserved. The hostility between staff and community ensures that they will not engage in nepotism or favoritism. Between these two extremes would be the insistence on the community's part of giving local boards of education rather than central boards veto power over hiring the principal or the teachers. If the task were a technical one, then the community could avoid contact with experts by having the bureaucracy handle its technical tasks. Where the bureaucracy and community are unfriendly, it is necessary for the community to hire its own experts to handle the technical problems. The fiercer the combat, the closer the community has to be with its own experts.

We have tried to do two things in this section. First we have suggested the two principles of linkages based on the balance theory: (1) linkages can be directly handled by the primary groups where the task is non-expert, and by advocate experts when they are expert tasks, and (2) linkages must keep community and bureaucracy isolated when they are too close and bring them closer together when they are too far. In addition, it was pointed out that there are at least two stages to any influence process—getting the bureaucracies' attention and producing change. These can demand entirely different linkages from a community.

A CLASSIFICATION OF LINKAGE MECHANISMS

On the basis of the above discussion we are now in a position to suggest some of the fundamental properties of linkages that enable us to anticipate whether they will permit the community to shrink social distance or maintain it. The underlying dimensions that have emerged from the above discussion are bureaucratic intensity, primary group intensity, interdependence of expert and non-expert tasks, and, one we have yet to discuss, scope (i.e., the extent to which the linkage mechanism permits one to reach many people or few). If our estimate is correct, these fundamental dimensions can be used to evaluate any empirical linkages as well as suggesting new ones. To illustrate this point we take a series of ways in which communities have sought to influence bureaucracies and roughly rank them on the proposed underlying dimensions. The following are some of the ways the community has influenced bureaucracies in the past.

1. *Advocate bureaucracy.* The primary group develops its own bureaucracy to deal with the target bureaucracy. It can either develop its own as the union did to deal with management, or it can, through political processes, take over an ongoing one as political parties take over governmental agencies, or it can seize one through force as happens in revolutionary movements.

2. *Delegated bureaucracy.* What characterizes this approach is that there is an already formed organization to which the community member can turn (e.g., a Race Relations Commission or an ombudsman).

3. *Voluntary association.* Communities may have voluntary associations rather than full-fledged bureaucracies represent them. Unions prior to their full-fledged bureaucratization were voluntary associations, the parents in Oceanhill-Brownsville had a voluntary association, etc.

4. *Mass media.* Frequently the community can best reach the bureaucracy through mass media. This approach is associated with public marches or riots, etc.

5. *Indigenous expert.* These are persons hired by a bureaucracy and who live in the immediate neighborhood, e.g. teachers who live in their school district.

6. *Proto-indigenous expert.* These are experts hired by the bureaucracy and who have backgrounds similar to the community, e.g., Black teachers in Black communities, or who have special training to make them sensitive to the local community, but do not live in the immediate neighborhood.

7. *Low-powered indigenous non-expert.* These are community members who act as street-crossing guards, lunchroom attendants, and as school and community aids in welfare agencies.

8. *High-powered indigenous non-expert.* These are members of boards of education who set policy or who have veto power over the hiring and firing of personnel.

9. *Systematic sustained boycott, strike, or violence.* Illustrations are long-term union strikes, bus boycotts, and the French Resistance movement. Usually these mechanisms must be associated with a bureaucracy or a voluntary association.

10. *Ad hoc riot, strike, boycott.* The big city "ghetto" riots, as well as spontaneous short-term boycotts or strikes by parents and students against schools.

11. *Mass march.* The peace marches and civil rights marches on Washington, and the Black organizations marching in Pittsburgh to attract attention to their demands for more skilled jobs are illustrative.

12. *Single person ad hoc contact.* The parent who comes in to complain about a teacher, or to get more information on a school program illustrates this mechanism.

It is clear that we have not exhausted all possible forms of linkage. It is also clear

Table 2 Hypothesized Rating of Some Linkage Mechanisms on Basic Underlying Dimensions of Linkages

VARIABLE	BUREAUCRATIC INTENSITY	PRIMARY GROUP INTENSITY	INTERDEPENDENCY OF EXPERT AND NON-EXPERT TASK	SCOPE
Advocate bureaucracy—community has its own bureaucracy—unions	Highest	Low	Mod-Low	High
Delegated bureaucracy—community borrows ongoing bureaucracy—lawyers	High	Lowest	Low-Mod	Mod-high
Voluntary association—community has its own voluntary association	Mod	Mod	Mod	Mod
Mass media	Mod-Low	Low	Low	Highest
Indigenous expert—teacher who lives in the area	High	High	Highest	Lowest
Proto-indigenous expert—Black teachers for Black children but not living in neighborhood	High	Mod	High-Mod	Mod-High
Low-powered indigenous non-expert—school-crossing guard	Low-Mod	High	Mod-Low	Mod
High-powered indigenous non-expert—board of education with veto power over hiring and firing	Low-Mod	Mod-High	Mod-High	High
Organized boycott, strike	Mod	Mod-High	Low-Mod	High-Mod
Ad hoc boycott, strike—one-day affairs, short-term riots	Low	High	Low	Mod-High
Mass marches—civil rights marches, peace marches	Low	Mod-Low	Low	High-Mod
Single person ad hoc contact—complaints or requests for information	Lowest	High	Low-Mod	Low

that the ones we have delineated can be combined in many different ways.

In Table 2 we list the mechanisms and their ratings on each of the underlying dimensions. The column headings are the underlying dimensions while the row headings are the empirical linkages. These ratings are rough approximations that suggest the logic of our procedure. The actual ratings would have to rest on empirical research.

With this in mind let us examine column one on bureaucratic intensity. Our ratings are based on the extent to which the linkage mechanism used by the community is itself a bureaucracy under the control of the community. Thus, the advocate bureaucracy has the highest ratings and is best represented in current American society by honest union bureaucracies and their membership. The linkages with the least bureaucratic intensity would be the single person contact.

In regard to the next column, labeled primary group intensity, the linkages in which community members are the major element, have the highest ratings. It is important to note that there are linkages such as the indigenous experts or proto-indigenous experts who are high on both primary group and bureaucratic intensity. Thus it is possible for one mechanism to be fairly high on both dimensions. It is also possible to think of degrees of primary group intensity. Thus a central city-wide board of education does represent community interests versus expert interests but the community it represents is a very large one and may lack the continuous contact and trust of a true primary group.

In examining the third column on the ability of the linking mechanisms to deal with interdependent expert and non-expert tasks, we suggest that all situations where the expert is indigenous to the community or where he had similar values and background to the community are rated high. We also hypothesize that a local board of education with veto power over hiring and firing of teachers is also high on this dimension. Individual contacts by themselves are not linkages that enable one to deal with both non-expert and expert tasks simultaneously. Where the community group engages experts on its behalf (e.g., advocate bureaucracies) there is some ability to handle both tasks but the rating is not necessarily high (e.g., a lawyer can sue in court without having to emphasize non-expert tasks).

The last column concerns the number of people that can be reached by a given mechanism. It is important to note that indigenous experts probably have the lowest scope in a society such as ours. The probability of funding indigenous experts progressively decreases the smaller the size of the community primary group and the lower the income of the neighborhood. By contrast it is more possible to find the proto-indigenous experts. The community-wide policy board has a wide scope but the local board has lower scope. The single person contact, in the same way as the indigenous expert, has a very low scope.

It can be seen how this classification of empirical linkages is highly suggestive as to when communities should utilize certain procedures. Thus we suggest that communities should resort to advocate bureaucracies or delegated bureaucracies when they are confronting massive resistance from their target bureaucracies and technical tasks are at issue. At the same time, it is clear that, where bureaucracies are highly vulnerable to primary groups, mechanisms utilizing simple primary group dimensions, such as a parent protesting or ad hoc boycotts or marches, can be very effective in changing the bureaucracies.

SOME GENERIC SOCIAL SITUATIONS AND IDEAL FORMS OF LINKAGES

With the above classification of linking mechanisms, we need only one more ingredient to pose a series of hypotheses or policy recommendations for ideal forms of linkages. What we need is a sufficient description of the environment to say whether the bureaucracy and the community are at some distance or not, whether the task to be changed involves experts or non-experts, whether the two types of tasks are heavily interdependent, which stage of the communication process we are in, and the structure of the target bureaucracy that the community seeks to influence. Ideally what one would like to do is to study all these factors simultaneously. However, for purposes of presentation we examine them three at a time. These initial discussions should permit a researcher, policy-maker, or community member to infer what types of linkages would be ideal for the more complex situations.

SOCIAL DISTANCE AND TYPE OF TASK

In our first analysis we simultaneously consider three factors—the social distance between the bureaucracy and the community, the type of tasks to be changed, and the sequencing of attention linkages and change linkages. In Table 3 the headings of each column indicate the degree of distance (i.e., bureaucracies friendly or not friendly), the headings of each row indicate the type of task and degree of interdependence (i.e., expert task, non-expert task, interdependent expert and non-expert tasks). For purposes of presentation we have simplified and dichotomized very complex continuums.

Within each cell we have indicated the sequence of mechanisms for getting attention and change. Putting all these variables together in this way reveals some relations that might not be obvious if each were considered separately. For instance, where the bureaucracies are friendly or vulnerable the community has only to use linkages with primary group intensity, even where expert tasks need to be changed; the rea-

sons being that where the bureaucracy is friendly or vulnerable the community primary groups can always borrow the bureaucracy's resources or experts to make changes. By contrast, where the target bureaucracy is hostile, the community always needs linkages with bureaucratic intensity (even for non-expert tasks) in order to get the attention of the target bureaucracy. With these thoughts in mind, let us briefly review some boxes in the table and see the kinds of predictions our theory suggests.

CELL IV—BUREAUCRACY IS NOT FRIENDLY AND THE TASK TO BE CHANGED INVOLVES EXPERTISE. This might be a situation where the bureaucracy resists any efforts on the part of the Black community to decentralize the school, introduce new courses, or change their staffing policy. In such a situation, we hypothesize that, to get the attention of the bureaucracy, the community primary group has to develop bureaucratic power of its own through an advocate bureaucracy or a delegated bureaucracy. The development of union bureaucracies was in part necessitated by the recalcitrance of management bureaucracies that refused recognition and were able to utilize their resources to enforce it. On the school scene it may involve Black parents going to the NAACP to sue the school system or forming their own organizations (e.g., Oceanhill-Brownsville) to produce a sustained and systematic boycott and going to churches for space to set up private classes so that their children will not lose by a systematic boycott. All of these procedures are designed to get the bureaucracy to pay attention. However, if the bureaucracy agreed to the changes, the community would insist on having its own experts draw up decentralization plans, write new texts for Black history, or ensure that new procedures on staffing were being followed, since a hostile bureaucracy cannot be counted on for this kind of expertise.

Table 3 Ideal Community Linkages Under Varying Conditions of Social Distance and Types of Task

TYPE OF TASK	BUREAUCRACY IS FRIENDLY OR VULNERABLE	BUREAUCRACY IS NOT FRIENDLY OR VULNERABLE
Task to be changed is technical involving expertise or large-scale resources, e.g., develop Black history curriculum; set up detailed decentralization plan; set up detailed desegregation plan.	I. Primary group intensity to attract attention and that is all the community has to do. The bureaucracy provides the expertise for the change, e.g., ad hoc group of parents petition school for Black studies program and the school provides the money and staff to set up the program and train the teachers.	IV. Bureaucratic intensity to attract attention and produce change, e.g., advocate or delegated bureaucracy threatens legal suit, systematic and prolonged disruption or setting up competitive system to get the attention of the target bureaucracy as well as employing experts to set up the curriculum to evaluate teacher-training.
Task to be changed is non-expert task, e.g., general racial policy on staffing; general curriculum policy on time to be spent on social studies, music, etc.; supervision of children crossing streets, or in the school during the lunch periods.	II. Primary group intensity to attract attention and produce change, e.g., parents get together to elect new central board members who represent their values and change policy accordingly. They recommend more Black teachers to be hired, Black history should be part of the curriculum, etc. One can rely on staff to implement policy.	V. Bureaucratic intensity to get attention and primary group intensity to get change, e.g., use advocate or delegated bureaucracy to organize systematic disruptions, institute suits in court to get attention of the bureaucracy to develop local boards of education that would ensure that parents' values are to be carried out in each school building.
Tasks to be changed are interdependent, e.g., assessing classroom disciplining behavior, classroom racial attitudes, etc.	III. Linkages with primary group intensity and some interdependence, e.g., parents have power to veto hiring and firing of superintendent and principal and leave it to their discretion to hire teachers.	VI. Linkages with both primary group and bureaucratic intensity as well as linkages that permit great interdependence for attention and change, e.g., advocate bureaucracy with threats of systematic disruptions, suits, etc., together with the demand that parents sit in on classroom sessions, have veto power over hiring and firing of teachers, as well as all other school staff, and the use of advocate bureaucratic sources to draw up decentralization plans.

CELL V—BUREAUCRACY IS NOT FRIENDLY AND THE TASK INVOLVES NON-EXPERTISE. We again might have a bureaucratic organization that is recalcitrant, but in this case the desired changes involve moving different community people into the bureaucracy. For instance, the community might want to have new people and different policies in the board of education. However, now they confront a determined opposition in the bureaucracy. This bureaucracy might be willing to put its professional resources into any battle for the board of education. In this case, for the community to win, it must have similar resources to hire newspaper space, to get out its constituency, etc. However, once in power they need a linkage with primary group emphasis to ensure that their policy is implemented. If the bureaucracy is really against the policy, then the primary group linkages must permit no delegation of authority to bureaucrats. For instance, if the board of education decides that it wants to experiment with decentralized systems and the teachers are against it, then the board has also to decentralize its activities (e.g., local board of education) in order to supervise the teachers. This is true because general policies have so many contingencies that a single central board could not begin to police them. From a theoretical point of view, the student of complex organization might note that this solution to policy is different from Weber's, which suggested that policy be made only at the top of the organization, as well as different from the human relations approach that suggests that the bureaucrat internalize the policy (Blau, 1955). It provides a theoretical rationale for the concept of participant democracy in a large-scale bureaucratic organization without having to imply that differences between experts and non-experts are trivial. The latter is often the rationale behind people arguing for such localized decision making.

Elaborations of Social Distance and the Use of Delegation and Scope-Secrecy

The concept of social distance can be elaborated and approached from a slightly different angle to highlight one of the implicit hypotheses in Table 3. In thinking of social distance, we suggest that the bureaucracy can be hostile to the local primary group or the larger community can be hostile to it or any combination of the two can occur. This elaboration of the situation permits one to highlight the role of scope in linkage mechanisms. Thus, where the larger community is in sympathy with the smaller community and the target bureaucracy is resistant, it is to the obvious advantage of the smaller community to concentrate on linkages that stress high scope. On the other hand, where the smaller community is facing a larger community that is hostile but has a target bureaucracy that is friendly, the smaller community must stress linkages that have low scope, i.e., reach only the members of the bureaucracy rather than the larger public. Thus, the smaller community might develop a volunteer organization that school staff can join as citizens and provide expert information. Or the school staff might surreptitiously leak information to the voluntary association. This might be the case where the larger community is for public aid to parochial schools while the public school staff and the smaller community oppose it.

Perhaps the situation that might trigger off the most secrecy is the one where both bureaucracy and the larger community are against the local community. Under these conditions the local community is likely to get squashed if it seeks change unless it initially operates very secretly (low scope) to build some organizational apparatus—usually a voluntary association and then a full-blown bureaucracy. Once the smaller community has developed its bureaucratic resources the situation is quite likely to lead to violence. Initially the violence is more like guerrilla warfare, but this can readily escalate into a pitched battle between two or more bureaucracies that might approach a more specialized military pattern. Thus, the UAW in seeking to organize the Ford Motor Company in the early 1940's was up against a trained private army and it developed specialized "flying squads" to deal with them (Bernstein, 1970). The sequence of linkages we have mentioned is typical of the development of trade unions in American society. It also can be seen emerging in the Black militant movement. To conclude these remarks on social distance, we point out that the greater the detail with which we can define the outer environment, the more we appreciate the theoretical importance of scope as a dimension of linkages. In this regard we must also note that people and organizations may not be free to alter their shapes at will. They might in turn be instruments of larger social change processes, e.g., class-conflicts, technological innovation.

Organizational Structure and Community Linkage Procedures

Another characteristic that is often related to social situations is the structure of the target bureaucracy. To make this point clear, let us examine three different types of bureaucratic structures: the rationalistic, rules-oriented structure; the collegial-human relations-democratic structure; and the laissez-faire structure. The first is the classical bureaucracy that we have described before. It has specialization and hierarchal authority for handling situations that cannot be specified ahead of time, rules and regulations for situations that can be specified ahead of time, administrative discretion within each specialty, but no role in policy-making, impersonal rela-

tions, etc. The collegial structure moves in the opposite direction, except it does not go as far as primary groups and very much retains merit as a basic criterion. Nevertheless, there is far less emphasis on specialization. Small family service agencies or psychotherapeutic treatment homes, advanced graduate departments in first-rate universities, advanced research institutes, all tend to follow this model (Litwak & Meyer, 1965; Perrow, 1967). In terms of educational philosophy the first model is consistent with a drill or learning machine approach, while the second is consistent with a pupil-centered approach. In contrast to either of these situations, the laissez-faire model is characterized by each individual doing his "own thing" with no common values or coordination. It is basically the collegial model without coordination.

Each of these structures has characteristics that suggest differential approaches if the community is to influence them. The rationalistic bureaucracy requires the outer community to have linkages with expertise to insure its message has been heard. This requirement is because this type of bureaucracy has much more specialization and rules and as a consequence the community can easily make a mistake as to the correct entry point. In contrast, the collegial structure—because everybody tends to do the same thing and because they tend to have face-to-face meetings of the staff—is easily reached by linkages with primary group intensity and low scope. Somewhat different in this respect is the laissez-faire system. Since each staff person does his "own thing" and there is little communication between each, it is necessary to have a linkage mechanism with high scope (i.e., one that will reach most members). Furthermore, it might be necessary to vary systematically the degree of bureaucratic and primary group intensity, depending on each member's definition of his job—as being more in the direction of experts or non-experts. Thus, some teachers in a school will be using a pupil-centered approach, others a drill, and still others may be doing nothing.

The problems of introducing changes are also different in each of the organizational structures. The rationalistic organization differentiates between policy and administrative decisions. In our scheme, the first is a non-expert task, while the second is an expert's task. This situation means that insofar as the community participates within the boundaries of the bureaucracy it can use linkages that do not simultaneously require bureaucracy and primary group intensity or close contact between primary group members and experts. By contrast, in a human relations-collegial-democratic organization, policy and administrative decisions are merged. Each expert is assumed to have internalized the policy of the organization. For the community it means that expert tasks and non-expert tasks cannot be separated and as a consequence heavy use must be made of mechanisms that permit both dimensions simultaneously (i.e., indigenous experts; experts with similar backgrounds; local policy boards, which have veto power over hiring, firing, and training of teachers). By contrast, in laissez-faire structures there is no way to know which linkages to use, since some teachers might operate as though administrative decisions and policy decisions are separate while others operate as though they are joined.

There is yet one final consideration of organizational structure. Up to now when we spoke of changes, we assumed that the administrative structures of the organization would be the same, but some specific activities would be changed. However, if we now consider administrative changes, it is hypothesized that where one is moving from a rationalistic to a human relations structure, it becomes increasingly important to utilize community linkages that have primary group emphasis and wide scope,

because central to the human relations structure is internalization of values on the part of all members of the bureaucracy. On the other hand, the move from a human relations to a rationalistic structure might emphasize more bureaucratic intensity since it no longer becomes central for the members of the bureaucracy to internalize community values. The task of policy-making is reserved for the community members. Table 4 summarizes this analysis.

We have now designated several key dimensions of the situation that, together with our theory of differential functions of primary groups and bureaucratic organizations, enables us to state more precisely which linkages can be used most effectively by the community to change bureaucratic organizations.

SUMMARY AND CONCLUSION

Let us briefly summarize the major points of our paper. First, we tried to make the point that the very structures of the bureaucracy and primary groups made them powerful within their respective spheres, i.e., expert tasks and non-expert tasks. Furthermore, these two types of tasks occur in most areas of life (e.g., government, health, business, military, police) and they cannot be isolated. At the same time, it was recognized that primary groups and bureaucracies have somewhat contradictory structures. From this analysis it was suggested that any time communities sought to change bureaucracies around expert tasks, they would have to have linkages that enabled them to have advocate experts. Where they sought to change bureaucracies in nonexpert areas they could utilize their own primary group members. We then went on to point out that interdependence of expert and non-expert tasks varies considerably, inside as well as outside the boundaries of the bureaucracy. As a consequence it was important to evaluate linkages on the basis of their abilities to

Table 4 Organizational Structure and Community Linkage Mechanism

STRUCTURE	COMMUNITY INITIATIVE	ORGANIZATIONAL CHANGE	ADMINISTRATIVE CHANGE
1. Rationalistic: specialization, rules, impersonal, separation of policy and administration.	Linkages with experts who know which part of the organization to approach. Need to have a person who is familiar with the system, e.g., ex-employee who now works for community.	Linkages where expert and non-expert tasks are clearly differentiated, e.g., centralized policy boards that are isolated from the bulk of the staff. The bulk of changes require technical expertise.	The move from a rationalistic to human relations structure will require linkages that combine expert and non-expert tasks, e.g., communities in local neighborhoods play a role in training teachers, hiring, and firing.
2. Collegial-human relations-democratic: move toward generalist, internalized policies, and committee meetings rather than rules.	Linkages with low scope and with primary group intensity. All people in organization do the same thing and meet with each other so community person has only to reach one person to ensure message will be heard. No detailed knowledge necessary.	Linkages that permit both expert and non-expert tasks to be evaluated simultaneously since members of bureaucracy need to internalize organizational policy to carry on their jobs. Thus decentralized boards with veto power over hiring and firing would be necessary.	The move from a human relations to a rationalistic structure will require linkages where expert and non-expert tasks can be separated. Move from local to central boards of education.
3. Laissez-faire: each person does his own thing. There is no central coordination.	Linkages with high scope are necessary because the community must reach most of the members of the bureaucracy to effect a change. For some the linkage ideally contains experts, for others non-experts, since they define their jobs differently.	No way to anticipate whether linkages with primary intensity or bureaucratic intensity are best since jobs are defined differently by each member of the organization. Community must be prepared to utilize several different approaches simultaneously.	The move from laissez-faire to rationalistic would require linkages that keep expert and non-expert tasks separate. The move from laissez-faire to human relations would require linkages that permitted both tasks to be looked at simultaneously.

handle both primary group and technical expertise. Finally, it was pointed out that it was necessary to take into account the number of organizations or people a given mechanism could reach. With these underlying dimensions in mind, we took twelve empirical linkages and suggested how they could be rated. We then took several aspects of social situations and showed what kinds of linkages would be optimal to both.

It is clear that our analysis is far from complete, for we are in a frontier area of sociological inquiry. Prior sociologists gave little thought to theories of linkages because they either assumed that bureaucratic structures and primary groups could not exist side by side in any strong form (i.e., they must be in conflict) or thought that primary group tasks could be isolated from bureaucratic ones so that the only forms of linkages one had to deal with were those that stressed isolation. It is quite clear that our formulation is far different in emphasis than either of the two prior theories. It provides a theoretical base for community participation in bureaucracies without denying that experts perform different tasks than community members. It stresses the need to develop a linkage theory between bureaucracy and community that goes beyond isolation and conflict.

There are several major gaps in our presentation. The assumption thus far is that the bureaucracy is sitting complacently by, while the primary groups seek to change it. In a prior work an attempt was made to show how bureaucracies change primary groups (Litwak & Meyer, 1966). The joint analysis of these two conceptual schemes must be undertaken in order to increase accuracy of prediction and policy formulation. Without going into details of other paths of inquiry that must be undertaken, we hope that this paper has been sufficiently suggestive to start others making their own inquiries.

NOTES

1. However, they are unlikely to be effective because community primary groups are likely to wane in influence where bureaucracies are strong. This analysis provides the theoretical underpinning for the kind of pessimism generated by people such as Marcuse (1966). It is clear that if any unscrupulous group seized control of the bureaucracies (as is suggested as being inevitable by such people as Michels [1952], Marcuse [1966], and C. Wright Mills) the bureaucracies would become a power unto themselves. Primary groups just do not have the organizational bases to compete with bureaucratic organizations and if they should somehow successfully intervene at any but the most general policy level they will destroy the bureaucracy. Put somewhat differently, this point of view suggests that parents can at best seek to control the board of education so as to set general educational policy but efforts on their part to deal with the everyday running of schools or the details or curriculum will either fail or, insofar as they succeed, destroy the educational system, i.e., replace expertise with nepotism. The same point can be made with regard to the police. The intuitive acceptance of this analysis is behind the "nihilism" of some student radical movements that suggest that we must reject technological priorities, bring the system down, and start afresh.

2. What we are saying is that for short-term treatment the expert is not the most effective. We might still want experts in the field because they might be better in the long run.

3. One of the characteristics of primary group relations is face-to-face contact in many areas of life and, all other things being equal, this means that primary group members are more often next to each other than are persons involved in secondary social relations.

4. There are some persons who, in their enthusiasm for participant democracy, assume the Marxian utopia has arrived (i.e., that anybody can substitute for anybody else and therefore everybody should have equal participation in all matters). What they are in effect doing is denying the role of experts. This kind of thinking leads one to patently false conclusions (e.g., saying that passengers should participate equally with airplane pilots in all decisions on landing airplanes, that patients should participate equally with doctors on where an incision should be made, etc.).

5. Kramer (1969) has an excellent description of the problems of too much closeness and too much distance. Thus he points out cases where too much closeness has led to nepotism and corruption, as well as cases where the bureaucracy did

not serve the goals of the poor that it was presumably set up to do.

SELECTED REFERENCES

BERNSTEIN, I. *Turbulent Years.* Boston: Houghton Mifflin, 1970.

BLAU, P. *Dynamics of Bureaucracy.* Chicago: University of Chicago Press, 1955.

HYMAN, H., & SHEATSLEY, P. Some reasons why information campaigns fail. *Public Opinion Quarterly,* 1947, 11, 412–423.

KAHN, A., GROSSMAN, L., BANDLER, J., CLARK, F., GALKIN, F., & GREENWALT, K. *Neighborhood Information Center.* New York: Columbia University School of Social Work, 1966.

KRAMER, R. M. *Participation of the Poor.* Englewood Cliffs, N.J.: Prentice-Hall, Inc., 1969.

LITWAK, E., & FIGUEIRA, J. Technological innovation and theoretical functions of primary groups and bureaucratic structures. *American Journal of Sociology,* 1968, 73, 468–481.

LITWAK, E., & MEYER, H. Administrative styles and community linkages of public schools: Some theoretical considerations. In A. J. Reiss, Jr. (Ed.), *Schools in a Changing Society.* New York: Free Press, 1965, Pp. 53–73.

LITWAK, E., & MAYER, H. A balance theory of coordination between bureaucratic organizations and community primary groups. *Administrative Science Quarterly,* 1966, 11, 31–58.

MARCUSE, H. *One-dimensional Man.* Boston: Beacon Press, 1966.

MICHELS, R. The conservative basis of organizations. In R. K. Merton, et al. (Eds.), *Reader in Bureaucracy.* Glencoe, Ill.: Free Press, 1952. Pp. 143–149.

OGBURN, W. F. The changing family. In R. F. Winch & R. McGinnis (Eds.), *Selected Studies in Marriage and the Family.* New York: Holt, 1953. Pp. 75–77.

PARSONS, T., & BALES, R. F. *Family Socialization and Interaction Process.* Glencoe, Ill.: Free Press, 1955, Pp. 3–33.

PERROW, C. A framework for the comparative analysis of organizations. *American Sociological Review,* 1967, 32, 194–208.

PURCELL, F. P., & SPECHT, H. Selecting methods and points of intervention in dealing with social problems: The house on Sixth Street. In G. A. Brager & F. P. Purcell (Eds.), *Community Action Against Poverty.* New Haven: College & University Press, 1967. Pp. 229–242.

REDFIELD, R. The folk society. *American Journal of Sociology,* 1947, 52, 293–308.

ROGERS, D. *110 Livingston Street.* New York: Vintage Books, 1969.

SIMMEL, G. *The Sociology of Georg Simmel.* Edited by Kurt H. Wolff. Glencoe, Ill.: Free Press, 1950. Pp. 409–427.

THEODORSON, G. A. Acceptance of industrialization and its attendant consequences for the social patterns of non-western societies. *American Sociological Review,* 1953, 18, 477–484.

TÖNNIES, F. *Fundamental Concepts of Sociology.* New York: American Book, 1940.

VINTER, R. Analysis of treatment organizations. In E. J. Thomas (Ed.), *Behavioral Science for Social Workers.* New York: Free Press, 1967. Pp. 207–221.

WEBER, M. The essentials of bureaucratic organization: An ideal-type construction. In R. K. Merton, et al. (Eds.), *Reader in Bureaucracy.* Glencoe, Ill.: Free Press, 1952. Pp. 18–27.

WILENSKY, H. L., & LEBEAUX, C. N. *Industrial Society and Social Welfare.* New York: Free Press, 1958.

WIRTH, L. Urbanism as a way of life. In P. K. Hatt & A. J. Reiss, Jr. (Eds.), *Cities and Society: The revised reader in urban sociology.* Glencoe, Ill.: Free Press, 1957. Pp. 46–63.

2

CITIZEN PARTICIPATION

If we were to limit our discussion to four key concepts central to the practice of community organization and social planning, they would surely be the following: *problem, purpose, power,* and *participation.* As noted in our introduction, there have been substantial changes in the purposes, forms, sponsors, and strategies of citizen participation over the last twenty years. Although the primacy of participation is widely recognized—it has even been called "the most vital organizational problem of our time"—the term continues to suffer from a high degree of ambiguity because of the ideological overtones which inevitably pervade any discussion of participation. Fueled by the opposing philosophies of representative or participative democracy, value judgments usually prevail over clarity and evidence in regard to actual experience with various modes of citizen participation. Frequently there is a mystique evoked by participation that draws on an antibureaucratic, antiprofessional ideology, which includes a rejection of bigness and the established institutions of representative government. The latter are assumed to have broken down and to be incapable of meeting the aspirations of "people who want to control decisions affecting their lives." Citizen participation, particularly at the grass roots, is thereby invoked as the *solution* to many social problems rather than as a preferred *means* for community problem solving.

Apart from these ideological aspects, there are numerous elements of participation which could become the basis of practice theory if they were studied more systematically. These include, for example, analysis of the multiple purposes of participation and their specific prerequisites, supports, and constraints.

In particular, the wide range of purposes, structures, and strategies for citizen participation needs to be distinguished because there is some evidence that different types of participation are suitable for different objectives and functions. Some of the major purposes include the provision of information and advice, consultation, support and sanction, problem identification and goal setting, planning, policy and program development. With respect to the means for selecting participants, there are issues pertaining to the degree of their authority, responsibility, power, accountability, and appropriate kinds of incentives and rewards. Other issues in regard to citizen participation are concerned with the power dimension. Some scholars view participation as a continuum which ranges from benign administrative involvement at one end to citizen control at the other end.

The selections in this section are concerned with the analysis of the role of citizens as service volunteers and as participants in planning bodies and neighborhood organizations.

Drawing mainly on research on participative decision making in organizations, Maryanne Vandervelde's "The Semantics of Participation" clarifies the concept as it is used in citizen involvement in community decision making. She finds considerable confusion in the social sciences. She proposes, in the interest of greater precision, that participation become a synonym for *involvement*, a term that should not connote any notion of influence, power equalization, or decentralization, three concepts with which *participation* has become unjustifiably entangled. Disentanglement of these disparate components would enable practitioners to focus their concern on questions about *who* participates in *what way, when, where,* and *how*. Participation then would be equivalent to involvement in a group decision-making process.

In "Citizen Participation: Characteristics and Strategies" Edmund M. Burke identifies three functions of citizen participation in planning: to serve as a constituency of support and as a source of information and to monitor the design and the implementation of social policies. Citizens can carry out the following kinds of tasks: to review and comment on programs and policies, consult, advise, share, and control decision making. Rather than furthering an elusive public interest, planning is seen as a means of furthering group interests on substantive issues. Five strategies of citizen participation are identified: education therapy, behavioral change, staff supplement, cooptation, and community power. Burke suggests that the appropriateness and the effectiveness of any particular strategy are related to the kind of organizational sponsorship that characterizes the planning process, its goals and resources, and the particular role sanctioned for citizen participation.

Health service planning organizations are the subject of "Representing Consumer Interests: The Case of American Health Planning" by James A. Morone and Theodore R. Marmor. Health service agencies may ultimately be primarily of historical interest, but the lessons to be learned from their experience and the consequent conceptual clarification are valuable. Morone and Marmor observe that the representation of consumer interests in planning was initially conceived as a means of challenging the domination of the provider (that is, physicians and hospitals) interests in the field of health. Despite the legislative requirement that over half the participants in a health service agency represent consumers, there were numerous legal challenges to this notion, and the results of this kind of participation fell far short of the expectations. In their perceptive analysis of participation, representation, and accountability, the authors show

how these ideas were conceptually muddled in the law itself. They identify different modes of accountability, participation, and representation. They conclude that unless the represented constituencies control some scarce resource such as votes, representatives cannot be held accountable and representation is essentially symbolic. Morone and Marmor recommend that the professional staff be placed under consumer control and assigned to provide support to the consumer effort and that consumer representatives be selected by organized interest groups.

There is a long tradition of faith in neighborhood groups as providers of social services. In the 1920s John Dewey in *The Public and Its Problems*[1] and Mary Parker Follett in *The New State*[2] presented the intellectual precursors of today's theories of empowerment in which neighborhood and other nongovernmental organizations are being rediscovered and proposed as "mediating structures between the individual and the mega-structures of public life."[3] As a means of recovering the lost sense of community and regenerating social institutions on the local level, Janowitz, among others, has called for "citizen participation in the management of social welfare institutions," adding that "the frontier in citizen participation rests on the specific local purpose voluntary association and on the direct involvement of local citizens in social welfare agencies."[4] The empowerment of neighborhood groups and primary social systems such as the family, peer, and other informal groups is advocated as a way of combating the inefficiency and undemocratic character of large public bureaucracies. Richard C. Rich, in "The Roles of Neighborhood Organizations in Urban Service Delivery," reviews the functions of locality based voluntary associations. He describes them as consumer cooperatives seeking to secure public service from other organizations, as alternative producers of desired services, and as organizations of citizen coproducers wherein service-delivery levels are determined in partnership between neighborhood residents and governmental agency staff. These three functions differ significantly in the effectiveness and the efficiency with which citizens can use them to secure services in large part because each kind of community association requires different kinds of resources.

The preceding readings deal with citizen volunteers performing essentially political roles as advocates and constituents in community decision-making processes. There is another function that volunteers perform in their capacity as citizens: They offer to others a wide range of person-to-person helping services, such as visiting, tutoring, trasnporting, shopping, giving care, offering advice, information, and emotional support, and providing social and recreational experiences. In the last decade there has been a resurgence of new forms of volunteer work in the fields of criminal justice, family violence, drug abuse, and community mental health. In addition, the character of volunteers has changed because more students, aged, retired, and professional persons are taking part, and governmental responsibility for the promotion of volunteerism has increased.

Professionals frequently work with citizen volunteers in their capacities as policymakers, fund raisers, advocates, and direct-service providers. In light of the cutbacks in staff and other resources in governmental programs, it is not surprising that some agencies have turned to volunteers to fill the gaps. But it is unwise to regard volunteers as a cheap substitute for professionals rather than as a supplement, and it is unlikely that volunteer effort can fill the gaps caused by reductions in governmentally supported programs. Harriet H. Naylor, in "Volunteers, Resource for Human Services," provides an overview of some of the principles that can be used in organizing and managing the employment of this important resource. Naylor discusses the special tasks that volunteers can assume in service delivery and as advocates, and she offers some guidelines for the effective performance of these functions in both governmental and voluntary nonprofit organizations.

NOTES

1. John Dewey, *The Public and It's Problems* (New York: Holt, Rinehart and Winston, Inc., 1927).
2. Mary P. Follett, *The New State* (New York: Longmans, Inc., 1918).
3. Peter L. Berger and Richard John Neuhaus, *To Empower People: The Role of Mediating Structures in Public Policy* (Washington, D.C.: The American Enterprise Institute for Public Policy Research, 1977), p. 3.
4. Morris Janowitz, *Social Control of the Welfare State* (New York: Elsevier North-Holland, Inc., 1976), p. 126; see also pp. 132–33.

Maryanne Vandervelde

The Semantics of Participation

The attention being focused these days on participative decision making (PDM) in organizations is part of a wider, democratic concern or value that people should be involved in decisions which affect them. Participation has been called "the most vital organizational problem of our time" (Mulder, 1971, p. 31); it is certainly an issue which concerns both superiors and subordinates. However, the definition of PDM is far from clear. Among the words used and confused in the context of PDM are: centralization-decentralization, involvement, influence, power equalization, and power equilibrium. These should all mean different things, but they are often used interchangeably and without proper definition in the literature. There has been little effort to differentiate the various components subsumed under PDM, and there has been

little concern about helping managers fit the concept to the need.

It is this author's contention that only one component of the usually confused PDM process deserves the PDM label. Participation is, or should be simply the act of participating—"to partake of, to share in" (Webster) the process of making decisions. A synonym for participation would be involvement—the who, how, when, and where parts of the decision-making process.

Participation, *per se*, says nothing about whether an organization is centralized or decentralized; participation does not indicate how much influence a person has on the actual decision that is made; participation does not point to any particular amount of power that that person has in the organization. In essence, an individual who participates in a decision-making process could be operating in a very centralized or decentralized system, could have very high or low influence, and could be in a group

Reprinted with permission of the author and *Administration in Social Work* 3:1, Spring 1979, pp. 65–78.

where power is equalized or where the power structure is quite hierarchical.

The purposes of this article are to explicate the current confusion in terminology in the literature; to offer a model of the group-decision process; to state what the strict definition of PDM should be; and to suggest the importance of including influence in a new concept of PIDM—participative and influence-based decision-making.

PDM REQUIRES "CONTINGENCY THINKING"

It is small wonder that attitudes about PDM vary widely; one person who says he/she is against PDM may have something quite different in mind from another person who says he/she is for it. The actual process of an employee's participation in decision making may mean anything from a man whose suggestion box idea is promptly put in the waste basket, to a worker who is designated chairperson of the organization's policy-setting body and actually wields a great deal of influence.

Organizational decision making can be viewed as a continuum—from totally authoritarian to totally delegated—in management practice, with PDM occupying a large central area on that continuum (see figure 1). Many people conceive of PDM as a static, unitary phenomenon near the right end of this spectrum, but participation does not usually mean that the manager totally delegates the decisions; there is nothing in the empirical studies of PDM that calls for the manager to be a "Casper Milquetoast." If one believes that participation means endless discussions by everyone about everything, the costs will

be seen as extraordinarily high: much expended energy, loss of time, diminished and confused responsibility, and unclear division of roles.

Rather, if PDM can be assumed to involve both superiors and subordinates in some kind of joint effort, it cannot be pictured at either extreme on the continuum, and the specific form of the process should be determined on a contingency basis. In general, the literature suggests that where the work to be done is complex, unpredictable, and less visible, organizations are better off using more decentralized decision-making structures and encouraging greater staff participation. Organizations operating in stable environments and dealing with relatively routine tasks, on the other hand, tend to lower efficiency and effectiveness by encouraging unnecessary participation.

In order for participative management to work, there must also be strong goal orientation, high standards, and clearly stated constraints (Bragg & Andrews, 1973; Hage & Aiken, 1970; Likert, 1967). Certain areas of responsibility and accountability can and must be retained for the manager without compromising the participative process (Hirsch & Shulman, 1976).

DEFINITIONS OF PDM IN THE LITERATURE

Some researchers never bother to define PDM at all, probably assuming that their own conceptions are shared by everyone. Those who *do* define PDM emphasize a wide array of facets in the decision-making process. These facets can basically be divided into four components, with several other factors influencing the entire process. Figure 2 is a model of the group decision-making process, including all four components extant in the literature on PDM. Only the area labeled involvement, however, is, to this author, the legitimate usage of the term "participation."

Figure 1

totally
authoritarian

totally
delegated

participation

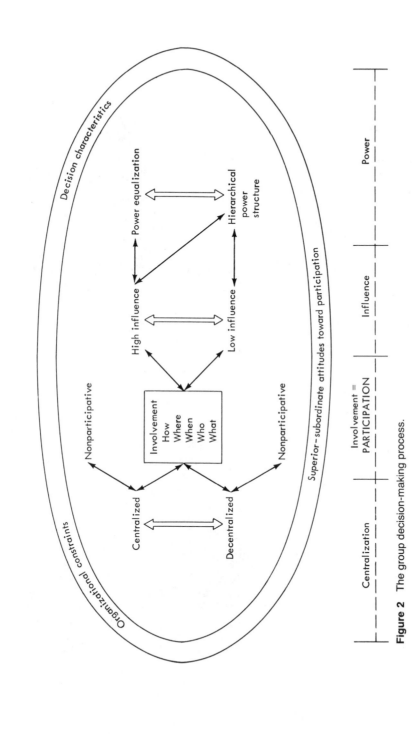

Figure 2 The group decision-making process.

Centralization-Decentralization

Many investigators have focused on centralization-decentralization, a structural component of organizations, in their definitions of PDM. Olmstead and Christensen (1973) conducted a national study of 31 social welfare agencies and found that the tendency for all agencies is toward unilateral (centralized) decisions. Ivancevich and Donnelly (1975) looked at 295 trade salesmen and found that those in flat (decentralized) organizations perceived more satisfaction and lower anxiety-stress and performed more efficiently than those in medium and tall (centralized) organizations. Hage and Aiken (1970) studied centralization, along with six other variables, in 16 health and welfare organizations and found that it was inversely related to high rates of program change; that is, decentralization allowed organizations to change more efficiently. Egan defined participation as a measure of decision-centralization, which he further defined as "an index of subordinate or leader ratings of perceived autonomy or influence in decisions of a group" (1974, p. 3). Starkweather's (1970) plea for decentralization in large hospitals is based on a "troika" of specialists in administration, nursing, and medicine; however, it is entirely possible that his decentralized system could be very nonparticipative.

Thompson's (1971) book argues that the more centralized an organization, the less innovative it will be in developing solutions to nonroutine problems and tasks. But the amount and kind of participation in decision making is not clear.

One attempt to differentiate centralization from participation has been made by McMahon and Camilleri (1975), who state:

> There appears to be no simple empirical relationship between "degree of centralization" of an authority system and participation rates. For example, our argument implies that in polar cases of centralization

the officers must be influenceable if members are to participate at all; but if they are, participation is not necessarily less than in decentralized organizations. This implies that participation rates are not likely to be an accurate index of decentralization (p. 640).

Decentralization is not a synonym for participation, although it is frequently used as such in the literature. Organizations can be: (1) centralized but participative; (2) centralized but nonparticipative; (3) decentralized but nonparticipative; and (4) decentralized and participative. Further, one should distinguish clearly between the premises and formulation of a decision versus its implementation. Often decisions are actually made in a centralized way, but subsequent decisions concerning implementation are decentralized.

Involvement

There are a few researchers who focus on the actual mechanics of participation—the how, what, when, where, and who kinds of issues. Hage and Aiken's measure of participation is "how much the occupants of various positions participate in decisions about the allocation of resources and the determination of organizational policies" (1967, p. 77). Mulder and Wilke see participation as "a process in which subordinates are allowed to contribute to decision making; the degree of involvement varying from consultation by the leader of the unit with his subordinates to real group decision making" (1970, p. 432).

The important work done by Vroom and Yetton (1973) and Vroom and Jago (1974) attempts to describe the circumstances under which participation should take place. To paraphrase Vroom et al., one can be autocratic when one has all the cards, but this very seldom happens in complex organizations.

The Bragg and Andrews (1973) study of a hospital laundry was concerned with the details of involvement—the role of the foreman, the process and content of group meetings, attitudes toward PDM, and absenteeism. But it also points to several situational factors which strongly favored success.

Influence

Campbell et al. (1970) use "influence in decision making" and "participation" interchangeably. Pennings (1976) subsumes under influence the following factors: participativeness, centralization, and organizational autonomy. Heller's definition of participation is "a process in which two or more parties influence each other in making plans, policies, or decisions" (1971, p. xxiv).

Tannenbaum and Kahn (1957) devised the control graph to show the averaged members' perceptions of the amount of influence exerted by different hierarchical levels. This graph measures the total amount of influence exerted (equated with degree of participation) as well as the manner in which the influence is distributed (by which they indicate the degree of power equalization).

Hrebiniak (1974) studied participation in terms of employee attitudes and perceptions of influence. He found much perceived deprivation in decision-making and also noted that subjects perceived a "fixed-pie" notion of power.

Comstock's work (1975) measures influence in organizations—the extent to which influence is distributed differentially for different types of decisions and the degree to which members from different positions perceive the same distribution of influence.

Power

One of the main characteristics of the participation concept is its relatedness to power. Viguers (1961) refers to the politics of power in a hospital, says that only the uninitiated believe that the organization chart shows where the power actually lies.

Prince (1972) talks of power sharing and says that it will facilitate growth and creativity of employees, while traditional management based on reward and punishment stifles initiative.

Social science professionals have talked for some time about the desirability of power equalization, but many would argue with Strauss' definition: "Participation, however defined, is well accepted as a form of power equilization" (1963, p. 60). Power equalization does refer to a process of reduction in the power differential between people, but to always equate participation with power equalization would be a mistake.

McMahon is one of the few researchers who are concerned with proper definitions, and he laments the confusion between PDM and power equalization: "The difference is that the main focus of power equalization is the *relative* amount of influence exerted by the lower organizational levels while participation deals with the involvement of all participants in decision making while ignoring the relative amounts of influence" (1976, p. 204).

A crucial question is posed by Mulder and Wilke: what is the meaning of "equals" in the context of equalization? One should not ignore the differences which exist in the amount of expert power held by individuals. Managers of organizations tend to have more information about the administrative, economic, technological, and social data relevant to that organization because they are constantly working with these data and are trained to handle them. Equally as important is having expertise in communications and human relations, and managers tend to have more experience in this area than subordinates.

Mulder and Wilke's (1970) experiment manipulated the influence process and drew conclusions quite opposite to the power equalization theme of Strauss and others: greater participation by subordinates in the decision-making process, combined with more expert power of superiors, results in a larger difference in superiors' effective influence on subordinates. Under certain conditions, then, participation leads to a widening of the power gap rather than equalization.

Mulder and Wilke cite many Dutch studies which indicate that even when participation procedures are instituted in good faith, most of the expert power is still concentrated in a small group of people. Differences between the various strata of society—between "haves" and "have-nots"—are very ingrained, and the costs of learning are veryhigh.

As Bacon stated many centuries ago, knowledge is power. It *is* possible that subordinates would have technological expertise and knowledge of detail not available to the superior. This is especially true in professional organizations. Furthermore, a subordinate, through working with his boss, might acquire more expert power than his superior. In either case, more participation would then lead to more influence of subordinate on superior and hence more power equalization.

It is a mistake, however, to assume that PDM is automatically a method of power equalization. A power equalized system is neither easy to accomplish nor a necessarily desirable achievement for organizations.

ATTITUDES AND PATTERN-MAINTENANCE MECHANISMS

A few researchers have been careful enough to consider PDM in the context of its environment, and semantics here too should not be ignored. Among all the factors that influence the entire process of decision-making (see figure 2), attitude is probably the most important. Several pieces of research have demonstrated the significance of (1) worker attitudes toward PDM, and (2) manager attitudes or attitudes in the work environment toward PDM.

On the subordinate level, Mulder (1971) cites many examples of research which show low levels of motivation to participate in decision-making, often coupled with low levels of expertise. Mulder suggests that participation is promoted primarily by members of the intellectual, often academic, levels of society. In other words, the intellectuals are making up the game and the rules, but the game will be played by others. Participation is not intrinsically benign. When people realize that they are participating in unimportant or incomprehensible matters, they will learn not to engage in any other possibly useful and productive participative activities. Dutch research confirms other findings that "bad participation was evaluated as worse than no participation at all" (Mulder, 1971, p. 36).

Joseph Alutto, in collaboration with other researchers, has studied in great detail decision preference (Alutto & Acito, 1974; Alutto & Belasco, 1972; Alutto & Vredenburgh, in press) and has noted the importance of differentiating (1) experiences of current decisional participation, from (2) statements of ideal or preferred rates of participation. Alutto and Vredenburgh's recent study of 197 nurses concludes: "Writers concerned with integrating the wide diversity of findings on causes and consequences of decisional participation would do well to question the generalizability of conclusions about patterns of current or preferred decisional participation" (p. 12). Clearly, few researchers have been as careful as they should be in differentiating these concepts when asking for subjective opinions about participation.

Lack of worker interest in participation can stem from many factors, including prior experience, personality characteristics (Vroom, 1960), age, etc. In human service organizations, there is the special phenomenon of "technical entrepreneurs"—professional artists, if you will, who are trained to help people and have no desire to be involved in the "dirty work" of administration.

Similarly, there are real intrapersonal barriers among managers. Krishnan (1974) found that a large majority of the corporate managers he surveyed believe that the traditional managerial prerogatives are desirable in decision-making. Argyris (1966) studied 265 decision-making meetings and found great discrepancy between executives' words and actions. In theory, they voted overwhelmingly for open systems, but in practice, they created decision systems that were the anathema of openness, trust, innovation, and flexibility.

Lowin (1968) says that both PDM and hierarchical systems have pattern-maintenance mechanisms which include selective intake and retention of personnel, implicit and explicit indoctrination (attitude change), and behavioral shaping within the organization. In a hierarchical system, PDM applicants, employees, and procedures will be discouraged. On the other hand, the pattern-maintenance system for PDM encourages and rewards suggestions from subordinates; pro-PDM attitudes and behavior are reinforced. Thus, researchers must be aware of the environment, the extant system in which PDM activities are supported or aborted.

Because motivational and environmental constraints are so important to the understanding of PDM, empirical demonstrations can be generalized only to populations that do not vary significantly in motive structure from the test population. Lowin cites many authors who question the validity of generalizing from PDM experiences abroad to those in the United States, or even from one subculture to another. Because of cultural differences in attitudes, expectations, and motive structure, "success in one climate may prove failure in another" (Lowin, 1968, p. 79). International comparisons indicate that the U.S. and other countries are quite different in their conception and implementation of participation (Tannenbaum et al., 1974).

And yet, despite the apparent importance of attitudes and pattern-maintenance mechanisms, these factors are all but ignored in much research to date. Hopefully, practitioners are more concerned about these situational factors than researchers have been.

ENDS AND MEANS

As Mintzberg (1973, p. 77) says, "the most crucial part of the manager's work—the part that justifies his great authority and his powerful access to information—is that performed in his decisional roles." The manager has many options in the decision-making structure he/she institutes and promotes within the organization; hopefully, the choice among these options is very carefully made in order to meet specific goals. Participation is not a unidimensional thing, and the strategies chosen by any manager will produce particular outcomes; the desired outcome, with recognition of external constraints, should determine the choice of decision strategies.

In Heller's (1971) study, 260 senior business executives were asked their reasons for using participation, and the following priorities emerged:

1. to improve the technical quality of decisions;
2. to increase satisfaction;
3. to improve communications;
4. to train subordinates; and
5. to facilitate change (p. xx).

These are to some extent different and separable goals which might involve quite different strategies of participation. The system may be centralized or decentralized;

involvement may take a variety of forms; influence may be anywhere on the continuum from high to low; and the power structure may be quite hierarchical or quite equalized. Nevertheless, the means or the process must be designed to fit the goals of decision quality, improved satisfaction or communication, training, change, or other such ends. Goals do and should suggest means. PDM can be many things, and it undoubtedly works best when its elements—as well as attitudes of both superiors and subordinates—are suited to the task at hand.

There are certainly problems with PDM or "groupthink" (Collins & Guetzkow, 1964; Allison, 1971; Janis, 1972; Van de Ven & Delbecq, 1974). Questions have been raised about the quality of group decisions and about individual behavior disturbances within the group (e.g., temporary states of elation, fear, or anger, which reduce mental efficiency; chronic blind spots arising from social prejudices; shortcomings in information processing). Crisis situations can lead to collective panic, scapegoating, or other forms of what might be called group madness. Group process can also lead to mindless conformity and collective misjudgment of risk (Janis, 1972). The implementation of PDM has its risks and can be an "awesome task" (Hirsch & Shulman, 1976).

Nevertheless, reviews of the empirical literature have by and large indicated a positive correlation between PDM and productivity (Campbell et al., 1970; Lowin, 1968; Ebert & Mitchell, 1975). There is considerable evidence that participation does enhance organizational effectiveness—under certain conditions. Why is this true? Ebert and Mitchell cite empirical evidence for their four conclusions: (1) organizational contingencies are clearer with PDM; (2) PDM increases the likelihood that employees will work for outcomes they value; (3) PDM increases the effects of social influence on behavior; and (4) PDM in-

creases the amount of control that one has over one's behavior (1975, p. 263). Participation also plays a role in controlling organizational conflict.

Human service organizations are especially suited for PDM because of their complicated environments, their problems of professionalism, and their complex technology. Many would argue that some level of PDM is simply mandated by these factors (Bucher & Stelling, 1969; Nagi, 1974; Morrissey & Gillespie, 1975; McWhinney, 1972; Dowling, 1972; Metsch & Levy, 1974; Neuhauser, 1972; Thompson, 1967; Hasenfeld & English, 1974; Demone & Harshberger, 1974). Health and welfare organizations have the precarious challenge not only to efficiently manage human resources, but also to produce for the most part an unquantifiable unit—increased human welfare at less expense. This requires "a more mature partnership between the . . . administrator and staff" (Hirsch & Shulman, 1976) than the traditional hierarchical model has allowed.

NEW DEFINITIONS: PDM AND PIDM

As resources become increasingly scarce, the investment on the part of both the individual and the organization in PDM deserves closer scrutiny. One aspect of that scrutiny should be the confusion and misunderstanding created by definitional and semantical problems. If the human service administrator thinks of PDM as a unified, static concept, it will either be used improperly or not at all. Many operational misjudgments may have been made in the past because the semantics of participation were unclear and confusing. Researchers have the obligation to be much more clear about definitions.

This review of the literature suggests that it is impractical, imprecise, and irrational to continue subsuming so many disparate components under the label "PDM."

Logically, participation should only mean the act of participating in, sharing in, and partaking of decisions that are made. This would include issues of who participates, in what way, when the participation takes place, and where. Participation would be a synonym for involvement. PDM would imply nothing about the centralization-decentralization of the organization, or the influence of individuals, or the power equalization or equilibrium of the group.

However, in this author's opinion, it would be a mistake for any researcher or manager to look at participation without also evaluating influence. As the research of Mulder and Wilke (1970) and others has shown, participation without influence can become a sham. This author's dissertation research with professional staff members in community mental health centers indicates that people have strong negative feelings about PDM in a situation where they know they have little influence; those negative feelings can, in fact, affect their performance levels. Nevertheless, it is not uncommon in organizations to find PDM existing where there is very little staff influence.

Therefore, it seems reasonable to suggest that the concept of PDM be replaced with the concept of PIDM—participative and influence-based decision-making. One would then look at both the process of participation and the level of staff influence in an effort to understand group decision-making.

Though often included in the definition of PDM, the structural concept of centralization-decentralization and the issue of power distribution or equalization do not really belong under this label. More accurately, participation should be defined precisely as involvement in, sharing in, and partaking of the group decision-making process—the who, what, when, where, and how aspects of involvement. And influence, which is a separable phenomenon but should really be considered along with

participation, might well be included in a new concept of PIDM.

Many strategies of participation are available. If definitions are thought through carefully, participative structures and processes can be developed which will meet the needs of subordinates, managers, and organizations.

REFERENCES

ALLISON, G. T.. *Essence of decision.* Boston: Little, Brown & Company, 1971.

ALUTTO, J. A. & ACITO, F. Decisional participation and sources of job satisfaction: A study of manufacturing personnel. *Academy of Management Journal,* March 1974, *17,* 160–167.

ALUTTO, J. A., & BELASCO, J. A. A typology for participation in organizational decision making. *Administrative Science Quarterly,* March 1972, *17,* 117–125.

ALUTTO, J. A., & VREDENBURGH, D. J. Correlates of current and preferred rates of decisional participation. *Academy of Management Journal,* (in press).

ARGYRIS, C. Interpersonal barriers to decision making. *Harvard Business Review,* March-April 1966, 44.

BRAGG, J. E., & ANDREWS, I. R. Participative decision making: An experimental study in a hospital. *The Journal of Applied Behavioral Science,* 1973, *9,* 727–735.

BUCHER, R., & STELLING, J. Characteristics of professional organizations. *Journal of Health and Social Behavior.* March 1969, 3–15.

CAMPBELL, J. P., et al. *Managerial behavior, performance, and effectiveness.* New York: McGraw-Hill Book Company, 1970.

COLLINS, B. E., & GUETZKOW, H. *A social psychology of group processes for decision-making.* New York: John Wiley & Sons, 1964.

COMSTOCK, D. E. *The measurement of influence in organizations.* Paper given at the Pacific Sociological Association Meeting, Victoria, British Columbia, April 1975.

DEMONE, H. W., & HARSHBERGER, D. (Eds.), *A handbook of human service organizations.* New York: Behavioral Science Publications, 1974.

DOWLING, W. L. Objective-setting and policymaking in hospitals. *Proceedings of the course on current trends in health care administration.* Ann Arbor, Michigan: 1972.

EBERT, R. J., & MITCHELL, T. R. *Organizational decision processes.* New York: Crane, Russak & Company, 1975.

EGAN, D. M. *Participative decision making and effectiveness of health organizations: A new method of assessment.* Paper presented at the First Annual Miami International Conference on Progress and Prospects in Health Care Distribution Systems, Miami Beach, Florida, November 1974.

HAGE, J., & AIKEN, M. *Social change in complex organizations.* New York: Random House, 1970.

HASENFELD, Y., & ENGLISH, R. A. (Eds.), *Human service organizations.* Ann Arbor: University of Michigan Press, 1974.

HELLER, F. A. *Managerial decision-making.* London: Tavistock Publishers, 1971.

HIRSCH, S., & SHULMAN, L. C. Participatory governance: A model for shared decision making. *Social Work in Health Care,* Summer 1976, *1*, 433–446.

HREBINIAK, L. G. Effects of job level and participation on employee attitudes and perceptions of influence. *Academy of Management Journal,* December 1974, *17*, 649–665.

IVANCEVICH, J. M. & DONELLY, J. H., JR. Relation of organizational structure to job satisfaction, anxiety-stress, and performance. *Administrative Science Quarterly.* 1975, *20*, 272–280.

JANIS, I. L. *Victims of groupthink.* Boston: Houghton Mifflin Company, 1972.

KRISHNAN, R. Democratic participation in decision making by employees in American corporations. *Academy of Management Journal,* June 1974, *17*, 339–347.

LIKERT, R. *The human organization: Its management and value.* New York: McGraw-Hill Book Company, 1967.

LOWIN, A. Participative decision making: A model, literature critique, and prescriptions for research. *Organizational Behavior and Human Performance,* 1968, *3*, 68–106.

McMAHON, A. M. & CAMILLERI, S. F. Organizational structure and voluntary participation in collective-good decisions. *American Sociological Review,* October 1975, *40*, 616–644.

McMAHON, J. T. Participative and power-equalized organizational systems. *Human Relations,* 1976, *29*, 203–214.

McWHINNEY, W. H. Organizational form, decision modalities, and the environment. In B. M. Bass, & S. D. Deep (Eds.), *Studies in organizational psychology.* Boston: Allyn & Bacon, Inc., 1972.

METSCH, J. M., & LEVEY, S. Organizational analysis: Theory or anecdotes? *A.U.P.H.A. Program Notes,* February, 1974.

MINTZBERG, H. *The nature of managerial work.* New York: Harper & Row, 1973.

MORRISSEY, E., & GILLESPIE, D. F. Technology and the conflict of professionals in bureaucratic organizations. *Sociological Quarterly,* Summer 1975, *16*, 319–332.

MULDER, M. Power equalization through participation? *Administrative Science Quarterly,* March 1971, *16*, 31–38.

MULDER, M., & WILKE, H. Participation and power equalization. *Organizational Behavior and Human Performance,* 1970, *5*, 430–448.

NAGI, S. Z. Gate-keeping decisions in service organizations: when validity fails. *Human Organization,* Spring 1974, *33*, 47–58.

NEUHAUSER, D. The hospital as a matrix organization. *Hospital Administration,* Fall 1972, 8–24.

OLMSTEAD, J. A. & CHRISTENSEN, H. E. *National study of social welfare and rehabilitation workers, work and organizational contexts, effects of agency work contexts: An intensive field study.* Vol. 1. Washington, D.C.: Government Printing Office, 1973.

PENNINGS, J. M. Dimensions of organizational influence and their effectiveness correlates. *Administrative Science Quarterly,* December 1976, *21*, 688–699.

PRINCE, G. M. Creative meetings through power sharing. *Harvard Business Review,* July-August 1972, *50*, 47–54.

STARKWEATHER, D. B. The rationale for decentralization in large hospitals. *Hospital Administration,* Spring 1970, 27–45.

STRAUSS, G. Some notes on power-equalization. In H. J. Leavitt (Ed.), *Science of organizations.* Englewood Cliffs, N.J.: Prentice-Hall, 1963.

TANNENBAUM, A. S. et al. *Hierarchy in organizations.* San Francisco: Jossey-Bass Publishers, 1974.

TANNENBAUM, A. S., & KAHN, R. L. *Participa-*

tion in union locals. New York: Harper & Row, 1967.

THOMPSON, J. B. *Organizations in action: social science basis of administrative theory.* New York: McGraw-Hill Book Company, 1967.

THOMPSON, V. *Bureaucracy and innovation.* University of Alabama Press, 1971.

VAN DE VEN, A. H., & DELBECQ, A. L. The effectiveness of nominal, delphi, and interacting group decision making processes. *Academy of Management Journal,* December 1974, *17,* 605–621.

VIGUERS, R. T. The Politics of power in a hos-

pital. *The Modern Hospital,* May 1961, *96,* 89–94.

VROOM, V. H. *Some personality determinants of the effects of participation.* Englewood Cliffs, N.J.: Prentice-Hall, Inc., 1960.

VROOM, V. H., & JAGO, A. G. Decision making as a social process: Normative and descriptive models of leader behavior. *Decision Sciences,* October 1974, *5,* 743–769.

VROOM, V. H., & YETTON, P. W. *Leadership and decision making.* Pittsburgh: University of Pittsburgh Press, 1973.

Edmund M. Burke

Citizen Participation: Characteristics and Strategies

When the planner (obviously, the planning organization, as well) intervenes into the decision-making process, collaboration is inevitable. By intervening into a set of existing or newly created entities, the planner and planning organization become enmeshed in a network of interpersonal and interorganizational networks. Individuals and organizations external to the planner and planning organization become involved in some or all stages of the planning process and consequently may and frequently do have an effect on the outcome of a plan. It is axiomatic to conclude that planning is *participatory.*

The issue, therefore, is not whether planning is participatory or not, but what is the nature of participation in planning?

Reprinted from Edmund M. Burke, *A Participatory Approach to Urban Planning* (New York: Human Sciences Press, pp. 65–88), with the permission of the author and Human Sciences Press, (Copyright 1979, Human Sciences Press) and the *Journal of the American Institute of Planners* 34:5 (September 1968), pp. 287–94.

Who are the participants? What roles do they serve? What is the process of decision making in planning with participants? And what functions do the participants in planning serve?

WHO ARE THE PARTICIPANTS?— TURNING POINTS IN THE PARTICIPATION OF CITIZEN IN PUBLIC PLANNING

Citizen Participation Prior to Legislative Prescriptions

Since the mid-1950s, the participation of citizens in planning has emerged as a matter of *right* whether acknowledged or not. Even prior to the mid-1950s, however, planners made an accommodation to the participatory character of planning. The nature of the response varied, however, and varied principally according to the planner's conception of the environment within which planning and decision making took place. A common and early response, for example, was to take into account tacitly the opinions of selected formal and informal community leaders either by associating with them or by presuming their needs and desires. For planning to be effective, as one planner boldly stated, "The planner must gain the confidence of important community leaders."[1] Effectiveness is defined, obviously, in terms of a plan's acceptance.

Basically the planner acknowledged the influence of community leaders. It was an informal mechanism of participation. The planner responded to elites for pragmatic reasons, that is, to achieve acceptance of planning goals.

Citizen Participation in Urban Renewal

The advent of urban renewal in 1954 brought about an outright rather than a tacit acknowledgement of participatory planning. Moreover, it widened the scope of participants and required a *formal* structuring of individuals and groups. Again, however, the response was primarily pragmatic in terms of achieving planning goals; not, incidentally, in response to specific federal legislation. It was basically a recognition of one more class of actors who were believed to have an influence on plan acceptance.

In the development of urban *redevelopment* legislation in 1949, no consideration was given to any role of citizens in the process. Authority boards were created composed of "leading citizens," but these were instituted to allow for a borrowing capacity outside of the state legislative requirements. Primary attention was devoted to developing a mechanism that would provide a planned unfragmented approach to slum clearance.

In the mid-1950s, the objective was changed from purely slum clearance and redevelopment to include rehabilitation of homes and businesses. To reflect this change, the name urban *redevelopment* was changed to urban *renewal*. The change also brought about a new relationship with individual citizens and groups. The Urban Renewal Administration insisted that local renewal agencies provide a means for citizen involvement. It is interesting to examine the substantive reasons.

A number of studies in the early 1950s began to question seriously the effectiveness of redevelopment. On the one hand it wasn't achieving the aims that it had set for itself. Slums continued to proliferate often faster than urban redevelopment programs could demolish them. Both Baltimore and Chicago, for example, had ambitious redevelopment programs between 1950 and 1955, yet the slum clearance activities could not keep pace with the rapidly deteriorating housing.

One of the administrative requirements which emerged out of the 1954 act was called "Citizen Participation." For most renewal agencies, however, citizen participation meant the creation or continuation of anywhere from a seven- to a fifteen-member advisory board composed principally of (again) "citizen leaders." For clearance objectives this made practical sense. So-called citizen leaders had access to those who could make development work; i.e., contractors, bankers, developers, legislators.

Grass roots, or any kind of broad scale citizen participation was negligible for a number of years. "In clearance areas," according to one urban renewal director, "you don't organize citizens, you prepare people for moving."[2] At the same time as urban renewal activities began to encompass rehabilitation objectives, the involvement of citizens in renewal planning began to emerge. One study of 95 renewal agencies conducted in 1965 reveals that grass roots citizen participation was confined almost exclusively to renewal agencies engaged in rehabilitation.[3] A little more than a dozen had any organized program involving citizens in planning agencies.

These few agencies accounted for two-thirds of all the nation's rehabilitation projects at that time.[4]

In this respect, citizen participation became less a value ideal than a practical necessity. To achieve rehabilitation goals, dwellings and businesses had to be fixed up and repaired. The citizens, in effect, controlled implementation of renewal goals. The renewal agency in order to achieve citizen cooperation held out the inducement of participation in planning. The involvement of citizens became a quid pro quo; the agency would take the deficiencies out of the neighborhood if the citizens would rehabilitate their houses.

Unlike participatory techniques prior to renewal, which aimed at developing sanction and legitimacy from among community leaders, the involvement of neighborhood groups in renewal planning sought two objectives: legitimacy and a change in citizen attitude. Prior to renewal, there was little necessity, pragmatically, to involve community leaders formally. A perception of community and political leaders' needs led the planner to devise courses of action beneficial to these groups. Community and political leaders benefited from the planner's efforts. This is not to suggest that the planner was a tool of the community and political leaders. Not necessarily. It occurred because the planner and the leaders shared the same value premises. The function of the planner was to improve the city and more often than not this meant improvement for business leaders, and it should be added, at the total community's expense.

Rehabilitation costs, on the other hand, cannot be spread across the community. Some can, of course. Public improvement is an example. But the main costs of rehabilitation are borne by the homeowners and the tenants. Techniques other than outright grants are necessary to induce them to make these improvements. Their

attitude has to be modified, changed to an orientation favorable to rehabilitation objectives.

Participation is used as the technique. By sharing in agency decision-making it was hoped that neighborhood citizens would come to share the aims of the planning activities. It was to be hoped that their attitudes would become positive toward the agency's goals. Indeed, the Urban Renewal Administration cited this as an objective of citizen participation: "The willingness of individuals to accept these [rehabilitation] standards and do their part in creating a better neighborhood can be stimulated if they have a part in the development of the standards."[5]

Despite the pragamatic nature of the response to participation, the urban renewal program was the first governmental program to broaden the scope of participation beyond the community elites. The urban renewal program, moreover, introduced into the lexicon of planning the term "*citizen participation.*"

Citizen Participation in Poverty Program

Beginning with the poverty program in the 1960s, the concept of citizen participation took on a new meaning. Newer actors were identified: the victims of poverty itself. It was a personal commitment, assured R. Sargent Shriver, the poverty program's first director, "that the poor themselves actively participate in the planning, implementation, and administration of these programs."[6]

The intention was less pragmatic than urban renewal. Where urban renewal described citizen participation as a means of gaining citizen cooperation, the poverty program announced that citizens should have a voice in programs and plans affecting their destiny. Citizens should also contribute substantively to the planning process by pointing out solutions and devising the means to solve problems. Other reasons were also offered. Some defined citizen participation as therapeutic for the poor; a way for the poor to learn how to overcome hopelessness and despair. Others saw it as a means for giving the poor power. In any event, the poverty program was the first federal program that stated clearly that a particular group of citizens should have a voice in planning.

From the outset the poverty program was marked by confusion and contention. It was doubtlessly the most controversial government program ever initiated. Disputes between mayors and local poverty officials marked the first sign of contention. The Bureau of the Budget, then Congress, and finally federal administrators lost their initial enthusiasm for the poverty program.[7]

While support was given to a number of programs, such as Headstart and Neighborhood Legal Services, begun by the Office of Economic Opportunity, support in the late 1960s began to diminish for the Community Action Program (CAP) agencies. The CAP agencies were the fundamental organs for involving the poor in planning.

Under Nixon, an outspoken foe of the "War on Poverty," the poverty program came under repeated attacks. A number of programs were transferred to existing federal agencies and departments. An attempt was made to phase out the CAP programs. The attempt failed. Two reasons can be offered.

After the initial conflicts that erupted in some of the nation's cities (Newark, Syracuse, Oakland, Pittsburgh, to name a few) the contention began to wane. The local CAP agencies began to find their way into the local structure of city government. The CAP agencies became an instrument for relating the poor to the programs of city government. Local mayors, once hostile, began to realize it might be difficult to live without CAP agencies, especially in administering a number of neighborhood programs that OEO had invented.[8]

Significantly, an amendment had been added in the 1967 Economic Opportunity Act providing that local governments would have the option of bringing their CAP agency under official control of city government. The purpose of the amendment was to assuage local officials and to serve as a threat to local CAP agencies that they could be taken over by local officials if they were uncooperative with City Hall. But the amendment was not needed. The conflict techniques that precipitated the backlash against the poverty program dropped out of use by local CAP agencies. In the six months following the passage of the amendment, only five percent of the CAP agencies were taken over by City Hall.[9]

A second reason for failure to wipe out community action agencies was the successful lobbying efforts by local constituents. The CAP agencies organized the poor not only for purposes of planning but also as a loyal constituency base. This was not an immediate objective, but served as an objective when the poverty program came under fire, particularly during the Nixon reign. The CAP agencies emerged as an interest group supported by a wide range of followers, who successfully defended the program in their local communities, before Congress and in the courts— a practical example of the behavioral hypothesis that if people are involved in a decision-making activity, they are likely to support and defend that decision.

The poverty program spawned three legacies for citizen participation in planning. One is that the base of participation has been legislatively widened to include specifically identified individuals and groups. In the case of the poverty program, this was originally defined as "residents of the areas and members of groups involved in local programs"; or, more simply, "the poor." Since the poverty program this definition has been broadened. Citizens are now defined as those who share an interest in a particular planning organization as well as those who would be affected by a plan or program of service. The latter are often referred to as "consumers."

A second legacy is that the purpose of citizen participation has shifted. Citizen participation is now seen as serving two purposes: one is organizational support. Citizens who are involved in planning activities will tend to endorse and support such activities. They become constituents of their own actions. The second is that the citizen participants are seen as a source of information and collective wisdom. Decisions tend to reflect widespread rather than narrow preferences. It will not ensure better decisions, nor, as Zbigniew Brzezinski advises, will it ensure political or social responsibility, "but it might make for a society that more readily approaches both."[10]

The third legacy is that citizen participation has become institutionalized. As each governmental planning program has emerged from Model Cities through health planning to human services planning, other legislation and federal regulations have required some form of citizen participation. It has become a normal part of the planning process, and as we noted in the Introduction, required in over 60 pieces of federal legislation.

Citizen Participation in Issue Politics

The civil rights struggle in the 1960s was instructive for Americans for a number of reasons. For one thing, it did awaken America to the contradictions between the promise of freedom and the practice of freedom. It not only brought about a wide number of legislative changes, but also changed the attitudes—albeit, still not sufficiently—of a significant number of people.

Another legacy was the dramatic illustration of the power of citizen participation. The participation was for the purpose of securing the rights of individuals in collective action. Marches, picketing, and sit-ins were the techniques of the collective action. The essence of the action was the organization of individuals around a common cause—an *issue*.

The 1970s witnessed the broadening of such participatory activities. There are organizations devoted to a wide spectrum of issues, such as women's rights, the protection of children, the legal rights of the mentally ill, the environment, disarmament, suburban rezoning, housing, and the like. Each defines its function as acting to protect the interests and aims of its constituency. The role of the organization is *advocacy*—promoting or proposing the adoption of an issue through judicial, legislative, or regulatory means. Frequently the organizations engage in adversary relationships with other organizations or governmental agencies.

Some issue-oriented organizations engage in planning—in the traditional sense of the term. The organization may initiate and develop a plan on behalf of its constituency. One example is a plan for public housing in a wealthy suburb proposed by a low income planning organization. An organization, on the other hand, may develop a plan as an alternative or competitive proposal to another organization's plan. A group, for example, may suggest an alternative income supplement proposal to that of the state welfare agency's proposal. A still further illustration is an organization that uses the courts to force another organization to develop a plan. A common example is when a mental health association gets a court order requiring the state department of mental health to develop more realistic plans for deinstitutionalizing state mental hospitals.

The significant factor in this development is that the operations of governmental agencies are more easily challenged. The citizen as a member of an issue-centered organization is provided an opportunity to influence decisions, to safeguard rights, or to force public organizations to initiate corrective action. The consequence is that the base of decision-making is even further widened. Citizens not only have the opportunity to influence decisions through the involvement in a planning agency's activities, but also citizens can influence decisions as members of organizations external to a planning agency.

This, of course, offers the potential, if not the actuality, of altering the "planning with citizens" orientation of planning agencies. Citizens active in planning agencies find their role to be not merely defending the planning agency and its plans before decision centers, such as legislators and city council members, but also before other citizen groups and organizations. More than one organization, all with citizen representation, may vie to influence decision centers over competing plans. The base and function of citizen participation has become expanded.

CITIZEN ROLES IN PLANNING

The roles citizens can and do play in planning organizations vary widely from one organization to the next. The lack of any consistent definition of citizen participation accounts for the variation. What determines the role is a variety of factors including organizational objectives and need, legislation and regulations, citizen pressures and demands, and, at times, issues of the moment.

Despite these variations, it is possible to identify a range of five roles. Each is based on the extent of influence the citizens have in deciding on planning issues and outcomes—from little influence to major or primary influence. They are a variation of the roles first proposed by Sherry Arnstein

in her widely quoted article "A Ladder of Citizen Participation."[11]

Although identified as discrete roles, they should be seen as part of a continuum. The roles, moreover, are additively inclusive; citizens, in other words, performing one role are assumed to be able to perform all predecessor roles. More than one role can be used in a planning organization.

Review and Comment

The role of citizens in the review and comment type of citizen participation is precisely as the title suggests. Citizens are given an opportunity to review proposed plans. Comments can be made, but the planning organization is under no commitment to alter or modify the plan.

It is a passive role designed primarily to provide information to citizens and groups.

This type of citizen participation is easily recognized because it relies on media techniques—newspaper advertising and radio announcements—and public hearings. The public hearings are formal, at which citizens are allowed to present testimony to a panel.

Consultation

The function of a consultant is to provide expert advice for the purpose of improving the effectiveness of a decision. Acting in this role citizens are recruited and asked for specific advice and information. The method for obtaining the advice is through meetings and questionnaires. The role of the citizen as a consultant is to be a part of framing planning decisions.

A secondary objective is to locate potential obstacles to planning issues and proposals. The use of meetings with a wide range of individuals and groups is a helpful technique in searching out attitudes toward a plan.

Similar to the previous role, the decision

to accept or reject the advice is the exclusive judgment of the planning organization. Unlike the review and comment role, however, the intent goes beyond just providing information to citizens. It is a two-way process of communications in which the main objective is to improve planning decisions.

Advisory

This is a formal organizational role. Citizens are recruited to the organization and placed on policy and planning committees within the planning organization. The committees, however, are *advisory.* Nonetheless, by virtue of membership in the organization, the degree of influence for citizens is greater than the degree of influence in the predecessor roles.

The objective of this role is to seek out both information and organized support for planning activities.

Shared Decision-Making

This role describes the participation of citizens and planners acting as partners in planning and decision making. The roles of each are recognized as essential in the planning process. The intention is to arrive at decisions that reflect the preference of the citizen-planner planning team.

This role is recognized by the formal participation of citizens in a wide variety of committees and tasks.

Controlled Decision-Making

In this role citizens exercise ultimate authority over all policy and planning decisions. The role of the professional staff is to facilitate decision-making—to act as advisers and provide information for citizen decision-making.

This role of citizen participation is common to voluntary organizations. There are some examples of the controlled decision-making role in public agencies, but they are rare.[12] It has been assumed that in public agencies ultimate decision-making is a responsibility of an elected legislative entity—city council, chief executive, state legislature, and the like.

DECISION-MAKING CHARACTERISTICS OF CITIZEN PARTICIPATION IN PLANNING

There are two processes for decision-making in planning with citizens. One is legislative and the other is interest group.

Legislative Decision-Making

The legislative or governing type of citizen participation is part of a historic tradition from the oligarchic conceptions of Athenian democracy through the broadening of the franchise arising out of the French and American revolutions to the emerging conceptions of "participatory" and "anticipatory" democracy. The long-held aim is a governing system in society in which the citizen shares in community and nation decision-making, or, in other words, sharing in *political power.* Because it typifies citizen and community control, the New England open town meeting is frequently held up as the ideal.

The ideal, however, has tended to be elusive, even in New England. Distrust of the masses and clear-cut prejudices have been persistent obstacles. In addition, the growing size and complexity of mass society has made the open town meeting concept difficult to fulfill.

The movement toward community control in the late 1960s arose out of the aim to share political power. Community control is primarily a mechanism for decentralizing political decision-making. It is the exercise of authority by a democratically organized government of a neighborhood jurisdiction.[13]

Alvin Toffler has argued for a variation of community control because of both the growing size of societies and the increased specialism of technology. Toffler proposes the development of constituent assemblies of nation, city, and neighborhood levels charged with social stocktaking and with defining and assigning priorities to specific goals. Toffler terms this *anticipatory* democracy. Equal representation cannot be guaranteed, but it does widen the base of participation in decision-making.[14]

Nevertheless, the governed under Toffler's new society, or under community control or under existing mechanisms of government are ruled by *representatives* (elected or chosen). The representative acts as the decision-maker. Political science textbooks cover this in adequate detail. It is the essential characteristics of the process that is of primary interest here.

First, of course, the constituency does not participate directly in the decision-making process. Each citizen supposedly has the capacity to influence the process. Some constituents have more influence than others, either through control of resources, institutions, knowledge, other constituents, or their own charisma. Decision-making frequently tends to respond to influential interests.

Admittedly, some legislators rise above interests and some indeed make decisions contrary both to influential constituents and their own constituency. These instances occur so rarely, however, that John F. Kennedy could only describe a dozen or so in his book *Profiles of Courage.*[15]

Despite the tendency to frame decisions around the interests of individual groups, the legislative decision-making process itself is designed to serve the "public interest." Indeed legislation is always propagandized as serving the public or national interest regardless of how shallow the piece of legislation. Oil depletion allowances are consistently upheld as serving the national interest. Welfare measures are advanced in terms of the public good. Ob-

viously, the public interest is not often served if only because it is not always possible, if possible at all, to determine the public interest. But what is of importance here is that the legislative decision-making process is *not* intended to serve the "private" interest.

Secondly, decision-making is determined by a voting preference. That is, a simple majority determines a legislative issue. Certainly an executive can veto a piece of legislation. But even in overriding a veto unanimity is not required. The essential issue is that consensus is *not* a characteristic of legislative decision-making.

Indeed, consensus is rare. Conflict, bargaining, negotiation, persuasion, and horse trading are the techniques of the legislative decision-making process. None of these techniques, incidentally, destroys the effectiveness of the legislative body's functioning. Conflict and at times heated argument, rarely if ever impair the relationship of the members with one another. Dispute is not just common, but viewed as healthy.

Thirdly, except in rare instances and only in instances affecting its own rules of conduct, the legislative body is not responsible for implementing the decision it makes. Once legislation is passed, whether by 51 percent or 98 percent of the body, the responsibility for implementing the decision falls to an administrative or executive group. An existing agency or a newly created agency is charged with carrying out the requirements of the decision.

Interest Group Decision-Making

If a public interest orientation and the absence of consensus are essential to the legislative process of participation, quite the opposite is necessary for the interest groups process of participation. Indeed, it operates for different purposes. First, it seeks to secure or protect a "private" interest, not a public interest. In its simplest form, it can be described as follows: A group of citizens come together around a common cause. They recruit others and persuade them to identify with their interest. They may even try to make their group "representative"[16] of the total population. But this is a technique, and a technique only, to provide sanction and legitimacy. The group, however, is still an interest group organized to achieve a cause that it alone feels is desirable.

Whether the cause is in the public interest or not is irrelevant. Sometimes it may be. Surely child labor laws and public education for the retarded, both of which arose out of the activities of interest groups, appear to have redounded to the interests of all. The inability to achieve gun registration laws and the continued support of oil depletion allowances on the other hand, appear not to have. The important point, however, is that in this context citizen participation is seen as a means for a group of citizens to obtain its own interests.

A second characteristic is the need for consensus in decision-making. An interest group is a means for organizing opinion and action either to achieve a specific goal or to protect an existing goal. In that sense, then, two functions are necessary. One is decision-making, the second is devising a course of action that will bring about the adoption of the decision. The latter is frequently the more formidable; and it is the latter that demands consensus and agreement during the decision-making phase.

Unlike a legislative body, which can delegate implementation, an interest group must rely on its own membership to achieve action. Members who are in disagreement with a course of action will be unwilling to assist in achieving the goal: The more disagreement, the more impotent the group becomes. Even though 60 or 70 or 80 percent of a group may vote in favor of a decision, they may still be unable to implement the decision. Those in op-

position may have the influence necessary to achieve action.

An interest group, consequently, struggles to achieve consensus and agreement. It is not, incidentally, a Quaker-like consensus that is sought. Some members may be cajoled into agreeing with a decision. Others may be pressured. There may even be conflict. But continued conflict destroys the process. It leads to splintering and therefore frustrating the goals of the groups.

A third characteristic is that interest groups have no authority. Despite the boastful tradition of interest groups in America, they are provided no special privileges of power. Indeed, even a commission appointed by a legislature must depend upon the persuasiveness of its case to commit legislators to agree with its recommendations. In the early 1960s, for example, a half dozen commissions and study groups were established by Congress to study the nation's public welfare system. None of the study groups' or commissions' major findings was implemented by Congress. The power of an interest group is the conviction of its case and the influence of its members.

For voluntary community planning agencies, the interest group process of decision-making is required. The absence of authority or positional legitimacy has required voluntary agencies to rely upon organizing individuals and groups to support planning activities. A basic principle of practice in the voluntary planning field, citizen housing agencies, conservation associations, settlement houses, and community welfare councils is that the planner and the agency are powerless. Planning goals, in other words, cannot be imposed on groups and communities merely for any value reason but simply because it would be unwise strategically.

Voluntary planning organizations, moreover, serve on behalf of a specified interest group. They may claim they serve the community at large, but this is a symbolic pronouncement, the function of which is to create a wider base of legitimacy for its actions.

In the voluntary social planning literature, a distinction is made between a "functional" community and a "geographical" community. The geograhical community is defined, as the term implies, by its geographical boundaries—neighborhood, city, metropolitan region, state, etc. A functional community, on the other hand, is composed of individuals and groups who share a common interest.[17]

This is a useful distinction, despite its obviousness. The voluntary planning agency emphasizes one set of objectives with its common interest group and another set with the geographical community. In working with the functional community, the objectives are to recruit and organize individuals to become a part of the common interest group, develop plans meeting the specific needs of the interest group and the general needs of the geographical community, to win support of such plans from the geographical community.

In relation to the geographical community, the objective is to identify specific needs of the geographical community, develop plans to meet these needs, and enlist support in the geographical community for implementation of these plans. In working with the functional community, the planning agency uses a community organization and planning method. In working with the geographical community, the agency uses a "community relations" or "public relations" method.[18]

Traditionally, an interest group orientation toward planning has been questionable for governmental planning agencies. Organizing interest groups to support a governmental agency is inconsistent with the public interest objective of government. Altshuler's case studies of planning

in the Twin Cities provides an interesting example. In one instance, the Minneapolis city planner established a citizen committee of business people to act as a sounding board for a master plan. The city council resented this tactic and interpreted it as a device to bring outside pressure on the council. This action, the council concluded, was alien to the practice of a planning professional whose primary function is to serve the public, or community-wide, interests.[19]

This conception of planning has been seriously questioned and is no longer considered valid. A number of studies, including the previously cited Altshuler study, report that however conscientiously planning agencies may try, they have considerable difficulty in defining the public interest. Given the diversity of interests in local communities, the search for a public, or community-wide, interest may be an elusive quest. It was this issue that served as a basis for Paul Davidoff's criticism of city planning in the mid-1960s and served as one of his premises for advocacy planning.[20]

Indeed advocacy planning essentially is interest group planning. Davidoff's suggestion that planners act on behalf of such groups as the Chamber of Commerce, labor organizations, antipoverty councils, and neighborhood organizations is a private-interest as opposed to a public-interest approach to planning. In Cleveland they have gone a step further and announced that the city planning agency is not only serving the physical development interests of the city (one development interest among others), but also serving the expressed interest of a singular group—the poor.[21]

Since the mid-1960s the growth in the number of specialized planning agencies further constrains the possibility of planning serving the public interest. Each planning agency is mandated to serve the interests of its own constituency. Community planning, it can be concluded, serves not the public interest, but the private interest of a group, or what Michael Fagence has identified as a "group interest."[22]

ASSUMPTION OF PLURALISM

To suggest that the function of a planning agency is to serve not the public interest but its own particular functional or group interest is not also to suggest that the public interest is achieved through the resolution of competing interests. This is the traditional conception of the private interest approach to governing and decision-making; that is, the interests of all are achieved through the free interplay of interests in the market place of ideas.[23]

However appealing this doctrine may be, it just does not seem to be consistently true. It assumes, obviously, that all interests are represented in the resolution process. It assumes, further, that all interests have equal information and equal access to information.

Even more significantly, the doctrine assumes that all interests have equal resources for influencing decisions. It would be simplistic to assume that all interest groups from bankers to neighborhood organizations have equal capacity to articulate issues, to utilize financial resources, and to organize constituencies. Some groups, in other words, are more equal than others.

Mazziotti has suggested that the assumptions of pluralism question not only the effectiveness of planning serving the interests of the powerless, but also the efficacy of advocacy planning. Advocacy planning, he argues, is premised on the conceptions of pluralism in decision-making. He suggests that the assumption of pluralism is a social myth designed to provide a rationale for instituting social programs that placate the politically and economically disenfranchised. The solution is a radical conception of planning that chal-

lenges not only current assumptions of planning but also the assumptions of the way power is structured in local communities.[24]

We are not so pessimistic as Mazziotti. Certainly the powerless are not always represented in the center of decision making. And certainly there is need for improvement. At the moment, however, the broader interests of a community, including the interests of the powerless, tend to be served over time by means of competing constituencies. The development of issue centered organizations and groups in the 1970s is an excellent example. Issue-centered organizations have broadened the base of community decision-making, as we noted earlier. They act as watchdogs over planning agencies' activities.

We would argue, too, that the *probability* of the public, or community-wide, interest being approximately served is achieved through citizen participation. Indeed, this is the essential function of citizen participation. It sets up the process for dialogue and thereby broadens the base of decision-making.[25]

SUMMARY

Planning is axiomatically participatory. Historically, however, the base of participation in public planning has changed from a small, informal elite to a formal broad base of constituents. The aims of citizen participation have also changed. Citizens now can serve three functions in planning. One is to serve as a constituency of support for the planning agency and its activities. The second is to serve as a means of wisdom and knowledge in the development of a plan and in identifying the mission of the planning agency. The third and emerging function is to act as a watchdog over one's own as well as others' rights in the design and delivery of policies.

There are five roles citizens can play in planning: review and comment, consultation, advisory, shared decision-making, and controlled decision-making. Citizens can be enacting more than one of these roles in an organization.

The emergence of a citizen role in planning, as well as the increasing specialized planning agencies, has changed the decision-making base of community planning from purely a public interest orientation to a private interest orientation. Planning agencies function on behalf of a substantive issue and a defined constituency.

CITIZEN PARTICIPATION STRATEGIES

Probably the most troublesome area of all is the choice of *strategy* objectives for citizen participation. Commonly advocated as serving fairly specific objectives, citizen participation is often predicated less upon value premises than upon practical considerations. In many cases, this is what makes it acceptable. It can, according to some claims, rebuild deteriorating neighborhoods, devise realistic and better plans, pave the way for the initiation of the poor and the powerless into the mainstream of American life, achieve support and sanction for an organization's objectives, end the drift toward alienation in cities, halt the rise in juvenile delinquency, and recreate small town democracy in a complex urban society.

This suggests that citizens can be used as instruments for the attainment of specific ends. Citizen participation, in other words, is a *strategy*. But the ends are sometimes conflicting. In one case, citizen participation is advocated as an administrative technique to protect the stability or even the existence of an organization; in another, it is viewed as an educational or therapeutic tool for changing attitudes; in still another case, it is proposed as a means for assisting an organization to define its goals and objectives.

To imply that citizen participation is a

single, undifferentiated, and overriding strategy is misleading. It is more accurate to speak of several strategies of citizen participation, defined in terms of given objectives. These objectives will be limited by available resources, as well as the organizational character of community activities, particularly community planning. Because planning operates through formal organizations, any strategy will be influenced by organizational demands—the necessity for coordinated efforts, the orientation toward purposeful (ideally, rational) action, and the demands of the environment, which, for public agencies, are often the requirements of extra-governmental jurisdictions. Thus, the relevancy of a strategy depends both upon an organization's abilities to fulfill the requirements necessary for the strategy's effectiveness and upon the adaptability of the strategy to an organizational environment.

. . . [C]itizen participation [can be analyzed] not as a value, but as the basis for various strategies. The more common uses of citizen participation will be reviewed, indicating the assumptions, conditions, and organizational requirements of each. Five strategies will be identified: *education-therapy, behavioral change, staff supplement, cooptation, and community power.*

Education-Therapy Strategy

A frequently proclaimed but rarely viable strategy of citizen participation focuses upon the presumed need for improvement of the individual participants. Accomplishing a specific task is irrelevant; rather, the participants become clients who are the objects of treatment. Consequently this strategy has often been defined as an end in itself.

One focus is education. In this context the act of participation is held to be a form of citizenship training, in which citizens working together to solve community problems not only learn how democracy works but also learn to value and appreciate cooperation as a problem-solving method. This would strengthen local government, spur community development, and create a sense of community or community identification.

Utilizing participation in community affairs as an educational device has had a profound and controversial impact on the practice of community organization employed by social workers. Early writers advocated participation not as the means but as the goal of community organization. At this stage there was a strong social reform orientation attached to community organization, and one of the pioneers in the field, Eduard Lindeman, termed it the Community Movement.[26] Later writers continued this emphasis but referred to participation as the "process goal" of community organization. Murray Ross, one of the principal spokesmen of this school of thought, explains that the aim of community organization is to help communities develop their own capacities to solve problems. Achievement of planning goals is secondary.[27]

More recently this view has come under criticism. Some maintain that process is secondary—in fact, not a goal at all but only a means. Cooperative attitudes, learned through the medium of participation, are preliminary to problem solving, and therefore are the means by which tasks are successfully undertaken.[28] One writer has suggested that in practice this takes place automatically—the goal of integration or process is abandoned as the demands of achieving specific tasks arise. "Broadly based decision-making must be replaced by decision-making by a few, who then 'sell' the task objective to others. The process of encouraging people to make their own decisions as to what is good for them thus gives way to the process of convincing them of what a change agent or a small group of 'leaders' thinks is good for them."[29]

Another way to focus this strategy is to use participation therapeutically as a means

for developing self-confidence, and, indeed, self-reliance—an underlying theme, incidentally, of the citizen participation objectives of both urban renewal and poverty programs. Individuals, according to this logic, will discover that by cooperating with their neighbors they can bring about changes affecting their community. More significantly, they will inspire each other, communicating an élan of hope and self-confidence. The participants will learn that they can reform their own lives: or, according to the hopes of OEO, turn away from the self-defeating and despairing culture of poverty; or, according to the Department of Housing and Urban Development (HUD), increase their sense of responsibility for their dwelling unit.

However meritorious the aim, there appears to be considerable difficulty in implementing this strategy. Admittedly, social group workers use participation as a device to achieve therapeutic or educational objectives. Then, too, those working with citizen groups report that positive changes do occur among individuals participating in community projects. Oscar Lewis, the anthropologist, has suggested that organizing the poor and giving them a sense of power and leadership through participation has been one method of abolishing the subculture of poverty in certain countries, notably Cuba.[30] Black Power advocates, as well, adopt as one of their premises that the organization of the black community will bring about the self-confidence and hope that American society has consistently denied its Negro citizens. But the formal and deliberate organization of citizens for this purpose has rarely been tried and if so, seldom for any appreciable time.

One such attempt was in Cincinnati more than fifty years ago. Called the Cincinnati Social Unit Plan, it organized a number of neighborhood districts and involved citizens in major health planning programs. The program engendered criticism from professional groups—chiefly medical—and local government officials. Some held the view that the citizens became *too* self-reliant. "There are still those who do not trust the voice of the people," commented Eduard Lindeman at the time.[31]

Mobilization for Youth in New York, a prototype of the Community Action Agencies, is another attempt, and similar in many respects to the Cincinnati program. It too defines participation as a means for increasing the independence of individuals in deprived areas. "Participation by adults," according to the Mobilization for Youth project, "in decision-making about matters that affect their interests increases their sense of identification with the community and the larger social order. People who identify with their neighborhood and share common values are more likely to control juvenile behavior."[32] But, like the Cincinnati program, it has run into difficulty with public officials and many of its goals have been emasculated.

What frustrates the use of this strategy in community planning is the inability to accommodate it to organizational demands. The focus is upon the means; participation is the overriding objective, not the accomplishment of goals or group tasks. The participants, therefore, must be determiners of decisions and policies, even to the point of allowing them to make unwise decisions or to create conflict and controversy. If, for example, the aim is to build self-reliance into the poor, any attempt to deter or inhibit their role in decision making will only reinforce their alienation and their belief that they are incapable of making decisions. Public officials in Cincinnati or New York would not take such chances. Similarly the Bureau of the Budget, governed by norms of efficiency and performance, has discouraged the use of this strategy by local antipoverty agencies.[33]

Behavioral Change Strategy

Group participation has been found to be a major force for changing individual behavior. Individuals tend to be influenced by the groups to which they belong and will more readily accept group-made decisions than lectures or individual exhortations to change. This has led to a strategy of participation which, although somewhat similar to the *education-theory* strategy, is sufficiently different to require a separate classification. The strategy is deliberately change oriented and is aimed at influencing individual behavior through group membership. It is a strategy commonly associated with community organization practice and more recently with increasing importance in certain schools of management science.[34] Moreover, it is a strategy reflected in much of the urban renewal literature on citizen participation and, in fact, is even enunciated in a President's Housing Message to Congress.[35]

Briefly, the objective is to induce change in a system or subsystem by changing the behavior of either the system's members or influential representatives of the system. The group is seen as a source of influence over its members. Therefore, by focusing upon group standards—its style of leadership, or its emotional atmosphere—it is considered possible to change the behavior of the individual members. The group itself becomes a target of change even though the goal may be to change individual behavior.[36] This particular emphasis distinguishes this strategy from the *education-therapy* strategy, for though many of the techniques may be similar, the objective is different. Whether an individual personally benefits from participating in the process is not necessarily relevant. The focus is upon the task and upon helping the group accomplish the task goal.

Two major premises underlie the *behavior change* strategy. First, it has been found that it is easier to change the behavior of individuals when they are members of a group than to change any one of them separately. Second, individuals and groups resist decisions which are imposed upon them. They are more likely to support a decision and, equally important, more likely to assist in carrying it out if they have had a part in discovering the need for change and if they share in the decision-making process. Participation in the decision-making process, in other words, can create commitment to new objectives.

The effectiveness of this strategy, however, depends upon the existence of certain conditions. In the first place, the participants must have a strong sense of identification with the group, and feel assured that their contributions and activities are meaningful both to themselves and to the group. There must, too, be some satisfactions or gains from participation, either through personal and group accomplishments or from the mere fact of the association with other members. The awareness of the need for change, and consequent pressure for change, must come from within the group as a shared perception. Facts, data, and persuasion are not enough.

There is a necessity, too, for participants to be actively involved in the decision-making process. The making of the decisions, the working through of the problem, so to speak, are the dynamic factors that change behavior. Communication channels, consequently, need to be open and undistorted. "Information relating to the need for change, plans for change, and consequences of change must be shared by all relevant people in the group."[37]

Planning agencies, particularly publicly supported ones, find it difficult to fulfill these conditions. Even though committed to the strategy, as many often are, intra- and extra-organizational demands often dictate a change in strategy. The complexity of many planning projects and, more important, the commitment of planners themselves, obstruct the citizen from becoming actively involved in decision-making. Citizens frequently complain that they are unable to understand the planners and consequently unable to become committed to a policy or goal they do not understand.

Extra-organizational demands have the effect also of closing off communication channels to the citizens. Organizations faced with adhering to performance norms, such as budget deadlines, discover that they are unable to apply the strategy. The demands for submission of program proposals (for example, the initial planning period in the poverty program is six months) or the priority demands emanating from a national agency, such as HUD or OEO, precludes the possibility of involving citizens for the purpose of changing their behavior. Local poverty agencies' staff complains that their time is spent in selling proposals to citizens to gain their support. They have neither the time nor the sanction to effectively foster group deliberation and initiative, however much they would like to.

A further difficulty is relating the participant group to other influential or decision-making centers of the community. It is rarely possible to include all members of a system in a community planning project. Frequently, then, the planning organization is dealing with system representatives. The group becomes not merely a medium of change, but also an agent of change—an action group designed to influence much larger systems. One example would be a representative neighborhood renewal committee attempting to influence other residents and city officials to improve its neighborhood area. But it is not always possible to assume that those involved are in a position to carry out the group's intentions. For the strategy to be effective in community planning, therefore, the participant must not only commit himself to a course of action, but also be in a position to commit others. This has been a vexing problem in community planning. It is not uncommon to involve someone who has little or no influence in the group he represents, or who may not be truly representative of his group.

If, on the other hand, the system representatives can influence change in their own reference groups, the strategy is a highly effective model for planned change. Experiments in industry with this strategy have been quite persuasive.[38] Moreover, a group highly committed to a change objective has proven to be a more effective change agent than an equivalent number of individuals.

Staff Supplement Strategy

Probably one of the oldest and certainly one of the most prevalent reasons for citizen participation is the simple principle of voluntarism—the recruitment of citizens to carry out tasks for an organization which does not have the staff resources to carry them out itself. This is a strategy basic to voluntary associations. Hospitals, family casework agencies, recreation services such as the YMCA and the Scouts, and fund-raising agencies rely upon citizen volunteers to perform many essential agency functions. In some instances, agencies depend entirely upon citizens to achieve their objectives. The clearest example is the voluntary fund-raising agency.

In community planning this strategy has been used to supplement the expertise of the planning agency's staff with the expertise of particular citizens. Basically, this is what Nash and Durden proposed in their suggestion to replace the planning commission with citizen task forces.[39] Moreover, it is a strategy widely used by Welfare Councils and a premise which underlies the Welfare Councils' reliance (over-reliance, some suggest)[40] on the committee

approach to social planning. The assumption of the Welfare Council is that its own staff need not be experts on substantive planning issues, rather they should be experts in knowing how to involve and work with citizens who are the presumed experts.

The objective of the strategy is to exploit the abilities, free time, and/or the expertise of individuals to achieve a desired goal. Ideally, it is a procedure whereby the citizen volunteer is matched with the specifications of the task. Interestingly, some agencies actually write up detailed job descriptions for volunteer roles. Much attention, therefore, has to be given to perfecting techniques for recruiting and holding volunteers. Incentivies to stimulate willingness to participate become crucial because of the desire to recruit specific individuals.

The use of skilled volunteers as supplementary staff is easily compatible with the requirements of many organizations. It is assumed that the volunteer is in agreement with the organization's objectives and is recruited to assist in carrying out those objectives. Few citizen participants are actually involved in policy-making roles. Scout leaders, case aides, and fund-raising solicitors, for example, are recruited to carry out the policies and directions of the organization. Incidentally, it is this auxiliary role which the Bureau of the Budget prefers for the poor in the poverty program.[41]

There are opportunities in community planning, nevertheless, for the participant to play a significant role in policy-making, and where in fact, this is the assumption upon which he is recruited.[42] The particular expertise of the citizen participant—a juvenile court judge in a study of delinquency, a public welfare recipient in an analysis of poverty, or a public health doctor in an air pollution study—is supposed to assist in determining policy. There is the possibility, however, that the citizen's expertise can become merely a sanctioning element; that is, a symbol through which in actuality the staff's voice becomes policy. But that is another strategy—*cooptation*—and is discussed later.

It is difficult to assess the usefulness of the participation of skilled volunteers in community planning. The overall strategy depends, of course, upon the classical notions of rationality in planning, about which there is now considerable doubt.[43] On many issues, particularly in welfare, urban renewal, and city planning, there are few "correct" decisions. The absence of any valid data, and more important, the ambiguity of assigning values, create a situation in which decision-making arises out of bargaining, negotiation, and compromise. The advice of an expert, whether he be citizen or professional, often becomes merely another opinion. And this is a decided limitation in relying upon this strategy exclusively in community planning. Additional strategies need to be employed which take into account the politics of decision-making or are aimed at overcoming value differences.

Cooptation

Another citizen participation practice is to involve citizens in an organization in order to prevent anticipated obstructionism. In this sense citizens are not seen as a means to achieve better planning goals nor are they seen as partners in assisting an organization in achieving its goal; rather, they are viewed as potential elements of obstruction or frustration whose cooperation and sanction are found necessary. This strategy, *cooptation*, has been defined as "the process of absorbing new elements into the leadership or policy-determining structure of an organization as a means of averting threats to its stability and existence."[44]

Cooptation is neither a new technique nor does it apply only to voluntary or welfare organizations. Corporations, for example, elect representatives of banking institutions to their boards of directors to provide access to financial resources. Politicians have been notably imaginative in this art. For instance, in order to ward off predictions that his administration would be fiscally irresponsible, President Kennedy appointed a highly respected Republican as Secretary of the Treasury.

Cooptation can take two forms, both of which are applicable to organizations involving citizens. One is employed in response to specific power forces. Certain individuals are considered to have sufficient resources or influence—financial, decision-making, legislative—to vitally affect the operation of the organization. To capture this influence or at least neutralize it, not only are they brought into the organization, but, more significantly, they are included at the policy-making level because their influence is crucial to the continuation of current organizational policy. This has been termed "informal" cooptation, and its key characteristic is that it is a technique "of meeting the pressure of specific individuals or interest-groups which are in a position to enforce demands."[45]

Although informal cooptation has obvious advantages, it also exerts its own toll. Choice becomes constrained. Those coopted will want to share in influencing policy and thus become one more definer of organization policy. Stability and security may be gained by cooptation, but frequently at a price. An organization will thus have to weigh the benefits against the costs.

A more prevalent practice of welfare and planning organizations is to rely upon what has been termed "formal" cooptation. It is a device for winning consent and legitimacy from the citizenry at large. The underlying belief is that the need the organization purports to serve is not in itself sufficiently persuasive to gain community support. Thus, groups who reflect the sentiments of the community are absorbed into the organization in order to gain legitimacy. Clergymen, for example, are inevitably involved in community projects because they bestow credibility upon the projects. Other groups reflecting community sentiments, who consequently are invariably involved, are representatives of labor, business, the professions, and women's organizations.

Formal cooptation also describes the practice of setting up and maintaining communication networks in a community. Any organization needs to establish reliable and readily accessible channels of communication through which information and requests may be transmitted to all relevant segments and participants. An organization depending upon community support and sanction is obliged to relate itself to the community as a participant. A common method is to tap into already existing citizen groups—neighborhood organizations or block clubs, for instance. In this way the local citizens, through their voluntary associations or committees, become identified and committed to the program and, ideally, the apparatus of the operating agency.[46]

The participants' ability to affect policy, according to Philip Selznick, is the basis for the distinction between informal and formal cooptation. Informal cooptation implies a sharing of power in response to specific or potential pressures. Formal cooptation, on the other hand, merely seeks public acknowledgement of the agency-constituency relationship, since it is not anticipated that organizational policies will be put in jeopardy. What is shared "is the *responsibility* for power," explains Selznick, "not the power itself."[47]

It is not possible to assume, however, that voluntary groups formally coopted by an organization will be willing to remain passive with respect to policy. Where citizen groups are in general agreement with the goals of the host agency, as may have been the case in Selznick's analysis of the TVA, the observation may be applicable. But with changing conditions and possible disagreement on goals, the citizen group may endeavor to capture or at least influence the policy-making centers to insure that policies are made in their interest.

Urban renewal is an example. On the whole, renewal agencies have tended to adopt the formal cooptation strategy. Relationships are established with neighborhood groups or block committees which serve both as a means for sanctioning renewal objectives and as a network of communication, especially in project areas marked for rehabilitation. Citizen groups, however, soon resist the role of sanctioning agents and information carriers, and push for more of a voice in planning decisions. Consequently, local urban renewal agencies have been hard pressed to establish procedures for citizen involvement, turning to trial and error applications of different practices.[48]

Yet, despite the usual disparaging connotation attached to cooptation it does provide a means for achieving social goals. Certain groups not normally included in community policy-making are given an entrance into the decision-making arena. Moreover, because it provides overlapping memberships, it is also a device that increases the opportunity for organizations to relate to one another and, thus, find compatible goals. From the organization's viewpoint, it provides a means for giving "outsiders" an awareness and understanding of the problem it faces.[49] At the same time, the strategy is an administrative device. Facilitating the achievement of social goals is incidental. The aim is to permit the limited participation of citizens as a means of achieving organization goals, but not to the extent that these goals are impeded.

Community Power Strategies

Power may be defined as the ability to exercise one's will even over the opposition of others. Individuals are capable of obtaining power and influence through the control of wealth or institutions. Whether such power can be exercised in all instances, or whether a small group can control all community decisions is a matter of dispute. Not disputed, however, is the fact that centers of power do exist outside the formal political structure of a community and such centers are influential in shaping community decisions.[50]

Most community organizations are interested in exerting influence. Frequently organizations come into being exclusively for the purpose of bringing their will to bear on community decisions. There are two strategies of citizen participation based on theories of community power, both designed to exploit community power. The first is to capture influentials by involving them as participants in the organization in order to achieve organizational objectives. This is the informal cooptation previously explained.

Another significantly different strategy accepts the premises of community power theories but not the conclusions. Change, it is suggested, can be caused by confronting existing power centers with the power of numbers—an organized and committed mass of citizenry. In effect, a new center of power is created, based not upon control of wealth and institutions but upon size and dedication.[51] This type of organization has the ability to obtain accommodation from existing power centers, both from its inherent strength and its choice of tactics.

Demonstrations, boycotts, and picketing are the common weapons of such mass organizations. Negotiation on issues is inevitable, but negotiation from strength is a prerequisite. The power structure must first be put into a position of willingness to negotiate and this occurs only after they have been pushed to do so. "When those prominent in the status quo turn and label you an agitator," says Saul Alinsky, the chief ideologist of the conflict-oriented strategists, to his organizers, "they are completely correct, for that is, in one word, your function—to agitate to the point of conflict."[52]

The conflict strategy works best for organizations committed to a cause rather than to specific issues or services. In securing the involvement of individuals identified with the basic cause, the organization serves as the unifying vehicle for achievement of individual aims. There is, then, little necessity to include the participants in the goal-defining process. Agreement is assumed. But on specific means to achieve the goal, disagreement may arise. Because the participants are emotionally involved in the ends, detached, pragmatic analysis of alternatives is difficult. Concerns are immediate and give rise to impatience, which, coupled with emotional involvement, can often lead to internal squabbling and dissension. Such conflict over means can immobilize an organization and lead to schisms. Certain race relations agencies have exhibited this difficulty.

Moreover, the effectiveness of the strategy appears limited in duration. Maintaining citizen interest appears to be the chief difficulty. The organization has only its goal, its idealized purpose, to sustain interest and create satisfactions. It is difficult to maintain interest in idealized goals over long periods of time. The emotional commitment required is too personally enervating. Often the leader of the organization is forced to depend upon exhortations or the manufacturing of crises to recharge interest. Membership dwindles or frequently the organization changes, tending to rely less upon conflict tactics and more upon cooperation. New classes of participants, reflecting community sentiments or power forces, are invited to join. Goals are modified and the organization becomes undistinguishable from other service-oriented organizations.

Conclusions

It is apparent that the effectiveness of a particular strategy of citizen participation depends upon certain conditions and assumptions peculiar to itself; likewise each strategy has its own advantages and limitations. The principal difficulty is in adapting a strategy or strategies to the demands of the particular type of organization and the environment within which it functions. Not all strategies are appropriate for all organizations. Conflict-oriented strategies, as many local anti-poverty agencies have demonstrated, are inappropriate in governmentally sponsored programs which demand coordination and cooperation.

A strategy of conflict appears best suited to social reform organizations which are privately supported, or, even more advantageous, self-supporting. Most disadvantaged groups seeking social change have had to depend upon either their own resources or the resources of groups highly sympathetic to their cause. The civil rights struggle is one good example; organized labor is another.

The *behavioral change* strategy and the *staff supplement* strategy appear to be the most appropriate for community planning. The latter permits the planning agency to employ on a voluntary basis the expertise of community individuals. Citizens are recruited for their particular talents—knowledge of the problem (and this can include people who are affected by the problem itself, such as clients of social welfare agencies), skill in publicity and promotion techniques, influence with community decision centers, and representation of community sentiment groups. Such people are recruited into the organization and encouraged to contribute their specialized knowledge to the solution of problems, functioning as full-fledged organizational participants.

The *behavioral change* strategy would appear to be useful in overcoming what is commonly referred to as the "politics" of the planning process. Given the debatable preference characteristics of planning goals and the free market concept of competing community organizations, it would seem advisable to employ a strategy of participation aimed at accommodating various interests. The *behavioral change* strategy has the advantage of subjecting value preferences to a dialogue, allowing them to be aired within the context of the planning process. Other involved organizations are also encouraged to participate in order to allay their fears, gain their advice, and seek their cooperation.

Obviously, this implies a more purposeful approach to citizen participation than is commonly assumed by planning agencies. One issue, of course, is the ability of the staff to work with citizen groups. The appropriateness of any strategy of citizen participation will depend in large measure upon the capabilities and knowledge of the staff to implement it. A strategy of *cooptation,* for instance, requires skill primarily in administration—relating citizen participants to the organization in such a way that they will not interfere with organization goal achievement. Power-conflict strategies appear to demand leadership of a particular type; often a charismatic leader is needed. He has to be skillful in exhorting his followers, giving them a sense of purpose, and helping them to identify with the goals of the organization.

The *behavioral change* and *staff supplement* strategies, on the other hand, require knowledge and skill in handling the dynamics of individual and group behavior.[53] While constantly seeking to maximize rationality, the staff needs to be sensitive to the individual differences of participants, enabling them to contribute to the planning process. The staff also must be able to analyze community systems in order to locate decision centers, identify representatives of community sentiment groups, and suggest individuals who can contribute knowledge and information to the solution of a problem. Moreover, the staff role is the direct antithesis of the executive leadership role. Although direction often is warranted, the aim is to give the citizen a sense of participation and an opportunity for leadership. The intention is to work *with* citizens in a collaborative process in much the same way that David Godschalk and William Mills suggest.[54]

Finally, there is the issue of organizational commitment to, but limited grasp of, citizen participation. The objective in this paper has been to provide an analytical understanding of citizen participation, in its various forms and functions. Clearly, understanding the particular conditions requisite for the success of a particular strategy frequently is a source of difficulty which contributes to the confusion and contention over the efficacy of citizen participation in general. Not clear about strategy implications of citizen participation, many planning organizations find a gap between what they purport to do and what they actually can do. Federally sponsored programs, such as urban renewal, the poverty program, and model cities, are a case in point.

Federal agencies at the national level, constrained by Congressional critics and bureaucratic practices, are forced to specify priorities and program guidelines, inhibiting participation by citizens on the local level. In turn, local staffs are often reduced to grinding out programs for Washington's approval. Many have been disillusioned and demoralized.[55]

Whether or not this is an inherent conflict is difficult to say. At this time it seems so. Yet, it is likely that within the constraints imposed on organizations at both national and local levels a new strategy of citizen participation may evolve. Too many federal agencies are too committed to the general principle of citizen participation not to find a solution.

To do so the premise that citizen participation is self-evident has to be discarded. Planning agencies must be more precise about what they mean by citizen participation, how they intend to implement it, what agency resources will be used to organize and involve citizens, and what voice citizens will have in planning decisions. This may mean a redefinition of planning agencies' goals toward a new focus where a citizen group assumes the responsibility for defining the goals and aims of the planning agency. But it also may mean less contentious citizen participation.

NOTES

1. Alan A. Altshuler, *The City Planning Process* (Ithaca, N.Y.: Cornell University Press, 1965), p. 55.
2. Edmund M. Burke, "Citizen Participation in Renewal" *Journal of Housing*, Vol. 23, No. 1, (January 1966), p. 20.
3. Ibid., pp. 19–21.
4. Ibid., p. 19.
5. Urban Renewal Administration, *Neighborhood Organization in Conservation Areas, Technical Guide 8*, (Washington, D.C.: U.S. Government Printing Office, March 1961), p. 3.
6. Quoted in Edmund M. Burke, "Have the Poor Wrecked Johnson's War on Poverty?" *The Antioch Review*, Vol. XXVI, No. 4, (Winter 1966–67), p. 443.
7. Ibid., pp. 443–458; and Daniel P. Moynihan, *Maximum Feasible Misunderstanding* (New York: Free Press, 1969), pp. 128–166.
8. Moynihan, op. cit., pp. 141–158.
9. Ibid., p. 158–159.
10. Zbigniew Brzezinski, *Between Two Ages* (New York: Viking, 1970), pp. 262–263.
11. Sherry R. Arnstein, "A Ladder of Citizen Participation," *Journal of the American Institute of Planners*, Vol. 35, No. 4 (July 1969), pp. 216–224.
12. Ibid., p. 223.
13. Alan A. Altshuler, *Community Control* (New York: Pegasus, 1970), p. 64.
14. Alvin Toffler, *Future Shock* (New York: Bantam, 1970), pp. 416, 430.
15. John F. Kennedy, *Profiles in Courage* (New York: Harper & Row, 1956).
16. The concept of "representativeness" is thoroughly explained in Michael Fagence's book on citizen participation. He outlines the various forms and types of representativeness. Michael Fagence, *Citizen Participation in Planning* (New York: Pergamon, 1977), pp. 50–69.
17. Murray G. Ross, *Community Organization* (New York: Harper & Row, 1955), pp. 40–44.
18. Ibid., p. 43.
19. Altshuler, *The City Planning Process*, op. cit., pp. 242–244, 267–270.
20. Paul Davidoff, "Advocacy and Pluralism in Planning," *Journal of the American Institute of*

Planners, Vol. XXXI, No. 4, (November 1965) pp. 331–338.

21. Norman Krumholz, Janice M. Cogger, and John H. Linner, "The Cleveland Policy Planning Report," *Journal of the American Institute of Planners,* Vol. 41, No. 5 (September 1975), pp. 298–304.

22. Fagence, op. cit., pp. 84–91.

23. G. David Garson, "On the Origins of Interest Group Theory: A Critique of a Process," *The American Political Science Review,* Vol. LXVIII, No. 4, (December 1974) pp. 1505–1519.

24. Donald F. Mazziotti, "The Underlying Assumptions of Advocacy Planning: Pluralism and Reform," *Journal of the American Institute of Planners,* Vol. 40, No. 1 (January 1974), pp. 38–47. See also Stephen Grabow and Alan Heskin, "Foundations for a Radical Concept of Planning," *Journal of American Institute of Planners,* Vol. 39, No. 2 (March 1973), pp. 106–114.

25. See also John Friedmann, "The Public Interest and Community Participation: Toward a Reconstruction of Public Philosophy" *Journal of the American Institute of Planners,* Vol. 39, No. 1 (January 1973) pp. 2–7.

26. Eduard C. Lindeman, *The Community* (New York: Association Press, 1921), pp. 58–76.

27. Murray G. Ross, *Case Histories in Community Organization* (New York: Harper & Bros., 1958), pp. 10–11; and Murray G. Ross, *Community Organization* (New York: Harper & Bros., 1955), pp. 13, 21–22, 48–53.

28. Bernard Coughlin, "Community Planning: A Challenge to Social Work," *Social Work* (October 1961), 37–42.

29. Roland L. Warren, *The Community in America* (Chicago: Rand McNally & Co., 1963), pp. 329–330.

30. Oscar Lewis, *La Vida* (New York: Random House, 1966), pp. xlii-lii.

31. Eduard Lindeman, "New Patterns of Community Organization," *Proceedings of the National Conference of Social Work, 1937* (Chicago: The University of Chicago Press, 1937), p. 321. See also, Roy Lubove, *The Professional Altruist* (Cambridge: Harvard University Press, 1965), pp. 175–178.

32. Mobilization for Youth, Inc., *A Proposal for the Prevention and Control of Delinquency by Expanding Opportunities* (New York: Mobilization for Youth, Inc., 1961), p. 126.

33. *The New York Times,* November 5, 1965, p. 1.

34. See, for example, Douglas McGregor, *The Human Side of Enterprise* (New York: McGraw-Hill Book Co., 1960).

35. John F. Kennedy, *Housing Message to Congress.* March 1961.

36. Dorwin Cartwright, "Achieving Change in People: Some Applications of Group Dynamics Theory," *Human Relations,* IV (1951), p. 387.

37. Ibid., p. 390.

38. See L. Coch and J. R. P. French, Jr., "Overcoming Resistance to Change," *Human Relations,* 1:4 (1948), pp. 512–532.

39. Peter Nash and Dennis Durden, "A Task Force Approach to Replace the Planning Board," *Journal of the American Institute of Planners,* XXX (February 1964), pp. 10–22.

40. Robert Morris, "Social Work Preparation for Effectiveness in Planned Change," *Proceedings of the Council on Social Work Education* (New York: Council on Social Work Education, 1963), pp. 166–180.

41. *The New York Times, loc. cit.*

42. This also holds true to some extent if the citizen is recruited to serve on a board of directors.

43. Richard S. Bolan, "Emerging Views of Planning in an Emerging Urban Society," *Journal of the American Institute of Planners,* XXXIII (July 1967), pp. 233–245.

44. Philip Selznick, "Foundations of the Theory of Organization," *American Sociological Review,* 13 (February 1948), p. 34.

45. Ibid., p. 35.

46. Philip Selznick, *TVA and the Grassroots* (Berkeley: University of California Press, 1953), pp. 224–225.

47. Ibid., pp. 34–35 (his emphasis).

48. Edmund M. Burke, "Citizen Participation in Renewal," *Journal of Housing* (January 1966), pp. 18–21.

49. James D. Thompson, and William J. McEwen, "Organizational Goals and Environment: Goal Setting as an Interaction Process," *American Sociological Review,* 23 (February 1958), p. 28.

50. For an excellent summation of power and influence see Dorwin Cartwright, "Influence, Leadership, Control," in James March, ed., *Handbook of Organizations* (Chicago: Rand McNally and Co., 1965), pp. 1–47.

51. Advocacy planning appears also to stress the concept of community power as a strategy of change. The power the advocate planner is stressing, however, is the power of knowledge—the technical apparatus that he can offer local interest groups which thus enables them to gain concessions from City Hall. See Lisa R. Peattie, "Reflections on Advocacy Planning," *Journal of the American Institute of Planners,* XXXIV (March 1968), pp. 80–88.

52. Quoted in Charles E. Silberman, *Crisis in Black and White* (New York: Vintage Books, 1965), p. 335.

53. Staff requirements for implementing the client-oriented strategy are difficult to define. In fact,

the advocates of using participation as an educational or therapeutic device have not been too clear on the requirements of the strategy itself. More emphasis has been placed on its merits than on its utility and consequences in community planning. Conceivably this is why it tends to be vitiated in practice.

54. David R. Godschalk and William E. Mills, "A Collaborative Approach to Planning Through Urban Activities," *Journal of the American Institute of Planners*, XXXII (March 1966), pp. 86–95.

55. For an unintentional indictment of citizen participation in the poverty program *see* Memorandum to Participants in ABCD (Boston) Staff-Community Conference, held on January 7, 1967, entitled "Evaluation of Conference" (mimeographed, February 10, 1967), p. 4.

James A. Morone and Theodore R. Marmor
Representing Consumer Interests: The Case of American Health Planning

I. INTRODUCTION

The National Health Planning and Resources Development Act of 1974 authorized a national network of local health planning institutions. The statute, Public Law 93-641, called for more than two hundred planning bodies—health systems agencies (HSAs)—which consumers were to dominate. The law required a consumer majority on each HSA governing board. These consumers were to be "broadly representative of the social, economic, linguistic and racial population of the area."[1] Consumer majorities, the program's framers assumed, would be powerful forces in shaping local health plans and thus in directing American medicine toward the wants, concerns, and interests of consumers.

The institutionalization of consumer participation accompanied an ambitious conception of health planning itself. The new program was to produce "scientific

Reprinted from *Ethics* 91 (April 1981), pp. 431–450, with permission of the authors and the University of Chicago Press. Copyright 1981 by the University of Chicago. All rights reserved.

planning with teeth," cut medical care costs, improve access to medical care, and assure its high quality. The HSAs were to pursue these ambitious aims through an unusual American mixture of plan-making and regulatory activities. The HSA plans would select local health priorities and identify proposals that satisfied community goals for medical care. Their way of working was envisaged as follows: hospitals or nursing homes intent on expanding would submit to the HSA detailed proposals taking into account the official HSA plan. The HSA decisions would be serial, one after the other, each expansion measured against the planning vision of the consumer-dominated agency. In theory, each proposal would either advance the pursuit of community health aims or be rejected.

In practice, however, the HSAs' regulatory authority is severely restricted, almost wholly negative in character, and almost certainly insufficient to reshape the local politics of medicine. The HSAs do review institutional proposals for capital expenditures over $150,000, but their role is in fact advisory to the state governments which are legally empowered to issue required certificates of need. The HSAs are also supposed to review the appropriateness of all medical facilities in their area, but they have neither the positive authority to make improvements nor clear sanctions by which to constrain present operations. Overall, HSAs exhibit a curious structure: decentralized planning bodies with consumer majorities, a highly rationalistic planning mission, and limited regulatory authority to deal with the pluralistic financing and delivery features of the American medical arrangements they are to reshape.

This is not a conception of governance likely to generate confidence among the skeptical. But it is precisely what one would have expected in the context of American health politics of the mid-1970s. At that time, there was widespread alarm about rising health expenditures. Whereas in the 1950s Americans spent 5 percent of GNP on medical care, a quarter of a century later expenditures had risen 50 percent, to some 7.5 percent of GNP by 1975. These increases, heightened in the wake of Medicare and Medicaid legislation in 1965, prompted near-panic in the early 1970s. The Economic Stabilization Program (1971–74) retained controls in medical care longer than other goods and services, but by 1974 and the end of price controls, it was clear another spurt of medical inflation was in progress. Prompted by inflationary fears, the Congress that year debated the broader question of national health insurance but was stalemated by the contending proposals of a Republican administration and a Democratic Congress. Watergate deflected congressional attention from forging new coalitions, so committees with newly expanded responsibilities for health confined their actions to reshaping health *planning* institutions amid intense but narrow political scrutiny.

What emerged as the new health plan-

ning program, then, was a compound of stalemate, a commitment to scientific planning, and a faith in democratic participation. That latter faith was central, as the law's words make plain. If consumers dominated and were broadly representative, how could health planning fail to reflect consumer interests? A microcosm of the community would act on the community's behalf. Making sure the HSA board is a microcosm was the rationale for the original insistence that racial, economic, social, geographic, and linguistic categories of constituencies be explicitly represented.

Whatever the intentions of the health planning legislation, the structure of HSAs promised operational problems. What the framers never considered were the implications of the jury model of representation that the microcosm idea expressed. They had no ready answers about how diverse consumer interests in health were to be either articulated or balanced. They presumed that the *representativeness* of HSA governing bodies was the crucial feature of their legitimacy. They failed to link the board's functional task—making choices about health resources—to the representational requirements. Set against the jury notion is what one might call the instrumental view of representation. How well, one asks in this connection, do given institutional practices express the interests of constituencies? What means do constituents have to hold their representatives to account? How well do representative institutions settle the policy problems they were designed to confront? Such questions are precisely what the descriptive model of representation—the model of the jury—neglects. The central HSA dilemma is that it employs a jury model of representativeness to assure the representation of consumer interests. As we will argue, the result is conceptual confusion and practical disappointment.

The next section briefly discusses the

terms of the law with regard to consumer representation and the legal cases that have practically illustrated the program's conceptual difficulties. The core of the paper sketches the competing notions of representation—and the associated ideas of participation and accountability. We think of this part as a philosophical map that analysts of consumer involvement in public policy-making should want to consider. In the particular case of health planning, we go on to discuss the kind of unbalanced political arena that promoters of policy change confront. Thus, when we turn at the close to prescriptions for improving the representation of consumer interests, it is in the light of practical constraints as well as philosophical considerations. The epilogue suggests what problems would remain with health planning even if the difficulties of its provisions for consumer representation were adequately worked out.

II. CONCEPTUAL MUDDLES, CONSUMER REPRESENTATION, AND HSAs

The health planning law was plain enough about consumer majorities on HSAs. Indeed, the statute required no less than 51 and no more than 60 percent of every board to be broadly representative of consumers. But the law and its regulations were silent on the details of implementing this microcosmic conception of representation. How representatives were to be chosen, for instance, was ignored. Which demographic groups should dominate under the broad headings of social, linguistic, and economic representation was not addressed. The clearest representational requirement was that metropolitan and nonmetropolitan representatives precisely mirror their proportions in the population at large.

What was explicitly addressed was the openness in which HSAs should conduct their business. Thus, there was a substitution of participatory conditions for clarity about consumer representation. Agencies, for example, were required to hold public meetings, with agendas widely available beforehand and the minutes available afterward. There were to be opportunities for public comment on almost every phase of HSA activity. All of these provisions—central to the acceptability of a legitimate substitute for representative government—failed to make the crucial connections between consumer interests and consumer representation.

Disputes over consumer roles in health planning reached the courts almost immediately and there exposed the conceptual difficulties of health planning's model of representation. Several suits claimed inadequate means for selecting consumer representatives. But a New York court ruled, in *Aldamuy* v. *Pirro*, that there were no criteria by which it could choose between two competing minority representatives even if one had been selected by election.[2] As long as the requisite *number* of a particular minority were board members, the law's representation requirements were satisfied. A district court in Texas determined that requisite number by referring to the census tract.[3]

In *Rakestraw* v. *Califano* and other cases, various social groups sued demanding seats on the local board; the law and its regulations incorporated no principles for differentiating those with valid objections from those with merely frivolous ones.[4] Across the nation, HSAs scrambled to find poor, even uneducated consumers in a legally mandated but conceptually misguided effort to mirror the demographic characteristics of their area. And after selection, the problems of effective consumer representation continued to bedevil the HSA boards. The technical details of health planning bewildered inexperienced board members. Many had no idea whom they spoke for and, in places, were unwilling to attend meetings. There were reports, particularly in the South, of HSA meetings attended only by provider representatives.[5]

III. REPRESENTATION'S CONCEPTUAL PUZZLES

Establishing representative institutions requires fundamental choices. Decisions must be made about the selection of representatives, what those representatives should be like, and the expectations that should govern their behavior. Whom to represent—the constituencies—is a central puzzle where geographic representation is abandoned. In addition, the organizational structures within which representatives operate must be specified. Do these structures enhance or impede effective representation? Is the tendency toward political imbalance redressed?

The character of consumer involvement in HSAs is contingent on the answers to these general questions. Indeed, many of the difficulties that plague the health planning act follow from a failure to consider most of them.

We consider these questions in this section through discussion of three topics: the distinction between participation and representation, several conceptions of representation, and their implications for democratic accountability.

A. Participation

Self-government can mean direct citizen participation in public decisions. But the conditions which make such participation feasible are largely absent in modern industrial societies. As a consequence, political representation often replaces direct participation as an operational expression of the principle that "every man has the right to have a say in what happens to him."[6] The rhetoric of the 1974 planning law emphasized consumer representation. The law itself, by contrast, concentrated on guidelines for direct public participation. Direct participation provisions tend to reinforce the political dominance of medical providers over consumers. Hospital administrators, state medical association officials, and other employed medical personnel are far more likely to pay the costs of participating in open HSA meetings. The general public is not likely to do so.

Furthermore, the difficulties of fostering direct consumer participation are aggravated by the nature of most health issues. Health concerns, though important, are intermittent for most people.[7] They are not as clearly or regularly salient as the condition of housing or children's schools—situations that citizens confront daily. Consequently, it is far more difficult to establish public participation in HSAs than in renters' associations or school districts.[8]

The point is not that participation is objectionable in health planning. Rather, we argue that, without being tied to accountability and the representation of consumer health interests, the provisions for participation are at best marginally useful to consumers. They are more likely to be utilized by aroused provider institutions.

B. Descriptive Representation

Descriptive representation—the type of representation required in PL 93-641—emphasizes the characteristics of representatives. Where constituencies cannot be present themselves for public choice, the descriptive model calls for a representative "body which [is] an exact portrait, in miniature, of the people at large." The argument is straightforward. Since all the people cannot be present to make decisions, representative bodies ought to be miniature versions—microcosms—of the public they represent.

The similarity of composition is expected to result in similarity of outcomes; the assembly will "think, feel, reason and [therefore] act" as the public would have.[9] A number of difficulties make this formulation problematic. First, "the public" is a broad category. What aspect of it ought to be reflected in a representative body? John Stuart Mill argued that opinions should be represented; Bentham and James Mill emphasized subjective interests; Sterne, a more ambiguous "opinions, aspirations and wishes"; Burke, broad fixed interest. Swabey suggested that citizens were equivalent units, that if all had roughly equal political opportunities, representatives would be a proper random selection and, consequently, descriptively representative. Whichever may be the case, a failure to specify precisely what characteristics are represented renders microcosm theories unworkable.

Even when the relevant criteria for selecting representatives are properly specified, mirroring an entire nation is impossible. Mill's "every shade of opinion," for example, cannot be reconstructed in the assembly hall on one issue, much less on every issue. One cannot construct a microcosm of a million consumers no matter which sixteen, seventeen, or eighteen consumers represent them on the HSA governing board. Competing opinions or interests can, of course, be represented. But the chief aim of microcosmic representation is mirroring the full spectrum of constituencies. Pitkin notes that the language in which these theories is presented indicates the difficulty of actually implementing them. The theorists constantly resort to metaphor: the assembly as map, mirror, portrait. They are all difficult to express in more practical terms.

Mirroring the community may be as undesirable a criterion for selecting decision makers as it is an infeasible one. The merriment that followed Senator Hruska's proposal that the mediocre deserved rep-

resentation on the U.S. Supreme Court suggests a common understanding of the limits of simplistic views of descriptive representation.[10]

In addition, if representatives are asked merely to reflect the populace, they have no standards regarding their actions as representatives. Descriptive representation prescribes who representatives should be, not what they should do.[11] Opinion pools measure public views more accurately than does descriptive representation.

Though exacting microcosm theories are not realistic, descriptive standards are relevant to the operation of modern legislatures. Legislators are commonly criticized for not mirroring their constituents' views or interests. In fact, John Adams's formulation might be recast as one guideline to selecting representatives—the public votes, essentially, for candidates who appear to "think, feel, reason and act" as its members do. But this broad conception of descriptive representation is sharply different from the utopian endeavor of forming a microscosm of the population in the HSA.

One contemporary version of the microcosm theory is what Greenstone and Peterson term "socially descriptive representation."[12] Rather than mirroring opinions or interests, this conception proposes mirroring of the social and demographic characteristics of a community's population. This amends Adams's syllogism: if people (*a*) share demographic characteristics, (*b*) they will "think, feel [and] reason" like one another, and (*c*) consequently, act like one another. Shared demographic characteristics, in this view, ensure like policy sentiments.

The problems with mirror theories, enumerated above, are all relevant to this version. Demographically mirroring a populace in an assembly is as unlikely as mirroring its opinions. Obviously, not all social characteristics can or ought to be represented. The problem of discriminating among them is particularly vexing. Common sense rebels against representing left-handers or redheads. What of Lithuanians? Italians? Jews? The uneducated? Mirror views provide few guidelines for selecting which social characteristics merit representation.

Even when the characteristics to be mirrored are specified, as regulations to PL 93-641 eventually did, problems remain. All individual members of a social group will not, in fact, "think, feel [and] reason" alike. And all will not represent their fellows with equal efficacy. Yet, by itself, mirror representation does not distinguish among members of a population group— one low-income representative is, for example, interchangeable with any other. As long as the requisite number of a population group is seated, the society is represented—mirrored—in the appropriate aspect. Such actors are not so much representatives as instances of population groups.

Socially descriptive representation is pernicious because it makes recourse to constituencies unnecessary. Attention to means of selection and accountability is reduced by emphasizing broad representativeness. Skin color or income, for example, mark a representative acceptable or unacceptable, regardless of what the constituency thinks. The result is that any member of the group is as qualified a representative as any other. It is a situation that invites tokenism. If the health planning law's only requirement is that a fixed percentage of a board be drawn from a specific group, there is nothing to recommend a black elected by fellow blacks or selected by the NAACP, or a woman elected by women or selected by NOW, over blacks and women drafted onto a board because they will not "rock the boat."

Aldumuy v. *Pirro,* cited earlier, illustrates the application of the theory of mirror representation. The court found no criteria in either the law or the regulations by which to appraise the representativeness of the HSA board except for descriptive characteristics. Since both the representatives of the board and their challengers satisfied the criterion of minority status, there was no way to choose between them. It was not possible to select one as any better or more representative than another.

It has been suggested that socially descriptive representation might be effective if representatives were tied to their constituencies by some mechanism of oversight. That stipulation, however, changes the theory of socially descriptive representation. Selected agents are then representatives not because they share a group's features but because they are acceptable to that group. As it has been interpreted in several of the cited court cases, PL 93-641 includes no such view. It requires only that the composition of the board be a statistical microcosm of the area's racial, social, linguistic, and income distribution. Still, for all its inadequacies, there is a kernel of truth in theories of socially descriptive representation. Obviously, social characteristics are sometimes related to interests, and, as the following section argues, interests are precisely what ought to be represented. Thus, religious affiliations bespeak clear interests in Northern Ireland, race affects interests in America, and poverty relates to interests everywhere.

C. Substantive Representation

The key issue in substantive representation is not what representatives look like but whom they look after, whose interests they pursue. Put simply, substantive representation means acting in the interests of constituencies. Doing so involves both properly apprehending those interests and effectively pursuing them.

The classic problem of ascertaining interests is immediately apparent. Are interests objective facts that intelligent leaders can best discern? Or are they more like subjective preferences that must be conveyed to representatives? The latter require a delegatory view where representatives follow constituent wishes. A more objective view of interests supports a trustee role, representatives acting in the constituency's best interest regardless of constituent desires.

In practice, substantive representation involves neither of these extremes. Representatives are neither unabashed messengers nor unfettered guardians, for interests are not completely objective or merely subjective. Various principles of representation are defensible within these broad limits—substantive representation is a general category rather than a particular principle. What we wish to stress is the change from the descriptive conception to a substantive one structured around the pursuit of consumer interests.

The nature of interests is easily caricatured in health politics. Health policy is often technical and complex. The guardian role is most often assumed not by the consumer representatives but by health professionals, accountable to professional norms rather than consumers' desires. The claim that they know the consumer's best interest is accurate, but only within the confines of the physician's office. For the issues that HSAs confront—such as the distribution of limited resources among competing, needy claimants—trusteeship on the basis of medical knowledge is inappropriate.

In practical politics, representatives regularly consider claims for which the interests of specified constituencies are no guide. Bringing the wants of various groups to the bargaining arenas of politics is insufficient; the consideration of ideal-regarding interests—for which there may be no organized constituency—is no less important in policy areas like the distribution and costs of medical care. Our emphasis on constituency interests—in contrast to

socially descriptive representativeness—should not be taken as indifference to the questions for which the representation of different interests is insufficient. The intellectual failings of descriptive representation, in short, are one subject; the proper design of institutions for resolving politically charged issues of medical care is another and one beyond our capacities here. But, for that design, attention to the representation of substantive interests is a crucial requisite.

The effectiveness of representatives is crucial to substantive representation. An eloquent speaker or a skillful political operator can be said to provide better substantive representation than another with an equal understanding of constituent interests but without the same skills. And representatives in influential positions—chairs of congressional committees, officers of HSA boards—may well be more effective than less well placed representatives. The reverse, representatives in positions of little influence, can provide only minimal substantive representation. A largely submerged issue for HSAs pertains to precisely this point. If HSAs are powerless and inconsequential bodies, the furor over representation is misplaced—consumer interests are substantively represented within the HSAs but not in matters of important health policy.

The drafters of the health planning act confused representativeness with substantive representation, mistakenly believing that socially descriptive representation would lead to effective representation of interests. They presumed that a local agency with a jury-like board would adequately represent the interests of consumers and legitimate their regulatory interventions in the medical care market. Although jury-like bodies serve a representative and legitimating function in some governmental contexts—notably determinations of guilt in criminal trials—their capacity for substantive representation of interests in circumstances requiring problem solving and complex conflict resolution is limited.

D. Accountability

Jurors have no constituencies to answer to. Substantive representation introduces constituencies and the necessity of means of making their representatives accountable. That link is the crux of accountability.

Put simply, accountability means "having to answer to." One is accountable to agents who control scarce resources one desires. In the classic electoral example, officials are accountable to voters whose votes are desired. Health officials may be accountable to legislatures that control funds, pressure groups that can extend or withdraw support, or even medical care providers who can choose whether or not to cooperate with health planning officials.

The crucial element in each case is that accountability stems from some resource valued by the accountable actor. Accountability is not merely an ideal, like honesty, that public actors ought to strive to achieve. Rather, the disposition of valued, scarce resources is manipulable by the relevant constituency.

We term the means by which actors are held accountable "mechanisms of accountability." These mechanisms can vary enormously in character and in the extent of control they impose. Voters occasionally exert some control with a yes or no decision, whereas work supervisors regularly monitor their subordinates' work, enforcing compliance with specific demands.

There is often, to be sure, a give-and-take process in which actors try to maximize their freedom of action and minimize accountability. And those indifferent to the scarce resources in question, such as officials with no desire to be reelected, are not, strictly speaking, accountable. But this illustrates the central point in speaking of accountability. One must be able to point

to specific scarce resources, particular mechanisms holding representatives to account.

Many of the HSA requirements expected to enhance accountability to the public are, in fact, necessary but not sufficient conditions for constraining HSA representatives. The emphasis on public participation and openness both legitimates HSAs and eases the task of reviewing HSA performance, as the following HSA requirements illustrate: a public record of court proceedings,[13] open meetings, with notice of meetings published in two newspapers and an address given where a proposed agenda may be obtained;[14] and an opportunity to comment, either in writing or in a public meeting, about designation,[15] or health system plans,[16] or annual implementation plans.[17]

Yet these requirements facilitate public accounting, not direct accountability. Since requirements for public participation and disclosure incorporate no formal mechanisms forcing boards to answer to consumers, there is little direct public accountability. Well-defined mechanisms of accountability are central to a strong conception of accountability. Propositions which substitute relationships described as "winning over" or "working with" the community for an identifiable mechanism are much weaker, conflating one common language usage of accounting for action with a stronger view of accountability to a constituency.[18]

Suggesting that HSAs would be ineffective without public support reflects an equally weak conception of accountability to consumers. The "say" of the citizenry is not expressed by "inhospitality" or "lack of trust" or "written protests" but by an authoritative decision institutionalized as a mechanism of accountability.

Accountability can be to more than one constituency. As health planning is now structured, the Department of Health and

Human Services (HHS), state government, local government, consumers, providers, and numerous other groups can all attempt to hold the HSA accountable. These competing claims introduce significant tensions. One especially problematic tension lies between accountability to local communities and to national government. Since the rules of HSA operations are decided locally, the potential for local accountability is present. Yet insofar as the law takes up the issue explicitly, it presses accountability to HHS.[19]

The department is responsible for reviewing the plans, structure, and operation of every agency at least once every twelve months.[20] Renewal of designation is annually at stake. This is accountability in every important sense. But it can be traced to the public only by the long theoretical strand leading through the presidency. From this perspective, HSA boards are no more accountable to the public than any other federal executive agency, certainly a far cry from the rhetoric that accompanied PL 93-641's enactment. As the law now stands, public accountability (either directly to constituents or indirectly through states and localities) is not prohibited or rendered impossible. But neither is accountability to the public institutionalized or even significantly facilitated.

The success of instituting accountability relates in large measure to the formal means of selecting representatives. But PL 93-641 and its regulations say little about selection. In the *Rakestraw case*, HHS was sued not only regarding the composition but also the selection of HSA boards. The plaintiffs demanded not the mere specification of formal selection procedures but a means that guaranteed accountability to the public. They were even willing to waive socially descriptive representation in favor of accountability through explicit selection provisions.

E. Who Is to Be Represented: A Prescription

Only one representational category is precisely delineated in the planning act—the public in nonmetropolitan areas must be represented on the board in proportion to their population. Otherwise, the National Health Planning and Resources Development Act cuts representation loose from geography; representatives stand for social groups rather than precincts, and difficult choices are avoided by entitling all groups to representation. However, the liberalism which provides the theoretical foundation of the act incorporates a vision of shifting, crosscutting interests that makes it impossible to name functional categories that enfranchise everyone equally. No matter what the representational categories, some groups will gain, others lose.

Considerable HSA litigation followed from insufficiently specified representational categories. It can be halted by changing the sweeping grant of representation that flows from the microcosm view to an enumeration of the interests to be represented. Rather than boards that are broadly representative of the population, we would suggest boards that represent specified interests in that population. The specification of interests that we urge must be made on the national level, either in amendments to the act or—as is more likely—in its implementing regulations. Decisions at the national level are crucial since Congress sought to bypass the local political process in the establishment of HSAs.[21]

The next obvious question is, which consumer health interests should be represented on the HSA board? There are groups that, while part of the population and therefore potentially included on a board constituted on the microcosm principle, do not have distinctive health care interests. For example, it is not clear that those with little formal education have the distinguishable health needs that characterize the low-income or aged populations.

Interests with claims to be heard vary by health issue. Regarding access, these are different problems for rural and urban populations, or for the chronically, as opposed to the intermittently, ill. The infirm could claim representation for each of their diseases whenever the issue of new facilities arises. So could every ethnic group regarding specific genetic diseases that disproportionately or exclusively afflict its members. The list of health interests is theoretically very long. However, Congress (or its delegate) must make these difficult choices and specify the various health interests that merit representation on HSA boards.[22]

Selecting the interests to be represented requires an assessment of the purpose of consumer involvement. Presumably, it is to facilitate the articulation and satisfaction of health needs now underrepresented in American communities. As an illustration of interests selection furthering this purpose, we suggest certain representational categories for the HSAs. Although there is no inherent symmetry or formal relationship between any two categories, there is a plausible, a priori justification for representation of the following interests:

a) *Payers.* The most pressing issue in health politics is rising costs. The interests with the clearest stake in controlling them are the aggregated health care payers—unions, large employers, insurance companies. In traditional markets, consumers are payers, but the dominance of indirect or third-party health payers has necessitated the distinction between payer and patient. Excluding the former is likely to result in biased boards, for payers have a clearly articulated financial interest that conflicts directly with that of most health care providers.

b) *The poor.* Reducing health services to control expenditures threatens groups that now receive insufficient care, most obviously the poor. Their interests—more and better care—conflict with those of the payers. Providing board positions for advocates of the poor may activate group interests that are difficult to organize and thus often overlooked.

c) *Racial minorities.* Many racial minorities have the same difficulty receiving adequate medical care as the poor because of poverty or discrimination or both.

d) *The elderly.* The old rely on health services more than any other age group. Despite a clear interest in medical care, their concerns about access, quality, and cost are easily overlooked in local politics.

e) *Women.* Women require a different mix of health care services from men. They too have clear health care interests that are not represented because of their near-exclusion from local political processes.

f) *Catchment areas.* Most health planning issues are, at bottom, issues of geography—where to introduce a new service or shut down an old hospital. With the exception of the criteria for metropolitan and rural representation, the planning act attempts to replace areal with functional representation. But the two are not incompatible. Indeed, the empirical evidence suggests that geographic categories are emerging on many boards as counties, towns, and neighborhoods win representatives. To carry the process further, each HSA area could be broken into large catchment areas corresponding to the distribution of hospitals and health services. Representatives could be drawn from the various areas in approximate proportion to the population.

g) *Special interests.* There should also be a miscellaneous category for interests that form a significant segment of the HSA's population—for example, migrant workers, black-lung victims, or other persons exposed to special occupational hazards. These interests would be specified by the secretary of HHS, either on the recommendation of the state or by appeal of the special interest. However, it is crucial that this be recognized as a residual category, filled by discretion of the secretary, not as a sweeping grant of representation to interests that count themselves a significant segment of some population.

Numerous objections can be raised to this specification of health interests that deserve representation on HSA boards.[23] People representing these interests may not value health in the same way as those having the same objective characteristics—whether they be related to sex, income, or minority status. They may also be members of a wide variety of groups, each with partially conflicting interests. This leads to two distinct problems: first, the temptation to multiply the number of interest groups represented until the board becomes unmanageable; and second, the tendency for representatives to neglect to speak for those interests which might be shared.

Admittedly, the notion of consumer interests in health is crude. And while we can state that some provider interests work against the interests of all consumers, we cannot unambiguously specify consumer interests because of their diversity. But this diversity of consumer interests is itself the strongest argument for interest-based representation as a necessary, if not sufficient, condition for substantive representation of consumers. Without the quasi-corporatist amalgamations that interest representation can engender, consumer interests will simply not be pursued.

Naming specific representational categories will resolve some political and legal confusion. However, it suggests a deeper dilemma. As the categories we propose illustrate, the public is not neatly divisible into broad, roughly equivalent functional categories. How can the HSA claim legitimacy to act as a public body when it does not equally enfranchise the entire population?

Following Charles Anderson, we suggest two criteria for assessing the legitimacy of such quasi-corporatist boards in a liberal setting.[24] First, the criteria for representation must be embedded in the board's function. Who is seated depends on what the body is expected to accomplish. Policy goals guide the selection of representational categories and constituencies. Interests are granted representation because it is reasonable to include them given the nature and goals of the program. Within this rubric, particular attention might be paid to interests that past politics have subordinated despite the importance of health programs to them.

More important, however, legitimacy does not flow from elaborate representational schemes. The HSAs are administrative agencies established by Congress. Their legitimacy to act as public bodies lies in that legislative mandate. Functional representation schemes may stave off provider dominance, promote sensitivity to previously overlooked interests, or engender some accountability to local groups; but such achievements make HSAs no more or less legitimate than other congressional initiatives. Ultimately, geographic majoritarianism is supplemented, not supplanted.

Of course, designation of interests deserving representation is only one part of the resolution of representational difficulties in HSAs. Another part relates to the mechanisms that will guarantee substantive and accountable representation. The treatment of such policies follows our discussion of political imbalance and health issues.

IV. IMBALANCED POLITICAL ARENAS

The puzzles of representation are exacerbated in circumstances that stimulate representation without explicitly structuring it—where there are no elections, no clearly defined channels of influence, or only vague conceptions of constituency. The politics of regulatory agencies or regional authorities provides examples of these circumstances. Though representatives of groups commonly press their interests within such contexts, there are no systematic canvasses of relevant interests such as are provided by geographically based elections. It is unclear who legitimately merits representation or how representation should be organized and operated.[25]

Interest-group theorists address the problems of representation in precisely such political settings. In their view, unrepresented interests that are harmed coalesce and seek redress through the political system. Despite the absence of electoral mechanisms of representation, the theorists' conception of representation is central to their view of legitimate governance; every interest that is strongly felt can organize a group to speak for it. And, at their most sanguine, group theorists suggest that "all legitimate groups can make themselves heard at some crucial stage in the decision-making process."[26] Politics itself, in this view, is characterized by legions of groups bargaining at every level of government about policies that affect them. Government is viewed as the bargaining broker, policy choices as the consequences of mutual adjustment among the bargaining groups.

The group model is now partially in eclipse among political scientists.[27] One criticism is relevant here: groups that organize themselves for political action form a highly biased sample of affected interests.[28] Furthermore, that bias is predictable and recurs on almost every level of the political process. We refer to it as a tendency toward imbalanced political arenas, the unequal representation of equally legitimate but differently affected interests.

Imbalance is present in part because organizing for political action is difficult and costly. Even if considerable benefits are at stake, potential beneficiaries may choose not to pursue them. If collective goods are involved (i.e., if they are shared among members of a group regardless of the costs

any one member paid to attain them), potential beneficiaries often let other members of the collectivity pay the costs and simply enjoy the benefits—the classic free-rider problem.

Free riders aside, the probability of political action generally varies with the material incentives. If either the benefits or costs of political action are concentrated, political action is more likely. A tax or a tariff on tea, for example, clearly and significantly affects the tea industry. To tea consumers, the tax is of marginal importance, a few dollars a year perhaps. The tea producers, with their livelihood at stake, are more likely to organize for political action, though even they are most likely to act if expected benefits outweigh costs. "The clearer the material incentives of the organization's members, the more prompt, focused and vigorous the action."[29]

The most common stimulant to group organization is threat to occupational status, as observers of American politics from de Tocqueville to David Truman have argued. If the group model overstated the facility and extent of group organization, some of its proponents isolated the most significant factor: narrow, concentrated producer interests are more likely to pay the costs of political action than broad, diffuse consumer interests.

Not only do concentrated interests have a larger incentive to engage in political action; they also act with two notable advantages. First, they typically have ongoing organizations with staff and other resources available. This dramatically lowers the marginal cost of political action. Second, most organizations have an expertise that rivals or exceeds that of any other political interest, even government agencies. Their superior grasp, and sometimes monopoly, of relevant information translates into political influence. The more technical an area, the more powerful the advantage, but it is almost always present to some extent.

In sum, two phenomena work to unbalance political arenas: unequal interests and disproportionate resources. The two are interrelated—groups with more at stake will invest more to secure an outcome. However, the distinction warrants emphasis for it has important policy implications. Attempts to stimulate countervailing powers by making resources available to subordinate groups will fail if they do not account for differing incentives in their employment. For example, even a resource such as equal access to policymakers (now the goal of considerable political effort) is meaningless if the incentives to utilize it over time are grossly unequal. The reverse case—equal interests, unequal resources—is too obvious to require comment. But that clarity should not obscure the fact that the dilemma of imbalance is deeper than the obvious inequality of group resources suggests.

Naturally, diffuse consumer interests are not always somnolent. There are purposive as well as material incentives to political action. A revolt against a sales tax might necessitate cuts in programs that benefit specific groups—diffuse payers defeating concentrated beneficiaries. Tea drinkers may be swept into political action, even to the point of dumping tea into Boston Harbor. Both are examples of diffuse interests uniting for political action. Such coalitions tend to have a grass-roots style of organization. Since sustained, long-term political action requires careful organization, they tend to be temporary. With the end of political deliberation, the group disbands or sets out in search of new issues. Concentrated interests, however, carry on, motivated by the same material incentives that first prompted political action.

The advantages of organized groups increase after a policy's inception. Such groups can be expected to pursue the policy through the stages of implementation and administration. Administrative politics are far less visible than legislative ones.

They are not bounded by discrete decisions, and they are cluttered with technical detail rather than the emotive symbols likely to arouse diffuse constituencies. The policy focus of program administration is dispersed—temporally, conceptually, even geographically. Concentrated groups are much more likely to sustain a commitment to participate.

Administrative processes may even grow biased to the point that other affected parties are shut out from deliberations that concern them. Important decisions are made in agencies and bureaus that define, qualify, or even subvert original legislative intent. For example, Congress included a consumer participation provision in the Hill-Burton Act, but the implementing agency never wrote the regulations for it. When consumers overcame the imbalance of interests and sued for participation, they were denied standing. Since the regulations had never been written, consumer representatives had no entry into the policymaking process.[30]

The major question for HSAs is how to overcome these tendencies and balance the politics of health or even promote consumer control. The law's emphasis on participation, its naive conception of representation, and the political economy of health all point to a continuation of imbalanced health planning arenas. The HSAs were created to exert control over health providers, yet the major issue concerning their governing boards is how to avoid provider domination.

V. REPRESENTING CONSUMER INTERESTS: OVERCOMING THE POLITICAL OBSTACLES

The task is overcoming political imbalance rather than just getting consumers on health planning boards. This section suggests how more effective representation of and accountability to local health interests might be established.

The HSA staffs could help consumers achieve political parity. Staffs have considerable expertise in issues of medical care and health. Occupying full-time positions in health planning, they have a concentrated interest in the industry. If they ally with providers or fail to take consumers seriously, they will surely undermine consumer representatives who cannot match the combined expertise of providers and staff. The support of the staff is essential to an active consumer role on HSA boards. The problem is systematically harnessing the market-balancing potential of the staff to consumer interests.

The most direct approach is to restructure the HSAs so that part of the professional staff is placed under consumer control—to be selected and accountable to the consumers. The tasks of these staff members could be specified in any number of ways, but the critical function would be providing professional (i.e., expert, full-time) support to the consumer effort.

Another potential for balancing the health planning market lies in organizations that already exist within the consumer population.[31] The very existence of these groups attests to a commitment to enhance the life circumstances of some part of the population. Furthermore, they have already paid the costs of organizing. We can expect them to devote attention to issues in a relatively sustained manner; and they can often overcome low expertise by redeploying their staff. Representatives from these groups will have clearly defined constituencies, experience in organizational politics, and resources at their disposal. These attributes will help them both in identifying group interests and in pursuing them, regardless of their other characteristics. Even minorities suing for representation in Texas, for example, were willing to accept whites representing blacks if the NAACP selected them. It is telling that much of the litigation challenging HSA boards comes from organizations formed to further the rights or general circumstances of disadvantaged groups within the consumer population.

The empirical evidence that exists supports our contention. The poverty boards of the 1960s (particularly the War on Poverty's Community Action Projects) tended to be most capable when their members were selected by organizations. Impressionistic evidence from some HSAs in which organizations have been involved in selection suggests similar experiences.

Ideally, then, the imbalanced political features of health planning will be tempered by two mechanisms—one internal to the HSA (staff assigned to the consumer representatives), the other external (selection of representatives by groups). We expect the former to facilitate organization and expertise among the consumer representatives, the latter to improve substantive representation and heighten their accountability.

Various reform groups have called for election of consumer representatives in a model roughly based on the selection of school boards. The surface plausibility of the proposal should not be permitted to obscure its difficulties. One problem with direct election of representatives to HSA boards stems from the failure of most Americans to consider themselves part of an ongoing health care community. They typically seek care sporadically and do not conceive of health care in terms of local systems. Both factors distinguish health planning from education or housing issues, where specific elections may be more effective.

Evidence from other programs supports the view that elections are problematic; less than 3 percent of the eligible population voted for local poverty boards in Philadelphia, less than 1 percent in Los Angeles. Those who did vote were moved to do so by personal, not policy, considerations. Overwhelmingly, they voted for neighbors and personal acquaintances. The policy formulated by these representatives was, predictably, particularistic. It helped their friends, not the community or the interests they ostensibly represented. Representatives generated little community interest or support. They tended to be ineffective advocates.

The evidence from HSAs that have held elections is strikingly similar—low turnout at the polls and high turnover among representatives. Representatives are uncertain of their task and their constituency. Furthermore, direct elections have facilitated the takeover of entire boards by single organizations. In northeastern Illinois, for example, abortion foes captured the HSA, linking every health concern to their own preoccupation; in Illinois, Arkansas, and Massachusetts, provider institutions chartered buses and flooded the polling places with hospital workers who voted for docile consumer representatives.[32]

Elections are appealing to reformers because they permit the public to choose health planning representatives directly; theoretically, the representatives can be held accountable with relative ease. In practice, the predictable electoral apathy of diffuse interests undermines direct elections as the mechanism of accountability to consumer constituencies.

VI. HEALTH POLICY AND THE HSAs

The National Health Planning and Resources Development Act's vision of representation is impossibly flawed but not irretrievably so. We have suggested one plan for achieving reasonably effective consumer representation and balancing provider dominance. But representing consumers, overcoming imbalance, even discerning the public interest in HSAs will not alter the American health system in any profound fashion. The HSA mandate—limiting costs, expanding access, and improving the quality of health—reaches far beyond the agencies' capabilities. Measured by these standards, the act's program is trivial—more symbol and rhetoric than significant potential.

Because the HSAs' planning functions are largely isolated from the process of health resource allocation, planning becomes too often a smoke screen, an empty symbol, or simply wheel spinning. The agency's difficulties of limited authority are compounded by the uncertain relationship between HSAs and the rest of government. In their reliance on "scientific planning," HSAs are yet another manifestation of the effort to find objective solutions to political choices. But scientific planning cannot relieve the tensions between national demands and local desires or between representing community interests and programmatic efficiency.[33]

Despite these problems, the health planning law does have significance, and that significance lies in its stimulation of a broad range of consumer interests. Viewed as an effort to organize communities into caring about their own health systems, it is the largest program of its kind. And one that could influence health politics long after its particular institutional manifestation—HSA planning boards—has been forgotten.

NOTES

1. PL 93-641 § 1512(b)(3)(c)(iii)(2).
2. Aldamuy et al. v. Pirro et al., C.A. No. 76 CV-204 (N.D. N.Y., April 7, 1977).
3. Texas Association of Community Organizations for Reform Now (ACORN) et al. v. Texas Area V. Health Systems Agency et al., C.A. No. S-76-102-CA (E.D. Texas, Sherman Div., March 1, 1977).
4. Rakestraw et al. v. Califano et al., C.A. No. C77-635A (N.D. Ga., Atlanta Div., filed April 22, 1977); The Louisiana Association of Community Organizations for Reform Now (ACORN) et al. v. New Orleans Area Bayou Rivers Health Systems Agency et al., C.A. No. 17-361 (E.D. La., filed March 15, 1977); Amos et al. v. Central California Health Systems Agency et al. C.A. No. 76-174 (E.D. Calif., filed Sept. 10, 1976).
5. See Wayne Clark, "Placebo or Cure? State and Local Health Planning Agencies in the South," photocopied (Atlanta: Southern Governmental Monitoring Project, Southern Regional Council, 1977), for examples of such reports.
6. H. F. Pitkin, *The Concept of Representation* (Berke-

ley and Los Angeles: University of California Press, 1967), p. 3.

7. This is not so for certain groups—e.g., the parents of children with special diseases—as our colleague Owen Fiss points out.

8. T. R. Marmor, "Consumer Representation: Beneath the Consensus, Many Difficulties." *Trustee* 30 (1977): 37–40.

9. John Adams, cited in Pitkin, *Concept of Representation,* p. 60.

10. For notable formulations of this common idea, see Edmund Burke. "The English Constitutional System," in *Representation*, ed. H. F. Pitkin (New York: Atherton Press, 1969); or Alexander Hamilton et al., *Federalist Papers*, no. 10, by James Madison (New York: Modern Library, Inc., 1937).

11. Judged by the model of a jury, such standards are unnecessary; representativeness is the condition for legitimacy. We want to thank Owen Fiss for stressing this competing model of representation.

12. J. D. Greenstone and P. E. Peterson, *Race and Authority in Urban Politics: Consumer Participation and the War on Poverty* (Chicago: University of Chicago Press, 1973), chap. 6. We have profited immensely from this analysis.

13. 41 Federal Register 12812 (March 26, 1976), § 122.114.

14. Ibid., §§ 122.104(b)(I)(viii) and 122.109(e)(3).

15. Ibid., §§ 122.104(a)(8) and 122.104(b)(7).

16. Ibid., § 122.107(c)(2).

17. Ibid., § 122.107(c)(3).

18. We are grateful to our colleague Douglas Yates for pointing out this distinction.

19. There are indications that precisely this tension is asserting itself as HHS, e.g., drafts guidelines and local communities protest that they do not apply in their specific situations.

20. PL 93-641 § 1515(c)(1).

21. Allowing local politics to define constituencies is fraught with trouble. Note the cycle: Congress, claiming that many interests were shut out of local politics, established entirely new governmental structures for health planning and mandated that they be "broadly representative." That requirement is itself so broad that it is unclear what interests qualify; the decision is left to the local political process which Congress sought to bypass in the first place. The vagaries of congressional consistency aside, local selection of the interests to be represented will not break the cycle of litigation. Interests that are shunned will sue, arguing that the local process which excluded them does not conform to the federal mandate to broadly represent.

22. As Owen Fiss has pointed out to us, the impossibility of mirroring a community's demography is equally true for specifying its health interests. But treating the selection of interests as a political choice need not reach the impossibility test of mirroring all interests.

23. We have profited particularly from Albert Weale's incisive comments on the topic of interests.

24. Charles Anderson, "Political Design and the Representation of Interests," *Comparative Political Studies* 10(1977): 127–52.

25. The problem is less nettlesome in legislatures. On a practical level, lobbying legislatures appears only marginally effective: analysts have generally found that politicans are most likely to follow their own opinions or apparent constituency desires. More important, there is at least a formal representation of every voting citizen. Of course, this does not minimize the complexities of electoral representation. But elective systems do afford a systematic canvas of community sentiment, however vague a guide it may be to policy formulation.

26. Robert Dahl, *A Preface to Democratic Theory* (Chicago: University of Chicago Press, 1964), p. 137.

27. See Andrew McFarland, "Recent Social Movements and Theories of Power in America," microfilmed (paper delivered at the American Political Science Association Convention, Washington, D.C., August 1979).

28. Recall the epigram, "The flaw in the pluralist heaven is that the heavenly chorus sings with a strong upper class accent. Probably about 90 percent of the people cannot get into the pressure system," by E. E. Schattschneider, *The Semisovereign People* (Hinsdale, Ill.: Dryden Press, 1960), p. 34.

29. James Q. Wilson, *Political Organizations* (New York: Basic Books, 1973), p. 318; T. R. Marmor and T. Heagy, "Politics of Medical Inflation," *Journal of Health Politics, Policy and Law* (Spring 1976), pp. 69–84.

30. Rand Rosenblatt, "Health Care Reform and Administrative Law, a Structural Approach," *Yale Law Journal* (1978), pt. 2, pp. 243–336.

31. P. C. Schmitter, "An Inventory of Analytical Pluralist Propositions" (monograph, University of Chicago, Department of Political Science, Autumn 1975).

32. See Mark Kleiman, "What's in It for Us: A Consumer Analysis of the 1979 Health Planning Amendments," *Health Law Project Library Bulletin* 4 (1979): 329–36; and Barry Checkoway, "Citizens on Local Health Planning Boards: What Are the Obstacles?" *Journal of the Community Development Society* 10(1979): 101–16.

33. For a fuller discussion of these issues, see the version of this paper published in *Health and Society* 58(1980): 125–65.

Richard C. Rich

The Roles of Neighborhood Organizations
in Urban Service Delivery

INTRODUCTION

The "neighborhood movement" of the 1960s and 70s established the political significance of urban neighborhoods, and resulted in the mobilization of a great many neighborhood associations that actively petition city government for services or attempt to organize residents to provide services directly.[1] While their effectiveness varies greatly, these associations often encounter difficulties which make the payoffs of their activities seem small in proportion to the resources channeled into them. Until means can be found to enhance their infleunce over community conditions, citizens will have little incentive to take part in these instruments of grass roots political participation.[2]

This barrier to participation is significant for two reasons. First, such organizations are necessary if citizens are to control the conditions of their participation in policymaking and implementation processes, rather than having the terms of this participation established by government officials. Second, citizen participation in the planning and delivery of services can enhance both the effectiveness and efficiency of those services by tailoring services to localized needs, mobilizing additional resources, and improving communications between consumers and producers of public services.[3] A first step in realizing these potential benefits from citizen involvement is the development of a theoretical understanding of the dynamics of neighborhood

Reprinted with permission of the author and *Urban Affairs Papers* 1 (Fall 1979), pp. 81–93.

organizations' roles in urban service delivery systems. If we can identify institutional barriers to effective citizen effort in the provision of public services, we may be able to design institutions and policies which will encourage extensive citizen participation and result in higher levels of consumer satisfaction at lower costs. Moreover, by providing citizens with an opportunity to shape service delivery, it may be possible to remove some of the major barriers to equitable distribution of public services in our urban centers.[4]

This paper offers a theoretical framework for analysis of voluntarily organized citizen participation in urban service delivery systems. It proceeds from a discussion of the nature of neighborhood associations to an examination of the major roles such organizations play in service delivery and concludes with an exploration of the relationships among public policy, the institutional design of service delivery arrangements, and citizens' opportunities for effective participation in public service provision. The primary focus of this paper is on assessing the potential influence over service levels which each role offers citizens' groups and on identifying the conditions under which each strategy is most likely to be effective in improving neighborhood services.

NEIGHBORHOOD ORGANIZATIONS AND COLLECTIVE ACTION

Community associations that actively attempt to influence service levels and other conditions affecting the quality of life in a given area can be viewed as institutions through which residents organize collective effort in defense of shared interests. As relatively large interest groups, urban neighborhoods may fall victim to what Mancur Olson terms the "logic of collective action" whereby common interests go unserved because each group member lacks an incentive to contribute toward the procurement of "goods" benefiting the entire group.[5] Neighborhood organizations may overcome this barrier to collective action by (1) acquiring some form of coercive authority, (2) dispensing individual benefits which will give members a personal incentive to contribute to group effort, or (3) providing residents with a dependable means of pooling their resources and sharing the costs of collective goods in such a way as to lead each to anticipate a net benefit from collective effort.[6]

Neighborhood organizations seldom have access to legal authority (though they may wield considerable moral authority) and generally do not control individual benefits similar to those dispensed through labor unions or professional associations. Consequently, the third option, serving as a resource-pooling, cost-sharing mechanism, is most likely to be the means by which organizations mobilize collective action. The viability of this strategy depends on the certainty with which community associations can exercise influence over events which produce benefits for residents and on the costs residents must bear in exercising that influence. The less certain and more costly the influence process, the fewer the anticipated net benefits of contribution to collective effort and the less attractive citizen participation will be for individual residents.[7]

From this perspective, neighborhood organizations may be seen as providers of collective goods, and the effectiveness and efficiency with which they perform this task becomes crucial in understanding the extent to which they mobilize citizens for political participation or self-help. We may examine the several potential and actual roles community organizations play in urban service delivery with an emphasis both on how much effective influence over neighborhood conditions each role allows citizens' associations and on how costly it is for residents to influence service delivery through each strategy. The greater the certainty of effectiveness and the fewer the demands made on each citizen, the higher the viability of any given role as a means of mobilizing meaningful citizen participation in service delivery.

Throughout the following discussion the term "effectiveness" is used to refer to the certainty of control over service conditions which a particular strategy offers. "Efficiency," by contrast, is used to refer to the ratio of the costs residents will bear as a result of using a given strategy to secure services to the value they receive from the resulting services. Purchase of supplemental patrols from a private security agency, for example, gives citizens fairly direct control over the frequency of patrol, but requires that citizens pay the full cost of the additional service. It is, therefore, an effective strategy (provided that residents have the collective resources necessary to purchase the desired services), but is not an especially efficient one, *as that term is used here.* On the other hand, petitioning the city to increase the frequency of police patrol provides a highly uncertain amount of control over service delivery for local residents. If they are successful, however, residents will enjoy improved services at a relatively low cost: the time spent persuading city officials. Remonstration to the city is, then, a relatively ineffective, but potentially efficient strategy. Whether or not any particular strategy is effective or efficient in any given situation is an empirical question.

Basically neighborhood organizations perform three broad functions with respect to public services. They act as (1) consumers' cooperatives, (2) alternative producers, and/or (3) coproducers of services. These roles can be examined separately.

THE CONSUMERS' COOPERATIVE ROLE

As consumers' cooperatives, neighborhood organizations perform two subfunctions. First, they act as *demand aggregating and articulating instrumentalities*. Individuals' preferences cannot produce a change in service delivery unless they are communicated to officials. Even then, they are not likely to produce changes unless they are communicated along with similar preferences on the part of a sufficiently large group. This is so for two reasons. First, services can seldom be practically provided to discrete individuals. (For example, the costs of a trash run to a single home at a different time from that made for the rest of the block would be prohibitive.) Second, officials must generally believe that failure to respond to demands will result in a significant sanction if citizens are to have any effective control over them, and control over such sanctions generally depends on numbers of people acting in concert. The role of demand articulation relies principally on traditional mechanisms of political accountability in order to bring bureaucrats' behavior into line with citizens' preferences indirectly by pressure on the elected officials who are in command of the agencies involved.

This aspect of the demand articulation function of neighborhood organizations is potentially important since it provides an alternative to the price mechanism in market exchanges. Most public services are "lumpy" in that their quality and/or quantity cannot generally be varied over time or geographic space with any ease.[8] As a result, policies are often supplied in packages for a taxprice and agency products cannot be marginally modified in response to consumer purchasing behavior. The absence of a price unit tied to the consumption unit means that marginal variations in demand do not become manifest in public enterprises as they do in private. The citizen/consumer who engages in political activity to influence agency service provision, however, may be conceptualized as exhibiting a willingness to pay a higher "price" in the form of time, resources, and energy expended in order to have an agency product which conforms to his or her preferences.

These sacrifices will serve the price function and induce alterations in bureaucratic behavior toward the geographic, ethnic, occupational, or social groups expressing exceptional demands only under certain conditions, however. First, the organized demand articulation must sufficiently influence elected officials so that they are *willing* to attempt to modify service delivery to accommodate the demand expressed. Where the group with an exceptional demand structure is a distinct minority in a constituency this influence will be difficult to achieve. Second, the elected officials must be *able* actually to effect a change in the relevant bureaucratic behavior. The loss of real authority in chains of bureaucratic control may inhibit effective response to the articulation of exceptional preferences.[9] Additionally, it may be extremely technically difficult to modify service delivery to a given geographically or demographically defined consumer group.

These weaknesses of the conventional demand articulation function of neighborhood organizations suggest that this function offers limited opportunities for bringing service bureaucracies under any sort of effective discipline. There are, however, other aspects of the demand articulation function.

One aspect is exemplified by the case where neighborhood organizations communicate the exceptional preferences of some group of citizen/consumers directly to agency personnel. If the personnel are devoted to the goal of public service and are not under legal, political, or technical constraints which prohibit their doing so, they may modify service delivery in response to this exceptional demand once they have been apprized of it. Instances of such modifications could doubtlessly be found but are equally doubtlessly rare.[10]

The more salient case is one in which persons within the agency, or in some governmental position with authority over the agency, seek to turn consumer dissatisfaction to their own gain. A city councilman, for example, may make disaffected consumer groups his constituency by championing their cause. When neighborhood organizations make these pockets of unsatisfied demand known to such persons, they contribute indirectly to making bureaucracy responsive. They turn atomized consumers into active clientele groups.

A final aspect of the demand articulation function relates to its effect on potential alternative producers of the services provided by urban governments. Private firms may be willing to produce these services, or some supplement to them if they feel certain that an effective demand exists for their potential product and can define the market for it. Additionally, adjoining or overlapping jurisdictions may be willing to undertake a new form of service delivery in order to increase their own standing or revenue if there is evidence that existing agencies are supplying the service in inadequate quantity or quality to satisfy the active demand.

By supplying evidence of an active demand for a specific type or level of service in a specific area, neighborhood organizations may reduce the risk involved in entrepreneurial undertakings and stimulate the development of alternative suppliers. This activity may contribute substantially to citizens' ability to achieve the level of service delivery they desire by means of purchase from alternative suppliers. It does *not* necessarily make existing agencies more responsive to citizen preferences. In fact, existing agencies may welcome the appearance of alternative producers through which citizens may satisfy exceptional demands since it will reduce the pressure on them to satisfy those demands. Because citizens cannot generally withhold taxes in order to compensate themselves for the necessity of purchasing desired service levels from alternative producers, urban agencies may not be hurt by the presence of other producers.

Alternative producers will threaten existing agencies only if they compete for the same tax dollars which fund the initial service-providing agency. Second, another, overlapping level of government could supply the service, and the taxpayers could shift their dollars to that level of government (say a county as opposed to a city) by their votes on bond issues, etc. Third, there is the possibility that citizens will compensate themselves for the purchase of services from private producers by refusing to vote [for] bond issues, or by electing public officials devoted to cutting back the budgets of agencies providing inadequate services. Finally, citizens can physically move from jurisdictions providing poor services to those providing more desirable ones, thereby reducing the former jurisdiction's tax base.

All of these situations provide only delayed, often indirect threats to the operating funds of urban agencies. This lack of effect is especially acute if the group with an exceptional demand is a small minority of the total population served by the agency, or if it controls few tax-generating resources. As a consequence, even this aspect of demand articulation by neighborhood organizations offers a rather restricted hope of disciplining errant service bureaucracies. Moreover, it places large demands on the time, energy, and resources of consumers.

The demand aggregation/articulation function is perhaps the most commonly recognized activity of neighborhood associations. Given the design of most urban service delivery systems (monopolistic provision of services by government agencies), this function may be the most immediately practical one for community groups.[11] Demand aggregation/articulation, however, is a highly costly strategy of uncertain effectiveness. It is, therefore, not likely to provide a basis for widespread, stable citizen participation in service delivery.

Neighborhood organizations may perform a second set of functions within their role as consumer cooperatives. These functions stem from their activities as *resource accumulators*. In this role, neighborhood organizations may make localized demands for specific services "effective." In economics, a demand is considered effective when the desire for a good is paired with the capacity to purchase it. Only if consumers can actually purchase a product can their preferences influence the allocation of resources among alternative goods in a competitive market. Individual consumers' demand for given public services often remains latent for two reasons. First, the cost of providing such services is often far beyond the financial means of single consumers. Second, the collective nature of these goods generally provides consumers with little incentive to enter into voluntarily organized joint purchasing arrangements.

Neighborhood organizations can make consumers' demand for specific services effective by overcoming these two conditions. First, they can often pool the resources of enough consumers to provide an aggregate capacity to purchase the goods. Second, they can ensure that contributions toward that purchase will be forthcoming by introducing an element of predictability into the contributory behavior of residents either through the exercise of formal or informal coercive power or by offering selective benefits for contribution

to collective effort. For more affluent communities, neighborhood organizations may make it possible for citizens to purchase additional services from alternative producers or governmental agencies on a contract basis. For the less affluent, they may make it possible to sustain enough pressure on existing agencies to elicit the desired service level. By pooling resources and insuring contributions (of time and effort as well as money) these organizations may enable lower class citizens to disrupt the orderly operations of bureaucracies and coerce agencies into modifying service delivery.

The task of resource pooling can allow community associations to make existing service agencies more responsive and to help citizens achieve the service levels they desire.[12] This strategy, however, will generally prove more effective for middle and upper class neighborhoods than for poor ones because its success depends on the adequacy of the resources mobilized by residents. Where residents cannot afford to purchase desired services collectively, resource pooling will not attract private providers of public goods. Where residents cannot muster the political influence necessary to persuade public agencies, service levels will remain unchanged.

Regardless of neighborhood affluence, the resource-pooling strategy places high demands on residents. If they purchase the desired goods and services directly, they must bear the full cost. If they persuade government to provide the services, they may be able to shift some of the costs to others (depending, of course, on the system of financing in use) and may realize a substantial return on a relatively small investment of time and money. If, for instance, citizens successfully petition city governments to resurface a street, the cost of the resurfacing and the benefits residents receive as a result will probably far exceed the value of the resources citizens put into their influence campaign. But

benefits will be realized in small increments over an extended period (through
reduced vehicle maintenance costs, for example), and the "price" of attaining the
service (e.g., time spent contacting citizens
to sign a petition) may seem prohibitively
high given the uncertainty of results and
delayed nature of the rewards. Moreover,
the costs of influence are not likely to be
evenly distributed among potential beneficiaries and the price that activists would
have to bear might far outweigh the individual benefits they would expect.

For affluent communities, the resource
pooling role may provide a greater certainty of payoff than demand aggregation/ar-
ticulation, but it imposes substantial costs
on participants. For poor communities, it
may be neither an effective nor an efficient
method of acquiring services. The extent
to which this is the case depends on the
responsiveness of service agencies to consumer demands and on the institutions
through which these demands are
communicated.

THE ALTERNATIVE
PRODUCER ROLE

In some cases, neighborhood *residents* can
produce the services they want. Citizens
may coordinate their efforts to establish a
day care center, arrange a taxi service, provide extra security through civilian patrols,
construct a playground on a vacant lot, or
clean up and landscape the community. If
they do these things, consumers' associations become alternative producers of public services.

As alternative producers, neighborhood
organizations may enable consumers to enjoy the type and level of services they desire. They may not, however, make existing agencies more responsive. Citizens
cannot generally withhold their tax dollars
from ineffective or unresponsive agencies
in order to compensate themselves for
their own productive efforts. As a result,

when neighborhood associations act as alternative producers, they do not confront
government agencies with authentic competition. They simply add to the costs of
achieving a given service level for the producing consumers who must "pay" twice;
once through taxes and once through their
coordinated efforts. In fact, city agencies
are likely to welcome consumers' productive activities. They can often use the
provision of services by this means as an
excuse for officially or unofficially reducing their own service delivery effort in the
area in order to shift scarce resources elsewhere or live more easily within their
budgets.

The role of alternative producer, therefore, offers citizens little opportunity to
improve bureaucratic responsiveness. It
may, however, allow them to enjoy improved services as a result of their own
efforts. Whether this is a viable strategy for
any given community will depend on the
nature of the collective goods it desires and
the resources it commands. Only if residents' combined resources are adequate to
produce desired goods and can be mobilized for that purpose is the role of alternative producer open to their neighborhood
associations. Affluent communities are
more likely to be able to purchase services
or persuade local government to deliver
them. As a result, the alternative producer
role will be most important for poor neighborhoods. There citizens' limited resources (e.g., free time, manual skills) may
be adequate to produce some of the labor
intensive services which residents cannot
"purchase" either with cash or political
influence.

Rich or poor, the neighborhood that
adopts this strategy for participating in
service delivery will find that its residents
must bear substantial costs since the full
responsibility of production and delivery
falls on their shoulders. Whether or not
these costs are acceptable to citizens will
depend heavily on the powers assigned to

the community association. If the association can guarantee resource mobilization and equitable sharing of costs among residents, expected benefits may exceed anticipated costs and indigenous production may be a logical response to perceived needs. If the association cannot guarantee participation and cost sharing, it will probably fall victim to Olson's logic of collective inaction.

The alternative producer role thus offers a potentially effective means of securing services, though this effectiveness will be restricted by the adequacy of neighborhood resources for producing specific services. Its costs to consumers, however, will be high and may be prohibitive if they cannot be shared widely enough among residents so as to make the benefits realized by each greater than his or her personal effort in producing the services. The strategy thus offers improved services to those communities that can afford to produce their own but offers little or no control over governmental service producers and may impose dual costs on citizens who both pay taxes and participate in neighborhood productive enterprises.

COPRODUCTION AND PUBLIC SERVICES

Apart from their activities as consumers' cooperatives and alternative producers, neighborhood organizations may serve to encourage citizens to act as coproducers of the public services they utilize. Many public services are provided through a process in which the service itself is jointly produced by the efforts of agency personnel and citizens.

The importance of this process of coproduction is widely recognized in the social or "soft" services.[13] For example, for a drug abuse or family planning service to be effective, consumers must be willing to heed the advice of counselors and exert some effort of their own. Coproductive processes similar to those operating in the social services also affect the quality and quantity of "hard" services delivered by municipal agencies. For example, citizens may act as coproducers of law enforcement services by being alert to and reporting suspicious events in their neighborhood, cooperating with police in investigations, and organizing efforts to prevent vandalism.[14]

Coproductive processes affect the delivery of municipal services even in the absence of citizens' awareness of their effects. For instance, the failure of citizens to take fire prevention precautions or to report fires at their outbreak can substantially increase the costs of providing adequate fire protection to an area. When citizens can be persuaded to actively engage in coproduction by removing fire hazards, preventing vandalism to fire alarm boxes, and maintaining casual surveillance, the total resources mobilized for the purpose of fire protection will be increased.

If individually small savings from active coproduction are realized across city services, they could constitute a substantial boon in the city budget. In an era of tight budgets, agency personnel should have a strong incentive to work with voluntary groups in order to produce a maximum amount of actual service delivery per tax dollar expended. The potential return on investment from resources put into organizing coproductive activity is probably greater than the return that can be expected from resources put into additional service delivery equipment, facilities, or personnel.[15] From the citizen's standpoint, small increases in the quality of the various municipal services delivered in his or her area can combine to make the neighborhood significantly more "livable" at relatively little cost to each resident.

Neighborhood organizations can facilitate active coproduction by coordinating the efforts of individual consumers and providing a liaison between officials and citizens. The federally funded Crime T.R.A.P. (Total Registration of All Property) program provides an excellent sample. Law enforcement personnel have found that registration and labeling of valuables both deters burglaries and facilitates investigations and prosecutions of burglaries that do occur. Contacting citizens and arranging the registration of property, however, is a costly job. A community association can take over this task in its neighborhood with little training or supervision from police. Moreover, the association may make the program more effective by lending legitimacy to the effort.

The benefits of active coproduction—which improves the services in an area—represent collective goods for residents. Coproduction will, therefore, be subject to the same logic of collective action as efforts at providing other collective goods. These efforts will be endangered by the possibility that some citizens will act as free riders unless institutional arrangements are devised to ensure participation.[16] Neighborhood organizations will be better able to secure participation if government agencies recognize community associations as citizens' representatives and support the coproductive efforts organized through them. In this way, residents can be assured of the effectiveness of their efforts and may be able to realize a substantial benefit from a relatively small additional investment.

Coproductive efforts may be organized in neighborhoods of any socioeconomic status since they often require little money and few special skills. The role of coproduction organizer, however, will generally be more important for less affluent communities because poor communities are least likely to be able to adopt either of the other major strategies effectively. Coproduction allows poor communities both to improve the quality and expand the range of services they enjoy without bearing the full costs themselves

and allows the costs that residents do bear to be shared widely. Coproduction efforts may also provide citizens with an increased influence over the behavior of service bureaucracies by giving these agencies an incentive to work with neighborhood groups in order to increase effectiveness and reduce costs.[17]

CONCLUSION

The foregoing evaluations of alternative roles for citizens' organizations may now be summarized. Figure 1 compares the probable effectiveness and efficiency of the three strategies for both affluent (middle and upper class) and poor neighborhoods. The figure postulates that high levels of both efficiency and effectiveness are associated only with the coproducer's role. The other roles promise either effectiveness or efficiency but not both.

Clearly, these conceptual roles are not mutually exclusive. The same organization can pursue each of the strategies, selecting that which seems most promising at any given time. Community associations can, however, expect varying degrees of success from the different strategies, and this analysis suggests that considerations of either effectiveness or efficiency (as defined here) will generally lead them to anticipate the greatest success from a coproductive strategy.

Coproduction offers a high degree of potential effectiveness because citizens need not depend totally on service agencies; rather they can initiate direct action, and also because it provides public officials with an increased incentive to respond to local demands. Coproduction can also be a relatively efficient strategy from the perspective of the individual citizen because it draws on resources from outside the neighborhood and allows costs to be shared widely among residents. It should, therefore, be easier to organize citizens for coproductive efforts than for other ac-

SERVICE ROLE	Effectiveness		Efficiency	
	AFFLUENT NEIGHBORHOOD	POOR NEIGHBORHOOD	AFFLUENT NEIGHBORHOOD	POOR NEIGHBORHOOD
Consumers' Cooperative (a) Demand Articulation	Uncertain	Uncertain	Potentially High	Potentially High
(b) Resource Pooling	Generally High	Uncertain	Low	Low
Alternative Producer	Generally High	Potentially High	Low	Low
Coproducer	Generally High	Potentially High	High	High

Figure 1 Effectiveness and Efficiency of Alternative Roles for Neighborhood Organizations in Service Delivery

tivities which offer more uncertain rewards and impose higher costs. Once organized, coproductive efforts have a high potential for influencing the community environment because they can produce both improved services and enhanced social relationships. The role of coproduction organizer thus promises neighborhood associations success both in mobilizing support and in influencing local conditions.

If citizen influence in service delivery is valued and if the coproducer role appears to be an effective means of obtaining this influence, then it is logical to ask what public policies might facilitate the adoption of this role by citizen groups. One category of policies which would have this effect is represented by the various reforms proposed by advocates of "administrative decentralization."[18] These policies involve the creation of institutions which allow regular consultation between citizens and service agencies, give citizens a formal role in planning and evaluation, or dispense administrative authority to neighborhood level officials who are more accessible to consumers. Citizens advisory boards, neighborhood service centers and similar

institutions can enhance the ability of community groups to play the demand aggregator/articulator role by improving their access to service officials and by increasing the flexibility with which services are provided in discrete geographic areas. These institutions may also encourage coproduction by improving the communication between citizens and administrators and thereby facilitate the coordination of governmental efforts with those of neighborhood residents. A number of U.S. cities have created neighborhood political institutions of this nature.[19]

Institutions of decentralized administration and citizen participation, however, do not provide local residents with direct access to public resources for service delivery. Nor do they provide public officials with any direct incentive to be responsive to citizens' demands. So long as final authority is vested in a central administrative agency, bureaucrats will have an incentive to respond primarily to the demands of their superiors' constituencies which may not include direct consumers of the services provided by bureaucratic agencies. Moreover, mechanisms of citizen participation and decentralized administration alone do not provide any means of coordinating citizen participation. The coordination of citizen participation remains a voluntary affair which imposes rather high costs on individuals and is likely to remain in the control of a relatively small number of activists.

As a result of these conditions, the effectiveness of citizen participation remains highly uncertain, especially for those communities lacking extensive monetary resources or political influence. If citizens take part in collective attempts to influence service delivery in response to their own calculations about the potential costs and benefits of that participation, anything which reduces the certainty of a positive result works against their decision to participate.

Another category of reform proposals would provide neighborhood level institutions with final authority over some services. These proposals are advanced by proponents of "neighborhood government."[20] They involve the creation of general purpose governments at the community level to plan and administer delivery of services which do not require metropolitan-wide coordination. These governments would have access both to funds transferred from higher levels of government and to the authority to tax their own citizens.[21] Such institutions could encourage sustained citizen input (since community decisions would be translated more directly into service modifications), thus raising the probability of a payoff and reducing the participatory costs to each citizen.

Neighborhood governments could improve the capacity of citizens' organizations for playing all three of the roles identified above but would be especially effective in encouraging coproductive activity. If neighborhood level institutions have final discretion over the use of resources that may be considered the common property of residents, citizens have an increased incentive to participate in deliberations which will determine that use. Moreover, small scale jurisdictions can make it easier for individuals to relate public expenditures to the services they receive. Public spaces and properties may come to be thought of as belonging to citizens. As a result, citizens may be willing to act to stop vandalism to public property and to encourage efficiency in service delivery. Inefficiency and ineffectiveness in public service delivery can then be viewed as direct costs to consumers because the relationship between neighborhood expenditures and local services is more immediate.[22]

Neighborhood-based service delivery could, for example, enhance program effectiveness in social services by removing the contradiction between administrative ease and consumer convenience which often inhibits coproduction in centralized systems. If service centers were locally based and locally controlled, citizens could reach them with less difficulty and could regulate their hours of operation to reflect the needs of users rather than the preferences of the middle class professionals who provide the services. In addition, local control could add legitimacy to service agencies' operations and create the good will necessary for coproduction in these fields.[23] Citizens could come to view the local health officer, family counselor, or housing inspector as their employee rather than as a representative of some distant government.[24] In this situation they are more likely to report problems, find their way to service centers, take advice, and cooperate in inspections, programs, and treatments.

Proposals for the creation of neighborhood governments to manage public service delivery must be viewed as an important policy option when local government seeks to encourage citizen participation and to enhance the potential effectiveness of that participation in redressing existing inequities in services.

NOTES

1. Janice E. Perlman, *Grassroots Participation from Neighborhood to Nation* in Stuart Langton, ed. Citizen Participation in America. (Lexington: Lexington, 1978), pp. 65–80; and Robert A. Rosenbloom *The Politics of the Neighborhood Movement,* South Atlantic Urban Studies, 4 (August, 1979), 103–120. On the range of citizen involvement in service delivery, see Frank S. Steggert, Community Action Groups and City Government (Cambridge: Ballinger, 1975).

2. Available evidence is sparse, but it suggests that membership in community-based citizens' groups is held by only a small minroity of urban residents. See Steggert, Community Action Groups.

3. For a review of the contributions of citizen participation programs to service delivery, see Robert K. Yin and Douglas Yates, Street-Level Governments (Santa Monica: Rand, 1974).

4. On the relationship between citizen involvement and the quality of public services, see Richard C. Rich, *Equity and Institutional Design in Urban Service Delivery,* Urban Affairs Quarterly, 12 (March, 1977), 383–410.

5. Mancur Olson, Jr., The Logic of Collective Action (New York: Schocken Books, 1965). Olson's theory depends on the concept of "collective goods" which can be defined as desirable structures of events which jointly benefit a group of persons under conditions that prevent the exclusion of those who do not contribute toward procurement of the goods from enjoyment of the benefits of the goods. For an application of Olson's reasoning to urban neighborhoods, see David J. O'Brien, Neighborhood Organization and Interest Group Processes (Princeton: Princeton, 1975).

6. For an elaboration of this argument with respect to all interest groups, see Norman Froblich, Joe A. Oppenheimer and Oran R. Young, Political Leadership and Collective Goods (Princeton: Princeton, 1971), pp. 20–23; and Robert I., Salisbury, *An Exchange Theory of Interest Groups,* Midwest Journal of Political Science, 13 (February, 1969), 1–32.

7. This reasoning assumes that participation is primarily an instrumental act rather than an affective or expressive one. Citizens are assumed to take part in collective effort principally for the purpose of creating or preserving desirable conditions. While there are clearly other motives for participation in neighborhood associations, they do not play an important role in this analysis.

8. See Elinor Ostrom, *Exclusion, Choice, and Divisibility: Factors Affecting the Measurement of Urban Agency Output and Impact,* Social Science Quarterly, 54 (March, 1974), 691–699.

9. William A. Niskanana, Bureaucracy and Representative Government (Chicago: Aldine-Atherton, 1971).

10. On the relationship between community groups and sympathetic bureaucrats, see Martin L. Needleman and Carolyn Emerson Needleman, Guerrillas in the Bureaucracy (New York: John Wiley and Sons, 1974).

11. Robert L. Bish and Robert Warren, *Scale and Monopoly Problems in Urban Government Services,* Urban Affairs Quarterly, 8 (September, 1972), 97–122; and E. S. Savas, *Municipal Monopolies Versus Competition in Delivering Urban Services* in Willis D. Hawley and David Rogers, eds., Improving the Quality of Urban Management (Beverly Hills: Sage, 1974), pp. 473–500.

12. The effectiveness with which neighborhood associations can play this role depends crucially on both the resources available to neighborhood residents, and the formal powers granted to the associations. If the organization cannot consistently raise sufficient resources to "purchase" desired goods (either directly or through pressure on public agencies), it cannot make neighborhood service demands effective. A lack of necessary resources in the community or an unstable mechanism of resource accumulation in the organization can prevent neighborhood associations from effectively serving as resource accumulators.

13. Victor R. Fuchs, The Service Economy (New York: Columbia, 1968); and Robert Perman, Consumers and Social Services (New York· John Wiley, 1975).

14. See Frances E. Pennell, *Private vs. Collective Strategies for Dealing with Crime, Citizen Attitudes Toward Crime and the Police in Urban Neighborhoods,* Journal of Voluntary Action Research, 7(January/April, 1978), 59–74.

15. T. H. Lederer and M. B. Badenhop, *Voluntary Effort as a Tax Substitute in the Revenue Sharing Formula,* paper presented at the annual meeting of the Southern Agricultural Economics Association, February, 1976; and Thomas F. Stinson and Jerome M. Stam, *Toward an Economic Model of Voluntarism,* Journal of Voluntary Action Research, 5(January, 1976), 52–60.

16. A free rider is one who enjoys benefits from a collective good without contributing toward its procurement. The availability of the free rider strategy endangers collective effort less because

large numbers of persons actually adopt the strategy than because the possibility that others will act as free riders makes each citizen uncertain as to the effectiveness of collective effort. This uncertainty could make citizens unwilling to risk making a contribution for fear that adequate support will not be forthcoming from others, and that their contribution will be wasted.

17. In existing service delivery systems, service agencies often find themselves in conflict with neighborhood organizations because they face the task of dividing limited resources among competing areas, and lack the capacity to meet the unique service demands of any given area. Organized coproductive efforts can alter this situation by placing citizens and public personnel in a cooperative relationship in which each has something to offer the other.

18. Douglas Yates, *Service Delivery and the Urban Political Order* in Willis D. Hawley and David Rogers, eds., Improving the Quality of Urban Management (Beverly Hills: Sage, 1974), pp. 213–240.

19. Richard C. Rich, *Neighborhood Governance Programs in the 1970s,* Neighborhood Organization Research Group Newsletters, 2 (July, 1979), 8–11.

20. Howard Hallman, Neighborhood Government in a Metropolitan Setting (Beverly Hills: Sage, 1974).

21. If adequate services are to be provided in deprived communities under a system of neighborhood government, there will have to be either extensive support for the localized governmental units from higher levels of government, or *significant* efforts at redistributing income among individual citizens so that the poor can afford to purchase public services with their tax dollars. On the relationship between the service demands of the poor and systems of neighborhood government, see Robert L. Bish and Vincent Ostrom, Understanding Urban Government (Washington, D.C.: American Enterprise Institute, 1973), p. 31.

22. See Jane Jacobs, The Death and Life of Great American Cities (New York: Vintage, 1961), pp. 29–73; and Oscar Newman, Architectural Design for Crime Prevention (Washington, D.C.: U.S. Government Printing Office, 1973), pp. 1–19.

23. This logic underlies the "team policing" concept in law enforcement. See Richard A. Myren, "Decentralization and Citizen Participation in Criminal Justice System," Public Administration Review, 32 (October, 1972), 721–722.

24. Yates, *Service Delivery and the Urban Political Order,* and Peter H. Rossi, Richard A. Berk and Bettye K. Edison, The Roots of Urban Discontent (New York: John Wiley, 1974).

Harriet H. Naylor

Volunteers, Resource for Human Services

INTRODUCTION

The demands on leadership in human services in the 1980s will be very different from most human service executives' expectations when they assumed management responsibilities. The shortage of money is not the single unanticipated factor, for novel working relationships have

Excerpted from *Volunteers, Resource for Human Services,* by Harriet Naylor of the Administration for Public Services, Office of Human Development Services, U.S. Department of H.E.W. Reprinted with permission of the author and Project Share—Occasional Paper Series, pp. 5–35.

also been incorporated into the dynamics of agency leadership.

Charles Hendry, as dean of the Toronto School of Social Work, described his *New Understandings of Leadership* to the American Camping Association in a meaningful way. He said, "*The head* is someone who got there by election or appointment; *a head* is a naturally influential person to whom people inevitably turn, no matter what the title; but the person who is *ahead* is the person who anticipates needs and fills them before they become crises." (1957, p. 15)

Hendry's views are especially relevant for human service professionals. Professional training has gone through many popular theories of management, some traditional and authoritatian, some scientifically specialized, and others more democratic. Until the 1970s most theories of administration assumed that executives would choose their staff members and that working environments would consist primarily of highly qualified, credentialed professionals.

In the 1980s, however, executives will also be expected to work with consumer public interest groups, fund monitors, working boards, and advisory committees. In short, the executive of the 1980s will have to be responsive to trends which began in the two previous decades.

The turbulent 1960s and the pragmatic 1970s moved several new constituencies into the decision-making process for program development and policy formulation. Ideas now came from the grassroots. Service consumers, mandated in Office of Economic Opportunity (OEO) programs for "maximum feasible participation of the poor," took part in significant numbers. Others, particularly the physically and socially handicapped, were speaking out on public policy and agency issues. Not willing to accept only those services that had been offered and concerned with inequities, many consumers were now seeking positions of influence in the planning process. They were learning to articulate their feelings concerning service deficiencies and delivery pattern shortfalls.

These groups, from which volunteers are increasingly drawn, will continue to present not only a challenge but also a valuable resource to the modern manager. Volunteers can play an active role, mediating between the agency and activist community elements. Many volunteers have evolved from the direct service environment to assume advisory and leadership roles. Often these volunteers represent the balance of power in decision-making groups, mediating between conflicting viewpoints and facilitating communication.

Volunteers are in a unique position to contribute valuable ideas since they are free to play advocacy roles unavailable to paid staff members. Within the agency they can represent the target population to the paid staff. Outside the agency, to legislatures, allocating bodies, and other agencies, they are able to influence decision makers who determine future patterns.

In spite of the volunteers' increased influence, many Americans are unaware how extensive volunteering has become and how important it is to the national life. According to a 1974 Census Bureau Survey commissioned by ACTION, almost one out of four Americans over the age of 13 does some form of volunteer work. That represents nearly 37 million people, of whom 41 percent are men. Volunteers average 9 hours a week on their individual projects. This is the equivalent of 3.5 million people working full time for one year. (*Americans Volunteer 1974*, p. 3) By applying a uniform wage rate of $4.76 an hour to this volunteer work, the monetary value comes to more than $33.9 billion. (Wolozin, 1976, p. 4) The survey also discovered that the percentage of Americans who volunteer increased between 1965 and 1974 from 18 percent to 24 percent. This was true for all categories of respondents, grouped by sex, marital status, and race. Since trends indicated by that study seem to be continuing, organized volunteering is soon likely to involve almost half our current population, including 12 percent of those with incomes under $4,000 per year. (*Americans Volunteer 1974*, p. 6)

Volunteers represent every level of professional skill, sophistication, and affluence. To ensure that their talents and experience are well matched to the agency needs, volunteers must receive adequate orientation and training. To develop the requisite competence, many organizations employ a volunteer director. Ideally, the agency's chief executive provides leadership and demonstrates support for the volunteers.

That leadership is essential. Organizations seeking to develop a really effective volunteer corps must be willing to provide the necessary psychological and financial support and recognize the true value of volunteer service. Most volunteers become interested in agency policy, goals, and decision making as their dedication grows. Hence opportunities for volunteers to become involved in these areas are essential. In summary, administrators must take their volunteers seriously, providing a visible, competent director of volunteers and facilitating orderly, meaningful participation in all facets of agency life.

In return, the volunteers will be able to offer constructive ideas and criticism based on direct service experience. Such internal sources can serve the agency as a valuable early warning system, alerting the agency to shifts in community and consumer attitudes. Volunteers, knowing the pressures on paid staff, can work to gain community support on behalf of the standards and ideals which they have learned from their staff partners. Serving the agency as at-large advocates to the community, volunteers can help mobilize the resources necessary to carry on the services the agency believes in and provides.

[Our] purpose . . . is to explore all these characteristics of volunteerism: to understand who the volunteers are, to present them in the myriad roles they can play, to study how they can be organized, to examine governmental attitudes toward volunteerism, and to look to its future.

I. WHO VOLUNTEERS AND WHY?

The Volunteers

Between 1965 and 1974, the number of volunteers in this country almost doubled. The ACTION/Census Bureau study *Americans Volunteer 1974* provides a profile of who volunteers and why. (p. 12) Although the largest group of volunteers falls into the 25 to 54 age bracket, teenagers and retired people also volunteer in significant numbers. According to statistics, one American man out of every five volunteers, and increasing numbers of nonwhites are volunteering. The ACTION survey revealed that more employed persons are active volunteers (25 percent) than unemployed persons (17 percent). (p. 4) There is also a positive correlation between volunteering and income level and length of formal education. (p. 5) This ever greater diversity of people willing and able to work without pay represents a rich staffing resource for human services administration and delivery.

Volunteering can serve to enhance the self-image of the one who volunteers . . . [and] offers diverse opportunities for self-discovery and learning. . . . Regardless of background, group identification is a significant factor in recruiting and especially in retaining volunteers. The peer group relationship made through participation with a school club, church group, older citizens' neighborhood center, Rotary Club, Junior Chamber of Commerce, or other organization is often a primary reason for volunteering. These relationships may replace some of the supports which the extended family used to offer. . . .

II. ROLES VOLUNTEERS ASSUME

. . . the activities which can be pursued by volunteers are as varied as the fields within which they can work. In most cases the boundaries of opportunity are defined only by the skills and aspirations of the individual volunteer. One can, however, systematize volunteer efforts into three broad categories: citizen participation, advocacy, and direct service delivery.

To be sure, these are not hard and fast delineations. Rather, they are conceptual frameworks for understanding. Any one volunteer can serve in any or all of the different categories, sometimes simultaneously. It is only necessary to realize that the modern volunteer represents a much more flexible resource than his counterpart of only a few years ago. . . .

Citizens with volunteer experience have an important perspective on goals and plans which it is their democratic right to express. The role of the volunteer administrator is to alert citizens to opportunities to influence change and to give them confidence to speak out in forums where their opinions are important. By becoming this type of active citizen, the volunteer can bridge the gap of differing, often diametrically opposed views.

The providers of services have their own perspectives: They tend to perceive needs in terms of professional interests. Educators, for example, want more education, and social workers more social services, not merely from self-interest but because these *are* the needs as they see them. Volunteers can offset this view with a more generalized approach, a vision of "how it ought to be" which cuts across discipline, technology, departmental, or agency lines to seek the *people* in need. In so doing, they help translate technical language and bring community wisdom to bear on social problems.

Consumers have quite different perceptions. They know what they want, which is not necessarily what the "experts" think they need. To reconcile wants and needs can often be the mediating role of the volunteer. Consumers may require volunteers as allies to change priorities developed from a "professional" need point of view.

In turn, to the extent he is perceived as altruistic, the volunteer tends to be trusted by providers, consumers, and contributors alike. This adds more weight to his opinions, and that influence becomes a professional responsibility. The forty million active volunteers who may today touch the lives of only one person each directly involve more than a third of the nation.

Their perceptions and opinions are important because their concern is real, their experience firsthand, and their influence persuasive.

Volunteers as Advocates

In the past, the staff of human service agencies . . . alone determine[d] the needs of clients and set about to provide for those needs as they perceived them. Within the last twenty years, however, clients have begun to demand services which are not necessarily those which the agencies thought appropriate. In an attempt to avoid an adversary situation, human service legislation began with the Economic Opportunity Act to mandate "maximum feasible participation" by representatives of the population served. While this brought the clients into the decision-making process, it did not ensure that conflicts would be resolved nor that new opinions would be based on solid information and an overall understanding of agency constraints. The legislation calling for citizen participation in program planning provides a new, important reason for human service administrators to make more use of volunteers in various roles.

Human service organizations are beset by economic and social pressures. Their clientele, more sophisticated than in earlier decades, is constantly reminded of the affluence around them. Miracle solutions on television have developed ever higher service expectations. Agency administrators would like their services to be responsive and effective in meeting their clients' needs. At the same time they must be sensitive to financial realities such as cost effectiveness, funding intentions, and inflation.

Effective leaders must be sensitive to public criticism. The public, conditioned by the facile solutions of television doctors, lawyers, and detectives, is often impatient with real life professionals who seem, by comparison, unsuccessful, overloaded, and constantly harried. In particular, public social services, the last refuge of persons for whom all other systems have failed, are frequently blamed for overall high government costs. Human service organizations might consider using a third-party interest group to interpret their needs and to educate the public. This new advocacy role might well be filled by volunteers familiar with agency policies and limits but without risk to job or need for service.

The possibilities for volunteer advocacy are growing in community action programs and governmental services as well as in the more traditional voluntary agencies. Acting as advocates or interpreters, volunteers can serve clients directly, help people find appropriate services, or mobilize resources in their behalf.

In all the types of human services, the volunteer advocate can serve individuals and their families from the earliest preventive efforts through treatment and rehabilitation. By articulating needs that victims of unfortunate circumstances may be unable to express and by communicating the nature of services and service providers to the user, the volunteer interpreter serves a dual purpose.

Volunteer advocates can extend staff outreach efforts to the community. They can persuade families to use services which may be new or those offered outside their immediate community. In this way, preventive services may be used early before situations become aggravated or chronic.

Volunteers can often help to allay the fears of patients and their families at the intake point. Since they are versed in all aspects of the program, they can aid the busy staff by explaining the program and reassuring the client. An ex-client is particularly valuable in this assignment as first-hand experience is considered authentic.

From another point of view, these same volunteer advocates may present the culture and tradition of a community to "outside staffers." Frequently, cultural patterns may influence perceptions which hinder

widespread and effective use of a service. Agency staff may, for example, jump to the conclusion that parents are not interested in their children when they do not follow their progress by visits and consultation. A volunteer can explain client difficulties with transportation, finances, or scheduling convenient appointment times. If paid staff understood cultural or traditional patterns unique to their communities, they might be helped to communicate more effectively.

Volunteer advocacy at the social action level can be called "class advocacy." Volunteer activities at this level can have an impact on community priorities and mobilize constituencies in support of special needs. This may involve expressing individual needs in such a way as to persuade service professionals to make themselves available and to tailor their service to those needs. It may involve persuading budget makers and decision makers at local, state, and even national legislative levels that services are needed and deserve budgetary support.

Volunteers may serve effectively as mediators between agency administrators and staff and community at large. They are members of the community, yet in their volunteer role they are also a part of the agency. The executive and board leadership would be wise to plan for and support volunteer development through providing educational opportunities so that volunteers can use their learning from this experience.

If volunteers are to be effective agency advocates, however, it is essential they be familiar with staff problems. Only then can they understand needs and frustrations as well as seek tangible accomplishments. Volunteers in this privileged position often assume these same staff goals and objectives. Volunteers may frequently be in a position to cut through protocol, red tape, and the limitations of position on an organization chart to approach the people who can effect real change in a community or who control support for the provision of services. The volunteer thus represents a possible source of strength in gaining public support for services, in ensuring that services are designed realistically, and in persuading the target group to use these services. Training staff to enlist volunteers as advocates is crucial to obtaining this fringe benefit of volunteer services. . . .

Volunteers in Service Delivery

The administrator who has become convinced that volunteers could further the work of his agency will be interested to know how volunteers, as individuals or in groups, have found creative ways to extend agency services. Community volunteers have brought together creative partnerships of government and the voluntary sector, using the special strengths of both.

Auxiliaries serve hospitals, schools, and social service agencies. They manage festivities and holiday gift giving, obtain tickets for sporting events, concerts, and plays. They sponsor fundraising activities. Some give materials for neighborhood beautification programs which involve youth groups in service projects. They pay for a trip to the beauty shop or for special clothing for special occasions. They organizae the collection, repair, and distribution of used toys to equip day care and nursery schools. . . .

III.   ADMINISTERING VOLUNTEER PROGRAMS

The Roles of the Administrators

Two people are crucial to the effectiveness of volunteer services, the agency executive and the director of volunteers. The agency executive is the person who leads staff in identifying the needs to be met by volunteers, has a vision of specific goals for a volunteer development system, appoints a volunteer director to accomplish these

goals, and provides ongoing support in the agency and in the community.

The director of volunteers is the other professional who, according to the 1977 Department of Labor *Dictionary of Occupational Titles* does the following:

> Directs activities of volunteer agencies and workers offering their services to hospitals, social service, and the community agencies. Confers with administrative staff to plan volunteer program consistent with needs of institution or agency. Recommends establishment of policies and procedures for inservice training, work hours, and types of service to be performed by volunteers. Secures services of volunteer workers. Organizes classes of instruction for volunteers to teach proper procedures and techniques. Suggests and directs projects to be carried out by volunteer workers. Assigns workers to various services with hospital or agency. Conducts surveys to evaluate effectiveness of volunteer service program. Arranges for appropriate recognition of volunteers for their services. (p. 128)

The agency executive and the director of volunteers perform complementary functions which require continuing communication, mutual support, and cooperation.

From the outset, the executive establishes the importance of volunteers to the agency, school, or department. This is, in essence, communicating awareness of the value of volunteers. A wise executive knows that the key to building volunteer participation is the identification of unmet needs which strike a responsive chord in everyone: consumers, paid staff, and the administrator. The greater the number of people aware of and sympathetic to these untended needs, the more likely volunteers will come forward and be accepted. . . .

The executive starts by setting up a steering committee to help the volunteer director carry out the initial exploration of possible opportunities for volunteers. Some original members may carry over to an advisory committee, but some may not. Representative consumers, staff workers and supervisors, community service club members or experienced volunteers, representatives of corporations and voluntary agencies, and community planners—each brings a distinctive and valuable point of view to the process of planning and implementing community volunteer involvement.

As the program unfolds, the executive director must be prepared for tensions which may arise when volunteers are brought into the program. A test of the effectiveness of the volunteer director may be the degree of acceptance shown the new volunteers by paid staff. In the helping professions, for example, volunteers may pose a very real threat, especially to inexperienced staff. These realities dictate frequent reassurance from the executive to preserve staff morale.

It must be made clear that volunteers are not necessarily taken on to save money. There are administrative costs entailed for training, staff supervision, program enhancement, and expense reimbursement. Thus volunteers perform not a "free" service but a "special" service, and, by definition, they cannot displace staff. In the long run, an effective program might save money by preventing recurrence of client problems, breaking the cycle of client dependency, and diverting clients from more expensive forms of care. The executive and the volunteer director must, however, assure staff that the intent is not to substitute volunteers for paid workers but to enrich the program. . . .

Close association with a volunteer may be interpreted as a threat by an insecure or immature staff person. Consequently, it is vitally important to delineate specific roles for volunteers and paid staff. New job descriptions may need to be developed for volunteer personnel. A seasoned staff member may enjoy the dependence of an inexperienced volunteer or a veteran volunteer the awe of a young professional partner. It may be necessary from time to time to review the rationale for both positions, redefine goals and objectives, and alter strategy to recognize individual growth of the changing needs of persons working together. Some agencies, for instance, find that a retreat, away from telephones and other distractions, renews the dedication and purposiveness of both volunteers and paid staff as they take time to build a creative partnership.

Another fear attending volunteers is the loss of confidentiality. Procedures can be drawn up which will protect the innocent and vulnerable without covering up negligence or malfeasance. Volunteers will respond well to trust and confidence expressed by paid staff. There is no reason why volunteers cannot maintain confidentiality as well as paid staff once the need and appropriateness of confidentiality are demonstrated.

Hesitant line staff and supervisors should be encouraged to examine how others work with volunteers. While keeping competition to a minimum, institutional rewards might go to those who demonstrate the best staff-volunteer teamwork. At best, a good staff-volunteer relationship is a truly mature interdependence, with accomplishments by both transcending those which could be realized independently. Volunteers often plan recognition for supportive staff because they grow to appreciate how little recognition is given in the daily grind.

The key to developing community involvement and support is the director of volunteer services. No program manager can possibly carry out all of the activities required: job development and design, recruitment, orientation, selection and placement, training, supervision, evaluation, promotion, and other recognition. Other components of a volunteer program include counseling, personnel administration, community relations, program development, recording, and reporting to various audiences. Academic credentials are not as important as such personality characteristics as intelligence, warmth, openness, integrity, optimism, flexibility, and a high tolerance for confusion.

The volunteer director has primary responsibility for overseeing the recruitment and training of volunteers. An excellent approach to early identification, recruitment, and screening of volunteers is a public education meeting to familiarize the community with an agency's program. Service club program chairmen should be invited, as well as church leaders, experienced clients, ACTION officers, and representatives of the media and civic organizations. The agency should be prepared to answer the following questions about its volunteer program: expense reimbursement, uniforms, training, insurance, out-of-town conferences, and advanced volunteer opportunities for community leaders. Recruitment may be considered the most difficult chore, but it need not be. Good programs have waiting lists—there are always people looking for an interesting volunteer assignment. A Gallup poll in November 1978 said that 69 percent of Americans would be willing to engage in specific neighborhood activities, including social services. The important factor is meeting *needs:* matching an agency or client need to a complementary volunteer need.

A reputation for good orientation and training attracts volunteers. A short but sincere welcome by the executive at the first meeting is desirable. Training is also critically important to keeping volunteers involved. Retaining volunteers is more difficult than recruiting them and requires the staff support and professional leadership of the volunteer director with reinforcement from the executive.

By supplementing basic knowledge with new information and skills, training increases the volunteer's confidence and competence and leads him from his first anxiety to wider interests. It encourages self-direction and creativity and fosters a desire to learn anew as problems demand alternatives and fresh insight.

Training is for staff, too. It helps staff understand volunteering and volunteers. It also helps staff and volunteers appreciate each other, gives them mutual confidence and respect and the ability to work together for common goals. This interaction tells the volunteer his accomplishments are valued and important. It offers a sense of real progress, often the crucial difference between dropping out and making a deeper commitment. . . .

Resource Organizations for Volunteer Administrators

In over 300 cities across the United States, Canada, Mexico, and Australia, community resources are available to agencies seeking to expand their use of volunteers. Nationally affiliated Volunteer Bureaus and Voluntary Action Centers (VACs), the Red Cross, County Extension Services, Social Services Volunteer Coordinators, and others are cooperative resources on which executives and volunteer directors can draw. They represent joint community efforts to bring together expertise in needs assessment, job design, recruitment, and training.

VACs, which are affiliated with the National Center for Voluntary Action,[1] link people needing service to experts in their fields of need and vice versa. . . .

Directors of Volunteers (or Coordinators) in Agencies (DOVIA) are membership organizations of professionals from all fields of human services. They serve as clearinghouses for program opportunities for volunteers, new training events or materials, and job opportunities for advancement. They offer developmental services not only for volunteers, but also for the volunteer director, the key person in a volunteer program. A committee searching for a director of volunteers would do well to start with the local VAC and its constituent organization, the DOVIA.

The Association on Administration of Volunteer Services is a national professional association with a certification system to raise standards of professional competence.

In March 1979 the Association of Volunteer Bureaus published *Standards and Guidelines for Volunteer Administration,* which apply to Volunteer Bureaus, VACs, and user agencies.

The Association of Voluntary Action Scholars consists of multidisciplinary scholars and practitioners and concentrates on research about volunteering and voluntarism.

The National Information Center on Volunteerism (NICOV), which recently merged with the National Center for Voluntary Action, is instituting a nationwide placement service which will link the placement services of local VACs and assist professional volunteer directors who want to move between cities or fields of service.

All of these organizations belong to the rapidly growing Alliance for Volunteerism, which is a loose coalition of approximately twenty volunteer-centered organizations representing a network of eighteen million volunteers.

IV. LOOKING TO THE FUTURE

Today's volunteers have backgrounds and motivation patterns more complex and diversified than yesterday's. Traditional volunteers tended to be affluent persons motivated by *noblesse oblige* to whom volunteering was an additional privilege often associated with class. Much has been written about psychic rewards, and very dedicated people were candid about enjoying feeling needed, finding friends with whom to work, establishing services, and enjoying the prestige attendant to volunteer activities.

During the so-called consumer revolution of the 1960s, however, other people, who had long been helping each other in a spirit of "neighborliness," began to enjoy the improved self-esteem, personal satisfactions, and social mobility associated with

more formal volunteering. At the same time, the beneficiaries themselves began to express resentment at having things done for them whether they wanted them or not. Organizations began to respond to the new realities by consulting consumers about what was wanted, by encouraging work *with* rather than *for* people, and by broading the base from which volunteers were drawn. The new attitudes were reflected in both the private and public sectors and at all levels of government. . . .

Any administration has to achieve objectives through the efforts of other people. To gain the cooperation of those necessary people, there must be established incentives. When the reward is monetary, the process of expressing appreciation is relatively simple. In contrast, volunteers' rewards must be tailored to their own unique situations. A late 1960s study of volunteering indicated that a sense of belonging, "full partnerships with staff," is a dominant factor in motivating volunteers. The experiences which a volunteer has with paid staff seem to determine how long he will stay with an organization.

Another factor, a voice in policy and planning, is increasingly important. Dr. Ivan Scheier of the National Information Center for Volunteerism considers a feedback system essential for the program evaluation process and with Babette Reigel and has devised instruments which quantify values in their *Basic Feedback System* (1977).

Unfortunately, many people in leadership positions still believe that volunteers cannot be supervised or held accountable. The trend, however, is definitely away from that feeling toward full accountability for volunteers. Volunteers seem to prefer specific indicators of their achievements rather than a blanket recognition which ignores individuality. Feelings of self-worth, a renewed sense of purpose and of energy are some of the rewards of volunteering. The climate of an organization can be greatly influenced by the enthusiasm of its volunteers.

It is up to the Volunteer Director or Coordinator to make certain that periodic reviews among volunteers, staff, and clients occur. General recognition events are also helpful in making volunteers feel appreciated. In the past six years the volunteer of the year awards given by the National Center for Voluntary Action have become increasingly important. Being nominated by one's peers and being recognized beyond the agency in which one works is in itself a gratifying experience. The attendant publicity stimulates other people to achieve similar goals.

The trend for working people to volunteer is increasing. A parallel trend is toward family volunteering on evenings or weekends. It is a challenge to human services to shift delivery patterns to fit needs after 5 P.M. and on weekends. It will require more flexible scheduling for paid staff and for volunteers to extend services for the times people need them and volunteers are available to serve. . . .

The most crucial problem facing voluntarism in the future may well hinge on economic realities. Service organizations may come to consider volunteers as primary care givers. Every human service executive, board, or advisory committee may have to consider many new ways to meet basic human needs. Which services to terminate or how to use volunteers more widely in order to deliver services may involve difficult choices. It might be wise to involve volunteers in primary care now so that they can become advocates for their staff partners, programs, and particular clients. Qualified staff members can assume supervision earlier and take on diagnostic and prescriptive functions while volunteers carry on the care giving and special services to maximize the effectiveness of paid staff time. In no way do volunteers want to be substitutes for qualified full-time paid professionals. They are the first to speak out for appropriate professional competencies. Being brought in as a cheaper worker is not inspiring, but doing important work which is very much needed is, indeed.

The ACTION census study (1974) cited impressive figures about volunteering, and if the 1965–74 trends continue, more than half of the United States population will be involved as volunteers. The challenge for the future is to devise ways to enable even more of the population to enjoy the benefits of having a volunteer and of being one, especially the elderly, the physically or mentally handicapped, children, and families. Volunteering is currently a means of broadening the scope of individual concern and understanding of all kinds of people. It may become a lifesaver if future economic and organizational needs so dictate. It would please volunteers to play such an important human services role. . . .

NOTES

1. [In] 1979 this organization merged with the National Information Center on Volunteerism and [is] known as VOLUNTEER—the National Center for Citizen Involvement.

REFERENCES

ACTION. *Americans Volunteer 1974*. Washington, D.C.: ACTION Pamphlet 4000–17, U.S. Government Printing Office, 1975–586–355/17, February 1975. (U.S. Bureau of the Census Statistical Study of Volunteering).

Annual Report for Volunteer Services (1978). Michigan State Department of Social Services.

Annual Report to the President and Congress of 1976. Federal Activities Related to the Administration of the Rehabilitation Act of 1973 as Amended.

Dictionary of Occupational Titles. Washington, D.C.: Department of Labor, March 1978.

HENDRY, C. E. AND ROSS, M. G. *New Understandings of Leadership*. New York: Associated Press, 1957.

National Governors' Association. *Voluntary Action and Citizen Participation*. (Proposal adopted at National Governors' Association Meeting, August 29, 1978) National Governors' Association, 1150-17th Street, N.W., Washington, DC 20036.

SCHEIER, I. H. AND REIGEL, B. *Basic Feedback System, A Self-Assessment Process for Volunteer Programs.* Boulder, Colo.: VOLUNTEER, 1977.

A Volunteer Development System. (Flier) Washington, D.C.: DHEW, Office of Volunteer Development, Publication No. (OHD) 76–10006, 1976.

U.S. Department of Health, Education, and Welfare, Rehabilitation Services Administration, Social and Rehabilitation Services. *Volunteers in Rehabilitation.* (A series of handbooks prepared as part of a research and demonstration grant, Project SRS grant 12 P550877/3/-03.) Rockville, Md.: Goodwill Industries of America, Inc., 1973. (See especially R. Griggs and S. Levin, *State of the Art.*)

WOLOZIN, H. *The Value of Volunteer Services in the United States.* Washington, D.C.: ACTION Pamphlet 3530.4, U.S. Government Printing Office, 909–188, September 1976.

3

PROFESSIONAL CHANGE AGENTS AND THEIR STRATEGIES

The readings in Chapter 1 are concerned with the community and organizational contexts for the practice of community organization and social planning. Those in Chapter 2 deal with various forms of citizen participation. The readings in this section focus on the roles of the professional change agent and analyze some of the key factors that determine the choice of an action strategy. They include an examination of the tension between generalist and specialist roles, the design of practitioner initiated change strategies within the organization, and the influence of community decision-making factors on change strategies. The final reading in this section provides some guiding principles regarding communication by professionals.

The concept of professional roles is generally used to describe the behavior of a change agent working with individuals, groups, organizations, and communities. The notion of "professional" role suggests a self-conscious and purposive utilization of a body of concepts and principles derived from the social sciences, along with practice wisdom. This combination of knowledge and wisdom helps the organizer/planner to guide an action system toward its goals. Somewhat less abstractly, the notion implies that the worker is educated and that professional organizers and planners know what they are doing and why they do it.

There is no one model of expected behavior for professional change agents. Instead, many different labels, such as *enabler, organizer, facilitator, expert, consultant, planner, educator, negotiator, guide,* and (although it has currently fallen out of favor) *therapist,* are used to describe the typical responsibilities assumed by practitioners. These roles are neither discrete nor static because the worker shifts from role to role as other elements in community organization change. Professional roles may vary from project to project and even from moment to moment within a particular project.

As professionals have become more involved in social action, new roles such as social broker and advocate have emerged, as did the more traditional ones associated with collaborative modes of work involving relatively homogeneous and more elitist groups. As a result, some roles are more directly related to particular forms of community organization than others. For example, the enabler role is especially relevant in community development; the expert and the consultant roles are especially important in social planning; and the organizer and the advocate roles are prominent in social action.

The critical issue in practice is, of course, how and when to play the appropriate professional role. Because of the absence of a coherent diagnostic and prescriptive framework for practice, many practitioners find it difficult to articulate the rationale for their particular role choices. Although it is possible to classify the multiplicity of roles according to such dimensions as directiveness or process orientation, no typology of roles has been developed which defines their distinguishing characteristics. One classification based on work with small groups (such as committees) interprets leadership as a set of multifunctional roles required for the attainment of the group's task goals and maintenance needs.[1] From this conception, it could be inferred that the professional usually plays the "missing member" role; that is, the professional tries to get the group to take responsibility for itself and intervenes when a needed function such as clarifying or expediting is not being performed.

Individuals and groups that deal with each other, whether within a network of organizations or in a community coalition, are continuously engaged in working out strategies, choosing and reassessing their objectives, and planning effective means of achieving them. Jim Torczyner, in "Dynamics of Strategic Relationships," seeks to understand the choice of strategies such as conflict, collaboration, and negotiation. Based on a review of the literature, he finds five interdependent factors based on mutual perceptions of respective interests and intentions which affect the establishment of strategic relations and account for their change over time. They are perception of the environment, power, issue priority, time, and legitimacy. After analyzing each one, Torczyner presents a series of hypotheses about the conditions under which these variables might be linked with the strategies of collaboration, conflict, and negotiation.

As a result of the proliferation of federally financed categorical programs during the 1960s and 1970s, distinctions between line and staff and direct and indirect modes of intervention in the social services have been augmented by the parallel development of two new professional roles. In "Generalists in Human-Service Systems: Their Problems and Prospects," Mark R. Yessian and Anthony Broskowski claim that much of the inefficiency, fragmentation, and ineffectiveness of the human services are caused at least partially by the excessive degree of specialization and the imbalance in power and perspectives between specialists and generalists. As planners, evaluators, and policy and program analysts, generalists are usually concerned with the internal integration of human-service organizations and with interorganizational relationships. The larger group of specialists take particularistic views of their agencies and their environments. They focus on single-service program areas or client groups and concentrate on the specific techniques of particular services. The authors believe the generalist role to be more capable of inducing badly needed changes in service systems. They propose a seven-point agenda for enhancing the effectivenss of generalists.

"A Process Model for Changing Organizations from Within," is an original article by George Brager and Stephen Holloway. Their discussion moves us from a broad view of the professional change agent to the view from below, that of the practitioner in an organization who attempts to initiate change. Brager and Holloway explain why internally stimulated change is necessary in human organizations. They suggest some of the practical methods included in the technology of a "bottoms up" change process. Using a case example in community mental health, the authors describe five sequential phases of change. In each phase there is a distinctive set of tasks to be completed, and they identify the forces for and against change which must be assessed and dealt with.

Another more theoretical approach is found in "Community Decision Behavior: The Culture of Planning" by Richard S. Bolan. Instead of planned change, Bolan starts with an initial assumption regarding the nature of the decision-making process and proposes four sets of independent variables that affect decision outcomes: (1) process roles, including the factors of motivation, opportunity, and skill; (2) the decision field in the community and in the target system; (3) planning and action strategies; and (4) issue attributes. Drawing on the social sciences and practice experience, hypotheses are offered regarding the relationship among these factors and decision outcomes. This complex, comprehensive framework has numerous implications for practice, research, and professional education.

From this concern with political strategies, we conclude with "Don't Slight Communication: Some Problems of Analytical Practice" by Arnold Meltsner. This selection deals with the usually neglected topic of communication. Some of the interactional and technical aspects of the practice of community organization and planning are seen in a new light. Eschewing the usual jargon of sources, messages, channels, and receivers, Meltsner discusses communication as a means of securing that another person's beliefs will be influenced by the results of an analysis or a plan. Although originally designed for policy analysts, the principles that Meltsner elucidates are very useful for community organization professionals. He notes common errors in communication and drawing on both experience and theory, he provides practical instructions which focus attention on the nature of the audience for a plan and the development of arguments that combine substantive aspects with social context. He also deals with some of the more technical ways of making effective presentations of programs.

NOTES

1. Edwin P. Hollander, *Leadership Dynamics: A Practical Guide to Effective Relationships* (New York: The Free Press, 1978), pp. 89–94.

Jim Torczyner
Dynamics of Strategic Relationships

The term *strategy* refers to the process by which individuals and groups choose their objectives and plan effective ways of achieving them. Strategic relationships are the positions such parties assume in relation to each other in the pursuit of these objectives. The variability of strategic relationships has been explored by scholars of diverse perspectives. Political scientists, economists, mathematicians, management consultants, and psychologists have used distinct terminologies and methodologies in their attempts to understand the way in which relationships of this kind are established and operate.

The present article relates some of these perspectives to a conceptual framework seeking to account for the variability of strategic relationships through the interplay of five variables. The author's analysis focuses on relationships within urban community politics because it is at this level that social work practitioners, particularly community organizers, are involved in and are affected by strategic relationships. However, the conceptual framework described may be applicable to other settings as well. Specific attention is given to Ilchman and Uphoff's (1969) analysis of political economy, Rapoport's (1960) examination of strategy, Walton and McKensie's (1965) work on bargaining, Walton's (1965) exploration of conflict and collaboration, and MacFarland's (1969) discussion of pluralism and power. Although these authors vary in viewpoint and approach, each empahsizes two related

Reprinted with permission of the author and *Social Work*, vol. 23, no. 6 (November 1978), pp. 467–74. Copyright 1978, National Association of Social Workers, Inc.

themes: the notion of exchange and that of interdependence.

According to the concept of exchange, parties form strategic relationships to maximize their gains. Individuals and groups can realize gains and minimize costs by exchanging resources with others or by withholding them. Whereas the principle of exchange explains why transactions between parties take place, that of interdependence implies that exchanges or transactions must take place because losses cannot be minimized, gains maximized, or desired results obtained without them. Dahl and Lindblom have described the fundamental principle behind the process as follows:

> The more the actions of one group are thought to be capable of adversely or beneficially affecting another, the more the second group is likely to protect itself by attempting to control the first. . . . Hence the interdependent groups must bargain with one another for protection and advantage [1953, p. 328].

Schelling, furthermore, has stated that strategy focuses on the "interdependence of the adversaries' decisions and on their expectations about each other's behavior" (1963, p. 3).

The present article continues this line of argument by drawing from the works of various authors and identifying five interrelated and interdependent variables: perception of the environment, power, issue priority, time, and legitimacy. These variables affect the establishment of strategic relationships and account for the variability of such relationships over time. The basic assumptions on which this article is based can be outlined as follows:

- Certain variables reappear in strategic relationships, and these relationships are formulated in relation to them.
- Since strategies are interdependent, these variables are interdependent as well.
- Since strategy represents a net calculation of these variables, they are not only interdependent but interrelated.
- The interrelationship and interdependence of these variables determine strategic relationships.
- Each variable is modifiable; consequently, the interrelationships are modifiable as well.
- Individuals and groups seek to manipulate these variables and interrelationships in favor of a desired outcome.
- As a consequence of initial strategic choices, the relationship among these variables takes new forms, affecting further strategic relationships.
- Because these unfolding relationships are predictable, individuals and groups can foresee successive responses and on this basis develop a general strategy for any given situation or set of circumstances that may arise.

STRATEGIC RELATIONSHIPS

The nature of the strategic relationship among individuals or groups indicates the degree to which the parties involved will cooperate with or oppose each other and minimize or intensify their differences. That is, strategic relationships provide a basis for predicting how parties will react to each other's actions, what parties are willing and not willing to do to attain their goals, and the scope of the boundaries and rules within which bargaining will take place.

The author will consider three primary strategic relationships, namely, conflict, collaboration, and negotiation. Various terms have been used in the literature to refer to these relationships. Strategy used during conflicts has been described as con-

test strategy by Warren (1969), individual rationality by Walton (1965), coercion by Dahl (1963), and as power-coercive by Bennis, Benne, and Chin (1961). Collaboration, furthermore, has been referred to as consensus by Warren (1969), cooperative rationality by Walton (1965), and peaceful adjustment by Dahl (1963). Given this range of descriptions, the use of any term, including those utilized by the author, reflects an arbitrary preference.

In conflict, the first relationship to be considered, the parties involved reject compromise and the pursuit of common interests and instead heighten their differences in pursuit of their ends and become polarized. In general, conflict strategy follows a particular course:

- Parties to a conflict state positions that they claim are irreconcilable and assert that the situation can be resolved only through the attainment of the objectives of one or the other party (Schelling, 1963).
- The parties become polarized, and each seeks to maximize its strength as it brings together resources and allies to promote its position.
- One party clearly becomes the winner in the situation, and the other attempts to save face, *or* neither party can decisively win because the costs of conflict exceed the gains to be made, and the parties seek to negotiate.

Conflict strategy differs from the concept behind zero-sum games, in which one party loses if the other wins. It is often used when the gains to be made by each party in a situation do not represent losses for the other parties. Winning, then, "does not have a strictly competitive meaning; it is not winning relative to one's adversary. It means gaining relative to one's own value system" (Schelling, 1963, p. 4). Moreover, the principle of interdependence dictates that "pure" conflict resulting in a totally warlike situation between parties is rare (Schelling, 1963). Such situations are not considered in this discussion. Situations in which compromise and negotiation are feasible are more characteristic of urban community politics and social work practice and are therefore given attention by the author.

Collaborative strategy follows a course that contrasts with conflict strategy. In collaboration, the parties involved minimize their differences and focus on common interests and benefits that can be realized through cooperation. Bennis, Benne, and Chin have stated that collaborative strategies are often used when a joint effort is made to determine goals and parties have "equal or almost equal opportunity to influence one another" (1961, p. 147).

Conflict or collaboration strategies are often used in situations in which negotiations become necessary. Thus, negotiations begin when conflict or collaboration is no longer desirable, and they may be used to end a conflict or to set the stage for collaboration. In either case, negotiation is employed to minimize certain differences between parties and to develop agreements whereby both parties achieve a desired result. Negotiations may conclude when goals aspired to have been fulfilled or when hostilities have been terminated. In addition, they may be used to determine the rules and scope of either conflict or collaboration and, consequently, to lock parties into an agreement.

The process of negotiation generally follows this course:

- Differences are stated.
- Common points of interest are identified and developed.
- Common interests take on greater importance than areas of conflict.
- Each party explicitly or implicitly agrees not to threaten these interests; the scope of the differences between the parties is thereby contained and reduced.
- Agreements are reached that resolve the

conflict by providing something of benefit to both parties.

The three strategic relationships described lend themselves to arrangement on a continuum. Conflict would fall at one end, accompanied by extreme differences and incompatible outcomes. Collaboration would fall at the other, accompanied by mutual interest and mutually beneficial outcomes. Negotiation would fall in the center, between these two ends.

It should be noted that the relationships described may involve two or more parties. In addition to engaging directly in conflict, collaboration, and negotiation with only one other party, individuals and groups may collaborate with each other, negotiate differences, or combine efforts in opposition to a third party to achieve the outcomes they desire. Such arrangements are known as coalitions and alliances, and they occur in strategic relationships when there are a minimum of three parties involved.

VARIABLES

The five variables of perception of the environment, power, issue priority, time, and legitimacy examined in this article have been derived from the literature, where they appear as they do in the present discussion, are referred to by other names, or are combined with other concepts. Operational statements for each of these variables will be presented, as well as a framework to investigate empirically hypotheses concerning the variables' interrelated effects.

The author acknowledges that basing his identification of variables on prior empirical work rather than on a review of the literature would have been preferable. However, no other method was possible because of the lack of consistent terminology and conceptualization and the unavailability of empirical data concerning the interrelated and interdependent effects of the variables. This lack of consistency reflects a diversity of perspectives that has resulted in the application of different concepts to explain the same phenomena and the use of different terms, operational statements, and definitions to describe the same concepts. Despite this diversity, certain variables that are generally recognized throughout the literature can be identified.

The author's emphasis on five interrelated variables represents a substantial departure from much of the literature, which focuses on one or two variables in the analysis of strategic relationships. Power and favored outcomes are the most frequently explored variables and are often seen as being singularly important in determining such relationships. Although these two factors are included in the author's analysis (in which the variable of favored outcomes is discussed in terms of the variable of perception of the environment), the present article argues that the establishment of strategic relationships and the changes in these relationships over time cannot be accounted for or explained in terms of power and favored outcomes alone.

If the various situations emerging from the interplay of these two variables are considered, it is not apparent which strategies will be selected in a given situation. That is, the interplay of power and favored outcomes cannot account for the choice by an individual or group of conflict, collaboration, or negotiation. For example, when one party has power and the other does not and each side prefers a different outcome, conflict strategy will not necessarily be employed. Furthermore, when both parties are powerful and favor the same outcome, collaboration is not the inevitable result. In both instances, more information is needed about the importance of the issue at hand to the parties involved, the urgency of the parties' goals, and the legitimacy of both parties before the strategic relationship that will be established can be predicted.

In the author's opinion, then, three additional variables must be considered if strategic relationships are to be understood. These five variables will now be operationalized and defined. Although many other variables are cited in the literature, none of them are as widely accepted as the five presented here. Since it is not the author's intention to present a typology of variables discussed in the literature, those variables excluded from this article's primary analysis will not be discussed further. However, if the premise is accepted that more than two variables and at least five should be considered in the study of strategic relationships, further work might determine whether additional variables should come under consideration.

Perception of the Environment

To what extent do the parties involved in a situation perceive each other as having similar or dissimilar objectives? The term "perception of the environment" refers to the perceptions that those in a situation have of the intent of other parties and the outcomes preferred by them. Emphasis is placed in the present article on the idea of perception because people often do not know with certainty the motivations and goals of those with whom they are dealing, and they consequently make decisions based on how they perceive the others' intent.

The importance of this concept in regard to strategic relationships is widely recognized in the literature. Game theory stresses that a party's preferences are dependent on how it perceives the preferences and intentions of other parties (Rapoport, 1960; Schelling, 1963). Schelling has explained this point as follows:

> . . . the best choice for either [party] depends on what he expects the other to do, knowing that the other is similarly guided, so that each is aware that each must try to guess what the second guesses the first will guess and so on, in the familiar spiral of reciprocal expectations [1963, p. 87].

Indeed, according to Schelling (1963, p. 86), this factor is actually the distinguishing characteristic of strategy.

The importance of the perception of the environment has been discussed by other authors as well (Dahl, 1961, pp. 330–40; Dahl and Lindblom, 1953, p. 324; and Apter, 1963). Ilchmann and Uphoff (1969) are among those who stress the role played in strategic relationships by expectations and perceived intentions. In discussing political environments and the relationships among the sectors of an environment and the central regime, they argue that mutual or divergent preferences are based on the anticipated exchange of resources between sectors. Two or more sectors that believe they can profit from an exchange are likely to collaborate. The less symmetrical the anticipated exchange between certain sectors, the more likely that conflict will characterize their relationships. In addition, Blau has suggested that intentions and preferences affect relationships because "social exchange requires trusting others to reciprocate. . . . the initial problem is to prove oneself trustworthy" (1967, p. 98).

To recapitulate, the perception of the environment is widely recognized in the literature as an important determinant of strategic relationships, and it concerns the degree to which parties perceive each other as sharing similar or dissimilar intentions and aspirations. This concept can be operationalized on a continuum as follows: The higher the positive value, the more one party perceives the other as sharing similar goals; the higher the negative value, the more one party perceives the other as holding dissimilar goals.

It should be noted that positive and negative values are assigned to the variables discussed in this article simply to express relationships and demonstrate relative differences between parties in regard to specific variables. In short, the values are not assigned for the purpose of calculating mathematical formulations and equations.

Power

The variable of power has been defined and conceptualized in a variety of ways and has been given particular attention in the analysis of strategic relationships (Walton, 1965; Walton and McKensie, 1965; Schelling, 1963; Rapoport, 1960; Gamson, 1968; Ilchmann and Uphoff, 1969; and Alinsky, 1971). Nevertheless, it retains a somewhat elusive quality because it is often broadly defined and is consequently difficult to operationalize. Weber, for example, defined power as the "probability that one actor within a social relationship will be in a position to carry out his will despite resistance" (1947, p. 152), but did not specify the constellation of factors or resources necessary for this to occur.

Other authors, however, have differentiated, categorized, and analyzed the composition of power, among them Etzioni (1961), Blau (1967), Chin and Benne (1961), Weber (1947), Ilchmann and Uphoff (1969), and Dahl (1963). Moreover, it is variously considered to be an expendable resource (Banfield, 1961), a resource that cannot be measured until it is applied (Newstadt, 1955), and a resource whose potential application is as important as its actual use (Schelling, 1963).

A comparative analysis of the concepts of power advanced by these various authors falls beyond the scope of this article. What the author instead seeks is an operational definition that lends itself to an analysis of strategic relationships at the level of urban community politics and in a context relevant to social work practice. The notion of independence and the works of Emerson (1962) and Blau (1967) seem particularly well suited for this purpose.

Interdependence is a prerequisite for the formation of strategic relationships. Both Emerson and Blau conceive of power as the degree to which one can act independently. In turn, independence is the degree to which one can act without fear of retaliation or the need for support. The degree of independence of an individual or group—or the degree of imbalance in interdependent relationships—is a measure of power. In reformulating Emerson's work, Blau has specified the conditions that produce such an imbalance. Individuals who need a service that another has to offer have the following alternatives:

1. They can supply this person with a service that he or she wants enough to offer his or her service in return.
2. They can obtain the needed service elsewhere, assuming that alternative suppliers exist.
3. They can coerce the person to furnish them with the service.
4. They can learn to resign themselves to do without the service.

Blau goes on to argue that power is attained and sustained by preventing others from exercising these four alternatives. By specifying how these alternatives may be countered, he develops the following strategy for the individual or group attempting to retain power:

1. Remain indifferent to the benefits others can supply in exchange by denying them access to resources.
2. Assure continued dependence of others by barring their access to alternative suppliers through monopolization.
3. Prevent others from using coercive force by obstructing the formation of coalitions among them.
4. Make certain that others need the benefits offered. Power depends on people's needs for the benefits those in power make available to them.

The variable of power can be operationalized by being plotted along a plus-minus continuum. The higher the positive value, the greater the power or independence of an individual or group relative to others. The higher the negative value, the lesser the power of an individual or group relative to others.

Issue Priority

The term "issue priority" refers to the relative importance placed by parties on the issue at stake. This importance may be directly related to the immediate consequences—gains or losses—that the resolution of the issue under consideration will have for each party. In addition, an issue's importance may be related to other concerns. For example, the direct outcome of a question may not be as important to a group as such secondary benefits as the effects of the situation on its organizational stability.

The variables of power and perception of the environment change relative to specific issues. That is, parties may favor similar outcomes in regard to one issue and dissimilar outcomes in regard to another. Similarly, a party may be powerful relative to the others in a situation concerning one issue and relatively powerless concerning another issue.

The importance of the variable of issue priority has been recognized by Blau (1967, pp. 97–98), who cites it as one of the three conditions that affect the process of exchange. In addition, Walton and McKensie (1965) specifically identify issue priority as a variable of great relevance to strategic relationships, and Thompson (1967) links it to the notion of domain. Domain consists of the claims an organization stakes out for itself regarding fields of activities, population served, and service rendered. An issue relating to this domain is, by definition, of high priority.

In the framework outlined in the present article, issue priority can be charted on a continuum. The higher the positive value, the higher an issue's priority as measured by possible benefits and costs regarding the resources to which an organization lays claims. The higher the negative value, the lower the issue's priority.

Time

Time plays a critical role in the variability of strategic relationships. As a variable, it encompasses the period in which the parties involved in a situation must act. Relative to time, short-term and long-term issues can be distinguished and operationalized. Short-term issues require parties to act quickly and decisively with relatively little time for deliberation. Long-term issues do not require immediate action, and decisions about them can be made in the future after considerable deliberation.

The effect of time on strategic relationships has been cited by Ilchmann and Uphoff (1969) and by Thompson, who states that "the dual search for certainty and flexibility [by organizations involved in strategic relationships] to a large extent revolves around the question of time" (1967, p. 150). In addition, Walton and McKensie have argued that "a longer time over which negotiations are scheduled allows more time for study and discussion of agenda items with beneficial effects for integrative bargaining" (1965, pp. 148–149). Blau (1967, p. 75), furthermore, has stated similar findings concerning the relationship of time to collaborative, consultative efforts. Finally, in citing a study by Douglas, Walton and McKensie have analyzed the dynamics of this variable, particularly in regard to the conclusion of negotiations, in the following way:

> The announcement of [a party's] final position has to be late enough to be believed and yet not too late to be heard . . . the timing of the final concession usually takes place within the shadow of the deadline. It is the deadline which gives the final phases of bargaining a characteristic quality of urgency [1965, pp. 91–92].

Time can be operationalized on a continuum. The higher the positive value, the more time parties have before they must act. The higher the negative value, the less time they have in which to arrive at a decision.

Legitimacy

As a variable in strategic relationships, legitimacy may either augment or detract from the resources that comprise power. It represents the extent to which an individual or group is considered to have inherent, legitimate, and acknowledged authority to act in regard to a specific domain. For example, a party may be relatively powerful but may not have sufficient legitimacy to exercise its power regarding certain issues. Conversely, a party may be powerless in relation to others but may play a critical role in a situation because of its legitimacy in regard to a particular issue.

Dahl defines legitimacy by giving the following example "When A commands or requests B, B feels that A has a perfect right to ask him and [that] he has an obligation to accept" (1963, p. 33). Thompson speaks of this variable as domain consensus and says that "it defines a set of expectations both for members of an organization and for others with whom they interact about what the organization will or will not do" (1967, p. 29). In line with these statements, Ilchmann and Uphoff (1969) claim that individuals and groups need or want legitimacy because it enables them to expend fewer resources to secure compliance with their desires or policies.

Legitimacy can be operationalized on a plus-minus continuum. The higher the positive value, the greater a party's legitimacy in relation to other parties. The higher the negative value, the lesser the legitimacy enjoyed by a party.

INTERACTION OF VARIABLES

Returning to the assumptions of this article concerning the interplay in strategic relationships of the variables described, the author will consider a recent situation in

Montreal involving the Committee for Safer Streets (CSS) and the city traffic department. CSS represents low-income citizens who live in congested communities having few recreational facilities. The children in these communities play in busy streets, and CSS was formed to take action about the high number of traffic accidents involving children. The traffic department is the city's legal authority responsible for road safety. The interaction between this department and CSS will be used as an example of the interplay of variables in strategic relationships.

Because the members of CSS believed they were not powerful enough to pressure the city to establish recreational facilities for their children, they selected as their objective the enforcement of existing traffic laws to correct the hazardous situation in the streets. They reasoned this objective would be easier to achieve because they would simply be asking the city to perform its duties. With this in mind, they outlined their first goal: to alert motorists to existing traffic laws by asking the city to post speed limit signs in their neighborhoods. They then sent a petition to the city traffic department. Their petition decried the recent accidents, demanded the immediate posting of speed limit signs and the enforcement of traffic laws, and asked for a meeting with a representative of the department without delay.

In terms of the five variables outlined, CSS members have little power (−) relative to the traffic department, and they are citing their own legitimacy (+) as parents of injured children. The issue in question is of high priority (+) to them, and they demand immediate action (−). Their perceptions of the city traffic department are favorable (+), as evidenced by their formulation of an objective they believed the department could and would support. It would seem that undertaking a collaborative strategy or negotiations would be appropriate under these circumstances, since CSS could, as a

bargaining point, cite the objectives it shared with the traffic department. However, predicting strategic options would be premature because more is needed to be known about the department in relationship to these five variables.

The city traffic department was not concerned about the problems of CSS because its attention had been directed toward plans for the upcoming 1976 Olympic Games to be held in Montreal. Already understaffed, it had little time to respond to other matters and a small number of employees available to post large numbers of speed limit signs. Although certainly having the power and legitimacy to act, it refused to do so because the issue did not seem important, nor was time pressing. In short, the department was sympathetic, chose not to act, did not respond to the petition, and consequently declared itself as having objectives different from those of CSS. The relationship between these two parties at this point is outlined in Table 1.

What constellation of variables would be necessary for CSS to achieve its objectives? At the minimum, the objectives of the city traffic department—which relate to the variable of the perception of the environment—would have to become favorable to CSS, and some agreement would be needed regarding when work on the signs would begin—which relates to the variable of time. Given this situation, several strategic options are available to CSS.

In the first strategy, CSS could attempt through reasoned discourse to convince the traffic department that this issue should be equally important to both parties, that change should occur immediately, and that the same outcomes are desired by both. In other words, the group could attempt to alter the constellation of variables in such a way that collaboration becomes possible. The pattern of variables that would emerge in this instance can be seen in Table 1.

Table 1 Conceptualization of the Variables Affecting the Strategic Relationship between CSS and Montreal Traffic Department

PARTY	VARIABLES				
	POWER	LEGITIMACY	TIME	ISSUE PRIORITY	PERCEPTION OF ENVIRONMENT
Initial Situation					
CSS	−	+	−	+	+
Traffic department	+	+	+	−	−
First Strategy					
CSS	−	+	−	+	+
Traffic department	+	+	−	+	+
Second Strategy					
CSS	−	+	+	+	+
Traffic department	+	+	+	−	+
Third Strategy					
CSS	+	+	−	+	+
Traffic department	+	+	−	+	+
Final Situation					
CSS	−	+	+	+	+
Traffic department	+	+	+	−	+

This strategy was rejected by CSS because it was clear that the issue was not one of high priority for the city and, consequently, that its goals and those of the city were not similar. Even if the two parties shared their goals, the city would not share CSS's sense of urgency. The group therefore considered a second strategy, in which it refrained from pursuing the matter at hand to wait until the Olympic Games passed and to attempt collaboration later. This strategy would provide both parties more time in which to plan and would thus reduce the pressure of the situation. Even though the issue in question might never be of high priority for the traffic department, the parties could collaborate because they ultimately share similar objectives. This relationship, which would favor collaboration, between the parties, is represented in Table 1.

This strategy was also rejected by CSS because it feared that any delay would weaken its organization and cause the interest of its members to diminish. Since it is not an organization involved in promoting or sponsoring a variety of programs, it could not postpone action in regard to traffic and initiate it again at a more appropriate time. It was not concerned about any other issues and, in fact, hoped to develop additional issues based on the anticipated success of its traffic sign campaign. It consequently considered a third strategy that involved the deliberate use of conflicts, in the hope that disruptive tactics might cause the issue to become one of high priority for the city traffic department. By applying enough pressure, CSS might succeed in preventing the department from adequately carrying out its other functions until the issue was resolved. The successful application of pressure would represent a change in the balance of power between the two parties. To force the traffic department to act differently, CSS would have to be able to choose tactics that would generate power for it. The pattern of variables that would ensue should all these developments occur is shown in Table 1.

The diagram of the third strategy considered depicts a situation that is ideal for collaboration: two parties have legitimacy and positions of power, agree that an issue is important and should be resolved quickly, and share similar principal objectives in a situation in which minor differences can be negotiated. CSS, however, was not in a position to generate power, although it tried to do so. At most, 100 people attended a series of sit-ins that it held at City Hall, and although the press had been alerted in advance, these actions received only minor notice. The group managed to obtain an appointment with a city official but by this time realized that its chances of success were nil. It wished to save face and announce some sort of victory to its constituency. It reduced its demands and asked the city to post signs in fewer areas than originally requested. The relationship of variables in this strategy is also shown in Table 1.

The experience of CSS demonstrates the interrelationships of the variables of power, legitimacy, time, issue priority, and perception of the environment in strategic relationships, the changing character of these variables, and the options that become available to individuals and groups as a result of changes occurring in them. In the case cited, little movement took place despite the activities of CSS because in using a conflict strategy it did not develop the kind of power that might have been effective in the situation. Moreover, the group had little choice except to undertake conflict because it vested too much of its future in one issue. A strategist working with CSS could have interpreted the strategic variables involved or intuitively understood them, would have suggested that the group expend little effort regarding the issue of traffic signs at present, and would have recommended the development of other programs.

The analysis of CSS's experience has attempted to show how strategic relationships are influenced by the five variables described. The possible combinations of these variables are manifold, and no instrument or empirical findings exist to help measure strategic relationships in terms of each possible configuration of variables. The author contends, however, that only a limited number of such configurations actually recur. These situations, in which conflict, negotiation, or collaboration may take place, consistently reappear because the arena in which planned change occurs is limited and because the proponents of change manipulate the environment to produce these situations in order to achieve certain ends. The concluding section of this article discusses this theme in terms of its implications for research.

RESEARCH IMPLICATIONS

The central premise of this discussion is that strategic relationships between parties are determined by the interplay of five interrelated and interdependent variables. The framework provided by the operationalization of these variables can be used to investigate empirically the particular conditions under which specific strategies are selected. Research undertaken in this direction could identify strategic options and delineate those situations in which conflict, collaboration, and negotiation are employed. Through the use of the framework outlined, research findings concerning the ideal conditions for employing these strategies could be made more specific. A study conducted by Warren and Hyman (1965) revealed that parties collaborate when they prefer the same outcomes and choose conflict when they have dissimilar preferences. These findings could be rephrased into the following hypotheses, whose operational statements are shown in Table 2.

COLLABORATION HYPOTHESIS 1: Collaboration will occur when two parties share similar objectives concerning an issue of high priority, are relatively equal in strength and legitimacy, and share time limitations that are similar.

Table 2 Operational Statements of Hypotheses Concerning Collaboration, Conflict, and Negotiation

HYPOTHESIS	PARTY	POWER	LEGITIMACY	TIME	ISSUE PRIORITY	PERCEPTION OF ENVIRONMENT
Collaboration						
1	A	+	+	+	+	+
	B	+	+	+	+	+
	A	−	−	+	+	+
	B	−	−	+	+	+
2	A	+	−	+	+	+
	B	−	+	+	+	+
Conflict						
1	A	+	+	−	−	−
	B	−	−	−	+	−
	A	−	−	−	−	−
	B	−	+	−	+	−
2	A	+	+	+	−	+
	B	−	+	−	+	+
Negotiation						
1	A	+	+	−	+	−
	B	+	+	−	+	−
2	A	+	+	−	−	+
	B	+	+	−	+	+
	A	−	−	−	−	+
	B	−	−	−	+	+

COLLABORATION HYPOTHESIS 2: Two parties, one holding power and the other legitimacy, will collaborate if the other strategic variables hold the same weight for both parties.

CONFLICT HYPOTHESIS 1: When one party is in a weak position and must act immediately on an issue of high priority, it will choose conflict if it prefers an outcome different from that desired by the other pary. If, in addition, the weaker party has legitimacy, it will seek to generate power by appealing to its recognized stake in the matter.

CONFLICT HYPOTHESIS 2: When a weak party considers important an issue that requires immediate action and the stronger party does not accept the urgency or importance of the issue, the weak party will choose conflict in an attempt to make the issue urgent and important to the stronger party, even if they prefer similar outcomes.

NEGOTIATION HYPOTHESIS 1: Parties will negotiate even if they disagree, if they are both in a position of strength and are approaching a final deadline.

NEGOTIATION HYPOTHESIS 2: Two parties who share similar objectives will negotiate support from one another, whether they are in a strong or weak position and even if the issue is important to only one of them. Such support represents a trade-off for the purpose of building a coalition.

In addition to being used to explore the conditions in which specific strategies are selected, this model can be utilized to generate consistent data. Research findings concerning strategic relationships often point to conflicting principles because the investigations from which they were derived dealt with different variables. At present, little unity exists in this area because an overall conceptualization is lacking regarding the variables that play a significant role in strategic relationships. Empirical investigations based on case analyses could determine the parameters for research design and investigation concerning this question.

Finally, the framework described can be used to qualify and test general principles set forth in the literature. Statements such as those made by authors cited in this article could be given greater precision. For example, when Ilchmann and Uphoff claim that "as a rule, the more quickly a regime seeks compliance with a given policy, the greater the expenditure of resources that will be required to secure compliance" (1969, p. 90), they imply a relationship between power and time that could be specified, qualified, and measured. Through research, the relationship between parties along all five strategic variables could be identified, and the conditions under which this rule applies could consequently be set forth.

In summary, the conceptual framework presented in this article represents an instrument for deriving more precise information and more detailed principles concerning the variability of strategic relationships. A great deal more work needs to be carried out in this area, and empirical investigations are necessary to determine the validity of the argument presented.

BIBLIOGRAPHY

Readers will note that bibliographical style has been used for references in this article. It is used only for reviews of the literature.

ALINSKY, SAUL D. *Rules for Radicals.* New York: Random House, 1971.

APTER, DAVID D. *Comparative Politics and Polit-ical Thought: Past Influences and Future Developments.* New York: Free Press of Glencoe, 1964.

BANFIELD, EDWARD, C. *Political Influence.* New York: Free Press of Glencoe, 1961.

BENNIS, WARREN G.; BENNE, KENNETH D.; AND CHIN, ROBERT. "Collaboration and Conflict," in Bennis, Benne, and Chin, eds., *The Planning of Change.* New York: Holt, Rinehart & Winston, 1961, pp. 147–53.

BLAU, PETER M. *Exchange and Power in Social Life.* New York: John Wiley & Sons, 1967.

CHIN, ROBERT, AND BENNE, KENNETH D. "General Strategies for Effecting Changes in Human Systems," in Bennis, Benne, and Chin, eds., *The Planning of Change.* New York: Holt, Rinehart & Winston, 1961, pp. 32–57.

DAHL, ROBERT A. *Modern Political Analysis.* Englewood Cliffs, N.J.: Prentice-Hall, 1963.

_____. *Who Governs?* New Haven, Conn.: Yale University Press, 1961.

_____, AND LINDBLOM, CHARLES E. *Politics, Economics and Welfare.* New York: Harper & Row, 1953.

DOUGLAS, ANN. *Industrial Peacemaking.* New York: Columbia University Press, 1962.

EMERSON, RICHARD M. "Power-Dependence Relations," *American Sociological Review,* 27 (February 1962), pp. 31–41.

ETZIONI, AMITAI. *A Comparative Analysis of Complex Organizations.* New York: Free Press, 1961.

GAMSON, WILLIAM A. *Power and Discontent.* Homewood, Ill.: The Dorsey Press, 1968.

ILCHMANN, W. F., AND UPHOFF, N. T. *The Political Economy of Change.* Berkeley: University of California Press, 1969.

MACFARLAND, ANDREW S. *Power and Leadership in Pluralist Systems.* Stanford, Calif.: Stanford University Press, 1969.

NEWSTADT, A. "An Introduction to the Theory and Measurement of Influence," *American Political Science Review,* 49 (June 1955), pp. 431–51.

RAPOPORT, ANATOL. *Fights, Games and Debates.* Ann Arbor: University of Michigan Press, 1960.

SCHELLING, THOMAS C. *The Strategy of Conflict.* London, England: Oxford University Press, 1963.

THOMPSON, J. D. *Organizations in America.* New York: McGraw-Hill Book Co., 1967.

WALTON, RICHARD E. "Two Strategies of Social Change and Their Dilemmas," *Journal of Applied Behavioral Science*, 1 (1965), pp. 167–79.

_____, AND McKENSIE, ROBERT B. *A Behavior Theory of Labor Negotiations*. New York: McGraw-Hill Book Co., 1965.

WARREN, ROLAND L. "Types of Purposive Change at the Community Level," in Ralph Kramer and Harry Specht, eds., *Readings in Community Organization*. Englewood Cliffs, N.J.: Prentice-Hall, 1969.

_____, AND HYMAN, HERBERT H. "Purposive Community Change in Consensus and Dissensus Situations." Waltham, Mass.: Brandeis University, 1965. (Mimeographed.)

WEBER, MAX. *The Theory of Social and Economic Organization*. New York: Oxford University Press, 1947.

Mark R. Yessian and Anthony Broskowski

Generalists in Human-Service Systems: Their Problems and Prospects

Next time you are in the company of human-service professionals and find the conversation running along the same old lines, you might ask what a regional director of HEW (the Department of Health, Education, and Welfare), an executive director of a community health and welfare planning council, a governor's human-service adviser, and a director of a neighborhood multiservice agency have in common. The question is bound to add a change of pace to the conversation. When after an appropriate interim you respond that they are part of a network of human-service generalists who could contribute greatly to the improved functioning of human-service programs you could, with a little luck, spark a lively discussion. It could go off in many directions, covering such areas as (1) the current status of generalists in the human-service environment, (2) the contributions which they can make in that environment, (3) the reasons for their limited impact to date, and (4) the ways in

Reprinted from *Social Service Review* 51:2 (June 1977), pp. 265–88, with permission of the authors and the University of Chicago Press. Copyright 1977 by the University of Chicago. All rights reserved.

which they could become more assertive and effective agents of change. Our aim here is to offer some insights in each of these areas and, in so doing, to provide some grist for discussions of this sort.

I. THE DIAGNOSIS

The Situation Today

Traditionally, the generalists who have played the most prominent part in the human-services field have been those working directly with people in need of service. These generalists, in their day-to-day work, have reflected a continuing concern for the overall well-being of clients and for the integrated delivery of services responsive to multiproblem client needs. In large part they have been trained social workers who have provided a broad range of personal-care services, but in their ranks there have also been many other professional and semiprofessional workers.

These clinically oriented generalists are still very much present, but in recent years they have been accompanied increasingly by another class of human-service generalists who are not directly involved with service recipients. These latter-day generalists do their work within organizational settings at all levels of government and in the private as well as the public sector. They are concerned with the internal integration of human-service organizations, with the interactions among these organizations, and, at bottom, with the responsiveness of the organizations to client needs. Some of them work as planners or evaluators, others as policy or program analysts, still others as managers. All function in a broad sense as human-service administrators.

This article is relevant to both classes of generalists, because they tend to share basic interests and to be quite dependent upon one another. Its focus, however, is on those whose jobs are oriented toward affecting the behavior of organizations. Throughout, the term "generalist" is used to refer to "organizational" generalists, unless otherwise indicated.

Personnel who work in organizational settings as generalists do not necessarily identify with the generalist label, nor do they necessarily associate much with one another or share any sense of group belongingness. They arrived at their present positions from a wide array of career backgrounds and for the most part without any specific career plans to become generalists. Yet they do appear to represent an affinity group (if not a distinct vocational breed), and they do share some basic characteristics. These include a concern with a wide range of both public and private human services covering different functional areas, different age groups, and different human problems; a view of the human-services environment which tends to be systemic and to reflect an appreciation for the interrelationships among human needs and among human-service programs; and a perspective which focuses in large part on planning and management issues as opposed to specific techniques or technologies of service delivery.

Within their organizational environ-

ments, these generalists work in proximity to many different kinds of human-service specialists. By far the more widely recognized participants in the human-service arena, these specialists are also much more numerous. In contrast to the generalists they tend to (1) focus on services covering a single major program area (e.g., health) or a single target group (e.g., the aged), (2) take a particularistic view of their enterprise and its environment, and (3) concentrate on specific techniques of a particular service. Although they, too, are concerned with organizational behavior, they are likely to concentrate their attention on only a small part of an organization's mission. For the most part they have line responsibilities and are directly concerned with the operation of individual programs, while the generalists have staff responsibilities and are indirectly concerned with the operation of many different programs.

Table 1 provides an illustrative listing of the places in which these human-service specialists can be found. A thoughtful comparison of the two listings will reveal that generalists are relatively minor actors in the current service-delivery system. In any community or at any level of government or within any organization they are apt to find themselves outflanked by specialists who have a firm grip on program dollars and authority, are tightly organized within their own professional societies, possess most of the program information and technical expertise, and enjoy a greater degree of public respect and support. At federal and state levels the imbalance appears to be particularly great, as specialists within the governmental bureaucracies join forces with their counterparts in Congress and private-interest groups to develop what often amounts to a monopoly of decision-making power in their immediate spheres of interest.[1]

In itself, this imbalanced situation need not be a major cause of concern. There is no body of knowledge that suggests that

Table 1 Selected Organizational Domains of Generalists and Specialists

GENERALIST DOMAINS	SPECIALIST DOMAINS
Office of the Secretary, U.S. Department of Health, Education, and Welfare	Public Health Service, U.S. Department of Health, Education, and Welfare
Office of the Regional Director, U.S. Department of Health, Education, and Welfare	Office of Education, U.S. Department of Health, Education, and Welfare
National League of Cities	American Medical Association
National Association of Counties	American Hospital Administrators Association
National Governors Conference	National Education Association
Federal regional councils	State public health agencies
Governors' offices	State mental health agencies
Offices of state human-service secretaries	State vocational rehabilitation agencies
Mayors' offices	Local school committees
County chief executives' offices	Local health departments
Community health and welfare councils	Community mental health centers
Neighborhood councils	Drug abuse prevention councils
Community action agencies	Child-care corporations

generalists deserve to be in ascendance. What is disturbing is the excessive specialization which has emerged as a result of this imbalance of power.

The high costs and inefficiencies that have been incurred by excessive specialization in the human-service field have been documented in other sources and need not be reiterated here.[2] It is worth emphasizing, however, that these costs and inefficiencies have had a very pronounced human impact. From the vantage point of the person seeking service, the current, highly fragmented human-service system presents great problems. It breeds uncertainty, leaves many important services inaccessible or only remotely accessible, and results in many service gaps and discontinuities.

In this context, the client who has three or more highly interrelated problems is at a particular disadvantage. Receiving highly specialized help for only one or two of these problems, no matter how effective this help may be in its own right, may turn out to be of little overall assistance if other related problems are not addressed. The situation is analogous to repairing a car with ten malfunctioning components by giving expert attention to the distributor and carburetor difficulties but ignoring the tires, axle, spark plugs, and other components which are in some way defective. As an operative system, the car must function as a whole, not just in a few places.

Many clinicians are quite aware of the interrelated nature of client needs and of the importance of fashioning integrative techniques and approaches at the delivery level. Some, in fact, have even been able to make some headway in this direction. But as long as integrative efforts within and among human-service organizations remain a rarity, and programs, especially at federal and state levels, continue to be developed and run within very narrow, specialized confines, these clinical efforts at integration are not likely to have much overall impact. Service providers are simply too dependent upon their organizations and programs to be able to function in any significant way outside their specialist sphere of influence.[3] Thus, for instance, the fragmentation that pervades HEW serves in a very real way to inhibit the efforts of the Peoria social worker trying to do her job in the most effective manner possible.

It is our contention that organizational generalists represent a vital counterforce to excessive specialization and can be key agents in making human-service organizations more responsive to the integrative impulses of the clinical generalists. In the succeeding pages, we hope to make it clear why they have this potential and how they can take advantage of it.

The Case for the Generalists

There are some obvious questions. Why the generalists? What is it that they have to offer? What roles can they be expected to play? The answers, for the most part, rest with the basic characteristics identified earlier. Because they deal with a broader universe than individual specialists, they are in a better position to see how programs relate to one another, to spot overlaps and duplications, to identify opportunities for coordination, and, at times, to determine the current relevance and effectiveness of individual programs. Less encumbered by the programmatic blinders which restrict the vision of so many specialists, they are in a better position to view the larger set of community needs and to see that programs and services are responding to these needs.

Furthermore, generalists are inclined to be much more flexible and responsive to change than are specialists. They are more likely to be able to shift perspectives and to look at the human-services environment from multiple vantage points, including those of the taxpayer, service recipient, service provider, third-party payer, legislator, program administrator, and policy planner. Specialists, as Sarason suggests below, tend to be more locked into their existing thought patterns: "In the short run specialization appears to have productive consequences in terms of new knowledge and practice, but in the long run it seems to render the individual, or field, or agency increasingly unable to assimilate and adapt to changes in surrounding social

events and processes. Worse yet, the forces (individual and social) which generate specialization unwittingly increase the extent of ignorance of the larger social picture so that assimilation and adaptation are not even perceived as problems."[4]

By making the case for the generalists, we do not wish to imply that generalists should engineer power plays designed to take control from the specialists. That would be foolhardy and probably lead to a more chaotic situation that now prevails. It is imperative, however, for the generalist to search for ways of realizing the potential afforded by their systemic perspectives. How can they promote the delivery of services that are targeted toward real needs? How can they serve as cohesive elements, influencing program agencies and providers to relate more effectively and imaginatively with one another? How can they trigger reform on behalf of service recipients? These are among the vital questions with which the generalists must cope. In this process, however, we must recognize they will inevitably address issues concerning the balance of power.

There are, of course, several ways in which generalists can confront these issues and exert leadership. What methods work best will depend on the time and circumstances. Among the types of roles which generalists can play in organizational settings are the following:

1. BROKER/FACILITATOR. Whether on behalf of other generalists trying to tap into needed services or on behalf of specialists trying to coordinate more effectively with other specialists, generalists are in a good position to provide valuable assistance. With their comprehensive view of the human-service environment, they can identify linkage opportunities and assist generalists and specialists alike to understand and to deal effectively with the complexities of that environment. In this sense, they can serve as brokers or facilitators for getting things done.

2. MEDIATOR. Generalists can play an important part in resolving disputes and conflicts which occur among providers in the human-services environment. Exercising this role successfully no doubt depends a lot on the personal skill of the individuals involved, but because they can relate more easily to the various needs of service recipients and are likely to have a broader (though not necessarily stronger) base of support, generalists are usually better equipped than individual specialists to promote negotiation and compromise.

3. INTEGRATOR/COORDINATOR. Left to themselves, program specialists cannot go very far in integrating or coordinating multiple and diverse services. As soon as they reach a point where their own immediate interests appear to be threatened, they quite expectedly tend to back away. It is apparent, therefore, that if substantial progress is to be made in this direction, generalists, who are more committed to the integration and coordination of services, must provide the leadership. They can do that in many ways, ranging from outside advocacy and identification of coordination opportunities, to provision of technical assistance, to direct involvement in the development and implementation of service linkages.

4. GENERAL MANAGER. Generalists can be given direct managerial responsibilities for the planning and delivery of certain human services so they can more easily and thoroughly exert an integrating influence on service operations. One of the dangers of this approach, however, is that a new and costly bureaucratic infrastructure can develop if general management is simply grafted on to the present categorical system.

5. EDUCATOR. Generalists can function in university or agency training programs to help educate categorical special-

ists on those aspects of integrated service delivery which will enhance the specialized services being provided to the citizen. Given a greater exposure to and understanding of systemic principles, professionals may become less resistant to and perhaps even supportive of the integration of certain activities.

6. ANALYST/EVALUATOR. By drawing heavily upon their systemic perspective and their concern for the overall impact of services on clients, generalists can play a very constructive part in the analysis and evaluation of human-service programs. They can generate information and raise vital questions on matters concerning program interrelationships or program impact which specialists are likely to overlook, and in so doing they can obtain useful feedback for subsequent planning processes. In the same context, they can serve as a significant source of information on client needs and on the type of programs necessary to meet these needs. Attkisson and Broskowski have argued that a generalist perspective is necessary for the tasks of program evaluation and planning.[5]

The Roots of the Problem

If the case for the generalists is as compelling as we believe it to be, why, then, do they have so little influence at the present time? Why are they relatively minor actors in the human-services arena? Although not professing to offer definitive answers to these questions, we identify below what we regard as four basic factors responsible for the current plight of human-services generalists. We feel strongly that these factors deserve more serious inquiry than they have received thus far and emphasize that though they affect the generalists directly it is the overall impact on the well-being of our society which provides the major cause for concern.

1. DIFFERENTIATION AND SPECIALIZA-
TION ARE COMMON HUMAN RESPONSES FOR
COPING WITH COMPLEX AND NOT VERY
WELL UNDERSTOOD PHEMONENA. Given
a complex matter, such as the human-service needs of people, it appears easier to
differentiate the separate parts and deal
with them as individual components rather
than trying to work with the whole or,
more precisely, with the interrelationships
among the components. It is this specialized approach, for example, which has
led to the enormous contributions in the
field of medicine during the twentieth
century.

As our knowledge increases in a given
field, however, differentiation and specialization in themselves emerge as less viable
approaches. As we become more familiar
with the bits and pieces, we find that integration and synthesis become increasingly
important as ways of dealing with high
rates of complexity and information overload. In fact, it could well be argued that
the recent major advances in science and
technology have depended on the efforts
of those who were able to integrate the
specialized research of many other specialist researchers.

It is sometimes argued that our current
level of understanding about the complex
human-services environment is insufficient to allow for bold strategies of integration and synthesis. Given the relative degree of specialization, however, we feel it is
time to search out aggressively those areas
in which integration may provide a reasonably better payoff. While differentiation
promotes rapid responsiveness to higher
specialization problems, its danger is that
the pieces may not be reunited for a more
powerful solution to a wider class of
problems.

Probably an even more relevant concern
is that we are becoming less able to afford
the luxury of excessive specialization,
whatever the state of our knowledge. Specialization prospers in rich and abundant
environments where there are enough resources to go around to let "everybody do
their own thing." In more barren environments the force of competition for limited
resources puts a greater premium on consolidation and efficiency. As our country's
growth rate slows and we become more
conscious of the limits of our resources,
this consideration becomes a most important one indeed.

2. GENERALISTS FIND IT DIFFICULT TO
DEMONSTRATE THE UTILITY OF THEIR
CONTRIBUTIONS. The benefits of integration do not tend to be immediately apparent. They are apt to take time, be
rather subtle, and appear less dramatic
than those achieved through specialization. The necessary patience is hard to
come by in a society that is enthralled by its
own rapid pace and "future shock"
environment.

Moreover, generalists, because they
tend to focus on large-scale problems
which no one person can fully comprehend or control, are likely to stimulate
our fears and insecurities and to leave us
uncertain about the worth of their efforts.
They do not provide us with quick, ready
reference points or easily identified products. For most of us the specialists are
more likely to provide immediate comfort
and security. They provide more easily
recognized goods and services, and they
seem to have better command of their own
environments.

In this context, there is a particular hazard associated with any significant reliance
upon the leadership of generalists. Because the contributions and standards of
generalists are much harder to define than
those of specialists, charlatans, particularly
smooth-talking charlatans, find it much
easier to penetrate their ranks. Few would
deny, for instance, that it is easier for one
with little or no knowledge in the given
area to function as a policy analyst or program coordinator than as a mental health

or vocational rehabilitation specialist. The extent of this problem is not known, but it does exist and does militate against generalists' efforts to gain greater legitimacy and respectability.

While specialists run programs and deliver services which have high external visibility and provide immediate and tangible contributions to an individual's well-being, generalists tend to work in more internal and inconspicuous capacities and to address, among other things, the ways in which specialist services can be provided more effectively. Though one can argue (convincingly, we feel) that the two functions are crucial and interdependent, the fact nevertheless remains that the services of specialists tend to be of more direct relevance to people in need of service than those of generalists. Many specialists, to extend the point, can assert, with a high degree of public credibility, that what they do can make the difference between an individual's life or death; few, if any generalists, can do the same. It is no wonder, then, the most generalists, be it consciously or subconsciously, are highly sensitive to criticisms from specialists. If generalists push an initiative that threatens the domain of specialists, they run the risk of a showdown, and in a showdown the specialists are the likely winners, both because they have more political power and because their services, in the final analysis, are more highly prized by the public.[6]

3. CAREER REWARDS GO TO THOSE WHO SPECIALIZE. Money, prestige, and advancement come through specialization. All of us learn these facts of professional life very early in our careers, and unless we are among the few willing to sacrifice these pursuits in favor of loftier purposes we gear ourselves accordingly.

It is unfortunate that universities and government agencies provide particularly strong stimulants to this passion to specialize. Although some reforms are now taking place, most educational systems, especially at the graduate level, continue to focus upon specialized components of that environment and to churn out graduates who are ready and anxious to carve out careers as specialists.

Those who choose government service, whether at the federal, state, or local level, are likely to find this orientation reinforced. The career paths they see before them all seem to go in highly specialized directions, as civil service regulations and job classification practices are heavily biased toward the virtues of specialization. For those who wish to work for government in a more diversified capacity, the only real alternatives are to run for elective office or to work as personal staff for elected or politically appointed generalist officials. The more secure and numerous jobs in the career service are almost completely in the province of the specialists.

4. LEGISLATORS AT THE FEDERAL, STATE, AND LOCAL LEVELS ARE EASILY INDUCED BY THE LURE OF CATEGORICAL LEGISLATION. What better way to appear responsive to a pressing human problem—such as alcoholism, drug dependence, mental retardation, or unwanted pregnancy—than to enact a law, with funding, specifically geared to that problem? It is a simple and direct approach, focusing public attention and resources on the problem. It enables legislators to take credit for a discrete, easily identifiable response to the problem. It gives an appearance of executive accountability to the legislature, and it satisfies the array of specialized interest groups concerned with the problem.[7]

The logic seems unassailable, especially to the U.S. Congress, which since the early 1960s has enacted more than 400 categorical programs designed to meet particular human problems. In so doing it has, of course, made available many valuable services, but it has also spawned and sustained numerous specialized constituencies, multiplied several times over the job opportunities available to human-service specialists, and added enormously to the complexity of the human-services environment. Faced with this situation and with relatively few resources allocated to broad-based, coordinative pursuits, human-service generalists find that the opportunities for constructive intervention on a system-wide basis are severely limited.

The executive branch of government has, of course, contributed heavily to the proliferation of categorical programs. It, too, is oriented primarily along specialist, program lines. But in this regard its excesses cannot begin to match those of the legislative branch, which in most cases does almost all of its significant work in specialized committees and in response to specialized interests. Generalist-oriented human-service staff assistants who are found (albeit not easily) in parts of the executive structure are rarely found in legislative settings, especially at the state and local levels.

II. THE CHALLENGE

What can be done to establish more appropriate roles for generalists? Are generalists inherently and inevitably minor actors in the often complex, highly differentiated organizations in which they work? Or can they become more influential in these organizations and in the human-services environment as a whole?

We feel there is no natural law or basic logic that confines generalists to a minor status. Although they may not or should not achieve the overall influence of specialists, they can assume much more constructive and significant roles. Moreover, we feel that generalists must move in this direction if significant corrective measures are to be taken in response to the ills of overspecialization.

Such a development, however, is not likely to happen by a sudden legislative or

executive decree or by the sheer force of logic. It will take concerted, forceful, and long-term action by generalists themselves. They must come to view themselves as key agents of change; they must begin to press vigorously for necessary reforms in their own and other human service organizations; and, in the process, they must start to think in terms of alliances of generalists—initially in conceptual terms but increasingly in organizational and political terms as well.

The Realities

The challenge facing generalists is a vast one, and they should address it energetically and with full confidence that it is a significant one. At the same time, however, they should not let their enthusiasm blind them to important realities. They should clearly recognize the following and, no doubt, many other such realities.

1. GENERALIST-SPECIALIST TENSIONS ARE AN INHERENT PART OF ORGANIZATIONAL LIFE. They are not unique to human-service organizations and will not be eliminated through reorganization or administrative reform. The important point is to see that an organization reflects a healthy balance between these tensions and is able to absorb them in a way that contributes to its basic mission. The concept of matrix organizations, applied in many business organizations but hardly at all, to date, in human-service organizations, is directed to the productive interplay of these generalist-specialist tensions.[8]

2. RESOURCES ARE SCARCE. The era of large-scale growth in the human-service field is over and not likely to be replicated any time soon. It is conceivable that in time this reality will result in a greater demand for the effective integration of existing services. On the other hand, in view of the vested interests and political power of spe-

cialists, this demand could remain latent or politically insignificant for some time to come. Whatever the case, it is clear that reform efforts which call for greatly increased expenditures are not likely to get far during the years ahead.

3. SOME HEADWAY IN GENERALIST DIRECTIONS HAS BEEN MADE IN RECENT YEARS. Most significant, perhaps, has been the headway made in recognizing the problems brought on by excessive specialization in the human-service field. Press accounts, congressional hearings, and scholarly studies afford ample testimony of these problems and of the need for reforms.[9] The actual reform efforts initiated over the past decade have been less impressive, but have nevertheless opened up many opportunities for generalists.

At the national level efforts have included the Community Action and Model Cities programs, the general revenue-sharing program, the community-development and manpower special revenue-sharing programs, and the Title XX social services program. At the state and local levels they have included the establishment of umbrella human-service departments and the initiation of many formal and informal coordinative efforts which cut across program lines. And at the university level they have included the formation at undergraduate and graduate levels of a number of multidisciplinary human-service programs.[10] Presently most generalists are more likely to look at these efforts in terms of the frustrations they have raised rather than the opportunities afforded. Although the frustrations have been very real and the gaps between promise and performance enormous, these efforts do represent a certain momentum upon which generalists should attempt to build.

An Agenda

We have outlined a seven-part agenda for reform which generalists might wish to consider. It is not a blueprint for action as much as a reference point intended to stimulate thought and constructive action. It is directed to human-service generalists in all types of organizational settings, at all levels of government, and in the private as well as public sector. In this sense it is largely innerdirected, in that it focuses on what generalists can do for themselves and among themselves.[11]

1. GET TO KNOW ONE ANOTHER. As indicated earlier, generalists do not necessarily associate with one another, recognize their commonalties, or, for that matter, view themselves as generalists. Yet, organizational loyalties notwithstanding, it remains that generalists in different organizational settings are likely to have more professional interests in common with one another than with specialists in their own organizations.[12] The job of a planner in the office of the HEW regional director, for instance, is too likely to bear a much closer relationship to that of a planner in the office of a state human-service secretary or in a nonprofit human-services planning and research organization than it is to that of any program planner in any of the categorical agencies within HEW. It makes good sense, therefore, for generalists to look beyond their own corridors and even beyond their own communities to search out and get to know one another. In so doing, they can find that there are many others who are concerned about and engaged in similar activities. They can obtain insights which will help them in performing their jobs; they can gain confidence in themselves and in the importance of their roles; and, not least of all, they can begin to gain more influence within their own organizational settings and within larger political settings.

It is no easy task to forge associations or alliances (formal or informal) which are geared to the generalist perspective. For those generalists who are inclined to move in this direction, therefore, we feel that the first efforts should be small and informal ones in which interested participants attempt to carve out approaches which are likely to appeal to a larger grouping of generalists. It may very well be that the best type of appeal is one based on certain issues (e.g., Title XX planning or multidisciplinary human-service training) rather than on the generalist identity per se. We do feel, however, that the territorial scope of any such effort should not be too expansive since identification with common turf can lend important specificity to discussions and can facilitate communication.[13]

In this context, the efforts of an informal, loosely affiliated network of generalists in New England are relevant. Known as the New England Human Services Coaliton, this group meets periodically to share experiences and to discuss issues which are of major interest to those who bring a generalist perspective to the human-services environment.[14] It has grown in about two years from a core of about ten to a "membership" of about 150 individuals who come from a wide variety of organizational settings, public and private, throughout the region. On the basis of our own participation in the effort, we can say that it has elicited an enthusiastic response from most of the participants and that it has promoted greater and more effective communication among generalists in New England. Evidence along this line is provided by the fact that many of the participants have begun to communicate with one another on other than group occasions and have come to rely upon one another as resources to draw upon in dealing with their own problems in their own organizational settings.

2. IDENTIFY COMMONALTIES WITH OTHER CLASSES OF GENERALISTS AND PURSUE CLOSER RELATIONSHIPS. Once organizational generalists begin to develop a sense of community in their own ranks, they should begin to look for allies, especially for other classes of generalists who share many of their basic interests and who

can contribute significantly to their understandings and to their political influence. There are at least four such classes of generalists to consider.

a) Clinical generalists. Clinical generalists, those who work directly with service recipients, can offer important client-level specifics which are often overlooked from more distant organizational posts. With their "bottom-up perspective" they can offer significant insights about how service delivery systems are and are not working and about how organizational changes can be made in the interests of service recipients. However, the dialogue may not always be an easy one. Clinical generalists do not tend to view the organizational generalists as generalists or as potential allies as much as cogs in the bureaucracy, too often unresponsive to the needs of their clients. Overcoming this perception could be one of the more difficult and important challenges facing the organizational generalists.

b) Elected officials. It is vital that generalists begin to develop closer alliances with representatives of general-purpose government (GPG); that is, with governors, mayors, county executives, legislators, and other elected officials who have broad governmental responsibilities. There are many good reasons for forming closer ties with these officials, but three are particularly compelling. In our form of government, these officials represent the "people" with more legitimacy and authority than is enjoyed by any other segment of our society. That does not mean that they are necessarily at the top of the ladder in terms of power or respect, but it does lend a special significance to their determinations of what is in the public interest. To the extent that generalists can draw upon such determinations in support of their efforts, their chance of succeeding, in the face of the inevitable pushing and pulling that takes place, is bound to increase.[15]

A second and more obvious reason has to do with money. It takes money to perform the roles indicated on the previous pages, and general-purpose government officials, through their control over the public purse, are in position to provide it. Yet, as many generalists have learned, this financial support is not easily obtained. It must be cultivated with care, over a long period of time, and in the midst of many competing demands. The fact that many state and local governments are being subjected to increased financial pressures because of economic and other conditions makes this job harder but no less important.

Finally, it is important to recognize the generalized orientation which is inherent in the positions occupied by GPG officials. Their legitimacy derives from their mandate to represent the general interests of the people, not the specialized interests of certain people or groups. As agents of the people, they must respond to many different types of citizen-needs demands and oversee a wide range of specialized programs and services. As such they, too, are generalists, albeit at a broad governmental level, and are concerned about many of the same kinds of issues. It follows that if human-service generalists recognize and attempt to take advantage of this basic affiliation they can gain some important reinforcement.[16]

For many generalists such political affiliations may appear amorphous, impractical, or perhaps even repugnant. What good, many of them are apt to ask, can come from drawing closer to the politicians and from injecting more politics into the human-services environment?

There is no conclusive evidence to date, but the service-integration and "capacity-building" demonstration projects funded by HEW over the past five years suggest that the benefits may be considerable. Many of them clearly indicate that without the support and participation of GPG officials, the opportunities for sustained progress in developing integrated service systems are minimal. Some of the projects show that with the commitment and leadership of such officials, particularly the chief executives, these opportunities are much enhanced.[17] It may very well be that what we need in the human-services environment is more politics, or at least more politics of the kind that involve elected officials.

In this context, generalists should address, in earnest, questions such as the following: How can they take better advantage of the generalist orientation of GPG officials? How can human-service generalists who function within the GPG orbit serve as more effective emissaries to elected officials? What lessons have been learned from previous efforts? To what extent and in what ways should they distinguish between chief executives and legislators?[18]

c) Academicians. Although academicians interested in human services tend to be as specialist oriented as those directly involved in the provision of services, there are some whose interests are similar to those of organizational generalists and who are inclined to work closely with them. These individuals can be very helpful not only in theoretical or conceptual terms but also in specific terms concerning such matters as training programs, evaluation technologies, and organizational linkage mechanisms. In fact, the potential in this area, which would encompass students as well as teachers, has hardly been tapped.

d) Functional generalists. Discussion of generalists and specialists along the lines presented in this paper, can have the unfortunate consequence of binding generalists to the importance of developing closer linkages with those who work in the organizational domains of the specialists. The dichotomy, we must emphasize, is not hard and fast. Some individuals, who would be categorized as specialists by our definition, may be receptive to closer associations with generalists. Such receptivity is especially likely to be present among specialists who, within the context of a broad program area (e.g., health) or target group (e.g., the blind, the elderly), conduct themselves in large measure as functional generalists concerned with the interaction and application of many specialist resources. These persons can make significant contributions to generalist deliberations and should not be overlooked.[19]

3. PROMOTE A BETTER PUBLIC UNDERSTANDING OF THE GENERALIST PERSPECTIVE. If generalists are to become more constructive and influential participants in the human-services environment, more people who are not directly a part of that environment must come to understand the roles of generalists. The necessity of generalists' roles and the dangers of excessive specialization must be presented to the public in terms that are meaningful to their present circumstances. Generalists, we feel, can make significant contributions to their own public images primarily through better performance (albeit in the midst of major constraints) but also through the ways in which they explain themselves and their missions to the public. If, as has been the case so far, they couch such explanations around terms like "services integration," "systems analysis," "information systems," and the like, they are not likely to get far. However, if they can develop explanations which indicate in relatively simple terms how they can and hope to influence organizational behavior and the delivery of human services, they may generate more understanding and a broader base of support. The generalist-specialist distinction would seem to help in this regard.

It is our feeling that generalists have been woefully lacking in this communications task and that they would have much to gain if they recognized and addressed the issue through collective efforts. The gains, in fact, could be much greater than

they would expect. For, in the process of trying to define their roles and objectives in simple terms understandable by the undoctrinated, they could very well begin to clarify their own understandings about what they are or should be doing as human-service generalists.

4. SEARCH FOR BETTER UNDERSTANDING OF GENERALIST POTENTIAL AND PERFORMANCE. Many people, both within and outside of the human-service field, view the generalist's job essentially as that of providing backup support to specialists. Those holding this view are not convinced that the job is of much intrinsic significance and, in fact, may feel that ascendance of generalist functions could create unnecessary and even harmful interference in the performance of specialist functions. This is a valid concern and one which generalists must confront. Edward C. Banfield, referring to the larger political environment, reflected such concerns in the following terms: "Despite the presumptions of common sense, it may be that under certain circumstances, the competition of forces which do not aim at a common interest produces outcomes which are more workable, satisfactory and effective than any that could be conceived by central decision-makers searching for solutions in the common interest."[20] Human-service generalists are not likely to diminish such concerns immediately, but as they seek to define their roles they should recognize and understand that many of the contemporary conceptualizations and descriptions are hardly convincing enough to inspire widespread confidence.

All too often, the generalist's job is a seat-of-the-pants operation, where "success" is determined by the incumbent's skill in improvising much more than in employing any existing body of knowledge. Generalists themselves should confront this situation and do some hard thinking, in practical terms, about how they can make better use of their generalist perspectives. In the process they should ask themselves many basic questions, including the following:

a) Why is the generalist perspective important? This question is perhaps obvious, but it is usually ignored. By addressing it seriously, generalists can begin to gain a better understanding of the contexts in which they work and of the type of initiatives they should and should not undertake.

b) In what ways and under what conditions can generalists best reflect a systemic perspective? The generalist roles posed earlier in this article may provide a starting point, but they certainly do no more than that. Generalists, drawing upon their own experiences and understandings of the human-services environment, should determine for themselves what types of roles and approaches are likely to have widespread meaning for those working in generalist capacities. In this regard they should examine carefully the relevance and use of system designs. Some very thoughtful and potentially significant designs, directed toward the human-services environment, have been developed, but to date relatively little attention has been given to the ways in which these ideal designs can be adapted to the less than ideal environments in which generalists and specialists must function.[21]

c) How can generalists begin to develop standards which can be used to guide and measure their performance? Given the state of uncertainty about generalist roles, the development of performance standards may be too ambitious a task at the current time. Yet the sheer importance of it seems to leave little choice. Such standards, even if relatively crude in nature, can provide much-needed reference points for generalists and can be instrumental in gaining more public legitimacy for generalist roles. It is no small matter to

recognize that standards can also help to defend generalists against charges of being charlatans or dilettantes.

5. PROMOTE OPPORTUNITIES FOR MULTIDISCIPLINARY HUMAN-SERVICES TRAINING. Both in universities and in public and private agencies, programs designed to train existing or potential human-service personnel are directed primarily along categorical, specialist lines. This orientation, obviously, promotes and reinforces highly specialized approaches to the planning, management, and delivery of human services.[22] As indicated earlier, there has been some movement in opening up more and better training opportunities for those inclined toward a generalist perspective. However, to date it has been slow and relatively inconsequential. For any significant level of activity to take place, it seems that generalists themselves must become the prime movers. They must recognize the crucial, long-term conditioning influence of training programs and begin to pressure forcefully and intelligently for the necessary reforms.

One line of activity in this regard is to prepare their case. They should be able to indicate, in some depth, why broad-based, multidisciplinary training programs are important and what types of skills and knowledge should be fostered through them. Such accounts, based as much as possible on the actual job demands of generalists, would provide valuable raw material for those planning or actually carrying out generalist-oriented training programs.

Finally, generalists can participate directly in efforts to initiate training programs or to revise existing ones by designing curricula and training experiences and by serving as instructors. In this regard, programs geared to generalists should be the major concern. At the same time, however, generalists can add to specialist training programs by addressing the integration of specialist services to reflect a total system viewpoint. Through exposure to such training, specialists can gain valuable information and may become more receptive to linkage efforts involving generalists or other specialists.

6. CULTIVATE ORGANIZATIONAL SETTINGS CONDUCIVE TO GENERALIST PERSPECTIVES. In order to apply their perspective, generalists must cultivate more supportive organizational settings. They must strive for the development of settings where there is more room for innovation, more receptivity to joint efforts involving specialists and generalists, and greater readiness to respond to the needs of service recipients in holistic rather than piecemeal fashion. For such movement to take place, however, generalists must develop some explicit and shared understandings about the particular elements of organizational settings which are vital to a generalist perspective and to the effective performance of generalist roles. What are these elements? To what extent and in what ways are they likely to affect generalist performance? Can more important elements be differentiated from less important ones? What are the hard political and financial realities likely to be met in trying to put them in place? By providing answers, even tentative answers, to these and other such questions, generalists can begin to develop some valuable guideposts for reform efforts in organizational settings of many different types.[23]

Many might argue that there is not enough knowledge upon which to base answers to such questions and that generalists, in any event, are not likely to reveal much agreement among themselves. This argument can be a very convincing one. Yet generalists have been coping in organizational settings for some time now, and though their "failures" are perhaps more notable than their "successes" they have

learned some important lessons in the process. Unfortunately most of these lessons have not been widely shared and have not become cumulative. Inevitably, this situation has meant that the same mistakes are being made repeatedly.

In this context, the services-integration and capacity-building demonstration projects sponsored by HEW over the past five years have provided a wealth of relevant experience. Funded with the major aim of generating increased knowledge about the development of integrated human-service systems and about the role of general-purpose governments in these systems, the projects have afforded significant opportunities for generalists. Although their overall funding level has been relatively meager,[24] they have placed generalists in important leadership positions and have enabled them to test innovative approaches and techniques in many different kinds of organizational settings. Assessments of these projects in terms of their lessons for generalists have been minimal—a situation which generalists themselves should try to correct before memories fade and relevant records and reports disappear. However, one recent report prepared for HEW by RAND does afford a very interesting, albeit tentative, conclusion. Looking closely at seventy local, comprehensive services-integration projects, not all of which were founded by HEW, RAND attempted to identify those types of linkages which were likely to foster the growth and development of an integrated service system. It found none. Such linkage mechanisms as interagency planning and budgeting, case management techniques, and information systems exhibited "a nonsignificant association with subsequent growth."[25] However, RAND did find that those integrative approaches which brought members of different agencies together fared better than those approaches which did not. The implication,

RAND speculates, may be that "the key to the evolutionary growth of services integration systems is that the links should require continuing interactions among personnel of the agencies involved."[26]

This is hardly an earth-shattering conclusion, but for generalists interested in cultivating organizational settings more conducive to integrative approaches, it offers food for thought. It may mean that a vital first step to take in cultivating such settings is to foster greater interaction among generalists and specialists, even if at the outset the purposes and expected outcomes of this interaction are not sharply defined. It may mean that the gradual development of a constituency for change may be worth more emphasis than a detailed specification of the type of change being sought. Such notions may contradict the rational, orderly inclinations of many of us, but they appear to be based on experience and quite certainly are worth further exploration.

7. SERVE AS EFFECTIVE AGENTS OF CHANGE. Most of the advice we have offered heretofore is of a long-term, background nature. It concerns actions which generalists can take to maximize their strengths and to promote conditions more favorable to them. As important as they are, however, such actions in themselves will not lead to the major changes which most generalists would like to see take place. For these changes to happen, generalists, individually and collectively, must be ready to enter the legislative and bureaucratic battlefields and fight intelligently and determinedly for what they perceive to be the necessary reforms.

However, it is one thing to be willing to enter these battlefields and quite another to be well prepared. The forces opposing change are in most places much stronger and more firmly entrenched. To confront them hastily and without a carefully prepared strategy is to undertake a course almost certainly destined to fail.

We do not enjoy the warfare terminology, but we use it to stress that if generalists intend to promote major changes in the status quo,[27] they must understand that sharp conflicts are inevitable and necessary. The ways in which generalists deploy their limited resources and power will be vital in determining how well they fare. These are hard realities which must be faced and anticipated. For those generalists who are not inclined to conflict there is, as we have indicated, more than enough work for them to do in other arenas. For those who are so inclined and able there are great risks, but with them come the prospects of making some significant breakthroughs and contributions.

To this activist band of generalists we offer four exhortations:

a) Be selective. At any given time and place there are likely to be numerous changes which must occur if generalists are to make significant contributions. Aside from the usual concerns for more money and authority, these are likely to involve a wide range of existing practices and requirements concerning civil service procedures, federal or state rules and regulations, and many other such factors which serve as constraints to more effective service delivery.[28] The important point here is that generalists in a particular time and place should make distinctions among these various constraints. They should identify those which are of priority concern, assess the strengths and weaknesses of the forces behind them, determine the support they could expect to obtain in opposing these forces, and, not least of all, think through the substantive grounds on which they would base their case against a given constraint. Through such considerations they can put themselves in good position to select and pursue those targets for reform in which the generalist case is strong and the chance of success reasonable.

b) Promote positive alternatives. Whether a reform is focusing on a type of change that would affect many generalists in many different settings or just some generalists in a particular setting, it is important for the generalist advocates to have a clear and convincing conception of what they are for (i.e., what it is they want to do and would do given the opportunity) as well as of what they are against. Without clear positive alternatives to replace existing procedures, advocates for change can lose credibility and become easy prey for the defenders of the status quo. Positive alternatives do not guarantee success, but they will increase one's chances, particularly if they offer specifics about how service systems would be improved and clients would be better off.

c) Use generalist allies. Generalists about to strike out at some existing constraints or about to advocate for some positive alternative should recognize that there are many potential allies and different ways in which they can help. For example, if a change is sought in a federal departmental requirement, generalists within that department could not be expected to help in the same way as could generalists in a governor's office or a private group. The latter types of generalists would probably have much more flexibility and be able to make much stronger and more open demands. As part of their homework, therefore, generalists about to go out in front on some reform issue would do well to identify their network of supporters, determine their distinctive contributions, and then, at least in some general way, try to orchestrate their actions.

d) Persevere. Most changes of any consequence are apt to take time, even under the best of conditions. Generalist architects of change, therefore, should be prepared to take a long-term view and to recognize the importance of patience and perseverance.

Valuable testimony of this sort is afforded by the experience of a Connecticut group which developed a truly innovative proposal calling for the provision of integrated, community-based services to a selected population of elderly people but which required HEW support in the form of money and waivers to myriad Medicare regulations. The story is a long one not easily told, but the salient point here is that although the HEW bureaucracy was strongly resistant to the proposal at the outset and at many intervening points during the next two years, the proposal was eventually funded essentially because the sponsors and the allies they cultivated refused to give up on it and continued to press HEW vigorously and intelligently for the necessary support. Perseverance in this case made the difference for the sponsors and we expect could do the same for other generalists who find themselves bucking the legislative or bureaucratic tide.

A Note of Caution

The agenda set forth in the preceding pages is, we believe, a full, exciting, and important one. However, because we have presented it in terms of what generalists can and should do for themselves, we feel compelled to close on a note of caution about generalists becoming too caught up in their self-interest. We do not expect generalists to be any more altruistic than any other participants in the human-service field, and we recognize that inevitably a good part of their energies are likely to be devoted to concerns about pay levels, working conditions, job benefits, and the like. Yet to the extent that they focus on such concerns at the expense of those dealing with the contributions they can make to the improved functioning of human-service systems, they tend to weaken their case. The strength of the generalist perspective and of the notion of an alliance of generalists lies in its relevance to these systems and, at bottom, to the overall well-being of service recipients, not in the inherent importance of generalists themselves. The distinction may be a fine one, but it is one that generalists would do well to keep in mind.

NOTES

The views expressed in this article are those of the authors and do not necessarily represent those of the institutions with which they are affiliated.

1. We do not mean to suggest that this concentration of power reflects a conspiracy lacking public support or legitimacy. In fact, at least in a general sense, quite the opposite is true. Specialists in all spheres of governmental activity have for some time enjoyed far-reaching public support and have been able to derive their power largely from that support. Herbert Kaufman, a political scientist, explains this state of affairs as a reflection of a popular long-standing quest for "neutral competence" in government; i.e., a longing to put government in the hands of experts who will make decisions on the basis of knowledge and objective standards rather than on the basis of political influences (Herbert Kaufman, "Emerging Conflicts in the Doctrines of Public Administration," *American Political Science Review* 50 [December 1956]: 1057–73).

2. The most comprehensive source for references to publications on the problems of the categorical system of service delivery is Project Share, a national clearinghouse for information on human-services integration (P.O. Box 2309, Rockville, Maryland 20852). Annotated bibliographies are available upon request.

3. This interdependence is addressed in a very convincing manner in Alfred J. Kahn, "Service Delivery at the Neighborhood Level," *Social Service Review* 50 (March 1976): 38–40.

4. Seymour B. Sarason, *The Creation of Settings and Future Societies* (San Francisco: Jossey-Bass Publishers, 1972), p. 121.

5. C. C. Attkisson and A. Broskowski, "Evaluation and the Emerging Human Service Concept," in *Evaluation of Human Service Programs,* ed. C. C. Attkisson, W. Hargreaves, M. Horowitz, and J. Sorensen (New York: Academic Press, 1976). For an excellent case study of the differences in evaluation and analysis when carried out under categorical as opposed to generalist auspices, see Joseph L. Falkson, "Minor Skirmish in a Monumental Struggle: HEW's Analysis of Mental Health Services," *Policy Analysis* 2(Winter 1976): 93–119.

6. In this regard, it is significant to note that one of the most widespread criticisms of a recent reorganization of the Florida Department of Human Resources is that giving generalists more decision-making power tended to dilute the autonomy of program directors and to inhibit the department's capacity to attract top-quality specialists. This information is taken from a case analysis prepared by K. G. Heintz under the supervision of Laurence E. Lynn, Jr., for use at the John F. Kennedy School of Government, Harvard University. It is entitled "Reorganization of Florida's Human Service Agency" and was prepared in 1975.

7. For an in-depth analysis of some of the major consequences of government's susceptibility to specialized interest groups, see Theodore Lowi, *The End of Liberalism* (New York: W. W. Norton & Co., 1969).

8. See Fremont A. Shull, *Matrix Structure and Project Authority for Optimizing Organizational Capacity,* Business Science Monographs, no. 1 (Carbondale: Business Research Bureau, School of Business, Southern Illinois University, May 1970); Duncan Neuhauser, "The Hospital as a Matrix Organization," *Hospital Administration* (Fall 1972), pp. 8–25; Robert W. Curtis, "From State Hospital to an Integrated Human Service System: The Management of Transition," *Health Care Management Review* 1 (1976): 39–50; Donald R. Kingdon, *Matrix Organization: Managing Information Technologies* (London: Tavistock Publications, 1973; distributed in the United States by Harper & Row).

9. See *Evaluation of Services Integration Projects,* Human Services Bibliography Series, no. 1 (June 1976), available from Project Share, P.O. Box 2309, Rockville, Maryland 20852.

10. Particularly notable in this regard are (1) the Community Allied Human Services Program at the College of Public and Community Services, University of Missouri, Columbia; (2) the efforts of the College for Human Services, 201 Varick St., New York, New York 10014; and (3) the Human Services Generalist Program in the Department of Psychology at the University of Minnesota.

11. This inner focus is not meant to suggest that a search for ways in which generalists can interact more effectively with specialists is not of great importance. Obviously, such a search is of considerable importance. However, such a search is not apt to be very successful if generalists do not have a sense of community among themselves, a sense of their own potential, and a sense of how

they can best take advantage of that potential. This section is thus devoted to the quest for these basics.

12. This is certainly true among specialists, who relate much more comfortably and easily with their counterparts in other organizations than they do with generalists in their own organizations. More often than not, it appears, they view the latter as outsiders and as threats to their professional interests rather than as members of the same team.

13. On the other hand, if the territorial scope is too limited, say, to a metropolitan area, discussions might become too detailed and might focus too heavily on personalities.

14. The central question posed at its fall 1975 conference, for example, was What are the major, underlying principles of services integration?

15. Such determinations, of course, can mean different things. In one instance they can be just that and little more; i.e., a determination, official or unofficial, that a particular objective or course of action is a desirable one. In another instance they can lead to a change in the rules of the game or in the distribution of authority characterizing generalist-specialist relationships. Or in still another instance, they can lead to the provision of funds in support of certain initiatives. The important point is that in any of these instances or others, generalists have much to gain if the determinations are supportive of their efforts.

16. We are not naive enough to suggest that because GPG officials are in positions which call for a generalized orientation, they always or even usually reflect this orientation. Obviously, many officials reflect specialized interests much more than they represent the public interest. The basic reason for this situation probably rests in the fact that the public or general interest is usually too fuzzy to be politically relevant in the midst of clear-cut and powerful specialized interests. However, at least part of the explanation, we feel, is that generalists have not been as adept as specialists in making their case in the political arena.

17. Most of this information appears in internal departmental reports. A national evaluation of the HEW general-purpose government capacity-building projects is now underway and is very much attuned to the political dimension of the projects. It should be completed in mid-1977. An assessment of some of the earlier HEW funded services-integration demonstration projects is less geared to political dimensions but does provide some pertinent information in this context (see Stephen D. Mittenthal, *Human Ser-*

vice Development Programs in Sixteen Allied Services (SITO) Projects [Wellesley, Mass.: Human Ecology Institute, 1975]).

18. It is interesting to note that in the case of the Florida reorganization which elevated the status of generalists in the state's Department of Human Resources, the legislative rather than the executive branch was the chief architect of the reform (see n. 6 above).

19. There is another element here meriting the consideration of organizational generalists. Functional generalists are often appointees (or the staff of appointees) of GPG chief executives. As such, they are likely to have closer ties with GPG generalists than are the true specialists who work in the bureaus and divisions under them. Moreover, quite a few of these functional generalists are likely to have broad-based generalist backgrounds rather than specialized backgrounds in the particular functional area in which they are currently employed.

20. Edward C. Banfield, *Political Influence: A New Theory of Urban Politics* (New York: Free Press, 1961), p. 327.

21. See Michael Baker, ed., *The Design of Human Service Systems* (Wellesley, Mass.: Human Ecology Institute, December 1974).

22. Frederick C. Mosher views the specialist biases of universities to be of major consequence to the public service and to be in substantial part responsible for the heavy emphasis on specialization within the public service (Frederick C. Mosher, *Democracy and the Public Service* [New York: Oxford University Press 1968], esp. pp. 24–52 and 99–123).

23. In this context, the mission of an organization may be a variable worth special attention. It may be that for generalists to come into their own, more organizations will have to redefine their missions in ways which give more emphasis to planning, evaluation, integration, cost saving, and other concerns which are central to the generalist's agenda.

24. Total funding between 1971 and 1975 for HEW's service-integration and capacity-building demonstration projects has been about $25 million.

25. William A. Lucas, Karen Heald, and Mary Vogel, *The 1975 Census of Social Services Integration: A Working Note*, prepared for the Department of Health, Education, and Welfare by RAND (Santa Monica, Calif.: RAND Corporation, 1975), p. viii.

26. Ibid., p. lx.

27. In this context generalists would do well to understand and reflect upon the inevitable tendency of established organizations and parts of or-

ganizations not only to resist change but also to act assertively in trying to remain the same. Donald Schon refers to this characteristic as "dynamic conservatism" (Donald A. Schon, *Beyond the Stable State* [New York: W. W. Norton & Co., 1971], esp. pp. 31–60).

28. A major and long-standing federally induced constraint of this sort is the single state agency requirement associated with many categorical programs. This requirement, which is usually reflected in statute as well as in administrative regulation, is a device to ensure that the relevant specialist professionals at the state level retain control over the categorical program and serve as the accountable agents to counterpart federal specialists. Although federal waivers to this kind of requirement are possible and have been made, they are very difficult to obtain, particularly in regard to the vocational rehabilitation program where HEW and Congress have been notably inflexible.

George Brager and Stephen Holloway
A Process Model for Changing Organizations from Within

Among the profound changes that mark the post industrial society is the shift in the functions of socialization, support, and control from the family to the community and state. Accompanying this shift has been the development of a range of social technologies that because they are costly, can only be implemented on a large scale. As a result, a vast array of formal organizations have come into being whose stated purpose is the enhancement of the social, emotional, physical and/or intellectual well-being of one or another component of the population.

These human service organizations, even the best led and most professional among them, are characterized by circumstances which compromise their stated purposes. There are many reasons why this is so: the fact that our society is ambivalent about the efficacy of institutional human services; that persons who need help are widely viewed as undeserving, unduly dependent, or deviant; and that human service agencies are charged with

conflicting mandates—for example, to cure but not coddle or to proffer services but to limit costs. Furthermore, the structure of formal organizations embodies inherent contradictions which bring conflict and problems in their wake. For example, hierarchical authority is necessary to unify and coordinate diverse organizational participants, but persons located at different places in a chain of command are privy to different information and develop different, potentially contradictory perspectives about organizational issues. Similarly, although specialization of task and function is a necessary feature of complex organizations, it also engenders clashes of position and competition for "turf."

The problems inherent in human service organizations affect the services that professionals are able to provide their clients. In some cases, the result is as profound as the service recipient's objectification or dehumanization.[1] In other instances, organizational problems result in subtle though significant service deficiencies. The agency does not "reach out" to potential clients; its intake procedures actively discourage its use; the agency is in-

Reprinted with permission of the authors and *Administration in Social Work* 1:4 (Winter 1977), pp. 349–58.

sensitive to client definitions of problems; it selects those for whom public sympathy is high and "de-selects" the others; it makes referrals for agency rather than client convenience; or it offers one modality to meet all needs.

A standard dilemma for human service professionals is to find themselves faced with organizational problems which sharply limit the quality of service they provide, yet lack the authority to change the situation for the better. Accommodations to this dilemma vary widely with individual workers and agencies. One adjustment common to traditional mental health settings, for example, is for the worker to engage in an unspoken compact with the administration in which the administrator grants the professional clinical autonomy in exchange for the professional's disinterest in organizational policy, the effect of which is the professional's lack of involvement in agency operations. Another accommodation is to allow service problems to go unrecognized or to become inured to them. An agency conducts an elaborate five-session intake procedure *before* it accepts clients for service, for example, but the worker either does not make the obvious connection between the agency's selection process and the type of clientele it serves or ignores its problematic aspects. Sometimes, too, workers become jaded, and morally or professionally unacceptable practices become gradually less vexing and accepted as a "fact of organizational life."

Other responses to the dilemma are available to client-oriented workers, however. These represent more socially desired adaptations to organizational reality, in our view. One, suggested by Gottleib, is for workers to develop areas of functional autonomy for themselves in order to promote the interests of their clients.[2] In the process they may manipulate the system to obtain client benefits. For example, a worker may make a not quite so accurate

diagnosis in order to ensure a client's eligibility for service, justifying the action as "situation ethics."[3]

Such a response may be the most a professional can achieve in attempting to humanize services in some organizations. When this is the case, it is, we judge, a professionally appropriate response to inequitable service systems. It is less effective, however, than a second alternative—the decision to work for change in those discrete aspects of the organization which workers find most problematic.

This paper focuses on the latter—that is, the change which may be induced by middle and lower level professionals from within the service organization which employs them. Such change, though ordinarily modest, is important nonetheless. Even modest change can have significant consequences in the lives of large numbers of people who are touched by the human services. Relevant, too, is the fact that engaging in organizational change efforts keeps alive a worker's commitments to high standards of service. Finally, skill in change practice, which is developed over time, tends to reinforce and refine service-oriented values, and this, combined with the natural progression of responsibility which accompanies career maturation, enhances the professional's opportunity to accomplish increasingly meaningful change.

Our focus on worker-initiated change does not stem from a romanticization of the lower-ranking practitioner, nor do we endorse the neo-populist notion that locates social concern and integrity invariably and exclusively in the lower reaches of the organization's order. Rather, our attention to practitioner-initiated change stems from two factors. Our primary interest is the provision of human services that are responsive to the needs and rights of the consumers of those services. It is an organizational truism that the closer organizational decision making is to the source of information, the more likely it is that the decision will accurately take account of the information. Since the staff members who interact with clients are line workers, one means of increasing an agency's responsiveness to client needs is to increase the impact of line staff on its programs and policies.

Secondly, our interest in worker-initiated change derives from the limitations of practitioner influence. Although low and middle level staff at times contribute to agency decision making, in general they are relatively powerless. This fact, too obvious to require documentation, makes increasing their impact on service provision a relevant professional concern. This is even more the case when one considers the paucity of both theoretical and practice attention which the subject has received in the literature.[4] What is urgently needed is an informed understanding of the processes of change and a practice technology of organizational innovation geared to maximizing the influence of professionals with limited formal power.

Such a task is beyond the scope of a single paper. It is our intention, rather, to outline our view of a "bottom up" change process and to identify some of the practice concerns which professionals need to consider at its various stages. We have selected five phases to characterize the change process: initial assessment, pre-initiation, initiation, implementation, and institutionalization. In each, there is a function or set of tasks that must be accomplished if the process is to move on to the next phase. When these tasks are not completed, the process runs down. Viewing the phases in terms of their intrinsic functions and the tasks that must be accomplished before the next phase can begin provides the practitioner with an agenda or approximate guide to issues in practice as the change process unfolds. In the balance of this paper, we indicate some of the tasks, practice concerns, and tactics which are relevant to each phase of the process.

INITIAL ASSESSMENT

Initial assessment, in our definition, is that phase of a change attempt in which the discrepancy between the actual and the desired state of affairs is recognized and some notions of what can be done about it are formulated. Relevant data are collected and organized, disciplined consideration is given to whether a change is feasible (and if so, *what* change), and a decision is made about attempting a remedy. If the decision is positive, the worker must consider the range of tactics he will use to advance the change.

An early task is to translate one's concern with current programs, policies, or procedures into a specific and operational objective. The characteristics of the chosen goal will, of course, affect the likelihood of its adoption.[5] The more a goal reflects current organizational values or the more directly it impinges on a generally recognized problem, the easier it is to win adoption. Similarly, its chances of acceptance are greater when a solution can be tested on a limited basis, such as in a demonstration program, or its implementation can be reversed if necessary. Chances for its adoption are also enhanced if the implementation of an innovation requires a lesser use of scarce resources. Conversely, goals which require highly technical operations, call for coordinating the efforts of various specialties, or have a widespread impact on other organizational actors are more difficult to attain than less complex innovations.

Once the worker has defined a tentative goal, he must assess the forces working for and against its adoption. By forces we mean the range of variables predisposing stability or change—or more specifically, those variables which have a probability of influencing the preferences of significant organizational participants with respect to the desired goal.

It is a truism of the literature that change in organizations represents their adaptation to external circumstances. Thus the organization's environment impels the major forces which lead to internal change, and the most potent of these forces are, in our view, economic and political. Obviously, such economic factors as agency financing and such political factors as the respective power position and prevailing values of an organization's various publics are critical variables in pressing for or against change. But environmental explanations are incomplete since organizations exposed to comparable external forces often respond differently.[6] The characteristics of the organization itself— for example, its ideology, goals, structure—also influence movement toward or away from particular change goals.

Finally, whatever environmental and organizational forces are at play, organizational change is *executed by people* whose action is governed by the meaning these forces have for them, their preferences for one or another outcome, and the intensity with which these preferences are held. Are various organizational members likely to be for the content of the change idea, against it, or neutral? Much, we believe, will depend on their organizational self-interest stemming from their role in the agency. How intensely will they favor or oppose the change, and what resources will they be prepared to use to support or resist it? Here the amount of influence an actor has is an important determinant since influence or its perception affects whether a participant will act on his commitments and with what success.

The essence of change strategy is found in identifying and weighing the potential impact of these variables stemming from the environment, organizational structure, or process and the meanings ascribed by participants.[7] Some of these variables constitute *pro-change forces* which, when increased, alter preferences in such a way that organizational participants act to support the proposed goal. Other variables constitute *restraining forces* which, when in-

creased, reinforce an actor's commitment to the status quo or move him to resist the change; conversely, when decreased, they modify actor behavior in the direction of the desired change. Change strategy consists essentially of enhancing or increasing the forces which are potentially supportive of the worker's goal and reducing or isolating the restraining forces which [mediate] against the change.

An example will make the point. A community mental health center—we shall call it Monrad—offered inpatient services and a lounge program for former patients. Clients who spent their day at the hospital but lived at home, however, fell through the cracks of the two departments. Although they were part of the inpatient program, their special needs were ignored. A mental health worker concluded that a day hospital was the most appropriate and feasible remedy for this group of clients.

There were a number of pro-change forces at work, but we cite only two for present purposes. First was an environmental force, the fact that Monrad's financial support faced constriction. The second related to the organization's ideology, its tradition as a leader in the mental health field. The goal of a day hospital was chosen in part because of its pro-change impact in that it would contribute increased funds. The worker's strategy to increase the second force—the center's tradition of leadership—was to make visible the development of day hospitals in other centers across the country.[8]

The mental health worker considered the varying potential preferences of Monrad's staff, and competition between the director of its hospitalization services and the head of the outpatient department was assessed as a potential restraining force. The worker's proposal called for the day hospital to be included within the hospitalization services (thus increasing the likelihood of the support of its director), and he also planned to neutralize the outpatient department head. In short, by identifying the pro-change and restraining forces, the worker began to develop an approximate blueprint for action.

Before a worker decides to proceed, however, there are further issues of a practical and ideological nature that must also be considered. He must, for example, weigh such matters as the potential risks and benefits to himself in proceeding. The role of clients in the change attempt—whether as active participants or as silent partners—must also be decided. Finally, value issues must be addressed as workers select a set of actions to influence a force—for example, whether and to what extent it would be appropriate for them to proceed in an unobtrusive or covert way. Although maneuvering within the organization may be justifiable *under certain circumstances* (e.g., when agency officials ignore client needs in the service of their personal interests; when other means of influencing are unavailable to workers without jeopardizing clients, colleagues, or themselves, and the like), the value dilemmas inherent in organizational practice must be considered as the worker moves beyond assessment to the next phase of the process.

PREINITIATION

Having decided to proceed, the practitioner must prepare the organization for the introduction of the change proposal. This is a frequently overlooked aspect of change practice. Once the worker gets his "bright idea," the temptation is to share it with colleagues and suggest that it be adopted at the next supervisory conference or staff meeting. Occasionally if the change is modest and the system predisposed to the proposal, this kind of single-step process is sufficient. Rarely does a change occur with such ease, however. Typically the field of forces impinging on the goal is complex, and the receptivity of decision makers cannot be counted on so readily.

Two major practice tasks should be noted in the preinitiation phase of the process. First, persons planning to initiate a change must develop "social capital"; that is, build their influence in the social system they intend to change.[9] Second, they must induce or increase system stress related to the change problem in order to increase the likelihood that decision makers will respond positively to its solution.

Practitioners may develop "social capital"—or "position" themselves—by seeking to enhance their attractiveness to others, dispensing social rewards such as recognition and approval, and highlighting shared values in interaction with others. Another means is to increase their network of contacts and political debtors. At one level the task is simply to know and be known by those who might ultimately have an impact on their goals. At another level, workers proffer support or grant favors to create a sense of obligation to reciprocate on the part of others, thus creating political debtors.

Establishing one's legitimacy to deal with a particular problem area is another means by which practitioners position themselves during the preinitiation phase. Legitimacy is ordinarily granted when an innovation falls clearly within the practitioner's function or jurisdiction. When it does not, however, the worker may attempt to enlarge his function or jurisdiction, sometimes imperceptibly by incremental degrees. Or he may try to gain knowledge and expertise in the subject matter so that, seen as an expert by other staff, he inspires others to rely on him in matters relating to the problem area.

The Monrad mental health worker gained the legitimacy to promote a day hospital program in this way. He describes his participation at the community meetings held by the Department of Hospitalization Services which were attended by the hospital's inpatients, the day patients, and clinical staff as follows:

During the community meeting, there were several issues raised which dealt with the use of leisure time at home, attempts at job hunting, and transportation problems, all matters affecting only the day patients at the meeting. I pointed out that this group of patients seemed to have several problems which are very similar to one another and volunteered to get together with them to continue talking if they wished. They agreed, and informal group meetings with the day patients were held after every community meeting thereafter.

. . . As a result of my close contacts with the day patients, I was able to make a point of reporting the difficulties facing patients who fell into this group. Staff began to look at me when some information about day patients was required, and even the director of the service started to seek out my advice when the treatment plan for a day patient was being discussed.[10]

A second practice task during preinitiation is to influence prochange and restraining forces so as to induce or magnify stress relating to the particular problem area. Unfortunately for change efforts, human service workers tend to perceive their function to be stress reduction. But change is unlikely to occur unless discomforting tension accompanies an attempt to change the status quo.

Organizations typically develop "defense systems" to avoid recognizing or acknowledging organizational problems. Making inroads into this defense system— and thus generating tension—may be accomplished by heightening problem awareness. Essentially, this entails introducing dissonant information—that is, information which reveals the inconsistencies between how the organization actually functions and how the participants believe it runs or how they would like it to run.

In bearing "bad tidings," the worker must understand the risk to himself and undertake the task with sensitivity. Thus, as he is making issues visible, the worker must try to avoid seeming to be dissident.

Indeed, he must find a way to be raising problems out of organizational loyalty— for example, by linking the problem with predominant organizational values— rather than as a criticism of current policy. Politically astute workers will also carefully ration the number of issues they identify and try to get others to be problem raisers along with (or instead of) themselves.

Heightened interaction within an agency diffuses problem awareness. Such interaction can be fostered informally (e.g., social contacts, partisan caucuses) or, when organizational protocol permits, through more formal devices (e.g., staff meetings, seminars). Structuring interaction among participants known to be discontented and encouraging them to bear witness to their discontent is a particularly effective means of magnifying stress.

The Monrad mental health worker skillfully orchestrated his goal of establishing a day hospital by using the various types of formal gatherings held at the center. He notes:

At the team meeting, ordinarily conducted by myself and the other team leaders, I brought up how overworked and overburdened staff were. Monrad's catchment area was due to be expanded, and I "wondered" how the new area would affect working conditions on the unit. We had a space problem as it was. With the possible increase of inpatients and "who knows how many more day patients there would be?" Where we would put everyone?[11]

Subsequently the Monrad worker encouraged one of the nurses whose work carried weight with the Director to raise the question of the impact of an expanded catchment area at an administrative staff meeting. And at an inservice training session, a partner in the change effort reported on a conference he had attended in which research findings regarding the beneficial effects on patients of day hospitals had been set forth.

It is worth noting that at each of these

meetings, a different staff member took the "front runner" position and that they avoided the premature introduction of their goal. Instead, they carefully set the stage for its initiation.

INITIATION

The introduction of the change goal into the organization signals the beginning of the initiation phase of change practice. An interactive process then ensues in which the innovation is adapted and diffused among the relevant organizational entities until it is either formally accepted or rejected.

The essential function of initiation is to make the change goal conform to the influence which can be mobilized to move its adoption. The two—change goal and influence—vary in tandem. The more an innovation is perceived to be consistent with the interests and values of those who must approve it, the less influence is necessary to ensure its acceptance. The more threatening the goal to their interests, the more resistance it will induce. And the greater the resistance, the more power which must be brought to bear by those promoting the change. Since an influence attempt is geared to a specific target, the identity of critical organizational actors—participants who *must* support the proposal for it to be realized—determines the worker's interventions. With those who are to be influenced as the focus, there are three practice questions to be considered: To whom should the appeal be made? Who should make it? And what arguments should be used?

Human service workers often give these questions insufficient consideration. Typically the decision maker is approached; the worker seeking the change is the one to raise the issue; and the argument is ordinarily made in terms of professional values. To introduce and diffuse a change goal effectively requires greater sensitivity to the dynamics of influence than these practices suggest.

In deciding to whom the appeal should be made, the practitioner must consider whether to go directly to the decision maker with the power to sanction the proposal, whether to introduce the idea to intermediates who may influence the latter's choice, or whether to first seek the support or decrease the opposition of organizational participants to whom the change goal is relevant. A general and prudent principle is to sequence one's steps to move from natural allies to probable proponents to uncertain but increasingly influential actors. This allows the practitioner to increase his resources for influencing as he moves through the process with less risk of either a premature veto or activating the opposition.

Organizing support from one's natural allies or other potential proponents is often critical to the success of a change attempt. The practitioner who has effectively stimulated problem awareness during preinitiation has taken the first step in forming such a coalition. If sufficient interest has been elicited, he may then "up the ante." One way is to fix the position by ensuring that the actor's stance is made public, if only within the confines of the budding coalition. The support of one actor, depending on who he is, may activate the support of others. Another way, once the position is fixed, is to make the requested assistance concrete—that is, to find something specific for the potential proponent to *do*, thereby increasing his commitment.

What makes for an effective alliance? Obviously, potential members who have influence with the decision makers are primary candidates, as, for example, the nurse in the Monrad example. Sometimes, too, participants have to be drawn into a coalition because they have a special interest in the change issue and their absence would challenge the legitimacy of the effort. Another significant consideration is the heterogeneity of the alliance. The more heterogeneous, the more powerful it is likely to be. Participants with differing sources of information, a variety of types of expertise, and links to different standing alliances, for example, make a more potent combination than coalitions in which the members' information channels, expertise, or informal relations are merely additive. Thus, the fact that the alliance at Monrad ultimately included actors of different hierarchical levels, professional backgrounds (i.e., medical staff, psychologists, social workers, paraprofessionals), and persons with lines into varying staff groupings made it a more potent coalition than had it been composed of a single professional group or of staff with equal authority.

With support in place, the next question is *who* should introduce the idea, a question which requires but does not always receive conscious determination. Its answer depends in large part on the audience to whom the change message is directed, as well as other tactical considerations. As the practitioner reviews the forces he hopes to impact, he finds that collaborative interventions are appropriate with some participants, other interventions require political maneuvering, and some forces may be subject to modification only by confrontation and conflict. By and large, however, the aim during the initiation phase is to educate and persuade rather than to threaten. Initiators, then, are selected for their credibility to the audience in question.

Finally, the practitioner must design his goal and its presentation so that the content of the change idea and the arguments favoring it maximize its potential for acceptance. Space does not permit detailing the ways in which this may be done, but we cite two for illustrative purposes. One technique is to minimize the threat or uncertainty inherent in most innovations by presenting the proposal as involving little or no change on the ground that it is related to the traditional values of the organization or more closely conforms to current programmatic directions than the policy it is intended to replace. Similarly, workers may define their goal as a procedural rather than a policy change, for procedural modifications are less threatening than policy changes and are typically decided at a lower level of the hierarchy. Second, and perhaps obviously, the goal must be justified by the target actor's interests and values. This, of course, must be done with grace and tact—since professionals are expected to act on normative grounds rather than political ones. Thus the Monrad worker describes the approach to the Director of the Hospitalization Services, a key decision maker, as follows:

> We assessed that Dr. N's primary concern would be how any projected change would affect his sphere of influence and that his favorable response was contingent on a day hospital's being administered by and located within his department. We knew that he also cared about the quality of patient care, and that our attempts to persuade him would have to emphasize patient welfare and make only oblique reference to "turf" issues.[12]

The adoption of a change proposal by key decision makers completes only the initiation phase of the process. It unfortunately does not ensure either its implementation or institutionalization. Practitioners with a skeptical bent will temper any self-congratulatory feelings they may have until the innovation is firmly in place.

IMPLEMENTATION

Implementation marks the period between the adoption of an innovation and its realization. A formal decision has been made, but a series of actions are now required to bring it into being. Three practice concerns are of special importance during this period. One is gaining or holding the support of staff actually involved in implementing the change, as well as handling old or emergent resistances. Another is to ensure that the implementers are clear about what is required of them since clarity is essential if they are to act as the innovators intend. The third—and perhaps most significant—concern is maintaining the commitment of organizational decision makers to the change proposal since the loss of their support is likely to signal its failure. It is this latter practice issue which we shall consider here.

Although the decision makers have endorsed the change before implementation begins, their attention may wander, and when they are inattentive, covert resistance becomes increasingly difficult to counter. Furthermore, the endorsement of important participants is not necessarily accepted as a binding commitment. As innovations require more effort, perserverance, or creativity on the part of implementers, it becomes more important for the commitments of decision makers to be concrete and visible.

As in all social processes, commitments shift with time, and the process of implementation itself encourages its erosion. There is, first, a honeymoon period. The energy invested in making the change reaches its "high" with the decision to go ahead, and as implementation begins, it draws from the energy generated by the acceptance of the change. In this initial period the attitudes of those who conceived the change and those who accepted it range from enthusiastic support to benign interest. Inevitably, however, the "bugs" inherent in any new operation begin to emerge. If there was significant resistance initially, the difficulties will be seized on and exaggerated as they occur. Even without opposition, time may be necessary for "debugging" the change, and as time elapses, agreements tend to get softer, the forces that impelled agreement alter, and negative reactions are likely to occur. The

honeymoon over, reconsideration of the change may result.

Knowledge of this process and the timing of worker interventions to coincide with it are central to assuring the implementation of a change. The practitioner must act when the decision maker's support is at its peak. It is then that elaborating support is most feasible. Decisions are made or resources proferred which might be unavailable once a counterreaction occurs.

When the decision maker is willing, a memorandum or statement is useful to mark the occasion of the change's adoption. Workers are not often in a position to exercise discretion over the content of a decision maker's announcement. Sometimes, however, busy decision makers are willing to share influence in terms of a statement's emphasis in exchange for the worker's volunteering to conduct the research and writing tasks necessary to develop and communicate new policy. Ideally, the statement should include the reasons for the innovation and its importance. In some circumstances, it might also cite problems raised by the change, along with why they were set aside in making the decision. In addition, the acts to be taken to begin implementing the decision might be specified, including an action-enforcing mechanism and the provision of future reports of progress. It may be recognized that some of the techniques of persuasion are incorporated in these suggestions (e.g., a high status communicator, a message which expresses confidence in its arguments, the contrary position included but effectively countered, the mild suggestion of threat in the request for reports of progress, and the means for reducing the threat by following the outlined steps).[13]

Workers must also take advantage of any events during the honeymoon period to reinforce commitment to the change. If clients respond favorably to the new policy or staff members react spontaneously to some elements of it, the practitioner will ensure that this feedback reaches those whose support is essential to the maintenance of the change. To the extent possible, the bearer of such glad tidings should not be an advocate already identified as a partisan of the idea.

There is likely to be some aspect or component of the change that is attractive to key organizational participants—for example, its cost reducing potential, its public relations value, or the like. An important element in maintaining early commitment is the facility with which the worker is able to keep the attractive aspects of the change central as the organization encounters the bumps and jolts of the implementation period.

If "bugs" are anticipated, they should be publicly identified *before* they occur since difficulties which are expected are not as likely to be experienced as major problems as unanticipated ones. Because commitment is difficult to maintain throughout the period of a long-range change, practitioners would be wise to identify readily achievable interim objectives against which to measure the innovation early in its implementation. One way of taking advantage of an innovation's credibility early in the implementation stage is to define what might be considered an immediate—if partial—success, achieve it, and make it visible.

Short of setting interim objectives, the worker may prevent premature judgment by setting a timetable for the evaluation of the change. To best protect the integrity of the trial period, the timetable should be incorporated into the proposal before implementation begins. But the worker must, in any case, maintain ongoing contact with decision makers and keep them informed of the process and its progress.

Paradoxically, a major concern throughout the implementation process is the reduction of stress. Thus interventions that were appropriate in one phase are con-

traindicated in another. Earlier we noted that the worker's task in the early stages was to influence working forces so as to upset the existent equilibrium and create stress. Once the innovation has been adopted, however, the task is to restore the equilibrium at the newly reached point. The very nature of implementation, however, creates disequilibrium since old procedures must be discarded, new relationships forged, new roles learned, and the like. Establishing a supportive environment for the implementers, expressing respect and approval, proffering help, and sharing concerns go a long way toward reducing the tensions which often accompany implementation.

INSTITUTIONALIZATION

Once a change is in place, it can be fully observed, permitting its evaluation. If the change has realized its original purposes, the final step of the process involves anchoring it into the system and assuring its permanence. In attempting to institutionalize the change, practitioners reverse their efforts. Earlier, their concern was to disrupt system stability; now it involves seeking stability rather than change.

Two tasks are uppermost. The first is to standardize procedures relating to the change, encouraging its routinization. The second—and more critical—is to link it with other organizational elements since, when linkages are established, a newly implemented change can more effectively ward off threats from contending ideas than changes that are less ingrained in the organization's fabric. As the change becomes interrelated with other organizational entities, forces for protecting the new state of affairs come into being.

The possibility of developing linkages with other organizational components depends, of course, on the content of the change, where it is located structurally within the agency, and how it impinges on these other components. As practitioners scan the organization for possible areas of connection between their change and other organizational elements, it is useful for them to consider linkages in terms of the three broad requirements that system theorists describe as essential to organizational maintenance and growth: the organization's need for input (e.g., to what extent can the change be linked to the agency's need for clients, funds, staff, or the like?); the organization's "throughput" or internal process (e.g., how can other subunits be made dependent on the innovation for their increased effectiveness?); and the impact of the organization's output or "finished" product on its environment (e.g., does the change have the potential of interrelating with special-interest groups, client organizations, legislative bodies, other competitive or cooperative agencies, or the like in ways that might be perceived by decision makers as advancing the agency's interests?). The change process is completed when the innovation, made to intermesh with these various components, becomes difficult to wrench from its organizational place.

It is perhaps fitting that we close, however, by noting that nothing within a formal organization is immune to the possibility of evolution and obsolescence, and as such, permanence is never more than relative and a matter of probabilities. The change process, as we have described it, begins with identifying a problem which impinges on the needs and rights of clients. It moves to designing a solution, assessing its feasability, preparing for the introduction of the change, seeking and winning its adoption, and finally, implementing and assuring the stability of the solution in the agency. But the process

does not end there. Forces within the environment and the organization continue to generate tensions for organizational actors, and as old problems are solved, new problems emerge. Thus does the process begin again.

NOTES

1. Naomi Gottleib, *The Welfare Bind* (New York: Columbia University Press, 1974).
2. Ibid., p. 130.
3. Harry Wasserman, "The Professional Social Worker in a Bureaucracy," *Social Work* 16, No. 1 (January 1971), p. 90.
4. Recent exceptions include Rino J. Patti and Herman Resnick, "Changing the Agency from Within," in Beulah R. Compton and Burt Galaway, eds., *Social Work Processes* (Homewood, Illinois: Dorsey, 1975), pp. 499–51; Rino J. Patti, "Organizational Resistance and Change," *Social Service Review* 48, No. 3 (September 1974), pp. 367–83; and Harold Weissman, *Overcoming Mismanagement in the Human Services* (San Francisco: Jossey-Bass, 1973).
5. Some of these concepts are detailed in Gerald Zaltman et al., *Innovations and Organizations* (New York: Wiley, 1973), Chapter 1.
6. For one example, see Gertrude S. Goldberg, "New Directions for the Community Service Society: A Study of Organizational Change" (Ph.D. dissertation, Columbia University 1976), pp. 189–233.
7. For a further discussion of these variables, see George Brager and Stephen Holloway, *Changing Human Service Organizations: Politics and Practice* (New York: The Free Press, 1978), Chapters 2, 3, and 4.
8. Alan Boyer, "Change at the Monrad Community Mental Health Center," unpublished paper, 1977.
9. C. P. Loomis, "Tentative Types of Directed Social Change Involving Systemic Linkage," *Rural Sociology* 24, No. 4 (December 1959).
10. Boyer, op. cit.
11. Ibid.
12. Ibid.
13. Herbert Abelson, *Persuasion: How Opinions and Attitudes Are Changed*, 2nd ed. (New York: Springer, 1970).

Richard S. Bolan

Community Decision Behavior: The Culture of Planning

Though planning has never operated in a vacuum, the scope of today's urban problems seems to impose special demands for awareness of the complex decision web in which the planner must function. The community decision arena could be considered the "culture" of planning since its rules, customs, and actors determine the fate of community planning proposals. Understanding the nature of this cultural envelope will help in determining appropriate strategies and techniques for planning and intervention. One way to extend understanding is through comparative examination of recently begun behavioral studies focused on this area.

Previous investigation of the character of urban decision making has been limited in a number of respects. Research has tended to proceed from relatively narrow viewpoints with major attention paid to idiosyncratic case studies often carried on with self-prophetic methods.[1] Examination of prior efforts shows strict respect for the limiting boundaries of disciplinary tradition. Little attention has been given to exploring the potential contributions of a rich variety of relevant social science disciplines. Perhaps most important, past research has been preoccupied with the concepts of power and influence and has failed to examine an equally interesting aspect of decision making—the quality and effects of the decisions themselves and the

planning process that contributed to such decisions.[2]

A corollary question relates to the efficacy of the planning process in urban government. Recent writings suggest that "rational" planning procedures bear little relation to the governing of cities: the time horizons and issues that have preoccupied planners are largely irrelevant and local urban governments are so disorganized, fragmented, dispersed and incompetent that no injection of "rational" planning (even when relevant) can survive such a political culture.

This paper attempts to formulate a conceptual framework for describing and understanding the relationships between planning and decision making in urban government. Variables of the framework are identified, and interaction between them is suggested by a series of interrelated hypotheses developed on the basis of past work in the field. Ultimately, following extensive empirical observation and testing, such a framework should prove useful in extending the theory and "state of the art" of urban planning in the sense that future planning practice might be more specifically adapted to the sociopolitical culture in which it operates. What is sought is not a normative or ethical theory as to how urban government or urban planning *should be* but rather a system for describing how urban government planning and decision making *do occur* and how they are influenced by the environmental and social structure that surrounds urban government. The approach, in short, is behavioral in nature.

Reprinted by permission of the *Journal of the American Institution of Planners*, vol. 35, no. 5, September 1969.

THE GENERAL FRAMEWORK

To begin, a classical model of rationality is described. Then this simplified rational model is adapted to succeeding levels of complexity to make it more realistic. For an individual, the classical model may be viewed as a series of steps:

1. The individual, in adapting to his environment, continually scans his surroundings and seeks to modify those parts that impinge on him in some fashion—offering either limitations or opportunities with respect to his needs or gratifications. He evaluates his environment in relation to a value set he has acquired from prior experience and cultural or social traditions.
2. After determining circumstances he seeks to modify (either to overcome a hardship or seize an opportunity), he establishes goals to be achieved.
3. From this, he designs as many alternative methods of achieving his goals as time and resources permit.
4. A full and complete set of probable consequences is predicted for each alternative means.
5. Each alternative means is evaluated to determine which method maximally accomplishes the desired goals with minimum cost or effort.
6. On the above basis, a method of goal achievement is selected and acted upon.
7. Over time each such rational process becomes a part of the individual's experiential makeup. Thus, either implicitly or explicitly, there tends to be a reevaluation of a past decision as a guide to the next.

This is, of course, an idealized sequence. Individuals seldom have the time or resources to carry out each step in fullest measure. Seldom is information wholly adequate; explicit specification of goals is often lacking; only a few alternative sets of means and ends can usually be considered; the ability to predict all possible consequences is highly restricted; meaningful evaluation for optimizing is difficult; and

prior decisions often serve as constraints on the decision at hand. Thus, rationality, at best, is an imperfect process for the individual.[3]

For a community of individuals seeking to make collective, or public, decisions the process is even more complex. However, many of the same elements are present. An intelligence system scans and evaluates circumstances and conditions in the community. This system must also have a capacity to set goals and plot schemes for achieving goals. It must have integrative mechanisms to handle conflicting demands and balance allocations of limited resources. It must possess some capacity to select among alternatives and take action. Thus, the *process steps* of rationality are similar whether an individual or a community is involved in decision-making.[4]

Multiplicity of participation and involvement introduces other dimensions as well. The presence of many actors creates the potential for specialization of *process roles*. Some persons, for example, excel at the identification of problems and opportunities; others perform publicist or popularizer roles; and others are brokers in the exchange of power and influence. How skillfully each actor plays his role, his ability to marshall and manipulate resources, his ability to enlist other individuals to play other roles, and the influences of motivation and self-interest have a bearing on the decision process and influence decision outcomes.[5]

In addition, the *decision field* has substantial impact on community decision-making, and the ability to make and implement social plans and programs. The term *decision field* is meant to describe organizational and institutional arrangements prevailing in a given community and their influence in structuring roles of actors and determining complexity of problem-solving arrangements. It is affected by the character and nature of structural differentiation in the community. Thus functional specialization, social differentiation, and degree and character of leadership and hierarchical structure all have a bearing on the outcomes of urban planning decisions. Moreover, internal characteristics of the specific decision units that ultimately vote on a given issue will also play a large role in determining decision outcomes.[6]

Similarly, *strategies of planning and intervention* have a substantial influence on the nature of community decision-making. These are the factors of prime concern to the planner. It is important to learn, for example, the degree to which one may exercise technical discretion in methods of solving problems and the relationship of

Figure 1 Diagram of the conceptual scheme for community decision making

Initial Premises
Process Steps

I. Structuring and defining ideas as proposals
II. Identifying the properties of alternatives
III. Structuring the decision field
IV. Engaging in the overt decision-making processes
V. Carrying out the consequences of decision process

Independent Variable Sets Influencing Decision Outcomes

Variable Set 1. Process Roles

a. Process role specialties

b. Process role measures
   Actor motivation
   Actor opportunities
   Actor skills

Variable Set 2. Decision Field Characteristics

a. Sociopolitical environment
   Formal structure
   Informal structure
   General policy structure

b. Decision unit character
   Source of power
   Accountability
   Group dynamics
   Group role

Variable Set 3. Planning and Action Strategies

a. Planning strategies
   Relation to decision focus
   Method strategies
   Content variables

b. Action strategies
   Reallocation of resources
   Institutional change
   Client change

Variable Set 4. Issue Attributes

a. Ideological stress
b. Distribution of effects
c. Flexibility
d. Action focus
e. Predictability and risk
f. Communicability

Dependent Variable

Decision Outcomes

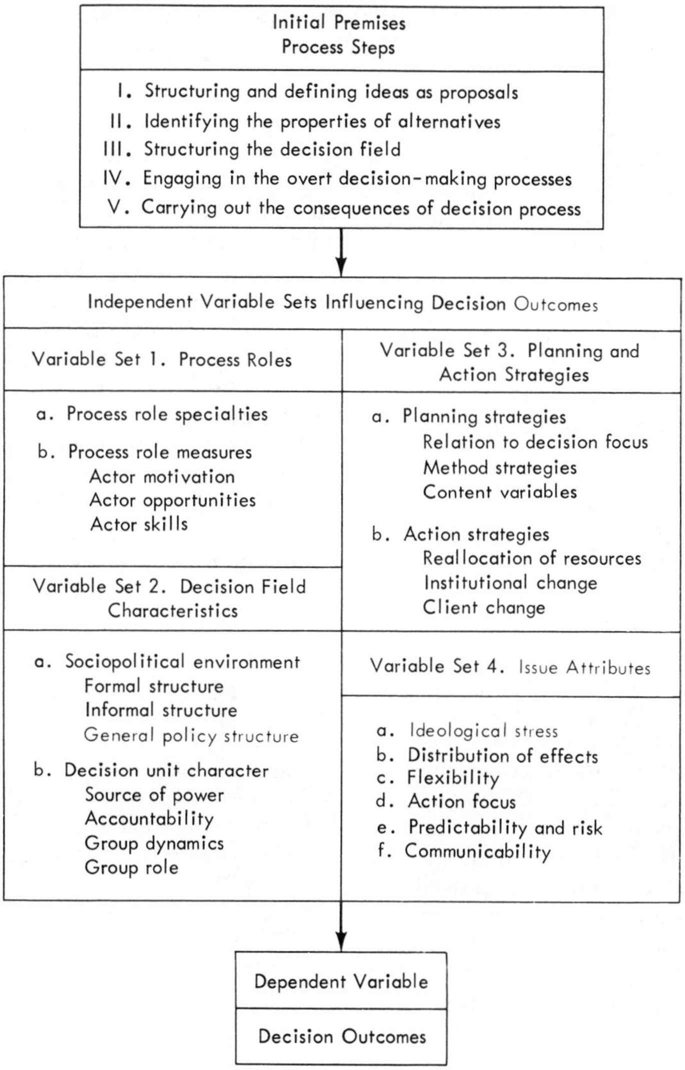

those methods to the community decision-making process and structure.[7]

Finally, *the character and origin of issues* or problems that a community undertakes to solve have a bearing on the nature of the decision-making process. Issues that create substantial ideological tension, that have significant and widespread impacts on costs and benefits, that suggest substantial changes in the distribution of power or wealth, or that entail high levels of risk are generally debated with greater intensity and over longer periods of time than are issues that are more incremental or of lesser consequence.[8]

These then, are the basic variable sets: (1) *process steps;* (2) *process roles;* (3) *a decision field* in which the decision-making process takes place; (4) *planning and intervention strategies;* and (5) *issue attributes.* The interactions of these basic sets of variables would seem to influence the character and quality of decision outcomes. (See Figure 1.)[9]

INITIAL PREMISES: THE PROCESS STEPS

Any community resolving an issue regardless of its nature must go through the decision process steps in order to reach a decision and undertake action.[10] A general outline of this process is (a) structuring and defining ideas as proposals; (b) identifying alternatives; (c) structuring the decision field; (d) engaging in social decision-making transactions; and (e) carrying out the consequences of the process. Figure 2 provides a detailed listing of the process steps. These steps are virtually identical to those in the classical concept of rationality with specific adaptations for group decision-making. Significant differences first appear after proposals and alternatives have been inserted into the system. Predicting consequences and calculating optima yield to a primary emphasis on managing and maneuvering the social processes intrinsic to collective decision making.

To one degree or another, it is assumed for the purposes of the conceptual scheme that most, if not all, of these steps must be undertaken if an urban government is to make any public policy decision. They chart the course of the process in the same manner that innings chart the course of a baseball game—although clearly in less rigid fashion. They are consequently viewed as the initial premises of the framework.

Variable Set 1: The Properties of Process Roles

Shown in Figure 1 are the major properties of process roles that actors play to carry out the process steps. The general impact of role relationships is that decision outcomes reflect the values, goals, and interests of those actors who possess the most resources, occupy a favorable position in the decision-making structure, possess the best skills in negotiating decision outcomes, and have the capacity for developing the best tactics and modes of influencing behavior.

The first major characteristic of role-playing deals with the nature of role specialization. As suggested by one recent research effort, a multitude of role specialists have been observed.[11] The listing of these key specialties for the purposes of this framework is as follows:

MAJOR PROCESS ROLES
Critic
Initiator
Planner
Technical Expert
Investigator, Analyst
Social-Emotional Expert
Strategist
Organizer
Spokesman, Advocate
Mediator, Arbitrator
Negotiator
Propagandist
Symbolic Leader
Enforcer
Evaluator

Process Step I. Structuring and Defining Ideas as Proposals
a. Recognition of discrepancy between desirable and current conditions.
b. Identification of the case as potentially actionable.
c. Formulation of possible and realizable solution(s).

Process Step II. Identifying the Properties of Alternatives
a. Inherent merits of alternative solution(s) as identified by experts.
b. The values held by individual actors.
c. The anticipated effect on the resources of the individual actors and the collectivity.[b]
d. The presumed effect on the position or status of individual actors in the social structure of the collectivity.[b]
e. The presumed availability of social support for alternative courses of action.[b]

Process Step III. Structuring the Decision Field
a. Identification of potential support and opposition.
b. Initial solicitation of support.
c. Initial negotiation informally offering the exchange of positive and negative sanctions.
d. Planning strategy for overt decision-making.
e. Organizing the necessary personnel and their resources.

Process Step IV. Engaging in the Overt Decision-Making Process (Possibly repeated at several levels or in other systems)
a. Acknowledgement of overt commitment and responsibility.
b. Involving the relevant audiences including manipulation of meanings.
c. Exchange of support and sanctions (including procedural and administrative facilitation or block).
d. Final negotiation.
e. Situated contingent action, commtting the collectivity to course of conduct.
f. Legitimation.

Process Step V. Carrying Out the Consequences of Decision Process
a. Implementation by designated persons or organizations.
b. Final application of positive or negative sanctions (payoff).
c. Appraisal of actors and power relations.
d. Appraisal of action and consequences.[b]
e. Reappraisal of program.[b]
f. Regeneration of process steps (if necessary as a result of appraisals).[b]

[a]See Reference (29) at end of article.
[b]Considered optional items, desirable and important to decision outcomes, but may be omitted. All other steps, it is assumed, must be taken if decision-making is to run its course from beginning to end.

Figure 2 Initial premises: outline of process steps.

There are many dimensions to actors' participation and skills. These involve a complete range of factors including expertise, friendship patterns, and the time and resources available to any actor in the light of competing matters requiring his attention. The specific hypothesis linking role and decision outcomes states:

An actor's ability to influence decision outcomes in a manner favorable to his own interests increases when the following attributes are present:

1. *Motivation:* The actor desires to participate because of needs for achievement, socialization, or status;
2. *Opportunity:* The actor has time, money, and situational factors that permit or require him to participate;
3. *Skills:* The actor possesses some or all of the following skill attributes:
   a. high intelligence;
   b. extensive experience in community decision-making activities;
   c. good interpersonal competence (warm, personable, well-liked);

d. good communications competence (speaks and writes well, makes effective use of symbols and media);

e. extensive knowledge of issue under discussion;

f. specific knowledge of contextual matters bearing on issue (legal background, legislative background, regulations, history, and the like); and

g. wide network of socioprofessional contacts.[12]

Variable Set 2: Decision Field Characteristics

The literature on the manner in which the decision-making environment affects decision outcomes agrees on many basic points.

Conclusions from this literature lend themselves to further synthesis. Two basic sets of factors and corresponding sets of hypotheses describing their probable influences are identified below and in Figure 3. A distinction between characteristics of the decision *environment* and characteristics of the decision *unit* is recognized. Evidence suggests the decision environment may influence a decision unit in a variety of ways. To the extent that a decision unit has identity, status, and independent power source, it will also be subject to independent internal forces.

DECISION ENVIRONMENT CHARACTERISTICS. Decision environment variables that effect decision outcomes include the following:

The formal legal structure has been well noted in the literature as being influential in urban decision-making. Generally, a highly focused and centralized decision center is more likely to produce action on a given proposal than a dispersed structure of many autonomous decision centers. Moreover, as Friedmann[13] has pointed out, a highly competent and stable bureaucracy is more likely to produce positive influences on decision outcomes than those

environments where bureaucracy is lacking or is relatively incompetent. A corollary hypothesis would be a structure with a highly articulated and respected hierarchy is more likely to produce positive action than a structure with no hierarchy.

The informal structure has been extensively described by many who have contributed to the body of political decision-making case studies of recent years. As Banfield[14] and Munger[15] point out, a community possessing a strong party mechanism is more likely to act on a proposal than a community which is nonpartisan (the party organization provides an informal mechanism for centralization). Moreover, the existence of strong private interest groups that dominate local politics means such groups will tend to influence decisions (in ways which coincide with their interests) much more than in circumstances where private interests are apathetic or dispersed. In short, as suggested by Clark,[16] communities with relatively strong integrative mechanisms for reconciling social stratification will tend to have a greater capacity for purposeful decision making.

Finally, the characteristics of the polity have a strong influence on decision outcomes for the public agenda. As Rossi[17] has pointed out, homogeneous communities tend to easily decide on goals and means to achieve them. Heterogeneous communities, where values and goals are numerous and usually conflicting, will find decision making relatively difficult. Rossi also makes a distinction between a "crystallized" community and a "noncrystallized" community. In the former, cleavages in values and public opinion tend to coincide with economic and class structure. Where this is true and where one class has clear political dominance over others, that class tends to dominate decision outcomes. A noncrystallized community (or a crystallized community in perfect political balance) tends to lead to indecision and inaction.

DECISION ENVIRONMENT CHARACTERISTICS	TENDING TOWARD ACTION	TENDING TOWARD INACTION
Formal-legal Structure	Focused decision center	Dispersed decision centers (22)[a]
	Highly competent bureaucracy	Incompetent or lacking bureaucracy (24)
	Articulated hierarchy	No hierarchy (8)
Informal Structure	Strong party machine	Nonpartisan (3,14)
	Elite or interest group dominance	Amorphous (32)
Characteristics of Polity	Homogeneous	Heterogeneous (8,32)
	Crystallized	Noncrystallized (6,32)
	Tradition free	Tradition laden (24)
	Striving	Prosperous or settled (24)

DECISION UNIT CHARACTERISTICS		
Source of Power	Appointed body	Elected body (16,30)
Accountability	Large clientele	Small or specialized clientele (18)
	Long term of office	Short term of office (18)
Group Dynamics	Socially cohesive	Socially heterogeneous (6)
	Significant reward-punishment schema	Insignificant reward-punishment schema (3)
	High status	Low status
	High functional role differentiation	Little or no role differentiation
Group Role	Focused	Comprehensive

[a]Numerals refer to references at end of article.

Figure 3 Hypotheses on the impact of the decision field on decision outcomes

As Friedmann[18] has suggested, a populace relatively free of long-standing traditions (such as urban areas on the U.S. West Coast) is more prone to action than a mature, settled, and tradition-laden community. A corollary hypothesis would suggest that a striving community is more likely to take positive action on issues and proposals than a prosperous or settled community. This hypothesis is clearly related to the degree to which a populace is aroused and concerned about the public agenda.

DECISION UNIT CHARACTERISTICS. As previously indicated, governmental decision-making is a function unlikely to be delegated to a single individual. The most usual circumstance is decision-making by groups of individuals. These groups may be relatively unorganized in any formal sense and brought together on a purely ad hoc basis. Conversely, they may be long-standing, highly organized units of government (such as a legislative body) with internal characteristics of their own, set traditions of procedure, and well-defined social mores. Some of the factors that would be influential are listed in Figure 3 and suggest the following hypotheses.

Of importance is the source of power for the decision-making unit. The more stable and unthreatened the decision unit, the more likely it is to take positive action on proposals. Thus an appointed body whose accountability is somewhat obscure is more prone to action than an elected body whose mandate is continually challenged at the polls. Accountability itself has an influence. One might expect a decision-making unit with a large clientele and long term of office to be more prone to positive action than a decision-making group with a specialized clientele and a short term of office (the upper house of a legislature versus the lower house, for example).

Internal dynamics greatly influence group actions.[19] Socially cohesive bodies are more prone to take action on issues within the group's value preference field than are socially heterogenous groups. This arises because of the pressures for conformity within such groups. For example, a legislative body, such as an upper house, whose members represent significantly large and heterogenous populations and hold long terms of office, becomes a socially cohesive organization. Consequently, it is more prone to positive outcomes than a legislative body whose members represent a wide variety of small populations and hold short terms of office.

Within groups where rewards and punishments are significant, one would anticipate a strong incentive for action. Conversely, if rewards and punishments are insignificant, one expects a stronger force for inaction. This suggests that the reward and punishment system represents a set of highly sensitive pressures on the behavior of group members.

Internal role differentiation might also tend to produce positive action. Examples of this are the highly structured committees of a legislative body (such as the Congress) whose individual members become specialists in the committee's work. The committee itself becomes a kind of interest group or spokesman for those who share the specialty. With strong role differentia-

tion, the recommendations of the smaller group (the committee) tend to dominate and sway the actions of the larger group.

Finally, the group role as seen by the group tends to influence its behavior. A group (such as a regulatory body) that sees its role as highly specialized and focused within a carefully circumscribed arena of action is more likely to act positively on proposals (which fall within that sphere of action) than a group that has a broader, more comprehensive area of responsibility (such as a legislative body).

Variable Set 3: Planning and Intervention Strategies

It is hypothesized that generally the manner and degree to which a public issue is seen and understood will influence the decision outcome. The amount of information brought to bear, the way it is introduced, and the actors involved in presenting information affect the kinds of decisions that might be expected. The detailed variables and their related hypotheses are outlined below and in Figure 4.

PLANNING STRATEGIES. Three general variables influence planning strategies as outlined in an earlier paper.[20] The first is the strategic variable of planning *position* in which attachment to a power center is hypothesized to be more influential in guiding or directing public decision making than independent and advisory planning bodies. A second factor is planning *method* where it is hypothesized that problem solving of an incremental or opportunistic character is more likely to guide or direct public action than comprehensive classical methods of planning that place great stress on identifying and quantifying interdependencies and related complexities among a variety of systems. The third variable influencing planning strategies is planning *content*. It is hypothesized that planning which deals with the immediate, focuses on means, and deals only with

PLANNING STRATEGIES	TENDING TO GUIDE OR DIRECT ACTION	TENDING TO MINIMUM EFFECT ON ACTION
Position Variable	Attachment to power center	Independent and advisory (3,15,23,24)[a]
Method Variables	Ad hoc opportunism	Comprehensive (24)
	Problem-solving	Classical focus on interdependencies (7,18)
	Incremental	
Content Variables	Immediate time horizon	Long-term time horizon (24)
	Means oriented	Goal oriented (7)
	Selected and focused information	Comprehensive information system (7)
Action or Intervention Strategies	Efforts to maintain distribution of resources	Efforts to reallocate distribution of resources (31)
	Efforts to change or modify individual behavior	Efforts to change or modify societal behavior (31)
	Efforts to bring about change with existing institutions and organizations	Efforts to alter existing institutions and organizations (31)

[a]Numerals refer to references at end of article.

Figure 4 Hypotheses on the impact of planning strategies on decision outcomes

highly selective and narrowly strategic information is more likely to guide or direct action than planning which looks to a long-term time horizon, is goal oriented, and focuses on comprehensive and complex systems of information. Most planners undoubtedly wish that these hypotheses could be proved incorrect, and determining the conditions under which they might be proved wrong is a key object of further

ACTION STRATEGIES. Three variables are at work here much in keeping with the action strategies recently outlined by Rein.[21] These strategies include (1) efforts to reallocate the distribution of resources; (2) efforts to change individual or societal behavior; and (3) efforts to change institutions and organizations within society. The guiding hypothesis is that action strategies which little disturb the status quo are more likely to be adopted by a political system. This would mean efforts to bring about social change that maintain the existing

distribution of resources and/or the present structure of institutions and organizations would more likely be accepted than those that seek major reallocation of wealth or power. Similarly, programs that are designed to change individual circumstances (such as social security) tend more toward action than programs that attempt massive changes in aggregate societal behavior (such as prohibition).

Variable Set 4: Characteristics of Public Issues

The general hypothesis relating to how public agenda characteristics influence decision outcomes is that positive action can usually be expected in any decision system where proposals are easily predictable in their consequences; are easily accomplished (both economically and administratively); and generally lie within a social value or preference field. What this means in specific terms lies in the influences of six basic variables affecting decision outcomes, shown schematically in Figure 5.

	TENDING TOWARD ACTION	TENDING TOWARD INACTION
Agenda Characteristics	Nonideological	Highly ideological (7, 13, 23)[a]
	Limited distribution of costs and benefits; limited scope	Wide distribution of costs and benefits; wide scope (7)
	Flexible over time	Irreversible; inflexible over time (7)
	Single focus for action programming	Dispersed focus for action programming (24)
	Consequences easily predictable	Consequences highly uncertain (1)
	Features of issue easily communicable	Features of issue abstract and complex (10)

[a]Numerals refer to references at end of article.

Figure 5 Hypotheses on the impact of the nature of the public agenda on decision outcomes

The ideological content of a proposal for change will influence the decision outcome. If there is little conflict over basic values implicit in a proposal, then it is hypothesized that there will be a greater tendency toward positive action. However, should a proposal seriously conflict with widely held values, then there will be a tendency toward rejection. If, for example, an urban government proposes to acquire all land and buildings by eminent domain and thereby eliminate private property within its borders, there would most likely be vigorous resistance in virtually all urban areas in the United States. In essence, communities are not likely to easily cut off widely held social values.

The second variable relates to distribution and scope of costs and benefits that are likely to occur if action is taken on a given proposal. This involves not only how many people are influenced by the proposal but how much they are influenced. Generally speaking, proposals involving wide and broad distribution and a substantial measure of intensity of costs and benefits are usually rejected in the political process. Proposals involving only limited costs and benefits as well as limited intensity are more likely to be accepted. More simply, political systems will tend to reject a proposal that costs a lot of people a lot of money and accept one that costs a few people a little money.

The third variable is the flexibility of action intrinsic to a proposal. If a proposal is irreversible or inflexible over time, it is more likely to be rejected than a proposal that can later be changed in proved inappropriate or in need of modification. Urban expressways provide an example of irreversible decisions, while a new educational program is an example of a decision that may be easily changed or adjusted in the light of later experience.

The fourth variable deals with the problem of programming action. If carrying out the proposal involves a great deal of coordination among a large number of dispersed and autonomous groups, it is more likely to be resisted and eventually rejected (largely because of uncertainty that it will actually be carried out as proposed). Even if adopted, it may easily be subverted in implementation. Proposals that concentrate or focus action within a single agency or a relatively few individuals and involve few external coordination problems will more likely be adopted.

Dealing with uncertainty clearly affects the decision-making process. This is true not only in political systems but in other more tightly controlled group circumstances as well. Where risks are high and consequences uncertain there is hesitancy to act. If on the other hand, consequences are easily predictable and risks minimized (and all other factors are favorable), positive decisions are readily reached.

Finally, ease of communication is a key variable. Issues that are abstract and require sophisticated power of conceptual reasoning are less likely to be communicated well (and are thus rejected) than issues that can be clearly perceived and understood by the actors who will have to deal with them. This is an important variable that is easily overlooked. Difficulty in communication can be equally, if not more, detrimental to decision making than lack of communication. A recent seminar at Boston College brought together a number of protagonists involved in an issue which generated one of the major riots in the ghetto of an eastern city (Newark, New Jersey) in the summer of 1967. Observing these actors was like observing those in the movie *Rashomon*. Each perceived and interpreted the same set of facts and circumstances in an entirely different way.

CULTURAL DYNAMICS

In any given governmental planning-decision-making environment, individual hypotheses are presumably exerting individual influences on decision outcomes. In addition, it could be expected that one might find interactions (and collinearity) between independent variables. Moreover, such interactions could occur at various levels. For example, an agenda item that is nonideological, predictable, inexpensive, and easy to accomplish may still be rejected because of interactions arising from particular interest group resistance. Moreover, interaction may occur on three different "vertical" levels with (1) formal public pronouncements and positions taken at formal ceremonies required by law (hearings, legislative sessions, and so on); (2) informal group activities (such as partisan cau-

cuses); and (3) independent activities of individual actors. In addition, "horizontal" influences may be present in which a given agenda item may be linked to another simultaneously occurring agenda item. This linking could occur in a variety of ways, such as a "technical" linkage (one issue is related to another in some logical, substantive way) or purely "political" linkage (such as log rolling—"You vote for my bill, and I'll vote for yours").

An additional complication in the dynamics of the structure occurs when more than one decision unit must act on a given agenda item. This provision is frequently built into federal grant-in-aid programs to ensure coordination; for example, a prerequisite for a water or sewer grant is approval of the local project by a metropolitan planning agency. In this instance, the process flow in Figure 1 would take on additional complicating elements; namely, the addition of more decision units—some at different levels of government—with different functions, different traditions and styles of operation, and different internal social attributes.

One can, in fact, envision for complex issues an entire network of decision units, including some completely outside the community. Thus for a given issue in a particular urban area, one would find a variety of circumstances with respect to issue attributes, planning and action strategies, and internal and external environmental pressures.

Another important dimension is the possibility of feedback throughout the system. For example, generation of issues has been suggested to occur through sources both internal and external to the system.[22] Thus an issue might be generated by planners and strategists, by actors within the decision field, or by actors within the general polity. Issues may be redefined or reformulated and consequently regenerated through the system before actual decisions are reached. Issues may experience unfavorable outcomes (inaction) at first and later be reintroduced with resulting favorable actions.

IMPLICATIONS AND CONCLUSIONS

This description of the conceptual framework of the culture of urban planning is, at best, a preliminary and tentative one in which many of the variables require more precise definition. It is also clear that development of objective measurement scales for each of the variables is an immediate and formidable task. Specific relationships between variables are not as yet seen precisely. The design of empirical research and analysis will be equally complex and demanding.

If, however, in advance of extensive empirical testing, the conceptual scheme can be imagined to reasonably reflect reality, it seems possible to formulate a number of potential implications for the urban planner if he is to adapt his theory and practice to the framework.

Process Versus Substance

The framework suggests very strongly the delicate nature of the relationship and balance between the substance and process of planning. It reinforces the notion that one cannot be emphasized at the expense of the other. The planner who approaches the cultural framework with technical expertise alone soon finds others' perception of his role quite narrow and his operating arena and impact highly circumscribed. He may be viewed as effective but only on certain restricted issues. On the other hand, focusing on process alone limits the planner to symbolic emotional support roles and unduly hampers his capacity for professional judgment as to feasibility of means and ends in any given problem situation. The framework points up the need for a planning function in the community

fully capable of effectively coping with both in proper degree and balance.

Impact on the Substance of Planning

The substance of planning is clearly affected by the scheme in quite serious ways. If the hypotheses in any way reflect actual tendencies, the thrust of such effects pushes toward developing a balance between short-run and long-run vistas, between selective and comprehensive prescription, and toward a deeper understanding of the importance of incremental decision making and negotiated conflict resolution. Since planning attempts to deal with rather profound policy matters for the urban community, it should come as no surprise that it has all the attributes of a legislative process even if in an administrative or even purely informal context.

Thus our concepts of optimality, our focus on an abstract welfare function, and our concern for an illusory greater good (or "public interest") is brought into serious question by the framework. Planning is being challenged more and more, not on its service to an overall public but rather on the differential and distributional aspects of its results affecting particular publics. Who actually pays and who actually benefits from community development programs are usually the crucial problems facing the decision-making apparatus of the urban community. Aggregate measures of this arouse only academic interest. Too often in the past the beneficiaries of a program have been an entirely different group than the group paying the price. We are generally unable to arrive at some means of restoring equity because in our preoccupation with an overall public interest, we have failed to explore and understand these distributional effects.

Reconciliation of conflicting goals, values, interests, and even drastically different concepts of discounting the future is an intrinsic part of planned social change. Thus analytical techniques emphasizing the concepts of marginality and differential incidence become paramount to the planner's kit of methodological tools. These will likely provide greater utility and relevance in the social transactions of a real-world planning process. The concept of suboptimality proved highly advantageous in the technological setting of the Department of Defense; in the social-cultural framework envisioned here, it would seem essential if the wide and complex array of publics in the urban community are to find any mechanism at all for decision making.

Authority for Planning

The conceptual scheme strongly suggests traditional notions of position and power as bases of authority and leadership cannot be divorced from less formal mechanisms for legitimating authority and exercising power.[23] With the multitude of roles and the complex array of skill dimensions, an urban planner is usually faced with an inability to assume all speaking parts in the play. Even assuming he had the skills, he would likely find it impracticable to assemble the necessary resources. Thus he is inevitably faced with the problem of *coordinating* and *motivating* others in their participation in the decision-making process.

With relatively few exceptions, the American urban community has so fragmented and dispersed authority that the proponent of any program or plan is forced into informal arrangements for exercising leadership and influencing decision making. It helps to be in a position of authority if this can be arranged, but it is still no guarantee of success. Thus skill in inducing motivation, in coordinating others' actions, and in building concensus in a contextually appropriate coalition (without recourse to coercion) is demanded of those

who wish to see a proposal through to a favorable decision outcome.

This clearly is a massive task, as anyone who is attempting to direct a Community Action Program or Model Cities effort can attest. It seems to have the best chance for success when the planner enjoys a wide range of social acceptability and is generally identified with the community's dominant norms and the values.[24] The conceptual scheme described here would also seem to suggest that the proposal itself cannot be too far removed from the norms and values of the relevant community.

Training of Planners

Finally, the conceptual framework seems to suggest training orientations in the education of planners quite different from those found in the traditional city planning curriculum. On the one hand, more sophisticated techniques in such areas as operations research, development of heuristic models, and other emerging planning tools still provide an essential element of planning training but with a new focus on subsystem analysis and . . . research into problems of incidence and differential effects of city-building activities. On the other hand, however, quite unlike the methods of architectural design, the development of social designs emphasizes training in interpersonal skills, social interaction theory, group dynamics, political theory, communications theory, and community organization. It suggests more effort at structured and supervised field or "intern" experiences in actual social decision-making settings.

In short, many of the educational thrusts suggested in a recent *Journal* article by Brooks and Stegman[25] are reinforced in our examination of the cultural setting. The Brooks and Stegman argument, however, suggests these educational reorientations *because* of the issues of the day. The conceptual scheme presented here implies these kinds of educational reforms are essential *regardless* of the issues of the day. This lack has contributed to many past failures when planning had no significant impact on urban policy-making.

Finally, to paraphrase Roscoe Pound, city planning, like law, is judged by its results, not by its logical processes. But results and logical processes are inextricably linked by the social milieu in which both are operating. The conceptual scheme presented here is an effort to develop a more detailed and useful understanding of these relationships. Built in are the mechanisms for beginning to examine and test alternative strategies and methods of urban planning with explicit recognition of process steps, process roles, and environmental and social climate influences. Even beyond this, however, it is hoped that the framework can provide a forward step in explanatory power in a highly complex area of human behavior that exerts crucial influences in restricting or expanding opportunities to develop better urban communities.

NOTES

1. See Lawrence D. Mann, "Studies in Community Decision Making," *Journal of the American Institute of Planners*, XXX (February 1964), 58–65.
2. The comments of Norton Long are appropriate to this outlook: "The question 'Who Governs?' has proved in the end rather less interesting than expected. In a sense it has been a blind alley arising from the obsession with when can it be shown that 'A' has power over 'B' and the understandable desire to refute the social science fiction of C. Wright Mills and Floyd Hunter. . . . This could lead to looking at the process of governing and its consequences rather than at the consequences of the specific acts of prestigious personages with top roles in the system." From "Political Science and the City," Leo F. Schnore and Henry Fagin (eds.), *Urban Research and Policy Planning* (Beverly Hills, California: Sage Publications, 1967), p. 252.
3. See Herbert Simon, *Administrative Behavior* (New York: The Free Press, 1965), chaps. 3–5.
4. Martin Meyerson and Edward Banfield, *Politics, Planning, and the Public Interest* (Glencoe, Illinois: The Free Press, 1955), pp. 312–22; David Braybrook and Charles Lindblom, *A Strategy of Decision* (New York: The Free Press, 1963), pp. 37–41; John Friedmann, "The Institutional Context" in Bertram Gross (ed.), *Action Under Planning* (New York: McGraw-Hill, Inc., 1967), p. 34.
5. Roscoe Martin, et al., *Decisions in Syracuse* (Bloomington: Indiana University Press, 1961), pp. 311–12; Ronald L. Nuttall, Erwin Scheuch, and Chad Gordon, "The Structure of Influence" in Terry N. Clark (ed.), *Community Structure and Decision-Making* (San Francisco: Chandler Publishing Co., 1968); and William A. Gamson, "Reputation and Resources in Community Politics," *American Journal of Sociology*, LXXII, No. 2 (September 1966), pp. 121–31.
6. See Ibid.; Clark, *Community Structure and Decision-Making*, chaps. 1–5; and Roland Warren, "The Interorganizational Field as Focus for Investigation," *Administrative Science Quarterly*, XII, No. 3 (December 1967), pp. 397–403.
7. Ibid., Friedmann, "The Institutional Context," pp. 31–41.
8. Richard S. Bolan, "Emerging Views of Planning," *Journal of the American Institute of Planners*, XXXIII (July 1967), 233–45.
9. The model is somewhat similar to that of Robert Alford in "Comparative Study of Urban Politics" in Schnore and Fagin (eds.) *Urban Research and Policy Planning*. Those classes of variables that he labels "structure" and "culture" are viewed here as a part of the general classes of variables of the decision field. The "situation" variables would be included here as part of the plan and action systems. See pp. 264–71.
10. These process steps are adapted from the process model described in Nuttall, Scheuch, and Gordon, "The Structure of Influence," pp. 351–52.
11. Ibid.
12. See, R. F. Bales, *Interaction Process Analysis: A Method for the Study of Small Groups* (Cambridge, Mass.: Addison-Wesley Press, 1950); John M. Pfiffner and Robert Presthus, *Public Administration*, fifth edition, (New York: The Ronald Press Company, 1967), chap. 5; Robert Presthus, "Authority in Organizations," *Public Administration Review*, XX (Spring 1960), 86–92; Ralph M. Stogdill, "Personal Factors Associated with Leadership: A Survey of the Literature," *Journal of Psychology*, XXV (January 1948), 60–66; Peter M. Blau and W. Richard Scott, *Formal Organizations* (San Francisco: Chandler Publishing Company, 1962), pp. 87–130; James W. Julian, Edwin P. Hollander, and C. Robert Regula, "Endorsement of the Group Spokesman as a Function of His Source of Authority, Competence and Success," *Journal of Personality and So-*

cial Psychology, XI (January 1969), 42–49; and various authors, "Personality and Politics: Theoretical and Methodological Issues," *The Journal of Social Issues,* XXIV, No. 3 (July 1968).

13. Friedmann, "The Institutional Context," chap. 2, p. 41.
14. Edward C. Banfield, *Political Influence* (New York: The Free Press, 1965), p. 237.
15. Martin, et al., *Decisions in Syracuse,* p. 46.
16. Clark, *Community Structure and Decision-Making,* chap. 2.
17. Peter H. Rossi, "Power and Community Structure," in Edward C. Banfield (ed.), *Urban Government: A Reader in Administration and Politics* (New York: The Free Press, 1961), pp. 418–19.
18. Friedmann, "The Institutional Context," chap. 2, p. 40.
19. Dorwin Cartwright and Ronald Lippitt, "Group Dynamics and the Individual," in Warren Bennis, Kenneth Benne, and Robert Chin (eds.), *The Planning of Change* (New York: Holt, Rinehart, and Winston, 1961), pp. 269–72; S. E. Seashore, "Group Cohesiveness in the Industrial Group" (Institute for Social Research, University of Michigan, Ann Arbor, 1954); and Leon Festinger, Stanley Schachter, and Kurt Back, *Social Pressures in Informal Groups* (New York: Harpers, 1950).
20. Bolan, "Emerging Views of Planning," pp. 237–43.
21. Martin Rein, "Social Science and the Elimination of Poverty," *Journal of the American Institute of Planners,* XXXIII (May 1967) 146–63.
22. Bolan, "Emerging Views of Planning," pp. 236–37.
23. Pfiffner and Presthus, *Public Administration,* chap. 5.
24. Presthus, "Authority in Organizations."
25. Michael P. Brooks and Michael A. Stegman, "Urban Social Policy, Race, and the Education of Planners," *Journal of the American Institute of Planners,* XXXIV (September 1968), 275–86.

SELECTED REFERENCES

Books

ALTSHULER, ALAN. *The City Planning Process: A Political Analysis.* Ithaca, New York: Cornell University Press, 1965.

BALES, ROBERT F. *Interaction Process Analysis: A Method for the Study of Small Groups.* Cambridge, Massachusetts: Addison-Wesley Press, 1950.

BANFIELD, EDWARD C. *Political Influence.* New York: Free Press, 1961.

BANFIELD, EDWARD C. (ed.). *Urban Government: A Reader in Administration and Politics.* New York: The Free Press, 1961.

BLAU, PETER M. and W. RICHARD SCOTT. *Formal Organizations.* San Francisco: Chandler Publishing Co., 1962.

BENNIS, WARREN, KENNETH BENNE, and ROBERT CHIN (eds.). *The Planning of Change.* New York: Holt, Rinehart and Winston, 1961.

BRAYBROOKE, DAVID and CHARLES LINDBLOM. *A Strategy of Decision.* New York: The Free Press, 1963.

CLARK, TERRY N. (ed.). *Community Structure and Decision-Making: Comparative Analysis.* San Francisco: Chandler Publishing Co., 1968.

DAHL, ROBERT A. *Who Governs.* New Haven: Yale University Press, 1961.

FAGIN, HENRY and LEO F. SCHNORE (eds.). *Urban Research and Policy Planning.* Urban Affairs Annual Reviews, Volume 1, Beverly Hills, California: Sage Publications, Inc., 1967.

FESTINGER, LEON, STANLEY SCHACHTER, and KURT BACK. *Social Pressures in Informal Groups.* New York: Harper, 1950.

GROSS, BERTRAM M. *Action Under Planning.* New York: McGraw-Hill, 1967.

MARRIS, PETER and MARTIN REIN. *The Dilemmas of Social Reform.* New York: Atherton Press, 1967.

MARTIN, ROSCOE, et al., *Decisions in Syracuse.* Bloomington: University of Indiana Press, 1961.

MEYERSON, MARTIN and EDWARD BANFIELD. *Politics, Planning and the Public Interest.* New York: The Free Press, 1955.

PFIFFNER, JOHN M. and ROBERT PRESTHUS. *Public Administration.* fifth edition, New York: The Ronald Press Company, 1967.

SIMON, HERBERT. *Administrative Behavior.* 2nd edition, New York: MacMillian Co., 1961.

WILDAVSKY, AARON. *The Politics of the Budgetary Process.* Boston: Little, Brown and Co., 1964.

Articles

ALFORD, ROBERT. "The Comparative Study of Urban Politics" in Fagin and Schnore.

BOLAN, RICHARD S. "Emerging Views of

Planning," *Journal of the American Institute of Planners,* XXXIII (July 1967), 233–45.

BROOKS, MICHAEL P. and MICHAEL A. STEGMAN. "Urban Social Policy, Race, and the Education of Planners," *Journal of the American Institute of Planners,* XXXIV (September 1968), 275–86.

DAHL, ROBERT A. "The Politics of Planning," *International Social Science Journal,* XI, No. 3 (1959).

FRIEDMANN, JOHN. "The Study and Practice of Planning," *International Social Science Journal,* XI, No. 3 (1959).

FRIEDMANN, JOHN. "The Institutional Context," in Gross.

GAMSON, WILLIAM A. "Reputation and Resources in Community Politics," *American Journal of Sociology,* LXXII (September 1966) 121–31.

JULIAN, JAMES W., EDWIN P. HOLLANDER, and C. ROBERT REGULA. "Endorsement of the Group Spokesman as a Function of his Source of Authority, Competence and Success," *Journal of Personality and Social Psychology,* XI, (January 1969), 42–49.

LONG, NORTON. "Political Science and the City," in Fagin and Schnore.

MANN, LAWRENCE D. "Studies in Community Decision-Making," *Journal of the American Institute of Planners,* XXX (February 1964), 58–65.

NUTTALL, RONALD L., ERWIN SCHEUCH, and CHAD GORDON. "On the Structure of Influence," in Terry N. Clark.

PRESTHUS, ROBERT. "Authority in Organizations," *Public Administration Review.* XX, (Spring 1960) 86–92.

REIN, MARTIN. "Social Science and the Elimination of Poverty," *Journal of the American Institute of Planners,* XXXIII, No. 3 (May 1967), 146–63.

ROSSI, PETER. "Power and Community Structure," in Banfield.

STOGDILL, RALPH M. "Personal Factors Associated With Leadership: A Survey of the Literature," *Journal of Psychology,* XXV (January 1948), 60–6.

WARREN, ROLAND L. "The Interorganizational Field as a Focus for Investigation," *Administrative Science Quarterly,* XII, No. 3 (December 1967) 396–419.

Various authors. "Personality and Politics: Theoretical and Methodological Issues," *The Journal of Social Issues,* XXIV, No. 3 (July 1968).

Arnold J. Meltsner

Don't Slight Communication: Some Problems of Analytical Practice

Analysis is a social process. Normative accounts implying that analysis is some objective exercise uninfluenced by human feelings, values, and beliefs could not be more mistaken. Analysis is produced by people operating in social contexts. Analysts work together as colleagues to produce analysis. They consult one another

Reprinted with permission of the author and The Regents from *Policy Analysis* 5:3 (Summer 1979), pp. 367–92. Copyright 1979 by the Regents of the University of California.

and review one another's work. They interact with many people besides analysts to secure data and to understand different perceptions of a problem. They report to a client whose values and predispositions strongly affect the conduct and outcome of analysis. With that client's support and sometimes without it, they disseminate their results to many people. That analysis is a social process is at no time more apparent than when we try to communicate the results of our work.

By *communication*, I mean the act of gaining acceptance and asserting a claim on another person's beliefs. Now this definition is inadequate, and I am sure it will not satisfy those who are used to the jargon of sources, messages, channels, and receivers. Its ambiguity allows me to stress a number of points, however. First, communication involves human interaction; in its simplest form, communication between an analyst and his immediate client is the relationship of two people.[1] Neither participant can completely control this relationship or determine its effectiveness. Second, my subject here is one side of this relationship—namely, the analyst and his means of gaining acceptance for himself and his work. Third, I interpret the results of analytical work to be "assertions" about reality or desirable changes to reality. These "assertions" may or may not be grounded in theory and evidence. In either case, the analyst makes a claim on his client or the person with whom he is trying to communicate. "A man who makes an assertion puts forward a claim," S. E. Toulmin informs us, "a claim on our attention and to our belief. Unlike one who speaks frivolously, . . . a man who asserts something intends his statement to be taken seriously."[2]

In making my own assertions about communication, I have felt the lack of empirical literature dealing with the communication of *analytical* information. Ideally I would have liked to discuss a range of behaviors associated with communication. This range could be determined by the kind of analyst (policy analyst, systems analyst, planner, and so forth), the analyst's role in a specific organizational context (say, a research technician working as a contractor for a large governmental agency), the type of client (perhaps a business executive with little patience), and the choice of different means of communication (such as memoranda, briefings, formal reports, movies). Instead I have fallen back on my own experience in working with governmental agencies and have sought to identify common errors in communication that cut across the wide range of possible analytical behavior.

Generally communication has two highly interrelated parts: social and substantive. One way to understand the distinction between them is to think of the skills of the analyst. Writing and speaking are social, while modeling and analyzing data are substantive; formulating and defining a problem require both substantive and social skills. The social part, the context in which communication takes place, encompasses such factors as the persuasiveness and credibility of the analyst, the feelings of trust between analyst and client, and the extent to which values and beliefs are shared by the analyst and his various audiences. The substantive part has to do with the logic and content of the study itself, with the validity and reliability of the knowledge it contains, and with its policy and organizational implications. When an adequate study is believed and accepted or when an inadequate study is not believed and is rejected, the substantive and social parts of communication usually are compatible—and the acceptance or rejection can be validated for the analyst by his peers. When the analyst perceives a problem of communication, the two parts usually are incompatible. This may mean, for example, that the analysis contains an adequate policy direction for the given context but fails to convince or gain the acceptance of the client. Or it may mean—a problem analysts sometimes ignore—that the analysis contains misleading information, yet the client accepts it.

In the situation of easy rejection the analysis fits the imperatives of the organizational context. It follows the canons of current analytical practice; it is adequate in the sense that most analysts would have done it in the same way if in the same environment. Yet the client and other organizational decision makers are not willing to accept either the study's assessment of a problem or its recommendations. In the situation of easy acceptance the study does not follow the standard practice; it is inadequate in the sense that other analysts would have done it in a different way if in the same environment. If they were asked to judge the study, they might call the analysis "sloppy" or "incomplete." Neither the analyst nor the client may be aware that the study's information is misleading and inappropriate for the organization. Nevertheless, the client and other organizational decision makers accept the implications of the study and act on them. For the client, the analysis as presented does fit the imperatives of the organizational context. Thus communication problems can be depicted simply, as in Figure 1.

Accepting inadequate information is a serious problem for the client. Of course, many clients are too intelligent and perspicacious to be easily deceived, but some can be. Other than developing the skills to evaluate analytical products, assessing analysts on the basis of their past records, and resorting to multiple and independent sources of information, a client can do little to protect himself against a social context that encourages his tendency to accept what he is being told. The analyst also has something to lose in this situation. In his desire to promote his study, he may be trading off short-term acceptance for long-term ridicule by his peers and abuse

Figure 1 Problems of communication occur when the social and substantive parts of communication are incompatible.

SOCIAL

		Credible	Noncredible
SUBSTANTIVE	Adequate	No communication problem	Easy rejection
	Inadequate	Easy acceptance	No communication problem

by his client if the recommendations of the study do not have the intended effect. In short, the social part of communication may have an empty victory over the substantive part.

A more familiar problem—and my chief concern here—is the domination of the social by the substantive: quality studies are rejected because the social part of communication is slighted. A number of years ago Kahn and Mann identified the pitfall of "hermitism": "The problems of communication and persuasion are often ignored though they are central to getting recommendations translated into policy."[3] According to them, the analyst must have the ability "to sell" his study and must spend a great deal of time doing so. Usually some member of an analytical team writes well, talks well, or has the personal attributes to secure the trust of a number of clients and decision makers. The ability is there, but what is often lacking is an appreciation of the extensive time and effort that must be devoted to communication if it is to be persuasive.

Besides underestimating the resource requirements for communicating—money, as well as time and effort—analysts frequently misunderstand when to spend these resources. All too often, only when a lengthy project nears completion does the analytical staff belatedly turn its attention to documenting results and disseminating recommendations. Considerable resources are expended on publications, illustrations, charts, slides, and other paraphernalia of professional systems and policy analysis. Yet much of this effort may be wasted because such communication is an afterthought of analysis. In order to be effective, communication must be an integral part of the analytical activity itself. As a relationship communication is a two-way process: the participants must have the opportunity to listen to each other. Therefore, to enhance the receptivity of an analysis and also to obtain information and other assistance, the analyst should involve the client and other likely members of the study's audience in the project from the beginning. Determining who will be members of the study's audience and sizing up their perceptions of the problem are communication strategies central to the initial steps of analysis.

Unfortunately, far too many analysts perceive communication as something outside analysis. Even such an experienced practitioner as Edward Quade makes this mistake when he identifies some failures of communicating with a client as "external pitfalls" or "factors or actions that handicap the analysis but do not originate within the analysis itself."[4] Some handicaps do result from the analysis itself; for example, a tight and logically structured analysis is easier to communicate than one that is loose and fuzzy. And a model that represents reality with simplicity but without doing violence to that reality will be easier for a client to understand and accept. For some purposes it is useful to make inside-outside distinctions, but in the case of communication to do so is dysfunctional to our understanding of the analytical process. Communication and analysis are interdependent activities. Not to recognize this interdependence and its social implications is a primary error. Difficulties in communication are inherent in situations where there is conflict over values, objectives, and beliefs. Although a certain amount of rejection of quality work is to be expected, the difficulties in communication should become less severe as the participants in analysis begin to appreciate the social context of their endeavors.

Having pointed out the importance of understanding communication as part of the social process of analysis, I will now discuss certain errors involved in the conception and choice of *audience* (recipients), *argument* (content and form), and *means* (techniques and media) of communicating analysis.

AUDIENCE

Although the choice of whom to communicate with is a central decision, it is one that analysts too often leave to the client. They may not be given a choice, but in order to improve the effectiveness of communication, analysts should not let this decision be made by default. Once they commit themselves to getting involved in the making of this decision, analysts will see that what is needed is a strategy for selecting and sequencing audiences. Such a strategy is not a simple matter to devise. It encompasses an appreciation of the organizational context of the analysis and of the fact that neither the client nor the analyst is the sole audience. The audience for analysis is seldom a single person.

Ignoring the Organizational Context

Analysis is conducted in an organizational context. All too often analysts sit "outside" the organization and have little exposure to the organizational imperatives that will influence their communications. To be outside means that the analysts are located so as to be *distant* from critical information and cues. Contractors and consultants often have this problem, but so do employees. For example, analysts who work, as employees, for the head of a large complex organization may be quite naive about the rest of the organization. They may not understand that the rest of the organization not only is a source of information but also has to be included, in some way, in the calculations about the audience for analytical communication. To convince the client is hardly sufficient when acceptance and implementation rest on these other members of the organization. What are some of the organizational factors that influence the conduct of analysis and its communication?

One important factor is time. Through its routines and rules the organization sets the schedule for the analysis. Such rules not only place constraints on performance but also establish when it will be best to communicate. For example, an analysis that is intended to influence a decision obviously should be presented before that decision is made and frozen. If the analysis is predicated on reallocating resources, it may be necessary to be aware of budgetary routines in order to catch the appropriate part of the cycle of financial management. Analysts can be highly proficient in the art of communication, but if they have little sense of time—that is, if they do not know . when it is opportune to communicate—their skills will not be worth much.

Another important factor is organizational structure and its capacity to absorb information. Over the years, an organization will develop a certain structure for the processing of work. Let us consider a fairly typical one, a hierarchy composed of many levels, specialized offices, and centralized decision making. As part of its processing of work, such a structure also processes large quantities of data. In so doing it also absorbs and filters that data. Hence an analytical report that is inserted into the organization will be modified as it goes through numerous levels before reaching its final destination. Modifications can take place as each level either rewrites the report or encloses transmittal memoranda that select certain aspects of the report for treatment. This digesting of data occurs simply to avoid placing an informational overload on central decision makers, but it also serves as a protective device to prevent damaging information from being communicated to one's superiors. In any event, organizational structure introduces a measure of distortion into the communication of analysis.

Analysts generally value their information more highly than do members of the organization. Not perceiving that the organization is already flooded with information, analysts are seldom sensitive to the costs of absorption. Of course a single report will not overload the informational capacity of an organization. Assuming that the communication of analysis takes place in an informational vacuum, however, can lead to miscalculation. One can easily forget, for example, that competing information is available from the communication lines of the organizational structure, that such information may be in conflict with the direction and findings of an analysis. Analysts have to take into account in their analyses and in their communication of them that their audiences will have received information that has been processed by organizational structures. Although analysts may circumvent the organizational structure to get their data, they will still have to contend with others' sometimes distorted views.

Circumventing a number of superiors to reach a sympathetic ear or reaching directly down several levels to a friend for data are common tactics for avoiding the effects of organizational structure. While such tactics can be effective, they also have high personal costs in terms of the analyst being marked as disloyal or being prevented access in the future. Analysts who have some perserverance might be better off by directly coping with the organizational structure in their conception of the audience and in the design of the means of communication.

Organizations also have a self-image that asserts: "This is what we are, this is what we do, and this is how we do it." In communicating to an audience, the analyst has to tailor the message so that it is consistent with this organizational identity. Suppose an organization's identity involves a conservative streak and a respect for traditional ways of doing things. Analysts, usually biased toward significant change, will have to cloak their recommendations for divergence from that tradition. What is new will have to appear old or only a slight change from present practices. Effective analysis is the product of a number of people and must be put into a framework consistent with the organizational identity.

Organizations also exist in a larger environment. They have permeable boundaries and are subject to the external influences of articulated interests. By acting as if these influences do not exist, as if the organization is a "closed" system, the analyst may make the mistake of concentrating his efforts at communication solely on sponsors and other members of the organization. Suppose the analyst is examining alternative early childhood development programs and focuses the report only in terms of the organization's perceived and stated interest in cognitive achievement, while downplaying or omitting his analysis of the other interests of parent and teacher groups. Such a report may not be well received by those groups when they review it; and, what is more important, the report may not be well received by the members of the organization because they also perceive the problem through the lens of these environmental influences.

Finally, the analyst should be sensitive to the variety of functions that a particular communication fulfills for the organization or a component of the organization. A common error is to assume that the communication of analysis serves only a single function—transmitting policy and programmatic information. Sometimes communication is used to establish the jurisdiction of the organization, to show that the organization has control over, and is working in, an area. Sometimes communication serves to maintain the analytical unit and to secure resources for its activities. Other times it is used to develop political support and to neutralize the opposition of the organization. And then there are times when the communication of analysis is strictly a symbolic act indicating concern for a problem about which the organization actually intends to do nothing.

In short, in choosing and calibrating their audience, analysts must be sensitive to the organizational context of communication—to such factors as timing, structure, competition of information, identity, environment, and functions.

Assuming the Client Is the Audience

Analysts would do much better at communicating if they used the notion of audience rather than of client. *Audience* is a neutral term; it does not prejudge the situation of decision making. The use of audience allows the analyst to regard potential recipients without bias and frees the analyst to attempt to influence the selection of the audience's members. Throughout this essay the word *client* is used to mean a member of the audience and a recipient of communication. Assuming that the client is the only member of the audience, however, can lead to serious errors.

One such error occurs when the analyst assumes that his client is *the* policymaker. Generally we think of clients as policymakers—persons who instigate analysis and are expected to use its results. They are our links to policymaking. Yet all too frequently, the person who sets the process of analysis in motion—the immediate client—is merely one link in a complicated chain of advisers and policymakers. Indeed that person may not be a policymaker at all, but a manager who has arranged and monitored an analysis for someone else. In complex organizations and political systems, the immediate client is, at best, only one of numerous policymakers who comprise the analyst's audience, and the analyst may be mistaken in focusing communication on that single client.

Related to this often erroneous idea of a single policymaker is the analyst's belief that his client will be the sole recipient of his communication. No completely foolproof way exists for preventing the dissemination of analytical information. Whenever the analyst commits his information to paper, the information takes on an independent existence. Any reader of a study can become a member of the analyst's audience by choosing to use the information. If the analyst recognizes that the material he is communicating is sensitive and can be used in adverse ways, however, he can take some small steps to restrict its utility to others. For example, a study can be written so that it applies only to a specific context from which it would be difficult to lift the findings.

Shaping analytical communication to fit the audience is a highly desirable practice, but one partially dependent on appropriate selection and understanding of that audience. Thus, as we have seen, concentrating on the immediate client as the sole member of the audience may lead to errors. In the first case, the analyst unduly restricts his communication so that it is not likely to appeal to other policymakers. In the second case, the analyst does not restrict his communication enough, and other policymakers misuse it.

Concentrating on the immediate client as sole recipient implies that the policy process is more or less constant. The analyst assumes that the person who contracted with him will be there to receive the product and that the decision will wait for his research. Yet all too often, when the analyst is ready, the immediate client has been replaced by an insensitive monitor, the key elected and administrative officials have left office, and the current crop of actors are on to another problem. Because policy and decision processes are fluid and dynamic, analysts cannot afford to fixate on singular conceptions of the audience. In order to connect with these processes, they have to be flexible and opportunistic in their conceptions.

In developing a strategy for the selection of the audience, the analyst should not get caught up in legal niceties. All too often, I have seen analysts restrict themselves and their communication because the contract called for so many copies to be delivered to a particular person. A contractual or formal arrangement may in fact exist between client and analyst; there is no reason to assume that such arrangements have to be breached, but there is every reason to augment them. No one is suggesting that the analyst ignore the wishes of the client, whether they be contractual or otherwise; it would be foolish to do so. Indeed, it is in order to protect the interests of the client that the analyst has to examine the potential audience for his work. Despite the sophistication and intelligence of the client, most of us would agree that in the practice of analysis it is inappropriate to accept only the client's definition of the problem without scrutinizing other definitions. The analyst's strategical leeway is also important in selecting the audience and in communicating the results of analysis.

Thinking strategically about the selection of the audience leads us to consider the sequencing of the audience. Sending the results of a study to the wrong person can cause the premature death of that study. The selection of the *initial* audience is crucial in this respect. Reaching a supportive staff person, for example, can do more to influence a decision maker than a more direct approach by the analyst. In a large agency with a well-established analytical office, the analyst sometimes can create a climate of receptivity for his work as he goes along. This process of building consensus can start quite modestly, with the analyst convincing first his fellow analysts, then the head of the analytical office. After having built up a cadre of supporters inside the analytical office, he can proceed to communicate with superiors and subordinates outside the office and eventually with peers and policymakers outside the agency.

In sum, when an analyst assumes that his immediate client is his audience, he gives up the opportunity to influence the choice of audience. From the viewpoint of communication, who is reached and when they are reached is as critical as what is said. Making up a distribution list for a report should not be treated as a trivial mechanical exercise. If analysis is to affect decisions, the analysis must reach the decision makers and those friends and enemies who can influence them. This is not to say that an analyst can always anticipate all those who will be in the audience, but that thinking strategically about the composition of the audience is essential for effective communication. The selection of the audience is not something to be left solely to the immediate client through either default by the analyst or his acceptance of erroneous assumptions. There are many clients to be reached; some may be peripheral, some remote, some in the future, yet all are part of a potential audience.[5]

Assuming the Client Is an Analyst

One of the common errors in communication occurs when the analyst assumes that his audience or client is like himself, sharing his beliefs and values, his definition of the problem, his language and education. With the particular client who requested the study he will expect a sympathetic and empathetic audience. Such expectations may be unrealistic. Running for office is not the same experience as running a computer. Policymakers and decision makers, while perhaps competent judges of analysis, have seldom been analysts. They may come from a different class and social background than the analyst. They may not even remember that they instigated a study. Even in situations where the client is a former analyst, the analyst should not assume that the client is *still* an analyst. True, the client and the analyst may share a common language, but it is unlikely that they will completely share policy preferences and definitions of the problem. Differences in perceptions and values are bound to arise because of the client's position in the decision-making system. Sitting where he does, the client develops different concerns than the analyst's—concerns about politics, administrative feasibility, and personal advancement.

The analyst should assess rather than assume the degree of similarity between himself and his audience. Two general situations can bracket this assessment, as Rogers and Shoemaker point out:

> *Heterophily* is the degree to which pairs of individuals who interact are different in certain attributes, such as beliefs, values, education, social status, and the like. The opposite of heterophily is *homophily*, the degree to which pairs of individuals who interact are similar in certain attributes. Generally, most human communication takes place between individuals who are homophilous, a situation that leads to more effective communication. Therefore, the extent of . . . heterophily . . . leads to special problems in securing effective communication.[6]

If Rogers and Shoemaker are correct in their inference that "most human communication takes place between individuals who are homophilous," the analyst's assessment should indicate the necessary specific elements for effective communication. If these elements are lacking, it is the analyst's responsibility to adjust the situation. Obviously the client does much to determine the effectiveness of communication; our focus here is on the analyst and what he should do—namely, increase the degree of similarity between himself and his audience. Analysts who have had experience in dealing with numerous clients usually do this without much thought: they listen sympathetically to the client, respect the client's knowledge of the situation and problem, and are able to convert the technical language of a report into the language of the client. They do not assume that the client is naive and easily manipulated but try skillfully to couch their arguments in terms that increase the appearance of shared values. They are so knowledgeable about their client that they read his mind. This ability to anticipate the reactions of a client is difficult to acquire and may depend on considerable prior exposure to the client. As the Chinese philosopher Han Fei Tzu reminds us:

> On the whole, the difficult thing about persuading others is not that one lacks the knowledge needed to state his case nor the audacity to exercise his abilities to the full. On the whole, the difficult thing about persuasion is to know the mind of the person one is trying to persuade and to be able to fit one's words to it.[7]

How to increase homophily between analyst and client is not at all clear. We seem to know what direction to take but not what steps will be effective in a variety of situations. The exact prescription rests on the skill of the analyst and the idiosyncratic aspects of the situation, not on empirically based generalizations. If the analyst stops attempting to make the client over in his own image and instead puts himself in the position of the client, communication will at least be enhanced.

ARGUMENT

Once the analyst knows his audience he can determine how to communicate. He will have to develop arguments that combine the substantive aspects of his study with its social context. An argument is the theme that holds the various parts of the study together and leads them to a particular conclusion. The conclusion may urge the acceptance of a specific policy alternative or of a novel way of perceiving the problem, or it may suggest promising avenues of research. When the argument is well executed, we usually say that the conclusions of the study followed from the analysis: the argument has been so constructed that the study appears to be correct and its conclusions compelling. In short, an argument should be persuasive.

Now when I say compelling and persuasive I do not mean that an argument as used in the practice of analysis is or should only be a strong appeal to the emotions of the audience. Commonplace techniques such as the use of analogy and comparison can also be persuasive. The use of a fortiori, where we disadvantage our preferred alternative to see if it is as good as we thought, is not only an analytical technique but also an effective argument in communicating with an audience.

Many mistakes in communication come about from the unwillingness of the analyst to recognize that his study's argument is not neutral, that it leads to some conclusion, and that it is meant to be persuasive. Other mistakes related to argumentation result from the difficulty of constructing an argument that tells a client something he does not want to hear or from the analyst's insistence on dragging the audience through an obscure methodological or mathematical line of reasoning.

Assuming an Argument Is Neutral

The argument of an analysis should be balanced, but this does not mean that it should not be persuasive. By definition, the communication of analysis is an act of persuasion. It is not the simple transfer of information from analyst to recipient—as if information could be aseptically transferred by itself and acceptance depended solely on the quality of information. Is it not false humility to assert—as many analysts do—that we merely provide information to help the decision maker or to improve the quality of decision making? Even in situations where the directional or steering content of the information is minimal, analysts are engaged in an act of persuasion. Our analysis has led us to accept an altered view of reality and that is the view we present to the recipient. We say: Here is our new reality; here is cause and effect; here is A, and if you do A, B will follow. We do not have to ask the recipient to choose A, only to accept that if A is chosen, B will follow. Essentially we are asking the recipient not necessarily to do something but to accept our view of reality and to change his framework of understanding. When we sincerely believe that our view is correct and not clouded with uncertainty and especially when we believe that our analysis indicates the correct path, what then? The most detached, unemotional, objective analyst cannot avoid seeking some confirmation from others. No matter how neutral he tries to be in his communication, he is engaged in persuading the recipient to believe him, and his problem is to do it well, convincingly, and evenhandedly.

Some analysts may object to the assertion that communication is an act of persuasion because to them persuasion implies a manipulative appeal to emotions, and they see themselves as appealing solely to reason. Appeals to reason can also be manipulative, but as long as analysts recognize that they are appealing to something, it will be sufficient for my purposes. Consider the scientific analyst who expects that giving his report to the decision maker is the end of his responsibility. Compare that analyst with one who advocates a particular policy and expects that with considerable activity and skillful communications the decision maker will adopt the policy. These analysts differ as to what is being communicated and they have different styles or employ different means of communication; but, oddly enough, they have similar expectations. They both expect the decision maker to embrace the communication and to behave differently because of it. In a sense, both analysts are advocates, although one of them is unaware of being so.

Telling the Client What He Wants to Hear

It is a sad commentary on the state of analysis, but all too often a client will listen if you tell him what he wants to hear and will not listen if you tell him what he needs to know. Why should this be so? It has to do with a person's tendency to select and distort what he perceives on the basis of his predispositions. Analysts of course are subject to the same tendencies, but norms of professional practice and review usually eliminate or modify many of the possible distortions. Perhaps clients do not like surprises.

Research on mass communications, in the laboratory and the field, has come up with several generalizations that seem applicable to the interpersonal communication between analyst and client. Consider these generalizations from Berelson and Steiner:

> People tend to see and hear communications that are favorable or congenial to their predispositions; they are more likely to see and hear congenial communications than neutral or hostile ones.
>
> People tend to misperceive and misinterpret persuasive communications in accordance with their own predispositions, by evading the message or by distorting it in a favorable direction.
>
> People respond to persuasive communications in line with their predispositions, and they change or resist change accordingly. Communications will be most effective—that is, will secure the response in line with the intention of the communicator—when they are in accord with audience predispositions; when they tell people what they (most) want to be told.[8]

Analysts clearly have a great deal to contend with if the behavior of clients is similar to that of most people. Of course sometimes the client's predispositions are congruent with the analyst's, and in such cases the problems of communication are fewer. But what about a client whose predispositions are in conflict with the recommendations of the analyst? No amount of prior consultation with the client about the definition of the problem can necessarily prevent such a situation from arising. What then can be done to ensure a fair hearing of an analysis and increase the chances of its acceptance? What alternatives are open to the analyst?

First, the analyst can decide to make no attempt to understand why the client's predispositions are in conflict with his recommendations. He can ignore the conflict and present his facts and recommendations with the expectation that the study will speak for itself. This alternative operates on the assumption that human beings are reasonable and that knowledge can prevail. Second, the analyst can recognize the conflict and present his study with the same facts and recommendations but do so using a personal style and form of communication that smooths out the abrasive aspects of the situation. This alternative operates on the assumption that human beings enjoy flattery and are prone to listen to those they trust. "The important thing in persuasion," Han Fei Tzu tells us, "is to learn how to play up the aspects that the person you are talking to is proud of and play down the aspects he is ashamed of."[9] Third, the analyst can recognize the conflict and modify his study so that the argument with its selected facts and proposed recommendations is more congruent, though not completely so, with the client's predispositions. This alternative operates on the self-preemptive assumption that it is preferable partially to compromise onself than to be completely compromised or not listened to at all. Fourth, the analyst can recognize the conflict and change his study so that it is completely consistent with the client's predispositions. This alternative operates on the assumption that future influence depends on present submission by the analyst and acceptance by the client.

As in many policy problems, not one of these alternatives is attractive. Each raises serious issues of both ethics and practicality regarding appropriate roles and standards for analysts. Yet surely we recognize that communication, by definition, does involve manipulation, anticipation of the client, and planned reaction by the analyst. Appropriateness of analytical behavior does not rest on whether to manipulate the client but on how much manipulation is acceptable. The first and the last alternative in all likelihood result in the client not hearing or accepting what he needs to know—a dubious ethical choice at best. The other alternatives, in which the analyst slightly changes his behavior or his study, offer the best chance for effective ethics and communication. Oddly enough, when viewed in this context, the second alternative, modifying the style of the analyst and the form of his presentation, seems most appropriate because it leaves the content and message of the study intact. The analyst does not have to settle for a less than preferable solution. Form is changed but not substance. Rather than telling the client what he wants to hear, the analyst tells him what he needs to know by making it appear that what is being said *is* what he wants to hear.

To do this involves tactics that orators and advisers have known and used throughout the centuries: making sure the time is right, stating the argument in terms familiar to the audience, presenting a departure from present policy as merely a slight extension of it, coupling the recommendation with the possibility of personal advancement for the client, and pointing out that the recommendation is really the client's and that he will be identified with it and get the credit for it. Add to this choice of clothes, haircut, and appropriate regional speech pattern, and the nuances of persuasion are endless. When John Stuart Mill was a young boy, he enjoyed reading the orations of Demosthenes. His father pointed out "the skill and art of the orator—how everything important to his purpose was said at the exact moment when he had brought the minds of his audience into the state most fitted to receive it; how he made steal into their minds, gradually and by insinuation, thoughts which, if expressed in a more direct manner would have aroused their opposition."[10]

No doubt many analysts will be uncomfortable with the notion that they may have to manipulate a client or audience. They will argue that it is impossible to change form without changing substance and consider attempts to do so expedient and unethical. They may well be right, but one thing is certain: If they do not use the manipulative arts of persuasion, their communications will be effective only in situations in which the values, attitudes, and beliefs of the participants are reflected in the analysis. With the exception of somewhat trivial and technical problems where such congruence by definition exists, such situations are not common.

Telling the Client What You Did

It is an axiom of the analytical world that clients are busy, impatient, and have short attention spans. They want to know only as much as they will need to explain their decisions to others. With the exception of crisis situations—where the demand for information is real and urgent—a client often reacts to the communications of the analyst with feelings of boredom and indifference. In a face-to-face situation, he may do so because he does not want to appear committed. Reading a report in the privacy of his office, he may easily be distracted by more pressing items on his agenda; even though he continues to read, his mind and heart are likely to be elsewhere. Keeping the client's attention is a struggle, and many an analyst loses it because he insists on telling the client what he did rather than what he learned.

It is true that a client will not completely understand the analyst's conclusions and recommendations if he does not know how they were reached, but is total understanding what we are after? I would suggest that often what we are after is acceptance. Now most of us would agree that acceptance with understanding is preferable. The two ends are not always compatible or obtainable, however, and thus we usually settle for acceptance with an illusion of understanding.

On the other hand, many analysts feel that acceptance itself is closely linked to a detailed documentation of methods. They reason that a presentation of methodology is one way of establishing the expertise of the analyst and the value of his analysis. The rationale here is legitimation and not necessarily enhanced understanding. The analyst believes that he will not be trusted or his work approved unless he presents his expertise in detail. How can one be viewed as an expert unless he shows the paraphernalia of his models, statistics, and the like? If the point of such demonstrations is to maintain one's reputation as an expert, then surely there must be other ways to do so. Association with a prestigious university or research firm, necessary credentials in terms of education and experience, and recommendation by former, well-known clients also contribute to the maintenance of reputation. Indeed, if one has to demonstrate repeatedly that he is an expert, he is likely not to be—at least in a reputational sense.

How an analysis is conducted can also affect the ease of communication. Consider the analyst who is taken with a new and sophisticated analytical method. He can hardly wait to try it out. When he does, he may find that he has trouble explaining it and why he used it. Generally, the analyst should choose a simple method that fits the problem and the quality of the data. The more obscure, specialized, and complex the method, the more difficult it will be to explain it and the more the analyst will be forced to provide detailed documentation so that the study can be validated by others.

The client is more likely to listen if the material is directly related to his concerns. If he wants to know how a program is operating, tell him about what contributes to the success and failure of the program. If he has to make a decision, concentrate on the policy choices and their consequences. If he wants to enhance his knowledge of underlying causes and relationships, show him the products of research, not the methods. Of course if he wants to hear about methods to enhance his knowledge or perhaps to calibrate the analysis, then it is appropriate to inform him. But even in such situations, the sequencing and the amount of attention devoted to methods should be carefully controlled. Generally, methodological details are better left for footnotes and appendices or for special meetings of staff and technicians.

MEANS

The many forms of communication include not only numerous media but the numerous ways of using them. All too often the analyst has a limited view of the available choices. He settles in with a particular method and makes do. Having learned that a communication technique worked in one situation, he somewhat slavishly continues to use it. The analyst seldom appreciates that he needs to develop multiple means of communication with diverse audiences, rather than simply following mechanical rules.

All too often the analyst is not given the time, money, and other resources to break out of prevailing communication practices. Audiences and clients want to swallow some "instant analysis" pill, yet they usually are not willing to pay for it. Both clients and analysts are too busy to make the effort that would improve the effectiveness of communication. What can be done about this neglect? I have no satisfactory answer other than that as analysts we must start with ourselves. We should not so overemphasize communication that our efforts are counterproductive, but we certainly can do more to seek new ways of reaching our audiences. At the same time we can educate our clients as to the importance of communication.

Assuming Once Is Enough

There is a trade-off between the resources used for the analysis and those used in communicating the results of the analysis. I have been arguing that analysts do not spend enough of their resources on communication and that they certainly do not make creative use of the resources they have allocated for communication. With a modicum of arrogance, analysts assume that the world of policy is anxiously waiting for their work. They put their results in one final report, do a few briefings, and assume that that will be enough. But how can one report be sufficient when the analyst is dealing with multiple audiences?

Usually the analyst is aware of at least two audiences, his client and his peers. In fact, the client represents a number of decision makers, and the peers represent numerous technically minded staffs, advisers, and fellow analysts. The former will participate in the formulation of a policy or the making of a decision. The latter, friendly or otherwise, will review the study for its technical competence and elegance. The informational needs and standards of the two audiences are in conflict and tension, yet, armed with a single report, an analyst attempts to cope with these different audiences. The logic of the situation would argue, however, that he should have multiple reports to communicate with multiple audiences. By this I do not mean a reshuffling of the material in a single report, but the actual execution of a number of separate communication products—different reports for different readers and different briefings for different audiences.

To many analysts multiple communication seems unnecessary work and a waste of time. Besides, they argue, the immediate client has not provided sufficient resources, in time and money, for them to do more. From the perspectives of most participants, a single product seems sufficient. Despite this erroneous consensus, it is up to the analyst to assert the need for additional resources for communication. By thinking strategically about the different audiences, analysts can reach effective compromises with their clients and make effective use of available resources. Audiences can be grouped and matched with particular communication media. Nor must analysts stay wedded to traditional reporting formats and briefings. Indeed, one analytical team, for example, made a documentary film to promote and disseminate its work.[11]

It may appear that such actions will cause redundancy and a clogging of communication channels with excess verbiage and paper. But while the analyst may find himself covering the same material, he will not do so in the same way. The language and the forms of communication will be different and the results will not be entirely repetitious. Redundancy in communication, in any event, is a practical means of dealing with the audience's tendency to selective perception. When the analyst couches his work in terms—language and form—that will appeal to a specific audience, his analysis is not as likely to be screened out by conflicting predispositions.

Actually what I am suggesting is only an extension of present analytical practice. Do we not create both reports and briefings? In reports, for example, do we not include a summary for the busy reader? Our reports also have a fairly stylized format: in the introduction tell the reader where he is going, take him there, and then conclude by telling him where he has been. In their efforts at communication, analysts often behave like the characters in Lewis Carroll's poem, "The Hunting of the Snark":

Just the place for a Snark! I have said it twice:
   That alone should encourage the crew.
Just the place for a Snark! I have said it thrice:
   What I tell you three times is true.[12]

I do not want to be accused of comparing the pursuit of analysis to a Snark hunt, and

I certainly do not believe that repetition creates truth. Yet redundancy, both within a communication product and through a number of such products, can facilitate acceptance of the analyst's message. Thrice may be silly, but once is not enough.

Following Mechanical Rules

Giving advice about communication is a hazardous business. Few people besides students of rhetoric and social psychology have studied what works in communication, and to my knowledge no major study or body of literature evaluates the communication of analysis. In addition, communicating the results of analysis is very much grounded in the specific situation. Few rules of writing and speaking are universally applicable. As we have seen, many idiosyncratic factors seem to influence the effectiveness of communication: the analysis, the conversion to an argument, the client and the audience, the organizational and social context, and the choice of media and technique. While it is easy to set forth some rules that work in some situations, it is easier to set forth exceptions. That is why no analyst should follow in a mechanical fashion a rule of effective communication from me or anyone else. A few examples will illustrate the problem.

I teach my students that using short declarative sentences in their writing allows easier communication with most audiences and clients. Simplicity usually pays. One of my ex-students is now experiencing a certain amount of frustration because she insists on following my rule while working for a client who does *not* prefer simple, straightforward sentences. In reviewing the work of other analysts, I usually urge that the analyst use ordinary language and get rid of the jargon and technical terminology. Such esoteric language can easily mislead nonexperts. Using ordinary language is a good rule when the policymakers in an audience do not share a common technical vocabulary, and, as Perelman and Olbrechts-Tyteca put it, "ordinary langugae can help to promote agreement on the ideas."[13] When the audience does share a technical vocabulary, however, using ordinary language is not a good rule because the technical vocabulary is a useful shortcut. I also believe in avoiding weasel words, such as *probably, tends to, perhaps, likely*. We use such words to qualify our inferences and to make up for some inadequacy in a study. If these words are used with skill, the reader will never know what the analysis is suggesting. Yet when the inference stands alone without the benefit of such trappings, it may appear not only naked but flat-footed to some. A client who, because of education or culture, is accustomed to convoluted and qualified language would never appreciate such a practice.

Because analysis is fairly abstract, I have found it helpful to supplement the definition of the problem with a vivid example or story. Making things as concrete as possible seems effective, particularly in an oral presentation. But a concrete example can also deflect an audience's attention or cause disagreement. An analysis that stays at an abstract level may be more difficult to understand, but it also promotes agreement.

Sometimes it is difficult to know operationally whether one is following a specific rule. Consider the rule that a study report should stand on its own, that the reader should be able to go from a statement of the problem to the recommendations without having to look at anything else. It would be silly to expect total self-sufficiency of a report; yet because communications are constrained—in terms of pages or time, for example—the rule hints at a degree of self-sufficiency. How much should be included? What should be excluded? Should topics generally known and agreed upon be omitted? How is the analyst to identify such topics?

In short, follow a rule if you can, but only if the rule is congruent with a specific communication situation. This last rule supersedes any other mechanical rule you may confront.

Overemphasizing Communication

An essay on communication all too easily overemphasizes the importance of communication at the expense of substance. The same sort of thing happens in the practice of analysis. Some experienced analysts are likely to appear too glib when communicating their results. Some analysts try to substitute communication for substance; words like *overselling* and *snowing* describe such a situation. As one perceptive reviewer of this essay recently told me:

> Many analysts, perhaps because of their own needs for esteem or prestige, perhaps from pressures by their oganizations, tend to pack or puff up analytic reports with unnecessary material which—it seems—is intended to impress but often has the opposite effect. It was a standing joke among my colleagues . . . that the fanciest "packaging" usually indicated the poorest substantive quality. Everything from the binding of the report to special type fonts gets used to dress up shabby work, and it's quite easy to spot the analysts who are trying this ruse.

What is needed is balance between skills of communication and skills of substance. Obviously, one depends on the other. Without some substance, there will be nothing to communicate. Without clear and reasoned thinking, the analysis will be very difficult to communicate. Frequently, for example, what is put forth as a communication problem is in reality a thinking problem: fuzzy thinking makes for fuzzy communication. For our purposes, however, let us assume that the substance exists. In what other ways does an overemphasis on communication lead us astray?

One way is by encouraging us to omit embarrassing information. Analysts are often reluctant to admit the weaknesses in their work. In our desire for a tightly reasoned argument in which data and analysis directly support conclusions, we may be prone to leave out nonsupportive information. We believe our conclusions to be correct; to ease the process of understanding and acceptance we want to leave out whatever detracts from that conclusion. Such a tactic may backfire, however; a third party to a communication may be delighted to point out the contrary evidence, thus undermining the main emphasis of the study and calling into question the honesty of the analyst. My own practice is to sacrifice a little on the communication side by preempting the future critic. It often pays to include the adverse example and to admit the limitations of one's work, regardless of the minor difficulty in communication this causes. Such "candor" provides a measure of balance and softens an unnecessary tone of advocacy.

Another quite different way we can be led astray is by overemphasizing a particular medium. We become media freaks. First, we narrow our choice . . . to written reports or briefings and tend to slight other forms of communication—such as writing memoranda, including analytical prescription in speeches, and using the telephone and social occasions. Then we put our energies into making sure our reports are neatly bound, with appropriate dividers in color. Or we develop briefings that make use of three projectors and artistic slides with numerous overlays, allowing easy digestion of complex information.

These techniques work fairly well with many audiences. The problem arises when technique displaces what we were trying to do in the first place—communicate. Consider that one central aspect of effective communication is feedback. The analyst has to know whether his message is getting across to his audience and if it is not, how to make suitable adjustments. The question then is not only which technique to use but how a particular technique en-

hances communication and provides the condition for feedback. Obviously, a face-to-face, informal situation would be best from this perspective. Both the analyst and his client could then engage the substance of the analysis and at the same time build mutual understanding and trust. Short of this ideal situation, the analyst has to ensure that his formal briefing, for example, is not so formal and simplistic that it entertains without engaging the audience or encouraging the audience's responses to substance.

CONCLUSION

Concern about communication usually masks concern about the lack of one's influence: "The analysis is sound. Why is it that no one pays any attention to it?" Worse than the analysis not being used is the analysis being misused or used in unintended ways. What can be done about this? Some would argue that the analyst must be his own client and assume a political role. In this vision, the analyst can become a master coalition builder, seeking allies and neutralizing enemies in the pursuit of a study's recommendations. Yet I do not think most analysts have the stomach for the rigors of politics. Some more modest prescription is needed.

Here is where an appreciation of communication and its social context comes in. Helping to choose the audiences, designing arguments to fit those audiences, and employing effective means of communication will increase the use of analysis. To this end, analysts will have to improve their understanding of rhetoric and the psychology of communication. They will also have to accept spending as much time on communication as they do on the analysis itself. Communication cannot be effective with meager resources or as an afterthought. Paying serious attention to communication is, so to speak, being political in the small, a sensible strategy consistent with present analytical practice and the analyst's limited resources. Analysts who then come to appreciate the art of effective communication will be in the good company of Aristotle, who pointed out the uses of rhetoric (*Rhetorica* I.1. 1355ª):

> Rhetoric is useful . . . because things that are true and things that are just have a natural tendency to prevail over their opposites, so that if the decisions of judges are not what they ought to be, the defeat must be due to the speakers themselves, and they must be blamed accordingly. Moreover, . . . before some audiences not even the possession of the exactest knowledge will make it easy for what we say to produce conviction. For argument based on knowledge implies instruction, and there are people whom one cannot instruct. Here, then, we must use, as our modes of persuasion and argument, notions possessed by everybody. . . . Further, . . . we must be able to employ persuasion . . . on opposite sides of a question . . . in order that we may see clearly what the facts are.

AUTHOR'S NOTE

I wish to thank Stuart Altman, Eugene Bardach, E. M. L. Beale, George K. Chacko, Christopher Bellavita, Giandomenico Majone, Milton Morris, David Selby, Allan Sindler, and Percy Tannenbaum for their helpful comments. A version of this paper has been published in Giandomenico Majone and Edward S. Quade, eds., *Pitfalls of Analysis* (Chichester, United Kingdom: John Wiley & Sons, 1979).

NOTES

1. For succinctness, I use masculine pronouns throughout this paper. They are intended to refer to both females and males.

2. S. E. Toulmin, *The Uses of Argument* (Cambridge: At the University Press, 1964), p. 19.

3. Herman Kahn and Irwin Mann, *Ten Common Pitfalls* (Santa Monica, Calif.: Rand Corporation, 1957), p. 45.

4. Edward Quade, *Analysis for Public Decisions* (New York: American Elsevier, 1975), p. 312.

5. Arnold J. Meltsner, *Policy Analysts in the Bureaucracy* (Berkeley and Los Angeles: University of California Press, 1976), pp. 200–10.

6. E. M. Rogers, with F. F. Shoemaker, *Communication of Innovations: A Cross-Cultural Approach*, 2d ed. (New York: Free Press, 1971), p. 39.

7. Burton Watson, trans., *Basic Writings of Mo Tzu, Hsün Tzu, and Han Fei Tzu* (New York: Columbia University Press, 1967), p. 73.

8. Bernard Berelson and G. A. Steiner, *Human Behavior: An Inventory of Scientific Findings* (New York: Harcourt, Brace and World, 1964), pp. 529–41.

9. Watson, *Basic Writings*, p. 75.

10. J. S. Mill, *Autobiography of John Stuart Mill* (New York: Columbia University Press, 1924), pp. 14–15.

11. Garry D. Brewer, *What Happens After the Reports Are Filed*, technical report no. 4 (New Haven: Yale University, School of Organization and Management, 1977), pp. 28–32.

12. *The Works of Lewis Carroll* (Feltham, England: Hamlyn Publishing Group, Spring Books, 1965), p. 731.

13. Ch. Perelman and L. Olbrechts-Tyteca, *The New Rhetoric: A Treatise on Argumentation* (Notre Dame, Ind.: University of Notre Dame Press, 1969), p. 153.

4

THE PROCESS OF
PROGRAM PLANNING

Knowledge and Technology

The era during which the first and the second editions of these *Readings* appeared coincided with the rise and decline of social planning. There has been a steady loss of faith in the desirability and feasibility of central, comprehensive forms of planning on a national and even on a community level. One of the early forms of social planning which referred to the human dimension of planning in such sectors as housing, transportation, and land use gradually evolved into the conception of planning as "a corrective in the service delivery system."[1] During the last decade, this version of planning was utilized in the mandated social planning of federal social service programs which, in a grants economy, was reduced to an allocational procedure. Consequently, little progress has been made in the further development of social planning theory. What has endured, however, is a conception of planning as a sociopolitical and technical process, an institutional or interorganizational activity under a variety of auspices with diverse goals, resting on an amorphous body of knowledge which has also not escaped criticism. This combination of future oriented technical and political knowledge and skills has been captured in the term *technipol*, reflecting the reasonable assumption that planning, like prayer, should lead to action. The analytical requirements of planning ideally suggest someone who is not only informed about the nature, the extent, and the impact of poverty, illness, delinquency, and housing but is also familiar with such fashionable tools as the indicators to be used in social accounting, cost-benefit analysis, data banks, and game simulation. Planning also suggests an ability to guide an action system through the planning process in which a problem is identified, data are analyzed, alternative policies are evaluated, and feasible programs are formulated in such a way that the collaborative competence of the participants is enhanced. These are indeed extraordinary expectations, and it is no wonder that most planning, particularly preventive and long-range efforts aimed at changing the structure of institutional systems, has foundered in the absence of adequate technical knowledge and/or the lack of the planner's power to implement.

The assumptions of prevailing theories of planning have been challenged for not reflecting adequately the actual environment for social planning both in organizations and at the community level. In the absence of an accepted theory of planning, we must continue to study the different, salient aspects of planning. In this section, in addition to a review of the current status of the art, the selections deal with problem analysis, program design, the concepts of needs and utilization, services integration, evaluation, and management information systems.

In "Comparsion of Current Planning Theories: Counterparts and Contradictions," Barclay M. Hudson describes and evaluates the relative strengths and weaknesses of five major schools of planning thought. They are synoptic (rational-comprehensive); incremental; transactive; advocacy; and radical planning. Each of these models of planning practice is assessed in the light of six criteria: public interest; human dimension; feasibility; action potential; substantive theory; and self-reflective capacity. Hudson concludes that the contradictions among models of planning reflect identifiable tensions and contradictions in our society. Therefore, he says, parallel applications of more than one model are usually necessary in order to arrive at a valid, three-dimensional perspective on social issues and appropriate action.

There are several questions that are central to all forms of community organization, planning, and policy analysis. They include the following: Who defines what is problematic; that is, what is the relationship between the conditions defined as problematic by the change agent and various interest groups? Because the relationships among goals, sponsors, participants, and methods are affected by the ways in which social problems are defined, the process and the elements of problem identification are of critical importance. Mark H. Moore provides a cognitive map of this kind of analysis in "Anatomy of the Heroin Problem: An Exercise in Problem Definition." Moore's paradigm is a useful one for analyzing many other similar problems. Moore analyzes the range of definitions of the heroin problem and the different policies the definitions suggest. He then proceeds to describe in detail eighteen attributes of the heroin problem along with social indicators by which they can be measured. Moore discusses how these attributes and indicators are related to appropriate objectives for public policy.

In "The Social Planning Design Guide: Process and Proposal," Franklin M. Zweig and Robert Morris describe some of the analytical aspects of program development. They discuss how one should think about the design of social service programs that are rational and that will have a high probability of utilization. They do not deal with the interactional or grantsmanship aspects of program development; instead, they consider questions about why certain steps should be taken in thinking through the problem and its solution. The ability to utilize a format of this kind is essential in planning because most funding bodies require a program proposal as a basis for support. Intended mainly as a prototype for the development of program proposals, the philosophical basis for Morris and Zweig's version of the rational model of planning is found in five classes of design elements: statement of the problem; theories of causation;

interventional alternatives and their consequences; the nature of the target population; and value considerations. These elements provide planners with a way of ordering their activities, together with built-in "branching mechanisms" which should stimulate the development of alternative explanations and interventions.

What would rational planning be without the concept of needs? The meeting of needs and the balancing of needs and resources are traditional goals and justifications for most social planning, giving it whatever theoretical coherence it may have. For example, needs assessments have been required by more than one-third of the federal categorical social programs created in the 1970s. Yet for some time there has been a suspicion that there were serious conceptual and methodological flaws in needs-assessment studies which might account for their seeming lack of influence. In "Needs Assessment: A Critical Perspective," Wayne A. Kimmel finds that *needs* is an empty and unbounded term and that all the methods used to measure it have serious weaknesses. He concludes that needs assessments are more suitable for program justification or advocacy than for analysis or systematic planning. Because needs assessment will probably continue to be requested. Kimmel poses a number of questions which should be considered.

One of the alternatives to needs assessment is the concept of "utilization" which is often found in studies of health services. In view of the widely perceived "need for health and welfare services," the prevalence of underutilization is surprising. Even in the United Kingdom, the low "take-up" of benefits is endemic in the personal social services despite the apparent universalism of these services. Why should this be the case? In "Health Services Utilization Models for Human Services Planning," Nancy W. Veeder reviews the development of models for measuring utilization in the field of urban health services over the last twenty years. She discusses the results of this work and explains utilization in terms of individual psychological states, group pressures, and institutional barriers. Four principal models that rely on psychological factors, socioenvironmental variables, family characteristics and life cycle stages, and behavioral components are evaluated in terms of their respective theoretical and empirical strengths and limitations. Veeder concludes on a rather encouraging note. These models, she says, demonstrate an increasing capacity to explain variations in behavior, and they can be extended even further.

Ostensibly, there is widespread agreement on the imporatnce of program evaluation to community planners. At the very least, it is required by virtually all funding sources. Yet there are problems in evaluating human services. Discouraging results are reported with great frequency. Although program evaluation, on which hundreds of millions of dollars have been expended, has become a major industry in the last decade, there is disagreement about the distinctive nature of the process and its products. The professional literature under the rubric of program evaluation is voluminous and covers a wide range of activities, including project monitoring, policy research, applied research, statistical recording, and management information systems. In "Evaluating Social Interventions: A Conceptual Schema," Dennis N. T. Perkins provides a taxonomy of assessment activities and alternative methodological procedures. Six assessment categories are identified, along with nine methods which are, in turn, dependent on the objectives of the evaluation. Perkins presents this schema as a means of establishing a common basis for communication as well as an aid in choosing an appropriate evaluation methodology.

Social planning at its core seeks to extend rationality over the diverse and sometimes seemingly unrelated activities of a nonsystem of human service providers. Historically, there has been a succession of community efforts to coordinate services, to eliminate duplication and gaps in services, and to balance needs and resources in response to the persistent deficiencies of service systems, such as fragmentation, discontinuity, inaccessibility, and unaccountability. Currently the term *human services integration* embodies these perennial aspirations. *Human service integration* differs from its predecessors in two respects: It refers to the human services, and it is concerned mainly with intergovernmental agency relationships. The term *human services integration* is used to describe a phenomenon that is more comprehensive than the social services. Indeed, it is sometimes difficult to know what does not fall within its synoptic purview. The concept of human services seems to have originated around 1967, and for some it still suggests the antiprofessional, antiservice bureaucracy ties of its founders who sought a closer link between paraprofessionals and consumers that would enable them to cope with individual, family and neighborhood, and community problems. However, the transformation of the Department of Health, Education and Welfare into the Department of Health and Human Services suggests that this ideology may have less significance for others.

Much of the interest in services integration stems from the recent involvement of local governments in the mixed social service economy promoted by the New Federalism of the 1970s. Spurred by the proliferation of federal categorical programs, governmental officials rediscovered the perennial problems of uncoordinated service programs delivered by a multiplicity of independent producers. These programs are characteristic of a market system of provider pluralism which does not acknowledge any central or integrating authority. Questions of efficiency and effectiveness as well as complex problems of interorganizational relationships are continually raised by the hundreds of specialized programs involving three layers of government.

Robert Agranoff, in his definitive essay "Services Integration," examines the history of the relationship of services integration to local government. Some sense of the complexity of these issues is revealed in his identification of thirty-seven forms of service integration, such as joint planning, the purchase of service, grants management, and case conferences. Experience with these various forms of services integration has been studied extensively in numerous local communities as well as at the state and federal levels, and Agranoff summarizes some of the leading research findings. It is particularly important to know the history of previous efforts to effect services coordination because of the cyclical nature of calls for more planning and coordination. It can be expected that in the decade of the 1980s, dominated by the scarcity of resources and efforts to decentralize decision making through block grants to the states, planners will be confronted by greater uncertainty, competition, and politicalization of the human service delivery system.

Despite the more modern vocabulary provided by social systems theory and the centrality of governmental agencies, most services integration efforts (like their predecessors) suffer from the liability of having to rely on voluntary coordination within the context of a local nonsystem. It is questionable that very much change or increased rationality can be expected under these circumstances, and the likelihood of there being developed a coherent national social welfare policy seems remote. Planners, therefore, may have to adapt themselves to exercising a more limited amount of leverage in the social services delivery system.

Among the highly touted devices for making human services planning and administration more efficient and scientific is a set of tools originally developed for use in policymaking in large organizations, such as PERT, MBO, and cost-benefit analyses. The transfer of this management technology to nonprofit organizations has often appeared faddish. Insufficient consideration has been given to the appropriateness of its use and adaptation in human services planning. Management information systems (MIS) are among the most recent innovations, and they have been adopted in many human service agencies in response to social and political pressures for greater accountability. In "Information Systems in Human Services: Misconceptions, Deceptions, and Ethics," James C. Noah presents a skeptical view. Noah states that MIS are designed to answer a multitude of questions for a variety of funding and licensing agencies, but these systems do not necessarily improve service delivery. Additional information, he argues, does not always lead to better decision making and may in fact deter the development of higher quality services. The measurement of process outputs is often a substitute for outcomes that are inherently difficult to specify and measure in the human services. More than an information processing device, MIS can be regarded as one component of a complex environment that comes to control the behavior of individuals in community and organizational systems. Noah proposes a framework for the analysis of MIS in which emphasis is put on the creation of an environment in which proper objectives are selected and relevant activities are generated.

NOTES

1. Joan Levin Ecklein and Armand Lauffer, *Community Organizers and Social Planners* (New York: John Wiley & Sons, Inc., and the Council on Social Work Education, 1972), p. 215.

Barclay M. Hudson

Comparison of Current Planning Theories: Counterparts and Contradictions

For sake of a place to start, planning can be defined as "foresight in formulating and implementing programs and policies." The overall purpose of this article is to replace this unitary definition by defining more specific categories of planning, some of them complementary, and some of them contradictory to a degree that scarcely permits an umbrella meaning of planning.

The first section of the article presents a simple classification of planning traditions. The second section provides a general set of descriptive criteria for planning theories and practices. No single tradition of planning can do everything, and the list of criteria serves as a framework to compare the relative strengths and limitations of different approaches. The criteria reflect some timeless debates in the field of planning: why to plan and how; for whom and by whom. Major issues of this type are briefly discussed in connection with the criteria proposed.

The concluding section suggests some implications for planning theory, practice, and further empirical research: the need for more systematic comparative study of different planning approaches; the relative validity of different traditions to different settings and problems; the internal cohesiveness of each paradigm with regard to methods, professional groupings, and social philosophies; the nature of resistances to parallel or mixed use of diverse

Reprinted from the *Journal of the American Planning Association* 45:4 (October 1979), pp. 387–98, with permission of the author and the American Planning Association. Copyright 1979 by the American Planning Association.

theories in tandem; and the extent of harmony or basic antagonism among the various traditions, both in theory and practice.

BASES FOR A CLASSIFICATION SCHEME

If planning consists of "foresight in formulating and implementing programs and policies," then planners were clearly in evidence four thousand years ago when King Hammurabi caused the laws of Babylonia to be carved on stone. Typical problems of twentieth century planning have had their counterparts throughout history, and professionals have been there to solve them—in urban design and public works programs; in regulation of coinage and trade; in foreign policy and military defense; in forecasting the future and preparing against calamity; in pushing back geographical frontiers and laying down transportation networks; and in devising laws for prevention of disease and disorder.

To understand planning, one has to look for the few abiding principles that underlie all purposeful action. The apparent diversity is mainly a matter of labelling and packaging, with subtle differences that are often exaggerated to achieve what salespeople are always seeking—"product differentiation" that will help sell the particular product each planner has to offer. For example, what yesterday was PPBS today is MBO (management by objectives), or ZBB (zero-based budgeting), or GAA (goals-achievement analysis), or logframe (logical framework programming. PPBS (the Planning-Programming-Budgeting System) is often cited as originating during

World War II as a means for allocating scarce resources for the war effort. Others claim it goes back to the auto industry in an earlier decade. Similarly, benefit-cost analysis came to prominence in public policy making during the sixties, yet it played an important role in planning the canal system in the American Northeast as early as the 1830s. Nor was that by any means the first time anyone had added up costs and benefits of acting on a proposal. Private businessmen and entrepreneurs were doing that long before Adam Smith. Almost any form of investment is a form of planning.

Clearly, then, planning covers too much territory to be mapped with clear boundaries. It overlaps far into the terrain of other professions, and its frontiers expand continually with the historical evolution of social problems to be solved. The way to grasp a layout of the planning field is not by reconnoitering from the periphery, but by drawing demarcation lines radiating out from the most familiar crossroads at the center. In other words, one needs a classification scheme that will highlight comparative distinctions among current planning traditions without necessarily pinning down their farther limits.

A number of classification schemes might serve: *procedural* theories versus *substantive* theories (Hightower 1969; Faludi 1973b,[1] or *algorithms* versus *heuristics*—that is, standardized problem-solving versus exploratory search procedures.[2] Another way of categorizing the field reflects different *sources of academic and professional literature*, entailing four major areas of concern: the tradition of rationalism, organizational development theory, empirical studies of planning practice, and philosophical synthesis relating to broad theories of social structural change (Friedmann and Hudson 1974).[3] These four "literary traditions" receive fairly balanced attention at the level of planning theory, but in planning practice, some far outweigh

the others. Planning efforts in the field rarely make overt reference to philosophical synthesis or organizational development theory, nor is much attention given to lessons of historical experience based on case studies of past planning efforts. Instead, predominant concern has generally centered on the tradition of rational comprehensive planning, also known as the synoptic tradition.

Because of its pre-eminence, the synoptic tradition serves as the centerpiece in the classification scheme to be developed below. The synoptic approach has dominated both American planning practice and the planning of development assistance programs overseas. The approach is well suited to the kind of mandate bestowed on government agencies: a set of constrained objectives, a budget, and accountability for not allowing one to stray too far out of line from the other.

There are, however, several other counterpoint schools of planning, most of which take their point of departure from the limits of the synoptic approach. The most important of these other traditions include *incremental planning, transactive planning, advocacy planning,* and *radical planning.* These by no means exhaust the range of contemporary planning traditions, but they cover enough ground to illustrate the major developments in planning theory and practice since roughly 1960, developments which have grown up in response to recognized deficiencies in the synoptic approach.

Each of the five traditions to be considered has an internally consistent, self-reinforcing network of methods, data requirements, professional skills, and working styles. Each has its own epistemology for validating information and its own institutional setting for putting ideas into practice. Each perceives the public interest in its own way, reflecting its particular assessment of human nature and its own sense of the legitimate range of interventions in social, economic, and political processes. The five traditions will be reviewed briefly in turn. Principal similarities and differences will then be discussed in terms of several descriptive criteria which have been chosen to highlight their relative strengths and weaknesses, their areas of complementariness, and their points of fundamental antagonism.

Synoptic Planning

Synoptic planning, or the rational comprehensive approach, is the dominant tradition, and the point of departure for most other planning approaches, which represent either modifications of synoptic rationality or reactions against it.

Synoptic planning has roughly four classical elements: (1) goal-setting, (2) identification of policy alternatives, (3) evaluation of means against ends, and (4) implementation of decisions. The process is not always undertaken in this sequence, and each stage permits multiple iterations, feedback loops, and elaboration of sub-processes. For example evaluation can consist of procedures such as benefit-cost analysis, operations research, systems analysis, and forecasting research. Looking closer at forecasting, one finds that it can be broken down into deterministic models (trend extrapolation, econometric modelling, curve-fitting through multiple regression analysis); or probabilistic models (Monte Carlo methods, Markov chains, simulation programs, Beyesian methods), or judgmental approaches (Delphi technique, scenario writing, cross-impact matrices).

Synoptic planning typically looks at problems from a systems viewpoint, using conceptual or mathematical models relating ends (objectives) to means (resources and constraints), with heavy reliance on numbers and quantitative analysis.

Despite its capacity for great methodological refinement and elaboration, the real power of the synoptic approach is its basic simplicity. The fundamental issues addressed—ends, means, tradeoffs, action-taking—center into virtually any planning endeavor. Alternative schools of planning can nitpick at the methodological shortcomings of the synoptic approach, or challenge its particular historical applications, or take issue with its circumscribed logic, yet the practical tasks it encompasses must be addressed in some form by even its most adamant critics. For this reason, there is a sustained dialectical tension between synoptic planning and each of the other counterpart theories; neither side of the debate feels comfortable with its opposite, yet they cannot do without each other. Each helps define the other by its own shortcomings; each sharpens the other's discriminatory edge of intentions and accomplishments.

Incremental Planning

A chief spokesperson for the incremental planning approach is Charles Lindblom, who describes it as "partisan mutual adjustment" or "disjointed incrementalism." Criticizing the synoptic approach as unrealistic, he stresses that policy decisions are better understood, and better arrived at, in terms of the push and tug of established institutions that are adept at getting things done through decentralized bargaining processes best suited to a free market and a democratic political economy. A good illustration of incremental planning is the apocryphal interview of a Yugoslavian official who was asked to describe his country's most important planning instrument. After a pause for thought the official replied, "the telephone." Yugoslavia in fact represents a blend of synoptic and incremental approaches. It promulgates national plans through a Federal Planning Bureau, but the country's economic and planning systems are composed of autonomous, self-governing working organizations. Plans are constructed by a mixture of "intuition, experience, rules of thumb, various techniques (rarely sophisticated) known to individual planners, and an endless series of consultations" (Horvat 1972, p. 200). This description might apply to planning anywhere else in the world as well. Lindblom calls it "the science of muddling through."

The case for incremental planning derives from a series of criticisms leveled at synoptic rationality: its insensitivity to existing institutional performances capabilities; its reductionist epistemology; its failure to appreciate the cognitive limits of decision-makers, who cannot "optimize" but only "satisfice" choices by successive approximations. Incrementalists also take issue with the synoptic tradition of expressing social values (a priori goal-setting; artifical separation of ends from means; presumption of a general public interest rather than pluralist interests). Finally, synoptic planning is critized for its bias toward central control—in the definition of problems and solutions, in the evaluation of alternatives, and in the implementation of decisions.

These criticisms are reflected in the countervailing tendencies of incremental planning, but also in the thrust of other planning approaches discussed below.

Transactive Planning

The transactive planning approach focuses on the intact experience of people's lives revealing policy issues to be addressed. Planning is not carried out with respect to an anonymous target community of beneficiaries, but in face-to-face contact with the people affected by decisions. Planning consists less of field surveys and data analyses, and more of interpersonal dialogue marked by a process of mutual learning.

> Transactive planning also refers to the evolution of decentralized planning institutions that help people take increasing control over the social processes that govern their welfare. Planning is not seen as an operation

separated from other forms of social action, but rather as a process embedded in continual evolution of ideas validated through action (Friedmann 1973.)

In contrast to incremental planning, more emphasis is given to processes of personal and organizational development, and not just the achievement of specific functional objectives. Plans are evaluated not merely in terms of what they do for people through delivery of goods and services, but in terms of the plans' effect *on* people—on their dignity and sense of effectiveness, their values and behavior, their capacity for growth through cooperation, their spirit of generosity. By contrast, incremental planning adheres more closely to the economic logic of individuals pursuing their own self-interest.

Advocacy Planning

The advocacy planning movement grew up in the sixties, rooted in adversary procedures modelled upon the legal profession, and usually applied to defending the interests of weak against strong—community groups, environmental causes, the poor, and the disenfranchised against the established powers of business and government. (Alinsky 1971; Heskin 1977.) Advocacy planning has proven successful as a means of blocking insensitive plans and challenging traditional views of a unitary public interest. In theory, advocacy calls for development of plural plans rather than a unit plan (Davidoff 1965). In practice, however, advocacy planning has been criticized for posing stumbling blocks without being able to mobilize equally effective support for constructive alternatives (Peattie 1968).

One effect of the advocacy movement has been to shift formulation of social policy from backroom negotiations out into the open. Particularly in working through the courts, it has injected a stronger dose of normative principles into planning, and greater sensitivity to unintended side effects of decisions. A residue of this can be seen in the increasing requirements for environmental, social, and financial impact reports to accompany large scale project proposals, whether originating in the private or public sector. Another result has been the stronger linkage between social scientists and judiciary processes in policy decisions. In the field of education, this alliance has left a mark in areas such as integration and busing, sources of school finance, equal provision for women in sports, disclosure of records, teacher training requirements, unionization, and selection of teaching materials. Advocacy planning has both reflected and contributed to a general trend in planning away from neutral objectivity in definition of social problems, in favor of applying more explicit principles of social justice.

Radical Planning

Radical planning is an ambiguous tradition, with two mainstreams of thinking that occasionally flow together. One version is associated with spontaneous activism, guided by an idealistic but pragmatic vision of self-reliance and mutual aid. Like transactive planning, it stresses the importance of personal growth, cooperative spirit, and freedom from manipulation by anonymous forces. More than other planning approaches, however, its point of departure consists of specific substantive ideas about collective actions that can achieve concrete results in the immediate future. It draws on varying sources of inspiration—economics and the ecological ethic (Schumacher 1973), social architecture (Goodman 1971), humanistic philosophy (Illich 1973), and historical precedents (Katz and Bender 1976, Hampden-Turner 1975).

This is radicalism in the literal sense of "going back to the roots," content to operate in the interstices of the Establishment rather than challenging the system head-on. The philosophy which underlies its so-

cial vision can also be found in the thinking of educational figures like John Dewey, Paul Goodman (*Communitas*), Ivan Illich (*Deschooling Society*), and others who share the view that education needs to draw on materials from everyday life of local communities, with minimum intervention from the state and maximum participation of people in defining, controlling, and experimenting with their own environment. Somewhat the same concerns find their way into conventional planning—for example, as reflected in the Bundy Report on decentralizing the New York City school system, and in the HEW-sponsored educational voucher experiments aimed at letting neighborhood committees take over planning functions usually vested in central bureaucracies.

The second stream of radical thought takes a more critical and holistic look at large-scale social processes: the effect of class structures and economic relationships; the control exercised by culture and media; the historical dynamics of social movements, confrontations, alliances, and struggles. The focus is less on ad hoc problem solving through resurrected community, and more on the theory of the state, which is seen to permeate the character of social and economic life at all levels, and in turn determines the structure and evolution of social problems (Gordon 1971. See also Ellul 1954). Radicals in this tradition view conventional planning as a form of Mandarinism, playing "handmaiden to conservative politics" (Kravitz 1970).

It is not the purpose of this paper to describe at length particular schools of planning thought. Any list of planning forms and styles could be extended almost indefinitely. Those discussed above are probably sufficient, however, to illustrate the variety of concerns that planners address and the range of conceptual tools they bring to their task.

The five approaches described above can be summed up in an acronym, SITAR, based on the first letters of Synoptic, Incremental, Transactive, Advocacy, and Radical planning. The *sitar* is a five-stringed musical instrument from India, a type of lute which can be played by performing on a single string at a time, or by weaving a blend of harmony and dissonance from all five. The same applies to SITAR as a taxonomy of planning theories; each can render a reasonable solo performance in good hands, but fuller possibilities can be created by use of each theory in conjunction with the others.

CRITERIA FOR COMPARATIVE DESCRIPTION AND EVALUATION OF PLANNING THEORIES

In judging the value of any particular planning tradition one can ask, how constrained are we to using one theory at a time? No single approach is perfect, but a particular theory can establish itself as "best" simply because there are no salient

options kept in view. The SITAR package suggests some of these options, but comparative evaluation requires another step—the establishment of criteria for comparison of different traditions' strengths and weakness, along with their varying intentions and accomplishments.

Table 1 presents a simple list of basic criteria that one might use for assessing the scope, character, and adequacy of the various planning traditions. The six criteria have been distilled from three independent selection processes; each process is somewhat subjective, but they overlap considerably in their results. First, the criteria were generated in part by *internal features* of the various SITAR traditions themselves, as expressed in the planning literature. Some criteria, such as definition of the public interest, reflect a common concern of all the SITAR traditions (although they differ considerably in their treatment of it). Other criteria, such as the use of substantive theories of political action and

Table 1 Criteria for Describing and Evaluating Planning Traditions

CRITERIA	CHARACTERISTICS AND APPLICATIONS
Public interest	Explicit *theory of the public interest,* along with methods to articulate significant social problems, and pluralist interests in outcomes. May include principles of distributive justice, and procedures for dealing with conflict.
Human dimension	Attention to the *personal and spiritual domains* of policy impacts, including intangible outcomes beyond functional-instrumental objectives—for example, psycho-social development, enhancement of dignity, and capacity for self-help.
Feasibility	*Ease of learning and applying* the theory. Implies the theory is practical to translate into policy implications, and adaptable to varying types of problems, scales of action, and social settings.
Action potential	Provision for carrying ideas into practice, building on experience underway and identifying new lines of effective solutions to problems.
Substantive theory	*Descriptive and normative theory* of social problems and processes of social change. Predictive capacity based on informal judgments, not just trend extrapolation; ability to trace long range and indirect policy consequences; historical perspectives on opportunities and constraints on action.
Self-reflective	Capacity for laying analytical assumptions open to criticism and counter-proposals; provision for learning from those being planned for; capacity for depicting concrete experience in everyday language, as well as conceptual models using aggregate data.

models of social change, represent a central concern—even a raison d'etre—of some traditions but are glaringly absent from others.

The second source of criteria was an informal review of *historical outcomes* from past planning efforts. Most of these cases are described in the literature;[4] some have been suggested by anecdotal sources and personal experiences shared with colleagues in the profession. The third source of nominations for criteria has been an advanced seminar in urban planning at UCLA, where over the years several cohorts of students have been posed the questions, "How do you judge a good planning theory? What planning experience can you cite that has been most successful, and what constitutes that success?" Their collated answers reflect considerable planning experience as well as academic grounding in planning theory, including general principles of policy science, social philosophy, and political economy.

From these various sources, roughly fifty different criteria were suggested, often overlapping, sometimes contradictory, occasionally esoteric. Winnowing and synthesis to a manageable set of criteria necessarily involves personal choices, and

probably reflects the author's own implicit philosophy of planning. It should be noted, though, that final choice of the six criteria shown in Tables 1 and 2 reflects, in part, a deliberate effort to balance strengths and weaknesses within and among the five SITAR traditions.

Table 2 is an attempt to evaluate the five SITAR traditions against the list of criteria described in Table 1. The purpose of this comparison is to suggest areas of similarity and difference among the various planning approaches, the relative strengths and weaknesses within each theory, and the overall pattern of emphasis and neglect found in the planning field taken as a whole.

The SITAR theories differ both in terms of their intentions and how well they have succeeded historically in fulfilling their chosen purposes. The table indicates for each theory at least one area in which it claims special strength, other areas in which it offers a partial or one-sided approach, and still other areas where clear shortcomings can be observed.

In any given area (for example, action potential) the theories provide different prescriptions for the planner—different analytical methods, varying substantive

Table 2 Relative Emphasis of SITAR Theories Based on Selected Criteria

MAJOR CRITERIA, OR DESCRIPTIVE CHARACTERISTICS OF PLANNING THEORY	THE SITAR TRADITIONS				
	SYNOPTIC PLANNING	INCREMENTAL PLANNING	TRANSACTIVE PLANNING	ADVOCACY PLANNING	RADICAL PLANNING
Public interest	○	○	○	•	•
Human dimension			•		○
Feasibility	•	•			
Action potential	○	○	○	○	○
Substantive theory		○	○		○
Self-reflective			○	○	○

Explanation of Table:
Characteristics are taken from Table 1
• indicates major strength or area of concern
○ indicates partial or one-sided treatment
blank cells indicate characteristic weaknesses

definitions of problems, different forms of action to consider. Consequently each of the six criteria included in the list presents an arena for debate on certain classic issues of planning theory and practice. The true meaning of the criteria is that they represent areas of philosophical choice in which planners must turn to one or another planning tradition for answers. Each tradition constitutes a body of foregone conclusions about problem definition and problem solutions. Planners can exercise better critical judgment about the assumptions they buy into if they consider the possibilities offered by a range of alternative candidate theories. A matrix like Table 2 may be simplistic for this purpose, but it is a place to start.

To give fuller meaning to the six criteria listed in Tables 1 and 2, it is worth discussing them briefly, with special attention to the kinds of issues that each one raises.

THEORY OF THE PUBLIC INTEREST. Definition of the public interest raises a fundamental planning issue: can goals be considered separately from specific options? Synoptic planning responds "yes," most other approaches, "no." Another key issue is: should conflicts that arise among groups in connection with planning be underplayed in favor of seeking a consensus? Or should they be focal points for defining communities of interest and promoting organized efforts to achieve a more just distribution of benefits? Radical and advocacy planning are based on conflict models of the public interest. Transactive and incremental planning are based on dialogue and bargaining among plural interests, although without an explicit treatment of power. Synoptic planning largely ignores or avoids issues of conflict by referring to a unitary concept of the public interest. For example, the synoptic tradition tends to rely on the Pareto optimum to deal with the problem of skewed incidence of benefits—a fairly lenient standard of social jus-

tice. Synoptic rationality also focusses primarily on technical relationships and objective realities, to the exclusion of subjective and emotional discussion sparked by divergent perceptions of problems being addressed. In addition, synoptic planning typically creates a division of labor between planners (experts) and politicians—a split which casts planners as technicians who can simply ignore political considerations of the public interest.

THE HUMAN DIMENSION. Major issue: should planning seek to provide a framework of objective decision rules (e.g., as benefit-cost analysis provides in synoptic planning)? Or should it aim at a more holistic context for judgment, referring not just to scientific and technical data but to subjective realities, including political concerns, cultural, aesthetic, psychological and ideological considerations, and controvertible theories of social, ecological, and historical processes? Transactive planning gives special attention to psychosocial and institutional processes which facilitate growth and mutual learning between the planner and his constituency. Radical planning emphasizes the role of human will and ideological cohesiveness which gives effective power to technical knowledge. Both radical and transactive planning raise explicit questions about the limitations of social science as an exclusive way of understanding social problems. Both give specific attention to alternative epistemologies, or bases for validating the uses and limits of knowledge. Both emphasize the role of personal knowledge, using concrete experience and direct participation as the point of departure for problem-solving and social struggle.

FEASIBILITY. The world is complicated, but planning methods need to be simple enough to make understanding manageable. How does one translate complexity into simplicity without falling into the trap of mistaking the model for reality itself: Indeed, planners tend to forget too often that the map is not the territory. Synoptic planning has the virtue of being easily grasped: its analytical techniques are fairly standard applications of social science, and its intentions are straightforward. Incremental and advocacy planning refer to the more subtle and complex processes of bargaining, but they come closer to what skilled entrepreneurs and politicians and social mobilizers do anyway, so they score fairly well on the criterion of feasibility. The operating principles of transactive and radical planning are less well known among planning professionals. Furthermore, both of these approaches call for the fostering and strengthening of community-based institutions which are presently overshadowed by centralized and bureaucratically organized agencies of government and corporate enterprise.

Another issue of feasibility revolves around a basic paradox of planning pointed out by numerous observers (Lindblom 1965; Caiden and Wildavsky 1974; Friedmann 1973). Where planning for the future is *feasible* (based on good data and analytical skills, continuity in the trends being extrapolated, and effective means to control outcomes), then planning is unnecessary—it is simply redundant to what already goes on. Conversely, where planning is most *needed* (where there is absence of data and skills and controls in the presence of primitive or turbulent social conditions), planning is least feasible.

ACTION POTENTIAL. Here the issue revolves around the meaning of "action." Synoptic planning addresses possibilities of large scale action and major departures from current strategies of problem-solving, based on fresh insight and thorough examination of goals and policy alternatives. By the same token, however, rational comprehensive planning is vulnerable to the criticism that its plans never reach the stage of implementation. Master Plans are written and filed away, except in rare cases when vast new sources of funding become available in lumps and allow the planner to design programs from scratch, thus putting real clout into Government-by-Master-Plan. Examples of this are the Tennessee Valley Authority (financed by the first surge of economic pump-priming under the New Deal); and large scale-projects undertaken in developing countries by OPEC governments or institutions like the World Bank.

Other planning traditions seek to reduce the gap between decision making and implementation by embedding planning processes in the common everyday practice of social management and experimentation. Only in synoptic planning is there major emphasis on producing "plans." Elsewhere, planning is more characteristically a process that consummates itself in direct action rather than production of documents.

The "structuralist" version of radical planning is similar to synoptic planning in presenting a major gap between analysis of problems and means for implementing solutions. Radicals would respond by saying that they are looking for long run, not short run results. If their effectiveness is not very visible, it is because most people are not educated in recognizing the contradictions within the system and the manifestations of growing tensions that will eventually lead to decisive transformations. Radicals also argue that significant change involves real but unrecognized forms of social, economic, and historical relationships which are being ignored by conventional social science and by the liberal philosophy that currently dominates social planning. Finally, the radicals would argue that radical change, when it comes, is rarely foreseeable; rather, it is a matter of being prepared for unique historical turning points. Other planning theories, in contrast, tend to focus exclusively on futures that are predictable on the basis of continuity in existing social structures and processes.

Outside of military science there is little writing in planning theory directly addressed to a theory of action. An important exception is the literature on "nonviolent alternatives," which explicitly takes on the problem of power and ways of realigning it toward practical, short-term objectives. Although the historical foundations of non-violent action have evolved mainly in situations of overt conflict and transient confrontation, this is not always the case. In many respects, this literature provides a missing link between theory and practice which other theories have not fully provided. In Table 2, all five SITAR theories are shown to address this problem, but without full success. This is not surprising because one definition of planning is that it is an activity "centrally concerned with the linkage between knowledge and organized action" (Friedmann and Hudson 1974, p. 2). All traditions of planning struggle with this relationship. If any had fully succeeded, there would scarcely be need for more than that one approach.

SUBSTANTIVE THEORY. Mainstream theories of planning are principally concerned with procedural techniques. Substantive content is usually left to secondary levels of specialization in sectorial areas such as education, housing, poverty, industrial development, or land use regulation. Exceptions are radical planning and, to a lesser extent, transactive planning. Both insist that planning styles and methods must adapt to correspond to the specific nature of social-problems being addressed. If they do not, our understanding of problems will be dictated by the arbitrary strengths and limits of our methodology, and not by an a priori appreciation of the substantive phenomenon. For exam-

ple, to understand what "poverty" means, it is not enough to simply look at census data, nor is it enough to simply experience it first hand. One needs a substantive theory of poverty, built up from comparative and historical study of its nature, as well as from principles of social justice and theories of transformation in economic structures. Otherwise, methodological bias or random availability of data or purely arbitrary perceptions from personal experience will dictate the way poverty is perceived. In this case one can easily become locked into a partial—hence erroneous—explanation of poverty, variously interpreted as the consequence of personal or genetic or cultural traits, or as a problem rooted in family structures, or in the physical infrastructure of communities, or in national policies of neglect, or in global dynamics of resource flows favoring industrialized economies at the expense of weaker peripheral areas. A planner who is primarily a methodologist will likely be stuck on one or another of these levels of explanation. A planner who is grounded in substantive theory, however, can press beyond the limits of particular methods to see problems in their entirety.

Most planning theories do not embody explicit world views on any particular subject. The issue thus raised is whether they are remiss in this respect or simply being open-minded and adaptable. A synoptic planner or incrementalist or advocate planner might argue that [his or her] methods serve equally well for most purposes—civilian as well as military applications, the needs of the poor as well as the rich, the problems of neighborhoods and the problems of the world. Radical and transactive planners would tend to argue, to the contrary, that no method is neutral, but that each has a characteristic bias toward one or another group's way of depicting reality. Objectivity itself is a biased frame of reference, excluding those qualities of experienced reality that can only be known subjectively, and must be validated on grounds where social science is reluctant to tread.

The issue manifests itself, for example, in the use of predictions. Forecasting can consist of purely descriptive analysis: extrapolation of trends, curve fitting, probability envelopes, contingency models to accommodate foreseeable variations in patterns. Alternatively, forecasting can incorporate a strongly normative element, designed to provoke corrective action on problems whose warning signs are feeble but urgent. This goes far beyond method, drawing on qualities of imagination, willingness to exercise moral interpretation of facts, and sensitivity to historical dynamics. Most planners would admit that their craft is one of art as well as science. Most are uncomfortable, however, with depicting the future in the full richness of subjective color and detail which they know gives meaning to the present. Works like the *Limits to Growth, California Tomorrow,* the *Crash of '79, The Year 2000, 1984, Looking Backwards,* or *The Shape of Things to Come* all address the same issues that planners deal with in the normal course of their profession. Yet planners are uncomfortable with the literary method, which may be a valid and accurate means of discussing social problems and solutions, but lacks the reliability and objectivity found in the more familiar tools of social science. Different schools of planning come down on different sides of this issue, but in the dominant synoptic and incremental traditions, theories of substance tend to be subordinated to theories of procedure.

SELF-REFLECTIVE THEORY. The central issue here is whether a planning theory needs to be explicit about its own limitations, and if so, how can the theory make clear what has been left out? Incremental planning is least explicit in this respect. The "science of muddling through" is full of hidden agendas and bargaining processes which encourage participants to keep their motives and means to themselves. In synoptic planning, there is far more emphasis on laying everything out on the table, but the rules of the game require that one deal with technical decisions on the basis of objective data. Corrections to the bias of neutral objectivity can be found, not within the synoptic tradition itself, but in the parallel applications of other SITAR traditions.

Etzioni (1968) has suggested a composite approach called "mixed scanning" which alternates between the synoptic approach to "fundamental" decisions and the incrementalist manner of dealing with "bit" decisions (see also Faludi 1973a; Allison 1968).

Transactive, advocacy, and radical planning each have specific procedures for pressing inquiry beyond the initial statement of a planning problem. Transactive planning emphasizes dialogue and development of trusting interpersonal relationships. Advocacy planning relies on the test of mobilizing people to challenge established procedures and institutions in protecting their collective interests. Radical planning calls for ideas to be tested in actions aimed at permanent change in social institutions and values. In contrast, synoptic planning refers to a more limited test of its adequacy in addressing problems: it creates a series of feed-back channels to correct errors in calculations, but the scope and substance of feedback are highly constrained. Like survey questionnaires, feedback channels are narrowly focused on the dimensions of outcomes defined a priori as important. Signals from unexpected quarters, carrying messages beyond the previous scope of understanding a problem, do not easily get through.

There exist certain procedures of critical analysis which might be included as optional components of the synoptic approach, that can be used to challenge the hidden assumptions of rational comprehensive planning. One example is Richard Mason's "dialectical approach to strategy planning" (1969). Another is the synectics procedure, a structured method of brainstorming that encourages divergent thinking in problem-solving.

Beyond this, there is a growing literature in the area of "critical theory" dealing with ways of bringing to light the logic and psychology of thinking about social problems, with a view to correcting its natural limitations and biases. This literature spans the sociology of knowledge, the philosophy of science, the effects of linguistic and cultural structures, the influence of conceptual paradigms, and other matters relating to planning epistemology (Mannheim 1949; Miller, Galanter, and Pribam 1960; Friedmann 1978; Polanyi 1964; Churchman 1971; Bruyn 1970; Hudson 1977). The majority of this writing, however, falls well beyond the scope of the synoptic tradition.

DIRECTIONS FOR FUTURE WORK

Beyond the SITAR package of planning traditions, one can identify additional schools of thought—indicative planning, bottom up planning, ethnographic planning methods, social learning theory, comparative epistemologies of planning, urban and regional planning, basic needs strategies, urban design, environmental planning, macroeconomic policy planning—the list goes on. A question this raises is whether SITAR depicts a fair sample of current thinking in planning theory. Readers can draw their own conclusions. For purposes of this article, the main function of SITAR is to pose key issues that emerge as points of contention among the various planning traditions. A different sample of comparative theories might bring other issues to [the] surface.

Another question concerns the choice of evaluative criteria used to describe and compare different planning traditions.

The choice depends on one's professional personality. The selection process is a kind of Rorschach test of one's own cognitive style, social philosphy, and methodological predilections. In this sense, one could probably devise an instrument to measure personal planning styles based on individuals' preference ranking for an extended list of possible criteria.

Particularly within the synoptic tradition, it is easy to overlook the importance of personal work style and theoretical orientation in determining the compatibility between individual professionals and their clients. Planning is not simply the exercise of a technical capacity involving objective requirements of data, skills, procedures, and institutional mechanisms. Just as important is the social philosophy shared by the planner, the sponsor, and the constituency they are addressing. For some purposes, it may be enough to assess objective needs and deliver solutions to a "target" community. In many cases, however, it is necessary to understand problems through face-to-face interaction with those affected. In such situations, the planner's effectiveness depends on sharing implicit grounds of communication with both colleagues and clients on the levels of information processing styles, value premises, political sensitivies, and other foundations of mutual understanding. Much planning effort is spent on building up this framework of communication and problem definition, but perhaps there is a short-cut. An instrument to test basic attitudes toward alternative planning styles might provide a way of matching clients with congruent professional modus operandi from the outset.

This raises a related issue: how well do clients perceive differences in planning traditions? Are they aware they have a choice? Do they understand the implications of their choice—for example, the relative strengths and weaknesses associated with different traditions? Could clients grasp the significance of evaluative criteria offered to compare traditions—for example, different treatments of the public interest?

One strategy for eliciting client preferences and testing their ability to perceive meaningful choices would be to initiate planning efforts with a "prelude" stage, consisting of a few days of intensive work exposing clients to alternative modes of approaching issues at hand. In a series of dry run exercises, representatives of different approaches could bring in hypothetical data, solutions, feasibility considerations, and unresolved issues bearing on decisions to be made. The clients would get more than a review of planning theory; the process would go a long way toward clarifying their own objectives and substantive policy options. At the same time, planners who participated would get a fast education in the client's own view of issues, based on reactions to the presentations.

It is not clear whether there exists a significant market for this kind of prelude analysis. Funding agencies tend to operate with their own particular style of planning, mainly the synoptic mode. Opening up choices would tend to confound standard operating procedures, reduce the predictability of outcomes, and weaken agency influence over determination of results.

On the other hand, the feasibility and usefulness of intensive short-term policy analysis—either as prelude or substitute for longterm planning efforts—is relatively well established. "Compact policy assessment" exists in the form of a wide variety of quick and dirty procedures for problem formulation, project evaluation, decision making, assumptions analysis, and feasibility testing of proposals. Both in community and organizational settings, there are various specialized methods for pooling judgment, fixing points of consensus, and isolating areas of uncertainty or disagreement for subsequent in-depth study (Hudson 1979). The problem is not so much availability of tools for compact policy assessment, but perception of the need for it. The SITAR package helps make explicit the possibilities of choice between alternative styles and methods of planning. Practical choices, however, will depend on effective procedures for concisely presenting different approaches within the specific problem-solving situations posed by individual clients.

Another question concerns the internal cohesiveness of each planning tradition, and the balance between each tradition and its counterparts. Some combinations appear fairly complementary; others may generate fruitful tension; a few might prove fundamentally incompatible. Defining conditions that facilitate the use of different modes in tandem will require further study.

One must also determine whether each tradition functions as a self-contained paradigm—not just a theory, but a tight and impenetrable mesh of conceptual models, language tools, methodologies, and problem applications, together with its own professional community of believers. It can be argued that a planning paradigm tends to create a determined set of procedures locked into a particular historical environment of problems and solutions (Galloway and Mahayni 1977). Yet there are reasons to think that people have a certain latitude for choice among analytical paradigms (Hudson 1975). Allison (1968) has shown that very different models of decision-making can be used to interpret a single scenario of crisis management. Etzioni (1973) has argued for a "mixed scanning" approach that incorporates both synoptic and incremental planning modes. Historically, advocacy, transactive, and radical planning practices have appeared on the scene as countervailing methods to ongoing processes of synoptic planning, not with the result of replacing the dominant paradigm, but of introducing a broader perspective on issues and another set of voices for articulating the public interest. Systematic evaluation of historical precedents like these would help create more realistic strategies for getting diverse traditions to work together. Such analysis would also help identify ways of encouraging clients to demand and exercise that option.

SUMMARY

Planning has come a long way in the last half century. The Great Depression and World War II provided decisive boosts to synoptic planning—the mandate for large-scale intervention in public affairs, a new repertoire of methods, general acceptance of deficit budgeting, and a firm belief that we can solve enormous problems with a little application of foresight and coordination in the public sector. In the last three decades, that promise has not been entirely fulfilled—either in subsequent wars or in resolving major social problems on the domestic front.

This paper has tended to focus on shortcomings of the synoptic tradition, yet the central problem is a more general one. The real issue is whether *any* planning style can be effective without parallel inputs from other complementary and countervailing traditions. The synoptic planning tradition is more robust than others in the scope of problems it addresses and the diversity of operating conditions it can tolerate. But the approach has serious blind spots, which can only be covered by recourse to other planning traditions. The world is not all that clear or consistent in presenting problems to be solved. Having planners with the ability to mix approaches is the only way to assure that they can respond with sensitivity to the diversity of problems and settings confronted, and to the complexity of any given situation.

The short list of planning theories just reviewed is more than anyone can feasibly apply in the course of daily professional practice. Nevertheless, it can provide a tool kit for many contingencies, and it can serve as a locator map to understand better where other people are coming from.

AUTHOR'S NOTE

Grateful acknowledgment is made to Drs. George Copa and Jerome Moss, who commissioned an earlier version of this paper for the Seminar on Planning and Vocational Education at the Minnesota Research and Development Center, Department of Vocational and Technical Education, University of Minnesota at Minneapolis, October 1978.

NOTES

1. *Procedural* theories of planning refer to techniques and conceptual models that define the work of planners themselves. In contrast, *substantive* theories concern the nature of problems and social processes which lie outside the profession, to which planners address themselves. Procedural theories would include principles of management and organizational development, communications skills for interacting with clients and communities, methods of data acquisition and analysis, historical knowledge of planning, laws and local regulations defining professional practice, and conceptual tools of sociology, economics, and other social sciences. Substantive theories, on the other hand, refer to specific problems or public policy sectors—for example, the nature of educational systems and issues, rural development policies, theories of poverty, future studies on energy policy, the politics of industrialized housing.

   The main problem with this dichotomous classification is that the line between substantive and procedural theories is blurry: procedures are often specialized in their application to particular substantive problem areas. Typically, in fact, a new procedure is invented to deal with a particular problem. Nevertheless, planning evolves through the continual application of old methods to new problems, and the discovery of new methods to deal with old problems. One of the distinctive features of planning is this reciprocal feedback between theory and practice, knowledge and action, conceptual models and the real world.

2. Algorithms versus heuristics. An *algorithm* is a set procedure for solving a known class of problems. It generally involves quantitative methods, and by definition it is capable of arriving at an optimal solution, based on specification of an ojective function, resources, and constraints. Examples are linear programming and input-output analysis, operations research, and trend projections. Most algorithms are backed up by theories. For

example, the S-shaped curve used in making growth forecasts reflects underlying premises about the nature of growth dynamics and the ceilings on expansion—a generalized pattern derived from statistics, general systems theory, and common sense. Algorithms also require characteristic skills, and professionals undertaking this kind of work can be clearly credentialled for degree of competence. *Heuristic* methods consist of more open-ended search procedures which apply to fuzzy problems, and which offer no optimal solutions but only approximations or judgmental trade-offs. Quantitative methods usually play a less central role although they can have important supporting functions, for example in gaming and simulation procedures to explore scenarios of the future policy situations. The result is not a specific solution, but better judgment about the sensitivity of outcomes to different action possibilities, or different environmental conditions.

Some organizational settings demand strict accountability in standard procedures, and thus rely on algorithms. (In some cases, the planner's role is to justify a particular project or policy dictated by prior reasons of ethics or politics, using selected algorithms that do not bring controversial issues into view.) Other organizations thrive on heuristics, for example those engaged in future studies or trouble shooting, where neither the problem nor the solution is well defined, and the client is more likely to be open-minded about surprise findings and unorthodox recommendations for action. Some planners feel that the really interesting problems are those being encountered for the first time and those which are too "wicked" to be reduced to a standard algorithm. (Rittel and Webber 1973; Friedmann 1978.)

Heuristics and algorithms each have their distinctive uses, but most planning methods can serve either purpose. It is important for planners to clarify with their clients whether the goal is to solve a problem that is clear in everybody's minds, using prescribed techniques and predictable types of answers or whether the task is to gain greater understanding of the problem itself, critically challenging the assumptions underlying past methods of problem-solving, keeping in play judgment and imagination, intuitive leaps and creative insights, to challenge the "givens" of a situation rather than accommodate them. The problem with algorithms and heuristics as a classification scheme is that they are very closely intertwined in specific planning procedures. Systems analysis, for example, has many elements of an algorithm, as in the use of statistical models to estimate input-output or cause-effect or cost-effectiveness relationships among the parts of a system. On the other hand, there are also heuristic

versions of systems analysis—the kind of procedure involving boxes and arrows, or a matrix format to array policy objectives against a list of strategy options, to gain a general impression of how well action choices stack up against the goals being sought.

3. Traditional divisions in planning literature refer to sources found in university-based planning programs, and reflected in the *AIP Journal*. Friedmann and Hudson (1974) have distinguished four broad categories of writing in this field:

Philosophical Synthesis (Mannheim, Lindblom, Etzioni, Schon, Friedmann, and others) attempts to locate planning within a larger framework of social and historical processes including: epistemological issues (relating to theories of knowledge and its limits); theories of social action and evolution; ideological contexts of planning; the tensions/reinforcements between planning and democracy; psycho-social development of communities; and social learning theory, which refers to society as a whole taken as a learning system.

Rationalism (Synoptic Rationality) is mainly concerned with procedural (as opposed to substantive) theories. Policy making is seen as a science, emphasizing econometric models and other algorithms for decision-making (Herbert Simon, Jan Tinbergen, C. West Churchman, Jay Forrester).

Organizational Development theory (Chester Barnard, Kurt Lewin, Warren Bennis, Chris Argyris, Lawrence and Lorsch) centers on management of institutions involved in planning and implementation of plans. Emphasis is on awareness, attitudes, behavior, and values that contribute to understanding, personal development, learning, and growth of effectiveness over time. Whereas the rationalist approach is addressed to allocative planning (efficient distribution of resources among possible uses), organizational theory has more to say about innovative planning—situations which call for mobilization of new resources, toward goals not strictly limited to considerations of economic efficiency, and requiring transformation of perceptions, values, and social structures to bring about needed change (Friedmann 1973).

Empirical studies of planning practice include literature on urban planning (Caro's study of Robert Moses, *The Powerbroker*, is a good example) and also on national planning, especially for lesser developed countries (works by Bertram Gross, Albert Waterston, Albert Hirshman, Guy Benveniste). Also included are some good analyses of regional planning efforts in the U.S., for example Selznick's study of the Tennessee Valley Authority, in which he coined the term "cooptation," or Mel Webber's evaluation of BART in the San Francisco Bay Area. Some of the best work has used the comparative case study approach, which captures enough richness of local detail to avoid the pitfalls of reductionist models and grand abstractions, but which also permits generalizations to be made, and lessons captured from past experience. Good examples of this are the studies of comparative strategies of non-formal education for rural development (Ahmed and Coombs 1975; see also Coombs and Ahmed 1974).

4. See references to empirical studies of planning practice cited in the preceding footnote, and the elaborated discussion in Friedmann and Hudson (1974).

REFERENCES

AHMED, MANZOOR AND COOMBS, PHILIP 1975. *Education for rural development: case studies for planners.* New York: Praeger Publishers.

ALINSKY, SAUL D. 1972. *Rules for radicals.* New York: Vintage Books.

ALLISON, GRAHAM T. 1968. *Conceptual models and the Cuban missile crisis: National policy, organizational process, and bureaucratic politics.* Cambridge, Mass.: Harvard University Press.

ARGYRIS, CHRIS 1965. *Organization and innovation.* Homewood, Ill.: Irwin Dorsey.

ARGYRIS, CHRIS, AND SCHON, DONALD 1975. *Theory in practice.* San Francisco: Jossey-Bass.

BARNARD, CHESTER I. 1938. *The functions of the executive.* New York: The Free Press.

BENNIS, WARREN G. 1969. *Organization development: its nature, origins, and prospects.* Reading, Mass.: Addison-Wesley.

BENNIS, WARREN G.; BENNE, K. D.; AND CHIN, R. EDS. 1976. *The planning of change,* 3rd ed. New York: Holt, Rinehart and Winston.

BENVENISTE, GUY 1972. *The politics of expertise.* Berkeley, California: The Glendessary Press.

BRUYN, SEVERYN T. 1970. The new empiricists: the participant observer and phenomenologist, and The methodology of participant observation, pp. 283–287 and 305–327. In *Qualitative methodology: firsthand involvement with the social world,* ed., William J. Filstead. Chicago: Markham Publishing Company.

BUNDY REPORT. New York City Mayor's Advisory Panel on Decentralization of the New York City Schools. 1967. *Reconnection for learning: A community school system for New York City.* New York: City of New York.

CAIDEN, NAOMI, AND WILDAVSKY, AARON 1974. *Planning and budgeting in poor countries.* New York: Wiley-Interscience Publications.

CARO, ROBERT. 1975. *The power broker—Robert Moses and the fall of New York.* New York: Vintage Books.

CHURCHMAN, CHARLES WEST 1968. *The systems approach.* New York: Dell Publishing Company.

CHURCHMAN, CHARLES WEST 1971. *The design of inquiring systems: basic concepts of systems and organizations.* New York: Basic Books.

COOMBS, PHILIP, WITH MANZOOR, AHMED 1974. *Attacking rural poverty. How nonformal education can help.* World Bank/ICED. Baltimore: Johns Hopkins Press.

DAVIDOFF, PAUL 1965. Advocacy and pluralism in planning. *Journal of the American Institute of Planners* 31, November: 331–38.

ELLUL, JACQUES 1954. *The technological society.* New York: Vintage Books, pub. 1964.

ETZIONI, AMITAI 1968. *The active society: A theory of society and political processes.* New York: The Free Press.

ETZIONI, AMITAI 1973. Mixed scanning. In *A reader in planning theory,* ed. A. Faludi. New York: Pergamon Press.

FABER, MIKE, AND SEERS, DUDLEY, EDS. 1972. *The crisis in planning.* Vol. 1: *The issues;* Vol. II: *The experience.* London: Chatto and Windus for the Sussex University Press.

FALUDI, ANDREAS, ED. 1973a. *A reader in planning theory.* New York: Pergamon Press.

FALUDI, ANDREAS 1973b. *Planning theory.* New York: Pergamon Press.

FORRESTER, JAY W. 1969. *Urban dynamics.* Cambridge, Mass.: The MIT Press.

FRIEDMANN, JOHN 1973. *Retracking America. A theory of transactive planning.* Garden City, N.Y.: Doubleday-Anchor.

FRIEDMANN, JOHN 1978. The epistomology of social practice: A critique of objective knowledge, *Theory and Society* 6, 1: 75–92.

FRIEDMAN, JOHN, AND HUDSON, BARCLAY 1974. Knowledge and action: A guide to planning theory. *Journal of the American Institute of Planners* 40, 1: 3–16.

GALLOWAY, THOMAS D., AND MAHAYNI, RIAD G. 1977. Planning theory in retrospect:

The process of paradigm change. *Journal of the American Institute of Planners* 43, 1:62–71.

GOODMAN, PAUL, AND GOODMAN, PERCIVAL 1960. *Communitas. Means of livelihood and ways of life.* Second Edition. New York: Vintage Books.

GOODMAN, ROBERT 1971. *After the planners.* New York: Touchstone Books.

GORDON, DAVID M. ED. 1971. *Problems in political economy: An urban perspective.* Lexington, Mass.: D.C. Heath and Company.

GRABOW, STEPHEN, AND HESKIN, ALLAN 1973. Foundations for a radical concept of planning. *Journal of the American Institute of Planners* 39:2: 106–14. Also "Comments" in *JAIP* 39:4 and *JAIP* 40:2.

GROSS, BERTRAM M. 1965. National planning: Findings and fallacies. *Public Administration Review* 25:4: 263–273.

HAMPDEN-TURNER, CHARLES 1975. *From poverty to dignity.* Garden City, New York: Anchor Books.

HESKIN, ALLAN 1977. Crisis and response: An historical perspective on advocacy planning. Urban Planning Program Working Paper, DP-80. Los Angeles: University of California at Los Angeles.

HIGHTOWER, HENRY C. 1969. Planning theory in contemporary professional education. *Journal of the American Institute of Planners* 35, 5: 326–329.

HIRSCHMAN, ALBERT O. 1967. *Development projects observed.* Washington, D.C.: The Brookings Institution.

HORVAT, BRANKO 1972. Planning in Yugoslavia. In *The crisis of planning,* Vol. II. ed., Faber and Seers. London: Chatto and Windus for the Sussex University Press.

HUDSON, BARCLAY 1975. Domains of evaluation. *Social Policy* 6, 3:79–83.

HUDSON, BARCLAY 1977. Varieties of science: not by rationalism alone; and Dialectical science: Epistemology for evolutionary systems. Los Angeles: UCLA Urban Planning Program (manuscript).

HUDSON, BARCLAY 1979. Compact policy assessment and the delphi method: Practical application of dialectical theory to educational planning and forecasting. Paper prepared for the Center for Studies in Education and Development. Harvard University, Cambridge, Massachusetts (February).

ILLICH, IVAN 1973. *Tools for conviviality.* New York: Harper & Row.

JANTSCH, ERICH, ED. 1969. *Perspectives of planning.* Paris: Organization for Economic Cooperation and Development.

KATZ, ALFRED, AND BENDER, EUGENE 1976. *The strength in us.* New York: New Viewpoints.

KRAVITZ, ALAN S. 1970. Mandarinism: Planning as a handmaiden to conservative politics. In *Planning for politics: Uneasy partnership,* eds., T. L. Beyle and G. T. Lathrop, New York: Odyssey Press.

LAWRENCE, PAUL R., AND LORSCH, JAY W. 1967. *Organization and environment. Managing differentiation and integration.* Boston: Harvard University Graduate School of Business Administration.

LEWIN, KURT 1948. *Resolving social conflicts: Selected papers on group dynamics.* New York: Harper and Bros.

LICHFIELD, N. 1970. Evaluation methodology of urban and regional plans: A review, *Regional Studies* 4: 151–165.

LINDBLOM, CHARLES E. 1959. The science of muddling through. *Public Administration Review* 19:79–88.

LINDBLOM, CHARLES E. 1965. *The intelligence of democracy. Decision making through mutual adjustment.* New York: The Free Press.

MANNHEIM, KARL 1949. *Ideology and utopia.* New York: Harcourt, Brace and Co.

MASON, R. O. 1969. A dialectical approach to strategic planning. *Management Science* 15: B-403-414.

MEYERSON, M., AND BANFIELD, E. C. 1955. *Politics, planning, and the public interest.* Glencoe, N.Y.: Free Press.

MILLER, GEORGE A.; GALANTER, EUGENE; AND PRIBAM, KARL H. 1960. *Plans and the structure of behavior.* New York: Henry Holt.

MILLS, C. WRIGHT 1959. *The sociological imagination.* London: Oxford.

PEATTIE, LISA 1968. Reflections on advocacy planning. *Journal of the American Institute of Planners* 34, 2:80–87.

POLANYI, MICHAEL 1964. *Personal knowledge: towards a post-critical philosophy.* New York: Harper Torch Books (orig. pub. 1958).

RITTEL, HORST, W. J., AND WEBBER, MELVIN M. 1973. Dilemmas in a general theory of planning. *Policy Sciences* 4: 155–169.

SCHUMACHER, E. F. 1973. *Small is beautiful.* New York: Harper & Row.

SCOTT, A. J., AND ROWEIS, S. T. 1977. Urban planning in theory and practice: A reappraisal. *Environment and Planning 9,* 1:1097–1120.

SCHON, DONALD 1971. *Beyond the stable state.* New York: Random House.

SELZNICK, PHILIP 1949. *TVA and the grass roots.* Berkeley: University of California Press.

SIMON, HERBERT 1957. *Administrative behavior,* 2nd ed. New York: The Free Press.

TINBERGEN, JAN 1964. *Economic policy: principles and design.* Amsterdam: North Holland.

WATERSTON, ALBERT 1965. *Development planning: lessons of experience.* Baltimore: The Johns Hopkins Press.

WILSON, JAMES Q. 1968. *City politics and public policy.* New York: John Wiley and Sons.

Mark H. Moore

Anatomy of the Heroin Problem: An Exercise in Problem Definition

The definition of a policy problem has more than semantic importance. If the purposes of a policy are too narrowly described, then important effects of policy proposals can easily be ignored or undervalued. If important variables affecting the behavior of the relevant system are overlooked, then significant opportunities or constraints on policy choices may be missed. In either case, the policy recommendations will be inappropriate.

For heroin policy, the definition of the problem is particularly critical. Consider alternative definitions and their implications for government policy.

Some see the objective of heroin policy as simply the reduction of heroin consumption. Abstinence is desirable, even if no other behavioral changes occur. Recommended policies include the establishment of detoxification programs, in-pa-

Reprinted with permission of the author and The Regents from *Policy Analysis* 2:4 (Fall 1976), pp. 639–62. Copyright 1976 by The Regents of the University of California.

tient psychiatric hospitals, and stringent restrictions on the supply of heroin. Excluded by the definition of objectives are methadone maintenance and the legal prescription of heroin.

For others, the objective is to improve the quality of the user's life. Any improvement in health, economic independence, or self-esteem is desirable, even if the individual continues to use heroin. Consequently, methadone maintenance and the legal prescription of heroin are seen as appropriate policies.

Still others define the objective as protecting others in the society from the dangerous behavior of users. Hence, all reductions in crimes committed by users are desirable. Jail and compulsory treatment become the appropriate instruments.

Similarly, some assume that the major variable influencing the behavior of users is their heroin consumption. If users suddenly stopped consuming heroin, their health would improve, their dignity and autonomy would be enhanced, and their crimes would be reduced. In this view, methadone maintenance and detoxification should secure broad, effective leverage on the behavior of individual users.

Others assume that the prohibition of heroin is the culprit. If users' real incomes were not drastically reduced by the high price of illegal heroin; if their control over their time were not disrupted by arrest, failure to make a connection, or intoxication from too heavy a dose of heroin; if they did not have to devote all their emotional energy to the compelling task of overcoming these obstacles—then they could lead self-controlled and dignified lives. Here, permitting the legal prescription of heroin is the recommended policy.

Finally, others assume that the set of opportunities confronting users is a major factor influencing both the predisposition to use heroin and much of the individual's behavior after he or she has become a user. In this view, policies that expand opportunities are necessary and sufficient both to prevent heroin use and to improve the behavior and condition of current users.

In the literature, these views have been disguised under a variety of slogans. The "law enforcement approach" is contrasted with the "medical approach." Policies attacking "symptoms" are contrasted with policies attacking "root causes." A narrow focus on heroin rather than on drug abuse in general is judged as obviously "suboptimal." These slogans, functioning as definitions of the heroin problem, have arbitrarily narrowed the range of reasonable objectives, created prejudices about effective policies, and led too quickly to overconfident conclusions.

The purpose of this article is to define the heroin problem in a way that avoids the narrow prejudices of the slogans. First I will list the attributes that should be included in any description of the heroin problem; and I will discuss the objectives that government should pursue in light of these attributes. Then, after identifying the major classes of policy instruments that

can wield some influence, I will present a simple, causal anatomy that allows us to reason from the proximate effects of policy instruments to their aggregate impact on the problem.

ATTRIBUTES OF THE PROBLEM AND THE GOVERNMENT'S OBJECTIVES

Table 1 identifies those attributes of the world that are significantly affected by heroin use or by the policies designed to control it; the table also gives some indications of the current state of the heroin problem in New York City.

It is not clear how many of these effects occur as a necessary consequence of heroin use in and of itself. It may be that heroin users[1] are people who would be unhealthy, poor, degraded, dangerous, and expensive to the public regardless of their addiction. If they all stopped using heroin tomorrow (or if they never had used it), their behavior and condition might be roughly the same as it is now.[2] It may also be that the only reason heroin users behave so badly and suffer such intolerable conditions is that they are forced to purchase heroin in an illicit market. If heroin were legally available in inexpensive, sterile, and predictable doses, the user's behavior and conditions might improve dramatically.[3]

The general issue of what causes users to behave as they do is encountered repeatedly in any analysis of the heroin problem. What is at stake in deciding this issue are presumptions about the ability of different policy instruments to improve the behavior and condition of users. If you judge that heroin use in itself determines much of the user's state, then you recommend policies that are designed primarily to reduce heroin consumption. If you judge that it is only the *illicitness* of heroin consumption that is at fault, then you recommend abandoning the current policy of prohibiting heroin use.[4]

I raise the issue here, not to resolve it, but to prevent misinterpretation of table 1. The assertion that the various effects are attributes of the heroin problem should not be read as an assertion that these effects occur largely as a result of heroin use in itself. We should make no presumptions about the efficacy of the various policy instruments until we have examined the behavior of users more closely. The purpose of the table is simply to provide a comprehensive and orderly accounting scheme for noticing important changes in the heroin problem or the effects of using any particular instrument to deal with the problem.

The government's objectives should comprehend all the attributes of the problem. More specifically, the government should seek to

1. improve the health of users;
2. enhance the dignity and autonomy of users;
3. reduce the crimes committed by users;
4. reduce the contagiousness of heroin use;
5. bolster the morale of the society;
6. reduce the public resources absorbed by heroin users.

It is in terms of these objectives and the more detailed attributes listed in table 1 that we should describe the state of the heroin problem and evaluate the impact of specific policies and programs.

I list six objectives, despite the controversy over which ones are the proper concern of government.[5] There are many who feel that government should intervene in private decisions only when these have a harmful effect on others. Those who hold strongly to this notion argue that government should be concerned only with the "external effects" of heroin use, such as crime and contagion. They insist that there is no effect of heroin on the individual user that justifies government intervention. Users may become diseased, may feel trapped in a life-style they do not like, may

be dependent both psychologically and economically on family and friends, but this is no cause for government intervention. People are free to choose their own roads to hell.

Others favor government intervention in private decisions when the decisions have significant consequences that the decision maker is either unable to determine or incompetent to evaluate. Thus the government is authorized to prevent children (and others who do not fully understand the consequences of heroin use) from gaining access to heroin.[6] Ordinarily, one assumes that denying access may be achieved by a "regulatory policy." Consequently, the government is authorized to have such a policy. But what if regulatory policy fails? In this case it is not clear whether the government should impose a "prohibition policy," for, while successful in denying access to children, such a policy would infringe on the decisional rights of presumably competent adults.

Still others feel that government has the obligation to motivate and help each of its citizens to enjoy a life that is consistent with current views of human dignity:

> In this conception of the public good, all citizens of a society are bound to be affected—indirectly but perhaps profoundly and permanently—if a significant number are permitted to go to hell in their own way. A society is therefore unworthy if it permits, or is indifferent to, any activity that renders its members inhuman or deprives them of their essential (or "natural") capacities to judge, choose and act.[7]

This view permits government intervention not only to reduce external effects and to prevent heroin use among those not able to estimate the consequences but also to enhance the dignity and autonomy of individual users.

If we were to strain to resolve this controversy, we might narrow the set of government objectives and simplify future

Table 1 Attributes of the Heroin Problem

Attributes of the Heroin Problem			Indicators of the Problem in New York City
Effects on Users	Health	Mortality	Mortality rate among users is approximately 1% per year;[1] 20-year-old user has the same life expectancy as a 50-year-old nonuser.[2]
		Morbidity	Nearly all tetanus cases are users;[2] Nearly all users contract clinical or subclinical hepatitis.[2]
		Intoxication	Roughly only 2 out of every 12 hours are spent being "straight";[3] Many users abuse alcohol.[4]
	Dignity and Autonomy	Economic Independence	Average income for users in legitimate work is estimated at $3,300;[5] 20-30% of users in New York City are on welfare; around 50-60% of users report borrowing from family as a source of money.[6]
		Conventional Responsibilities	Over 50% of cases of child abuse in New York City involve families of users;[2] ⅓ of users never help out former wife or family.[7]
		Satisfaction with Life	

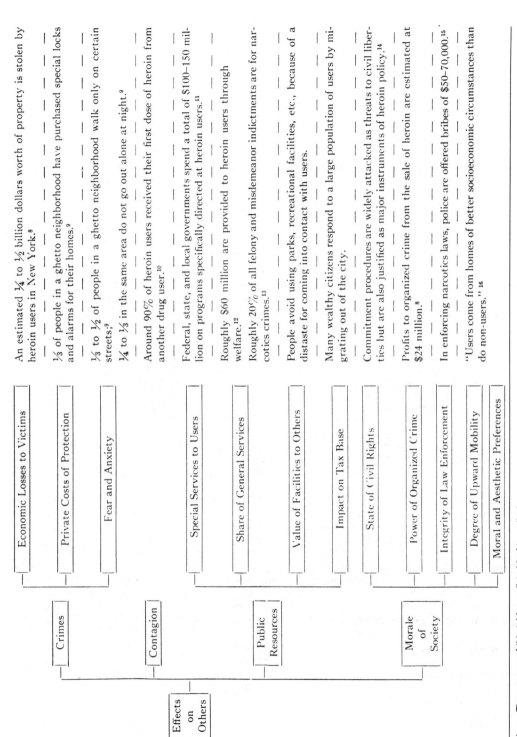

Effects on Others		Description
Crimes	Economic Losses to Victims	An estimated ¼ to ½ billion dollars worth of property is stolen by heroin users in New York.[8]
	Private Costs of Protection	⅓ of people in a ghetto neighborhood have purchased special locks and alarms for their homes.[9]
	Fear and Anxiety	⅓ to ½ of people in a ghetto neighborhood walk only on certain streets;[9] ¼ to ⅓ in the same area do not go out alone at night.[9]
Contagion		Around 90% of heroin users received their first dose of heroin from another drug user.[10]
	Special Services to Users	Federal, state, and local governments spend a total of $100–150 million on programs specifically directed at heroin users.[11]
	Share of General Services	Roughly $60 million are provided to heroin users through welfare.[12]
Public Resources	Value of Facilities to Others	Roughly 20% of all felony and misdemeanor indictments are for narcotics crimes.[13]
	Impact on Tax Base	People avoid using parks, recreational facilities, etc., because of a distaste for coming into contact with users.
	State of Civil Rights	Many wealthy citizens respond to a large population of users by migrating out of the city.
Morale of Society	Power of Organized Crime	Commitment procedures are widely attacked as threats to civil liberties but are also justified as major instruments of heroin policy.[14]
	Integrity of Law Enforcement	Profits to organized crime from the sale of heroin are estimated at $24 million.[8]
	Degree of Upward Mobility	In enforcing narcotics laws, police are offered bribes of $50–70,000.[15]
	Moral and Aesthetic Preferences	"Users come from homes of better socioeconomic circumstances than do non-users."[16]

NOTE: The sources of this table are listed in Appendix A.

analysis. However, I am not willing to decide on the appropriate set of government objectives until I see what the consequences of having a limited set would be. Since we are still uncertain about the precise effects of various policies and about the importance we should attach to the various effects, it seems best to let the ones presented in table 1 remind us of everything that might be at stake in choosing (or keeping) any specific policy toward heroin use.

POLICY INSTRUMENTS

The policy instruments that the government can use to manipulate the attributes of the heroin problem are numerous and diverse. In this section I sort the hetero-

geneous set of instruments into subsets about which I can make general observations. Within these subsets, the comparisons of specific instruments are simple and revealing.

Differences in Scope

One of the most important differences among policy instruments is their relative breadth or narrowness of scope. Some policies are designed to influence a broad range of behavior; others are not. Some are designed to influence only those people who are currently using heroin; others target a much larger segment of the total population. Thus we can define the scope of a policy in terms of (1) the range of behavior the policy is designed to influence; and (2) the population group the

Table 2 Scope of Alternative Policy Instruments

POLICIES THAT INFLUENCE THE BEHAVIOR OF THE GENERAL SOCIETY		POLICIES THAT INFLUENCE THE BEHAVIOR ONLY OF PEOPLE ALREADY USING HEROIN	
POLICIES THAT INFLUENCE A BROAD RANGE OF BEHAVIOR 1	POLICIES THAT INFLUENCE HEROIN CONSUMPTION ONLY 2	POLICIES THAT INFLUENCE A BROAD RANGE OF BEHAVIOR 3	POLICIES THAT INFLUENCE HEROIN CONSUMPTION ONLY 4
Macro employment policies	Prohibition of all sales and use of heroin	Therapeutic communities	Ambulatory detoxification
Welfare programs	Drug education programs	Individual psychotherapy	"Bare bones" methadone maintenance
Public health programs	Early detection and quarantine programs	Methadone maintenance with ancillary services	
Anti-poverty programs	Antagonist immunization programs	Probation and parole	
Job-training programs		In-patient psychiatric hospitals	
Prohibiting discrimination in hiring		Sheltered work programs	
Juvenile delinquency programs			
Jails and prisons			

policy affects. Table 2 presents a large number of policy instruments and distinguishes among four subsets of policies according to differences in scope.

Policies Attacking "Symptoms" vs. Policies Attacking "Causes"

Policies that differ in scope are sometimes loosely distinguished as those that attack "symptoms" of the heroin problem and those that attack its "root causes." Presumably, policies attacking symptoms are those designed primarily to reduce heroin consumption among people currently using the drug (see the fourth column of table 2). Policies attacking causes have broader scopes: They seek to influence more aspects of behavior than simply heroin consumption and generalize their influence to a larger portion of the total population (column 1).

The classification in terms of symptoms and causes produces ardent judgments about the relative merits of specific programs: it strongly implies that policies attacking symptoms are cynical, impermanent, inefficient, or otherwise undesirable, and that policies attacking causes are self-evidently superior.

There is a sound instinct in this. If you define the objectives of heroin policy as broadly as I have done, you must intuitively judge that a policy restricted to reducing the heroin consumption of current users will not have a substantial impact on the problem. Too much of the user's adverse behavior and unhappy condition will persist despite the reduction in heroin consumption. Too many people whose behavior we would like to influence—siblings, parents, spouses, neighbors—will remain out of reach.

But if a sole reliance on narrow policies would be a mistake, so might a sole reliance on broader ones. There are two reasons to believe that the broader policies would fail. First, such policies in general have had much weaker effects than expected on the overall behavior and condition of people: Many of the great social programs of the sixties failed to improve the lives of those they were designed to serve. The time for great confidence in the magical effects of antidiscrimination laws, job training, and antipoverty agencies has passed. Second, because heroin users are separated from society by racial discrimination, by discrimination against people with criminal records, and by their own poor attitudes, health, and skills, they tend to be among the last aided by expansion in employment or extension of general social services. Even when broad policies are aggressively pursued, users require special attention and support to overcome the remaining barriers. Such attention and support can be provided only by policies with somewhat narrower scopes: In some cases, the very narrow policies will be sufficient for this; but in others, more comprehensive and intensive programs (column 3) will be required. Thus there is an important complementary effect among programs with different scopes: Combinations are likely to provide greater leverage than any one class of policy pressed alone.

Note that the programs listed in column 3 raise a special issue: Why should a program designed to do much more than simply reduce heroin consumption be restricted to heroin users? Many of the rehabilitative techniques employed by these programs are *generally* applicable. Presumably, there are other disadvantaged, degraded, and dangerous people in the world who might benefit from them as much as or more than heroin users could. Consequently, equity might demand that these programs be accessible to nonusers as well as users.

There are two arguments for restricting them to heroin users. First, one can argue that heroin users are generally much more degraded, unhealthy, and dangerous than other poor people; because they are among the worst off in society, they deserve special attention. Second, one can argue that heroin users are unusually susceptible to treatment in social programs: While it is hard to have any impact on the habits, attitudes, and skills of ordinary poor people, there is something about heroin users that makes it easier for them to make dramatic improvements in their behavior and condition. Once we relieve them of the compulsion to use heroin, they spontaneously rehabilitate themselves or become more amenable to guidance that leads to rehabilitation. Since we know that methadone maintenance programs are much more successful than manpower programs in obtaining employment for their clients and much more successful than most probation systems in reducing crime, there is some reason to believe the second argument.

It is not important to *resolve* this issue. But it is important to keep it in mind. If heroin users are not necessarily "worse off" than the general population of poor people and if they do not improve unusually dramatically in social programs, then the restriction of programs may be difficult to justify. But if they are "worse off" or if they do show dramatic improvements in treatment, then the justification is easier.

The Scope of Prevention Programs

The policy instruments listed in the second column of table 2 affect the general population and seek to influence behavior only with respect to heroin consumption. By definition, programs with this particular scope are prevention programs: They are aimed at people not now using heroin and seek to reduce the probability of their using it in the future.

The very scope of such programs points to the central problem in their design: How can we concentrate them on those vulnerable to heroin use rather than diffuse their effects to the general popula-

tion? It is difficult to distinguish the vulnerable from the immune, and failure to do so leads to unavoidable mistakes in deciding when and where to begin the prevention program. Many vulnerable groups will be ignored. Thus, although we would like to narrow the scope of prevention programs to affect only potential heroin users, such programs are, in fact, directed at a relatively undifferentiated general population.

Supervised Programs: Custody vs. Treatment

The policy instruments in the last two columns of the table are similar in two important respects. First, they concentrate their effects on people who are currently using heroin; this distinguishes them from the general policies (column 1) and the prevention policies (column 2). Second, they achieve their effects by combinations of rehabilitative services and direct supervision of the user's behavior.

The differences among these programs are equally important and are not all captured by the distinctions in table 2. The table indicates that the programs differ with respect to the range of behavior they are designed to influence. A second difference has to do with the extent of the programs' direct supervision and rehabilitative services. For example, therapeutic communities offer extensive supervision and extensive rehabilitative services. Jails offer extensive supervision but few rehabilitative services. Ambulatory detoxification programs offer little of either. A third major difference concerns durability of improvement: Virtually all the programs can improve the user's behavior and condition while he remains under direct supervision; but relatively few (perhaps none) can claim that these improvements persist for extended periods after supervision is removed.

A natural distinction that many draw among these supervised programs is between those that provide "treatment" and those that are "custodial." There are several strong connotations associated with this classification. One is that treatment programs are more likely to bring about broad, durable improvements in the user's life. Custodial programs can achieve either broad or narrow influence, but the effect is assumed to last only as long as the user remains a participant and under direct supervision. A second connotation is that treatment programs are concerned primarily with the individual user's health and dignity and only secondarily with protecting others in the society from the effects of his unfortunate situation. Consequently, they are assumed to provide extensive rehabilitative services and only minimal custody. Custodial programs are assumed to be concerned mainly with protecting society and only secondarily with the health and dignity of the individual user; accordingly, they are assumed to provide more control over the user's life and less rehabilitative service. Finally, a third connotation is that while users voluntarily seek treatment programs, they must be coerced into entering custodial programs.

Again, there are sound observations and judgments captured by this natural distinction. However, the distinction can also be misleading. Hasty classification of a program can lead us to assume the presence of characteristics that the program does not in fact have; or it can lead us to make these assumptions with more confidence than is merited. Table 3 presents a conventional classification of programs under the treatment and custodial categories and then explores the nature of the programs far more explicitly by attending to the following five questions:

- How broad is the achieved change in behavior?
- How durable is the achieved change in behavior?
- Does the program affect primarily the

user's health and dignity or his impact on others in the society?
- What is the relative investment in rehabilitation compared with custody?
- Is participation in the program voluntary or compulsory?

While the judgments revealed in the table are all debatable, they suggest that the conventional classification creates distinctions among programs that may actually have roughly comparable effects and blurs distinctions among programs that may be quite different.

The detailed analysis of these programs will be left to another paper. It is sufficient here to note that the five questions listed above can be used in evaluating supervised programs that compete as alternative instruments for directly influencing the behavior of individual users.

A SIMPLE MODEL OF THE HEROIN PROBLEM

The Need for a Model—The large number of objectives and the diversity of policy instruments complicate the design of heroin policy. There are too many things to take into account. Consequently, we need a model of the heroin problem that allows us to concentrate on small components without losing sight of how these components fit together to make the larger problem. Ideally this model would

1. suggest simple terms for summarizing and comparing the effects of diverse policies;
2. identify the major, distinct components of the heroin problem that can be attacked by government intervention;
3. facilitate the sorting of policy instruments into subsets that attack the same component of the problem;
4. alert us to interdependence among attacks directed at different components;
5. explicitly introduce the dynamics that cause the size and character of the problem to change over time.

Table 3 Similarities and Differences among Supervised Programs: Conventional and Unconventional Views

CONVENTIONAL VIEW TREATMENT PROGRAMS	SUPERVISED PROGRAM	VIEW WHEN ATTRIBUTES OF PROGRAM ARE EXPLICITLY DESCRIBED			
		BREADTH AND DURABILITY[1] OF INFLUENCE	LEVELS OF SERVICES AND SUPERVISION	EFFECTS ON USERS VS. EFFECTS ON OTHERS	WILLINGNESS OF USERS TO VOLUNTEER
1. Therapeutic communities	1. Therapeutic communities	Broad and short	High levels of both	Large effects on both	Low
2. NACC rehabilitation facilities	2. NACC rehabilitation facilities	Moderately broad and short	Modest services; high supervision	Primarily on others	Low
3. Methadone maintenance	3. Methadone maintenance	Moderately broad and short	Modest services; modest supervision	Moderate effects on both	High
4. Methadone maintenance without ancillary services	4. Methadone maintenance without ancillary services	Moderately broad and short	Low services; modest supervision	Moderate effects on both	?
5. Ambulatory detoxification	5. Ambulatory detoxification	Very narrow and short	Low levels of both	Small effects on both	High
CONTROL PROGRAMS					
1. Jails and prisons	6. Jails and prisons	Broad and short	Low services; high supervision	Primarily on others	0
2. Probation	7. Probation	Broad and moderately long	Modest services; high supervision	Moderate effects on both	0
3. Parole	8. Parole	Broad and moderately long	Modest services; high supervision	Moderate effects on both	0

[1]Durability refers to the period of time over which changes in behavior are maintained *after* direct supervision ceases.

We can construct a simplified but useful model from a few basic observations.

Strategic Objectives of Heroin Policy: Reducing the Number of Users and Improving Their Behavior and Condition

A heroin problem begins with a population of people who use heroin. It is largely their behavior and condition that generate the adverse consequences of heroin use. If these people did not commit crimes, recruit new addicts, purchase heroin from an organized criminal industry, loiter in parks, kill themselves with overdoses, start fires in abandoned buildings, suffer withdrawal symptoms, beg money from friends and relatives, and so on, there would be no heroin problem. If they did them less frequently, the problem would be less severe.

The seriousness of the heroin problem is also affected by the *number* of people who use heroin. If there were no heroin users, there would be no problem. If there were fewer users, there would be a smaller problem.

These basic observations imply that the strategic objectives of heroin policy should be to (1) reduce the number of people who use heroin; and (2) improve the behavior and condition of current users.

Indeed, we should be able to summarize virtually all the important effects of heroin policy in terms of changes in the number of users or changes in the behavior and condition of users. These are the simple terms we need to summarize and compare the effects of widely divergent programs.

Given our two strategic objectives, the factors that determine the number of users and influence their behavior and condition should be the targets of government policy. To the extent that these factors can be manipulated by policy instruments, they represent opportunities for successful government intervention. To the extent that they lie beyond the reach of policy instru-

ments, they will frustrate and constrain government efforts.

Factors Determining the Number of Users

The factors that determine the number of users are the rates at which people become and cease being heroin users. One can think about these rates as flows into and out of the population of users. The important flows *out* of the population include

1. the rate at which users voluntarily abstain from heroin use;
2. the rate at which users die;
3. the rate at which users participate (voluntarily or involuntarily) in various kinds of supervised programs;
4. the rate at which users are "cured" by various kinds of programs.

The important flows *into* the population of users include

1. the rate at which nonusers become users;
2. the rate at which users abandon, escape, or are released from supervised programs;
3. the rate at which users who have been "cured" or who have voluntarily abstained relapse into heroin use.

Small changes in the relative sizes of these flows can lead to surprisingly large differences in the number of users to be tolerated over the next five to ten years. Consequently, each of these flows should be an important target of government programs and policies.

In general, the government's objectives should be to expand flows out of the population and reduce flows into the population. The obvious exception is the objective to reduce the rate at which users die: Deaths among users constitute a major cost of the heroin problem and signal the failure of government programs.

Factors Influencing the Behavior and Condition of Users

Ordinarily we assume that a major factor influencing the behavior and condition of the heroin user is his level of heroin consumption. If he suddenly stopped using heroin, we reason, he would enjoy better health, have more money to spend on rent and food, and commit fewer crimes. This belief—that heroin use in itself exerts a pervasive influence on the user's behavior—is the major reason why we see the consequences of his behavior as the cost of heroin use rather than of poverty, discrimination, or unequal educational opportunity. But while it would clearly be wrong to assume that heroin use has *no* effect on the user's behavior and condition, it seems even more mistaken to assume that the use of the drug, in and of itself, accounts for *all* of his state.[8]

A second major factor influencing the user's behavior and condition has to do with the habits, skills, and attitudes that shaped his life before he went on heroin. While heroin use, compared with other occupations and hobbies, imposes a fairly rigid structure on the individual's life, it does not completely transform it. Even among those who become desperately addicted, significant elements of their lives prior to addiction remain a part of their lives following addiction. And for the many who avoid becoming deeply involved with heroin, the influence of their pre-addiction life on their present life is much stronger. Thus much of the user's behavior results simply from continuation of the attitudes, skills, and habits that marked his life before he became a user. Presumably, his behavior will not change unless his attitudes, skills, and habits change.

A third influential factor is the set of opportunities accessible to users. The conventional wisdom is that users are trapped by their dependence on heroin: If only they could rid themselves of it, they would enjoy much better lives. An alternative view is that they have significant discretion over whether they remain heroin users and that the reason they so often do is that the alternative careers and lives available to them are not more attractive. Adopting this view, one would expect that changes in their level of unemployment, changes in the degree of discrimination against them (as either addicts, ex-cons, or members of minority groups), and even changes in their marital status would have some important effect on their behavior and condition. Of course, the extent to which any one user responded to a change in opportunity could be significantly influenced by his level of heroin use and by his attitudes, habits, and skills; but given any level of heroin consumption and any set of attitudes, habits, and skills, one would expect to see some change in the user's behavior and condition in response to a change in his set of opportunities.

A fourth factor is the user's participation in supervised programs. To some extent, these programs influence the individual's behavior by changing factors we have already identified—that is, by reducing his consumption of heroin; by altering his skills, attitudes, and routines; and by enlarging the set of opportunities available to him. However, they also influence his behavior simply by achieving some level of supervision over a portion of his day. Consequently, even if a supervised program were to fail in all its efforts to change the other factors governing the user's behavior, it would probably achieve some change simply by interrupting the user's daily routine.

Of profound impact, finally is the fact that the manufacture, distribution, and possession of heroin are prohibited throughout the United States. Because of this policy, the user faces high prices, unpredictable quality, and irregular access in trying to buy heroin; these difficult supply conditions significantly reduce his autonomy, increase the crime rate, and often result in death. In addition, the user is subjected to arrest, bears the stigma of those who are arrested, and is barred from many opportunities by his own desire for anonymity and by the desire of those who control the opportunities not to associate with criminals. While there is room for disagreement about the policy's precise effects and their desirability, there is no doubt whatsoever that prohibition has an enormous impact on the behavior and condition of users.

There are significant interdependencies among all these factors. For example, supply conditions have an impact on the user's behavior only as long as he continues to consume some amount of heroin; so if a program were to eliminate his consumption of heroin, the addition of a policy to improve supply conditions would have no additional impact on his behavior and condition. I have already suggested other interdependencies: The set of alternative life-styles available to the user is influenced by his level of heroin consumption, his individual skills and attitudes, and the policy of prohibiting heroin use; and the influence of supervised programs derives partly from their success in changing the user's level of heroin consumption, his skills and attitudes, and his set of opportunities. The extensive interaction among these factors implies that when a change occurs in a user's behavior and condition, it will be difficult to discover which of the factors has changed or which changed first.

A Simple Diagram Illustrating the Targets of Government Action

I have identified the major factors determining the number of heroin users (the various flows into and out of the population of users), and I have identified the major factors influencing the behavior and condition of users. Figure 1 comprehends

Figure 1 A Dynamic Model of the Heroin-Using Population . . . Types of users are described in Appendix B.

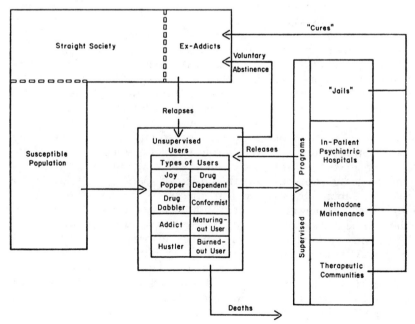

most of these factors in a simple diagram, the purpose of which is to help us organize our analysis of the heroin problem.

The factors determining the number of users are straightforwardly represented by the arrows connecting the various states in the model. You can visualize the government's objectives as contracting the arrows *into* the population and expanding the arrows (but not the death arrow) *out* of the population.

The factors influencing the behavior and condition of users are represented much less straightforwardly. Indeed, two of the major factors (the set of opportunities and the prohibition of heroin) are not explicitly represented at all. Perhaps the easiest way to think of these factors in terms of the diagram would be to imagine a box drawn around the entire system, with these factors influencing that box.

The influence of levels of heroin consumption and the pre-addiction life-style of users is captured by distinguishing among eight different types of users. These types represent different combinations of heroin consumption and pre-addiction life-styles. The government's objective is to increase the proportion of users who have relatively good life-styles (for example, maturing-out users and conformists) and to reduce the proportion who have relatively poor life-styles (for example, burned-out users, hustlers, and drug dependents).

The diagram captures the influence of supervised programs by distinguishing between users participating in these programs and users on the street. The government's objectives in this area are to increase the number of users in supervised programs, increase the numbers in specific kinds of supervised programs, and exploit the comparative advantages of programs in treating special types of users.

The failure of the figure to represent the prohibition policy and the set of opportunities available to users is dangerous to the extent that we are led to ignore the possibility of improving heroin policy by manipulating these factors. The danger is particularly grave because both factors influence not only the users' behavior but also their number. Consequently, in any analysis of the problem, one should take care to consider the impact of these factors and the potential for manipulating them.

Relationship between the Model and the Effects of Heroin Use

Table 1 described a variety of adverse effects that are ordinarily assumed to flow from heroin use: the poor health of addicts, their loss of autonomy, and so on. It is these effects that ultimately matter to society. Consequently, they are the criteria by which we should *ultimately* evaluate the impact of policies to deal with the heroin problem.

However, they are *not* the proximate targets of government policy instruments. Indeed, by suggesting that all the effects that concern us are caused directly by heroin use, Table 1 implies that there is only one target of heroin policy—the level of heroin consumption. In this section I have suggested that there are many factors besides the level of consumption that determine the ultimate magnitude of the heroin problem. Identifying these other factors broadens the array of opportunities for government intervention. In addition, I have indicated the interdependence of the various factors. Thus figure 1 offers a strategic view of opportunities for attacking the heroin problem, while table 1 defines the terms in which we must ultimately evaluate the impact of specific strategies or policy instruments.

We should use the simple model to order the sequence in which we analyze diverse policy instruments, to alert ourselves to forgotten opportunities and important interdependencies that can be exploited, and to develop rough notions of how specific policy instruments can be packaged into concerted overall strategies. We should use table 1 as a guide for detailing the effects of specific programs and making the final choice among overall strategies.

CONCLUSIONS

The appropriate way of testing the definition of a policy problem is to see if it has heuristic value for investigating the problem and making policy recommendations. Often this heuristic value derives from the specification of "intermediate" analytic categories and an explicit identification of the logical and empirical relationships that link them. The "intermediate" analytic categories expose and suggest differences in detail but organize the rules of comparison. The specification of the logical and empirical linkages alerts the analyst to redundancies, important complementary effects, and missed opportunities. If there are many suggestive categories and if the logical and empirical links are intricate but well defined, then the analyst's agenda is filled with interesting questions to consider and important effects to trace. Whether he marches through the agenda with intelligence and imagination is another matter; but we will not be able to attribute his failure to a superficial, ad hoc definition of the problem. I hope that the definition proposed in this paper will create as interesting and compelling an agenda for other analysts of the heroin problem as it has for me.

APPENDIX A
SOURCES FOR TABLE 1

1. Alan Thalinger, "A Study of Deaths of Narcotic Users in New York City—1969" (New York: Health Service Administration, New York City Department of Health, Health Research Training Program, 1970).
2. U.S. Congress, House, Select Committee on Crime, *Drugs in Our Schools, Hearings* before the Select Committee on Crime, 92d Cong., 2d sess., 1972. Testimony of Michael M. Baden, M.D.
3. Vincent Dole et al., "Narcotic Blockade," *Archives of Internal Medicine* 118 (October 1966): 305.

4. John Langrod, "Secondary Drug Abuse among Heroin Users," *International Journal of the Addictions* 5, no. 4 (December 1970): 614.
5. Alan Craig Leslie, "A Benefit/Cost Analysis of New York City's Heroin Addiction Problems and Programs—1971," Teaching and Research Materials (Cambridge, Mass.: Public Policy Program, John Fitzgerald Kennedy School of Government, Harvard University, 1972). The estimate is made by taking the distribution of occupations in a sample of addicts in Addiction Services Agency treatment programs, multiplying by the median U.S. income, and then adjusting for an assumed bias in the sample.
6. Richard D. Brotman and Alfred M. Freedman, *Continuities and Discontinuities in the Process of Patient Care for Narcotic Addicts* (New York: New York Medical College, 1965), p. 105.
7. Ibid., p. 114.
8. Mark H. Moore, *Economics of Heroin Distribution*, Teaching and Research Materials (Cambridge, Mass.: Public Policy Program, John Fitzgerald Kennedy School of Government, Harvard University, 1971). See also Max Singer, "The Vitality of Mythical Numbers," *The Public Interest*, no. 23 (Spring 1971).
9. Paul Kleinman and Deborah S. David, "Protection against Crime in a Ghetto Community" (New York: Columbia University, July 1972), table D–1.
10. William H. McGlothin et al., *Alternative Approaches to Opiate Addiction Control: Costs, Benefits and Potential* (Washington, D.C.: Bureau of Narcotics and Dangerous Drugs, U.S. Department of Justice, 1972), Appendix B, p. 10.
11. New York City Addiction Services Agency, *Comprehensive Plan for the Control of Drug Abuse and Addiction* (New York, 1973), pp. 13–14.
12. New York City Human Resources Administration, *Narcotic Addicts on Public Assistance* (New York, October 1973), p. 22.
13. New York City Criminal Justice Co-ordinating Council, 1972 *Criminal Justice Plan* (New York, 1973), pp. 6–9.
14. See generally: Dennis Aronowitz, "Civil Commitment of Narcotic Addicts," *Columbia Law Review* 67, no. 3 (March 1967); Albert B. Logan, "May a Man Be Punished because He Is Ill?" *American Bar Association Journal* 52 (October 1966); "Due Process for the Narcotic Addict? The New York Compulsory Commitment Procedures," *New York University Law Review* 43, pp. 1172–93; "Civil Commitment of Narcotic Addicts," *Yale Law Journal* 76 (1967): 1160.
15. New York State Commission on Investigation, *Narcotics Law Enforcement in New York City* (New York, 1972), pp. 138–39.
16. Isidor Chein et al., *The Road to H.* (New York: Basic Books, 1964), pp. 126–27.

APPENDIX B
FIGURE 1: TYPES OF USERS

Joy Poppers use heroin regularly but not intensively, reserving weekends or special occasions for their sprees. Included are most young, beginning users from lower-class families (white, black, and Puerto Rican), who become interested in heroin during adolescence because it is risky, precocious, and potentially pleasurable. Many have delinquent orientations and skills before starting on heroin; others will become delinquent around the time they begin use. Practically none will significantly increase their criminal activities solely because of a desire for more heroin. A large minority of the group will stabilize at low rates of consumption for long periods of time and thereby gain status for having avoided "getting hooked." Another large minority will give up heroin use because it frightens them or becomes inconvenient. A bare majority will advance to higher rates of use in one of the behavioral patterns described below.

Drug Dabblers use heroin in the context of experimenting with a variety of drugs. Most suburban and college heroin users are in this category. Their affluence and casual drug use make it unnecessary for them to become criminals. They substitute among drugs freely according to availability and fads. Most (those who have no psychological problems, suffer few stresses, and never get close to reliable sources of heroin) will stabilize at infrequent, low levels of use or abandon heroin entirely. But some will find drug use in general and heroin in particular satisfying and advance to intensive use of drugs of all kinds.

Addicts (high drugs, high crime) fit the usual stereotype of heroin users. They consume heroin frequently enough to spend a large part of each day "on the nod"—and the rest of the day "hustling" for the next fix. They hustle more energetically and persistently than the hustlers described below, committing risky crimes if necessary to stay slightly ahead of their tolerance. They substitute other drugs for heroin because they like being stoned, but the skill and energy they devote to illegal activities usually provide them with enough money for heroin. Many go into dealing at one time or another. Eventually, after seven to ten years, they get tired of hustling for heroin. Whether they also

lose interest in getting stoned at that time will largely determine whether they become "maturing-out" or "burned-out" users.

Drug Dependents (high drugs, low crime) use heroin in a pattern of intense use of drugs of all kinds. Their major motivation is to be stoned for as much of the day as possible. Although they may prefer heroin, they will eagerly consume other drugs when heroin is not available or too expensive. Since they are stoned most of the time, they are unlikely to be energetic, aggressive criminals. Some become sellers, but their careers end quickly when they consume more drugs than they sell. Of all heroin users, they have the most serious psychological and physical problems. Most will become "burned-out" users. Few will be able to resume a normal life, even with extensive government efforts.

Conformists (low drugs, low crime) are heroin users almost by accident. They experimented with heroin and became mildly dependent on it, psychologically and physiologically. They do not have long histories of use and rarely use other drugs. Their moderate use of heroin and conventional attitudes imply that they are able to retain legal jobs. They may have criminal records for drug use but are rarely arrested for crimes against people or property. Included are many weekenders who never developed a strong yen to hustle or be stoned; a lot of veterans who became addicts in Vietnam, where life was boring and heroin easily available; and some drug dabblers who accidentally became mildly "hooked." They frequently undertake detoxification voluntarily, at home. While they are most likely to become cured or mature out, some may become more interested in heroin or in hustling and become one of the other types described above.

Hustlers (low drugs, high crime) enjoy the excitement of earning an illegal income almost as much as they enjoy the direct physiological effects of heroin. They use heroin regularly but are attracted less to getting stoned than to the incentives that heroin use provides for developing and using criminal skills. Typically, they begin using heroin only after they have become hustlers and criminals. Many also use cocaine to indicate the wealth that derives from their skillful hustling and to show their independence from heroin. Some begin dealing in heroin and then tend to become more dependent on the drug and less motivated to "hustle." Many of the young, lower-class delinquents who have been using heroin for more than one year and less than seven fit into this category.

Maturing-Out Users have tired of the risk of heroin use and no longer enjoy the euphoria or analgesia of being stoned. They maintain moderate levels of heroin use by habit. Those who were previously aggressive criminals tend to become more careful or try to obtain legitimate employment. Those who once used many drugs in an undiscriminating way reduce their consumption and become more careful about the drugs they use. This group includes most people who have used heroin for ten years or more or who have reached age 35. The prognosis is very favorable. Members of this group often do very well in supervised programs of all types.

Burned-Out Users have become old, tired, and passive but have not relinquished the desire to be stoned. Because of their high visibility to police (due to many previous arrests), they find criminal activities unattractive; but their poor work records keep them from legitimate employment. Consequently, they tend to be very poor: they work as informants, do petty services for the drug trade (e.g., steering users to dealers), and engage in a few small hustles. Thus they can afford heroin only occasionally. Most use inexpensive drugs. Indeed, many become alcoholics. Included are a large minority (perhaps a bare majority) are the users who survive past the age of 40 or 45. They are in desperately poor health, physically and mentally. They have a very poor prognosis, regardless of government efforts.

For a full description of the different types, an estimation of their representation, and an analysis of the sources of the typology, see Mark H. Moore, "Policy towards Heroin Use in New York City" (Ph.D. diss., Harvard University, 1973).

NOTES

1. I will generally refer to "heroin user," not "heroin addict," to signal clearly that I do not accept uncritically the old stereotypes about how users behave or the old beliefs about the physiology of heroin use. Later in the paper I propose a typology of users that includes eight different types. Only one of these is called an "addict"—his behavior most closely resembles the behavior of the stereotypical addict—and while I estimate that this type accounts for a substantial proportion of all users (around 30 percent), it still represents only a minority. Consequently, when speaking of the entire population of users, I will say "user"; and when speaking of "addicts," I will mean that one type of user.

2. This hypothesis clearly leads to the judgment that it is pointless for a user to stop taking heroin. The same judgment follows from a second hypothesis: if the users had never taken heroin, they would now be in good condition, but since their deterioration comes from long periods of heroin use, it cannot be dramatically changed simply by their giving up the drug. Both hypotheses generally suggest that the user's condition is influenced more by previous behavior than by current heroin consumption.

   But the hypotheses differ significantly in their implications for the value of preventing heroin use. The first implies that prevention is not important; the user would be the same with or without heroin. The second implies that prevention is very important: While it does little good for the user to stop now, he would have enjoyed an attractive life if he had never started. This is a kind of "virginity principle": the value is in preventing initiation; once initiated, the person can hardly be retrieved. I lean toward the second hypothesis. I see the long-run effects of heroin use as critical—opportunities are lost, attitudes change, legitimate skills become obsolete, health deteriorates, relations with family and friends become unpleasant, etc. After eight years of use, a person simply does not have the capabilities and opportunities he had before he started.

   Preventing initiation remains vital even if you believe that many of the long-run effects of heroin use are bad *only* under a prohibition policy, particularly since the policy stigmatizes users by giving them criminal records: if it looks like the prohibition policy will be continued, it is essential to prevent new people from becoming users.

3. See, for example, A. R. Lindesmith, *The Addict and the Law* (New York: Vintage Books, 1965). In another paper, where I examine the issue closely, I find that there is a reasonable chance that legal prescription would have very good effects *or* very bad effects. Thus, while the expected value of the policy may be great, I argue for both additional experimentation and a continued reliance on policies that may have lower expected values but also smaller variances. See my "Policy towards Heroin Use in New York City."

4. Note that if you think *illicit* heroin consumption is the problem, you should be satisfied not only with policies that make all heroin use legal but also with policies that (a) reduce heroin use entirely or (b) reduce illicit heroin use by substituting the legal consumption of something else for the consumption of heroin. All three types of policy would presumably obviate the problem of high

prices, irregular access, and unpredictable quality attending illegal heroin use. You should recommend the legal prescription of heroin as the sole policy only if you believe that it is easier to legalize heroin than to reduce all heroin consumption or to replace heroin with some other legal good *and* if you believe that legalization will not change other objectives of the society. But while these views about implementation and the other objectives of society seem reasonable, they should not be accepted as true *a priori.* They should be subject to argument and evidence.

5. I am deeply indebted to Professor James Q. Wilson for emphasizing the importance of this controversy, for neatly delineating the sources of the controversy, for providing eloquent language to express the alternative views, and for persuading me that the third view (that society may have an obligation to enhance the quality of a citizen's life) is a reasonable one, particularly in the area of heroin addiction.

6. One way of justifying intervention in the decisions of children is to argue that a 15-year-old will not be the same person when he reaches 35. But the 15-year-old's decisions and actions, the argument continues, affect the set of opportunities and hence the utility of the person aged 35. Thus the behavior of one person (the person at age 15) has an important external effect on a different person (the same person at age 35), and government intervention is rationalized as a way of controlling the production of negative externalities. I am indebted to Richard Zeckhauser for pointing this out to me.

7. James Q. Wilson, Mark H. Moore, and I. David Wheat, "The Problem of Heroin," *The Public Interest,* no. 29 (Fall 1972).

8. I identified this issue earlier as one that will persistently intrude into any analysis of the heroin problem and affect presumptions about the efficiency of various policy instruments. To recapitulate briefly, if the user's bad behavior is caused largely by heroin consumption, then the policy should be simply to reduce consumption through detoxification and methadone maintenance. If it is caused by the user's previous skills, attitudes, and habits, then we may have to invest in training, remotivation, and the provision of detailed daily routines through therapeutic communities and sheltered work. If the available set of opportunities determines the user's behavior, we may have to expand that set through macro-employment policies, antidiscrimination efforts, and improved education. If the illicitness of heroin use is at fault, then we might consider the legal prescription of heroin.

In my "Policy towards Heroin Use in New York," I argue that for many users, heroin use is less important in determining behavior than the junkie stereotype would lead us to believe. This places an upper bound on what can be accomplished with policy instruments that succeed only in reducing heroin consumption. Even so, it seems clear that compared to other ways of influencing a person's behavior, simply reducing heroin consumption is relatively effective and easy. But this is truer for some types of users than others. Moreover, it is less certain than we would like. Consequently, there are strong reasons to begin experimenting with programs that have somewhat broader scopes in dealing with individual users.

Franklin M. Zweig and Robert Morris

The Social Planning Design Guide: Process and Proposal

One of the most salient features of social work practice at the community level is the virtual absence of capacity to formulate comprehensive social plans. The literature of community organization, even as it has

Reprinted with permission of the author and National Association of Social Workers from *Social Work.* Vol. 11, No. 2 (April 1966), pp. 13–21.

been modified in recent years, reflects a singular preoccupation with social process and a nearly complete neglect of the technological aspects of social planning.[1] Whatever factors may be cited as playing a part in this situation, it is apparent that the avoidance of plan-making in the curricula of professional schools and in the practice of professional social workers places them in a weak position with respect to formulating designs for social problem solution and prevention.

Unfortunately, this shortcoming exists at a time when innovation aimed at solving massive social problems at the local, metropolitan, and national levels is going full steam ahead. The organizations responsible for the management of innovation—such as those operating antipoverty and community mental health efforts—have created many . . . roles that place a premium on planning technology. These innovating roles cry out for broad scope and effective imagination. In short, they require practitioners to adopt a planning stance and technological skills beyond those they generally now possess.

AN APPROACH TO PLAN-MAKING

Noting that the frame of reference for the ensuing discussion is the individual social work practitioner performing an innovating role in an innovating organization, it is possible to cite three canons that constitute a planning stance.

The primary canon of the stance is that the social worker must adopt a problem focused approach to plan-making.[2] This means that he initially explores the nature of the problem at issue, that he does not permit consideration of what to do about the problem to interfere with his full assessment of it, and that he frees his observational capacities to the greatest possible extent.

A second, derived canon is that the social worker will take nothing for granted about the target social problem. By not allowing his perceptions to be limited by his current knowledge, by the mythology surrounding a given problem, or by the perceptual biases of his close associates, the practitioner opens up an expanded arena for objective analysis.

A final canon relates to the planner's view of the plan. He must be able to view a

plan as a rational, deliberate scheme for solving a social problem—an expert's design for intervention and solution. The plan, therefore, must possess the necessary components to describe the target problem, to assess it, to set objectives for its solution, and to set forth the means by which such objectives may be accomplished. Since the nature of the problems with which the social planner deals is never unitary or amenable to simple cause-effect analysis, the plan must set forth the entire range of available alternatives for problem solving, and the planner must be prepared to select among the alternatives according to his best judgment or according to a standardized decision-making scheme.

A particular set of biases, or stance, is to be attributed to the plan itself. The plan created by the expert cannot be merely a statement of Utopia, although it must be at least that. While it must reflect the Utopian objectives of the planning effort, the plan must be geared to offer realistic courses of action. It must hone its ideal types as closely as possible to the margins of reality. The design cannot be perceived as a theory in itself. It must be a design for solution that specifies the theoretical framework upon which it is based. It must constantly guide action, but such guidance must be based on the reality of the target problem rather than on its mythology. The plan must specify in a clear fashion its inputs and outputs, and it must structure the expectations of the planner for feedback. Finally, the plan must be specialized according to the problem addressed but must also be developed within a mosaic of broad economic, social, and political forces.

SOCIAL PLANNING DESIGN GUIDE

The social planning design guide is a concept that can be expressed as a plan-making process. It is a means for providing boundaries for professional judgment for social welfare planners who perform innovating roles at the community level.

As a plan-making process, the design guide is a systematic means of citing the relevant tools that can be used in plan-making and for ordering the sequence in which these tools are used. The guide is viewed as a process for integrating different classes of design tools. It is viewed as a means by which the cognitive processes of the planner are mobilized so as to produce problem-specific plans that meet the innovative role expectations for both specialism and holism.

Five classes of design tools appear to exist. They are, in sequential order of input, (1) the statement of the problem, (2) the theories of causation relevant to the problem, (3) intervention alternatives and their possible consequences, (4) information about target population, (5) value considerations. Each will be discussed briefly, the purpose being to describe its "essence." Detailed elaboration of each class is necessary, but expanded discussion must await subsequent efforts.

STATEMENT OF THE PROBLEM

The statement of the problem sets the conditions for all the additional classes and categories of design tools subsequently to be selected. The statement should explicate the problem, providing answers to the questions "who? what? where? how? and under what conditions?" as they pertain to the problem. The statement should be brief enough to provide a succinct, descriptive overview yet elaborate enough to describe the problem fully as it is manifested in a particular time and place.[3]

Using the definition of social problem cited earlier, the statement should begin with declarative statements in answer to the following questions: (1) What is the nature of the situation brought to the planner's attention? (2) Which social values are being threatened by the situation? (3) What kind of group recognition and action regarding the problem is extant? More-

over, the statement should include three descriptive elements that can constitute a synopsis of the situation: time scale, geographic scale and locus, and extent of the problem.

Time scale refers to the duration of the problem. Geographic scale refers to its spatial location, specyfing both horizontal boundaries and vertical scale.[4] Extent refers to the number of people affected by the problem, including those directly and peripherally affected.

An example is in order. Let us suppose that a planner in an innovative planning role has been told that a horrible situation at the community level exists in *x* neighborhood: Mothers are working full time, and young children are left unattended, often from early morning to late evening, to roam the streets and create confusion and mischief. Having engaged in preliminary exploration, the planner sets up the following statement:

Situation. Interviews with fifteen residents of *x* neighborhood, with the precinct police chief, with social agency leaders, and with city and state political representatives from the neighborhood disclose that there is widespread concern about lack of care for children of a large number of working mothers. These children are sometimes expected to be on their own, sometimes are left with neglecting friends or relatives. Concern is evidenced on the part of several mothers interviewed; they claim there is no way to provide adequate care, yet they feel they must work.

Further work using an exploratory, purposive-sample survey indicates that this situation has existed for about six years and has accompanied the high immobility of one-parent families replacing many two-parent families who moved to the suburbs.

In *x* neighborhood, composed of some 11,500 persons and some 4,200 households, 1,300 one-parent families are resident, and of these, 726 female heads of households are employed full time. These families average about 2.6 children per family. It is estimated that only about half of these families have permanent care arrangements for their school-aged and preschool children.

Moreover, this situation has been found to exist in two other areas of the community, in y neighborhood and in the semiindustrial area bridging the melting points of census tracts 21, 23, 25.

In all three areas the police have taken 32 different preschool children and 47 school-aged children into protective custody in the last three months.

Values threatened. (1) Local merchants complain about increased petty thievery on the part of unsupervised children. (2) Many working mothers express guilt about inadequate arrangements for these children; some are fearful they may have to quit work and rely on public welfare; some feel that the care arrangements are adequate. (3) Police are annoyed with after-school vandalism and attribute this to unsupervised children. (4) Several social agencies are concerned that these unsupervised children, especially preschoolers, are deprived of important family relationships. (5) Local school officials feel that widespread neglect curtails preschool children's later ability to use elementary education. (6) Local political leaders feel the "good name" of the neighborhood is being seriously undermined by "these kinds of people."

Recognition of need for collective action. All of the above groups expressed the necessity of "doing something about the situation" although none could map a particular course of action which he could call effective.

Summary. Neglect of children of working mothers is a problem in three areas of the central city. There seems to be widespread recognition of the problem and the situation threatens the interests of some institutional units by reflecting poorly on their ability to keep the situation under control.

It is clear that the statement of the problem can be tailored to fit several levels, for example, family, neighborhood, organization, city, state, region, and nation. It would seem to be good practice to attempt to generalize to the level at which the planner's position is located in order to establish horizontal relevance of the problem in terms of intervention resources which the planner may wish to enlist in his plan-making process.

A statement of goals—objectives to be reached by the plan—should accompany the statement of the problem. The goals statement serves by sheer contrast to the problem to highlight the state of affairs desired after the plan has been implemented. Objectives would, of course, be general at first formulation and would be refined increasingly as the plan-making process continues. Initially the statement of objectives serves to explicate terminal goals—ideal end situations. As plan development proceeds, objectives will be increasingly specified and differentiated into terminal and instrumental goals.

Recognition that a given social problem has vertical impacts is an important component in the planner's thinking.[5] A problem located at a neighborhood level, in the example used, will certainly have connections with the larger community and external jurisdictions of government and voluntary associations at state, regional, and federal levels. Conversely, a general problem in the national scale will have its impact for communities and neighborhoods. As a rule of thumb, then, the planner might do best to formulate goals for every level with relevance for the problem at hand, ordering them in terms of their relevance to the locus of his innovating organization. With respect to the problem "neglect of children of working mothers," the planner would order goals (1) at the community level, (2) at the neighborhood level, (3) at the next most relevant upward vertical levels.

THEORIES OF CAUSATION

The second class of design tools is the causal explanation of the problem. The entire *perspective* of the plan is oriented [toward] how the planner explains the etiology and dynamics of the problem.

The casual explanation lends meaning to the statement of the problem by providing an analytical vehicle, a cause-effect interpretation.

Theories of causation available to social work are the products of various branches of social science. The term "theory" may be overstating the case a bit, however. *Completed* conceptual schemes are a rarity in social science, and an accepted theory of causation pertaining to a given social problem would obviate the need for a social planning design guide by providing an explanation so complete that the subsequent classes of design tools—modes of intervention and the like—would automatically be prescribed by the very nature of the theory itself.

As the situation now exists, there are a variety of conceptual tracks that aim at explaining a part of the problem. Every planner, then, has his choice of conceptual stances, and each stance dictates a slightly different direction for the making of his plan.

What explanation, for example, can be given for the working mother phenomenon? One conceptual track will hold that mothers work in response to a cultural readjustment of the role of women in Western society; another track will hold that women work in order to meet personal-financial and societal-economic exigencies; still another track will hold that women work because they have not resolved their own feelings about their sexual identity. Which one is right? Perhaps all are to some degree, but the choice of any one predisposes the planner to a particular stance with reference to modes of intervention and other classes of design tools to be utilized according to the sequence outlined above.

The major point is that in a planning process the causal explanation of the problem implicitly shapes the plan. Tracing out the available explanations utilizing the best available social science orientations provides motive force for different directions for action. Scarcity of resources often makes mandatory a selection of a few solutions from a large range of solutions. When the social planning practitioner makes such a choice, it is his professional responsibility to select alternatives that can be based on the most clearly stated conceptual formulations of problem causation.

MODES OF INTERVENTION

Once the statement of the problem and a given range of causal explanations have been formulated, the planner faces the task of choosing an appropriate mode (or modes) of intervention. For example, if neglect of children of working women is the problem and if the causal explanation of the working women phenomenon holds that women work in order to overcome financial deficits in family income, a whole series of possible interventions is opened up. At one end of the series, an intervention might be applied by subsidizing the wages of low-income breadwinners, thus "freeing" women to stay at home. At the other end of the series, intervention might be achieved by paying women to stay at home and care for their children. A mid-series intervention might be retraining of women to qualify them for better-paying jobs so that they in turn can afford to buy child care services for their children.

Analysis of modes of intervention should do more than indicate to the planner a possible course of action. This design tool should indicate "that, given a course of action, the consequences are likely to be these." Elaboration of modes of intervention, then, gives the planner some basis for expecting results and consequences from a given course of action.

The statement was made above, as an example, that one of the possible courses of action that is feasible as an intervention mode is the subsidizing of families with preschool children by government if the woman chooses to remain at home. The consequences—social, psychological, economic, and political—of this course of action may be determined by examining outcomes of previous similar efforts. Insofar as this level of information is available, possible consequences can be made manifest to the planner.

Thus, this class of design tools provides the means whereby the planner can outline the strengths and weaknesses of a given course of action. Studies may have demonstrated, for example, that a given course of action may be quite unacceptable for one social class segment of working women but acceptable to a different social class segment of working women. In recommending a mode (or several modes) of intervention, the planner can be secure in the knowledge that a differential outcome prediction has been attempted.

Two dimensions of intervention are suggested without elaboration: intervention with the client system and with the service system. Intervention with the client system aims to deal with the conditions of the client system that accommodate or block actions aimed at improvement. Intervention with the service system aims to deal with bureaucratic and interorganizational conditions in the community that accommodate or block actions aimed at improvement. Both dimensions are necessary for the innovating planning professional.

A brief note on intervention theories seems in order. Intervention theories are virtually nonexistent as explicit frameworks.[6] Implicit theories of intervention hover around various scales of human systems. Psychosocial therapy and psychotherapy are implicit intervention theories aimed at personality systems. "Institutional change" is aimed at community subsystems and their vertical counterparts at the national level. Nonviolent protest is implicitly aimed at modifying the national system. Revolution is an attempt to replace an existing national or societal system with

a substitute. While the explication of interventive theories is primitive, the planner must constantly check himself in selecting an intervention mode for an underlying implicit theory of intervention, attributed by himself or by others.

INFORMATION ABOUT TARGET POPULATIONS

The fourth class of design tools falls under the heading "Information About Target Populations." Without discussing this aspect in detail, this class would appear to include the following subclasses: (1) knowledge of population, e.g., culture and life styles, race, religion, income characteristics, shape and trends of movement and growth, households and their formations, density, housing and neighborhood characteristics, and so on; (2) analysis of resources, e.g., state of the economy, industrial development and investment phenomena, manpower utilization trends, public expenditure patterns, private consumption patterns, land use patterns, and so on; (3) knowledge of social standards, e.g., minimal health and welfare standards formulated by the community, forms of organization for enhancing or policing standards, and so on. In one sense, this class of design tools might be termed "tempering items," that is, with respect to the three classes of design tools discussed above, information about target populations provides an important correction factor. These "tempering items" closet the design guide at the appropriate point with information about reality, thus relieving it of an entirely utopian character.

VALUE CONSIDERATIONS

Value considerations constitute the fifth and final class of design tools. Evaluative biases will always be expressed by the planner, by the reviewers of the plan, and by the community that will be asked to accept it. Such underlying values as are not expressed in preceding classes should be expressed in this class. This is the final tempering item and should provide a guide to the possible as well as the desirable. In a way, it is the transitional zone between plan-making and plan-carrying out, that is, it constitutes the last analytical category of a plan and it also is the first order of information input into a strategy of implementation. The context of this category largely holds promise of answering the questions, "Is the plan appropriate" and "Will it go?"

A "BRANCHING MECHANISM"

Beginning with a statement of the problem and moving through the subsequent classes of design tools has the function of expanding the basis for the concrete conclusions that constitute the social plan. The test of the design guide is the degree to which a unitary problem statement can be built up into multiple explanations and interventions. The design guide, then, possesses a built-in "branching mechanism" which can be schematically presented. (See chart below.)

The general value of the branching characteristic is this: a unitary, initial problem item is developed by the planner to yield multiple solutions. And the primary professional importance of the branching characteristic is this: the planner is constrained from taking anything for granted and is impelled to employ the limits of exploration.

SOCIAL PLANNING DESIGN GUIDE

Beyond its service as a guide for ordering activities by the practitioner, the design guide can be viewed as an entity, a technical-mechanical aid to the professional planner. It is, in this sense, a plan-making instrument.

As a plan-making instrument, the guide consists of three components:

1. AN INPUT COMPONENT consisting of all available written information pertinent to each class of design tools. For example, the problem statement class would include an encyclopedia of problem situations set forth as problem statements, alphabetically arranged and justified in terms of meeting

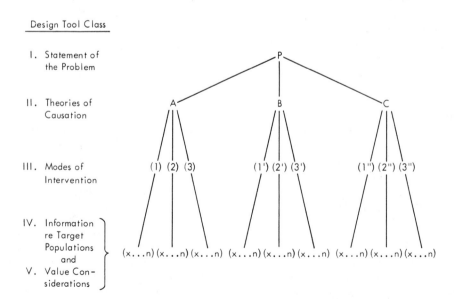

Design Tool Class

I. Statement of the Problem

II. Theories of Causation

III. Modes of Intervention

IV. Information re Target Populations and
V. Value Considerations

the model criteria for designation as a problem; the theories of causation class would include a compilation of existing theories of causation keyed to the compendium of problem statements and containing the history, basic premises, and empirical basis for each theory; the models of intervention class would be comprised of a compilation of intervention approaches and experiences appropriately keyed to both problems and theories of causation. The final two classes, target population information and value elements, are self-explanatory, empirically collected data.[7]

2. A STORAGE-RETRIEVAL COMPONENT. Employment of an electronic device for storing and obtaining classes and items of information is essential, given the geometric progression of possibilities once the statement of the problem has been formulated. The technical problems pertaining to this component, it will suffice to say, would require the full-time attention of computer technicians and programming experts.[8]

3. AN OUTPUT COMPONENT. Because the design guide is a utilitarian instrument geared to assist the social planner, the final product must be a usable aid for decision-making. The following format could constitute a report outline capable of meeting that criterion.

a. Statement of the problem and goals of the planner encompassed in a statement of the antiproblem.
b. Propositions of a causal nature: Given the statement of the problem, if *such and such* holds true than it occurs or reacts *in such a way* due to *such and such* factors.
c. Propositions of an interventive nature: Given the causal proposition, then approaches to intervene in *such and such* ways will have *such and such* consequences.
d. Tempering items of a realistic nature: Given the above, differences or sim-

ilarities between theory and practice or between previous tests and an anticipated test based on this plan are, by virtue of the target population and other ecological factors, *such and such*.
e. Tempering items of a value nature: Given the above, the information thus far refined must be viewed in light of the *such and such* values of the planner, of the client or service system as were not heretofore stated, and of other relevant persons or groups.

In order to gauge the utility of the instrument, an evaluative system could be applied as a further aid to decision-making. One evaluative system often referred to but rarely utilized is cost-benefit analysis. This approach, recently and experimentally adapted from economic and physical planning techniques, provides a more quantitative basis for judging the relative merits of the many possible alternatives generated in the design process. Were a truly useful version of this approach operational, it could constitute an excellent supportive component for the basic instrument.

It is envisaged that the social planning design guide, as an instrument, would be available to planners working on several scales of problem-solving, from neighborhood scale to the national scale. How this can be done realistically—through a university, foundation, or governmental agency—warrants the concerted attention of the social work profession.

SUMMARY

A major problem not addressed in the preceding text concerns the decision-making tasks facing the planner who utilizes either process or instrument without aids such as cost-benefit analysis. The major unanswered question is this: How is the practitioner to choose from among the many alternatives yielded by the branching mechanism? This question can be addressed in terms of the notion of priorities, in the value sphere, and in terms of the notion of feasibility, in the reality sphere. Answers to this question, as they evolve from subsequent work, are necessary to adequately provide plan-making capacities among social workers.

It must suffice to say that the design guide can provide parameters for judgment. It constitutes a mechanism against which the planner can pit his judgment and experience, a means for checking his own professional diagnosis.

The guide is *not* a substitute for professional expertise. It is a superrational, systematic means for quickly refining the content and delineating the boundaries of a pressing problem. Used at the outset of the task, the guide offers a group of directions for possible pursuit. Used after considerable cultivation of the problem, the guide provides a means whereby the planner may check his judgment for gaps or needed supplementation.

The social planning design guide provides a challenge to social work. It is the projection of one means to enhance the plan-making capacities of those members of the profession who seek to move boldly ahead in the solution of broad-scale social problems.

NOTES

1. Alfred J. Kahn, "Social Science and the Conceptual Framework for Community Organization Research," in Leonard S. Kogan, ed., *Social Science Theory and Social Work Research* (New York: National Association of Social Workers, 1960), pp. 64–80; Jack Rothman, "An Analysis of Goals and Roles in Community Organization Practice," *Social Work,* Vol. 9, No. 2 (April 1964); Thomas D. Sherrard, "Planned Community Change," *The Social Welfare Forum,* 1964 (New York: Columbia

University Press, 1964); Charles F. Grosser, "Community Development Programs Serving the Urban Poor," *Social Work,* Vol. 10, No. 3 (July 1965).

2. A special definition of the term "social problem" is used throughout this discussion. As a point of reference, the definition used is by Robert Merrill: "A social problem is a situation which threatens an established societal value with the concomitant realization by some sub-group of that society of the need for taking collective action with respect to the threatening situation." (Paraphrased.) "The Analysis of Social Problems," *American Journal of Sociology,* Vol. 30 (April 1924).

3. A different, complementary approach to social problems is contained in Herman Stein and Irving Sarnoff, "A Framework for Analyzing Social Work's Contribution to the Identification and Resolution of Social Problems," in *The Social Welfare Forum, 1964* (New York: Columbia University Press, 1964).

4. The terms "vertical" and "horizontal" are used here and later in this discussion in the sense developed by Roland A. Warren in his book *The Community in America* (New York: Rand-McNally, 1963), especially chaps. 8 and 9.

5. Ibid.

6. The beginnings of an explicit theory of intervention is provided in the elaborated concept of "institutional change" developed by Lloyd Ohlin and Richard Cloward in *Delinquency and Opportunity* (Glencoe, Ill.: Free Press, 1961). See also Lloyd Ohlin and Martin Rein, "Social Planning for Institutional Change," in *The Social Welfare Forum, 1964* (New York: Columbia University Press, 1964).

7. Some of these have already been evolved in at least primitive form. Bernard Berelson and Gary Steiner, in *Human Behavior* (New York: Free Press of Glencoe, 1964), have assembled much data regarding causation and intervention; the Bureau of Census reports more data about populations than are commonly used, and even more are available for analysis but not published.

8. A start has already been made to store and retrieve complex data about human problems. The MEDLARS Program for quick retrieval of vast stores of medical data and the Yale Area Studies Program dealing with human cultures are two examples.

Wayne A. Kimmel

Needs Assessment: A Critical Perspective

INTRODUCTION: THE PROBLEM

Federal requirements for an assessment of "need" to be met by programs began to appear in legislation in the mid-sixties. By the early to mid-seventies the frequency of these requirements seemed to have increased. By now presumably thousands of "needs assessments" have been created in response to federal requirements. With the growth in the number and potential cost of needs assessments, however, their methods and utility began to draw attention and critical scrutiny. Questions have been raised about what is going on under the rubric "needs assessment," and critical commentary and articles have begun to appear. Commenting on "problems and deficiencies in the needs assessment process," for example, Shapek (1975) observed:

> A host of federally funded studies have assisted state and local officials in creating priority listings of needs. The supposition is that once these listings have been created, such ordering will permit decision makers to plan and manage resources and programs more effectively as well as to formulate more significant, long-range policy initiatives. Unfortunately, there is little evidence that this occurs. Needs listings are largely ignored and ridiculed (p. 754).

In a recent attempt to locate basic materials on needs assessment, Varenais (1977) sampled the available literature. She concluded that the writing on the subject constitutes "a semantic jungle," that definitions are vague, and that discussions of the

Excerpted from *Needs Assessment: A Critical Perspective*, prepared by Wayne A. Kimmel for the Office of Program Systems, Office of the Assistant Secretary for Planning and Evaluation, Department of Health, Education and Welfare, December 1977.

subject are "confused." Commenting on a preoccupation of the literature with methods rather than results, she concluded:

> Many sources suggest intricate sets of activities to produce information but omit satisfactory explanations of *what* these processes are directed toward or *how* the data would be used (p. ii).

Similarly, a recent examination (Zangwill, 1977) of a large collection of HEW statutes and regulations which call for needs assessment concluded:

> . . . it is clear that the department, in its official instructions to recipients of its funds, provides no clear conception of the what, why, and how of needs assessment (p. 5).

After noting that resource allocation decision making in public agencies is complex and based on the political and value-laden competition of interested parties for scarce resources, a federal official recently cautioned a national conference on needs assessment:

> I don't think we ought to be lulled by the fact that data and needs assessment are going to give us our priorities and our choices (Peterson, 1976, p. 27).

What are the criticism and doubt about? What is needs assessment? Why should it be done? What good will it do? The remainder of this paper attempts preliminary answers to these questions.

FEDERAL REQUIREMENTS FOR NEEDS ASSESSMENT

Laws and Regulations

Since the mid-sixties the amount of federal legislation which includes references to or requirements for "needs assessment" has grown. An assessment, or evidence that one was conducted, is often required as part of a planning process, a component of a plan, or a precondition for grant support. Relatively prominent programs which require a needs assessment include Vocational Education, Social Services (Title XX of the Social Security Act), Health Planning and Resources Development, Community Mental Health Centers, and Aging programs.

Provoked by the spread of what appeared to be a vague, ambiguous, and potentially expensive set of requirements, the Office of the Assistant Secretary for Planning and Evaluation conducted a broad but partial examination of the laws and regulations of HEW programs which contain a need assessment reference or requirement (Zangwill, 1977). The report of that examination includes [this] conclusion:

> . . . while NA requirements play a major role in the Federal grant-in-aid mechanism, the requirements are very poorly defined. A grantee could easily follow the formal requirements without using the results to design or improve its own program. If this situation is common HEW could eliminate regulation-required NA altogether in the many programs without clear requirements in their legislation. On the other hand, if the Department believes NA is useful, it could provide clear directions and/or technical assistance to enable grantees to make it a meaningful part of their program planning. Following either course would improve the present situation, in which it is clear that the Department, in its official instructions to recipients of its funds, provides no clear conception of the what, why and how of needs assessment (Zangwill, pp. 4–6).

Why Does the Federal Government Require Needs Assessment?

The answers to this question are probably as mixed and variable as the motives and interests of the individuals and groups who initiated, participated in, or promoted

the requirements in the first place. Though we cannot trace the ten-to-twelve year federal history of needs assessment requirements, discussions with a variety of federal officials yield a mosaic of opinions and interpretations which can be characterized this way:

1. Assessing need is a natural *first step in planning*. If you do not know "what the need is," so the argument goes, how can you figure out what to do? According to this view, the rationale for needs assessment is apparently self-evident. The intended function appears to be basically analytical.

2. Needs assessment will presumably contribute significantly to a broad range of other useful activities, including planning, priority setting, evaluation, resource allocation, decision making, and policy formation. Like the first rationale, this one poses needs assessment as a rational, analytical tool.

3. The focus on "need" is basically a response to increasing pressure over the past ten years for cost reduction, accountability, and demands for justification (frequently of an economic and quantitative variety) of many existing and new public programs. According to this view, the increasing demands for economic justification provoked program advocates and officials to respond by sponsoring or conducting studies of their own. Needs assessments are used to "justify" the existence and proposed growth of programs by underscoring that "need" does in fact exist and that it is frequently far greater than the coverage of existing services. This rationale suggests that assessments are inspired for advocacy purposes. It also implies that there [is] sometimes an attempt to "fight fire with fire," studies with studies, "cost" data with "need" data.

4. Needs assessment is basically a reflection of the desire of social scientists (other than economists, who do not use the term "need") to use their tools to participate in social program planning. Rightly or not, the field of psychology is usually identified

as the likely professional source of the concept "need." Abraham Maslow's humanistic psychology is based on a theoretical notion of a "hierarchy of human needs" and is frequently referenced when this rationale is offered. In addition, the needs-assessment literature frequently urges the use of formal surveys as the preferred method. Survey researchers sometimes have backgrounds in psychology or opinion research. In this view, support for needs assessment is support for some academic disciplines and their techniques.

5. Needs assessment is another reflection of the common but misguided call for "more data for decisions." According to this interpretation, technocrats with a bent for numbers are responsible for the promotion of needs assessment. "More data" is a commonplace, knee-jerk response to perplexing problems of public policy which are poorly understood. Data is assumed to clarify understanding.

6. Needs assessment is an additional tool of "participatory democracy." It is a way to "by-pass" bureaucrats by "going directly to the people" to ask them what they need and want. According to this interpretation, its primary purpose is not analytical but political. It is purportedly a way to gather information "directly" from citizens and provide it "directly" to decision makers.

7. In a final alternative rendering of a rationale for the growth of needs assessment, the trend is characterized as a new fad, even a new ideology. Several participants in a recent conference alluded to the needs assessment "movement."

There are no means to weigh the alternative proposed rationales for the growth of federal needs assessment requirements. The explanations have, however, all been tendered by thoughtful individuals, some of whom were involved in the actual formulation of needs assessment requirements. Most, if not all, of these alternative rationales also appear in the proceedings of a recent conference on "Need Assessment in Health and Human Services" (Bell

et al., 1976). Like most other trends which draw wide attention and varied adherents and spokesmen, this one is probably actuated by a broad range of motives and intents.

VIEWS AND CLAIMS

Alternative Views of Needs Assessment

The literature contains many varied views of needs assessment. It appears that needs assessment can be almost anything: a change-oriented *process*, a *method* for enumeration and description, an *analytical procedure*, a *decision-making* process, a process for the "resolution of many viewpoints," etc. If there exists an underlying conception of "need," it is rarely explicit and never specific. The literature speaks for itself. . . .

(Bowers and Associates; Centr for Social Research and Development, 1974; Florida Department of Health and Rehabilitative Services, 1975; Human Services Institute, 1975; Hargreaves et al., 1974; Minnesota State Planning Agency, 1974).

Claims for Needs Assessment Are Ambitious

Like views of the purposes of needs assessment, the claims for it are broad and ambitious. . . .

. . . (Booz, Allen Public Administration Services, Inc., 1973; Warheit et al.; Siegel, 1974; Scheff, 1976). . . .

If one were to believe the many and ambitious claims, needs assessment is good for planning, evaluation, priority setting, resource allocation . . . and for many other purposes.

What Does Needs Assessment Mean?

Since there are so many federal requirements and so many claims for needs assessment, one might conclude that this straightforward question has a simple answer. It does not. . . .

Of the two words, "assessment" is the least troublesome. Leaving aside the tax related meanings of the term, the dictionary indicates that "assess" means "to evaluate; appraise—see synonyms at estimate." Assessment, then, means the act of evaluating, appraising or estimating. However common it may be, the concept "needs" is more troublesome. A large share of the literature does not even bother to discuss or attempt to define the word. The meaning is assumed to be clear and obvious. After all, we all have needs.

Unfortunately, "need" is a word with variable meaning because it does not have a specific referent. It does not refer to something in particular but rather to *something which does not exist. . . .* In short, *"need" is basically an empty term, one without conceptual boundaries. If the term is to have operational meaning it must be defined in a specific context, usually by the use of absolute or relative (comparative) criteria.*

If we combine the basic meanings of the two words "need" and "assessment" we have this rough but open ended definition of needs assessment:

Act of estimating, evaluating or appraising a condition in which something necessary or desirable is required or wanted.

. . . In this *relative* meaning of "need" we have one of the major keys to the confusion about needs assessment. Needs do not show themselves. Someone must establish what constitutes a need. The needs assessment literature implies that in practice needs will not only show themselves but will also show their relative importance (priority). The relative character of "need" is reflected in the fluctuating and debated nature of that widely cited global measure of need, the so-called "poverty line." A recent HEW report noted that:

Measures of poverty used for national policy purposes require fundamental social, political and ethical judgments. . . .The official measure of poverty has a number of limita-

tions, some of which stem from the fact that *there are no commonly accepted standards of need, other than for food.* (U.S. DHEW, April 1977, p. xxii, emphasis added.)

When we speak of need(s) in a human resources context we often think of basic human needs, subsistence needs, survival needs. The word rapidly becomes suffused with emotion, feeling, urgency and passion. It also becomes loaded with cultural, normative, philosophical and political overtones. Because it is both emotion-laden and value-loaded, "need" is subject to many shades of meaning, intent and interpretation. The emotive and mercurial attributes of the word "need" follow the term into activities called "needs assessment."

APPROACHES TO NEEDS ASSESSMENT

There Is No Single or Preferred Approach

Those who are looking for a single or preferred approach to needs assessment will be disappointed. A sampling of the literature indicates that proposed approaches and methods are many, heterogeneous, and without practical or conceptual links or unifying logic. . . .

The [outline following] lists the several methods which have been suggested for needs assessment. Other methods or approaches could probably be added.

Alternative Approaches to Needs Assessment Identified in the Literature

I. Gathering Opinions and Judgments:
   A. Key Informants (Knowledgeable individuals and experts)
   B. Community Forums (Discussion meetings of any set of community members)
   C. Public Hearings (with any set of lay or expert witnesses)
   D. Community and Political Leaders

 E. Group Processes (e.g., a semi-structured process such as the nominal group method)
II. Collecting Service Statistics:
 A. Utilization data and rates
 B. Caseload and workload data
 C. Grievance and complaint data
 D. Wait-list data
 E. Service data in existing Management Information Systems
III. Epidemiological Studies (Systematic studies of the origins of problems, especially health problems)
IV. Studies of the Incidence and Prevalence of Problems (e.g., of disease or handicapping conditions or defects)
 V. Social Indicators—Use of quantitative measures of the variables, e.g., unemployment, crime, schooling, income, prices, housing, etc.
 NOTE: "Indicators" can be derived from descriptive sociodemographic data like census data.
VI. Surveys:
 A. Formal *general* population sample survey (. . . may be conducted through direct, telephone or mail questionnaire)
 B. Formal *subpopulation* sample survey (e.g., of a locality, an age group or a service population)
 C. Selective special interviews with service clients, providers, practitioners, agency officials, etc.
VII. Secondary Analysis of Existing Studies or Sets of Organized Data
VIII. Combinations of the Above

It is not the purpose of this paper to describe or critically evaluate the individual approaches listed in the table. That has been done elsewhere (e.g., see Francis (1973) and Schneider (1976) on the limitations of social indicators and the Conference Proceedings (Bell, 1976) mentioned earlier for a critique of a number of the others). There are, however, several observations worth making about the *set* of approaches and methods.

First, none of them is new. They are all *borrowed* for use in needs assessment. Most are traditional approaches which have been employed by public agencies for years: experts (key informants), community meetings (forums), public hearings, community and political leaders, workload, grievance, complaint and utilization data. One, social indicators, is "new" within the past ten years, though indicators like unemployment rates, consumer prices and inflation rates have been used for decades. The so-called "nominal group process" method for getting convergent results out of group discussions is of recent vintage, but deriving group choice or preference through discussion and voting has been going on for thousands of years.

Second, with perhaps the exception of epidemiological research studies, all the approaches are ways to collect data or opinions. None has a well developed set of analytics, models or theoretical procedures associated with it beyond standard statistical procedures which exist for manipulating data. The approaches do not include guides for data interpretation and analysis in the context of resource allocation or priority-setting.

Third, all the methods except epidemiological research and the use of experts are sources of *descriptions* of needs and not explanations of why and how they arise or what could be done about them.

Fourth, there do not exist systematic procedures for relating data from one approach or method to the next. There is no method for synthesis.

Fifth, beyond the Roman Numeral classification into which we have arbitrarily cast them, there is nothing unifying or common about the approaches apart from the fact that they represent alternative ways to gather data, opinions and judgments.

Sixth, it is a commonplace observation in the literature that *single* approaches to needs assessment will not do, because they are all limited. Most advocates claim that multiple approaches must be employed, presumably in the belief that the weaknesses of one method will be canceled out by the strengths of the next.

Seventh, in terms of their logical distance from those "in need" the set of approaches includes at least three types:

1. Approaches for direct queries of individuals which include surveys and interviews of existing and potential clients.
2. Approaches for direct queries which include the use of experts, informants and knowledgeable individuals who are reporting on the perceived needs of others.
3. Indirect approaches from which inferences must be made about needs which include the use of sociodemographic data sources and derived social indicators.

All the methods require inferences from descriptive statements of need to the "causes" or sources of those needs. Dealing with needs appears to be like dealing with symptoms of problems rather than with their underlying "causes." *Finally, none of these proposed approaches constitutes a way of "assessing" needs. At best, the approaches lead to descriptive statements of needs but none of them provides a way to "assess" them.* How does the assessment (valuing and weighing) of needs occur? Are we thrown back to the political process which needs assessment is intended to improve? Or to experts? Or to advocates? It appears that the proposed methods are not needs *assessment* methods at all, but needs *description* methods at best. One observer has argued that the proponents of needs assessment got off on the wrong foot when they tried to give the activity the appearance of an "analytic technique" when it is not.

The Emphasis of Needs Assessment

Every major method and approach to "improving" organizational performance focuses on, emphasizes or accents some aspects of an organization's behavior, structure, functions or processes (see, for example, Kimmel et al., 1974). Management By Objectives, for example, focuses on internal short-range management goal and objective setting. It is intended to induce joint objective setting between superiors and subordinates and thereby increase communication between them. PERT is intended to improve an organization's capacity for defining and relating tasks, for work scheduling and for determining optimal or critical paths through complex interrelated activities by estimating and comparing their cost and time requirements. Organizational Development (OD) is intended to improve organizational performance by improving employee self-consciousness and interpersonal relations.

When it is not silent on its purposes the literature states that needs assessment is intended to improve an agency's capacity for planning, priority setting and resource allocation decision making. Another, but broader, approach directed to the same types of improvements is the Planning-Programming-Budgeting (PPB) approach introduced to the Federal government in the mid-sixties. Because they are billed as similar in intended purposes, a brief comparison of the two approaches will help define the dominant features and limits of needs assessment. . . . [A selective comparison of] the two approaches suggests [the following] contrasts.

The *major conceptual or philosophical sources* of PPB are the fields of economics (primarily micro-economics), decision-theory and theories of public or collective choice. There are *no* clear conceptual sources for needs assessment. The summary of the national conference proceedings identified earlier (Bell, 1976) makes the point plainly:

Needs assessment has risen from opportunistic and empirical sources. It is not "owned" by any one discipline. As a result, it has no unique theoretical frameworks. Also, perhaps as a result of its "odd" birth, it is not well grounded in either a theoretical literature or in research findings. There is missing the scholarly first step of finding out what went before (p. 316).

The *major concepts* of PPB include a heavy emphasis on (a) cost and budgetary constraints and on the relationship between the expenditure of resources (input) and the production of services (output); (b) the development and evaluation of *alternative* program and policy actions in terms of their *cost, efficiency* and *effectiveness;* and (c) the importance of *time* reflected both in a multi-year time horizon for planning and in a concern for estimating the effects of future uncertainty on the cost and feasibility of alternative courses of action.

By contrast, the concepts of needs assessment probably came from psychology and social casework. There is little if any attention paid by the needs assessment literature to the cost and budgetary constraints on choice. Emphasis is on the consideration of a broad spectrum of unconstrained needs as they are articulated by individuals, experts and leaders or inferred from data. The focus is clearly on increasing the amount of detail (descriptive) about the conditions, defects and "unsatisfied needs" of individuals and groups. Whereas PPB carried with it techniques for gauging price, cost, and benefits, needs assessment is preoccupied with identifying "gaps" between estimates of need and the capacity of existing services to meet those needs. Assessing need is necessarily forced into processes and activities of valuing and judging the comparative claims of different sets of needs. By contrast, the analytical studies of PPB were to accept the goals and objectives of agencies (though critically examining them) and to assist in accomplishing them through programs with least cost or maximum output. While there is no question that PPB analysis cannot be free of value judgments, needs assessment thrusts the assessor and user into the very heart of value judgments without the benefit of the disciplining effects of costs, resource constraints, program objectives or the limits of available know-how and technology. *The needs assessment literature misses or dismisses the key and commanding fact that "need" satisfaction is not free.*

MAJOR TOOLS: The major tools of PPB are basically of three types. First, a budget cast in a program classification framework. Second, the development and use of a multi-year program and financial plan developed under funding constraints or ceilings. Third, a set of analytical techniques and approaches for analyzing data which include cost-benefit, cost-effectiveness and systems studies. Finally, it is significant that emphasis on data collection methods and procedures are not a part of the PPB analytic toolkit.

By contrast, data *collection* procedures are the dominant types of method associated with needs assessment. Though some few have a minimum amount of methodological rigor (e.g., survey research), on the whole the techniques are not analytic. They are not designed to assist in directly structuring problems, tracing their causes or assessing their effects. They are primarily devoted to collecting opinions, expert judgment and data for subsequent use in whatever analysis or evaluative interpretation might be applied.

DOMINANT FOCAL POINTS: Needs assessment is characterized in a very major way by a look *away* from existing programs and *away* from an agency's goals and objectives . . . toward the community, especially toward the conditions and "needs" of the service and risk populations. In this sense it is very "market oriented," very "target group" oriented. This dominant preoccupation of needs assessment keeps the literature and the practice of needs assessment distracted from the operations and requirements of real public choice processes and from the economic political and bureaucratic constraints under which all program planning, budgeting and policy-making occur. These blind spots of need assessment contribute to insulating the activity from "realities" of collective choice and from the large body of existing writing on systematic techniques of analysis. The problem is only partially knowing our "needs." It is also understanding *problems* which create needs and formulating effective ways to solve or reduce them.

Finally, the preferred *organizational location* of PPB analysis and planning has always been in a staff location serving decision makers directly. The needs assessment literature and practice is quiet or indeterminate on where the function of need assessment should be located. In fact, a large share of past needs assessments have been conducted by groups "outside" the formal framework of a public agency.

USE MADE OF THE RESULTS OF NEEDS ASSESSMENT

If needs assessment pays off as an aid to policymaking (a prime claim of proponents), the payoff should be shown through the use made of assessment results. Yet despite the fact that thousands of "needs assessments" have been conducted, documentation of their use is scant. . . .

Five Manpower Needs Assessments

During 1973–77 the National Institute of Mental Health sponsored five contract projects to stimulate the development of manpower-planning capacity at the state level. Each of the projects contained a needs-assessment component. The impact of these assessments was evaluated by the author as part of a larger study of the overall projects (Kimmel, 1977). The projects suggest the wide range of activity which is included under the label "needs assessment" and the variability in their use and impact. . . .

Major conclusions which can be drawn from the set of five projects appear to be these:

> The label "needs assessment" may be applied to any approach, procedure, or method, ranging from "thinking sessions" to technically complicated surveys.
>
> Needs assessments which are conducted without assumptions about future resource, budgetary, or funding constraints are likely to be judged "blue sky" and unrealistic.
>
> Needs-assessment results which fit the political predispositions of policymakers are more likely to be used than those which do not.
>
> Assessments which use multiple and existing sources of data and information are likely to be low in cost and still yield information precise enough for most agency purposes.
>
> Assessments conducted by outside groups (e.g., research groups or universities) are more likely to be oriented toward technically elegant issues of interest to intellectuals than to practical issues of more interest to program and policy officials.
>
> There are political and ideological issues at stake in the selection of needs assessment approaches. . . .

Summary

The available evidence suggests that activities carried out under the label "needs assessment" are diverse, rarely judged directly useful for policymaking purposes, and inspired or rationalized by reasons which are often only vaguely related, if at all, to resource allocation decision making in public agencies.

LIMITATIONS OF ONE APPROACH TO NEEDS ASSESSMENT: FIELD SURVEYS

One method of generating data for needs assessment, the field survey, deserves special mention because surveys are frequently mentioned in the literature and are often promoted vigorously in practice. State-wide surveys conducted by Florida and Oregon are referenced because they were large, and relatively expensive, laid claims to basic validity and utility, were judged by some worthy of export to other states, and illustrate well the pitfalls of attempting to use surveys to improve allocation decisions among competing claims in a public agency context.

To some (usually survey researchers) a field survey is the preferable (superior) method for needs assessment. Yet surveys have been in use for a long time and they are not magical. The typical limitations and problems of a survey are several.

1. The cost of a survey can be high, especially when a detailed questionnaire is administered to a relatively large sample dispersed over a large geographical area. A survey of any significance will probably be more expensive than any of the alternative approaches to needs assessment.

2. While samples can be drawn with statistical rigor, sample attrition and non-response rates may affect substantially the representativeness of an actual set of respondents.

3. A survey typically relies on self-report data. Self-reporting about complicated individual and social problems is frequently unreliable. Individuals may have mental health problems, for example (or hypoglycemia or dietary deficiencies), and not be aware of them. Similarly, they cannot be expected to know of subtle physical, psychic, or social problems unless the problems have been reliably diagnosed by competent specialists. Even experts disagree over the diagnosis and treatment of a wide variety of human problems. In addition, some subject areas are extremely sensitive and do not lend themselves readily to reliable exploration through a survey interview; for example, marital problems, child abuse, alcoholism, drug use and abuse, abortion, etc. In short, surveys are not likely to be effective instruments for gathering reliable perceptions of some important and basic human problem (need) areas.

4. Survey researchers tend to prefer prestructured and close-ended questionnaire formats because data is then easier to tabulate (although not necessarily easier to interpret). Pre-structured, alternative answers to questions also speed an interview which must stay within the constraints of time, cost, and the patience and time of the interviewee. But semi-structured and open-ended questions are often more effective vehicles for exploring life habits, styles, and circumstances which create or intensify many human needs and problems. The exploration of "causes" of problems (and thus effective remedies) rather than symptoms requires more time and the skill of an experienced and sensitive interviewer. Anyone who has filled out, designed, or read the results of survey questions has probably wondered about what difference it would make if a given question had been asked in a different way or had been preceded or followed by related or more probing questions.

5. If it is used to estimate the incidence of needs in a population, a survey depends in part on the extent to which the sample of respondents is "representative" of the larger population. Actual field surveys must rely on voluntary cooperation and cope with a mobile and changing population, many of whose problems are "one-time" or transient. "Representativeness" may be hard to achieve. Several observers have warned against the seemingly commonplace "ecological fallacy" associated with surveys and social indicators; i.e., attributing to individuals within a community the characteristics of a community as a whole. . . .

PRIORITY RANKING OF NEEDS

According to many advocates, needs assessment is designed to guide resource allocation decisions, partly through ranking needs in priority order. The Florida surveys provide a concrete example, though the problems we will highlight are endemic to all survey assessments. An attempt was made in each of the three surveys (client, resident, and key informant) to have individuals select from a list and rank order the five most pressing unmet needs or target groups. [Table 1] compares the rankings of the three groups. As might be expected the rankings varied from group to group, confirming what has been called "Mile's Law: Where you stand depends on where you sit."

The table indicates that the clients and residents identified four out of five of the same priorities but they ranked them differently. The key informants selected and ranked areas that were, with one exception (transportation), different from the areas selected by the other two groups. Similarly, when key informants ranked both "unmet needs" and "pressing problem areas" only three of the five areas were common (unemployment, child abuse, and malnutrition) and these were ranked in different order. "Mental health problems" were among the top five areas only in the list of the key informants. Finally, regardless of whose priority list you inspect, some problem areas appear interdependent in cause and remedy. Some portion of common dental problems (identified by clients and residents) are surely [caused by] poor diet and malnutrition (identified by key informants). The reported needs for food stamps and financial assistance (identified by clients and residents) are caused in part by unemployment (identified by key informants). Some child abuse is probably caused or triggered by the circumstances of unemployment or welfare status. . . .

The key point should be clear: while "priority lists" are appealing on their face, they are of little direct help in actually deciding upon reasonable resource allocation strategies.

SELECTED ISSUES AND PERSPECTIVES RELATED TO NEEDS ASSESSMENT

Efforts to "assess need" in a *technical* way are not new. They bear a strong family resemblance to earlier and similarly unsuccessful historical attempts like those of Jeremy Bentham who, in the nineteenth century, tried to develop a "felicific calculus" by which one could gather and synthesize diverse individual preferences into consistent group choices which would supposedly ensure maximum happiness and human welfare. Since then there has accumulated a large body of technical, esoteric,

Table 1 Comparison of Rank Order of Top Five Unmet Needs by Residents, Clients, and Key Informants, State of Florida

COMMUNITY RESIDENT SURVEY[1] (n = 1,187)	CLIENT SURVEY[2] (n = 1,769)	KEY INFORMANT SURVEY[3] (n = 1,154)	
		UNMET NEED	MOST PRESSING PROBLEM AREA
Routine Dental Care	Routine Dental Care	Unemployment	Child Abuse
Food Stamps	Financial Assistance	Child Abuse	Abuse of Elderly
Financial Assistance	Food Stamps	Malnutrition	Unemployment
Information and Referral	Utility Problems, including telephone	Transportation	Malnutrition
Transportation Problems	Transportation Problems	Low-income Medical Care	Mental Health Problems

[1]Department of Health and Rehabilitative Services, July 1976, pp. 35–36.
[2]Department of Health and Rehabilitative Services, July 1976, pp. 32–33.
[3]Department of Health and Rehabilitative Services, February 1976, p. 31.

and often unproductive speculation and writing on this subject. In a seminal analysis of the general problem, Arrow (1970) concluded that aggregating individual preferences into collective choices or decisions cannot be done *technically* in a reasonable and satisfactory way. There have since been no compelling rebuttals to Arrow's conclusion. Arrow was dealing with "preferences." The current concern is with "needs" which are analytically even more evasive and intractable. Here are some of the reasons.

A Merging of Needs and Wants?

Some of the obvious confusion associated with needs assessments arises from a lack of clarity about the differences between needs and wants or, indeed, preferences. Except in extreme cases (e.g., abject poverty), the distinction is no longer easy to make. Commenting on this contemporary dilemma, Bell (1976) recall[ed] that when Aristotle spoke of man's "natural needs," he meant sufficient food, clothing, shelter from the elements, care during sickness, sexual intercourse, companionship, and the like. These needs are *biologically* derived and are *limited and satiable*. The use of the word *need* was then simple. Bell argues that times have changed. The *"private* household" where these early notions of need applied has been displaced by the *"public* household" where they do not. We now have a political economy which is a mixture of government and a modern "bourgeois" market economy. Now the motives for the acquisition of goods are no longer exclusively *needs* but also *wants*. "In bourgeois society, psychology replaced biology as the basis of 'need' satisfaction. . . . In Aristotle's terms, *wants* replaced *needs*—and wants by their nature are unlimited and insatiable."

> . . . the public household now becomes the arena for the expression not only of public needs but also of private wants. . . . Above all the basic allocative power is now political

rather than economic. . . . The fact that the public household becomes a "political market" means that the pressure to increase services is not necessarily matched by the mechanism to pay for them, either a rising debt or rising taxes. (pp. 222–27)

This historical movement from a notion of needs as biologically based and limited to one which is psychologically based and unlimited is part of the current cultural backdrop of social or human resources programs. The boundary between wants and needs has always been hazy because individuals are not always clear about their "real" needs versus their wants. Except in extreme cases, their formulations change depending on their circumstances, available choices (including resources), and preferences. The overlap, [the] merging and confusion of need and want (and sometimes preference), is one reason why there are often differences between self-perceived and self-reported needs of, say, a client of a social welfare program, on the one hand, and needs perceived (or diagnosed) and reported by an expert (e.g., a clinical psychologist, caseworker, etc.) on the other.

The intertwining and mingling of needs, wants, and preferences can be demonstrated in a simple way: Do a needs assessment on yourself. How sure are you that your needs are not your wants? Are not your preferences? Discuss your self-assessment with someone else. How sure are you now? The merging of needs, wants, and preferences is a basic reality. . . .

Philosophical Premises

There appear to be several implicit philosophical premises on which the needs-assessment literature rests. First, the search for needs is an implied argument for "more" services rather than less. The premise appears to be expansionist. It seems unlikely, for example, that a needs assessment would be conducted unless there were some prospect of uncovering *more* needs. It also seems unlikely that program officials would sponsor a needs assessment if there were a real prospect that the assessment would disclose either that a set of specified needs were already satisfied or that existing service capacity already exceeded the demand from all those "in need."

Second and linked to the first premise, there seems to be an implicit assumption in the needs literature that *government* should provide whatever additional services are required. (See, for example, Levitan, Lewis, and U.S. DHEW, July 1976). This pro-government bias of needs assessment is interesting in light of rising public sentiment over the past eight to ten years that government is too big, too inefficient, and too expensive. It is also a premise which is subject to basic disagreement on the grounds of both political philosophy and service effectiveness. It is not obvious that even if there were collective social agreement that a new service should be provided or an old one expanded, provision of that service should be made by government bureaucracy. A grand alternative to government provision of more services to the poor, which has been proposed with some force over the last few years, for example, is a so-called incomes policy. Under this approach, the poor would receive a minimum guaranteed income to be spent at their own discretion. Government would not be called upon to expand further the narrow, categorical support for services which grew up in the late fifties and early sixties and resulted in the overlapping, redundant, and fragmentary service system we now have. In most areas there are plausible if not preferable alternatives to direct government intervention and subsidy. The needs-assessment literature automically assumes that the preferred provider is the government.

A third assumption seems to be hidden only in that portion of the needs-assessment literature which proposes a survey as the preferred method. That assumption is that *new* data is better than existing or old data. The assumption is a push toward new data collection as the only reasonable course of needs assessment. . . .

The Context Is Political

Needs assessment does not occur in a vacuum. If the results of an assessment are to be useful and used, they must fit the context in which all public agencies operate. That context is inherently political. . . .

In this system, public agencies are not mere machines that follow rationalistic recipes of choice. Decisions do not occur in a one-time fashion but in intricate streams over long periods of time. Programs do not appear by virtue of "big decisions" but rather evolve through decentralized and fragmented processes of competition and adjustment among partisan interests. Programs, like budgets, grow incrementally and slowly, not in great leaps or quantum jumps. . . .

A RECAPITULATION

This paper has drawn on a sampling of the literature to expose the anatomy, espoused purposes, claims, criticisms, and uses of needs assessment. Major conclusions can be summarized briefly.

First, the federal government has prescribed that needs assessment be conducted as a precondition for grant support or as part of a plan or planning process. Federal laws and regulations, however, are always silent on what "need" means and usually silent on what methods or procedures should be employed to conduct a needs assessment. Tellingly, HEW does not make decisions based on national needs assessments. This approach is left to state, regional and local governments, and agencies.

Second, an examination of the meaning of the terms "need" and "assessment" and of the definitions and characterizations given in the literature lead to the conclusion that "need" is an empty and unbounded term. It takes on meaning only in a specific context when someone or some group establishes an absolute (e.g., an income-related poverty line) or relative (e.g., the needs of group A compared to those of B) criterion or standard for gauging need. These criteria are themselves value laden and subject to philosophical and political debate and dispute. (See, for example, the provocative discussion of the "wavering poverty line" in U.S. DHEW, April 1976).

Third, the methods proposed for the conduct of needs assessment are many and borrowed from other places. They consist of heterogeneous, mixed methods for (1) eliciting opinions or judgments of need from a variety of sources, (2) collecting data directly from the field (e.g., through a field survey), (3) inferring need from indirect indicators (e.g., social indicators), or (4) inferring need from the secondary analysis of existing data (e.g., utilization data already collected on the use of services in existing programs). Experts tend to agree that all the individual methods have weaknesses. As a way to partially overcome these weaknesses they urge the use of multiple approaches but have never shown how any single approach or combination of approaches can actually be used in priority-setting.

Fourth, there is no theory or organized analytics which lie behind the methods of needs assessment. [There] are instead, only tools for descriptive data collection, not for data analysis or interpretation.

Fifth, self-conscious advocates of needs assessment realize that undifferentiated data on needs stand a small chance of influencing decisions and they therefore urge simplistic "convergent" models for data reduction and synthesis and "a proc-

ess" (undefined) for bringing needs data to the attention of decision makers.

Sixth, the tools and concepts of needs assessment were compared with those of Planning-Programming and Budgeting which is directed toward the shared purposes of influencing resource allocation decisions. The comparison revealed that needs assessment is generally "market" or "target group" oriented and conducted without explicit regard for resource, budgetary or funding constraints. PPB by contrast takes such constraints as [points] of departure and relies on an additional set of constraints in the form of articulated program and policy objectives. PPB carries with it tools for *analysis*. Needs assessment does not.

Seventh, an examination reveals that the evidence on the actual utilization of the results of needs assessments is spotty, scant, uneven and not encouraging. A very small percentage of needs assessments appear to have been used in an actual decision-making setting and the evidence suggests that much of that use [might have been based on] the utility of needs data for purposes of program justification and advocacy rather than analysis and systematic planning.

Eighth, although surveys are sometimes promoted as the preferred approach to needs assessment, an examination of a statewide survey in Florida exposed several of the typical limitations and problems with this approach. Self-reporting on serious, subtle, and sensitive psychic, social, and physical problems is difficult and often unreliable. Sampling, questionnaire design, and item construction involve *selection* and thus the exercise of values over what is and is not important. Sample "representativeness" is hard to accomplish in real field surveys, especially those directed toward large-scale population groups subject to mobility and change in circumstances. Prestructured surveys are weak instruments for investigating the "causes" or sources of needs and problems and thus for formulating effective remedies.

Ninth, while "priority lists" are appealing in principle they are of little help in formulating strategies for investing budget resources.

Finally, a brief identification of the issues and operating context of a public agency suggested that there is often a merging of needs and wants (and indeed preferences); existing knowledge about the causes of and effective remedies for a large number of important social problems is partial, bounded, and fragmentary; and the needs-assessment literature seems to rest on a set of arguable philosophical premises, including the notion that remedies for all social problems should be undertaken by government.

In sum, the conceptual, methodological, and practical limits of proposed approaches to needs assessment suggest that most assessments will have only a small chance of impacting on policy and resource allocation decisions. . . .

SOURCES

ANONYMOUS. *The Policy Analysis Source Book For Social Programs.* Washington, D.C.: GPO, 1976.

ARROW, KENNETH J. *Social Choice and Individual Values.* New Haven and London: Yale University Press, 1963.

BELL, DANIEL. *The Cultural Contradictions of Capitalism.* New York: Basic Books, Inc., 1976.

BELL, ROGER A., MARTIN SUNDEL, JOSEPH F. APONTE, AND STANLEY A. MURRELL *Need Assessment in Health and Human Services.* Proceedings of the Louisville National Conference. Louisville, 1976.

BELL, ROGER A. "The Use of a Convergent Assessment Model in the Determination of Health Status and Assessment of Need," in Roger A. Bell, *Need Assessment in Health and Human Services,* already cited.

BOOZ, ALLEN. Public Administration Services, Inc. *Assessing Social Services Needs and Resources.*

Final Report. Washington, D.C., August 15, 1973.

BOWERS AND ASSOCIATES. *A Guide to Needs Assessment in Community Education Programs.* Reston, Virginia, January 1976.

CAPLAN, NATHAN. "Factors Associated with Knowledge Use Among Federal Executives," in *Policy Studies Journal.* Urbana, Illinois: University of Illinois, Spring 1976.

CENTER FOR SOCIAL RESEARCH AND DEVELOPMENT. *Analysis and Synthesis of Needs Assessment Research in the Field of Human Services.* Denver, Colorado: Denver Research Institute, University of Denver, July 1974.

DAVIS, JAMES A. "On the Remarkable Absence of Nonacademic Implications in Academic Research: An Example from Ethnic Studies." San Francisco: Academic Press, Inc., 1975. Reprint from *Social Policy and Sociology* by N. J. Demaerath and others.

DEPARTMENT OF HEALTH AND REHABILITATIVE SERVICES, PROGRAM PLANNING AND DEVELOPMENT, OFFICE OF EVALUATION, STATE OF FLORIDA. *Statewide Systematic Needs Assessment Project: Community Resident Survey,* July 1976.

———. A Florida Key Informant Needs Assessment for Title XX, February 1976.

———. Statewide Systematic Needs Assessment Project: Client Survey, July 1976.

FLORIDA DEPARTMENT OF HEALTH AND REHABILITATIVE SERVICES, DIVISION OF PLANNING AND EVALUATION, BUREAU OF RESEARCH AND EVALUATION. *Annotated Bibliography of Needs Assessment,* April 1975.

FRANCIS, WALTON. "A Report on Measurement and the Quality of Life and the Implications for Government Action of The Limits to Growth." Washington, D.C.: U.S. Department of Health, Education, and Welfare, January 1973.

FRANCIS, WALTON. Unpublished letter to HEW Region X Office reviewing the Oregon Needs Assessment Project (November 1977).

GERONTOLOGY PROGRAM, UNIVERSITY OF NEBRASKA. "Public Opinion and the Making of Social Policy." Omaha, March 31, 1976. Prepared for the Office of Human Development, Department of HEW, Region VII Office.

HARGREAVES, WILLIAM A., C. CLIFFORD ATTKISSON, LARRY M. SIEGEL, AND MARGUERITE H. MCINTYRE. *Part II: Needs Assessment and*

Planning. San Francisco: National Institute of Mental Health, 1974.

HATRY, HARRY, LOUIS BLAIR, DONALD FISK, AND WAYNE KIMMEL *Program Analysis for State and Local Government.* Washington, D.C.: Urban Institute, 1976.

HITCH, CHARLES J., AND ROLAND N. MCKEAN. *The Economics of Defense in the Nuclear Age.* New York: Atheneum, 1965.

HUMAN SERVICES INSTITUTE FOR CHILDREN AND FAMILIES, INC. *Needs Assessment in a Title XX State Social Services Planning System.* Location unstated, April 1975.

KIMMEL, WAYNE A. "Mental Health Manpower Development at the State Level: Five Pilot Projects." Washington, D.C.: National Institute of Mental Health, June 1977 Draft. A contract study.

KIMMEL, WAYNE A., WILLIAM R. DOUGAN, AND JOHN R. HALL *Municipal Management and Budget Methods: An Evaluation of Policy Related Research,* Final Report—volume I: Summary and Synthesis. Washington, D.C.: The Urban Institute, December 1974.

KIMMEL, WAYNE A. "PPB: Analysis, Planning, and Processes of Choice." Cambridge, Massachusetts: Harvard University, June 1968, unpublished paper.

KNOWLES, JOHN H. (ed.). *Doing Better and Feeling Worse.* New York: W. W. Norton & Company, 1977.

LEAGUE OF CALIFORNIA CITIES. *Handbook: Assessing Human Needs.* Sacramento, August 1975.

LEVITAN, SAR A., AND ROBERT TAGGART. *Jobs for the Disabled.* Baltimore, Md.: Johns Hopkins University Press, 1977.

LEWIS, VIVIAN. "Day Care: Needs, Costs, Benefits, Alternatives," in *Studies in Public Welfare,* Paper no. 7: Issues in the Coordination of Public Welfare Programs. Washington, D.C.: U.S. Government Printing Office, July 2, 1973.

MCKENZIE, RICHARD B., AND GORDON TULLOCK. *The New World of Economics: Explorations Into the Human Experience.* Homewood, Illinois: Richard D. Irwin, Inc., 1975.

MINNESOTA STATE PLANNING AGENCY. *Needs Assessment: A Guide For Human Services Agencies.* St. Paul, Minnesota, January 1977.

MURRAY, THOMAS, AND RICHARD WEATHERMAN. *Educational Needs Assessment and Program Development for Child Caring Institutions.*

Minnesota: State Department of Education, Reprint, November 1973.

MUSTIAN, DAVID R., AND JOEL J. SEE. "Indicators of Mental Health Needs: An Empirical and Pragmatic Evaluation," *Journal of Health & Social Behavior,* March 1973.

PETERSON, ROLAND L. "Social Mandates and Federal Legislation: Implications for Health and Planning," in Roger A. Bell, *Need Assessment in Health and Human Services,* already cited.

PROJECT SHARE. *Human Services Bibliography Series: Needs Assessment.* Rockville, Maryland, August 1976.

REDICK, RICHARD W. "Annotated References on Mental Health Needs Assessment." Rockville, Maryland: National Institute of Mental Health, February 1976. Typescript.

REGION X, U.S. DEPARTMENT OF HEALTH, EDUCATION AND WELFARE. *Ties That Bind . . .* HEW National Management Planning Study—1976. Seattle, Washington, July 4, 1976.

RIVLIN, ALICE M. *Systematic Thinking for Social Action.* Washington, D.C.: The Brookings Institution, 1971.

SASLOW, MICHAEL G. "Needs Assessment," A Statewide Survey of Local Social Service Problem Areas, Draft Final Report. A Contract Study for HEW Region X. Seattle: HEW/OHDS Public Services Division, October 1, 1977.

SCHEFF, JANET. "The Use of Client Utilization Data to Determine Social Planning Needs," in Roger A. Bell, *Need Assessment in Health and Human Services,* already cited.

SCHNEIDER, MARK. "The 'Quality of Life' and Social Indicators Research." *Public Administration Review,* May/June 1976.

SHAPEK, RAYMOND A. "Problems and Deficiencies in the Needs Assessment Process." *Public Administration Review,* December 1975.

SIEGEL, LARRY M., AND C. CLIFFORD ATTKISSON. "Mental Health Needs Assessment: Strategies and Techniques," in Hargreaves and others. *Part II: Needs Assessment and Planning,* already cited.

THOMAS, LEWIS. "On the Science and Technology of Medicine," in John H. Knowles, *Doing Better and Feeling Worse,* already cited.

U.S. DEPARTMENT OF HEALTH, EDUCATION AND WELFARE. *A Five-Year Plan for the Development of Community Mental Health Centers.* A Report to the Congress Pursuant to the Community Mental Health Centers Amendments of 1975, July 1976.

U.S. DEPARTMENT OF HEALTH, EDUCATION AND WELFARE. *The Measure of Poverty: A Report to Congress as Mandated by The Education Amendments of 1974.* Washington, D.C.: GPO, April 1976: GPO Publication no. 017-046-00039-0.

VARENAIS, KRISTINA. *Needs Assessment: An Exploratory Critique.* Washington, D.C.: Office of the Assistant Secretary for Planning and Evaluation, HEW, May 1977. HEW Publication number: OS-77-007.

WARHEIT, GEORGE J., ROGER A. BELL, AND JOHN J. SCHWAB. *Planning for Change: Needs Assessment Approaches.* Rockville, Maryland: Department of Health, Education and Welfare, Alcohol, Drug Abuse, and Mental Health Administration, undated.

ZANGWILL, BRUCE. *A Compendium of Laws and Regulations Requiring Needs Assessment.* Washington, D.C.: U.S. Department of Health, Education and Welfare, May 1977. HEW Publication number: OS-77-006.

Nancy W. Veeder

Health Services Utilization Models for Human Services Planning

Planning of urban services has relied heavily on the use of mathematical models to predict the behavior of prospective users of such services. The most prominent example of this in urban planning has been the transportation model. The basic goal of such efforts has been to provide urban services in such locations and having such capacities and delivery features that the services will be optimally used by the target populations.

In early transportation models, predicted use usually greatly underestimated actual use. In the United States, such has been the rush to use whatever highways could be provided that most contemporary models have had to build in provision for capacity constraints.

Other urban service utilization models have also missed the mark, but in the di-

Reprinted with permission of the author and *Journal of the American Institute of Planners* 41:3 (March 1975), pp. 101–09.

rection of underutilization. Underutilization has been a key problem in many social services; for example, underutilization traditional neighborhood recreation facilities was recently analyzed by Gold (1972). Underutilization of health services has been a major difficulty for health planners and providers (McKinlay, 1972). Such services require extensive capital investment and the availability of highly trained professionals. Deficiencies in their planning and use can be measurable factors in the cost and quality of health care.

This paper reviews recent model building efforts in the utilization of urban health services in the hope that these efforts will stimulate future research about service utilization with reference not only to health but also to mental health, education, recreation, employment, and other urban social services. Examination of the health utilization models indicates their sensitivity to the role of psychological states, social group pressures, motivations, beliefs, and institutional barriers to service utilization. Unlike the more typical and mechanical supply–demand models, efforts to understand utilization of health services have attempted to cast the widest conceptual net of behavior variables. The successes and failures of such efforts can thus be seen as vitally important to the future effectiveness of the entire range of social service planning.

The following discussion focuses on four models which have been theoretically and empirically evolved to explain the utilization patterns of health service consumers. These models represent some of the more conceptually sophisticated thinking and fairly well summarize health services utilization thought and research for the past twenty years.

HEALTH SERVICES UTILIZATION MODELS

The Rosenstock Model: Psychological-Motivational Determinants of Health Services Utilization

CONCEPTUAL BASES OF THE MODEL. The Rosenstock model is based upon Kurt Lewin's theoretical and empirical work within the context of "field theory." Rosenstock's model postulates that a person is likely to take a "health action" (that is, take steps to use a health care facility) if

1. he believes himself susceptible to the disease in question;
2. he believes that the disease in question would have serious effects upon him if contracted;
3. he is aware of certain actions that can be taken (that these avenues are available and accessible) and believes that these actions may reduce his likelihood of contracting the disease or reduce the severity of (or cure) the disease should he contract it;
4. he believes that the threat to him of tak-

ing the action is not as great as the threat of the disease itself.

(Rosenstock, 1960, p. 20)

A key concept in the model is the "cue" or trigger which trips appropriate action. In a later work, Rosenstock (1966) posits a "psychological state of readiness to act" which [is comprised of] susceptibility and severity factors; this state provides the backdrop against which a "cue" is processed and acted upon. The preferred path of action is determined by the individual's perception of potential barriers and benefits in terms of availability and accessibility of resources (the decision to act being based on some assessment of benefits minus barriers or costs). Combinations of these variables (susceptibility, severity, benefit, barrier) can exist in extreme intensity without resulting in observable acts, "unless some instigating event occurs to set the process in motion" (Rosenstock, 1966, p. 101).

Rosenstock notes that health cues may be internal or external to the individual and that "the required intensity of a cue that is sufficient to trigger behavior presumably varies with differences in the level of readiness. With relatively low psychological readiness (i.e., little acceptance of susceptibility to or severity of a disease), rather intense stimuli will be needed to trigger a response. On the other hand, with relatively high levels of readiness even slight stimuli may be adequate" (1966, p. 101). However, cues to action have not been empirically assessed.

Rosenstock emphasizes emotional, rather than cognitive, aspects of beliefs. The focus of the model's application is "to link current subjective states of the individual with current health behavior" (Rosenstock, 1966, p. 98). However, when deriving intervention possibilities, Rosenstock focuses on environmental and cognitive, rather than psychological, attempts to modify health behavior: minimizing barriers to action, increasing opportunities to act, providing cues to trigger responses. Some ways he suggests to do this include reducing costs, reducing distances, setting convenient service hours, reminders from physicians, and mass media announcements.

EMPIRICAL ASSESSMENTS OF THE MODEL. The greater number of research efforts in health service utilization have taken Rosenstock's model as the theoretical framework for data collection and analysis. Results of studies which examine concepts posited in the model (severity, susceptibility, availability, and accessibility) suggest that the choice of explanatory variables has met with varying success empirically.

A person's perception of actual or potential *severity* of symptoms was found to be positively related to health care seeking in only one of five studies which examined this concept, a study by Kegeles of dental care seekers. However, a replication study failed to support these findings (Kegeles, 1963). Three other studies found severity perceptions to bear little or no relationship to health-care-seeking actions (Kirscht et al., 1966; Hochbaum, 1964; Leventhal, 1960).

Belief in potential or actual *susceptibility* to illness fared better than did severity in most research. Of nine studies which examined this concept, five found positive relationships between belief in one's susceptibility to a disease entity and health-care-seeking actions (Borsky and Sagen, 1959; Gochman, 1970, 1971; Hochbaum, 1956; Kegeles, 1963). Inconclusive data concerning both severity and susceptibility beliefs were generated by Kirscht et al. (1966) and Leventhal (1960).

Only one study addressed itself to the *availability* of resources concept. Kegeles (1969) found little association between beliefs concerning the availability of paths to alleviate serious consequences of cancer of the cervix and obtainment of an examination for cervical cancer.

The *accessibility* of health care resources was found to be important in the two studies that addressed this issue. Rosenstock (1959), in an examination of six studies of use and lack of use of polio vaccine, found that one key factor in seeking vaccine was convenience or proximity of facilities. Borsky and Sagen (1959) also found that convenience was an important factor in obtaining preventive health examinations.

In addition to the four concepts specifically stressed in the Rosenstock model, two other concepts recurrently appear in studies: *demographic characteristics* of education, status, and income; and group influences. Hochbaum, Kegeles, Rosenstock, and Glasser all found education to be associated with motivation to seek health care; and Kegeles, Rosenstock, and Glasser also found a positive association with income. Hochbaum (1956) determined that the group influence (particularly opinions of family and friends) on tuberculosis X-ray seeking behavior was considerable. Heinzelmann (1962), in a comparative exploratory study of 284 college students' rheumatic fever prophylactic beliefs and behavior, noted that the study could not differentiate which knowledge and belief patterns specifically led to prophylactic behavior. However, he observed that social group influences on behavior should be explored in future research. Rosenstock (1959) also found social pressure to be an important factor in obtaining Salk vaccines. Glasser (1958), in another survey of Salk vaccine use, noted that a large percentage of those who obtained Salk vaccines knew friends who had also obtained vaccines.

One theme clearly emerges from studies employing the Rosenstock formulation: Social group factors are important health action expedients and deterrents. Rosenstock includes "interpersonal influences" cursorily in the "barriers and benefits to action" part of his formulation; however, he plays down the influence, or potential influence, of such factors. Empirical tests of his model rarely give those factors an important place in design, yet data indicate that they may be important in determining health behavior.

The Suchman Model: Socioenvironmental Determinants of Health Services Utilization

THEORETICAL BASES FOR THE MODEL. Edward Suchman posited a sociologically oriented model for health-care-seeking behavior. Suchman's major hypothesis, that "the selection of the source of care will reflect the knowledge, availability, and convenience of such services, and social group influences upon the individual," is similar to Rosenstock's in the variables and concepts included within it; however, the major emphasis is different in that Suchman stresses "social group influences" and deemphasizes the inner psychological "state of readiness" (internally derived motivation). Specifically, Suchman poses the following hypotheses.

1. Significant variations exist in knowledge about disease, attitudes toward medical care, and behavior during illness among different ethnic groups;
2. significant variations among ethnic groups are related to the form of social organization within the ethnic group;
3. lower socioeconomic and minority groups are more socially isolated or ethnocentric than are upper socioeconomic and majority ethnic groups and this ethnocentricism is highly related to lower level of disease knowledge, fearful or skeptical attitudes toward medical care, and dependency upon lay support during illness;
4. those individuals who belong to relatively more homogeneous and cohesive groups will be more likely to react to illness and medical care in terms of the social group's definition and interpretation of appropriate medical behavior

rather than more formal and impersonalized prescriptions of the official medical care system;

5. the more ethnocentric and socially cohesive the group on a community, friendship, or family level, the more likely are its members to display low knowledge about disease, skepticism toward professional medical care, and dependency during illness;
6. a cosmopolitan social structure is related to a scientific health orientation; and a parochial, or local, structure is related to lay, or popular, health orientation.

(Suchman, 1964, 1965a, 1965b, 1965c, 1966)

EMPIRICAL ASSESSMENTS OF THE MODEL. Suchman (1964, 1965a, 1965b, 1965c, 1966) in a series of exploratory studies and substudies of a sample of 5,340 adults in the ethnically mixed area of Washington Heights in New York City, found the following.

1. The type of social group structure was not found to be related to either health status or source of medical care;
2. [the] form of social organization is found to be more important than ethnicity or social class in relation to sociomedical responses;
3. lower socioeconomic and minority groups are significantly more socially isolated or ethnocentric; ethnocentricism is, in turn, highly related to a lower level of knowledge about disease, fearful or skeptical attitudes toward medical care, and dependence upon lay support during illness;
4. a more cosmopolitan social structure is related to a more scientific health orientation, whereas a parochial social structure is related to a more popular, or lay, health orientation.

Other investigators have addressed themselves to social group influences on health care seeking. In a preliminary report of an ongoing study of the Kaiser Foundation Health Plan (Oregon Region), Pope et al. (1971) note findings that seem to confirm the hypothesis that the more cosmopolitan person with a more scientific health orientation is more likely to use the telephone for symptom reporting than is the less cosmopolitan person with a less scientific health orientation. Nolan et al. (1967) found key variables in utilization of prepaid pediatric services to be organization of services, availability and accessibility of services, and socioeconomic status. However, Battistella (1971) found location in the social structure to be less important in delay of medical care seeking than was individual orientation to medical care. Zola (1964) highlighted the multiplicity of factors which trigger medical-care-seeking actions by working-class adults: interpersonal crisis, social interference, presence of social sanctioning for the action, perceived vocational or avocational threat, and nature and quality of symptoms.

The Andersen Model: Family Life Cycle Determinants of Health Services Utilization

THEORETICAL BASES FOR THE MODEL. Ronald Andersen (1968), in emphasizing family life cycle stages as determinants of utilization, posits the model shown in Figure 1 to explain family use of health facilities and services. According to Andersen's model, "a sequence of conditions contributes to the volume of health services used. Use is dependent on (1) the predisposition of the family to use services; (2) their ability to secure services; and (3) their need for such services. Further, the importance of each component depends on the discretion exercised by families in using services" (1968, p. 8).

Predisposing factors include family composition (age, sex, and marital status of the head of the family; family size; age of the youngest family member; and age of the oldest family member); social structure (employment, social class, occupation, and education of the head of the family; race, and ethnicity); and health beliefs (belief about medical care, physicians, and disease). The enabling component in the model includes family resources (family income, family savings, health insurance, regular source of care and welfare care) and community resources (physician-population ratio, hospital bed-population ratio, residence, and region). The need component includes illness (health level, symptoms, disability days, and free care for major illness) and response (seeing doctor for symptoms and regular physical examinations). Andersen divides utilization behavior into two major types, discretionary and nondiscretionary: "Behavior which is highly discretionary involves considerable choice on the part of the family. Non-discretionary behavior is primarily dictated by the physical condition of the family member. Decisions in the latter instance are usually made by providers of services" (Andersen, 1968, p. 18).

EMPIRICAL ASSESSMENTS OF THE MODEL. The model of families' use of health services awaits empirical test in studies other than the one by Andersen. Andersen's results indicated that there was

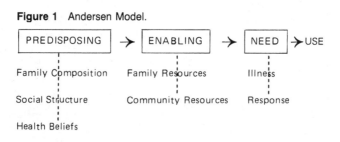

Figure 1 Andersen Model.

"considerable variance in family use of health services (which) was not accounted for in this study" (1968, p. 56). Accordingly, Andersen suggests that the original sequential model (predisposing → enabling → need → use) be modified inasmuch as "there are some differences in the relationships of the components for different types of services (hospital, physician, dentist) which should be considered in models for future studies" (1968, pp. 55–56). In general, Andersen's data indicate that the need variables (illness and response) were the most powerful use predictors within the 43 percent of utilization variance accounted for by the variables included in the model.

The Gross Model: Behavioral Components in Health Services Utilization

A fourth health services utilization model has been recently designed. Gross (1972), working within a behavioral frame-

Figure 2　The Gross Model.

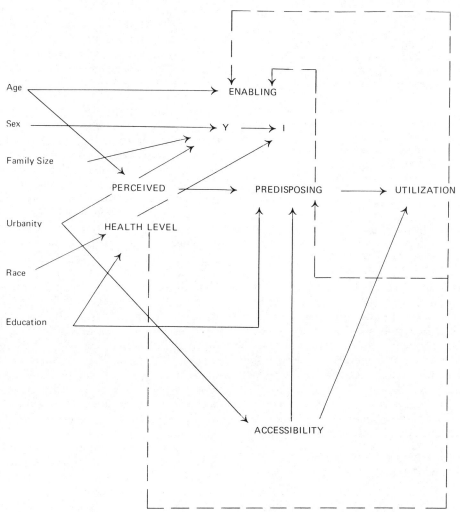

work for explaining utilization, sets forth the causal model shown in Figure 2. Gross delineates the following formula to explain the diagram in Figure 2.

$$U = f (E; P; A; H; X; \epsilon)$$

where

U = utilization of various services reported by the individual interviewee;

E = enabling factors (income, Y; health insurance status, I; family size, S; occupation of head of family; sex of head of family; education of head of family);

P = predisposing factors (attitudes of individual toward health care, services, and physicians; health values; health behavior when symptoms of health disorder are recognized; use of regular source of care; knowledge of existence of various services);

A = accessibility factors (distance and/or time of individual from facility; appointment delay time; waiting times; availability of hospital, physician, and dental services at varying distances from household; availability of a regular source of care);

H = perceived health level of individual and/or his family as assessed from health interview survey (disability days, restricted days, sick days);

X = individual and area-wide exogenous variables (age, sex, family size, race, education, location);

ϵ = residual error term.

This model certainly appears to be more comprehensive than the other three. Nonetheless, the variables are not more explicit in definition, despite the seeming precision of the formula. It remains to be seen whether this model will serve to enhance understanding of health services utilization behavior. Gross (May 3, 1974) has indicated that the model is in the process of test and refinement and that results should be available in the near future.

Summary of Strengths and Limitations of the Models

The criteria for empirically useful models are that they possess "deployability" (be capable of application in different settings), "scope" (number and extent of data which may be derived by use of the model), and "precision" (the replicability and validity of data derived through application of the inference rules provided by the model) (Lachman, 1963). The four models discussed show comparable strengths and limitations to other urban planning models (Lee, 1973) with respect to these criteria.

The four models are similar in many respects, with some important differences. All four employ similar terminology for variables; however, concepts and variables are organized along somewhat different lines and definitions are frequently at variance, making replication problematic. Figure 3 depicts comparisons in concepts and variables selected in the four models. For example, Rosenstock's key concepts of severity, susceptibility, availability, and accessibility are touched upon by the other three formulations. However, Rosenstock (a psychologist) emphasizes individual psychological beliefs about actual or potential severity of illness and susceptibility to illness, whereas Suchman and Andersen (sociologists), and Gross (health services administrator, planner, and researcher) emphasize availability, accessibility, interpersonal/social influences, and demographic factors, along with generalized "health values and/or beliefs." In short, where the four models differ most is in the importance given to individual beliefs concerning severity and susceptibility in determining utilization behavior. Where the models are in greatest agreement is in the importance of availability, accessibility (cost and distance) of health care services, and social group influences (family and peer), combined with demographic variables.

Empirical assessments of the models have produced similar snags. It is difficult to assess whether these snags are a function of lack of methodological rigor and comparability or failings inherent in the

SOURCE	SEVERITY	SUSCEPTIBILITY	AVAILABILITY	ACCESSIBILITY
ROSENSTOCK	Individual perceptions of actual or potential severity	Individual perceptions of actual or potential susceptibility	Environmental barriers to health action	Environmental barriers to health action
SUCHMAN			Availability	Convenience
ANDERSON			Community resources	Family resources
GROSS	Perceived health level of the individual		Knowledge of existence of services Availability of hospitals, doctors, clinics Availability of regular source of income	Income Distance/time from facilities Appointment delay Waiting time

SOURCE	SOCIAL INFLUENCES	DEMOGRAPHIC	HEALTH BELIEFS AND ATTITUDES
ROSENSTOCK	Interpersonal influences		
SUCHMAN	Reference group opportunities and influences; role	Status Ethnicity	Psychological factors (past experiences, beliefs, personality motivation)
ANDERSON		Family composition Social structure	Health beliefs Illness and response
GROSS		Family size Occupation Education Sex of head of family Race Residence	Attitudes toward health care Health values Health behavior

Figure 3 Comparisons in concepts selected by four health services utilization models (Rosenstock, Suchman, Andersen, Gross).

models or both. Those studies which emphasize attitudinal-motivational factors (belief in severity and susceptibility, faith in medical care) emerge with rather low empirical yield. This observation can be explained perhaps by the fact that attitudes as measured often bear little relationship to actions or perhaps by the realization that there exist few methodological tools with sufficient precision to measure attitudes and beliefs with validity. Rosenstock (1966) has summarized many of the methodological weaknesses in studies employing his model. These include lack of comparability in operational definitions; measurement and quantification problems; small sample sizes; the potential applicability of the model only to preventive health actions taken by middle-class adults;

and exploratory, rather than experimental, research design strategies. Suchman also noted the limitations of exploratory design for the purpose of establishing an hypothesized causal sequence among variables and the disadvantages of "the broad and superficially defined concepts employed" and "the relatively non-rigorous and imprecise measures of the operational indices used" (Suchman, 1965c, p. 13). These definitional and measurement difficulties were recently encountered in a study of prenatal care utilization which attempted to combine aspects of all four models for study (Veeder, 1973).

One major limitation of all four models is that they provide a static-structural explanation (Marx, 1963) for an essentially dynamic decision-making process. These are static models which confine the relevant variable field and posit relationships between variables which are believed to contribute to a decision that becomes apparent at an outcome point—the point of use or nonuse. In none of the utilization literature is there a concomitant model which attempts to generalize the steps in the consumer's health-decision-making process. What is missing is a description of decision-making factors which occur between cue and utilization action (Rosenstock), between group affiliation and influence and action (Suchman), between family life cycle stages and discretionary action (Andersen), and between enabling/predisposing factors and utilization outcomes (Gross). McKinlay has recently highlighted the need for "detailed empirical information relating to the number and various types of stages typically passed through in the use of some services; whether different stages involve different types or orders of decisions; and the extent to which different orders or types of contingencies or parameters operate to affect decisions at different stages" (1972, p. 140).

Decision theory offers one possibility for theoretically delineating and empirically testing the steps in the process of making choices between urban service alternatives (Veeder, 1972). Etzioni has outlined three basic decision-making strategies: rationalistic, incremental, and mixed-scanning (1968, p. 249–305). Rationalistic decision making is predominantly deductive, incremental decisions are exclusively inductive, and mixed-scanning combines elements of both. Although Etzioni focuses on macro-decision making, the mixed-scanning decision-making model appears to have heuristic value for explaining individual decision making. Thus decision theory, and, in particular, the mixed-scanning model, may provide an explanatory system with potential for activating static or, at best, "pseudodynamic" (Lee, 1973) models.

IMPLICATIONS FOR HUMAN SERVICES PLANNING

The litany of limitations inherent in health services utilization models appears to be long; however, their promise for more enlightened human services planning appears to be great. First, the four models discussed are cumulative, that is, each model building effort subsequent to Rosenstock's adds certain variable clusters which previous empirical work has shown to have greater predictive potential in relation to service utilization. Second, the definitions taken in the models acquire greater precision as the four models develop. Hence the analytic techniques applied to data generated by the models are increasingly sophisticated, growing from largely qualitative analysis in Rosenstock's and Suchman's work to use of multivariate and path analysis techniques in the work of Andersen and Gross. Third, it appears that greater amounts of utilization behaviors are explained.

It has been suggested in this discussion that predictions about service utilization behavior might be increased if future model building attempts incorporated a process, or decision-making-over-time component. Future human service utilization research efforts should be geared not only toward refining factors which go into a decision to use or not use a service and toward increasing the predictive power of these selected factors but also toward devising means to assess those factors which go into decisions at different points in time. In other words, what may be a constraining cluster of factors at one point in the service utilization decision-making process may be an enabling set at another point in time. Future research efforts should include an activating decision-making component.

The applicability of these health services utilization models may well extend beyond the specific context within which they were generated to areas such as recreation, housing, education, mental health, and employment, for example. Factors such as family size and composition, education, peer influences, cultural constraints, individual belief systems, organizational policies, and personnel may, singly or in concert, determine utilization behavior across contexts. Factors such as these must be considered both quantitatively and qualitatively. For example, accessibility factors of cost and distance may be seen not only in terms of "amount" but also in terms of an individual's "beliefs" about how much and how far. Further, individuals may define "cost" not merely in terms of money and time but also in psychological terms. The availability of resources in sheer numbers does not explain the tendency of persons to fail to utilize services even when available (McKinlay, 1972). The knowledge factor is key to the availability concept since lack of knowledge about the existence of a service or its focus renders that service unavailable.

Model building efforts in the social sciences, such as health services utilization models, may serve to expand the understanding of planners for human services in a range of areas. If such understanding is not gained and applied, "incautious interventions will continue to be immodestly applied" (Alexander, 1972, p. 148), and consumers of services in a range of health, education, recreation, counseling, and other urban service sectors will continue to be short-changed.

REFERENCES

ALEXANDER, TOM (1972). "The Social Engineers Retreat Under Fire," *Fortune* (October):132–48.

ANDERSEN, RONALD (1968). *A Behavioral Model of Families' Use of Health Services.* Chicago, Ill.: Center for Health Administration Studies, University of Chicago.

BATTISTELLA, ROBERT M. (1971). "Factors Associated with Delay in the Initiation of Physician's Care Among Late Adulthood Persons," *American Journal of Public Health* 61 (July):1348–61.

BORSKY, PAUL N., AND OSWALD SAGEN (1959). "Motivations Toward Health Examinations," *American Journal of Public Health* 49 (April):514–27.

ETZIONI, AMITAI (1968). *The Active Society.* New York: The Free Press.

GLASER, MELVIN A. (1958). "A Study of the Public's Acceptance of the Salk Vaccine Program," *American Journal of Public Health* 48 (February):141–46.

GOCHMAN, DAVID S. (1970). "Children's Perceptions of Vulnerability to Illness and Accidents," *Public Health Reports* 85 (January): 69–73.

———(1971). "Some Correlates of Children's Health Beliefs and Potential Health Behavior," *Journal of Health and Social Behavior* 12 (June):148–54.

GOLD, S. M. (1972). "Non Use of Neighborhood Parks," *Journal of the American Institute of Planners* 38 (November):369–78.

GROSS, P. F. (1972). "Urban Health Disorders, Spatial Analysis, and the Economics of Health Facility Location," *International Journal of Health Services* 2 (February):63–84.

———(May 3, 1974), personal communication.

HEINZELMANN, FRED (1962). "Factors in Prophylaxis Behavior in Treating Rheumatic Fever: An Exploratory Study," *Journal of Health and Human Behavior* 3 (Summer): 73–81.

HOCHBAUM, GODFREY M. (1956). "Why People Seek Diagnostic X-rays," *Public Health Reports 71* (April):377–80.

———(1964). "Public Participation in Medical Screening Programs: A Socio-Psychological Study," U.S. Department of Health, Education, and Welfare, Public Health Service, Public Health Service Publication no. 572.

KEGELES, S. STEPHEN (1963). "Why People Seek Dental Care: A Test of a Conceptual Formulation," *Journal of Health and Human Behavior* 4 (Fall):166–73.

———(1969). "A Field Experimental Attempt to Change Beliefs and Behavior of Women in an Urban Ghetto," *Journal of Health and Social Behavior* 10 (June):115–24.

KIRSCHT, JOHN P., ET AL. (1966). "A National Study of Health Beliefs," *Journal of Health and Human Behavior* 7 (Winter):248–54.

LACHMAN, ROY (1963). "The Model in Theory Construction," in Melvin H. Marx, ed., *Theories in Contemporary Psychology.* New York: Macmillan.

Lee, Douglass B. Jr. (1973). "Requiem for Large-Scale Models," *Journal of the American Institute of Planners* 39 (May):163–78.

Leventhal, Howard (1960). "Epidemic Impact on the General Population in Two Cities," in Irwin M. Rosenstock, et al., eds., *The Impact of Asian Influenza on Community Life.* Department of Health, Education, and Welfare, Public Health Service.

Marx, Melvin H. (1963). "The General Nature of Theory Construction," in Melvin H. Marx, ed., *Theories in Contemporary Psychology.* New York: Macmillan.

McKinlay, J. B. (1972). "Some Approaches and Problems in the Study of the Use of Services—An Overview," *Journal of Health and Social Behavior* 13 (June):115–52.

Nolan, Robert I., et al. (1967). "Social Class Difference in Utilization of Pediatric Services in a Prepaid Direct Service Medical Care Program," *American Journal of Public Health* 57 (January):34–47.

Pope, C. R., et al. (1971). "Determinants of Medical Care Utilization: The Use of the Telephone for Reporting Symptoms," *Journal of Health and Social Behavior* 12 (June):155–62.

Rosenstock, Irwin M., Mayhew Derryberry, and Barbara K. Carriger (1959). "Why People Fail to Seek Poliomyelitis Vaccination," *Public Health Reports* 74 (February):98–103.

Rosenstock, Irwin M., et al., eds. (1960). *The Impact of Asian Influenza on Community Life.* De-partment of Health, Education and Welfare. Public Health Service.

———(1966). "Why People Use Health Services," in *Health Services Research 1, The Milbank Memorial Fund Quarterly* 44 (July):94–127.

Suchman, Edward A. (1964) "Sociomedical Variations Among Ethnic Groups," *American Journal of Sociology* 70 (November):319–31.

———(1965a). "Stages of Illness and Medical Care," *Journal of Health and Human Behavior* 6 (Fall):114–28.

———(1965b). "Social Factors in Medical Deprivation," *American Journal of Public Health* 55 (November)1725–33.

———(1965c). "Social Patterns of Illness and Medical Care," *Journal of Health and Human Behavior* 6 (Spring):2–16.

———(1966). "Health Orientation and Medical Care," *American Journal of Public Health* 56 (January):97–105.

Veeder, Nancy W. (1972). "Prenatal Care Utilization Decisions: Linkages Between Decision Making Theory and Health Services Utilization Models," manuscript, Brandeis University.

———(1973). "Prenatal Care Utilization and Persistence Patterns in a Developing Nation," Ph.D. dissertation, Brandeis University.

Zola, Irving Kenneth (1964). "Illness Behavior of the Working Class: Implications and Recommendations," in Shostak and Gomberg, eds., *Blue-Collar World.* Englewood Cliffs, N.J.: Prentice-Hall.

Dennis N. T. Perkins

Evaluating Social Interventions: A Conceptual Schema

Although millions of dollars are expended annually on activities described as evalua-

Reprinted from *Evaluation Quarterly*, vol. 1, no. 4 (November 1977) pp. 639–56, by permission of the author and the publisher, Sage Publications, Inc.

tion research, there is substantial disagreement about the characteristics of evaluative activities and the technical methods used in their implementation. The kinds of projects commonly undertaken under the aegis of evaluation constitute a disparate group, including such varied activities as policy research, project monitoring, applied research, descriptive statistical reporting, the development of management information systems, and many others.

The intent of this paper is to provide a set of conceptual reference points that may be helpful in distinguishing among such evaluation activities. Specifically, it proposes a broad taxonomy of potential assessment types and identifies a number of methodological alternatives that are available to the researcher. It is hoped that such a framework will provide a vocabulary for describing evaluation activities and will assist in the choice of an appropriate methodology.

BACKGROUND

While part of the confusion over the nature of evaluation research is purely semantic, emanating from a proliferation of terms and labels, other disagreements result from substantive differences. Some researchers are concerned principally with the accomplishment of specified programmatic goals. Wholey et al. (1971: 23), for example, provide the following definition:

> Evaluation (1) assesses the effectiveness of an on-going program in achieving its objectives, (2) relies on the principles of research design to distinguish a program's effects from those of other forces working in a situation, and (3) aims at program improvement through a modification of current operations.

Critics of the goal-attainment model hold other conceptions of the evaluation role. Like Etzioni (1960), Schulberg and Baker (1971: 77) propose a "system model" in which the point of departure for the evaluator is not simply the program goal but rather the development of an operational model of the internal processes of the organization or social unit that is attempting to achieve the goal: "Instead of simply

identifying the goals of the organization and proceeding to study whether they are attained, the system model requires that the analyst determine what he considers a highly effective allocation of means." Similarly, Scriven (1976: 133) points out that focusing on stated objectives may obscure unintended consequences of the program being evaluated. He proposed, therefore, a "goal-free" evaluative procedure in which the evaluator examines formal goals only after an independent examination of program activities.

There are also those who distinguish the evaluation activities associated with classical research from those of program evaluation. According to Steele (1973), evaluative research should be aimed at contributions of new knowledge, while program evaluation is said to address existing questions about specific programs. Moreover, Steele argues that the methodologies employed in traditional social science research may be inappropriate for the unique problems encountered in program evaluation, suggesting that, in the latter case, one must question the traditional ".05" level of significance.

Each of these conceptions of evaluation has some merit, and it is not the purpose of this paper to advocate a single, exclusive view of evaluation research. It does seem that Steele's distinction between research and program evaluation is misleading since the .05 criterion is, of course, a purely discretionary measure which might be excessively rigid in some exploratory studies, yet too liberal for some applications in medical research. Further, Campbell (1971) contends that the scientific methods that have been developed for classical research are equally appropriate for evaluation, and Rossi (1971:97) writes:

> There are no formal differences between . . . "research as such" and "evaluation research." Research designs, statistical techniques, or data collection methods are the same whether applied to the study of the

most basic principles of human behavior or to the most prosaic of social action programs.

But the central point here is that researchers have developed evaluation schemata that fit their own needs and, as a result, the typologies associated with these conceptions are necessarily circumscribed. What is needed, therefore, is a framework that integrates the plethora of activities currently identified as "evaluation research."

TOWARD AN EVALUATION TAXONOMY

A taxonomy of evaluation types might be empirically derived from previous evaluation studies using multivariate statistical techniques, such as inverse factor or cluster analysis (Frederickson, 1972). More deductively, a classification system might be based on any one of a number of characteristics that have been suggested as organizing dimensions (e.g., subject matter, timing, unit of analysis, and so forth). The typology developed in this paper follows the implications of Weiss's (1972: 6) observation that "what distinguishes evaluation research is not method or subject matter but intent—the purpose for which it is done." Thus the schema that follows is derived from the first-order characteristic of assessment purpose, employing a theoretical model of program development to discuss six generic evaluation types. Although the divisions suggested in this conceptualization are clearly not the only means of classification, it will be proposed that the following evaluation types may be identified: strategic, compliance, management, intervention effect, and program impact. These six evaluation classes will be examined in the context of a theoretical model which describes the inception and implementation of a social program.

With this preface, then, the evolution of a federal program can be depicted as beginning with the identification of a social problem, or issue of public policy (Figure 1). Programs to address such problems are legislated by Congress, often with goals that are sufficiently general that they must be made "operational" by an administering agency; that is, the fundamental intent

Figure 1 Theoretical Model of Program Development

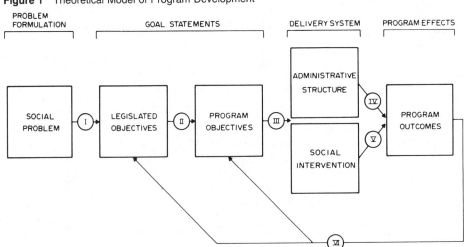

of the legislative language must be translated into programmatic objectives and guidelines that are suitable for day-to-day administration and evaluation.

Next, a delivery system must be established to accomplish the programmatic goals and objectives. In some programs, such as School Assistance in Federally Affected Areas, the delivery system is simply the administrative structure that oversees the distribution of resources. In other instances—Head Start, for example—the administrative structure is coupled with a deliberate social intervention. In both cases, the output of the delivery system may be characterized in terms of a specific set of program outcomes that, at least theoretically, are consonant with the goals and objectives originally set forth by those who conceived the program.

At the "front end" of the program development process, evaluation efforts are largely diagnostic, directed toward greater understanding of the dimension of a social problem, including its origin, scope, and susceptibility to federal intervention. These efforts are analogous to those characterized by Anthony et al. (1965) as strategic planning studies: that is, studies that involve deciding on basic organizational objectives, on changes in these objectives, and on policies used to govern acquisition and disposition of resources.

Such *strategic* evaluations may be concerned with the etiology of social problems, focusing on the "implicit theories" that lie behind ameliorative programs. A strategic assessment, for example, might test Ryan's (1972) contention that social interventions typically blame the victim for problems that are systemic in character. Strategic evaluations may also suggest new legislative initiatives (Linkage I of Figure 1), as in the case of the Coleman et al. (1966) examination of educational opportunity, or Armor's (1972) research on the effects of busing. Studies conducted by the Educational Policy Research Centers are typically of the strategic genre, along with the policy research activities proposed by the Office of Research, Evaluation, and Data Systems, HEW, and the planning studies conducted by the Office of Education.

A second class of evaluative effort deals with the issue of *compliance*. One may ask, for example, whether the programmatic objectives established by an administering agency are consistent with the aims of Congress, as reflected in the legislative goals (Linkage II of Figure 1). Although individual members of Congress and their staffs are acutely aware of this linkage, private citizens and special interest organizations may also be concerned with the relationship. The National Committee on Education Change, for instance, employed a full-time Washington representative to serve in a "watchdog" role vis-à-vis the National Institute of Education. His sole function was one of assessing the extent to which the new agency's activities were directed toward the mandated goal of improving equality of educational opportunity.

Compliance evaluations may be conducted at other points in the process as well. Within the administrative structure of the delivery system, such assessments are frequently made to ensure that funds are allocated according to program guidelines; under the regulations of the Emergency School Assistance Program, for example, the expenditure of funds for busing was strictly proscribed. Compliance evaluations may be conducted at the program level or within individual projects where such assessments are often referred to as "monitoring." The term "monitoring," however, may also imply concern for the outcome of the delivery system. In this schema, compliance evaluations are conducted exclusively for the purpose of assessing adherence to legislative goals or program objectives.

A third category of evaluative effort concerns the logic inherent in program design. The evaluability assessments advocated by Horst, Nay, Scanlon, and Wholey (1974) would fall into this category since they are intended to examine the linkages among the objectives identified by the program manager, the implementation activities undertaken to achieve those objectives, and the anticipated program outcomes (Linkages III, IV, and V of Figure 1). Specifically, such program design evaluations may ask the following questions.

(1) Are the problems, intended program interventions, anticipated outcomes, and the expected impact sufficiently well defined as to be measurable?

(2) In the assumptions linking expenditure to implementation of intervention, intervention to the outcome anticipated, and immediate outcome to the expected impact on the problem, is the logic laid out clearly enough to be tested?

(3) Is there any one clearly in charge of the program? Who? What are the constraints on his ability to act? What range of actions might he reasonably take or consider as a result of various possible evaluation findings about the measures and assumptions discussed above? [Horst, Nay, Scanlon, and Wholey, 1974: 20]

Other less comprehensive program design evaluations deal with single dimensions of the evaluability issue—whether, for example, program objectives are stated in measurable terms.

The fourth and fifth evaluation types are associated with the functioning of the program delivery system, one addressing itself to the administrative component and the other to the intervention itself. Assessments dealing with the first issue focus on the efficiency and effectiveness with which managers deploy the resources at their disposal to achieve program objectives (Linkage IV of Figure 1). Such *management* evaluations are part of the management

control process and generally assume that such factors as objectives, facilities, financial resources, and the policies of top management are—at least in the short run—fixed elements (Anthony et al., 1965).

The fifth class of evaluation addresses the issue of *intervention effect*. Such assessments attempt to establish the relationship between program interventions and outcomes (Linkage V of Figure 1) or, in some cases, the processes involved in producing those outcomes. Smith (1974) has further classified such evaluations at three levels of complexity (1) assessments of the effects of entire systems—for example, do schools make a difference?; (2) assessments of the elements of a system—such as teacher characteristics, school resources, and student-teacher ratios; and (3) assessments of programs or configurations of elements—such as a mathematics program, which is expected to have a specified effect on student outcomes. Intervention-effect evaluations are analogous to the research component that is found in classical scientific experimentation. Here, the principal foci are internal validity (Campbell and Stanley, 1966), that is, determining whether the experimental intervention made a difference and construct validity (Cronbach and Meehl, 1955), that is, identifying the "active ingredient" that accounts for observed intervention effects.

Intervention-effect evaluations frequently include some form of "process evaluation" or analysis of the transformation system by which programmatic resources are converted to outputs. Although such process analyses can be employed in formative evaluations to guide the development of emerging programs (Scriven, 1972), this is not their only purpose. A process evaluation—which might be viewed as an analogue of the laboratory experimenter's "manipulation check"—frequently provides the only means of assessing which, if any, field interventions were actually implemented. As

Guttentag and Struening (1975) have observed, the precise nature of the "independent variable" that comprises a social intervention is typically difficult to specify and may be more accurately represented as a complex "set" of events. Thus a process evaluation is typically needed to identify the relationships between individual components of an intervention and observed outcomes and to ensure that the evaluator is not unknowingly assessing the effects of "non-events" (Charters and Jones, 1973: 5).

Finally, a sixth class of evaluation deals with the net output of the program delivery system (Linkages IV and V, combined) and with the relationships between these outcomes and legislated goals and program objectives (Linkage VI). Often termed *program impact* evaluations, these studies are less concerned with administrative activities or a specific intervention than with the actual attainment of program goals.

Some have argued that many such studies are doomed to provide little useful information. Timpane (1974), formerly Deputy Assistant Secretary for Planning and Evaluation at HEW, comments:

> Millions of dollars are spent on studies such as Title I with little or no chance of success. Because of ambiguous goals, treatments which can't be identified, or inadequate controls, one might know at the outset that such studies are simply a waste of time.

Similarly, in his analysis of Head Start and Title I, Smith (1974: 11–24) argues:

> In neither type of study is any attempt made to implement particular treatment types (e.g., particular Head Start curricula) or to assign subjects to treatment and control groups. If the program being evaluated is universally applied to the target population, no control groups are possible. . . . The lack of control groups precludes information about overall program "effects" and differential treatment effects are confounded to an unknown extent with other treatments

and with subjects exposed to the treatments. Information is thus confined to a descriptive and hypothesis generating type.

A different view is held by evaluators in the Office of Education, who contend that program impact evaluations are not only desirable but legally required. Mogin (1974), for example, contends:

> The Commissioner of Education is required by the General Education Provisions Act to report to Congress on each and every program, and the requirements of H.R. 69 are even more stringent. Although there are serious methodological problems with impact evaluations, there are also ways around them; for example, Title I is a complex program, but 60% of all Title I projects have reading as an objective. Baseline data can be collected and progress evaluated; we feel such impact evaluations can and should be conducted.

The desirability of program impact studies—or any other class of evaluative activity—is a function of the objectives and constraints placed on the evaluator, and it is not the intent of this paper to resolve the issue in any ultimate sense. The preceding analysis would simply suggest that six distinct evaluation classes may be identified, with three important caveats. First, any typology involves a number of rather arbitrary distinctions, and a paradigm that is lucid for one observer may be far less intelligible to another. Second, it is simply infeasible to partition the world of evaluation into mutually exclusive and exhaustive sets; overlap often occurs, and new categories must be continually invented if one is to capture precisely the character of any particular activity. Finally, it is important to recognize that many evaluations are complex enterprises, and it is neither necessary nor desirable that their scope be limited to a single category. With these reservations in mind, however, it is proposed that evaluative activities may be usefully classified as strategic, compliance, program design, management, intervention effect, or program impact.

EVALUATION METHODOLOGIES

Associated with the preceding evaluation types is a variety of analytical and research methods. Methodology, in fact, might have been chosen as an alternative means of classification. In this analysis, however, technique is viewed as a second-order characteristic of interest primarily for its contribution to the fulfillment of evaluation objectives.

A number of research strategies have been described in the literature (e.g., Campbell and Stanley, 1966; Runkel and McGrath, 1972; Suchman, 1967; Tripodi et al., 1971), and it is apparent that conceptions of analytical techniques are every bit as diverse as views on other facets of evaluation. Table 1 displays a number of the more prevalent of these techniques, summarizing the key characteristics of each.

As in the previous typology, certain qualifications are in order. Although the tabular summary reflects a number of common distinctions, there are other ways of conceptualizing analytical techniques, and the list could certainly be extended or collapsed. Bayesian methods, for example, have been suggested as a promising analytical approach (e.g., Pratt, 1965; Riecken and Boruch, 1974), and techniques such as the multiattribute utility model (Edwards and Guttentag, 1975) might profitably have been included. Terms that are frequently associated with each method have been included where appropriate, although it is important to recognize that "related or equivalent" does not necessarily mean identical. True experimental designs, for instance, are often used in laboratory studies that can be closely controlled by the experimenter. Yet experimental designs have also been used in field studies (e.g., Morse and Reimer, 1956), and there is no theoretical reason why true

experiments need be confined to the laboratory (Cooke and Campbell, 1976; Riecken and Boruch, 1974).

Each method has its constituency, and preferences often are deeply entrenched and value laden. Campbell and Stanley (1966: 6), for example, characterize the one-shot case study as "of almost no scientific value," and Campbell (1971: 11) advocates the "greatly expanded use of experimental evaluations." At the same time, Dukes (1965) provides a rationale for studies involving single individuals, Walton (1972) defends the use of the case study in analyzing organizational behavior, and Weiss and Rein (1969) contend that the controlled experiment is inappropriate for the evaluation of broad-aim programs. Their analysis—which is based on a case study—argues for a more qualitative, process-oriented methodology.

Many researchers see the methodological issue in terms of a series of polar alternatives, suggesting that evaluations must be "hard" (based on quantitative data) or "soft" (based on qualitative information), experimental or naturalistic, rigorous or anecdotal, and so forth. Advocates typically conclude with prescriptive statements about the "right" design—that is, a normative model which is to be universally applied.

There are, on the other hand, those who view methodological alternatives in less absolute terms. Runkel and McGrath (1972: 116–17), for example, write:

> Too often in behavioral science the choice of strategy is made first, based on the investigator's previous experience, preferences, and resources, and then the problem is chosen and formuated to fit the selected strategy, rather than the other way around. . . . The trick is not to search for the right strategy but to pick up the strategy that is best *for your purposes and circumstances.*

The assertion that an appropriate choice of research strategy can only be made in light of a particular set of research objectives is supported by other theorists, and Willems (1969: 46) argues that research strategies are more accurately conceptualized as continuous—rather than dichotomous—alternatives:

> . . . the set of activities an investigator actually engages in while conducting his research falls somewhere in a two-dimensional descriptive space. The first dimension, which is most frequently thought of in differentiating research activities describes *the degree of the investigator's influence upon, or manipulation of, the antecedent conditions of the behavior studied.* . . . The second dimension, which is less commonly considered than the first, describes *the degree to which units are imposed by the investigator on the behavior studied.*

To illustrate, the extent of manipulation may be very small in a naturalistic study conducted by an evaluator concerned with understanding the operation of an educational program. On the other hand, an experimenter intending to demonstrate the effects of instituting a token economy in a community treatment center would attempt to influence strongly the behavior of center residents. Along the second dimension of structure, studies may range from unstructured observation, through open-ended interviews, to fixed-alternative questionnaires in which the respondent is required to choose from a limited set of performed answers.

To Willems' framework might be added a third dimension: the *intensity* of measurement, an elaboration that subsumes both time span and frequency of data collection. This addition becomes useful if one wishes, for example, to distinguish between a cross-sectional survey and a longitudinal study using similar instrumentation. In both cases, the investigator engages in little experimental manipulation but provides considerable structure to potential responses. In the latter case, however, flexibility may be enhanced through analytical techniques—such as cross-lagged panel correlations—that permit more extensive

exploration of causality (Campbell, 1963; Lawler, 1968; Pelz and Andrews, 1964).

These three dimensions define a descriptive space within which individual designs can be located (Figure 2). An interrupted time series analysis, for example, would typically be characterized by extensive investigator intervention, relatively structured response categories (e.g., frequency of specific behavioral events), and measurement of high intensity reflected in the repeated assessment design. A cross-sectional survey, however, would involve little active intervention by the researcher, a highly structured response (e.g., a Likert-type questionnaire), and low intensity of measurement (data collected at a single administration). The locations shown in Figure 2 illustrate modal types, but numerous variations are possible. For example, Campbell's (1973) time-series analysis of the Connecticut speeding crackdown involved no active experimenter intervention and would therefore be located on the low end of the "degree of manipulation" axis.

The implication of this representation is

Figure 2 A Space for Describing Research Strategies (adapted from Willems, 1969)

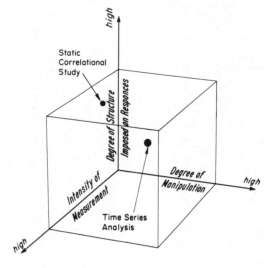

Table 1 Summary of Principal Evaluation Methods

METHODOLOGICAL TYPE	EQUIVALENT OR RELATED TERMS	CHARACTERISTICS	EXEMPLAR
Experimental Design (Campbell and Stanley, 1966)	Laboratory Study	Full control over scheduling of experimental stimuli (the "when and to whom of exposures and the ability to randomize exposures").	Pretest-Posttest Control Group involves prior measurement of two randomly constituted groups, introduction of experimental treatments to one group, and subsequent comparison of control and experimental scores.
Quasi-experimental Design (Campbell and Stanley, 1966; Caporaso and Roos, 1973)	Field Experiment	Partial control over experimental stimuli (e.g., the "when and to whom of measurement")	Time Series: involves the periodic measurement of some variable, the introduction of an experimental event, and the identification of a discontinuity in the measurement pattern.
Preexperimental Design (Campbell and Stanley, 1966)	Naturalistic Observation Case Study	Relatively little control over rival explanations of hypothesized treatment effect.	One Shot Case Study: involves the analysis of a single group, drawing inferences based on expectations of what might have occurred without experimental intervention.
Survey Research (Babbie, 1973; Runkel and McGrath, 1972)	Sample Survey	Static correlational studies, typically employing multivariate techniques to analyze data collected from large samples	*Equality of Educational Opportunity* (Coleman et al., 1966); *Bureaucratic Encounters: A Pilot Study in the Evaluation of Government Service* (Katz et al., 1974)

Approach	Method	Description	Example
Benefit-Cost Analysis (Schultz, 1967)	Systems Analysis PPBS	Evaluation of the relative effectiveness of alternative programs (expressed in dollar terms), judged in relation to economic costs	HEW Analysis of the Work Incentive Program, 1968 (Rivlin, 1971); Evaluation of the Costs and Benefits of Human Resource Development Program (Mirvis and Macy, 1976).
Cost-Effectiveness Analysis (Levine and Williams, 1971; Tripodi et al., 1971)	Systems Analysis Cost-Outcome Analysis	Comparison of alternative programs on the basis of program costs, and results measured in equivalent units	Comparative analysis of two programs, both of which are designed to attain a nondelinquency rate of 90% for a target population (Tripodi et al., 1971)
Administrative Audit (Tripodi et al., 1971)		Evaluation of program policies and practices in terms of compliance with internal and external standards	Studies typically conducted by the General Accounting Office
Operations Research (Churchman et al., 1957)	Systems Analysis Management Science	Application of scientific quantitative methods to develop optimal solutions to problems of program operation	Development of a model for optimizing staffing through work sampling and multiple regression analyses (Halpert et al., 1973, PH-43-68-1325)
Formal Theory (Runkel & McGrath, 1972)	Means-Ends Analysis (Porter, et al., 1975) Reconstructed Logic (Kaplan, 1964)	Construction of abstract models of behavior systems, performing logical manipulations to adduce new insights.	Evaluation Planning at the National Institute of Mental Health: A Case History (Horst, Scanlon, Schmidt, and Wholey, 1974)

that a particular research strategy can be viewed in the context of a broad range of potential alternatives. Each dimension is theoretically independent of the other, and the design of choice may be radically different from the restricted analytical approaches found in common practice. Such a schema avoids the dichotomous thinking frequently imposed on the research process, makes explicit the range of methodological options available to the evaluator, and challenges the belief in a preeminent evaluation strategy.

The fallacy of insisting on a single analytical technique is further illustrated by an elaboration of the evaluation taxonomy presented earlier. When the six categories of evaluation are arrayed in relation to methodological alternatives (Figure 3), the necessity for judicious matching becomes apparent. While the true experiment is perhaps the most powerful method for assessing the effects of social intervention, situational factors can render the experimental design infeasible (Timpane, 1970). Moreover, the logic of program design can be analyzed without regard to randomization and control groups, management evaluations may be best accomplished by operations research or case study methods, and strategic evaluations can be based on correlational or cost-benefit analyses. Fur-

ther, it is likely that complex evaluations will require several methodological approaches, with each analytical technique tailored to a specific facet of the assessment effort.

In conclusion, then, the course proposed in this paper might be characterized as a "contingency approach" to evaluation methodology. Rather than defending a single, ideal evaluation strategy, this precept suggests a comparative analysis of alternative techniques, ultimately directed toward achieving an optimal fit between evaluation objective and assessment method.

SUMMARY

The preceding discussion has attempted to provide a framework for conceptualizing a range of evaluation research activities. It was argued that a principal consideration should be the purpose of the endeavor and that methodological choices should be made only after clear specification of the type of evaluation being implemented.

For those who have not been baffled by the semantic complexities of evaluation terminology, the call for an integrating framework may not be particularly compelling. Yet a taxonomy of evaluation types might be considered as but one of a number of classificatory systems employed in research, and such schemata have demonstrated their utility in a variety of contexts. Woods (1974:584), for example, describes the value of classification systems in organizing our knowledge of the world:

> Before Mendeléeff arranged the elements according to their atomic weights, the discovery of new elements had been essentially "accidental." The classification by atomic weight, however, allowed the known elements to be grouped into families provided that empty cells were left in the table. Mendeleeff not only successfully predicted that elements would eventually be discovered to

Figure 3 Evaluation Types and Methodological Alternatives

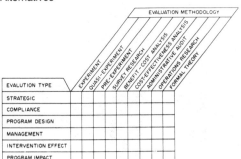

occupy these empty spaces but he also was remarkably accurate in predicting many of the properties of these yet-to-be discovered elements.

It seems unlikely, of course, that an evaluation typology could be used in precisely the same way. Classification frameworks have typically been associated with tangible objects (Woods, 1974), and paradigms for interpreting their properties may be more evident than those used to classify abstract phenomena. On the other hand, the discovery of physicalistic "objects" or the development of a perfect system of classification are not the only purposes of taxonomy. Allen and Biglan (1972), for example, have shown that agreement on a disciplinary paradigm facilitates collaboration and communication in research, and Kuhn (1962: 108) describes the "normative functions of paradigms" in scientific progress. Thus a shared typology may provide a basis for the communication of ideas, serve as a conceptual shorthand for observation and discussion, and assist in the choice of an appropriate research methodology.

REFERENCES

ALLEN, D. B. AND A. BIGLAN (1972). "The characteristics of research in different academic areas." USOE Technical Report 72-35. Seattle: University of Washington.

ANTHONY, R. N., J. DEARDEN, AND R. F. VANCIL (1965). Management Control Systems. Homewood, IL: Richard D. Irwin.

ARMOR, D. J. (1972). "The evidence on busing." Public Interest 28:90–126.

BABBIE, E. R. (1973). Survey Research Methods. Belmont, CA: Wadsworth.

CAMPBELL, D. T. (1973). "Reforms as experiments," pp. 187–225, in J. A. Caparoso and L. L. Roos (eds.), Quasi-Experimental Approaches: Testing Theory and Evaluating Policy. Evanston, IL: Northwestern Univ. Press.

———(1971). "Methods for the experimenting society." Preliminary draft of paper presented at a meeting of the Eastern Psychological Association, Washington, D.C.

———(1963). "From description to experimentation: Interpreting trends as quasi-experiments," pp. 213–42, in C. W. Harris (ed.), Problems in Measuring Change. Madison: Univ. of Wisconsin Press.

——— and J. C. STANLEY (1966). Experimental and Quasi-Experimental Designs for Research. Chicago, IL: Rand-McNally.

CAPORASO, J. A. AND L. L. ROOS [EDS.] (1973). Quasi-Experimental Approaches: Testing Theory and Evaluating Policy. Evanston, IL: Northwestern Univ. Press.

CHARTERS, W. W. AND J. E. JONES (1973). "On the risk of appraising nonevents in program evaluation." Evaluation Researcher 11: 5–7.

CHURCHMAN, C. W., R. L. ACKOFF, AND E. L. ARNOFF (1957). Introduction to Operations Research. New York: John Wiley.

COLEMAN, J. S., ET AL. (1966). Equality of Educational Opportunity. Washington, DC: Government Printing Office.

COOKE, T. D., AND D. T. CAMPBELL (1976). "The design and conduct of quasi-experiments and true experiments in field settings," pp. 223–326, in M. D. Dunnette (ed.), Headbook of Industrial and Organizational Psychology. Chicago, IL: Rand-McNally.

CRONBACH, L. J., AND P. E. MEEHL (1955). "Construct validity in psychological tests." Psych. Bull. 52: 281–302.

DUKES, W. F. (1965). "N = 1." Psych. Bull. 64: 74–79.

EDWARDS, W., AND M. GUTTENTAG (1975). "Experiments and evaluations: A reexamination," pp. 409–63, in C. A. Bennett and A. A. Lumsdaine (eds.), Evaluation and Experiment. New York: Academic Press.

ETZIONI, A. (1960). "Two approaches to organizational analysis: A critique and a suggestion." Admin. Sci. Q. 5: 257–78.

FREDERICKSON, N. (1972). "Toward a taxonomy of situations." Amer. Psychologist 27: 114–23.

GUTTENTAG, M. (1975). "The handbook: Its purpose and organization," pp. 3–7, in M. Guttentag and E. L. Struening (eds.), Handbook of Evaluation Research, vol. 2. Beverly Hills, CA: Sage.

———— AND E. L. STRUENING [eds.] (1975). Handbook of Evaluation Research. Beverly Hills, CA: Sage.

HALPERT, H. P., J. W. HORVATH, AND J. P. YOUNG (1973). An Administrator's Handbook on the Application of Operations Research to the Management of Mental Health Systems (PH-43-68-1325). Washington, DC: National Institute of Mental Health.

HORST, P., J. N. NAY, J. W. SCANLON, AND J. S. WHOLEY (1974). "Program management and the federal evaluator." Paper prepared for the Public Administration Review Symposium on Program Evaluation.

HORST, P., J. W. SCANLON, R. E. SCHMIDT, AND J. S. WHOLEY (1974). Evaluation Planning at the National Institute of Mental Health: A Case History. Washington, DC: The Urban Institute.

KAPLAN, A. (1964). The Conduct of Inquiry. New York: Chandler.

KATZ, D., B. A. GUTEK, R. L. KAHN, AND E. BARTON (1974). Bureaucratic Encounters: A Pilot Study in the Evaluation of Government Service. Ann Arbor, MI: Institute for Social Research.

KUHN, T. S. (1962). The Structure of Scientific Revolutions. Chicago: Univ. of Chicago Press.

LAWLER, E. E. (1968). "A correlational-causal analysis of the relationship between expectancy attitudes and job performance." J. of Applied Psychology 52: 462–68.

LEVINE, R. A., AND A. P. WILLIAMS (1971). Making Evaluation Effective: A Guide (HEW 5-70-155). Santa Monica, CA: The Rand Corporation.

MIRVIS, P. H., AND B. A. MACY (1976). "Accounting for the costs and benefits of human resource development programs: An interdisciplinary approach." Accounting. Organizations and Society 1: 179–93.

MOGIN, B. (1974). Personal communication, August 13.

MORSE, N., AND E. REIMER (1956). "The experimental change of a major organizational variable. J. of Abnormal and Social Psychology 52: 120–29.

PELZ, D. C., AND F. M. ANDREWS (1964). "De-

tecting causal priorities in panel study data." Amer. Soc. Rev. 29:836–48.

PORTER, L. W., E. E. LAWLER, AND J. R. HACKMAN (1975). Behavior in Organizations. New York: McGraw-Hill.

PRATT, J. W. (1965). "Bayesian interpretation of standard inference statements." J. of the Royal Statistical Society, Series B (Methodological) 27: 169–203.

RIECKEN, H. W. AND R. F. BORUCH (1974). Social Experimentation: A Method for Planning and Evaluating Social Intervention. New York: Academic Press.

RIVLIN, A. M. (1971). Systematic Thinking for Social Action. Washington, DC: The Brooking Institution.

ROSSI, P. H. (1971). "Evaluating educational programs," pp. 97–99, in F. G. Caro (ed.), Readings in Evaluation Research. New York: Russell Sage Foundation.

RUNKEL, P. J., AND J. E. MCGRATH (1972). Research on Human Behavior: A Systematic Guide to Method. New York: Holt, Rinehart and Winston.

RYAN, W. (1972.) Blaming the Victim. New York: Vintage.

SCHULBERG, H. C., AND F. BAKER (1971). "Program evaluation models and the implementation of research findings," pp. 72–80, in F. G. Caro (ed.), Readings in Evaluation Research. New York: Russell Sage Foundation.

SCHULTZ, C. L. (1967). "Why benefit-cost analysis? Paper presented to the Subcommittee on National Security and International Operations of the Committee on Government Operations, U.S. Senate, Washington, D.C.

SCRIVEN, M. (1976). "Evaluation bias and its control," pp. 119–39, in G. V. Glass (ed.), Evaluation Studies: Review Annual, vol. I. Beverly Hills, CA: Sage.

————(1972). "The methodology of evaluation," pp. 123–36, in C. Weiss (ed.), Evaluating Action Progams: Readings in Social Action and Education. Boston: Allyn & Bacon.

SMITH, M. S. (1974). "Large-scale 'experimentation' in education." Unpublished manuscript, Harvard University.

STEELE, S. M. (1973). Contemporary Approaches to Program Evaluation: Implications for Evaluating Programs for Disadvantaged Adults. New York: ERIC Clearinghouse on Adult Education.

SUCHMAN, E. A. (1967). *Evaluative Research.* New York: Russell Sage Foundation.

TIMPANE, P. M. (1974). Personal communication, August 22.

———(1970). "Education experimentation in national social policy." *Harvard Educ. Rev.* 40: 547–66.

TRIPODI, T., P. FELLIN, AND L. EPSTEIN (1971). *Social Program Evaluation.* Itasca, IL: F. E. Peacock.

WALTON, R. E. (1972). "Advantages and attributes of the case study." *J. of Applied Behavioral Sci.* 8: 73–78.

WEISS, C. H. (1972). *Evaluation Research: Methods for Assessing Program Effectiveness.* Englewood Cliffs, NJ: Prentice-Hall.

WEISS, R. S., AND M. REIN (1969). "The evaluation of broad-aim programs: A cautionary case and a moral." *Annals of the Amer. Acad. of Pol. and Social Sci.* 385: 133–42.

WHOLEY, J. S., J. W. SCANLON, H. G. DUFFY, J. S. FUKUMOTO, AND L. M. VOGT (1971). *Federal Evaluation Policy: Analyzing the Effects of Public Programs.* Washington, DC: The Urban Institute.

WILLEMS, E. P. (1969). "Planning a rationale for naturalistic research methods," pp. 44–70, in E. P. Willems and H. L. Raush (eds.), *Naturalistic Viewpoints in Psychological Research.* New York: Holt, Rinehart and Winston.

WOODS, P. J. (1974). "A taxonomy of instrumental conditioning." *Amer. Psychologist* 29: 584–97.

Robert Agranoff

Services Integration

What is "services integration" and what is its significance for the informed local government manager? Services integration is a new name for an old attempt to bring together the many agencies and programs that deliver human services to our citizens. At one time that concern was primarily in the private sector, but the expansion of the public sector as a dominant force in human services has made it a public management issue. In particular, the two decades since the 1950s have been marked by a rapidly expanding role for local, state, and federal governments in the areas of funding and delivery of services to people in need. This, in turn, paved the way for a

Exerpted with permission of the author and publisher, from *Managing Human Services* (Washington, D.C.: International City Management Association, 1977), pp. 527–64.

complex network of public and private funding and operation of human services programs. Since the late 1960s and early 1970s, the very extensiveness of the evolving network of human services has generated a movement to achieve some overall responsiveness and coherence in this public enterprise.

Services integration is the movement which coordinates public and nonpublic agencies and programs, consolidates related public programs, and creates administrative relationships among the various organizations delivering human services. As of the later 1970s, the services integration movement was still relatively new, and definition of the "traditional" or "best" integration systems was not yet possible. In its broadest sense it includes any attempt by political decision makers, administrators, planners, or service providers to develop and implement coherent policies. This process includes activities such as passing new legislation, creating new organizations, and delivering services that address the needs of human service clients. An integrative approach to human services problems proceeds from the standpoint that the most effective way to meet people's needs overall will come from broad concern with the needs of the entire governmental system or the entire set of a client's individual needs rather than from concern based on a single problem or the demands of a single advocacy group or in response to a single categorical agency.

The historical antecedents [of] public services integration in the United States stem from the voluntary (that is, the private and/or charitable) sector, from local health and welfare councils, and from local unified fund organizations. The earliest attempts at coordination date back to the nineteenth century central case registries and service inventories performed by the charitable organization societies in major cities.[1] In the twentieth century, local health and welfare councils established in many cities were responsible for producing the first plans in the United States outlining broad human needs and developing strategies for fulfilling those needs. Unified funding agencies such as the United Way and United Fund organizations were also established to centralize funding, establish program priorities, and disperse priority-determined resources. These organizations, which still exist in many American cities, were made up of representatives of such individual agencies and programs as the Lighthouse for the Blind, the Legal Aid Society, the Jewish Vocational Service, local speech and hearing societies, the Family Service Agency, and dozens of others. Their purposes included the sharing of information, the joint raising of funds, the avoidance of unnecessary duplication, the service of unmet needs, and a general goal of working together.

The voluntary sector has been overshadowed by public sector program growth in recent decades. The federal and state governments enacted legislation funding new programs to be delivered at the local level. They did not, however, always go through city and county decision makers in arranging for the implementation of these programs. Often new units of government were set up or local program directors made directly responsible to their professional peers at the state or federal level. The result was administrative confusion. Local government leaders found themselves faced with a bewildering array of programs. They generally had little or no influence regarding the adoption of the programs, possessed little operational knowledge of them, and, most pertinently, had little capacity for control over them. Subsequently, however, federal money of a more discretionary nature began to come into the picture. The mechanisms have been such programs as the Office for Economic Opportunity, the Model Cities program, general revenue sharing, and block grants for community development. These allowed for local decisions regarding allocation of resources and engendered a local advocacy process for human services, often focusing attention on previously unserved needs and constituencies. As a result, the provision of human services at the local level became more than just an outlet for state and federal health and welfare programs. Local governments became responsible for assessing needs, making choices, and allocating resources across a broad spectrum of issues. As these programs grew, it became important to local government managers to put together into a functional human services policy the independent and local discretionary programs. The interest in human services integration burgeoned as a result.

How can human services integration specifically be defined? Essentially, services integration includes three major components (1) *a policy development/policy management capability cutting across independent programs and categories* of human services, such as a comprehensive approach to the rehabilitation of injured persons, meeting their financial, legal, medical, therapeutic, and training needs; (2) *a services delivery system designed to meet the needs of clients whose problems go beyond a single agency or program,* such as the tying together of agencies through an information and referral network; and (3) *an organizational structure supportive of the policy management capability or the service delivery system or both,* such as a consolidated human services department.

Most services integration efforts selectively stress one or two of these three components at the expense of the others. There are those who correctly argue that true, or pure, services integration is not possible without all three. However, many political, constitutional, legal, and technical barriers stand between the present array of human services programs and complete services integration. Therefore, this discussion will encompass all types of movements toward local governments services integration, ranging from voluntary coordination of existing programs to the creation of entirely new human services systems. This inclusive approach is consistent with the definition of human services integration used in a mid-1970s census of local services integration: "An innovative organizational effort to coordinate or consolidate human services activities at the local level in traditional agencies as a means of enhancing the effectiveness, efficiency, and/or continuity of comprehensive service delivery."[2] . . .

THE NEED FOR HUMAN SERVICES INTEGRATION

Five major factors can be associated with the movement toward the integration of human services. First, *the expansion of categorical human services programs* in the public sector has made the array of services more striking and the responsibility for their management more difficult to avoid. Second, *the role of government in human services has become multi-faceted;* it now goes beyond the operation of services to funding, to regulation, to the purchase of services, and to other functions. Third, the way these expanded services have generally been organized and operated (that is, categorically and under public, proprietary, and voluntary auspices) has led to *generic problems in service delivery, including fragmentation, discontinuity, inaccessibility, and unaccountability.* Fourth, questions have begun to surface as to *whether the services provided are really meeting the goals* on which their design and implementation [were] based. It is now felt that programs and clients should be measured against levels of expected attainment. And fifth, there is a desire in local government to develop *a policy management capacity*—to put it all together, to see what it means, to be responsive to needs, and to be efficient and effective. The following discussion will focus on each of these elements in turn. . . .

The number of programs administered by the U.S. Department of Health, Education and Welfare (HEW) expanded to over three hundred by the later 1970s. . . .

The development and implementation of this expansion through independent channels [are crucial factors] for understanding the move to services integration. Nearly every program came about in response to the needs of a distinctly identifiable group. Ordinarily a group of persons in need or their advocates perceiving a failure to meet a specified set of needs petitioned the government to support their program, usually for research, training of professionals, and aid to the states for service provision. Each group wanted its own agency to minister to the perceived needs. . . .

There were few expenditures—of money or personnel—geared to the development of general social services approaches.[3] Thus human services activities have typically been part of a categorical system of agencies and programs that are relatively independent of each other.

The Changing Role of the Public Sector

Unlike the defense, postal, or highway systems in the United States, which have always been dominated by the public sector, human services systems evolved out of the proprietary and voluntary sectors. . . .

In the late nineteenth century, there was considerably more human services activity under private than public auspices. The "for-profit" sector only expanded in areas such as health, where there was a widespread demand for services and where delivery of such services was profitable. In the twentieth century, there was a gradual public takeover of many voluntary social programs. This was due to increased demand for a greater number of services as target populations also grew in number and as the need for broader geographic coverage made the cost of service provision beyond the ability of any private entity to handle. Until the 1960s, a "takeover" usually meant public operation of services, sometimes parallel in nature to operations of the voluntary and proprietary sectors but usually financially and administratively independent of them. In general, however, a program was either public, voluntary, or proprietary.

This pattern has since changed: Public involvement need no longer be restricted to delivery of services, and the distinction between public and nonpublic activity has become blurred. Governments have become involved in different mechanisms for human services provision in addition to the operational provision of services. A city, for example, can also become involved in the following ways.

1. As a funder—through direct grants to voluntary programs, through purchase of services from voluntary or private agencies, by matching voluntary agency deficits, or by providing third party matching funds for a formula grant program.
2. As a facilitator/coordinator—by using its influence, management expertise, and staff resources to bring together various organizations for coordination of existing programs and development of new programs.
3. As a capacity builder—by using its skills and knowledge in planning and evaluation in order to improve human services program effectiveness.
4. As a regulator/taxer/employer—through tax and regulatory policies and through its economic influences as a major employer to facilitate resolution of human problems.[4]

Other governments also have these nonoperational options, and they too have chosen to take advantage of them. Therefore, publicly generated human services programs can now include any (or a combination) of these options. When government is granting funds to voluntary agencies, purchasing services from for-profit providers, or helping voluntary and proprietary agencies plan, evaluate, and regulate nonpublic programs, it becomes less meaningful to speak of public and nonpublic programs. Instead, it is more suitable for local government managers to think of contemporary human services programs as a continuum, each with some degree of a public-nonpublic relationship. The implications for services integration are obvious. With a greater, almost universal, involvement in programs, many administrators agree that it has become imperative that they, their staffs, and elected officials all think in terms of managing the array of programs from the standpoint of some public purpose.

Generic Problems in Service Delivery

Categorically funded programs administered under various auspices have led to some serious problems in service delivery. As programs were independently established, they were usually organized for the purpose of delivering a single service. Such basic program requisites as eligibility determination, physical location of programs, professional staffing, service approaches, and lines of responsibility were established along vertical functional program lines. This categorical system for human services programming has contributed to what many social policy analysts consider to be the four key problems in service delivery:

1. *Fragmentation*—separate organization of services due to location, specialization, duplication, or lack of cooperation;
2. *Inaccessibility*—obstacles for a person trying to make use of the network of local social services, such as restrictive eligibility on the basis of social class, race, success potential, or other exclusionary criteria;
3. *Discontinuity*—obstacles to clients moving from provider to provider or other gaps in assistance that appear as an agency tries to match resources to needs, such as when communication channels or referral mechanisms are lacking; and
4. *Unaccountability*—a lack of interactive relationships between the individuals being served and the organizations' decision makers, such as inability of clients to influence decisions that affect them or the insensitivity of service providers to clients' needs and interests.[5]

Thus persons who enter the categorical services system may discover (often to their distress, frustration, or anger) that they must first wend their way through an intricate maze of social services and then, when they have ascertained which service they need, that they are not able to get it because eligibility requirements exclude them from the program for some reason. Finally, if they wish to find some resolution of their problem, they may well have no viable course of redress. . . .

Achieving Goals

One might facetiously conclude at this point that if the clients do not get the services needed, then the implicit aim of human services programs must be to foster the vertical functional system and provide occupational outlets for professionals. Indeed, many observers do feel this way primarily because professionals have never been held accountable for the services they deliver. Traditionally, funding and accountability systems have been tied to specific programs rather than geared to specific outcomes. Programs were budgeted on the basis of delivery of relatively discrete services to an estimated number of clients. The auditing process then accounted for these previously specified items. It was always vaguely understood that based on their condition, clients were to be restored to some level of self-sufficiency, but the expected outcomes were never measured.

It also became apparent that clients did not always reach the promised objective. Welfare recipients were not removed from the unemployment rolls; they remained, sometimes for more than one generation, creating a "culture of poverty." Mental hospital patients were not successfully treated before being discharged to communities, only to be readmitted, creating a "revolving door" situation. . . .

The prevalence of these conditions has

led to considerable cynicism about social programs generally and to greater concern on the part of policymakers, asking whether social programs actually accomplish any of what they are supposed to.

In order to prevent "cultures of poverty," "revolving doors," "creaming," and "tender loving greed," programs will have to be measured on the basis of outcomes. At the policy level, the greatest concern has been for measurements of clients' functioning levels—can they hold jobs, stay off welfare, live independently in the community, and so on? On the whole, there has been a shift in interest from the number of clients served to what happens to the clients that are served.

The interest in outcome measures has led to a concern for a "total system intervention" on clients. The measurement of social program interventions against desired future states of affairs tends to be independent of programs. The aim is to look at what happened to clients rather than how many were served and at what cost. The outcome question has, in turn, led to a whole series of related human services questions. Are services cost effective? Are they equitable? Do they meet reasonable standards of quality? Do they have any impact on community incidence rates (extrusion from the community, divorce, delinquency)? Do programs meet expected goals? It is believed that cross-program questions such as these, focusing on outcomes of individuals and program achievements, can best be answered through an integrated planning and evaluation capacity where there is an overall perspective and a capacity for independent assessment.

The Search for a Policy Management Capability

The enormous size and diversity of human services programs, the varied roles of government, the problems generated by the categorically organized system, and the need to measure overall accomplishment all suggest the conclusion that human services policies are in need of some management independent of and at a higher level than any individual program. . . .

The growth of a policy management role is a logical stimulant to services integration. As one assesses needs, analyzes options, selects programs, and allocates resources on a broad scale, it becomes more difficult to justify the existence of independent agencies performing similar services, duplicating programs, generating service gaps, leaving needs unserved, and producing cost-ineffective programs. Given such circumstances, the logical "next step" to coordination, consolidation, and unification becomes more apparent. . . .

SERVICES INTEGRATION IN THE INTERGOVERNMENTAL CONTEXT

Before proceeding to a discussion of the practices employed in the search for local human services integration systems, it is helpful to outline and discuss the broader questions of services integration, particularly insofar as they relate to the major components of our governmental system. The following discussion first identifies some of the basic activities relating to services integration. Both state and local-level operations, however, have a direct relationship to federal initiatives in this area, so the discussion then proceeds to take a look at the thrust of federal programs. The third section considers the role of state and county activity, particularly as it impinges on local-level operations. This portion of the chapter ends with an analysis of some general questions stemming from or appropriate to this intergovernmental context.

Services Integration Mechanisms

Efforts employed to accomplish combined efforts in the human services ordinarily involve an integrating agent. This integrator is charged with coordinating or otherwise jointly operating the services or functions of autonomous units or providers and integrating linkages or mechanisms that maintain the joint or unified endeavors. An integrator can be a governmental executive, board, staff, or individual within an agency. Linkages tie together, consolidate, or unite various administrative, fiscal, and service delivery functions providers ordinarily perform separately.[6] . . .

The more common services integration linkages and their definition would include

Joint planning—the joint determination of total service delivery system needs and priorities through a structured planning process.

Joint development of operating policies—a structured process in which the policies, procedures, regulations, and guidelines governing the administration of a project are jointly established.

Joint programming—the joint development of programmatic solutions to defined problems in relation to existing resources.

Information sharing—an exchange of information regarding resources, procedures, and legal requirements (but not individual clients) between the project integrator and various service providers.

Joint evaluation—the joint determination of effectiveness of service in meeting client needs.

Coordinated budgeting/planning—the integrator sits with all service providers together or individually to develop their budgets but without any authority to ensure the budgets are adhered to *or* the traditional service agencies develop their budgets together.

Centralizing budgeting—a centralized authority develops the budgets for the traditional service agencies with the authority to ensure that they are adhered to; may or may not include central point funding.

Joint funding—two or more service providers give funds to support service, most often in a broad programmatic fashion.

Purchase of service—formal agreements that may or may not involve a written contract between the integrated system and some other party or among agencies to obtain or provide service; generally a fee-for-service arrangement.

Transfer of budget authority—funds are shifted from one agency within the integrated system to another agency in that same system.

Consolidated personnel administration—the centralized provision of some or all of the following: hiring, firing, promoting, placing, classifying, training.

Joint use of staff—two different agencies deliver service by using the same staff; both agencies have line authority over staff.

Seconding, cross-agency assignment—one or more employees are on the payroll of one agency but under the administrative control of another.

Organizational change across agencies—service agencies in the integrated system or newly created agencies receive staff or units from another agency in the system *and/or* an umbrella organization is created.

Organizational change within the agency—reorganization of agency staff or organizational units involving changes internal to each organization only (may be similar changes in each agency).

Co-location of central offices—central administrative offices for two or more agencies at the locale are relocated at a single site.

Co-location of branch functions—several agencies co-locate personnel; performing branch as opposed to centralized administrative functions at a single site.

Outstationing—placement of a service provider in the facility of another service agency: no transfer of line authority or payroll responsibility takes place.

Record keeping—the gathering, storing, and disseminating of information about clients.

Grants management—the servicing of grants.

Central support services—the consolidated or centralized provision of services such as auditing, purchasing, exchange of material and equipment, and consultative services.

Satellite services—are provided whenever per-

sonnel from one service agency are resta-
tioned so as to increase the number of site
agencies in the integrated network.

Outreach—the systematic recruitment of
clients.

Intake—the process resulting in the admission (including determination of eligibility) of a client to the provision of direct
service.

Transportation—provision of transportation
to clients.

Referral—the process by which a client is directed or sent for services to another provider by a system that is in some way
centralized.

Diagnosis—the assessment of overall service
needs of individual clients.

Follow-up—the process used to determine
whether clients receive the services to
which they have been referred and to
shepherd the client through the service
delivery system.

Case conference—a meeting between the integrator's staff and staff of agencies who
provide service to a given family for the
purpose of discussing that family either
generally or in terms of a specific problem, possibly determining a course of action, and assigning responsibility among
the agencies for implementing the
solution.

Case consultation—a meeting of staff members of agencies who provide service to a
given family for same purposes as specified in "case conference" above.

Case coordinator—the designated staff member having prime responsibility to assure
the provision of service by multiple autonomous providers to a given client.

Case team—the arrangement in which a number of staff members, either representing
different disciplines or working with different members of a given family, work
together to relate a range of services of
autonomous providers to a given client.
The primary difference between case conferences and case teams is that the former
may be ad hoc, whereas the latter involves
continuous and systematic interaction between the members of the team.

Data system—any machine or computerized
record keeping system containing at a
minimum information regarding patients
contacted and clients treated.[7]

These examples of linkages are taken from
actual services integration mechanisms undertaken by state and local governments.
While improving the local service delivery
system is the intent of integration, such
efforts have not come without federal
influence.

Federal Initiatives in Services Integration

While most of the experiments with
creating integrated human services systems have come at the state, substate, or
local level, the movement has not been
without federal government influence.
Dissatisfaction with increasingly expensive
and difficult to manage social programs
has led federal government officials—particularly in the Department of Health, Education, and Welfare—to support programs that would aid in the coherent
delivery of services. Because these supportive efforts have stemmed from a desire to
overcome the effects of the federal government's pattern of categorical programming, each federal initiative shares the
common thread of attempting to link together one or more federal program (or
previously organized single program) and
to facilitate area-based planning for policy
development, organization building, and
development of service delivery systems.
Although the more recent attempts to integrate services have been direct research
and demonstration efforts, other stimuli
have been indirect, such as revenue sharing, and earlier programs such as economic opportunity and Model Cities
shared similar linkage goals. . . .

RESEARCH AND DEMONSTRATION
EFFORTS. The 1970s has proved to be a
decade of experimentation with various
forms of services integration. These
efforts were spurred by federal efforts to
get local communities to try different approaches. Service delivery aspects of integration were developed under the Services
Integration Targets of Opportunity

(SITO) program, which ended in 1975. SITO was designed to seek demonstration results on components and for techniques that are critical to the delivery of integrated and comprehensive approaches. This focus was predicted on the assumption that no single uniform model existed and that it is entirely possible that a variety of approaches and models could be applied, with elements applicable in differing environments and situations. In all, nearly fifty projects were funded at different levels of government organization, of different sophistication and technical expertise and with differing techniques and approaches to services delivery.[8]

The ongoing HEW Partnership Grants program is intended to develop methods of strengthening the capacity of state and local general purpose government chief executive officials in planning and managing the delivery of human services. The Partnership program is aimed at a number of specific objectives, including assessment of needs, planning, and priority setting; technical assistance; and managing, defining, and rationalizing the roles of general purpose governments in human services delivery. While the SITO and Partnership programs are different, the latter is supposed to build on the knowledge of the former. They are linked through the goal of improving services delivery through coordinative and integrative means.

These two programs have been shepherded by a relatively new unit in HEW, the Office of Intergovernmental Systems. This office is specifically charged with developing alternative strategies to services integration, with developing means of breaking down the barriers of categorical programming and with fostering cooperation with state and local governments. In addition to administration of the SITO and Partnership projects, the office is evaluating the effectiveness of information systems; studying the technology as applied to services integration planning and evaluation; and studying effectiveness measures to identify how to measure what works in order to assist local governments in determining funding priorities.

HEW has also initiated national legislation that would facilitate state and local planning and management of human services in a more coherent manner. While presented to Congress in various forms, basically the "allied services" concept is to support grants to the states and through states to localities for the development of "allied services plans," providing for the coordinated delivery of human services. Included are special implementation grants to states and localities to assist in covering the initial costs of consolidating or allying administrative support services and management functions. Allied services would also permit those states which have approved allied services plans to transfer funds from one HEW program to another for similar uses. At the national level, allied services would empower the secretary to waive administrative and technical barriers applying to categorical programs when they impede the allied or coordinated delivery of services. At an early period in HEW's attempt to secure passage of allied services, entire states were to be divided up into human services planning units, and a wide range of HEW programs were to be included. As a result of sustained opposition from categorical groups, professionals, agency administrators, and members of Congress, the program has been modified. Instead of including a wide range of HEW programs on a statewide basis, only demonstration areas of states need be selected out, and only two required and three additional optional programs need be covered, apparently reducing allied services to a research and demonstration effort.

SUMMARY. While noteworthy antecedents, none of the federal initiatives discussed has had the effect of transforming the old human services into comprehensive integrated systems. With varying weight, each has had an indirect influence at the local level by demonstrating and encouraging city hall to understand the existing state of services, setting policy goals, and mapping out how to get there in a reasonable fashion.

State and County Activity

As new federal social programs are enacted, they generally are implemented by state plans and through states to independent county departments or county level offices of state departments. The states and counties have thus also undertaken services integration. The states and counties, however, are faced with more independent categorical human services than cities, and integration has necessarily been a prime concern at these levels.

REORGANIZING THE STATES. As of the late 1970s, over thirty of the states have developed some form of linking activity, ranging from small coordinating offices attached to the governors' staff to completely unified departments, merging administration and service delivery. Most states fall somewhere between, with a comprehensive human resource department which administers public assistance-social service programs and at least three other major human service programs.[9] Each state's organizational form is somewhat different, being a product of its own history, its political environment, and its geographical, demographic, and socioeconomic characteristics. Each state, in turn, puts a somewhat different emphasis on the dimensions of services integration. Since most of these departments came about as a part of general state reorganization, they tend to emphasize organizational form. Many states have adopted different patterns for organization at the state level and for service delivery at the local level, making it very difficult to categorize them into a particular model. Within these limitations, a study by the Council of State Governments has nev-

ertheless divided the states that have reorganized into three categories: *confederated* agencies, where organizational or legal authority remains in line departments, but a new agency, program, or function is created to coordinate human resource programs (Virginia, Minnesota); *consolidated* agencies, where all or most administrative and planning/evaluation authority rests in a newly created human services agency, but programs are developed and services are delivered along traditional agency or divisional lines (North Carolina, Oklahoma); and *integrated* agencies, where a vertical structure is created, responsible for both management and operations, (Florida, Arizona).[10]

EXPERIMENTATION AT THE COUNTY LEVEL. There is a greater variety of integration approaches at the county level. Indeed, much of the experimentation at the city level, to be illustrated in this chapter, is similar to county human service innovations. Polk County, Iowa, under the directorship of the manager's office, has placed responsibility for coordinating human services into twelve lead agencies that cover major human services at the county level. In addition, they have developed a case manager system for client tracking, problem diagnosis, service coordination, and monitoring. In Lancaster County, Pennsylvania, the county government, Lancaster city government, and a voluntary service agency council have combined, under the leadership of the latter, to encourage citizen participation and engage in needs assessment and planning for human services. Its emphasis, therefore, is primarily on the policy management component. . . .

Many other county human service organizations have been created as they become absorbed into state and regional structures created under state reorganizations, thereby becoming local administrative units of a state department of human resources. However, the degree of consolidation is usually more minimal than that of the state structures. Few states have actually merged an entire state's county agencies into human resources programs. . . .

Integrated Services As a Service

At this point it is helpful to step back from the intergovernmental context and note the important fact that human services is an emergent service strategy employed in many of the categorical services; that is, to many a professional, one approaches the client as a whole individual with multiple needs, all or most of which must be addressed if one is to restore the client to the highest possible level of functioning or self-sufficiency. Indeed, some would argue that this approach to service would be an additional component of services integration to be added to the three listed at the beginning of this chapter. If a provider adheres to such a service ideology, it implies that one must think in terms of linking the client with the services of others.[11]

THE CONCEPT OF THE WHOLE INDIVIDUAL WITH MULTIPLE NEEDS. It has been found that persons disabled by injuries more readily adapt to the community if they receive medical, social, and psychological services along with their vocational training. It has also been found that the tendency to fractionate services to mentally ill clients [militates] against successful job placement. Mental health and vocational training workers once thought that vocational rehabilitation should come after treatment, whereas the emergent approach is toward simultaneous services. Immediate involvement of the client in the two services results in a higher rate of self-sufficiency than with a two-step procedure. . . .

IMPLICATIONS FOR SERVICES INTEGRATION. Recognizing this as a common situation with many clients, the service provider sees that the solution to the problem involves going beyond his or her agency or program. One must provide for a range of services: providing linkage on income support, arranging for the rehabilitative service of another agency, informing of the availability of legal services, and/or intervening on behalf of the client. Thus the service worker becomes more than a direct service provider; he or she links, advocates, expedites, and monitors.[12] The approach to the service is to build these additional activities into the client's service plan. . . .

Any service worker who brings such a complex set of community forces into his or her approach to service will be aided by a more integrated human service system.

"Bottoms Up" Integration

The approach to dealing with clients depicted in the previous section should have suggested to local government managers why it is important to incorporate modes of service delivery into human services integration. It is difficult to foster a multiservice concept by focusing attention on organizing administrative structures and building policy management capacities alone. That is why many have concluded that successful integration must therefore deal with questions of service delivery as well. It is important to provide coherent services to the individual as well as reducing fragmentation and duplication of agency activities.[13]

COHERENT SERVICE DELIVERY: THE EXAMPLE OF SPINAL INJURY PATIENTS. In approaching integration at the service delivery level, one is allowed to assess individual needs, search for resources across agencies, arrange for service, follow up these services, and monitor the impact of these services. A prime example, related by Perry Levinson, is the spinal cord injury projects sponsored by the Rehabilitation Services Administration of HEW, which attempts to coordinate the sequencing of services from the moment of the accident to re-entry of the patient into an active community existence, including a steady job. Many people must be trained, preplaced, and integrated into a reasonably smooth delivery system. [They] include police personnel, National Guard helicopter pilots, private physicians, ambulance drivers, architects designing barrier free building and transportation systems, recreation facility leaders, volunteer groups, and vocational rehabilitation counselors. All of their roles and services must be anticipated and properly sequenced if the spinal cord injured are to have any chance of returning to a "normal" life.[14] Creating a working system of services such as this, involving numerous actors and programs, logically begins with clients and their needs.

ORGANIZING AROUND CLIENT NEED SETS: THE "BOTTOMS-UP" APPROACH. Approaches such as that just described have led to what is commonly known as the bottoms-up mode of human services planning. Rather than looking at agencies and agency functions for purposes of linking, one plans by organizing around sets of client needs. For example, the Olympic Center in Bremerton, Washington, planned and organized its services around clusters of client needs rather than categorical or program structures. They analyzed the various presenting problems into client types—"individual adults" eligible for a limited number of services, "individual children" eligible for limited services, and "services for families" not made available to the other two—and established the fundamental components of the service delivery system around these three client types.[15] Promoting a multi-service approach at the point where the services meet the clients can eliminate situations where program gaps exist, cases are inade-

quately evaluated, services offered are inadequate or in conflict, and/or simultaneous services are not meshed.[16] "Bottoms-up" planning is as necessary to avoid these problems as top-down planning is to promote program coherence.

THE SEARCH FOR LOCAL SERVICE INTEGRATION SYSTEMS

The following discussion outlines and analyzes components of what might be termed the search for managerially viable local human service integration systems. The approach taken is to take an introductory overview of the basic managerial approaches involved and then to consider the role of such elements as informal cooperation; coordination within services; linking independent agencies and programs; creating new departments; developing new systems; a concluding section on pooling the experiences. . . .

Overview: The Search As Subsystem of the Organized Community

The establishment of integrative mechanisms is the development of systems. Each of the services brought together has its own interrelationships of agencies, supporting groups, clientele, and interactions. They tend to be isolated from one another, with a network for the income poor, a network for the mentally disabled, a network for the physically disabled, a network for the blind, and so on. Services integration works toward combining these networks into a functioning system meeting human needs.

The search for a community human services system should be conceived as a subsystem of the organized community. The human services subsystem deals with how human input is received, directed to community goals, transformed into policies, and delivered as services. . . .

Informal Cooperation

As a precursor [of] any formalized human services system, one must take note of the thousands of informal cooperative activities that are regularly undertaken between agencies as service workers deal with multiproblem clients. Some of these relationships are formalized but are so regular they can be patterned. Others are formalized to the point where working agreements for certain types of clients have been established between agencies. Many developmental disabilities agencies, for example, have worked out arrangements to have psychological testing and psychotropic ("acting on the mind") medications dispensed at the mental health center or family service agency. Still other arrangements are based on the purchase of services across agencies. A growing number of school systems have opted to purchase social work and speech and hearing services rather than operate them in their own departments. Other cooperative arrangements are required by administrative rule as stipulated by law or a condition of a grant or purchase. The local mental health center in many states is charged with monitoring and coordinating the efforts of public assistance, Social Security (SSI), vocational rehabilitation, and other programs to support former mental hospital patients in the community. Federal welfare program recipients must link up with employment services, and they are entitled to a range of social and medical services as a condition of their eligibility. These working relationships between agencies are not systematic, but they could be used as basic building blocks of more formalized human services networks, particularly if client flow through the system is used as a basis of organizing.

Coordination Within Services

Not only is there a need to link fragmented categorical programs, but many of the categories themselves represent a multiplicity of agencies and programs. In the health field, there are the local health department, public and private hospitals, private physicians and group practices, neighborhood health centers, and school health programs. In the employment and training field, there are the public employment agencies, private employment agencies, Urban Leagues, job training centers, sheltered workshops, vocational rehabilitation programs, job counseling programs, and employer-based, on-the-job training programs. . . .

The key components of creating and maintaining a comprehensive human services system for a local community need not be complex (although the process of developing and managing it may be). A comprehensive system would bring all of the elements of the community mentioned into an interrelated structure that would perform the necessary policy development, organizational, and service delivery functions. One such ideal human services system includes

1. the identification of community members who have been, who are, or who may be candidates for service;
2. a governance body, controlled by community members, to develop policies related to desired effects on the target population;
3. the enumeration of desired effects on the population, which can be assessed by performing a measurement on individuals;
4. a system manager to provide interface between governance and the system, providing a single point of accountability;
5. the organized human service system, which acts on the target population by providing services;
6. a system audit, which will measure the actual "delivered" status of target populations, that is, what has actually happened to clients; and
7. system funding that flows through governance to the system manager, provid-

ing energy which enables the system to operate.[17] . . .

The development process for services integration experiments has been found to involve essentially the same four phases of system building, the components of which may be summarized as follows:

1. *Phase one*—capacity building and analysis of the existing system—including integrators organizing their own staffs and developing the political support and strength needed for reform, definition of populations, needs assessment, services inventories, operations analysis associating costs with services, and possible analysis of client through-put, or pathways, through the system.
2. *Phase two*—design and feasibility study for the changed system—including the development of measurable objectives and accountability systems; design and implementation of specific governance changes; actual development of linkages; and estimation of system investment costs and benefits, including such process variables as accessibility of service and continuity of service and such output variables as change in client dependency status.
3. *Phase three*—development and implementation of the integrated system—including similar attention to objectives and accountability, governance, linkage development, and cost-benefit, as [in] phase two.
4. *Phase four*—documentation and evaluation, which is an ongoing, feedback cycle—including similar attention to objectives and accountability, governance, linkage development, and cost-benefit, as [in] phase two.[18]

Services integration experiments have varied in the quality of performance in these phases, but progress in adhering to these steps has proved to be an important evaluative device for investigating services integration progress. It may be that any community will have to consider this process.

Linking Independent Agencies and Programs

The bringing together of autonomous units need not start with an elaborate structure. In many city governments, such as Dayton, Ohio, the role of "city coordinator of human resources" may be a part-time assignment, allocating a portion of someone's time in the mayor's or city manager's office to routinely maintain liaison, continuity, and consistency with policy. In small cities it may be the manager who takes on this responsibility. . . .

One of the more concerted attempts to coordinate human services may be seen in the overall policy, planning, and management functions engaged in by San Jose, California, through its office of intergovernmental affairs, which is a part of the office of the city manager. The three divisions of the intergovernmental unit and their functions are as follows:

1. *Program review and coordination,* which is responsible for maintaining systems for tracking pending and active federal and state programs; coordinating individual grant applications; operating the municipal systems related to the A-95 review process; and routing of project notifications through the city system of review.
2. *Program development and coordination,* with prime responsibility for relating city policy to programs and projects outside of City Hall, development and evaluation of program proposals to carry out city developmental policies, coordination of grant applications by outside agencies with city departments, working with various planning groups and agencies (manpower, CAA, county departments, etc.), and development and maintenance of a community participation structure.
3. *Community planning and management,* which is responsible for developing a

body of policy and an overall development strategy by which priorities can be generated and proposed projects measured, including integrating planning and program development activities of all service delivery systems, [providing] the strategy and framework for new project applications, [exploring] the impact of the HUD Annual Arrangement process on health, education, employment and training, transit and criminal justice, and [applying] the experiences from the latter to the development of similar systems for defining needs, setting objectives, and developing mutually supportive projects for other service delivery systems.[19]

Each of these functions represents a specific division, having responsibility for human services and non-human services programs. The San Jose plan emanated [from] the "planned variations" program of Model Cities. Its structure is one of the most comprehensive approaches to policy planning and coordination.

In some cases, human services coordination has been shifted from city hall to a lead agency. Under this form, a single operating agency is designated to take on certain policy management, planning, and coordination activities in addition to [its] service role. Service delivery remains in the individual agencies. . . .

Colocation of human services agencies is another emergent form of coordination. Location of categorical agency field operations in the same place is designed to facilitate coordinated service delivery. . . .

One of the most interesting modes of linkage is the Louisville-Jefferson County nonlocational model, which links city-county public and voluntary human services agencies through an on-line computerized information system. The program, called the Human Services Coordination Alliance, is governed by a policy board comprised of agency executives, representatives of city and county governments, and a representative from the regional area development district. The operational mechanisms of the system have been developed by a central staff and technical representatives from each agency. It is comprised of an intake, screening, and referral network containing an agency resource file, a service selection system, a standardized referral system and a client tracking system, and a human services information system—a software system providing agency and client data for needs assessment, planning, and evaluation.[20] The system operates by having each client-contact professional fill out a simple information form, enter it into the system, and retrieve any necessary information; all in their own agency. . . .

Reflecting the diversity of city human services programming, the linking of independent agencies and programs has taken a variety of forms. They range from coordination of programs inside and outside city government by a designated executive level coordinator to the actual operation of a delivery system—including public agencies—by a private body. They share the characteristic of leaving existing organizations as they are, focusing on interrelationships.

Creating New Departments

Decision makers in a number of governments have decided that coordination does not go far enough in solving human services problems. They have gone on to create departments of human resources or human services [from] existing departments and old divisions. The primary motivation for city-level consolidation appears to be . . . planning and policy management, with consolidation of administration as a secondary concern and, to a lesser extent, service delivery. Cities usually consolidate around Community Action, Model

Cities, revenue sharing funded human services, youth, and aging. The federal Housing and Community Development Act has been an added impetus to consolidation, under requirements to define the role of human services as the social services support for community development activities and subsequent allocation of funding. Bringing the activities together in a single unit, with an overall planning and management capacity, was a major aim of this legislation. . . .

Developing New Systems

Few instances exist of a government at any level creating an entirely new human services system. Ordinarily the political and organizational problems involved with numerous existing agencies present significant obstacles, particularly with the existence of many loci of operation and control. For a city this problem is particularly acute because the bulk of the human services are delivered under the auspices of other governmental units or by quasi-public or voluntary agencies within the city. Also, services integration is in such an experimental phase, as of the later 1970s, that it is not clear what an appropriate system is. Nevertheless, there have been a few illustrative attempts to approach human services from a more systemic viewpoint.

Several cities, [including San Diego, Washington, D.C., New Haven, Conn., and Seattle], have attempted to work toward completely integrated delivery systems on a developmental basis. Project 86+ in San Diego is representative of these efforts. It is based on the development of interdisciplinary teams of social service practitioners whose primary function is the utilization of comprehensive social services. This sixteen-member team, which includes public assistance, social services, probation, employment and training, mental health, public health, youth em-

ployment, and probation services, is involved in planning and delivering integrated services within a pilot area.[21] Staff have been deployed to the project from the participating departments, and their activities are supported by the planning and management activities of the San Diego County human resources agency, a consolidated department. . . .

Conclusion: Pooling the Experiences

The [recentness] and variety of services integration projects have led to considerable interest in assessing their impact. Thus HEW has commissioned a series of studies that attempt to develop generalizations [from] these experimental efforts. None of the completed studies represents an organizational process or impact study. They merely attempt to pool the experiences into a common framework.[22]

Service integration projects have occurred in all types of communities: almost one-third in major population centers, two-fifths in small and medium-sized cities, and one-fourth in small towns and rural areas. Although considerable support and encouragement for local integration experiments [have] come from the federal and state governments (most were federally funded), this support is ordinarily not crucial to getting started. Not surprisingly, state encouragement for local services integration was more likely to be found in states with some form of state-unified human services agency.[23] Generally, the impetus for services integration is local.

Few local services integration projects attempted to create new systems of human service delivery. Rather, the dominant strategy was to bring together the existing elements into a more coherent system, adding support or joint administrative services. With a single exception (New York

City neighborhood governments), all projects undertook centralization strategies. This is undoubtedly due to the major emphasis of services integration on using organization design to overcome the effects of decentralization.[24] Few projects start new direct service organizations, offer new services, or serve new locales. The extent of "pure" integration is quite minimal. Therefore local services integration can best be characterized as system development rather than creation of entirely new human service systems.[25]

Almost all the projects have been initiated by local public agencies. The support of local general purpose government is very important for getting a project off the ground, but not absolutely crucial. Few projects precisely followed the comprehensive planning model depicted earlier, including needs assessment, a service resource inventory, interagency planning, preparation of planning documents and evaluation, but most took one or more of these steps along the way.[26]

Although most projects included both service delivery and administrative changes, ordinarily a single objective was dominant. The major reasons for initiating a project are building planning capacity, administrative consolidation, improvement of case services, bringing a variety of services to a neighborhood, and/or the development and planning of coordinative mechanisms. The nature of the objective obviously affects the allocation of resources devoted to and the approach taken in developing linkages and differentially impacts a new structure accordingly.[27] Continued system growth, that is, the ability to pursue additional linkages beyond initial objectives, is apparently not positively associated with any particular approach. The establishment of coordinated planning and budgeting mechanisms, case management techniques, and

data systems exhibited a non-significant association with subsequent growth. Projects emphasizing centralized outreach, transportation, and support services are even less likely to develop further system growth.[28] The authors presenting these findings suggest that because these latter three links do not involve agency personnel directly, it could be that the key to the growth of human services systems should require continuing interactions among agency personnel, thereby ensuring continuing dialogue, making each other aware of service gaps and duplications and of opportunities for further integration.[29]

One very significant shortcoming of the experiments with services integration is that few have undertaken an evaluation strategy that can define outcome changes. Most projects have established general organizational or service objectives rather than specific goals or effects on clients they wish to attain.[30] Thus one can conclude that new services integration linkages have made new services available to clients, the clientele for existing services has been expanded, the service network has become more continuous, and the services are more efficient, but one cannot as yet make definitive statements about whether these innovations have led to higher rates of self-sufficiency, rehabilitation, or adaptability.[31] There are many other unanswered questions about service integration, and some are quite complex. For example, to the extent that centralized core services reduce duplication and result in cost savings, such savings are "traded off" by administrative costs for the implementation and maintenance of complex management systems. Yet these investments can be said to be a protection of a public investment in human resource development, contributing to efficiency. Clearly, many local government managers will agree that a research agenda on services integration is necessary, incorporating such assumptions and trade-offs, and measuring outcomes against goals.

PROBLEMS AND ISSUES IN LOCAL GOVERNMENT SERVICES INTEGRATION

Services integration at the city level, like that at any other level, operates within a context. A services integration context would include the existing structure of government, the political configuration, the type and extent of services offered, the role and attitudes of service providers and provider agencies, and available technologies. Each setting provides a different configuration of the elements of the context, and thus there has not proved to be a single way to deal with the problems. There are, however, some commonalities and experiences at each level that provide a context of considerations for integration, including those for cities. As with any emergent concern in local government, the problems encountered in generating appropriate managerial, administrative, and operational roles should not be underestimated. The following discussion focuses on three items: the limited role for cities; the importance of government structure; and the all-important role of political factors.

Limited Role For Cities

The limited role of cities in human services compared to other governments is clearly of primary concern. Federal and state legislation restricts the role of cities in many human resource functions. Most HEW federal-state programs are operated at the local level by counties or state subunit organizations. To the extent that municipalities are involved in such programs, support often comes indirectly through grants or purchase of services. In only a few instances have operational responsibilities for state programs been trans-ferred to the cities. Some cities are involved in joint city-county departments, usually with the county as the lead or operational agency. This means that service delivery "systems" are split between direct state, county, and local entities, plus the voluntary agencies. Thus Gans and Horton conclude that the concept of local human resources agencies in municipal governments has stemmed from the consolidation concepts that give rise to community development departments, but it is a concept far from reality because of the very real jurisdictional limitations on cities in human services.[32] . . .

Yet the city is the highly visible entity wherein the most complex human problems are embedded and is the location where most programs meet people. Any attempt to foster a multi-service concept, whether planning, organization, or delivery, must come to grips with a role for cities. . . .

The Importance of Government Structure

The structure of government is a very important consideration for human services integration. As will be elaborated upon in the discussion of political factors which follows, federal government organization itself stands as a prime example of significant barriers. Many conflicting rules and regulations of categorical programs present roadblocks to integrated planning and delivery, which perpetuate the informal vertical-functional system. It is hoped—from the perspective of the later 1970s—that Title XX of the Social Security Act, providing social services to a broad population on a flexible basis, will serve as a catalyst for further unification.[33] At the local level, the ability of a unit of government to effect integration is related to its structure. Generally the human service structure one can create is dependent on the amount of self-determination granted by the state. The greater the amount of self-determination, for example, through home rule, the more flexibility a city will have in responding creatively to problems in human services delivery.[34]

Another structural factor is the configuration of human services within a local area. In states that have reorganized, they have rationalized service boundaries of various programs, making it easier to work with programs, if not units of government. . . .

Political Factors

Last, but certainly not least, it is vitally important to consider the political dimensions of services integration. The foremost political consideration is that services integration always involves a struggle for power. Its primary effect is to transfer control from the advocates of narrow interests to those with broader interests, from specialists to generalists, and from the managers of programs to the managers of policy. . . .

Many local government managers would agree that another consideration in services integration is that it is not to be understood as a popular movement. Ordinarily, services integration has no constituency to speak of. Indeed, the major constituencies for human services programs generally align with the opposition to integration. . . .

The key problem, then, is to preserve the special mission and unique contribution of the independent categorical agency yet meet the concerns that services integration addresses. Specialists and the specialities are obviously needed. Services integration suggests they are needed within a new, coherent framework. It is a significant boundary problem, raising many questions. When is the problem something beyond the agency's expertise? When does the client need other services? When is the agency using public funds for purposes

out of tune with public intent? When is the configuration of programs contributing to waste, inefficiency, and duplication? These questions are significant "turf" or "public interest" questions, depending on whose ox is gored. What to one side is preserving the professional mission of serving a need is to the other side managing public policy in the public interest.

Funding is another issue connected to specialization. The system of fragmented categorical funding, going directly to service departments and agencies, supports the existing system. More than 99 percent of federal project and formula grants administered by HEW are channeled to individual agencies. The integrating agents have to rely on the goodwill of the service providers because rarely do they have the fiscal weapons to accompany the organizational ones. There is little discretionary money to speak of; most of the consolidated departments depicted here really combine categorical programs. Title XX is a new tool for cross-category funding, but it is largely in the hands of state planners. If all or most of the money would go through the integrators, service providers would be dependent on them for their budgets, and integrators would have more control, and they could ensure greater cooperation. A series of national-state changes in funding patterns [away from provider organizational and professional loyalties to client needs] to a more centralized human services function should result in basic changes in accountability and organization.

Categorical funding patterns, however, are only one among several federal barriers placed before managers in general purpose governments as they deal with human services programs. In a survey of planners, budget officers, and program administrators investigating federal-state-local interrelationships in administering HEW programs, it was revealed that in addition to funding rules, compliance requirements, categorical eligibility and service restrictions, organizational and structural requirements, geographical districting requirements, advisory group requirements, sign-off regulations, out-of-sequence application times, difficulties in anticipating federal resources, and difficulties in locating federal responsibilities also present significant barriers to services integration.[35] The survey was appropriately titled, *Ties That Bind.* Thus, despite the federal encouragement of integration described above, one must conclude with Sidney Gardner that "the policy environment for HEW's efforts to expand general purpose government involvement in human services integration was mixed, . . . characterized by both new managerial incentives and some sizeable political *disincentives* to seek such involvement."[36]

Anyone who has concluded that most services integration efforts have thus far relied on voluntary coordination and its attendant administrative weaknesses has arrived at the correct conclusion. Few local experiments have the benefit of mandated linkages or the support of meaningful legislative changes. Independent programs that are linked give the integrator only the modest tools of being at the center of information, operation of the linkage mechanisms, and perhaps the support of the top political leadership. The departments and agencies have the operating resources, the clients, and their own sets of political supporters. New departments are constrained by the categorical funding and rule-making patterns which make it necessary to perpetuate "divisions," with their own sets of operating resources and clientele. To be sure, a new department may be able to assess needs, plan, allocate resources, evaluate and perform central administrative services on a more comprehensive and efficient basis, but it almost always is within the context of predetermined operations. As any administrator knows, only a small proportion of the resources [is] committed

to non-operational functions. This reduces the role of the integrator to that of an informer, negotiator, bargainer, and facilitator of cooperation within a system rather than that of a director of a new authority structure.

It appears that more fundamental systems change may be necessary to achieve the aims of services integration. The illustrations of services integration presented here reveal that managing the local human service matrix has been largely within the system as it now exists. It is basically tinkering with the old system, relying on the existing agncies to continue to deliver their services. Whether a series of coordinative linkages between free standing agencies are established or programs are consolidated into a new department, little has been done to alter the basic operations of individual programs. Unified budgeting, joint funding, purchase of services, fund transfers, joint planning, mutual operating policies, joint programming, and the like are largely built upon what is there. It is easy for the reader to conclude that few, if any, changes have been made. From the standpoint of the organizational designer, the innovations are weak structural solutions.

From the standpoint of the realities of the American system of administrative organizations, these linkages are, however, a step in the direction of "public" management. The juxtaposition of multiple categorical agency responses to various clientele interests with the need to manage an integrated human service system is a reflection of the ambivalence between a more executive leadership (managerial-centered) philosophy and a more representative, democratic bureaucracy that is part of public administration theory and practice.[37] One can argue that the intent of services integration is to facilitate executive leadership, support policy development, create a semblance of public accountability, move toward rational organization, meet public needs, and attempt to match public programs with public goals within a framework of democratic administration. Using these principles as standards of achievement, one cna say that we are, indeed, achieving some success with services integration.

Fundamental success will ultimately rest on the adoption of national social policy. Until the myriad of human services programs are turned into coherent policies, reflecting comprehensive approaches to agreed upon goals, service integration will be difficult. Despite problems in inconsistency and lack of coordination of component units, it is much easier to identify a national security policy, an economic policy, a transportation policy, or an agricultural policy than it is to think in terms of policies that support human development. Instead of programs, policies are needed that are targeted to maintenance of self-sufficiency, preservation of living in the community, maintenance of given levels of health, and retention of employment over time, independent of categorical services. Only linkage mechanisms—coordinative devices, cooperative endeavors, review and sign-off procedures, central clearance—not programs that are based on the primacy of reaching national goals, presently exist.[38] If social programs followed policies, it would be easier to plan, organize, and develop accountability at all levels.

NOTES

1. Walter I. Trattner, *From Poor Law to Welfare State* (New York: Free Press, 1974), p. 84.
2. William A. Lucas, Karen Heald, and Mary Vogel, *The 1975 Census of Local Services Integration*, working note prepared for the Department of Health, Education and Welfare (Santa Monica, Calif.: Rand Corporation, 1975), p. 2.
3. Ibid., p. 62.
4. *Opportunities for Municipal Participation in Human Services* (Durham, New Hamp.: New England Municipal Center, 1975), unpaged.
5. Neil Gilbert, "Assessing Service Delivery Methods: Some Unsettled Questions," *Welfare in Review* 10 (May/June 1973):25.
6. Sheldon P. Gans and Gerald T. Horton, *Integration of Human Services: The State and Municipal Levels* (New York: Praeger Publishers, 1975), p. 36.
7. Gans and Horton, *Integration of Human Services*, p. 36; Lucas, Heald, and Vogel, *The 1975 Census*, pp. 70–71.
8. Several overviews of SITO projects are referenced in this chapter, including those in notes 2, 6, 9, 10, and 17.
9. Council of State Governments, *Human Services Integration: State Functions in Implementation* (Lexington, Ky.: Council of State Governments, 1974), p. 1.
10. Ibid., pp. 24–25. For a detailed analysis of states representative of these models, see Robert Agranoff, ed., *Coping with the Demands for Change within Human Service Administration* (Washington, D.C.: American Society for Public Administration, 1977), chaps. 3–7.
11. Frank Baker, "From Community Mental Health to Human Services Ideology," *American Journal of Public Health* 64 (June 1974): 577.
12. For further details on these activities, see Robert Agranoff, "Human Services Administration: Service Delivery, Service Integration and Training," in *Human Services Integration*, ed. Thomas J. Mikulecky (Washington: American Society for Public Administration, 1974), pp. 43–44.
13. Lucas, Heald, and Vogel, *The 1975 Census*, p. 37.
14. Perry Levinson, "A Management Strategy for Departments of Human Resources: The Indirect Line Authority/Decentralization Principle," in *Human Resource Administration*, ed. Beryl Radin (Washington: Section on Human Resources Administration, American Society for Public Administration 1975), pp. 3–4.
15. Carsten Lien, *A Design for a Multi-Service Delivery System*, report prepared for the Department of Social and Health Services, State of Washington (Menlo Park, Calif.: Stanford Research Institute, 1973), p. 19.
16. Alfred J. Kahn, "What Is Social Planning?" in *Readings on Human Services Planning*, ed. Gerald Horton (Arlington, Va.: Human Services Institute for Children and Families, Inc., 1975), p. 13.
17. Stephen D. Mittenthal et al., *Twenty-Two Allied Services (SITO) Projects Described as Human Service Systems* (Wellesley, Mass.: The Human Ecology Institute, 1974), pp. 6–9.
18. Lyle M. Spencer, Jr., "Planning and Organizing Human Service Delivery Systems," *Proceedings of a Seminar on Human Services Integration*, sponsored by the Social Welfare Research Institute (Denver: University of Denver, 1973).
19. Department of Housing and Urban Development. *Changing Demand for Local Capacity*, pp. 73–74.

20. Human Services Coordination Alliance, "An Overview of the Human Services Coordination Alliance" (Louisville, Ky.: Human Services Coordination Alliance, 1975), pp. 4–7.

21. Human Resources Agency, "A Report on Proposed Agency Reorganization and Integration of Human Services," Human Resources Agency, County of San Diego, California, 1976, pp. 23–24.

22. William A. Lucas, *Aggregating Organizational Experience with Services Integration: Feasibility and Design* (Santa Monica, Calif.: Rand Corp., 1975), pp. 16–20.

23. Lucas, *Census of Local Services Integration*, pp. 14–26.

24. Robert Agranoff, "Organizational Design: A Tool for Policy Management," *Policy Studies Journal* 5 (Autumn 1976), p. 15.

25. Gans and Horton, *Integration of Human Services*, p. 11; Lucas, *Census of Local Human Services Integration*, p. 32; Mittenthal, p. 51.

26. Lucas, *Census of Local Services Integration*, p. 30.

27. Gans and Horton, *Integration of Human Services*, p. 14.

28. Lucas, *Census of Local Services Integration*, pp. 42–43.

29. Ibid., p. ix.

30. Mittenthal, p. 53.

31. Gans and Horton, *Integration of Human Services*, p. 10.

32. Department of Housing and Urban Development, *Changing Demand for Local Capacity*, p. 6.

33. Robert Morris, "Public Administration Responsibility for the Evolution of Human Resource Services," in Agranoff, *Coping with the Demands for Change within Human Services Administration*.

34. National Association of Counties, *Human Services Integration at the Community Level*, p. 15.

35. U.S., Department of Health, Education and Welfare, *Ties That Bind: HEW National Management Planning Study* (Seattle, Wash.: HEW Region X, 1976), passim.

36. Sidney Gardner, *Roles for General Purpose Governments in Services Integration* (Rockville, Md.: Project Share, 1976), p. 18.

37. Herbert Kaufman, "Emerging Conflicts in the Doctrines of Public Administration," *American Political Science Review* 50 (December 1956): 1057; Vincent Ostrom, *The Intellectual Crisis in American Public Administration* (University, Ala.: University of Alabama Press, 1974), pp. 110–11.

38. Melvin Mogulof, "Elements of a Special Revenue-Sharing Proposal for the Social Services: Goal Setting, Decatorization, Planning and Evaluation," *Social Service Review* 47 (December 1973): 599–602.

James C. Noah

Information Systems in Human Services: Misconceptions, Deceptions, and Ethics

In recent years, management information systems (MISs) have become widely implemented in human service agencies. One major impetus for this growth has been legislation such as Public Law 94-63, which requires community mental health centers to evaluate their programs. Unfortunately, the increased utilization and dependence on MISs [have] continued without any serious examination of what an MIS can accomplish.

Reprinted with permission of the author and *Administration in Mental Health* 5:2 (Spring/Summer 1978) pp. 99–111.

tually do to help achieve organizational goals. Moreover, there are many misconceptions about the utility of MISs for solving agency problems. Misinterpretations have arisen because agency administrators have failed to (1) adequately define their information needs, (2) distinguish between the hardware and software features of an MIS, and (3) recognize that the information generated by an MIS does not necessarily control the behavior of individuals within or outside the agency.

This article will describe the usual operational assumptions of an MIS, to distinguish between MISs used in profit, as opposed to nonprofit, human service enterprises, and to look at MISs functionally, including some ethical considerations.

DEFINITION AND MAJOR ASSUMPTIONS

The literature is replete with definitions of MISs, most of which propose that an MIS is a series of reports designed to provide pase, present, and projected information to *assist* in the decision-making process. A usual requirement is that the information be relatively complete and timely. There is generally *no specific* requirement that an MIS be comprehensive in design. For example, one can establish an information system for children's services without developing a system for an entire community center. However, partial MISs rarely exist. The assumptions for developing an MIS in the first place argue against fragmented efforts.

Ten years ago Russell Ackoff delineated five major assumptions of management information systems.

1. Managers operate with a deficiency of relevant information. There is information that decision makers should have that is not available to them. The task is to design a system to generate, store, and retrieve such information.
2. Decision makers should be asked what information would be beneficial for improving decisions. The assumption is that they know best what decisions must be made and which information would be helpful.
3. Decision making will improve if information is provided. This assumption rests on three suppositions: (1) the decision making of a particular manager can improve; (2) relevant information will assist in that improvement; and (3) decision makers will use information if it is provided. A corollary of these assumptions is that sound information is eagerly awaited by potential users.
4. Information allows better communication between managers and, consequently, results in improved organizational performance. If decision makers have the same information available to them, decisions in and among various departments will improve because they will have a better idea of what controls the entire decision-making process.
5. Managers need only know how to use the information generated by the system and not how it works. How information is coded, collated, and stored is less important than having easy access to it.

To these assumptions of Ackoff, another common one may be added.

6. Total systems are better than fragmented systems. Having information from every aspect of the operation allows better decisions to be made with benefit to the entire organization.

Again, information systems are viewed as a way of collecting, collating, and reporting information to enhance the decision-making process. Having information available for assisting the decision maker is viewed usually as extremely positive. Information can alert decision makers to any number of discrepancies between the intent of an effort and actual results and can point out areas in need of investigation and correction.

These assumptions of MISs have been employed by most developers and users of information systems over the last twenty years. Interestingly, however, Ackoff's paper was entitled "Management Misinformation Systems" and was concerned primarily with exposing the fallacies and misconceptions of MISs so conceived. A brief comment on a few assumptions should illustrate some common misconceptions about MISs.

Regarding access to relevant information, Ackoff argues that although decision makers (DMs) may lack such information, they also have an overabundance of irrelevant information; that is, DMs are exposed daily to information irrelevant for their use. The designer of the MIS could opt to increase relevant information, decrease irrelevant information, or pursue both courses of action. The content of the information system would, of course, change correspondingly, depending on which assumptions were made. In fact, the intent of the information system could be reversed completely if too much irrelevant information was available. Condensing information, as opposed to generating more information, would then be the goal of the system.

The assumption that decision making will improve if information is provided is perhaps the most serious misconception of management information systems. Let us give the DM the benefit of the doubt and assume that decision-making behavior can improve; that is, ability is not the question. Two other premises, however, must be considered. They are obviously related. Will relevant information assist in improving decision making? Only if the decision maker knows how to use the information. It is a common experience to be provided with all the facts necessary for arriving at the correct solution to a problem. But all the information is of little use if one does not know how to use it correctly. Even assuming that the decision maker knows how to use the information, will it be used? Perhaps but not necessarily because it is readily available or because one has the knowledge of how to use it. There is a great deal of evidence to show that managerial behavior is not solely under the control of available information. It is a relatively common experience to have presented a decision maker with the facts, processes, etc., necessary for making a particular decision with little or no resultant action. Decision-making behavior is usually under much more complex control. There is a principle to all of this—facts may never stand in the way of decisions being made.

To complete the demise of the assumptions mentioned previously, W. M. A. Booker provided a similar analysis of the "total system" in a paper entitled the "Total Systems Myth." The total systems concept essentially states that information from every functioning aspect of an organization is necessary for better decisions to be made. Information systems should be designed to provide comprehensive and complete data from each element of a service delivery system. The myth is that decision makers rely on such complete information for making a decision and, furthermore, that they are able to integrate information for the "betterment of all." Included in the myth is the belief that such complete information can be provided. John Dearden (1966) "put the icing on the cake," so to speak, by illustrating the absurdity of a total systems concept. Can a single integrated system be designed to fit all of management's information needs? In his words, "only if Superman lends a helping hand."

Critiques of management information systems, such as Ackoff's, Booker's, and Dearden's, have had relatively little impact on either the design or use of such systems. In fact, the use of MISs has, if anything, increased. Although intended originally for use in profit-oriented enterprises, information system concepts and procedures are being applied increasingly to endeavors, such as mental health, where profit is not the primary objective. Systems analysis, it should be remembered, received most of its impetus from the field of engineering. Consequently, less attention has been paid to the human components of a system. When human factors are considered, they seem to arise as an afterthought to "reflect the engineering community's quest for a social role" (Hoos, 1974, p. 23). Methods that have been successful in improving hardware oriented systems are assumed to be valid for conceptualizing human behavior in organizations. The dangers of extending concepts and procedures developed for more hardware-oriented systems to nonprofit-oriented human service systems have been discussed in greater detail elsewhere (Noah, Krapfl, and Maley, 1977) and will not be considered here. But just as MISs appeared to be a boon to the competitive, profit-oriented market of the business world, so do they seem to be serving [as] a similar impetus for generating accountability in delivery systems where the service rendered is more difficult to specify.

PROFIT-ORIENTED AND NONPROFIT-ORIENTED SYSTEMS

Service agencies are highly dependent on federal and state institutions as sources of income. For example, in mental health, NIMH and state departments of mental health are common funding sources. As public funds and purchasing power have dwindled, there has been an attempt to broaden the funding base of most programs. Consequently, service delivery agencies are competing for federal, state, local, contractual, third-party payer, and philanthropic funds. In response to these demands, social and political pressures for accountability have increased. Concomitantly, reporting requirements and information requirements have multiplied (Elpers, 1972). Managers of service agencies anticipate often that an MIS will satisfy the demands for accountability by answering all their information needs. Moreover, the MIS is sometimes seen as a means of facilitating the capture of third-party payments, ensuring continuity of service, and reducing duplicated efforts (Driscoll, Broskowski, Friedman, and Pisciotta, 1974). Because of these anticipated and sometimes promised advantages, the MIS has become a popular management tool in nonprofit human service delivery.

In practice, the MIS has not been as advantageous as promised. Even though facilitated record keeping and data flow,

centralized information collection efforts, and improved communication of information may result from the use of an MIS, these are successes in mechanization that may not necessarily affect selected managerial behavior. Dearden and McFarlan (1966), for example, discuss the unexpected effects that occur in many organizations using an MIS: Records move faster, but there are more of them; clerical staff increases to support the immense amount of paperwork that the MIS produces; and centralized information does not result in improved decision making.

The failure of some MISs to improve management functions has been discussed earlier relative to prevalent misconceptions of the relationship of information to management functions (e.g., managers assume that the more information they have concerning the operations they manage, the better their decisions affecting those operations will be) (Ackoff, 1967). The demand for more information is made easier by available technology. The computer, for example, permits the processing of many more categories of information than does a manual system or one supported by office machines and calculators (Hagedorn, Beck, Neuber, and Werlin, 1976). However, the ability to provide information reinforces administrative behavior that although beneficial in the short run, may have long-term negative consequences. Ackoff states: "The less we understand a phenomenon, the more variables we require to explain it. Hence, the manager who does not understand the phenomenon he controls plays it 'safe' and, with respect to information, wants 'everything.' The MIS designer, who has even less understanding of the relevant phenomenon, . . . tries to provide . . . the information."

This is particularly true in nonprofit-oriented service delivery where the phenomenon, not well understood, is the outcome of services. The MIS is designed to answer a multitude of questions from a variety of funding and licensing agencies and, as such, becomes a heavily burdened reporting vehicle and not necessarily a means of improving service delivery.

Relatively little attention has been accorded the manner in which a MIS controls data collection, data recording, or managerial decision making. Computer hardware may be a useful element in a MIS, but it is not the panacea for management problems. Hardware does not guarantee the collection of valid data or guarantee that data will come to control, let alone improve, decision making and services.

The MIS in nonprofit service delivery does not guarantee improvement any more than the MIS in profit-oriented enterprises does. More information, including the quantities measured as dictated by funding and licensing agencies, will not necessarily result in higher quality services and may in fact deter such improvement. The model of traditional MIS has been purchased with little effort to analyze or modify the contingencies operating for its use in a profit-oriented environment. Critical aspects of the MIS have been ignored in nonprofit-oriented systems, as they have been in other enterprises.

In profit-oriented enterprises, management measures success in terms of monetary profit. In mental health, the profit objective, for the most part, is missing. The often stated objective of mental health is to improve the "quality of life" of the persons served. Defining the quality of life requires value judgments and considerations of cultural norms unnecessary in profit-oriented systems (Simon, 1976). The product of nonprofit service delivery systems is far less amenable to specification than that of profit-oriented systems. In order to meet the public demands for accountability in mental health, variables such as process costs, the amount of staff time utilized in direct and indirect services, and the number of consumers (clients) served are measured to provide an indication of "success."

Obviously, quantity variables are more easily specified and defined than those of quality. The MIS provides a means of collecting such information in a generally applicable format for both processing and reporting to other agencies. However, even though measures of quality are often inferred from quantitative data, measures of quantity do not necessarily reflect the quality of service provided to the consumer. If the object in human service delivery is to improve the client's quality of life, for example, measures of the quantity of services per consumer, per catchment area, and per delivery system are inadequate. A MIS that reports such information may not provide management with the information necessary to monitor the quality of services. The MIS acts simply as a "how many" reporting device and not as a mechanism by which to improve either the quality of service or the quality of managerial decision making (Cohen, Noah, and Pauley, 1977).

A FUNCTIONAL ANALYSIS OF AN MIS

For an MIS to be beneficial in meeting objectives other than reporting requirements in the field of human service delivery, the MIS should be conceptualized as more than an information-processing device. This MIS is one component of a complex environment, or system. The task of a systems developer is not to develop a MIS but to arrange an environment to select proper objectives, to generate activity that accomplishes those objectives, to provide a continuous monitoring system to assess results, and to reevaluate and rearrange the system as a function of information generated by the analysis. Such a system must be viewed as extremely fluid. None of its features can be assumed to remain fixed.

Feedback from systems operations may require changes in those operations, but it also may require changes in the specification of objectives or in the measurement and monitoring strategies themselves. Such operating systems are affected not only by restrictions outside the systems boundaries (e.g., by a state legislature) but also by the internal operations of the system itself (e.g., the behavior of other individuals in the environment).

Behaviorally, a system should be viewed as a complex of behavior-environment relationships. When one focuses on the behavior of any one individual (e.g., manager, employee), the behavior of all other individuals plus work rules, salaries, interpersonal relations, information systems, etc. define the controlling environment. The control works two ways. For example, the behavior of the manager is influenced by the data from the information system or by employee reaction, but both of these can be altered by the manager. That complex of rules, operations reporting systems, and fellow employees' performances is the system. The task is to define those aspects of the environment that control the behavior(s) of interest; that is, in addition to the specification of the target behavior, one must specify the antecedent conditions and consequences that control behavior (i.e., a three-term contingency). The analysis of behavior and environment in terms of the three-term contingency can deal with any aspect of the system and need not be limited to use only when dealing with techniques of measurement or in specifying outcomes. This analysis is to be accomplished when dealing with any aspect of the system, including the analysis of information collection and usage. This is not to say that the specification of antecedents, consequences, and, for that matter, behaviors of interest is easily accomplished. In-

stead, the point is that any analysis other than a functional one complicates the definition and subsequent analysis of the system.

Analyzed in this manner, the functional aspects of the MIS rather than the hardware assumes priority. The MIS is simply one tool utilized by the systems developer.

The MIS collects, processes, and outputs data, but monitoring the reliability of the information reported and measuring the correspondence between the reported data and actual events must also be built into the service delivery system. In effect, the MIS must effectively change and/or maintain individuals' behavior if the MIS is to provide an appropriate data base for decision making. Decision making, in turn, must affect the functioning of the MIS in order that a feedback system will develop between managerial behavior and the data system.

This approach to the MIS is very different [from] the traditional concept of a centralized, computerized, total MIS. When the MIS is viewed as part of a complex interaction [among] people, behavior, and machinery within a service delivery system, the essential element, and one that differentiates this view from the traditional view, is the element of behavior control.

THE ISSUE OF CONTROL

Many of the criticisms of management information systems are related to concerns about the general issue of control. Information systems are, in effect, intended to bring employees' behavior under the control of data, even though the results of contingencies established by the design of the information system are often unanticipated. Managerial control and performance outcomes both are influenced directly by the consequences of information usage requirements. The major difficulty, it seems, is not with the use of information systems to gain control but rather with what is being controlled by the information system. What information is gathered, how information is gathered, and how information is used are all related to the target of the control process.

In point of fact, there is seldom a single target for which information is used. The same information is amenable for documenting a myriad of reporting requirements. Is the target NIMH? The board of directors? Civic groups? Potential consumers? Political interest groups? For what purposes will the information be used? *What* goals are being served by using the information? *Whose* goals are being served by using the information?

Reporting activities to NIMH, for example, is a requirement for funding and one for which specified consequences exist. Reporting requirements for community mental health centers request staff to document how many clients are seen per unit of time, the length of treatment, the proportion of time spent in direct and indirect services, etc. Little, if any, attention is paid to the consequences (outcomes) of such services or the consequences of the reporting requirement per se. If outcome is not consequent and process is, staff behave predictably. More clients may be seen, the same clients may be seen more frequently, the length of each treatment may be limited, etc. With regard to information, staff furnish reports documenting their activities, and the information is used to satisfy the reporting requirements of funding agencies. The accuracy of the information or the relevancy of the information for determining client benefit is seldom disputed.

When discussing information requirements and reporting contingencies of this type, I think of similar contingencies controlling the behavior of pilots and other military personnel during the Vietnam War. Contingencies were arranged to reinforce pilots for reporting the number of bridges destroyed and soldiers for reporting the number of enemy wounded or killed. You may recall the daily and/or weekly body counts and bridge counts collected by the Army and Air Force and reported by the news media. As a result of the contingencies, we managed to destroy ten million bridges and wound or kill twice the population of North Vietnam. Reporting requirements were satisfied, and short-term consequences were quite positive. However, the long-term payoff to those responsible was decreased credibility.

Our efforts to shape accountability in human services by requiring and reinforcing the documentation of quantity may have similar long-term negative consequences. Staff and managers reinforced for unverified services or reinforced for providing services, regardless of the quality of service, are being reinforced for the wrong behaviors.

Process accountability or "What did you do?" is a far cry from answering questions such as "What was the benefit to the client and other purchasers of your service?" "Were the benefits temporary or permanent?" "How much did it cost to effect change?" Reinforcing *just* process and not outcome will not allow funding and evaluation agencies to return to baseline when the emphasis of evaluation criteria changes from process to outcome. The baseline has been changed as a function of current evaluation practices.

The question whether shaping accountability in this manner will prove to be beneficial and/or economical must be reserved for a later time. A major problem in human service delivery is that little is known about the environmental arrangements under which the consequences of a particular action outweigh the consequences of inaction and vice versa. There is an immediate need for a systematic, scientific basis to plan behavioral interventions in such a way that unanticipated negative costs in behavior-environment systems will not occur (Willems, 1977). The use of information systems to document services toward meeting the demands of accountability is no exception.

ETHICAL CONSIDERATIONS IN THE DESIGN AND USE OF INFORMATION SYSTEMS

Before closing, I would like to mention a few ethical considerations for designing and using information systems in human service delivery. Some of these considerations are obvious but others may not be immediately apparent.

1. RESPONSIBILITY. Inherent in the collection, evaluation, and interpretation of information is responsibility. The designer of a system is responsible for understanding the objectives of the system, for ensuring the reliability and validity of information with respect to the objectives of the systems purchaser, and for ensuring that conclusions based on these data are valid and reliable. Additionally, responsibilities include those of the system designer to the organization. When information is used outside of the organization, the systems designer is responsible to the systems purchaser. The designer is also obliged to ensure that users of the system understand the limitations of that system.

2. CONFIDENTIALITY. The notion of confidentiality of information has recently received a great deal of publicity related to other areas and, correspondingly, deserves a great deal of scrutiny related to human service information systems. Not only must the limits of confidentiality be specified to the individual providing information, but a clear specification of confidentiality requirements must be available to those receiving information. Safeguards must be taken to ensure that confidentiality from

independent examination of information records will be maintained. When information is to be used for documenting responsibility for services, individuals must be aware that often some disclosure of personal data is necessary. Information-collection procedures must ensure the non-disclosure of nonessential personal data. Consequently, it is necessary to define the relationship between the information collected and information usage prior to dissemination.

3. CLIENT WELFARE. Two ethical issues regarding client welfare are noteworthy. The first concerns the relationship between the systems designer and systems purchaser. Because external sources, such as government agencies, often require that some information system be invented and maintained for reporting purposes, it is important to evaluate the information system relative to the achievement of specific goals. Well-defined exit criteria must be specified to protect both the systems designer and systems purchaser(s). The second issue occurs when the clients are defined as management and staff personnel. Specification of the relationship between them and the use of information must be precise enough to ensure that both management and staff are protected.

4. CAUSING CHANGE. This final concern is less obvious than the preceding ones. When functionally analyzing an information system, I stated, such a system is only one component of a complex environment controlling behavior. The decision to change the controlling environment by implementing an information system should be taken seriously. Information systems are designed to affect behavior change and constitute an intervention into an existing system.

Successful interventions just don't happen—there is method to the madness. Promoting an innovation works best when shaping methods are employed; changing organizational goals requires a power base from which to operate; and getting individuals to increase participation and effectiveness is a complicated behavioral change process. There are not startling, unusually sophisticated, or esoteric ideas. They are ideas easy to forget and neglect when dealing with behavior controlled by a complex environment.

The decision to design and use an information system for purposes of documentation or more expanded purposes may drastically change the environmental arrangements controlling the behavior of individuals, and old ways of doing things may no longer be effective. These changes, in turn, may result in other changes both inside and outside the organization. For example, the decision to change an aftercare service by providing a greater correspondence between patient skills and placement settings affects not only the program designer and other behavior change agents but social workers, other placement service activities, etc. It is naive for either the systems designer, systems purchaser, or systems user to assume only limited effects of an intervention attempt.

The point is that most interventions have unintended consequences. Information systems are no exception. Specifying the possible consequences of an information system for those the system is both intended and not intended to affect must be assessed.

Information systems can be useful devices for achieving accountability, promoting evaluation, and disseminating information. However, things are typically more complicated than they seem. Like most everything else, so are information systems.

REFERENCES

ACKOFF, R. L. Management misinformation systems. *Management Science,* 14: 147–56, 1967.

BOOKER, W. M. A. The total systems myth. *Systems and Procedures Journal,* 28–32, July–August 1965.

CALLAHAN, E. *Education and the Cult of Efficiency.* Chicago: University of Chicago Press, 1962.

COHEN, S., NOAH, J. C., AND PAULEY, A. *New ways of looking at MISs in human service delivery.* Submitted for publication, 1977.

DEARDEN, S. Myth of real-time management information. *Harvard Business Review,* 68: 123, 1966.

DEARDEN, J., AND MCFARLAN, F. W. *Management Information Systems: Text and Cases.* Homewood, Ill.: Richard D. Irwin, 1966.

ELPERS, J. R. *Management information systems: Tools for integrating human services.* Paper presented at the 24th Institute on Hospital and Community Psychiatry. St. Louis, September 1972.

HAGEDORN, H. J., BECK, K. J., NEUBERG, S. F., AND WERLIN, S. H. *A working manual of simple program evaluation techniques for community mental health centers.* DHEW Publication (ADM) 76-404, 1976.

HELLER, K., AND MONAHAN, J. *Psychology and Community Change.* Homewood, Ill.: Dorsey Press, 1977.

KORCHIN, S. J. *Modern Clinical Psychology.* New York: Basic Books, 1976.

NOAH, J. C., AND CANNON, S. *Accountability and human service delivery: A review.* Manuscript in preparation, 1977.

NOAH, J. C., KRAPFL, J. E., AND MALEY, R. F. *The notion of accountability.* Unpublished manuscript, West Virginia University, 1976.

NOAH, J. C., KRAPFL, J. E., AND MALEY, R. F. *Behavioral systems analysis: An integration of behavior analysis and systems analysis to meet the demands of accountability.* Submitted for publication, 1977.

PETER, L. J., AND HULL, R. *The Peter Principle,* New York: William Morrow, 1969.

SIMON, H. A. *Administrative Behavior.* New York: The Free Press, 1976.

WEISS, C. *Evaluation Research.* Englewood Cliffs, N.J.: Prentice-Hall, 1972.

WILLEMS, E. Behavioral ecology. In: Stokols, D., ed. *Psychological Perspectives on Environment and Behavior.* New York: Plenum Press, 1976.

5

SOCIAL POLICY ANALYSIS

The relationship between community organization and social planning presents many terminological ambiguities because multiple meanings attach to both terms. We have chosen to define social planning as a major mode of community organization practice which focuses on a range of interventions at the level of organizations and institutions rather than directly on the population group affected by a social problem. Although some may view the two terms as synonymous, others regard social planning as a loosely defined field of practice especially concerned with the prevention or the reduction of a social problem through analysis of social conditions, policy formulation, and program administration.

There is, in addition, considerable overlap between social planning and social policy analysis. Both are professional disciplines that share a common conceptual base, methods, and modes of analysis which are traditionally rooted in a rational, comprehensive model of decision making. Policy formulation and planning both involve choices. Policies have been described as "standing plans . . . general guides to future decision making.[1]" . . . There has also been a recent convergence of policy analysis and planning because of their mutual concern with implementation, accountability, and evaluation and the assessment of political factors in determining feasibility. Although they share similar methods of analysis, in actual practice, planners are expected to promote citizen participation in the process and are much more likely to have responsibility for implementing the products of their work. Thus the planning role tends more to be that of a technipol. The role of a policy analyst is more of a staff position. A planner is expected to design feasible social plans and organize the relevant community elements to ensure their realization. As Abraham Kaplan has described the function, the social planner must delineate *compossible* plans, that is, those that are *com*patible with the facts and *possible* to implement. This means that the practitioner must have substantive expertise about the nature of social problems and the origins and the effectiveness of various social policies and institutional arrangements. He or she must also know how to mobilize sufficient influence to bring about the changes required. A policy analyst, on the other hand, is more concerned with the intellectual substance of community organization and planning.

This section is composed of selections pertaining to different perspectives on policy analysis. It includes articles that deal with the principles of accountability and policy implementation and concludes with examples of two policy issues of special interest to community organization practitioners and planners: community mental health and deinstitutionalization with reference to the relationship between community care and family policy and the policy choices associated with the direct provision or the purchase of service contracting by governmental agencies.

"Policy Analysis Methods and Governmental Functions" by Duncan MacRae, Jr. is a presentation of his view of the state of the art. He defines his subject as "the choice of the best method among a set of alternatives with the aid of reason and evidence." According to MacRae, the method of policy analysis consists of four elements: definition of the problem: criteria for choice; comparison of expected consequences of alternatives using models of causation expressed in terms of previously specified values, and the political feasibility of implementation. He develops a typology relating the models to seven types of governmental functions.

A more political and strategic perspective is proposed by Dennis A. Rondinelli in "Urban Planning as Policy Analysis: Management of Urban Change." He summarizes his arguments in a series of nine propositions which emphasize the conception of planning as analysis, intervention, and the management of the political conflict that is inextricably part of urban change. Rondinelli's hypotheses about the nature of urban policymaking are supported by considerable empirical evidence. He also makes a strong case for modifying the professional education of planners to provide them with knowledge and skill to design and implement political strategies.

Despite tendencies to justify some forms of planning on the basis of such process values as increasing the civic competence of the participants, the ultimate test of plans and policies generally resides in their implementation. The rather sparse studies of local planning and its results are not as instructive as the extensive literature on social policy implementation which burgeoned during the 1970s. Most studies of policy implementation and program evaluation lead one to a pessimistic view of the capacity of important policy initiatives to achieve desired social change. The extent to which methodological constraints and/or the inherent nature of the human services are responsible for these failures is not clear. Yet some federal programs have been more successful than others. What are some of the conditions associated with the more effective policy initiatives and their implementation? In "The Conditions of Effective Implementation: A Guide to Accomplishing Policy Objectives," Paul Sabatier and Daniel Mazmanian review empirical research on a wide range of policy initiatives that sought social change through regulation, legal directives, and conditional disbursement of funds. They discover five necessary conditions for the achievement of policy objectives: the soundness of the technical theory underlying the programs; the clarity of the policy directives; the commitment and the managerial and political skill of the leadership of the implmenting agency; the active support of the community constituency and key governmental and legislative officials; and a relatively stable policy and socioeconomic environment. The authors suggest several strategies to be followed if these conditions cannot be met. For example, they deal with the question of how to increase the probability of effective implementation even under suboptimal conditions.

Among the values expected to be optimized by policies and programs is that of accountability. The popularity of this idea in the human services is exceeded only by the lack of agreement about its meaning. It has been viewed as both an end and a means; it has been defined in terms of procedures, results, disclosure of information, recourse, and compliance with regulations; and it is often indistinguishable from such concepts as evaluation, efficiency, effectiveness, control, and responsibility. At a minimum, accountability means, as Marone and Marmor have shown, having to answer to those who control a necessary and a scarce resource. Therefore it involves the obligation to report in appropriate detail on how the organization is discharging its service and fiscal responsibilities so that decisions can be made. This kind of reporting, or "public accounting," which is essential to accountability, should, however, be distinguished from restrictions on agency functioning that might limit its autonomy. Although reporting requirements and red tape may be costly nuisances and may even deflect agency resources, they do not necessarily impair an agency's freedom. These questions are discussed in "Social Program Implementation: The Demand for Accountability" by Bruce L. Gates. Gates distinguishes between accountability and responsibility and analyzes the external sources of accountability, which include the use of citizen participation. Characteristically vague policy mandates in the human services and the multiplicity of groups with legitimate authority over some aspect of program performance make accountability a continuing and complex issue. The particular role and the choices confronting organizations responsible for direct services delivery are singled out by Gates for special attention.

With the slowed growth of the welfare state and with mounting resistance to taxing and public spending, service delivery issues in government-voluntary relationships have taken on a new importance. There are greater pressures for public policymakers to find alternative means for planning and delivering public services in a cost-efficient and equitable manner. The increased use of voluntary, nonprofit agencies is being advocated as an effective means of avoiding the deficiencies of governmentally provided services. In this view, contracting with the voluntary sector is a solution to the dilemma posed by people who want more services and less government.

Despite the enormous growth in the purchase of service contracting during the 1970s, there is scarcely any information about its consequences for the clientele and the organizations involved. In fact, there is virtually no knowledge about the differences between services delivered by a governmental agency, a voluntary, nonprofit, or proprietary agency, and more primary social systems such as the family and informal networks. In "Contracting for Human Services: An Organizational Perspective," Ralph M. Kramer summarizes the potential advantages and disadvantages of the policy of purchasing services from the perspectives of both the government and the voluntary, nonprofit provider. Based on a review of national experience in the human services, a series of factors are explored that should be taken into account in decisions about whether to purchase or provide services. Some basic guidelines for contracting are proposed. Underlying the option for contracting are issues relating to the organizational interests of the government and its nonprofit service providers. The paper concludes with a reevaluation of the concepts of autonomy and accountability.

The relationships between planning and social policy in the field of community mental health constitute the theme of the article by Steven P. Segal, "Community Care and Deinstitutionalization: A Review," which deals with the implications of family policy for community care of the deinstitutionalized mentally ill. The policy of deinstitutionalization adopted by many states in the last decade has revived the belief in the capacity of the family to resume its major function as a care giver for the mentally ill. Segal analyzes the role of the family in tertiary, secondary, and primary prevention roles with respect to the mentally ill in the context of the development of other programs of community care. Drawing on research on the family as a helper, he proposes a range of policies that would support these roles. Community organization practitioners and planners who are responsible for the design and the implementation of viable programs of community care should find these perspectives useful.

NOTE

1. Preston P. LeBreton and Dale A. Henning, *PlanningTheory* (Englewood Cliffs, N.J.: Prentice-Hall, 1961), p. 3. Quoted in Alfred J. Kahn, *Theory and Practice of Social Planning* (New York: Russell Sage Foundation, 1969), p. 3.

Duncan MacRae, Jr.

Policy Analysis Methods and Governmental Functions[1]

The field of policy analysis combines valuative judgments, technical calculations, and politically oriented action. Practitioners often learn these ingredients of the

"Policy Analysis Methods and Governmental Functions" by Duncan MacRae, Jr., is reprinted from Stuart S. Nagel, ed., *Improving Policy Analysis* (Sage Focus Editions, vol. 16, 1980), pp. 129–51, by permission of the publisher, Sage Publications (Beverly Hills/London).

field through eclectic combinations of material from various disciplines and professions, together with experience on the job. A more systematic definition of the field is needed, however, both to fill gaps in practitioners' preparation and to establish a solid basis for instruction in the field. Major intellectual contributions to policy analysis have been made by economics, operations research, and applied statistics; but I shall argue here that a broader alternative framework may be preferable.

As this field develops, it must regulate its relations with the political system in which policy choices are made and the academic system in which the quality of recommendations is controlled. Such a field, if it exists within a democratic polity, must avoid contributing to an increased domination of decisions by experts. It must not be an occult administrative science but must frame its recommendations in terms intelligible to citizens and public leaders. Its principles and procedures must be widely disseminated among citizens rather than restricted to the staff of government and powerful private organizations.

A tension exists between the requirements of such a field for citizens and for staff analysts. Citizens must be concerned with broad questions of value and political philosophy; staff analysts must often take their superiors' values as given. Citizens must be concerned with what government *is* as well as with what it *does;* thus their education must deal with constitutional and institutional change. On the other hand, the acceptance of this new field by academics as well as employers can be fostered by stress on technical and quantitative skills in which expertise can more easily be demonstrated and quality more easily reviewed by expert peers.

I shall center my discussion on the "methods" or "methodology" of policy analysis as a collection of procedures that can be taught and reviewed so as to establish an academic definition for the field. We must recognize, however, that "methods" potentially encompass much more than procedures for the gathering and statistical manipulation of data. They extend to procedures of logical criticism that may be directed at theories or at systems of valuation. They include the systematic components of "soft" aspects of policy analysis, such as the assessment of political feasibility. They extend, in fact, to any sys-

tematic procedure shared by members of an expert community in their published work and in their critical judgment of one another's work (Ziman, 1968).

Taking this broad view of methods, I shall ask whether the discourse of policy analysis can eventually resemble that of an academic discipline or subdiscipline so that its quality can be monitored by a group of trained experts (MacRae, 1976a, ch. 9; MacRae, 1976b). This question, concentrating on the community of experts, is distinct from that of the relation of policy analysis to *political* communities; questions concerning the interests, privileges, and power of analysts must also be examined if we propose that the field be a discipline. I shall deal here with the internal intellectual relations of such a discipline, not its external or political relations; but by defining "methods" broadly, I am advocating the instruction of citizens and not merely of government officials.

I shall present a general classification of methods in relation to a systematic view of the elements constituting policy analysis. Within this general classification I present two approaches to the classification of one of these elements, models of causation: a more conventional one based on their forms and procedures and another related to the functions of government. This last classification suggests the possibility of a distinctive field of policy analysis with close connections to political science.

THE ELEMENTS OF POLICY ANALYSIS

Policy analysis may be defined as the choice of the best policy among a set of alternatives with the aid of reason and evidence. Its methods may be organized [according to] a set of elements or parts.

(1) DEFINITION OF THE PROBLEM. We need to learn how the various preexisting definitions of our problem may be trans-

formed into our "analyst's problem" (Mac-Rae and Wilde, 1979, ch. 2), which is rephrased in precise enough terms to permit analysis, is related to a system of values providing criteria for choice, and yet can be introduced in the processes of enactment and implementation of a particular political community.

(2) CRITERIA FOR CHOICE. Whether we use "objective functions" of operations research or systematic ethical criteria such as those of equity or cost-benefit analysis, we must formulate and use clear valuative criteria for comparing the results of policies. Precise valuative discourse, such as that of philosophy and economics, can reshape and ambiguous values of citizens' discourse, but eventually the results of this technical discussion of values must be reintroduced in the discourse of citizens and understood by them.

(3) ALTERNATIVES, MODELS, AND DECISIONS. Policy analysis involves comparison among possible alternative policies. The expected consequences of these policies are compared after being predicted by models of causation and are expressed in terms of the valuative criteria we have previously specified.[2] On the basis of the values or disvalues of the alternatives, we then choose among them. One model of particular importance is the economic model of the free, competitive market, including possible departures from this model and means of coping with them. Numerous other relevant models exist, drawing on knowledge from various natural and social sciences and combinations of them. These models differ in their forms, in the procedures used for testing them, and in their relations to governmental functions; I shall classify them below in these respects.

(4) POLITICAL FEASIBILITY. Analysis of the prospects for [enacting and implementing] a chosen policy is an essential feature of the larger analytic process. This topic draws on both political science and sociology, but also involves much information that is specific to particular political situations as well as skills of non-academic practitioners.

Each of these elements of policy analysis, as we shall show, involves some aspects that can be criticized as part of an academic literature; other aspects, however, vary with the particular problem at hand and with the analyst's role and are less easily subjected to reasoned public criticism.

Definition of the Problem

The choice of the analyst's problem illustrates an aspect of analysis in which skill or art predominates over formal methodology. Even in scientific research, the art of choosing problems that are theoretically significant and feasible to investigate is largely a matter of experience and talent rather than of formal procedure. In policy analysis there is even greater room for individual judgment since the significance of an analysis depends on the feasibility not only of processing information but also of action on the recommendation that is made—not to mention significance for a particular system of values. There may be checklists that will provide some guidance in the choice of problems for analysis, but we cannot easily speak of a "methodology" for this purpose.

The definition and redefinition of a policy problem depend on the analyst's learning at the start the various definitions of the "problem situation" that are held by significant participants. He must learn to inquire directly and indirectly, to listen, and to read between the lines. He must judge what elements of a group's position are unalterable and which are possibly subject to bargaining or compromise. His choice is not only whether to work in a given problem area but how to reshape its definition in a way that is consistent with his capacities for analysis and with the expected response of the relevant actors to his proposals. The definition of the problem thus overlaps with the assessment of political feasibility, to which we return below.

Formulating and Measuring Valuative Criteria

The first element of policy analysis for which we may consider a "methodology" is the development of criteria for choice. Although in a positivist perspective our basic values are mere givens, insusceptible to debate or reasoned discussion, I have proposed (MacRae, 1976a, ch. 4) that we follow a systematic method in putting forward and comparing the values on which policy analysis is based. This method involves first rendering any proposed system of values clear, consistent, and general and then comparing two or more such systems in terms of particular moral convictions shared by the participants in the discussion. Valuative discourse of this sort is not easy to carry out; but the value system developed in welfare economics stands as an example challenging the proponents of other values to formulate theirs with equal precision. It is conceivable that academically public discourse of this sort could be extended to include other value systems concerned with the general welfare and mutual criticism among them.

Not every policy decision will involve value systems of this degree of systematization. In actuality, analysis may be based on multiple values that have not been rendered consistent. It may involve very specific values specified by an employer, the law, or community consensus. But insofar as a "methodology" of valuative discourse is possible, it is likely to involve not only careful verbal logic but also mathematics or formal logic, such as we see increasingly in the valuative discussions of philosophy, economics, and public choice (e.g., Harsanyi, 1978).

The "methodology" of valuative discourse may be extended from the conceptual and logical definition of the values used to their measurement. The specification of a procedure for measuring a valuative criterion is one way of defining it clearly. In economics the principal methods of measurement have been introduced in benefit-cost analysis or applied welfare economics. Conventions have been introduced for defining and measuring costs; for avoiding double counting of benefits; for comparing increments of change under resource constraints in terms of benefit-cost ratios; and for choosing among alternatives given their streams of benefits and costs over time (Stokey and Zeckhauser, 1978, chs. 9 and 10). Survey methods may also be adaptable to the measurement of demand for publicly supplied goods and services (McKinney and MacRae, 1978).

Measurement cannot, however, be separated from the more basic question [of] whether the things measured are really the values we wish to achieve. Economic values, for example, rest on the assumption of fixed preferences, the satisfaction of which is by definition equivalent to an increase in welfare; but the mere fact that this assumption has been formalized elegantly does not require us to accept it.

An alternative "methodology" for the measurement of well-being, which is relevant to this discussion even though it is not widely used in policy choice, is being developed in the field of "subjective social indicators" (Campbell, Converse, and Rodgers, 1976). Here the satisfaction or happiness of individuals is measured directly by questioning them. Such measurements then allow us to raise the question [of] whether the possession of goods and services does indeed lead people to say they are happier or more satisfied—a question that cannot be answered in the economic perspective where preference satisfaction is tautologically equivalent to welfare.

The comparsion of these two methods of measuring welfare is of special interest as regards the valuation of human life. If policies are to be judged in terms of their effects on human beings, their consequences must be compared in terms of their effects on human welfare. Insofar as welfare is viewed as extending over time, then an extreme case of difference in welfare is that in which various policies lead to differences in the expected length and quality of human lives. Cost-benefit analysis typically assesses the value of human life in terms of a stream of earnings discounted over time. Some studies of health policy have made use of the notion of "quality-adjusted life-years" (Weinstein and Stason, 1976) based in part on comparisons that individuals make of the quality of life under different circumstances and partly on a notion of discounting. In addition, individuals may be questioned after experiencing various life conditions, and their reported levels of satisfaction or happiness may be compared. Comparison of these methods may give rise to fruitful discussions of the philosophical notions on which these measurements rest.

When particular outcomes of decisions may be assigned numerical values and when they are expected to occur with known probabilities, methods for [computing] statistical expected values may be used. For discrete alternatives, these methods of choice may be expressed in the form of decision trees (Raiffa, 1968). This procedure includes the calculation of the numerical value of a criterion function, but the probabilities and the form of the tree also express the causal model involved; we return below to the relation between decision trees and models.

The maximization of a value such as net monetary benefit or happiness is one form that a consistent ethical system may take. Often, however, such maximization is constrained by unconditional or non-teleological values that correspond to moral prohibitions, laws, rules, or contractual agreements. A set of methods exists for choosing the best alternative under conditions of constrained maximization; they include linear programming (Stokey and Zeckhauser, 1978, ch. 11; Gupta and Cozzolino, 1974, chs. 6–8). These methods in effect provide an operational definition of the consistent valuative system that combines the variable to be maximized and the constraints. They also involve models of causation, which may be involved in the equations that define the value at a point in terms of the spatial coordinates.

The combination of two or more valuative criteria entertained by a particular decision-maker has also been approached through multiattribute decision analysis (Keeney and Raiffa, 1976). A partial reconciliation of two incommensurable criteria is also made in cost-effectiveness analysis. This method is used for [comparing] a set of alternatives (e.g., policies expected to produce certain amounts of change in health or knowledge), each of which is characterized by a value of "effectiveness" and a disvalue of "cost." When effectiveness cannot be translated into monetary terms, these pairs of numbers have no simple ordering. Nevertheless, procedures exist for ordering them to some extent (Quade, 1975: 94).

Specific and distinct criterion variables are also often measured without an explicit formal method for reconciling them. Such a disparity of criteria often arises when various public programs (e.g., health, education, social services) are being compared. For any one such program, we may attempt to measure the need for it (Carter, 1966), its effectiveness (Morse, 1967: 5–6), or citizens' satisfaction with it (Webb and Hatry, 1973). "Methodologies" exist for measurements of this sort even though the underlying values are not parts of general ethical systems. These methodologies lead, in turn, to diverse notions of how the resulting analyses should be related to the political systems in which they function. The reconciliation of various specific values, corresponding to particular measures, may take place through pluralistic political decisions (Gates, 1975) or through assignment of numerical values by a group to possible outcomes of policy alternatives, producing a "social welfare function" for the particular problem at hand (Odum, 1976: 167–177).

So far we have considered the formulation and measurement of values that exemplify shared concepts, such as the public interest or the general welfare. Such formulations can be compared and discussed publicly in terms of their adequacy. Some approaches to policy analysis, however, include in the criteria for choice aspects of the chooser's personal welfare (Vaupel, 1976: 190–197). In this case the values of various choosers differ in part because they include a diversity of "tastes," and public discussion in order to reconcile them seems pointless.

Models: Form and Procedure

The best known and most extensive domain of methods in policy analysis concerns models of causation, relating policies to their expected consequences (Quade, 1975; Stokey and Zeckhauser, 1978: Part II). Two main bases [for classifying] these models are available (1) their form and the procedures for testing them, and (2) their relation to functions carried out by governments. The first sort of classification, treated in this section, is not specific to *public* policy; it is found in fields such as operations research and management science or, as regards procedures, in evaluation research or applied statistics. The second, which we shall discuss in the following section, is more specific to analyses of public policies and has some affinity with political science.

We first set aside the possibility that knowledge generated by preexisting academic disciplines is automatically optimal for policy analysis, needing only to be "ap-plied." Knowledge generated by basic natural science is indeed often appropriate for policy choices, being applied by engineering and health sciences. Even in natural science, however, there are models that derive directly from an effort to predict valuative variables rather than seek knowledge for its own sake. This approach has been proposed for biological research in agriculture (Levins, 1973).

For policy choices relating to social processes it is all the more necessary to seek the relevant models directly rather than expect them to develop from basic science. Much basic research, at least in sociology and political science, deals with variables over which policymakers have no control, unrelated to explicit valuative concerns. The generalizations that arise from this research are far less precisely verified than those of natural science (Almond and Genco, 1977), and parameters in them may even change over the years. As Foote (1975: 329) expresses it, "Sociological generalizations do not cumulate; they obsolesce." This difficulty may well hold for other social sciences.

Many of these models of causation are subject to quality control and review through publication for expert scrutiny. Some, however, are not; the models used in concrete policy choices always involve some degree of conjecture or subjective assessment. Policy choices are made with a finite time horizon, in contrast to the indefinite time horizon of pure science. Unless the decision-maker is extremely fortunate, he must always engage in probability judgments, and even the necessary probabilities cannot be known with certainty by the use of standard methods. He must conjecture not only about probabilities but about the form of the model (what variables are really relevant?) and its applicability to the concrete case at hand. The concern of decision theorists with Bayesian prior probabilities (Raiffa, 1968) is thus a manifestation of an essential and unavoidable feature of policy analysis. The subjective character of these probabilities has contributed to the reluctance of many statisticians to accept the Bayesian approach; their concern with the objective bases of their scientifically public discourse leads to this position. Nevertheless, when the necessity of making public decisions is considered, we have no choice but to admit these judgments.

CLASSIFICATION BY FORM.   Some bases for classifying models by form concern whether they are simple or complex; represented explicitly or by simulation; discrete or continuous in the alternatives presented; based on adversary assumptions like games; homeostatic or not.

The *complexity* of a model concerns the number of variables it contains, or the related question [of] whether it encompasses a segment of a system or a larger system. Procedurally, we here distinguish between models that may be formulated in explicit mathematical terms, and those whose complexity requires simulation.

The distinction between *discrete* and *continuous* alternatives may be illustrated by the types of models related to decision trees, on the one hand, and maximization problems using calculus, on the other. Continuous alternatives are also involved in linear programming. Problems of optimal allocation of resources may involve alternatives of either type; for example, choice of paths of travel can involve discrete alternatives, and choice of amounts of factors of production can involve continuous ones.

Models in which we face an opponent require that we take into account his possible anticipation of our choices. This anticipation leads to *games;* to human simulation as in war games; and in decision trees, to assignment of probabilities that take the opponent's tactics into account.

Homeostatic models are those that return to a desired equilibrium when disturbed.

Some undisturbed ecological systems have this property. The model of a perfect competitive market has an analogous property; a change in the exogenous variables of supply, technology, or taste leads to a new equilibrium but one that is again Pareto efficient (Bator, 1958: 351). Some models of political systems—two-party competition or pluralistic interaction of groups—have been alleged to have similar properties, but these models have been formulated more often verbally than mathematically. The implicit policy prescription, when a homeostatic model is claimed to apply to a segment of reality, is to do nothing; thus free-market and pluralistic models have been associated with conservatism.

A wide variety of non-homeostatic models have also been proposed: Keynes' general theory, the Richardson (1939) arms-race model and contemporary models of future world population growth and energy shortage, are among them. Simulations of river basins, weapons systems, and urban development are also usually non-homeostatic. Such models are complex; insofar as they predict extreme and undesirable results, they may be used as calls for innovative interventions—provided that they include relevant manipulable variables.

CLASSIFICATION BY TESTING PROCEDURE.   The methods discussed so far, in connection with models, concern the combination of presumably known information and relationships so as to predict the consequences of policies. Many methods deal, however, with the ascertainment of relationships or the testing of models.

The *procedures* used for testing or verifying models distinguish such approaches as the true experiment, the quasi-experiment, and nonexperimental inferences of causation. Related to this classification is the question whether we "verify" assessments of feasibility at the same time as we verify models or separately; Braybooke and Lindblom (1963) have proposed an incremental procedure that combines both testing processes.

The most general approach to testing procedures is that which regards the gathering of information as itself a decision, made so as to further a value or values. [From] this perspective, our choice whether or not to engage in analysis, including the gathering of information, is weighed in terms of its expected benefits and costs estimated in terms of prior probabilities. Vaupel (1976: 202–204) has used a decision tree to derive the criterion for analysis pd > c, where

> p = the probability that analysis will make a difference,
> d = the difference that it will make if successful, and
> c = the cost of analysis.

If the inequality is satisfied, analysis is worth the cost. Raiffa (1968: 27, 42) introduces the notion of the value of information assessed in terms of outcome values for a given decision tree. This notion may also be applied to the choice of optimal sampling designs when various elements in the design have different benefits or [contribute to reducing the] variance in an estimate (Neter, 1972) or different costs (Rossi and Lyall, 1976: 20).

The gathering of information to test models is most rigorously done by means of experiments; in the social sciences, [such experiments] normally require randomized controls (Gilbert, Light, and Mosteller, 1975). Techniques of experimentation, including their organizational and professional sources of support, are analyzed in Riecken and Boruch (1974). The relation between experimental and quasi-experimental designs is discussed in detail in Campbell and Stanley (1966).

Two important nonexperimental procedures are those of path analysis (structural equation models) and time-series analysis. Path analysis has been developed extensively by sociologists, with contributions from econometrics (Goldberger and Duncan, eds., 1973). It permits a systematic test of linear causal models, some of which involve dozens of variables. The results of such tests need to be cross-checked, however, by experiments and actual policy interventions.

The analysis of time series interrupted by policy interventions provides another opportunity for testing models in a way that goes beyond cross-sectional path analysis. Even when these interventions do not involve randomized controls, time series provide useful information, including information about delayed effects, gradually disappearing effects, and other time dependencies. A comparison between empirical time-series analysis and structural equation models has been presented by Hibbs (1977).

Models and Governmental Functions

Another major basis for classification of models concerns the *functions* that governments perform. *Public* policy analysis is concerned with governmental actions—the conditions under which they should be undertaken, conditions for their efficiency, conditions for their implementation, and the possible establishment of structures that will facilitate the proper choice and implementation of policies. We thus consider the relation of policy-analysis methods to the substantive functions of government. This sort of classification may allow us to organize models of effects or policies in a way that will help to distinguish policy analysis from other fields, while drawing its component parts together.

We shall classify the functions of government in relation to the models necessary to analyze them. We conceive of government as performing seven types of functions that correspond roughly to different types of models:

(a) direct monetary transactions including taxes and subsidies;

(b) production and delivery of goods;
(c) delivery of services;
(d) regulation;
(e) monitoring and enforcement;
(f) persuasion and socialization; and
(g) meta-policy.

We shall discuss each [function] in turn, defining it and indicating the types of models that seem appropriate to it.

DIRECT MONETARY TRANSACTIONS INCLUDING TAXES AND SUBSIDIES.

The other functions that government performs are supported by taxes (if not by direct participation as in the case of the military draft). A particular type of expenditure together with an earmarked tax can bring about redistribution of income, but that redistribution appears in its purest form if tax receipts are given to lower-income persons or families as direct monetary payments. One form of such redistribution is a negative income tax, which may be evaluated in terms of both vertical equity and efficiency. Experimental studies of the negative income tax have focused on its efficiency in providing work incentives, however (Pechman and Timpane, 1975); consideration of vertical equity has not been analyzed directly as an ingredient of optimum policy but has simply been taken to be limited by political feasibility.

The design of tax systems has been a major concern of the field of public finance (Musgrave and Musgrave, 1973). This concern has been directed largely [toward] efficiency in relation to production possibilities and consumer demand, but much less systematically [toward] vertical equity, which is seen as involving arbitrary valuative judgments or social welfare functions.

Taxes or subsidies that are conditional on certain activities by payer or recipient are considered below as means of regulation.

Horizontal equity in the collection of taxes has also been the subject of systematic research, as in the case of real property taxation (Rackham and Smith, 1974). Analytic methods have also been used to assess horizontal equity in the distribution of municipal aid to Minnesota counties (Brandl, 1980). This type of study of equity has analogies in the distribution of goods and services.

PRODUCTION AND DELIVERY OF GOODS.

The first question that must be asked about governmental production of a good (or service) is whether and how much it should produce. The question whether government should be involved at all is paramount in the analysis of "market failure," centering [on] a model of the free, competitive market. Departures from this model create a *prima facie* case for government intervention. The development of public-choice models of government behavior, however, has led some to question whether governments may not themselves be susceptible to "failure," i.e., to less-than-efficient production (Niskanen, 1971).

There are other grounds than economic efficiency, however, on which government production or supply of goods has been justified, notably equity, rights and needs. Justification in terms of rights or needs makes it difficult to allocate scarce resources among different programs at the margin, since various rights or needs constitute incommensurable criteria. Considerations of equity may be included in a general "social welfare function," either by assigning priority to certain persons or groups or by weighting the consequences to them more heavily, in terms of specific operational definitions of equity.

If we can demonstrate that government should produce or supply a good (or service), we next face the question as to how much should be produced. One way to estimate the proper scale of production is to compare demand with cost, if these functions can be estimated accurately (McKinney and MacRae, 1978). Such comparisons are further complicated if the basis for justifying governmental production is a criterion other than economic efficiency, for in that case the economic method of calculation is less well developed. Equity adjustments, for example, involve equity not only among those receiving the good, but also among taxpayers.

Problems of spatial and temporal distribution of supply lead to a number of models that have been studied in the application of operations research to public systems: degree of decentralization; optimum location; allocation of supply and consumption over time; speed of response; and problems of congestion and queuing (Beltrami, 1977).

Delivery or availability of goods involves the closely related question of who should receive them and how this distribution is to be implemented. A special problem arising [from the] government supply of goods or services is that of determining eligibility. Goods may be made available on the market with a user charge and subsidy (the amount of which must be chosen), or given free to all as a right, in which case these problems do not arise. But if given to some and not all, they have to be distributed through a process that determines eligibility, leading to problems of monitoring and enforcement such as we mention below.

The distribution of goods, when only some receive them, also leads to problems of vertical and horizontal equity. If the poor are provided with food or housing, for example, then the measure of poverty that determines eligibility may be scrutinized in terms of its relation to the needs of family units. Not only income but family size and composition and sometimes savings are considered. These considerations of equity and need are over and above the problems of disincentives to earn that exist when goods are made available only below a threshold value of income.

So far, in speaking of "goods," we have referred to problems that exist for the fur-

nishing of services as well. We have, nevertheless, distinguished goods from services in order to distinguish those methods appropriate to technologies of material production from those involving human relationships. "Goods," in this connection, refer to transportation, utilities, weapons, health technology, and other things requiring organization and technology to produce; many of the corresponding models lie in operations research and engineering. Analyses of such processes for the private sector are largely adaptable to the public sector provided that we substitute some measure of the general welfare for private profit as a criterion or objective function.

As we move to the more labor-intensive production of services such as fire protection or the removal of solid waste, the necessary models are less technical and more social in nature. Each of these examples, however, involves some technology; we must stress, therefore, that our distinction between "goods" and "services" is in some respects a continuum.

DELIVERY OF SERVICES. Here we are concerned with the delivery by a government agency of a service, often including personal interaction between the deliverer and the client or beneficiary. Estimating the consequences of policies involving services includes sociological studies of the ways in which professionals act (Freidson, 1970). It may also involve studies of the ways in which clients, individually or in groups, participate in service delivery (Whitaker, 1978). These models are thus more likely to involve other contributions from the social sciences than operations research or management science in a narrow sense. Problems of equity, availability, and distribution of services also arise that are similar to those mentioned above for delivery of goods. An example of statistical analysis to estimate degrees of equity in the delivery of police services is given by Bloch (1974).

REGULATION. In contrast to the provision of goods or services, we see regulation models as involving prediction[s about] the functioning of a larger system, including the regulated person or organization. Regulation ordinarily involves the provision of a "bad," rather than a good, to the persons whose activities are affected. [It is assumed that they will] take steps to reduce the undesirable consequences of this "bad" if possible, e.g., by shifting taxes to consumers or renters, by changing production technology to reduce concentrations of specific effluents, or by changing modes of transportation when regulation makes one mode more expensive. Effects analogous to those of conditional taxation can also be brought about by subsidies; family allowances have been introduced to stimulate fertility, and industries may be encouraged by subsidies. Tariffs, or the taxation of competitors, can have a similar effect.

The general type of model that seems appropriate for the study of consequences of regulatory policy is then one of a system that may be altered by the reactions of those affected. We assume that they comply with the legal requirement but adjust some of their other activities as a result; in the next section, "monitoring and enforcement," we consider the possibility that those potentially affected may not comply. In addition to the desired effects of compliance, regulatory policies have also involved costs in their implementation (Miller and Yandle, 1979).

System[s] models or simulations are also relevant to prediction of the results of plans that are to be put into effect over time. Here again, even if there is compliance, the functioning of a larger system may affect the results. A plan for attaining a given spatial allocation of functions in a city, or for furnishing a supply of manpower over a decade, may well be affected by other variables that change during that period, such as changes in population composition and location, demand, and al-

ternative sources of supply. To anticipate these changes a "social indicator model" (Land, 1975) may be desirable, provided that it takes into account the manipulable variables through which policies work. Analogous models of expected changes in natural systems are also useful, e.g., in projecting quantities and compositions of waste water in a watershed system. Models of this sort have broader application than to regulatory policies; they are relevant, for example, to forecasting need or demand for given types of governmental production—e.g., waste removal or purification, social services, or schools.

MONITORING AND ENFORCEMENT. We classify as a separate function the assurance that those who are regulated actually comply with a policy once it is enacted. This compliance may be either implementation by government employees (Kaufman, 1973), or obedience to laws or regulations by citizens. This category of government functions resembles regulation, in that a "bad" is being delivered; but we are dealing here with possible deviance from an instruction or law rather than with legally permitted avoidance or shifting of costs. Simulation models related to regulatory policies typically assume that the regulation is successful (at least to a specified extent) in obtaining legal compliance—that speed limits are obeyed, that taxes are collected, that agricultural production or airport noise is reduced to within a prescribed limit. Models of monitoring and enforcement deal, however, with the possibility that some of those affected do not comply, and with policies to increase compliance.

There is a superficial similarity between these types of models and the statistics of quality control, which provides guidance as to how many items emerging from a productive process should be inspected and how they should be chosen in order to maintain given quality standards. The problem is complicated, however, by the fact that sanctions are involved, e.g., for health conditions in restaurants or for the safety of buildings. The result is in part a game-type situation in which those affected seek to avoid inspection, anticipate it, or circumvent the results (e.g., by modifying the indicators that measure compliance). Modeling such processes is more complex than modeling industrial processes for quality control; in addition, it involves political elements, in that the person inspected or monitored is a citizen of a free society who claims rights against unannounced government searches, electronic eavesdropping, and the like.

A general abstract model for estimating the optimal level of such policy variables as severity and certainty of punishment has been proposed by Becker (1968); but many problems are involved in translating it into practice. A related question concerns how "finely tuned" sanctions should be in view of their cost and complexity. In addition, a factor neglected by economic models is the degree to which norms are internalized by the public, leading to compliance without sanctions; this possibility leads us to the following type of governmental function, persuasion and socialization.

PERSUASION AND SOCIALIZATION. In a free society, as well as in economic models, we tend to assume that government does not persuade citizens or change their preferences. Such activities are associated with totalitarian regimes and are seen as incursions on citizens' freedom. Yet one reason that has been advanced for having a public school system, aside from its provision of job opportunities, is its contribution to citizenship. Citizenship consists not merely in political skills or capacity to seek one's self-interest through the political process, but involves civic obligation, devotion to the general welfare, and willingness to abide by procedural rules that govern collective decisions. Whether schools actually produce these values is an empirical question; possibly the study of political socialization could throw light on the effectiveness of various public policies in this respect.

Some governments go farther [than others] in socializing and persuading their citizens, in the service of goals that may be argued to be in the general interest. Instruction centered about a particular notion of human development or perfection may be of this sort, though it cannot easily be undertaken by public policy in a pluralistic society and may be more appropriate to religiously based states. Some governments have urged their citizens to curtail their reproduction rates, and public exhortation is also a possible means for reduction of demand for energy as the supply dwindles. If models of these social processes were available, they would deal with the formation of social norms (MacRae 1976a, ch. 8) as well as with the persuasion of individuals.

META-POLICY. Governments not only tax, subsidize, provide specific goods and services, regulate, enforce, and persuade; they also make policies that affect the making of decisions themselves. It is in this aspect of policy analysis that the traditional concerns of political science are most relevant. The assessment of regimes, constitutions, political party systems, legislative procedures, electoral laws, jury procedures, and other procedural policy alternatives is a major concern of applied political science, and was so before the "behavioral revolution." The general values that are discussed in normative political theory, as well as more specific values of interest to political science, are often most relevant to choices of this sort: Do these meta-policies provide for innovation, consensus, support, participation? Do they protect against tyranny, or encourage the development of character and personality? Changes in decision systems may also be assessed in material or economic terms; Dye's (1966) efforts to relate state welfare expenditures to party competition show, however, that this relation is not always easy to demonstrate.

Other meta-policies involve altering the structure of the organizations that supply goods and services, [and] that also make decisions: [The] creation of a Department of Energy, for example, involved a structural decision as well as a substantive one of allocating goods and services. Organizational change often makes available a new "bundle of products" that may be provided more or less efficiently, in greater or lesser quantity, under the new organizational form than under the old. Conceivably, such changes can be evaluated in terms of outputs and their costs.

Predictions of the consequences of changing political institutions or organizational forms seem considerably less certain than operations research on management problems. Abstract models have been developed for assessing constitutional arrangements in terms of preference satisfaction (Buchanan and Tullock, 1962), but such models seem somewhat removed from the concrete detail of specific choices among political institutions.

The seven types of governmental functions we have distinguished correspond roughly to types of policy related models. Our typology of government functions corresponds at some points to a typology advanced by Lowi (1972). Our categories (b) and (c), corresponding to the provisions of goods and services, correspond roughly to his "distributive" policies; (d) and (e) correspond to aspects of his "regulative" policies; and (f) and (g) [correspond] to his "constituent" policies (in which he includes "propaganda"). His category of "redistributive" policies relates primarily to our category (a) but also enters somewhat into the delivery of goods and services to particular groups, (b) and (c). There seems to be a lack of systematic

methods for dealing with redistribution. We may need to supplement analytic methods developed for the private sector to reflect specific concern for the redistributive function of government.

Feasibility

We now return from our discussion of models of the effects of policies to methods for estimating whether the policies will be enacted and implemented. We have dealt in part with feasibility of implementation . . . in connection with monitoring and enforcement. But for most of our analyses of feasibility, precise and systematic models are hard to find. Indeed, much of our discourse about feasibility is relatively inaccessible to the criticism of an expert community because of its links to highly specific situations that are of limited general and theoretical interest.

A major effort to predict the type of politics that will be associated with a policy proposal has been that of Lowi (1972). His approach "begins with the assumption that *policies determine politics*" (1972: 299). Even if this determination is subject to the influence of other variables and only approximate, insofar as it exists it can help us to chart our course toward feasibility. In proposing a systematic classification of policy processes, Lowi asserts that this procedure "converts ordinary case studies into chronicles and teaching instruments into data" (1972: 300). To the degree that this claim can be sustained, it may move case studies of policy analysis into the domain of analysis and criticism by experts in general terms.

The enterprise, however, is not an easy one. Much of the literature on feasibility and implementation consists of accounts relatively unilluminated by predictive theory. Other useful approaches consist of checklists or characteristic patterns for guidance in our quest for feasibility (Meltsner, 1972; Bardach, 1977). They cannot thus easily enter the scientific discourse that consists of verified general propositions. In one sense, it is a challenge to political science to find generalizations about feasibility; but the very fact that such generalizations, once found, would be known to opponents as well as proponents of a policy would lead to counterstrategies and perhaps change the character of the generalizations themselves. A "methodology" for feasibility will not be easy to find.

CONCLUSION

This discussion, ranging across various disciplines and fields, has been directed [toward] the formation of a domain of discourse concerning policy analysis, monitored and criticized by a community of experts. But in putting forward the ingredients of this domain, I have also tried to distinguish between those that are most fully developed and those least developed.

Methodology as we know it pertains best to models of production and distribution. These models have been developed in economics, operations research, and applied statistics. There are, nevertheless, numerous other ingredients of policy analysis that are essential to its conduct, whether [or not] they can be rendered as precise as economics. They include the assessment and reformulation of problems as presented; the development of consistent and operational ethical criteria for choice (for which welfare economics provides only one type); the choice among political institutions and organizations; and the assessment of feasibility. If the field of public policy analysis is to be directly applicable to concrete policy choices, then all these considerations must be combined. Just as in basic social research, quantitative methods must be combined with qualitative, participant-observer, and historical analyses, in the methodology of policy analysis we need to combine a variety of methods aimed at our substantive goal of successful analysis.

NOTES

1. A revised version of the paper published in *Society* as "Concepts and Methods of Policy Analysis"; an earlier version was presented at the annual meeting of the American Political Science Association, New York City, September 3, 1978. I am indebted to Robert P. Strauss for a helpful suggestion.
2. Non-teleological valuative criteria, independent of consequences, are also used in evaluating policies, but they do not require the same concern with methods or with models of causation.

REFERENCES

ALMOND, GABRIEL A., AND STEPHEN J. GENCO, 1977. "Clouds, Clocks, and the Study of Politics," *World Politics* 29, no. 4 (July 1977): 489–522.

BARDACH, EUGENE, 1977. *The Implementation Game* (Cambridge, MA: M.I.T. Press).

BATOR, FRANCES M., 1958. "The Anatomy of Market Failure," *Quarterly Journal of Economics* 72, no. 3 (August 1958): 351–79.

BECKER, GARY S., 1968. "Crime and Punishment: An Economic Approach," *Journal of Political Economy* 76, no. 2 (March/April 1968): 169–217.

BELTRAMI, EDWARD J., 1977. *Models for Public Systems Analysis* (New York: Academic Press).

BLOCH, PETER B., 1974. *Equality of Distribution of Police Services* (Washington, D.C.: Urban Institute).

BRAYBROOKE, DAVID, AND CHARLES E. LINDBLOM, 1963. *A Strategy of Decision* (New York: Free Press).

BUCHANAN, JAMES M., AND GORDON TULLOCK, 1962. *The Calculus of Consent* (Ann Arbor, MI: University of Michigan Press).

CAMPBELL, ANGUS, PHILIP E. CONVERSE, AND WILLARD L. RODGERS, 1976. *The Quality of American Life* (New York: Russell Sage).

CAMPBELL, DONALD T., AND JULIAN L. STANLEY, 1966. Experimental and Quasi-Experimental Designs for Research (Chicago: Rand McNally).

CARTER, GENEVIEVE W., 1966. "Measurement of Need," in Norman A. Polansky, ed., *Social Work Research* (Chicago: University of Chicago Press).

DYE, THOMAS R., 1966. *Politics, Economics, and the Public* (Englewood Cliffs, NJ: Prentice-Hall).

FOOTE, NELSON N., 1975. "Putting Sociologists to Work," in N. J. Demerath, III, Otto Larsen, and Karl F. Schuessler, eds., *Social Policy and Sociology* (New York: Academic Press).

FREIDSON, ELIOT, 1970. *Profession of Medicine* (New York: Dodd, Mead).

GATES, BRUCE L., 1975. "Needs-Based Budgeting: Considerations of Effectiveness, Efficiency, and Justice in the Delivery of Human Services." Paper presented to APSA annual meeting, San Francisco.

GILBERT, JOHN P., RICHARD J. LIGHT, AND FREDERICK MOSTELLER, 1975. "Assessing Social Innovations: An Empirical Basis for Policy," in A. A. Lumsdaine and C. A. Bennett, eds., *Evaluation and Experiment* (New York: Academic Press).

GOLDBERGER, ARTHUR S., AND OTIS DUDLEY DUNCAN, EDS., 1973. *Structural Equation Models in the Social Sciences* (New York: Seminar Press).

GUPTA, SHIV K., AND JOHN M. COZZOLINO, 1974. *Fundamentals of Operations Research for Management* (San Francisco: Holden-Day).

HARSANYI, JOHN, 1978. "Bayesian Decision Theory, Rule Utilitarianism, and Arrow's Impossibility Theorem." Center for Research in Management Science, University of California, Berkeley.

HIBBS, DOUGALS A., JR., 1977. "On Analyzing the Effects of Policy Interventions: Box-Jenkins and Box-Tiao vs. Structural Equation Models," in David R. Heise, ed., *Sociological Methodology 1977* (San Francisco: Wiley).

KAUFMAN, HERBERT, 1973. *Administrative Feedback: Monitoring Subordinates' Behavior* (Washington, D.C.: Brookings).

KEENEY, RALPH L., AND HOWARD RAIFFA, 1976. *Decisions with Multiple Objectives: Preferences and Value Tradeoffs* (New York: Wiley).

LAND, KENNETH C., 1975. "Social Indicator Models: An Overview," in Kenneth C. Land and Seymour Spilerman, eds., *Social Indicator Models* (New York: Russell Sage Foundation).

LEVINS, RICHARD, 1973. "Fundamental and Applied Research in Agriculture," *Science* 181, no. 4099 (August 10, 1973): 523–24.

LOWI, THEODORE J., 1972. "Four Systems of Policy, Politics, and Choice," *Public Administration Review* 32, no. 4 (July/August 1972): 298–310.

MACRAE, DUNCAN, JR., 1976a. *The Social Function of Social Science* (New Haven, CT: Yale University Press).

———. 1976b. "Technical Communities and Political Choice," *Minerva* 14, no. 2 (Summer 1976): 169–90.

———. 1978. "Introducing Undergraduates to Public Policy Analysis by the Case Method," *Policy Studies Journal* 6, no. 3 (Spring 1978): 353–59.

——— AND JAMES A. WILDE, 1979. *Policy Analysis for Public Decisions* (North Scituate, MA: Duxbury Press).

MCKINNEY, MICHAEL W., AND DUNCAN MACRAE, JR., 1978. "Survey Assessment of Monetary Demand for Publicly Provided Goods: Recreation." University of North Carolina at Chapel Hill, Institute for Research in Social Science, discussion paper.

MELTSNER, ARNOLD J., 1972. "Political Feasibility and Policy Analysis," *Public Administration Review* 32, no. 6 (November/December 1972): 859–67.

MILLER, JAMES C., III, AND BRUCE YANDLE, EDS., 1979. *Benefit-Cost Analysis of Social Regulation* (Washington, D.C.: American Enterprise Institute for Public Policy Research).

MORSE, PHILIP M., ED., 1967. *Operations Research for Public Systems* (Cambridge, MA: M.I.T. Press).

MUSGRAVE, RICHARD A., AND PEGGY B. MUSGRAVE, 1973. *Public Finance in Theory and Practice* (New York: McGraw-Hill).

NETER, JOHN, 1972. "How Accountants Save Money by Sampling," in Judith M. Tanur et al., *Statistics: A Guide to the Unknown* (San Francisco: Holden-Day).

NISKANEN, WILLIAM A., 1971. *Bureaucracy and Representative Government* (Chicago: Aldine).

ODUM, EUGENE P., ET AL., 1976. "Totality Indices for Evaluating Environmental Impact: A Test Case—Relative Impact of Highway Alternatives," in Marlan Blissett, ed., *Environmental Impact Assessment* (New York: Engineering Foundation).

PECHMAN, JOSEPH A., AND MICHAEL TIMPANE, EDS., 1975. *Work Incentives and Income Guarantees* (Washington, D.C.: Brookings).

QUADE, E. S., 1975. *Analysis for Public Decisions* (New York: American Elsevier).

RACKHAM, JOHN B., AND THEODORE REYNOLDS

SMITH, 1974. *Automated Mass Appraisal of Real Property* (Chicago: International Association of Assessing Officers).

RAIFFA, HOWARD, 1968. *Decision Analysis* (Reading, MA: Addison-Wesley).

RICHARDSON, LEWIS F., 1939. "Generalized Foreign Politics," *British Journal of Psychology:* Monograph Supplements, vol. 23.

RIECKEN, HENRY W., AND ROBERT F. BORUCH, EDS., 1974. *Social Experimentation* (New York: Academic Press).

ROSSI, PETER H., AND KATHERINE C. LYALL, 1976. *Reforming Public Welfare* (New York: Russell Sage Foundation).

STOKEY, EDITH, AND RICHARD ZECKHAUSER, 1978. *A Primer for Policy Analysis* (New York: Norton).

VAUPEL, JAMES W., 1976. "Muddling

Through Analytically," in Willis D. Hawley and David Rogers, eds., *Improving the Quality of Urban Management* (Beverly Hills, CA: Sage Publications).

WEBB, KENNETH, AND HARRY P. HATRY, 1973. *Obtaining Citizen Feedback* (Washington, D.C.: Urban Institute).

WEINSTEIN, MILTON C., AND WILLIAM B. STASON, 1976. *Hypertension: A Policy Perspective* (Cambridge, MA: Harvard University Press).

WHITAKER, GORDON P., 1978. "Citizen Participation in the Delivery of Human Services." Presented at the conference on Participation and Politics, Tutzing, Federal Republic of Germany.

ZIMAN, JOHN, 1968. *Public Knowledge* (London and New York: Cambridge University Press).

Dennis A. Rondinelli

Urban Planning as Policy Analysis: Management of Urban Change

The American planning profession is undergoing a traumatic transformation. Despite the expenditure of millions of dollars over the past fifty years to produce a myriad of master plans for urban development, few cities in the United States have been developed or substantially redeveloped in accordance with a comprehensive plan. Large-scale policies designed to ameliorate major urban social and economic problems have been either ineffective or perverse (Banfield, 1970). Attempts to require comprehensive planning in federal housing, transportation, regional economic development, antipoverty, and community development programs have not succeeded. Academic curricula dedi-

Reprinted by permission of the author and *Journal of the American Institute of Planners*, vol. 39, no. 1, January 1973, pp. 13–22.

cated to teaching plan making are questioned and repudiated by a sizable element of the profession and its critics. The "noiseless secession from the comprehensive plan" (Perin, 1967) is forcing planners to redefine their goals and objectives and to search for new roles and functions. Alternatives range from national environmental and physical planning, through a wide variety of social, economic, and technical planning specialities, to neighborhood and minority group advocacy. Concepts, styles, and methodologies run an equally broad gamut (Bolan, 1967).

A consensus is developing within one wing of the profession that planners can perform an important role as urban policy analysts. With the increasing complexity of urban decision making, political leaders and urban administrators are demanding from planners pragmatic assistance with policy formulation and implementation. The cities "want advice on how to choose the right goals and the most effective policies for every function of government," claims Gans (1970:224), "and similar advice is being sought by all institutions and groups who seek to frame their goals and policies in a deliberate manner from federal agencies, civic groups, and protest organizations to corporations and semi-public institutions."

Underlying the pressures to transform planning into a policy science is a widely held assumption that planners can bring order and rationality to urban policy-making. Friedmann (1969:316) challenges the profession "to undertake the courageous and systematic evaluation of societal performance and to identify the strategic points for massive innovation in the guidance of the system." Bolan (1969) argues that planners, operating within the behavioral parameters of the community decisionmaking process, must adapt their functions to the procedural steps of urban policymaking: structuring and defining proposals, identifying the properties of alternatives, structuring the decision field, and engaging in and implementing decisions. New demands are made on the form and content of planning education. New missions will be required, predicts Altshuler (1970:186), "the purpose of which will be to provide men who have emerged as potentially important decision makers with some broad planning perspectives and a capacity for systematic analysis of policy options."

Unlike traditional comprehensive planning that sought to devise a long-range ideal end state for urban development in the framework of a synoptic master plan, policy planning seeks to deal with pressing problems of urban life by influencing the substance and direction of on-going public decisionmaking. Policy planning is action oriented. It attempts intervention rather

than mere prescription. Policy planning is concerned with making an incremental impact on national as well as local policies affecting the quality of urban services and the rate and distribution of urban growth. It involves the organization and evaluation of the programs as well as policy design. Urban policy planning is the management of urban change.

While much has been written about the need for innovation and experimentation to overcome critical urban problems, neither planners nor public administrators have, as Hyman (1971:365) notes, answered the question of who "is competent to plan and direct the revisions necessitated. . . . There appears to be little understanding that a nation in flux requires administrators trained to deal with change." Little evidence exists that planning curricula impart the skills and knowledge needed to analyze policy alternatives, provide training and experience in techniques of intervention in the policymaking process, or generate relevant research into mechanisms of policy formulation and implementation. Few planning education programs focus on the nature of policy innovation, mobilization and utilization of policy-influencing resources, or the management of political conflict necessary to achieve social change in urban areas.

Recent evaluations of the past decade's experience with federal urban and regional development policy not only add empirical evidence to theoretical criticisms of traditional comprehensive planning but may also assist planners to avoid the pitfalls of venturing into the uncharted field of policy planning. The New Frontier—Great Society decade produced the largest quantity of policies designed to ameliorate urban and regional development problems since the New Deal. But careful evaluations of the processes by which these policies emerged reveals the complex interrelationships and narrow parameters within which policy planners must work. This paper aims to characterize, through a series of empirically supported propositions, the nature of urban policymaking and to outline implications for educating planners in analyzing, intervening, and managing policy for urban change.

CHARACTERISTICS OF URBAN POLICYMAKING

Proposition 1

Policymaking is an inherently political rather than a deliberative process. Policy is made through sociopolitical processes—resolution of conflict among groups with divergent interests—rather than by intellectual and deliberative choice (Banfield, 1961; Bauer, Pool and Dexter, 1963; Bauer and Gergen, 1968; Braybrooke and Lindblom, 1963). As a process of political interaction, policy evolves from a process of interorganizational conflict over a wide variety of values, criteria, ends, means, and interpretations of rationality. It is a generator as well as a product of conflict, evolving through a process of "social weighting" that rarely can be comprehensively planned or centrally guided. Groups seeking particular goals or allocations of resources induce response from other groups that stand to gain or lose from enactment of the policy proposals. Through political interaction and social adjustment, the decisions and priorities of the participants in policymaking are ratified, altered, compromised, or rejected (Lindblom, 1959). In some cases, as Bachrach and Baratz (1970) note in their study of antipoverty programs in Baltimore, policies evolve from a history of actions that restrict the choice of alternatives and the margin of acceptable change. Policy can be made through "nondecisions" by the unchallenged drift of events or by deliberate attempts to repress conflict. It may evolve indirectly, generated by unanticipated results of previous decisions. Indeed, policymaking often transcends deliberative problem solving; as a process of political interaction, it is more complex and distinctly different from individual decision making.

Proposition 2

Policy is formulated and implemented through highly fragmented and multinucleated structures of semi-independent groups and organizations in both the public and private sectors and through a complex system of formal and informal delegation of responsibility and control. If Great Society policymaking taught one lesson, it is the difficulty of controlling either the evolution of policy proposals through legislative enactment or the implementation of policy through administrative management. Power resources are fragmented and widely dispersed. Points of leverage are multiple and decentralized. Policy is formulated and implemented by a multitude of organizations with highly specialized personnel, information, technical expertise, analytical skills, and influence resources. Each group pursues its own perceptions of its interests and its own conception of the public interest. A potentially large number of them gain veto or delaying power over enactment of urban policy proposals and carve out domains or spheres of influence over program implementation. The history of the Model Cities program, antipoverty legislation (Donovan, 1967), the Area Redevelopment Act (Levitan, 1964), the Public Works and Economic Development Act (Rondinelli, 1969), the Appalachian Regional Development program, and Federal Highway assistance (Morehouse, 1969; Levin and Abend, 1971) document the complex interaction of groups at all stages of policy formulation.

Once enacted, policies must be implemented through a highly decentralized governmental structure (Grodzins, 1966). Discretionary authority, regulatory control, allocational responsibility, and approval powers are fragmented through systems of interagency, intergovernmental, and intersectoral delegation. At the federal level, for example, when the Economic Development Administration provides business loans to private firms in economically depressed areas, it must submit the applications to the Small Business Administration for clearance. SBA reviews the proposals and performs credit investigations and market feasibility studies. EDA has little control over the time SBA takes to review the applications, the criteria it uses in the review process, or the people making decisions. EDA supplementary technical assistance programs, moreover, are related to programs administered by other federal agencies. Congress decreed in EDA's enabling legislation that grant proposals dealing with specialized aspects of area development must be reviewed by the Department of Labor's Manpower Training Development Office, the Community Facilities Administration of the Department of Housing and Urban Development, the Farmer's Home Administration in the Department of Agriculture, health facilities program agencies within the Department of Health, Education and Welfare, and the Bureau of the Budget.

Regional development policy is implemented through a quagmire of intergovernmental hybrids. In the Appalachian Regional Commission, for instance, administrative power is shared among a federal cochairman appointed by the President, the governors of twelve states, and an executive staff responsible to the commission as a corporate body. Substantial influence over decisions is delegated to state government agencies and semi-independent local development district corporations. In Pennsylvania, responsibility for implementation of Appalachian Regional Development Policy is delegated by the Governor to the Commonwealth's Department of Commerce, which redelegates planning, clearance, allocation, and review powers to more than a dozen specialized agencies, departments,

and commissions over which the Department of Commerce exercises little direct control (Commonwealth of Pennsylvania, 1967).

The reticulated pattern of delegation and fragmentation of power extends beyond government into the private sector. The policy boards of the Model Cities, antipoverty, and Economic Development District agencies are composed of local special interest groups, neighborhood target groups, business and labor representatives, civic and service organizations, as well as local, state, and other government officials. In the traditional sense of administrative responsibility, federal departments providing urban development assistance cannot be held accountable for the outcomes of policies they are assigned to implement. They must rely increasingly on state and local government officials to define local problems, formulate appropriate policy responses, and interpret and implement federal guidelines. Administrative accountability in the Model Cities program, for instance, is shifted almost entirely by formal contracts from HUD to local government agencies. "We are spelling out in clear terms," notes Secretary Romney, "that local government officials must exercise final control and responsibility for the content and administration of a local Model Cities program" (U.S. Congress, 1969). Lines of power and responsibility are intertwined by interdepartmental agreements, delegate agency mandates, and intergovernmental contracts, most of which are nearly impossible to enforce formally and have little legal standing. Enforcement comes through informal pressure and manipulation. The ability to guide, let alone comprehensively plan, national development policies, is highly complicated and narrowly constrained by delegation.

Proposition 3

Policy problems are complex, amorphous, and difficult to define concisely. Urban policy planning is limited, moreover, by political parameters on defining the problem. Problems become the focus of policymaking to the extent that specialized groups and coalitions can bring public attention to them. Few issues are defined in the same way by all who participate in the policymaking process. Each interested organization places a different emphasis on a different component of the problem or defines the whole problem in terms of a part. Interest groups proposing legislation to assist urban depressed areas in the 1960s, for example, saw the problem as one of high unemployment, declining physical plant, changing technological and economic advantages, and obsolete infrastructures in industrial communities. A strong coalition of southern congressmen, who significantly amended the original policy proposals, viewed the problem as underemployment, inability of rural areas to mobilize resources, outmigration of unskilled labor from rural areas to urban centers, and failure to exploit natural resources in agricultural areas. The Appalachian governors saw it as multistate competitive disadvantage. The Department of Labor defined it in terms of the need for massive manpower retraining. Social welfare groups were sure that the crux of the problem was racial injustice, discrimination, lack of educational opportunities, and the need for both "black capitalism" and economic development of center city ghettos. Each group mobilized support for its own definition of the problem (Rondinelli, 1969).

Proposition 4

Problem perception, policy response and program implementation are characterized by long lead and lag times. Comprehensive analysis and coordinated control of policy implementation are constrained further by the long lag and lead times inherent in political interaction. Lags develop between emergence of a problem and public recognition. Acknowledgement of a problem's

existence does not assure allocations of public resources for its solution. A lag exists until proponents can mobilize a coalition of support, resolve conflicts with opponents, and gain consensus on appropriate policy responses. The ARA, Public Works and Economic Development, and Appalachian Regional Development acts of the 1960s were policies designed to ameliorate problems of urban and regional economic decline that first arose prior to the 1930s depression. Lags exist, moreover, between the proposal of policies and their legislative enactment. The initial proposal for creation of ARA was made in late 1954; the bill creating the agency was not signed into law until 1961. Although proposals for an Appalachian Regional assistance program first appeared in the mid-1950s, the Appalachian Regional Commission was not created until a decade later. Many components of the Economic Opportunity Act of 1964 were initially introduced during the New Deal. Furthermore, long leads occur between organization of the programs and identification and evaluation of their effects. Thirty years were required to recognize publicly the failure of New Deal social welfare policies. Conditions under which programs were formulated change during both lag and lead times. Perceptions and definitions of the problem, personalities, and motivations of participants change; the strengths of demands and support of sponsoring and opposing interest groups shift. The problem itself may be partially or totally displaced from public attention.

Proposition 5

Systematic analysis and evaluation are complicated by the difficulty of determining real policy output. Dror's (1968) distinction between the nominal output of a program (reports, projects, rules, trained manpower, and so forth) and the real output (substantive effects of policies on conditions they were designed to correct) has significance for policy planning. The experience of ARA, EDA, OEO, and Model Cities is one of extreme difficulty in identifying and measuring real policy outputs. By the end of its first year in operation, EDA found it had no way of proving that its activities were responsible for bettering conditions in areas where unemployment rates fell below 6 percent, the termination level for EDA assistance (Rauner, 1967). In order to justify its program to Congress and the Bureau of the Budget, EDA was forced to adopt a "worst first" strategy. Investments were concentrated in areas with the highest rates of unemployment and lowest family incomes—those least likely to be affected by national economic growth. Only in this way could EDA isolate the influence of its program on regional recovery. But the "worst first" strategy raised claims by other federal agencies that EDA's policies obstructed their own plans. The co-chairman of the Appalachian Regional Commission testified to Congress on the difficulties encountered by EDA's plans for development of the most hopeless regions, while the Appalachian Commission was attempting to concentrate resources in the areas of highest growth potential (U.S. Congress, 1967b). Systematic analysis and quantitative evaluation yielded to political and social subjectivity: "Ultimately a value judgment is required to decide whether one unemployed person in Lowville, New York, is equivalent to one low-income family in Wolf, Kentucky," argues a former EDA assistant administrator. "In the same view, determining how much of EDA's program appropriation should be assigned to each of its seven program sets is properly a matter of administrative judgment. No mathematical computations or maximizing formula can solve this problem" (Rauner, 1967).

Proposition 6

Facts, information, and statistics used to analyze policy alternatives are subjectively interpreted through preconceived, specialized

interests. Even if "objective" indicators of "optimal" courses of action could be determined, the data would not be treated objectively. Not only the substance of policy but facts and statistics also become the subject of debate and conflict. Quantitative data are rarely interpreted by participants independently of their role perceptions, subjective expectations, preconceived interests, and ideological predispositions. Congressional hearings on regional economic development legislation reveal that neither supporting nor opposing policy analysts allowed facts to complicate the preconceived logic of their arguments. Experts provided congressional committees with analyses yielding diametrically opposed conclusions. Some used the same set of data to support different arguments before different committees. Provisions to prohibit industrial piracy-subsidies that would induce industries to move from one urban area to another—were written into ARA, EDA, and Appalachian bills largely because of the "evidence" presented by national business lobbies that opposed passage of the legislation. "Is it not ironic that the same witnesses who tell us that this legislation is bad because it will be so effective that it will lead to pirating are invariably the same witnesses who tell us that this legislation is bad because it will not help the depressed areas at all?" asked Pennsylvania Representative William W. Scranton at a congressional hearing on the EDA bill. "These arguments, frequently offered by the same witnesses, are not even consistent" (*Congressional Record*, 1961). A favorite tactic of congressional committee members themselves is to invite policy analysts and experts who will present evidence favorable to their own predispositions toward a policy proposal.

Proposition 7

The number of possible alternatives for ameliorating policy problems is indeterminate. Alternatives evolve through processes of political interaction. Traditional planning theory requires systematic evaluation of alternatives in order to make optimal choices. Gans (1970:223) defines planning as a "method and process of decision making that proposes or identifies goals (or ends) and determines effective policies (or means)—those which can be shown analytically to achieve the goals while minimizing undesirable financial, social, and other consequences." Yet, in reality, the choice of alternative means is dictated by the possibilities evolving from political interaction rather than from deliberative, a priori, design and analysis. Alternatives are gradually invented out of compromises among participants with different perceptions of the problem, interests, and criteria. Acceptance of one alternative—optimal to one set of interests—need not result in the rejection of others. Mutual adjustments result in creation of new courses of action from combinations of existing alternatives (Diesing, 1955). A priori delineation and evaluation of alternatives is complicated, moreover, by the fact that groups participating in policymaking rarely perceive their goals clearly or define their objectives explicitly. Goal formation is often situational, that is, dependent on expectations of what can actually be achieved under given political conditions at a particular point in time. As expectations change, goals are altered. In most cases, the ends means chain of which Gans and others speak is not a chain at all. Goals may be instrumental rather than terminal. Ends become means: Attainment of one set of goals may merely pave the way to pursue another set. Thus the number of possible permutations and combinations of feasible or potentially feasible alternatives can be enormous. The alternatives given priority depend in part on the groups drawn into policymaking conflicts and on the strength of their influence.

Evaluation and choice are twice confounded by substantive and political spillovers. Initial policy conflicts often expand into intricate, extended networks of secondary conflicts over values, ideology, and socioeconomic and political costs and benefits. Spillovers occur from and to related policy problems. Participants in policymaking often come into conflict over questions that have little to do with the substantive content of the problem. They become enmeshed in arguments involving personal political ambitions, personal and organizational prestige, control over funds and other resources, and philosophical doctrine.

Finally, political parameters may make consideration of a wide range of alternatives impossible, limiting evaluation to a restricted set or to only one. The running conflict over delegation of functions and authority in the ARA, EDA, and OEO programs strongly reflected the power of the Budget Bureau to restrict consideration of other forms of organization. Senator Paul Douglas and his associates on the Banking and Currency Committee, for insance, favored creation of independent regional development assistance agencies capable of performing their own planning and operational functions. But the Budget Bureau and some specialized federal departments insisted on delegation of ARA and EDA powers. The intensity with which the Bureau of the Budget fought for delegation foreclosed the possibility of dispassionate, objective analysis and choice of the optimal alternative. "I originally favored a single agency operation," Douglas recalls, "but I was overruled by the bureaucracy downtown in the Budget Bureau, and my head was so bloody after that encounter that I gave up" (U.S. Congress, 1965:107).

Proposition 8

Each participant in policy formulation and implementation has limited evaluation capacity. Even when the number of alternatives is large, the ability of any participant in policymaking to evaluate them comprehensively is limited. In reality, as Simon (1958) notes, decision making often reduces to a choice between two alternatives: "doing X" or "not doing X." "Not doing X" may represent the whole set of possible alternatives that decision makers lack the resources, interest, information, or power to evaluate. These courses of action may be considered vaguely in terms of the opportunity costs of rejecting "doing X" or considered serially and incrementally only if alternative "doing X" is rejected or if it is accepted and later proves to be ineffective (Braybrooke and Lindblom, 1963). But if "doing X" is considered satisfactory to the participating interest groups, alternatives may never be explicated.

The limited evaluation capacity of one congressional committee working on economic development legislation is not untypical. When a bill to amend the Appalachian Regional Development Act and Title V of EDA legislation was introduced in 1967, minority party members of the House Public Works Committee strongly opposed further expansion of these programs. They were at a loss, however, to offer positive alternatives to the amendments. They noted:

> When faced with the monumental task of searching and collecting information and data, visiting representative areas of the country to determine their problems and needs, conferring with state and local officials and business leaders in an effort to develop a really workable and effective program, we soon came to the conclusion that our limited, though capable, staff could not even make a dent in this work load in the time available to us. Reluctantly, we were forced to abandon, at this time, the development of a constructive alternative. (U.S. Congress, 1967a: 90).

Proposition 9

Policy planning is done under conditions of uncertainty, risk, incomplete information, and partial ignorance of the situation in which problems evolve, the resources of interested groups, and the effectiveness of proposed solutions. Professional planners and public administrators have done little better than legislators in comprehensive policy analysis. Studies of the Federal Aid Highway Act of 1962— a law requiring that assisted highway projects be the result of a "cooperative, comprehensive and continuing planning process"—indicate that the Bureau of Public Roads lacks the political power to impose comprehensive analysis requirements (Morehouse, 1969). State, local, and metropolitan planning agencies lack the information, political resources, and analytical ability to comply with areawide planning provisions of later transportation programs (Levin and Abend, 1971). Greer (1965) suggests that local planners often found themselves in the same situation with the Federal Workable Program for 701 Assistance.

The Area Redevelopment Administration's attempts to implement congressional requirements for submission of overall economic development programs (OEDP's) by depressed areas as a condition for financial support were obstructed by uncertainty over congressional standards, lack of competent analysts at the local level, and by political pressures from congressmen themselves to speed up the process of aid distribution. ARA was not able to specify the requirements for comprehensive planning or even to evaluate the OEDP's that were submitted. Most local planning groups, therefore, simply filed superficial reports filled with masses of badly analyzed data to satisfy minimum standards. ARA could not disqualify localities for not performing a task that it could neither define nor evaluate. "The agency resolved this dilemma," reports Levitan (1964:200), "by accepting each OEDP submitted by communities as a token of good faith and an indication that the community desired to plan its economic future on a sound basis."

Attempts to formulate Model Cities guidelines to allow maximum freedom for analysis and planning by localities failed miserably. "They did no good," one former Model Cities Administration deputy director complained. "Most of the cities didn't understand the process but were willing to play our silly little game for money. What was meant as a challenge, a prod, was interpreted as a regulation, a cage. Regulations you can relate to; freedom is something else" (Jorden, 1971:46).

IMPLICATIONS FOR PLANNING

Policy analysis requires drastic modifications in the concept of and approaches to planning and fundamental changes in planning education. Research, analytical techniques, and skills required for traditional plan making are not adequate for policy planning. Planners trained as policy analysts must develop a view of the planning process that is substantially different from that of comprehensive planning. While existing planning curricula focus heavily on substantive urban problems, few provide the knowledge and skills required for effective intervention in the policymaking process. Conflict resolution and the management of social change are intrinsic to policy planning.

A Political Interaction View of Policy Planning

Comprehensive planning was prescriptive—seeking to design an ideal end state for urban development—rather than interventional. The plan-making approach to education stressed objective, synoptic analysis, the search for endless numbers of alternatives and a combination of best choices into a long-range master plan for urban growth. Details of "routine" decisions were relegated to politicans and administrators. But grand schemes, long-range comprehensive plans, and systematic policy scenarios were ignored conveniently in a political system that renders rational, comprehensive evaluation of urban policies highly improbable and synoptic policy changes nearly impossible.

Analysis, to be of value to policymakers, must isolate components of urban problems and reduce them to calculable proportions. Policy planners must indicate how resources can be mobilized and focused on remediable aspects of problems in such a way that urban areas can be moved marginally, through successive approximation, away from unsatisfactory social and economic conditions. Policy planners must delineate those alternatives upon which a variety of interests can act jointly and seek ways of binding together some of the disparate participants in policymaking to promote mutual cooperation along lines of specialization and common interest. An integral part of policy analysis is the search for ways of reconciling differences among specialized interests, where possible, and evaluating compromise positions, bases for mutual exchange, incentives, and instruments of manipulation and persuasion.

A political interaction view of policy planning defines one of the planner's roles as that of identifying "strategic factors." Strategic factors, Barnard (1938:203) notes, are those "whose control, in the right form, at the right place and time, will establish a new system or set of conditions which meet the purpose." Policy planning must search out limiting factors inhibiting desired social change and delineate the types of complementary factors needed to enact and implement appropriate programs or controls. Given the complexity of the pluralistic political system in which he must operate, the policy planner may focus on calculating the opportunity costs of pursuing alternative courses of action or of taking no deliberate action. By explicating the losses incurred by urban interests from the lag between socio-economic change and the public response to that change, strong incentives might be provided for the formation of effective coalitions to reduce their losses from inaction, delayed action, or inappropriate action. Policy planning is adjunctive—a process of facilitating adjustment among competing interests within a multinucleated governmental structure to encourage policy outputs of marginally better quality measured against the status quo. (Rondinelli, 1971).

Research Needs and Planning Skills

The characteristics of public policymaking have been explored by the social sciences in recent years, but little thought has been given to manipulating processes of political interaction in order to plan urban policy more effectively. Nor have the skills and knowledge needed by policy planners been identified. Research is scarce on the relationships among the policymaking structures, the characteristics of the policymaking process, and techniques of interaction and knowledge needed to manage urban change and to design strategies of intervention. The attempt here is to raise research questions and to suggest some categories of skills and knowledge needed by policy planners to intervene effectively in urban policymaking (See Figure 1).

Adaptive adjustments among groups seeking to influence policy through tacit interaction (Schelling, 1960; Lindblom, 1965) strongly characterized the evolution of urban development legislation during the 1960s (Rondinelli, 1969; Cleaveland, 1969). Indirect adjustments often take place without direct communication among policymaking participants, either because they cannot or do not want to communicate with each other. Each participant, instead, takes an action that he believes will avoid or resolve conflict based on expectations of what other participants will do or what they have done in the past.

To some degree, it is based on intuitive rapport, "second guessing," or mutual recognition of a desirable goal. In other cases, it arises from uncoordinated reactions to the same basic conditions or perceptions of the same problem.

How do these techniques influence the content of policy proposals? How do they affect the structure and dynamics of conflict resolution? Are adaptive, noncentrally coordinated processes of interaction more successful in implementing policy proposals than techniques of direct coordination? In what types of issues are they least effective? Can groups be induced to tacit agreement by third parties? A planner attempting to use adaptive adjustment techniques to guide urban policies through formulation and implementation must understand processes of small group decision making, organizational behavior, intragroup dynamics, and interorganizational interaction.

The pluralistic, multinucleated structure of policymaking involves vast networks of specialized groups linked together in intertwining "decision chains" (Wheaton, 1964). Through decision chains, coalitions create and participate in spheres of influence over specific types of issues and programs. To enact a policy or reform a program often requires that multiple consent be obtained from the myriad of interests composing an organized sphere of influence. Indeed, failure to seek approval from the clientele of an established program, as proponents of a Federal Department of Urban Affairs discovered in the early 1960s (Parris, 1969), may activate a coalition of opposition to plans for policy change. What are the techniques of obtaining mutual consent? How do the techniques of obtaining formal, legal consent ("review and approval," "sign-off consent") differ from those of obtaining informal, political consent (logrolling, reciprocity, vote-swapping). What trade-offs, exchanges, and spillovers arise

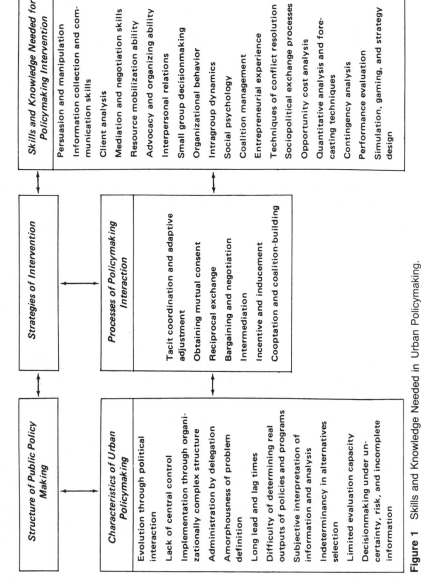

Figure 1 Skills and Knowledge Needed in Urban Policymaking.

Structure of Public Policy Making	Strategies of Intervention	Skills and Knowledge Needed for Policymaking Intervention
Characteristics of Urban Policymaking	**Processes of Policymaking Interaction**	Persuasion and manipulation
Evolution through political interaction	Tacit coordination and adaptive adjustment	Information collection and communication skills
Lack of central control	Obtaining mutual consent	Client analysis
Implementation through organizationally complex structure	Reciprocal exchange	Mediation and negotiation skills
Administration by delegation	Bargaining and negotiation	Resource mobilization ability
Amorphousness of problem definition	Intermediation	Advocacy and organizing ability
Long lead and lag times	Incentive and inducement	Interpersonal relations
Difficulty of determining real outputs of policies and programs	Cooptation and coalition-building	Small group decisionmaking
Subjective interpretation of information and analysis		Organizational behavior
Indeterminancy in alternatives selection		Intragroup dynamics
Limited evaluation capacity		Social psychology
Decisionmaking under uncertainty, risk, and incomplete information		Coalition management
		Entrepreneurial experience
		Techniques of conflict resolution
		Sociopolitical exchange processes
		Opportunity cost analysis
		Quantitative analysis and forecasting techniques
		Contingency analysis
		Performance evaluation
		Simulation, gaming, and strategy design

in the act of obtaining mutual consent? Can some links in the decision chain be avoided or neglected in certain types of urban issues without jeopardizing the policy outcome? Can the process be standardized for particular issues to reduce lag and lead times in policy ratification and implementation? To deal effectively with decision chains in urban policymaking, planners must possess persuasion and manipulation skills, experience with client analysis, and information and communication skills. Knowledge of general principles of social psychology can assist in designing tactics of influence and manipulation (Mehrabian, 1970).

Policy conflicts are settled through processes of reciprocal exchange, negotiation, intermediation, and bargaining. The complex delegate agency arrangements characterizing urban policy implementation mandate the use of exchange-bargaining techniques among proponents and opponents of urban assistance policies. Failure to negotiate settlements among disparate groups—federal departments, state and local government agencies, clientele and target groups, and political factions—has led to serious complications in implementing Model Cities programs. What are the channels of exchange and bargaining among participants in urban policymaking? What groups and organizations serve as intermediaries in urban policy conflicts? What functions can the planning agency play in facilitating processes of exchange and negotiation? Which inputs into the bargaining processes influence policy decisions? Do quantitative analysis, evaluation of data, and trend projection play an important role in influencing the environment for negotiation and bargaining? What are the terms of and parameters on bargaining and exchange among opposing groups in urban policy formulation? Mediation and negotiation skills become important for planners involved in bargaining-exchange relationships in urban pol-

icymaking. Knowledge of organizational behavior, processes of conflict resolution, sociopolitical exchange processes, and strategy design is imperative. The ability to simulate and design games of strategy involving urban issues could provide a means of assisting political and administrative decision makers to test alternative proposals and political tactics.

Coalition building is the essence of conflict management. Ultimately, urban policies evolve from compromises among groups with sufficient power and resources to persuade other participants of the desirability of a particular course of action. Incentives and inducements change both the parameters of decision making and the costs and benefits of policy alternatives to interested groups. What are the techniques of coaliton building? How are interested groups brought together? How can initial policy proposals be designed so as to control the scope of conflict and attract allies into a coalition strong enough to ensure enactment and effective implementation? How can conflict that is being repressed by groups attempting to prevent an issue from being discussed be socialized to ensure that the issues become the focus of public attention? Alternatively, how can issues that are being socialized to the point that effective coalition formation becomes impossible be repressed? What are the costs of building urban policy coalitions? What are the dynamics of interaction among coalition participants? Which techniques are necessary to maintain a coalition of support for urban policies? The use of incentives requires enterpreneurial experience. Skills in organizational leadership, advocacy, resource mobilization, and coalition management are essential to this aspect of policy planning.

Intervention in policymaking is a continuous process of strategic analysis. Forecasting, quantitative measurement, contingency planning, and identification of opportunity costs are integral parts of strategy design. Monitoring and performance evaluation skills are as necessary for effective policy planning as substantive expertise in the urban problem issues. If planners are serious about redirecting the profession's energies toward policy planning, curricula must be redesigned to provide the skills, knowledge, and experience necessary for effective management of urban change.

SELECTED REFERENCES

ALTSHULER. A. (1970). "Decision-making and the Trend Toward Pluralistic Planning" in E. Erber, ed., *Urban Planning in Transition.* New York: Grossman, pp. 183–86.

BACHRACH, P., AND M. S. BARATZ (1970). *Power and Poverty.* New York: Oxford University Press.

BANFIELD, E. C. (1961). *Political Influence.* New York: The Free Press.

_____ (1970). *The Unheavenly City.* Boston: Little, Brown.

BARNARD, C. I. (1938). *The Functions of the Executive.* Cambridge, Mass.: Harvard University Press.

BAUER, R. I. DE SOLA POOL, AND L. DEXTER (1963). *American Business and Public Policy.* New York: Atherton.

BAUER, R., AND K. GERGEN (1968). *The Study of Policy Formation.* New York: The Free Press.

BOLAN, R. S. (1967). "Emerging Views of Planning," *Journal of the American Institute of Planners 33* (July): 233–45.

_____ (1969). "Community Decision Behavior: The Culture of Planning," *Journal of the American Institute of Planners 35* (Sept.): 301–10.

BRAYBROOKE, D., AND C. E. LINDBLOM (1963). *A Strategy of Decision: Policy Evaluation as a Social Process.* New York: The Free Press.

CLEAVELAND, F. (1969). *Congress and Urban Problems.* Washington, D.C.: The Brookings Institution.

Commonwealth of Pennsylvania, Governor's Office of Administration (1967). Executive Directive no. 18. "The Administration of the Appalachian Program in Pennsylvania," mimeographed, April 13.

Congressional Record (1961).   107, no. 4 (March 29): 521.

DIESING, P. (1955). "Noneconomic Decision Making," *Ethics* 46 (Oct): 18–35.

DONOVAN, J. C. (1967). *The Politics of Poverty.* New York: Western Publishing Company.

DROR, Y. (1968). *Public Policy Making Re-examined.* San Francisco: Chandler.

FRIEDMANN, J. (1969). "Notes on Societal Action," *Journal of the American Institute of Planners* 35 (Sept.): 311–18.

GANS, H. J. (1970). "From Urbanism to Policy Planning," *Journal of the American Institute of Planners* 36 (July):223–26.

GREER, S. (1965). *Urban Renewal and American Cities.* New York: Bobbs-Merrill.

GRODZINS, M. (1966). *The American System.* Chicago: Rand McNally.

HYMAN, A. A. (1971). "The Management of Planned Change," in S. E. Seashore and R. J. McNeill, eds., *Management of the Urban Crisis.* New York: The Free Press.

JORDAN, FRED (1971). "The Confessions of a Former Grantsman," *City* (Summer): 45–47.

LEVIN, M., AND N. ABEND (1971). *Bureaucrats in Collision: Case Studies in Area Transportation.* Cambridge, Mass.: The MIT Press.

LEVITAN, S. (1964). *Federal Aid to Depressed Areas.* Baltimore, Md.: Johns Hopkins Press.

LINDBLOM, C. E. (1959). "The Handling of Policy Norms in Analysis," in M. Abromovitz et al., *Allocation of Economic Resources.* Stanford, Calif.: Stanford University Press.

_____ (1965). *The Intelligence of Democracy.* New York: The Free Press.

MEHRABIAN. A. (1970). *Tactics of Social Influence.* Englewood Cliffs, N.J.: Prentice-Hall.

MOREHOUSE, T. A. (1969). "The 1962 Highway Act: A Study in Artful Interpretation," *Journal of the American Institute of Planners* 35 (May): 160–68.

PARRIS, J. H. (1969). "Congress Rejects the President's Urban Department," in F. Cleaveland, ed., *Congress and Urban Problems.* Washington, D.C.: The Brookings Institution.

PERIN, C. (1967). "The Noiseless Secession from the Comprehensive Plan," *Journal of the American Institute of Planners* 33 (Sept.): 336–46.

RAUNER, R. M. (1967). "Regional and Area Planning: The EDA Experience." Washington, D.C.: U.S. Department of Commerce, Economic Development Administration, mimeographed.

RONDINELLI, D. A. (1969). "Policy Analysis and Planning Administration: Toward Adjunctive Planning for Regional Development," Ph.D. dissertation, Cornell University.

———— (1971). "Adjunctive Planning and Urban Development Policy," *Urban Affairs Quarterly* 7 (Sept.): 13–39.

SCHELLING, T. C. (1960). *The Strategy of Conflict*. New York: Oxford University Press.

SIMON, H. A. (1958). "The Role of Expectations in an Adaptive or Behavioristic Model," in M. J. Bowman, ed., *Expectations, Uncertainty and Business Behavior*. New York: Social Science Research Council.

U.S. CONGRESS (1965). Senate Committee on Banking and Currency. "Public Works and Economic Development." Hearings on S. 1648, 89th Congress, 1st Session (May).

U.S. CONGRESS (1967a). House Committee on Public Works. "Appalachian Regional Development Act, Amendments of 1967 and Amendments to the Public Works and Economic Development Act of 1965." Hearings, 90th Congress, 1st Session.

U.S. CONGRESS (1967b). Senate Committee on Government Operations. "Creative Federalism." Hearings, 89th Congress, 2nd Session.

U.S. CONGRESS (1969). Testimony of George Romney. Senate Committee on Banking and Currency. "Progress in the Model Cities Program." Hearings before the Subcommittee on Housing and Urban Affairs, 91st Congress, 1st Session.

WHEATON, W. L. C. (1964). "Public and Private Agents of Change in Urban Expansion," in M. Webber et al., *Explorations into Urban Structure*. Philadelphia: University of Pennsylvania Press.

Paul Sabatier and Daniel Mazmanian

The Conditions of Effective Implementation: A Guide to Accomplishing Policy Objectives

The capacity of public policy to alter social behavior is a complex process that should be seen in historical perspective. In any specific policy area, the basic policy orientation often remains fairly constant over time, with change coming in small increments as a result of adjustments made by relevant agencies, interest groups, and legislative committees.[1] In this paper, however, we examine the conditions under which a statute or other major policy action (such as an appellate court decision) that seeks to alter significantly the historical evolution of policy can actually achieve its objectives.

Reprinted with permission of the author and the Regents from *Policy Analysis* 5:4 (Fall 1979), pp. 481–504. Copyright 1979 by the Regents of the University of California.

The bulk of the literature on policy implementation that has developed over the past decade is generally quite pessimistic about the ability of important policy initiatives actually to effect the desired social changes. Studies of Title I of the Elementary and Secondary Education Act of 1965, efforts to create jobs in Oakland, California, under the Public Works and Economic Development Act of 1965, the 1970 Clean Air Amendments, the New Towns In-Town program, and the Comprehensive Employment and Training Act (CETA) of 1973 have all concluded that these programs have had only very limited success in achieving their stated objectives.[2] In fact, a recent review of federal social programs suggests that such programs must be altered to fit within the constraints of local political systems if they are to be implemented at all.[3]

On the other hand, some federal statutes—most notably, the 1966 Voting Rights Act and the 1964 Civil Rights Act—have been effectively implemented.[4] In addition, a recent study indicates that the California legislation creating the Bay Conservation and Development Commission has been quite successful in drastically reducing the historical trend of dredging and filling in San Francisco Bay.[5]

Clearly some programs are much more able than others to fulfill their legal mandates. The purpose of this paper is to identify and explain a set of five (sufficient and generally necessary) conditions under which a policy decision that seeks a substantial (non-trivial) departure from the status quo can achieve its policy objectives. Recognizing, however, that all of these conditions are probably seldom met in practice, we also suggest a number of strategies available to legislators and other policy formulators for overcoming specific deficiencies. Our objective throughout the paper is to maximize the congruence among policy objectives, the decisions of the implementing agencies, and the actual impacts of those decisions.

The paper is addressed to two different audiences: scholars interested in developing a general theory or conceptual framework of the implementation process (in which respect our work builds upon the earlier efforts of people [such as] Van Meter and Van Horn, Bardach, Hargrove, Williams, and Berman) and policy formulators (such as legislators) and their staffs who wish to estimate the implementability of various policy alternatives and to understand the manner in which they can structure the implementation process so as to maximize the probability that statutory objectives will be attained.[6] For this purpose, it is important that the proposed framework provide not only a clear understanding of what is crucial but also distinguish those factors under the control of policy formulators from those over which policy formulators have only a very limited influence.[7]

One final introductory note: We feel that the literature on policy implementation has become unduly fragmented, both between types of policies—with some authors limiting their scope to social (distributive) programs, while others are concerned only with regulatory policies—and between types of policymaking institutions, with very little integration between studies of the implementation of legislative and judicial decisions. While such fragmentation can be partially attributed to scholars' traditional caution concerning the generalizability of their conclusions, it is nevertheless inimical to the heuristic value of comparative studies and to the norm that theories should apply to as wide a range of phenomena as possible. Therefore we shall throw modesty to the wind and argue that our framework applies to all governmental programs that seek to change some target group's behavior, either as an end in itself or as a means to some desired end state. At the very least our framework applies to traditional regulatory programs governing private behavior, attempts to change the behavior of private actors through the conditional disbursement of funds, and attempts to change the behavior of field-level public officials (such as school boards, teachers, police) through legal directives or the conditional disbursement of funds. Moreover, although our focus throughout is on the implementation of statutes, the framework also applies to appellate court decisions.[8]

THE CONDITIONS OF EFFECTIVE POLICY IMPLEMENTATION

It is our contention that a statute or other major policy decision seeking a substantial departure from the status quo will achieve its objectives under the following set of conditions.

1. The program is based on a sound theory relating changes in target group behavior to the achievement of the desired end-state (objectives).
2. The statute (or other basic policy decision) contains unambiguous policy directives and structures the implementation process so as to maximize the likelihood that target groups will perform as desired.
3. The leaders of the implementing agencies possess substantial managerial and political skill and are committed to statutory goals.
4. The program is actively supported by organized constituency groups and by a few key legislators (or the chief executive) throughout the implementation process, with the courts being neutral or supportive.
5. The relative priority of statutory objectives is not significantly undermined over time by the emergence of conflicting public policies or by changes in relevant socioeconomic conditions that undermine the statute's "technical" theory or political support.

The conceptual framework underlying this set of conditions has been presented elsewhere in greater detail and is based upon a (proto) theory of public agencies that views them as bureaucracies with multiple goals that are in constant interaction with interest (constituency) groups, other agencies, and legislative (and executive) sovereigns in their policy subsystem.[9]

Before elaborating on each of these conditions, we should note that obtaining target group compliance is obviously much more difficult in some situations than in others. The greater the difficulty, the greater the legal and political resources that must be marshaled if compliance is to be achieved. In the terms of our framework, the required "strength" (or degree of bias) of the last four conditions is a function of several factors, including the amount of change required in target

group behavior, the orientation of target groups toward the mandated change, and the diversity in prescribed activities of target groups. In other words, the greater the mandated change, the more opposed the target groups, and the more diverse their prescribed activities, the greater must be the degree of statutory structuring, the skill of implementing officials, the support from constituency groups and sovereigns, and the stability in socioeconomic conditions if statutory objectives are to be attained. Within this context, the set of five conditions should always be sufficient to achieve policy objectives. Moreover, each condition is probably necessary if the change sought is substantial and requires five to ten years of effort; in easier situations, however, it may be possible to omit one of the last three conditions.

CONDITION 1: *The program is based on a sound theory relating changes in target group behavior to the achievement of the desired end-state (objectives).*

Most basic policy decisions are based upon an underlying causal theory that can be divided into two components—the first relating achievement of the desired end-state(s) back to changes in target group behavior, the second specifying the means by which target group compliance can be obtained.[10] Both the "technical" and the "compliance" components must be valid for the policy objective(s) to be attained.

At this point, we are concerned only with the former ("technical") component, as the remaining four conditions in our framework relate primarily to the latter. In particular, we wish to emphasize that target group compliance—and the costs involved in obtaining it—may be wasted if not correctly linked to the desired end-state. For example, the "technical" component of the theory underlying the 1970 Clean Air Amendments relates air quality levels back to emissions from various stationary and mobile sources (the target groups). It assumes that human activities are the major source of air pollutants and that pollutant emissions from various sources within an air basin can be related, via diffusion models, to air quality levels at specific locations. To the extent that non-human sources, such as volcanoes, constitute a major emission source or that little is known about pollutant interaction and transport in the atmosphere, target group compliance with legally prescribed emission levels will not achieve air quality objectives (or will do so only very inefficiently). Moreover, the administrative and other costs involved in obtaining compliance are likely to be resented—with a corresponding decline in political support for the program—to the extent that promised improvements in air quality are not at least approximated. In short, an invalid technical component has both direct and indirect effects on the (non)achievement of policy objectives.

We should note, however, that there are some programs for which target group compliance can be interpreted as *the* policy objective. In such instances, the absence of any explicit attempt to link target group behavior to some subsequent end-state means that the first of our five conditions would not apply (as the underlying "technical" component deals directly with that linkage). For example, the goal of desegregation policy in the South could be construed as the elimination of dual schools—in which case the compliance of local target groups (school boards) would be tantamount to successful implementation. Insofar, however, as the goal of desegregation was not simply the elimination of dual schools but also the improvement of black children's reading scores, the "technical" assumption that unified schools improve reading scores would have to be valid for the policy objective to be attained.

CONDITION 2: *The statute (or other basic policy decision) contains unambiguous policy directives and structures the implementation process so as to maximize the likelihood that target groups will perform as desired.*

This is the condition most under the control of policy formulators (such as legislators). Unfortunately, its importance has often been overlooked by behaviorially oriented social scientists. For these reasons, we will briefly examine its constituent parts.

(a) The policy objectives are precise and clearly ranked, both internally (within the specific statute) and in the overall program of implementing agencies. Statutory objectives that are precise and clearly ranked in importance serve as an indispensable aid in program evaluation, as unambiguous directives to implementing officials, and as a resource available to supporters of those objectives both inside and outside the implementing agencies.[11] For example, implementing officials confronted with objections to their programs can sympathize with the aggrieved party but nevertheless respond that they are only following the legislature's instructions. Clear objectives can also serve as a resource to actors outside the implementing institutions who perceive discrepancies between agency outputs and those objectives (particularly if the statute also provides them [with] formal access to the implementation process, such as via citizen suit provisions).

While the desirability of unambiguous policy directives within a given statute is normally understood, it is also important that a statute assigned for implementation to an existing agency clearly indicate the relative priority that the new directives are to play in the totality of the agency's programs. If this is not done, the new directives are likely to undergo considerable delay and be accorded low priority as they struggle for incorporation in the agency's operating procedures.[12]

(b) The financial resources provided to the implementing agencies are sufficient to hire the staff and conduct the technical analyses involved in the development of regulations, the administration of permit/service delivery pro-

grams, and the monitoring of target group compliance. Although this condition is fairly obvious, ascertaining what constitutes "sufficient" resources presents enormous difficulties in practice. As a general rule, however, a threshold level of funding is necessary for there to be any possibility of achieving statutory objectives, and the level of funding above this threshold is (up to some saturation point) proportional to the probability of achieving those objectives. Financial resources are perhaps particularly problematic in labor-intensive service delivery programs and in regulatory programs with a high scientific or technological component, where implementing agencies often lack the funds to engage in the research and development necessary to examine critically the information presented by target groups and, in some cases, to develop alternative technologies.[13]

(c) Implementation is assigned to agencies supportive of statutory objectives that will give the new program high priority. Any new program requires implementing officials who are not merely neutral but also sufficiently committed and persistent to develop new regulations and standard operating procedures and to enforce them in the face of resistance from target groups and from public officials reluctant to make the mandated changes.[14]

Thus it is extremely important that implementation be assigned to agencies whose policy orientation is consistent with the statute and which will accord the new program high priority. This is most likely when a new agency is created with a clear mandate after an extensive political struggle, as the program will necessarily be its highest priority and the creation of new positions opens the door to a vast infusion of statutory supporters. Alternatively, implementation can be assigned to a prestigious existing agency that considers the new mandate compatible with its traditional orientation and is looking for new programs. In addition to selecting gener-

ally supportive agencies, a statute can sometimes stipulate that top implementing officials be selected from social sectors that generally support the legislation's objectives.[15] Even if this cannot be done through legislation, legislative supporters can often play a critical role in the appointment of noncivil-service personnel within the implementing agencies.

In practice, however, the choice of implementing agencies and officials is often severely constrained. In many policy areas (such as education) there is little option but to assign implementation to existing agencies that may well be hostile or whose personnel may be so preoccupied with existing programs that any new mandate tends to get lost in the shuffle. In addition, most positions within any governmental agency are occupied by career civil servants who are often resistant to changes in existing procedures and programs and only moderately susceptible to the sanctions and inducements available to political appointees. In fact, the generally limited ability of policy formulators to assign implementation to agency officials committed to its objectives probably lies behind many cases of suboptimal correspondence of policy outputs with statutory objectives.[16]

(d) The statute (or other basic policy decision) provides substantial hierarchical integration within and among implementing agencies by minimizing the number of veto/clearance points and by providing supporters of statutory objectives with inducements and sanctions sufficient to assure acquiescence among those with a potential veto. Surely one of the dominant themes in the implementation literature is the difficulty of obtaining coordinated action within any given agency and among the numerous semiautonomous agencies involved in most implementation efforts. The problem is particularly acute in federal statutes that rely on state and local agencies for carrying out the details of program delivery and for which some field-level implementors and/or target

groups display considerable resistance toward statutory directives. Thus one of the most important attributes of any statute (or other basic policy decision) is the extent to which it hierarchically integrates the implementing agencies. To the extent the system is only loosely integrated, there will be considerable variation in the degree of behavioral compliance among implementing officials and target groups—as each responds to the incentives for modification within its local setting—and thus a distinctly suboptimal attainment of statutory objectives.[17]

The degree of hierarchical integration among implementing agencies is determined by the number of veto/clearance points involved in the attainment of statutory objectives and the extent to which supporters of statutory objectives are provided with inducements and sanctions sufficient to assure acquiescence among those with a potential veto. Veto/clearance points involve those occasions in which an actor has the capacity (quite apart from the question of legal authority) to impede the achievement of statutory objectives.[18] Resistance from specific veto points can be overcome, however, if the statute provides sufficient sanctions and/or inducements to convince role occupants (whether implementing officials or target groups) to alter their behavior. In short, if these sanctions and inducements are great enough, the number of veto points can delay—but probably never ultimately impede—behavioral compliance by target groups.[19] In practice, however, the compliance incentives are usually sufficiently modest that the number of veto/clearance points becomes extremely important. As a result, the most direct route to a statutory objective—such as a negative income tax to provide a minimum income—is often preferable to complex programs administered by numerous semiautonomous bureaucracies.[20]

(e) The decision rules of implementing agencies are supportive of statutory objectives. In addition to providing unambiguous objectives, generally supportive implementing officials, few veto points, and adequate incentive for compliance, a statute (or other basic policy decision) can further bias the implementation process by stipulating the formal decision rules of the implementing agencies. The decisions of implementing agencies are likely to be consistent with statutory objectives to the extent, for example, that the burden of proof in permit/licensing cases is placed on the applicant and that agency officials are required to make findings fully consistent with statutory objectives. In addition, a statute can assign authority to make final decisions within implementing institutions to those subunits most likely to support statutory objectives. Finally, when multimembered commissions are involved, the statute can stipulate the majority required for specific actions. In the case of regulatory agencies that operate primarily through the granting of permits or licenses, decision rules that make the granting of a permit contingent upon substantial consensus, such as a two-thirds majority, are obviously conducive to stringent regulation.

(f) The statute (or other basic policy decision) provides ample opportunity for constituency (interest) groups and sovereigns supportive of statutory objectives to intervene in the implementation process through, for example, liberal rules of standing to agency and judicial proceedings and requirements for periodic evaluation of the performance of implementing agencies and target groups. While a statute can take steps to assure that implementing officials are generally supportive of statutory objectives and that the decision process involving implementing agencies and target groups contains few veto points, adequate incentives for compliance, and supportive formal rules, we nevertheless contend that implementing officials cannot necessarily be trusted to act in a manner consistent with statutory objectives. What is also required is constant oversight and interven-

tion from supportive constituency groups and legislative (and executive) sovereigns.

A statute (or other basic policy decision) can take a number of steps to maximize the probability of such intervention. First, it can require opportunities for public input at numerous stages in the decision process of implementing agencies and even require that the agencies take positive steps to assure the participation of unorganized potential beneficiaries. Second, it can provide for liberal rules of standing to appeal agency decisions to the courts. For example, the citizen suit provisions of the 1970 Clean Air Amendments have been used on several occasions to compel the U.S. Environmental Protection Agency to carry out statutorily mandated provisions that it had failed, for one reason or another, to do.[21] Third, requirements for periodic reporting of agency performance to legislative and executive sovereigns and for evaluation studies by prestigious independent organizations (such as the National Academy of Sciences) are conducive to external oversight of the implementing agencies and probably to the achievement of statutory objectives.[22]

In sum, a carefully formulated statute (or other basic policy decision) should be seen as a means by which legislators and other policy formulators can structure the entire implementation process and maximize the probability that the policy outputs of the implementing agencies and the behavior of target groups (whether outside or inside those agencies) will be consistent with statutory objectives. This requires, first, that they develop unambiguous policy objectives and incorporate a valid technical theory linking target group compliance with the desired impacts. In order to maximize the probability of such compliance, they should then assign implementation to supportive agencies, provide implementing officials with adequate financial resources, hierarchically integrate the implementation process through mini-

mizing veto points and providing sufficient incentives to overcome resistance, bias the formal decision rules of implementing agencies, and provide opportunities for outsiders to participate in the implementation process and to evaluate accurately agency (and target group) performance.

But a statute, no matter how well it structures implementation, is not a sufficient condition for assuring target group compliance with its objectives. Assuring sufficient compliance to actually achieve those objectives normally takes at least three to five and often ten to twenty years. During this period, there are constant pressures for even supportive agency officials to lose their commitment, for supportive constituency groups and sovereigns to fail to maintain active political support, and for the entire process to be gradually undermined by changing socioeconomic forces. In short, while a statute can go a long way toward assuring successful implementation, there are additional conditions that must be fulfilled if its objectives are to be attained.

CONDITION 3: *The leaders of the implementing agencies possess substantial managerial and political skill and are committed to statutory objectives.*

As already indicated, legislators and other policy formulators can take a number of important steps—both in the drafting of a statute and in the subsequent appointment of noncivil-service personnel—to increase substantially the probability that the leaders of implementing agencies will be supportive of statutory objectives. In practice, however, statutory levers are often somewhat limited (except where creation of a new agency is feasible), and the process of appointing political executives is heavily dependent upon the wishes of the chief executive and important legislators—several of whom may well not be committed to implementation of the basic policy decision. In short, the support of top implementing officials is sufficiently important and problematic to warrant being highlighted as a separate condition for successful implementation.

Moreover, policy support is essentially useless if not accompanied by political and managerial skill in utilizing available resources. Political skill involves the ability to develop good working relationships with sovereigns in the agency's subsystem, to convince opponents and target groups that they are being treated fairly, to mobilize support among latent supportive constituencies, to present the agency's case adroitly through the mass media, and so forth. Managerial skill involves developing adequate controls so that the program is not subject to charges of fiscal mismanagement, maintaining high morale among agency personnel, and managing internal dissent in such a way that dissidents are convinced they have received a fair hearing.[23]

Finally, there is some evidence that maintaining high morale, commitment, and perhaps even skill becomes increasingly difficult over time. Innovative policy initiatives often attract committed and skillful executives to implementing institutions, particularly in the case of new agencies. But such people generally become burned out and disillusioned with bureaucratic routine after a few years, to be replaced by officials much more interested in personal security and organizational maintenance than in taking risks to attain policy goals.[24]

CONDITION 4: *The program is actively supported by organized constituency groups and by a few key legislators (or the chief executive) throughout the implementation process, with the courts being neutral or supportive.*

It is absolutely crucial to maintain active political support for the achievement of statutory objectives over the long course of implementation. If the first three conditions have been met, this essentially re-

quires that sufficient support be maintained among legislative and executive sovereigns to provide the implementing agencies with the requisite financial resources annually, as well as assuring that the basic statute is not seriously undermined but instead modified to overcome implementation difficulties.

This seemingly rather simple requirement is, however, exceedingly difficult to accomplish, for a variety of reasons. First, the rather episodic issue-attention span of the general public and the mass media tends to undermine diffuse political support for any particular program among both the public and legislators.[25] Second, there is a general tendency for organized constituency support for a wide variety of programs—including environmental and consumer protection, as well as efforts to aid the poor—to decline over time, while opposition from target groups to the costs imposed on them remains constant or actually increases. This shift in the balance of constituency support for such programs gradually becomes reflected in a shift in support among members of the legislature as a whole and the committees in the relevant subsystem(s).[26] Third, most legislators lack the staff resources and/or the incentives to monitor program implementation actively.[27] The exception is constituent casework, which tends to be heavily skewed toward complaints. Without active political support from a few key legislators, implementing officials supportive of the program find it difficult to overcome the constant drumbeat of constituent complaints, as well as the delay and resistance inherent in implementing any program requiring substantial behavioral change (except in those instances where target groups support such change).

Despite these difficulties, the necessary infusion of political support can be maintained if two factors are present. The first is the presence of a "fixer" (or fixers)—that is, an important legislator or executive official who controls resources important to other actors and who has the desire and the staff resources to closely monitor the implementation process, to intervene with agency officials on an almost continuous basis, and to protect the budget and the legal authority of the implementing agencies.[28] Except in very unusual circumstances, however, any particular "fixer" is unlikely to occupy a crucial position and/or to maintain an interest throughout the long process of implementation. This brings us to the second and ultimately the most important requirement, namely, the presence of an organized supportive constituency (interest) group that has the resources to monitor closely program implementation, to intervene actively in agency proceedings, to appeal adverse agency decisions to the courts and to the legislature, and to convince key legislators that the program merits their active support,[29] for the paramount advantage of any organization over an individual is continuity. If the supportive constituency is present, "fixers" can generally be found and/or nurtured.

Programs involving intergovernmental relations, however, pose additional difficulties to the maintenance of political support. On the one hand, programs of intergovernmental "subordinates" (such as localities vis-à-vis states and the federal government) are often subject to revision and/or emasculation by superordinate units of government.[30] Unless a program's representatives occupy important positions at the superordinate level, there is little that can be done to maintain its legal (and sometimes financial) integrity. Conversely, superordinate levels are usually confronted with substantial local variation in political support for program objectives and, consequently, in the compliance of local implementing officials with program directives. While such variation can, in principle, be overcome if the superordinate statute provides very substantial incentives for compliance and sufficient fi-

nancial resources to enable superordinate officials essentially to replace local implementors, in practice the system is seldom structured to that degree, and thus superordinate officials are forced to bargain with recalcitrant local implementors.[31] The result is greater sensitivity to local demands and generally a suboptimal achievement of statutory objectives.

The discussion thus far has focused on the need for political support among the legislative and executive sovereigns of implementing agencies. But one must not neglect the courts. In most cases, the contemporary deference of most federal and state courts to agency decision making means that they play a rather minor role in the implementation process except on procedural issues and to assure conformity with explicit statutory directives.[32] But courts strongly opposed to a given statute have the authority to emasculate implementation through delay in enforcement proceedings, through repeatedly unfavorable statutory interpretations, and, in extreme cases, by declaring the statute unconstitutional[33] On the other hand, there have been some instances where courts have substantially strengthened programs through favorable rulings.[34] Given the enormous potential role of the courts, we argue that successful implementation of statutory objectives requires that they be either neutral or supportive.

CONDITION 5: *The relative priority of statutory objectives is not significantly undermined over time by the emergence of conflicting public policies or by changes in relevant socioeconomic conditions that undermine the statute's "technical" theory or political support.*

Change is omnipresent in most contemporary societies in part because most countries are immersed in an international system over which they have only modest control, in part because policy issues tend to be highly interrelated. Pollution control, for example, is linked to energy, to inflation and national monetary policy, to transportation, to public lands, and to numerous other issues. As a result of this continuous change, any particular policy decision is susceptible to an erosion of political support as other issues become relatively more important over time. Obvious examples would be the effect of the Vietnam War and inflation on many Great Society programs and the effect of the energy crisis and inflation on pollution control programs.[35] Change can also be so extensive as essentially to undermine the technical assumptions on which a policy is based, as when the migration of poor people from the South and Puerto Rico to northern industrial cities brought into serious question the ability of state and local governments to provide matching funds for welfare programs.

It is in responding to such changes that support for a particular program from key legislators, organized constituency groups, and implementing officials becomes crucial. If they are sensitive to the effects that changes in seemingly tangential policies and in technical assumptions can have on "their" program, they can take steps to see that these repercussions are addressed in any new legislation.[36]

This concludes our discussion of the conditions of effective policy implementation. To recapitulate: A statute or other basic policy decision will achieve its objectives if (1) it incorporates a valid "technical" theory linking target group behavior to those objectives; (2) it contains unambiguous policy directives and structures the implementation process so as to maximize the probability of target group compliance; (3) the leaders of implementing agencies are supportive of those objectives and skillful in utilizing available resources; (4) the program is supported by active constituency groups and a few key legislators throughout the implementation process, with the courts being neutral or supportive; and (5) the program is not undermined by

changing socioeconomic conditions. If all of these conditions are met, then any statute—no matter how ambitious—will be effectively implemented. In most cases, each of the conditions will have to be met if effective implementation is to take place; the exception would involve policies that seek only modest changes in target group behavior and/or in which target groups are amenable to mandated changes.[37]

Throughout this discussion, however, we have been somewhat vague about the actual process of policy feedback and evaluation. Moreover, while the set of conditions should (at the very least) serve as a useful checklist to policy formulators and to scholars, it provides little guidance about what can be done when one or all of the conditions cannot in practice be met. If this paper is to serve as a useful guide to implementation analysis and assessment, it must at least briefly address these two topics.

POLICY FEEDBACK AND EVALUATION

Thus far our attention has been focused on the extent to which implementing agencies and target groups act in a manner consistent with statutory objectives and ultimately on the extent to which those objectives are actually attained. In this respect we have mirrored the focus on formal goals of much of the literature on implementation assessment and program evaluation.[38]

But if one is interested in the evolution of policy and particularly with the political feedback process, a much wider range of impacts (or outcomes) needs to be considered. Of particular importance are unintended impacts that affect political support for the program's objectives. For example, any assessment of the implementation of school desegregation policy should be concerned not only with the amount of desegregation achieved but also with the effect of desegregation on "white flight" and ultimately on the amount of political and financial support for the public schools. Moreover, there is some evidence that political feedback is based primarily upon perceived, rather than actual, impacts and that policy elites evaluate a program not in terms of the extent to which it achieves its legal mandate but rather in terms of its perceived conformity with their policy preferences.[39]

The actual process of policy evaluation and feedback occurs continuously on an informal basis as the implementing agencies interact with concerned constituency groups, legislative (and executive) sovereigns, and the courts. At periodic intervals, however, the process normally becomes more formal and politically salient as attempts are made to revise substantially the basic statute. For example, major efforts to amend federal air pollution control law seem to occur every three to four years. Some of these revisions can be attributed to continued resistance from affected target groups, while others can be traced to significant changes in relevant social and economic conditions. Whatever the source of proposed changes, it is important that supporters of the original objectives provide for independent evaluation studies to accurately assess the actual impacts of the program. Such systematic evaluation serves both to correct imperfections in program design and performance and to counteract the tendency for complaints to dominate the informal feedback process.

IMPLEMENTATION UNDER SUBOPTIMAL CONDITIONS

A frequently voiced criticism against both legislators and scholars is that they have been far more concerned with the passage of legislation than with its effective implementation. Over the past decade, however, a burgeoning interest in policy implementation and evaluation has occurred in the academic community. This has matched a corresponding shift of emphasis among legislators from the passage of major new policy initiatives to more effective implementation and oversight of existing programs. One of the principal purposes of this paper is to provide both communities [with] an understanding of the conditions under which statutes (and other basic policy decisions) that seek to change the status quo can be effectively implemented—that is, can achieve their policy objectives.

Our discussion has shown that legislators and other policy formulators can go a long way toward assuring effective policy implementation if they see that a statute incorporates a sound technical theory, provides precise and clearly ranked objectives, and structures the implementation process in a wide number of ways so as to maximize the probability of target group compliance. In addition, they can take positive steps to appoint skillful and supportive implementing officials, to provide adequate appropriations and to monitor carefully the behavior of implementing agencies throughout the long implementation process, and to be aware of the effects of changing socioeconomic conditions and of new legislation (even in supposedly unrelated areas) on the original statute.

In practice, of course, even those legislators and other policy formulators concerned with effective implementation operate under substantial constraints that make it extremely difficult for them to perform all these tasks. Valid technical theories may not be available. Imperfect information, goal conflict, and multiple vetoes in legislative bodies make it very difficult to pass legislation that incorporates unambiguous objectives and coherently structures the implementation process.[40] Implementation must often be assigned to agencies that are not supportive of the policy objectives. Supportive interest groups and legislators with the resources to serve as "fixers" may not be available or may go on to other things over the long course of implementation.

Nevertheless, even under such suboptimal conditions, several steps can be taken at least to increase the probability of effective implementation.

1. If a valid "technical" theory linking target group behavior to policy objectives is not available or is clearly problematic, then the authors of the statute should make a conscious effort to incorporate in it a learning process through experimental projects, extensive research and development, evaluation studies, and an open decision process involving as many different inputs as possible.

2. If the legislature insists on passing legislation with only the most ambiguous policy directives, then supporters of different points of view can initiate litigation in the hopes of finding a court that will invalidate the law as an unconstitutional delegation of (legislative) authority. While not very promising, this strategy has been employed successfully at least once in a California case, with subsequent legislation providing much clearer guidance to the agency.[41]

3. If implementation cannot be assigned to strongly supportive agencies, then it is absolutely crucial to provide for intervention by outsiders through citizen suit provisions, periodic reporting to sovereigns, evaluation studies by prestigious and relatively independent outsiders, and perhaps special legislative oversight committees.

4. If there are no active supportive interest groups with the necessary resources to monitor implementation carefully, then identification and mobilization of such a group must be a major priority of supportive legislators and implementing officials—as any program is doomed in the long run without one. While it is occasionally possible to create new organizations from scratch, a more feasible strategy is to convince an existing organization with the requisite resources to expand its program to make program monitoring a major responsibility.[42]

5. If a "fixer" is not readily available, then program supporters must make a major effort to find or develop one. This may involve convincing a competent new legislator to specialize in this area or convincing an existing legislator that constituents strongly support the program and thus require it being given higher priority. If legislators in the relevant committees having jurisdiction over the implementing agencies are apathetic (or, worse, hostile) toward the new program, then efforts should be made to reorganize committee jurisdictions or perhaps to create a special oversight committee with a program supporter as chairperson. Whatever the means, however, finding a "fixer" is of paramount importance for effective implementation.

In short, even if the conditions for effective implementation are not met at the time of the basic policy decision, policy formulators and other program supporters can still take a number of steps to approximate the ideal over time.

AUTHOR NOTE

We would like to thank several people for their advice and criticism on previous versions of this paper: Larry Baum, Paul Berman, Don Brown, Charles Bullock, Paul Culhane, George Downs, Len Goodwin, Irwin Hargrove, Helen Ingram, Karl Kurtz, Dale Marshall, Phyllis Moen, Arnold Meltsner, Roger Noil, Nelson Rosenbaum, Judy Rosener, Carl Van Horn, and Lettie Wenner. This research was sponsored by the National Science Foundation under grant ENV77-20077. NSF is, of course, not responsible for the views expressed herein.

NOTES

1. In such cases, policy implementation is relatively unproblematic, as change is incremental, and there is a high degree of consensus among the major actors. See A. Lee Fritschler, *Smoking and Politics*, 2d ed. (Englewood Cliffs, N.J.: Prentice-Hall, 1975), ch. 1; and Charles Lindblom, *The*

Intelligence of Democracy (New York: Macmillan Co., 1964).

2. Jerome Murphy, "Title I of ESEA: The Politics of Implementing. Federal Education Reform," *Harvard Educational Review* 41 (1971): 35–63; Milbrey McLaughlin, *Evaluation and Reform: Title I* (Cambridge, Mass.: Ballinger Publishing Co., 1975); Jeffrey Pressman and Aaron Wildavsky, *Implementation* (Berkeley and Los Angeles: University of California Press, 1973); Henry Jacoby and John Steinbruner, *Clearing the Air* (Cambridge, Mass.: Ballinger Publishing Co., 1973); Charles Jones, *Clean Air* (Pittsburgh: University of Pittsburgh Press, 1975); Martha Derthick, *New Towns In-Town* (Washington, D.C.: Urban Institute, 1972); Carl Van Horn, "Implementing CETA: The Federal Role," *Policy Analysis* 4 (Spring 1978): 159–83.

3. Paul Berman, "The Study of Macro- and Micro-Implementation," *Public Policy* 26 (Spring 1978): 172–79.

4. See Harrell Rodgers and Charles Bullock, *Law and Social Change* (New York: McGraw-Hill, 1972), and *Coercion to Compliance* (Lexington, Mass.: D. C. Heath, 1976).

5. Gerald Swanson, "Coastal Zone Management from an Administrative Perspective: A Case Study of the San Francisco Bay Conservation and Development Commission," *Coastal Zone Management Journal* 2 (1975): 81–102. For another example, see Robert Johnston, Seymore Schwartz, and Thomas Klinkner, "Successful Plan Implementation: The Growth Phasing Program of Sacramento County," *AIP Journal* (October 1978): 412–23.

6. See Donald Van Meter and Carl Van Horn, "The Policy Implementation Process: A Conceptual Framework," *Administration and Society* 6 (February 1975): 445–88; Eugene Bardach, *The Implementation Game* (Cambridge, Mass.: MIT Press, 1977); Erwin Hargrove, *The Missing Link* (Washington, D.C.: Urban Institute, 1975); Walter Williams and Richard Elmore, eds., *Social Program Implementation* (New York: Academic Press, 1976); Berman, "Macro- and Micro-Implementation"; Martin Rein and Francine Rabinovitz, "Implementation," working paper no. 43 (Cambridge, Mass.: Joint Center for Urban Studies, 1977); Harold Luft, "Benefit Cost Analysis and Public Policy Implementation," *Public Policy* 24 (Fall 1976): 437–62.

7. See Victor Nielsen, "Input-Output Models and the Non-Use of Policy Analysis" (Paper presented at the 1974 Annual Meeting of the Western Political Science Association, Denver, Colo., April 1974); James Coleman, "Problems of Conceptualization and Measurement in Studying Policy Impacts," in *Public Policy Evaluation*, Sage Yearbooks in Politics and Public Policy, vol. 2, ed. Kenneth Dolbeare (Beverly Hills, Calif.: Sage, 1975), pp. 24–26.

8. For an excellent comparative analysis of the ability of legislatures and appellate courts to structure the implementation process, see Lawrence Baum, "Implementation of Legislative and Judicial Policies: A Comparative View," in *Effective Policy Implementation*, ed. Daniel Mazmanian and Paul Sabatier (Lexington, Mass.: Lexington Books, 1980).

9. Paul Sabatier and Daniel Mazmanian, *The Implementation of Regulatory Policy: A Framework of Analysis* (Davis, Calif.: Institute of Governmental Affairs, 1979); and Paul Culhane, "Bureaucratic Politics Theory and the Open Systems Metaphor" (Paper presented at the 1978 Annual Meeting of the Southwestern Political Science Association, Houston, Texas, April 1978).

10. For related discussions, see Berman, "Macro- and Micro-Implementation," p. 163; and Pressman and Wildavsky, *Implementation*, "Preface." In principle, a valid technical component should (*a*) incorporate all major factors directly contributing to the problem within the purview of the program and (*b*) correctly relate each of these factors to the desired end-state(s). Leonard Goodwin and Phyllis Moen, for example, suggest that one of the major reasons for dissatisfaction with American welfare policy is that at any point in time, it has addressed only a very limited subset of the factors affecting income disabilities and thus has had little effect on the overall problem ("On the Evolution and Implementation of Welfare Policy," in *Effective Policy Implementation*, ed. Mazmanian and Sabatier).

11. For general discussions of the importance of unambiguous objectives as requisites of program evaluation and as political resources, respectively, see Leonard Rutman, ed., *Evaluation Research Methods* (Beverly Hills, Calif.: Sage, 1977), ch. 1; and Theodore Lowi, *The End of Liberalism* (New York: W. W. Norton, 1969).

We would like to suggest that the clarity and consistency of statutory objectives be conceptualized along the following ordinal scale. (1) Ambiguous objectives. These include both meaningless injunctions to regulate "in the public interest" and mandates to balance potentially conflicting objectives—such as air quality and industrial employment—without establishing priorities among them. (2) Define "tilt." This involves a relatively clear ranking of potentially conflicting, rather general objectives—such as to improve air quality even if it results in some unemployment. (3) Qualitative objectives. These involve a rather precise qualitative mandate—for example, to protect air quality so as to maintain the public health, including that of susceptible populations. Note that this qualitative objective is considerably more precise than that under a "tilt." (4) Quantiative objectives, such as to reduce automotive emissions from 1970 levels by 90 percent by December 31, 1975. Clearly, the last objective constitutes a greater resource to proponents of change than the first.

12. For examples in which vague and/or inconsistent objectives have hampered the achievement of behavioral change, see Murphy, "Title I of ESEA," pp. 38–44; Richard Weatherly and Michael Lipsky, "Street Level Bureaucrats and Institutional Innovation: Implementing Special Education Reform," *Harvard Educational Review* 47 (May 1977): 180–96; Pressman and Wildavsky, *Implementation,* pp. 25–26, 71–77, 87–90; and Richard Johnson, *The Dynamics of Compliance* (Evanston, Ill.: Northwestern University Press, 1967), pp. 58–59. In contrast, clear standards facilitated implementation of the 1965 Bay Conservation and Development Act (Swanson, "Costal Zone Management," pp. 81–102).

13. This has, for example, been a substantial constraint on the acquisition of information concerning offshore petroleum resources and in the development of low-emission motor vehicles. See U.S. Senate, Committee on Interior, *Hearings on the Energy Information Act,* 93d Cong., 2d sess., 1974; and Jacoby and Steinbruner, *Clearing the Air,* ch. 3–4.

14. For reviews of the reasons for bureaucratic resistance to change, see Richard Elmore, "Organizational Models of Social Program Implementation," *Public Policy* 26 (Spring 1978): 199–216; Herbert Kaufman, *The Limits of Organizational Change* (University, Ala.: University of Alabama Press, 1971); and Anthony Downs, *Inside Bureaucracy* (Boston: Little, Brown and Co., 1967), ch. 13, 14, 16, and 19.

15. For example, several studies of state and regional land use agencies have shown that local elected officials are generally more likely than appointees of state officials to approve proposed developments—thereby suggesting that a land use statute can significantly affect the probable policy orientation of the implementing agency through the distribution of appointees from these two categories. See Edmond Costantini and Kenneth Hanf, *The Environmental Impulse and Its Competitors* (Davis, Calif.: Institute of Governmental Affairs, 1973), pp. 55–58; and Judy Rosener with Sally Russell and Dennis Brehn, *Environmental vs. Local Control,* mimeographed (Irvine: University of California, 1977).

16. See, for example, Murphy, "Title I of ESEA," pp. 35–63; Pressman and Wildavsky, *Implementation,* ch. 3–5; Bardach, *Implementation Game,*

ch. 5; Rodgers and Bullock, *Coercion to Compliance,* ch. 2; N. Milner, *The Court and Local Law Enforcement: The Impact of Miranda* (Beverly Hills, Calif.: Sage, 1971); and Hugh Heclo, *A Government of Strangers* (Washington, D.C.: Brookings, 1977), ch. 3–6.

17. See Elmore, "Social Program Implementation," pp. 199–216; Berman, "Macro- and Micro-Implementation," pp. 166–79; Rodgers and Bullock, *Coercion to Compliance;* Pressman and Wildavsky, *Implementation,* ch. 5; Frederick Lazin, "The Failure of Federal Enforcement of Civil Rights Regulations in Public Housing, 1963–1971: The Cooptation of a Federal Agency by Its Local Constituency," *Policy Sciences* 4 (September 1973): 263–74.

18. This is a slightly more restrictive notion of veto/clearance point than that used by Pressman and Wildavsky (*Implementation,* ch. 5). In calculating the total number of such points, one must add those involved in the development of general rules and operating procedures, in the disposition of specific cases, and in the enforcement of those decisions. One must also consider the possibility that implementing agencies are not given adequate legal authority to achieve mandated objectives. Thus any purely cooperative arrangements needed with other agencies must also be included in the number of veto points; in such cases, of course, the implementing agencies are likely to possess very few incentives to induce compliance, and thus the system can be said to be poorly integrated.

19. For an example of the ability of sanctions to bring about behavioral compliance over the strong resistance of target groups (in this case, southern school officials), see Rodgers and Bullock, *Coercion to Compliance,* pp. 36–45.

20. For discussions of the advantages of simplicity, see Pressman and Wildavsky, *Implementation,* ch. 7; Bardach, *Implementation Game,* pp. 250–53; and Charles Schultze, *The Public Use of Private Interest* (Washington, D.C.: Brookings, 1977).

21. See Bruce Kramer, "Economics, Technology, and the Clean Air Amendments of 1970: The First Six Years," *Ecology Law Quarterly* 6 (1976): 161–230; and Marc Mihaly, "The Clean Air Act and the Concept of Nondegradation: Sierra Club v. Ruckelshaus," *'Ecology Law Quarterly* 2 (Fall 1972): 801–36. For general discussions of legal standing, see Karen Orren, "Standing to Sue," *American Political Science Review* 70 (September 1976): 723–41; and Kenneth Stewart, "Environmental Law: Standing to Sue," 30 *Vanderbilt Law Review* (1977): 1271–95.

22. While these mechanisms can increase the probability of favorable oversight, they are certainly not cure-alls. Evaluation studies by prestigious

external sources are likely to aid implementation effectiveness because of the difficulties of agencies to evaluate critically their own programs (see Rodgers and Bullock, *Coercion to Compliance*, ch. 6, and Murphy, "Title I of ESEA," pp. 42–44). Nevertheless, there are a wide variety of reasons why both agencies and legislatures conduct evaluation studies—only some of them relating to improving program performance (see Martin Rein and Sheldon White, "Policy Research: Belief and Doubt," *Policy Analysis* 3 [Spring 1977]: 239–71).

23. For discussions of leadership and illustrations of its importance, see Heclo, *Government of Strangers*, ch. 5–6; Francis Rourke, *Bureaucracy, Politics, and Public Policy*, 2d ed. (Boston: Little, Brown and Co., 1976), pp. 94–101; Richard Bolan and Ronald Nuttall, *Urban Planning and Politics* (Lexington, Mass.: D. C. Heath, 1975); Eugene Bardach, *The Skill Factor in Politics* (Berkeley and Los Angeles: University of California Press, 1972); Andrew McFarland, *Power and Leadership in Pluralist Systems* (Stanford, Calif.: Stanford University Press, 1969), ch. 8; Phillip Selznick, *Leadership in Administration* (New York: Harper and Row, 1957); and Victor Vroom and Philip Yetton, *Leadership and Decision-Making* (Pittsburgh: University of Pittsburgh Press, 1973).

24. Marver Bernstein, *Regulating Business by Independent Commission* (Princeton, N.J.: Princeton University Press, 1955), ch. 3; Downs, *Inside Bureaucracy*, ch. 2, 8, and 9. For some ambivalent evidence, see Kenneth Meir and John Plumlee, "Regulatory Administration and Organizational Rigidity," *Western Political Quarterly* 31 (March 1978): 80–95.

25. Anthony Downs, "Up and Down with Ecology—the Issue-Attention Cycle," *Public Interest* (Summer 1972): 38–50.

26. See James Q. Wilson, "The Politics of Regulation," in *Social Responsibility and the Business Predicament*, ed. James McKie (Washington, D.C.: Brookings, 1974), pp. 135–68; Paul Sabatier, "Social Movements and Regulatory Agencies," *Policy Sciences* 6 (Fall 1975): 301–42; and Barry Weingast, "A Positive Model of Public Policy Formulation: The Case of Regulatory Agency Behavior," working paper no. 25 (St. Louis: Center for the Study of American Business, 1978).

27. See Hargrove, *Missing Link*, pp. 112–17; Morris Oguls, *Congress Oversees the Bureaucracy* (Pittsburgh: University of Pittsburgh Press, 1976); Malcolm Jewell and Samuel Patterson, *The Legislative Process in the U.S.*, 3d ed. (New York: Random House, 1977), ch. 18; and John Johannes, "Congressional Caseworkers: Attitudes, Orientations, and Operations" (Paper presented at the

1978 Annual Meeting of the Midwest Political Science Association, Chicago, Ill., April 1978).

28. Bardach, *Implementation Game*, pp. 268–83. For example, Bardach describes a case in which this function was ably performed with respect to an important 1967 mental health law in California by a legislator who was the ranking Republican on the California Assembly Ways and Means Committee, who was widely acknowledged as the legislature's expert in this area, and who, moreover, viewed this legislation as the crowning achievement of his career. One might also cite the efforts of Senator Edmund Muskie with respect to federal pollution control legislation (see Bernard Asbel, *The Senate Nobody Knows* [Garden City, N.Y.: Doubleday, 1978]).

29. See Sabatier, "Social Movements and Regulatory Agencies," pp. 317–27; Walter Rosenbaum, "The Paradoxes of Public Participation," *Administration and Society* 8 (November 1976): 355–83; and B. Guy Peters, "Insiders and Outsiders: The Politics of Pressure Group Influence on Bureaucracy," *Administration and Society* 9 (August 1977): 191–218.

30. Probably the most extreme case is federal preemption of nuclear safety issues in power plant siting. For examples of the sometimes deleterious effects of new federal pollution control statutes on state programs, see Jones, *Clean Air*, ch. 8; and Harvey Lieber, *Federalism and Clean Waters* (Lexington, Mass.: D. C. Heath, 1974), ch. 7.

31. For examples of the effects of variation in local support on the implementation of federal programs, see Murphy, "Title I of ESEA," pp. 35–63; Rodgers and Bullock, *Coercion to Compliance*, ch. 2–4; Paul Berman and Milbrey McLaughlin, "Implementation of Educational Innovation," *Educational Forum* 40 (March 1976); 345–70; and Rufus Browning, Dale Rogers Marshall, and David Tabb, "Implementation and Political Change: Sources of Local Variations in Federal Social Programs," in *Effective Policy Implementation*, ed. Mazmanian and Sabatier. See also Berman, "Macro- and Micro-Implementation," pp. 168–79; Elmore, "Organizational Models of Social Program Implementation," pp. 199–216; Jeffrey Pfeffer and Gerald Salancik, *The External Control of Organizations* (New York: Harper and Row, 1978); and Helen Ingram, "Policy Implementation through Bargaining. The Case of Federal Grants-in-Aid," *Public Policy* 25 (Fall 1977): 499–526.

32. See Louis Jaffe, *Judical Control of Administrative Action* (Boston: Little, Brown and Co., 1965); and Edward White, "Allocating Power Between Agencies and Courts," *Duke Law Journal* 1974 (April 1974): 195–244.

33. The locus and scope of judicial review can, how-

ever, be regulated by statute. For example, judicial review of the decisions of the Illinois Pollution Control Board is limited to the appellate courts and to rather narrowly defined procedural issues. See Elizabeth Haskell and Victoria Price, *State Environmental Management* (New York: Praeger, 1973), pp. 17–20.

34. One of the best examples is the effect of *U.S. v. Georgia* (1969) in accelerating southern school desegregation (see Rodgers and Bullock, *Coercion to Compliance*, ch. 2–3).

35. See J. Clarence Davies and Barbara Davies, *The Politics of Pollution*, 2d ed. (Indianapolis: Pegasus, 1975), pp. 52–60, and Henry Aaron, *Politics and the Professors: The Great Society in Perspective* (Washington, D.C.: Brookings, 1977).

36. An excellent example was the effort of Senator Muskie in resisting the efforts of the auto companies and utilities to use the energy crisis to emasculate the 1970 Clean Air Amendments.

37. In the case of special education reform in Massachusetts, for example, the ultimate target groups (teachers and other local school officials) were apparently generally supportive of the mandated changes in their behavior. This essentially eliminated the need for a very hierarchically integrated decision process, and the program was rather successfully implemented despite a decided lack of skill on the part of state implementing officials. Nevertheless, uncertainty concerning the adequacy of financial resources and the relative priority of special education in the total educational program created significant obstacles to effective implementation. See Weatherly and Lipsky, "Implementing Special Education Reform," pp. 171–97.

38. See, for example, Rutman, *Evaluation Research Methods*, pp. 28–29; and David Nachmias, *Public Policy Evaluation* (New York: St. Martin's, 1979),

pp. 13–15. For a somewhat more inclusive view of impact analysis, see Frank Levy, Arnold Meltsner, and Aaron Wildavsky, *Urban Outcomes* (Berkeley and Los Angeles: University of California Press, 1974).

39. While the literature on policy evaluation deals primarily with the correspondence between actual impacts and policy objectives, from the standpoint of political feedback it is perceived, rather than actual, impacts that are crucial. See Daniel Mazmanian and Paul Sabatier, "The Role of Attitudes and Perceptions in Policy Evaluation by Attentive Elites: The California Coastal Commissions," in *Public Policy Analysis*, Sage Yearbook in Politics and Public Policy, vol. 8, ed. Helen Ingram and Dean Mann (Beverly Hills, Calif.: Sage, 1979).

40. See Rein and Rabinovitz, *Implementation*, pp. 11–14; Carl Auerbach, "Pluralism and the Administrative Process," *Annals of the American Academy of Political and Social Science* 400 (March 1972): 1–13; and Nelson Rosenbaum, "Statutory Stringency and Policy Implementation: The Case of Wetlands Regulation," in *Effective Policy Implementation*, ed. Mazmanian and Sabatier.

41. In 1971 a California appellate court held the Forest Practices Act of 1945 unconstitutional on the grounds that it improperly delegated its lawmaking authority without adequate standards (*Bayside Timber v. San Mateo County*, App., 97 Cal. Rptr. 431), which led to major amendments to the legislation, including considerable clarification of the policy directives. This is, of course, a perfect example of what Lowi would term an application of the "Schechter Rule" (Lowi, *End of Liberalism*, ch. 10).

42. For an example, see Sabatier, "Social Movements and Regulatory Agencies," pp. 310–17.

Bruce L. Gates

Social Program Implementation: The Demand for Accountability

. . . A social program [is] identified by some combination of decisions regarding

Excerpted from Chapter 3 of *Social Program Administration* (Englewood Cliffs, N.J.: Prentice-Hall, Inc., 1980) with permission of the author and the publisher.

who was to get what and how. While this combination of decisions generally defines what the program is supposed to do as a single element in the total realm of redistributive strategies, it often fails to specify exactly how these decisions are to be implemented. Given an eligibility criterion, for example, using what specific information and by what specific procedures shall program staff actually determine who is eligible for program allocations? In the absence of detailed procedural plans governing such day-to-day program decisions, there may be abundant opportunity for the exercise of discretion by administrators and providers responsible for the program's implementation.

Because discretionary behavior may lead to decisions and actions detrimental to the achievement of desired program outcomes, it is common for policy makers to impose a bureaucratic structure upon program activities, which is designed to limit discretion and channel behavior. To be effective, however, bureaucratic controls like specialization, routinization, and standardization require an element of certainty that, for a variety of reasons, is often lacking in the social welfare enterprise. First, social policy goals and program purposes are seldom stated clearly and are subject to wide degrees of interpretation by different groups in the policy-making community; hence, the ultimate objectives of the program may be uncertain. Second, the results of social programs are seldom amenable to precise verification; in even the simplest of programs there may be substantial disagreement regarding the nature of program results. Third, policy makers often lack the theoretical relationships linking actions with results and thus lack the basis for determining what specific set of actions and decisions is to be preferred. And fourth, even when the preferred set of responses may be known, policy makers often lack the necessary controls to ensure that actual responses are in compliance with those that are preferred.

In varying degrees, these problems will confront any program in any organizational setting; such is the nature of efforts to define and ensure purposeful organizational and individual behavior. But they are exacerbated in the social welfare enterprise because program implementation oc-

curs by "remote control"; the substantive parameters of the social program—which define what it is supposed to do—are generally determined by central authorities in pursuit of national goals, but program implementation—the actions and decisions that determine what the program actually does—occurs in the local community. Both conceptually and organizationally, the circuitous channel from central policy to decentralized implementation is riddled with ambiguity and uncertainty. It affords those groups and individuals in positions of power, and upon whose cooperation and support successful implementation depends, substantial opportunity to influence program operations and hence the substance of social policy. What some of these principal forces are, how they may attempt to influence program operations, and the possible roles of the program administrator in the implementing process are the major questions addressed in this chapter.

VAGUE POLICY:
THE GENESIS OF
THE ACCOUNTABILITY DILEMMA

. . . In an effort to deal actively with a large number of complex foreign and domestic problems, various administrations have proposed and Congress has adopted a multitude of policies that leave many substantive, procedural, and organizational issues surrounding their implementation unanswered. . . . Because many public policies concern the redistribution of power and wealth from one group to another, the political relationships among contending interests have become increasingly interdependent and complex. . . . Often overlooked, state and local governments are no longer the relatively soverign political entities of earlier days but have increasingly become the instruments through which national public policy—but particularly social policy—is implemented. . . .

Policy making in America today is generally characterized as a pluralist process of bargaining, compromise, and coalition building among individual and institutional actors who may possess divergent and even incompatible goals and fundamentally different views on the nature of the problems that policy is to address. Particularly in the arena of social problems, this process generates policies that for a variety of reasons are inherently vague.[1] In dealing with complex problems it is impossible to specify in advance either precise goals or the exact course of action to be followed because sufficient knowledge of cause and effect does not exist. Congress possesses neither the time nor the staff to create precise policy. Language itself is insufficiently precise, with laws always subject to some degree of interpretation. And it is often beneficial within implementing organizations, especially if the environment is characterized by instability, complexity and uncertainty, to avoid being locked in by a fixed set of goals and strategies.

All of these factors no doubt contribute to the dilemma. But by far the most persuasive reason behind vague social policy rests in the simple fact that legislators find it politically expedient to intentionally avoid clear statements of policy. Abstract thinking about problems and their solutions is one thing, but the legislative adoption of written policy often requires the establishment of coalitions with different and conflicting interests; vague written policies offer the advantage of allowing each actor in the coalition to *interpret* the policy (both individually and on behalf of his constituents) as promoting his own interests. Thus, much more may be lost than gained by attempting to formulate clear legislation, because such efforts may easily upset the delicate balance and fragile associations that permit the legislature to act.

At some point, however, vague intentions must be translated into concrete actions, oftentimes discretionary actions undertaken by persons responsible for policy and program implementation. But the exercise of such discretion leaves the implementing organizations vulnerable to scrutiny and challenge by interests who claim that discretionary decisions are not consistent with *their* interpretation of policy intent. Written policy and implementing procedures may be altered as a result and challenged by another group; and the process continues. The result is that policy is not *made* but rather *emerges* through the process of implementation, and a key factor in understanding this process is the notion of accountability.

When organizations, programs, and organizational actors are responsive to legitimate sources of authority and influence it is said that their behavior is *accountable*. When organizations, programs, and organizational actors are unresponsive to legitimate sources of authority it is said that their behavior is *unaccountable*. If no legitimate source of authority exists or none chooses to exercise its influence, it is said that behavior is *discretionary*. Although sometimes used interchangeably, the terms *accountability* and *responsibility* are not the same and should not be confused. Whereas the organizational actor may be responsible *for* the performance of a task, the actor may also be accountable *to* some group or individual possessing legitimate authority over its performance. Accountability, then, explicates a specific source of power, authority, or influence.

For a *given aspect* of organizational performance, the analysis of accountability raises two questions. First, what groups and individuals have legitimate authority over that aspect of organizational performance? And second, through what mechanisms do they exercise authority and control? If the program is seen as a complex series of interrelated activities, the issue of accountability raises a third fundamental question. What effect does a multitude of legitimate authorities, each focusing upon a particular aspect of organizational performance, have upon the integrity of the program as a whole?

Volumes have been written in regard to the first issue, and the various views on what constitutes a legitimate source of authority in the American political system will not be recounted here.[2] In a sense, however, we are captives of our perspective, for if the social program is viewed as an open system, it is presumed that groups and individuals having control over the resources necessary for program operations and survival—or other groups who are able to influence them—possess legitimate control over program operations. Simply, those who can influence its resources—its legal mandate, its finances, its clients, its personnel, and its information—can influence the program. Given this, our interest here is with the second and third questions regarding accountability.

THE EXTERNAL LOCUS OF ACCOUNTABILITY

The combination of vague policy mandates and a multitude of groups and individuals possessing legitimate authority over some aspect of program performance—frequently providing program decision makers with mixed and conflicting signals as to what shall be considered accountable program behavior—requires a revision in the way we normally think about organizational and program goals. In the real world, it seems far less appropriate to assume that behavior is governed by a singular, official goal that is revealed by mandate than by a complex set of contending influences that will "emerge as a set of constraints defining acceptable performances."[3] Moreover, as Graham Allison has noted:

> [t]he set of constraints emerges from a mix of expectations and demands of other organizations in the government, statutory authority, demands from citizens and special interest groups, and bargaining within the organization.[4]

Few of us as individuals, much less as members of large complex organizations, are able to accommodate simultaneously multiple constraints upon our behavior. Rather our attention is selective; we tend to do the work, to accommodate the constraints that seem most immediately pressing. Likewise, it has been noted that an organization's multiple but competing goals and constraints can be made somewhat compatible by treating them *sequentially* in response to continuously changing demands. Allison comments:

> As a problem arises, the subunits of the organization most concerned with that problem deal with it in terms of the constraints *they* take to be most important. When the next problem arises, *another* cluster of subunits deal with it, focusing upon a different set of constraints.[5]

Note that the organizational leadership does not tell its membership that, for example, "This week we will abandon efficiency and focus upon equity as our major constraint"; neither people nor organizations are so malleable. Rather, leadership shifts authority and responsibility to various organizational sub-groups known to be in support of and possibly better able to implement, the constraint of current importance.

Alice Rivlin has noted that the beginning of the newfound concern with accountability coincided with the many social program reforms that occurred during the 1960s.[6] This seems natural in view of the nature of those reforms, many of which were based upon new and unproven theories of societal and individual change, many of which were designed to alter traditional power relationships, and most of which were accompanied by only the vaguest of congressional mandates. Using some of these reforms as a backdrop, in this section we shall investigate three political and administrative mechanisms used to ensure program accountability: the formal rules and guidelines that emanate from social legislation; the constraints provided through the process of citizen participation; and those issued by the courts.

Legislation, Rules, and Guidelines

. . . Within the legalistic model, the implementation of policy is centered upon the creation of a set of rules which serve two important functions: to ensure that administrative actions are equitable and nonarbitrary and to ensure further that those actions are in compliance with the statutory provisions in the legislation. . . . The purpose of these rules and procedures is to limit agency discretion. . . .Rules are key elements in the implementation of national policy through state and local governmental operations; . . . various rules often accompany the grants-in-aid that are a primary source of funds in the social welfare enterprise. To understand the difficulties in formulating clear, concise rules through which to control the behavior of state and local implementing organizations—especially when the policies governing rule generation are vague—the recent history of the federal government's attempt to establish a national social services policy is especially instructive. Of particular significance are the rules implemented in an effort to control the actual implementation of both the need and the allocation parameters of social programming. . . .

[President John F.] Kennedy's staff initiated and Congress ratified what were popularly known as the Public Welfare Amendments of 1962. These amendments created a distinct category of grants to the state for caseworker provided services, an adjunct to the grants for cash assistance already in existence under the original public assistance programs. Neither the statute nor the administrative guidelines, however, clearly specified what "services" were to qualify for the 75 percent matching federal funds to be made available to the states under the amendments. Instead, both bureaucratic and legislative decision makers were prepared to let the defini-

tions "emerge from experience."[7] This was accomplished by giving the secretary of HEW, the agency responsible for implementation, the statutory authority (i.e., discretion) to define what services were to be funded under provisions of the new law. Policy was initially vague because the definition of services was vague.

A second goal of the amendments was to *prevent* dependency. To implement the preventative strategy, eligibility for federally supported services was extended to include, not only current welfare recipients, but also former and persons "likely to become"[8] welfare recipients. By implication, the authority to determine who was "likely to become" a welfare recipient was vested in the state and county welfare bureaucrats already implementing the AFDC program, particularly the intake workers. Eligibility determination had always allowed intake workers substantial discretion within the state-operated programs; the vague statutory specification of potential recipients further increased it.

Finally, as was federal practice with respect to the grants to states for cash assistance under the public assistance programs, Congress placed no ceiling on the federal dollars to be allocated to the states for services. Provided that the states submitted a general plan and provided that services were judged by HEW to qualify for funding, the federal government would match $3 for every $1 the states spent.

Almost immediately both administrative and congressional leaders realized that the strategy of using services to reduce dependency had been oversold. Despite dramatically improving economic conditions, the welfare rolls continued to grow; the service strategy, whatever good it might be achieving, was not reducing public dependency. In 1967, under the leadership of House Ways and Means Chairman Wilbur Mills, Congress moved to further tighten the definition of services and to further strengthen work requirements.

A major result of the 1967 amendments was the creation of the Work Incentive Program (WIN), in which the Congress *attempted* to condition welfare benefits on the recipient's willingness to work. Under the provisions of WIN, HEW was required to refer all welfare recipients to the Department of Labor to register for work. This was implemented by giving HEW the authority to require state and county welfare offices to refer recipients to state employment service agencies, the latter the responsibility of the Department of Labor. There welfare recipients would receive job counseling, would be referred to training programs, or would receive on-the-job training in federally subsidized jobs.

The law did not require, however, that *all* individuals be referred. Those whom Congress deemed "inappropriate" for referral, nonetheless, were rather well defined under statutory provision. Nevertheless, HEW and a large number of states *interpreted* the statute far more liberally than was apparently intended; as a result, state welfare offices were actually required to refer comparatively few recipients. Additionally, the Department of Labor, through its guidelines issued to the state employment offices, did not require its state counterparts to accept the referrals if there was "good cause" for refusing.[9] The net result was that between October 1968, when the program began, and September 1971, slightly more than 300,000 persons had been enrolled in WIN projects.[10] In one not atypical month during that period, WIN enrollees represented less than 8 percent of the total adult AFDC population.[11] . . .

In 1972 Congress attempted to further strengthen the work requirement; still the welfare rolls continued to grow and service expenditures for the following year were projected to reach $4.7 billion.[12] In exasperation, Congress succeeded in curbing the growth of social service expenditures by doing what it had never done in the history of the public assistance grants; it placed a yearly ceiling of $2.5 billion on grants to the states for social services.

Ultimately, HEW and the Congress got out of the business of attempting to define and to implement a national social service policy through the states. With the exception of some child family planning and job-related services, grants to the states for social services are now governed by the provisions of Title XX of the Social Security Act adopted in 1975. The central thrust of Title XX maintains that federal social service dollars will be allocated to the states on the basis of a population formula. The exact nature of services the states will provide with these dollars is to be a state decision to be based on and accountable to the implementation of a statewide needs assessment process. . . .

There are many explanations for the astronomical growth of both the welfare rolls and social service expenditures during the late 1960s and early 1970s; some are attributable to government policy and operations, others to factors beyond its control. Some say that the growth of welfare rights organizations and an advocacy-oriented social work profession increased the enrollment of those already eligible for but not claiming benefits.[13] Others argue that an increasingly attractive combination of benefits with interrelated eligibility provisions—AFDC cash payments, food stamps. Medicaid, and other social services— helped to induce dependency.[14] Some will argue that the growth in service expenditures, especially during the latter period, was the result of the Family Assistance Plan, which most expected to become law; within that legislation, grants to states for services were to be tied to 1971 spending levels, thereby providing states with a strong incentive to spend as much as possible.[15] The fact is, the lack of reliable statistics and sound accounting procedures reduce these explanations to the status of speculation. Nonetheless, the policy did not fulfill public or congressional expectations that dependency would be reduced.

While it is tempting to look for a scapegoat, to isolate the blame, it is not as simple as it might seem. Let's look at the results; were the results accountable to the "intent" of Congress? There are differing opinions as to what the intent of Congress really was. It has been noted, for example, that conservative congressional decision makers intended that the service strategy would reduce the welfare rolls, while liberals saw it as a means of providing greater benefits to the poor, regardless of their impact on the rolls.[16] On the one hand, it does not appear that the conservative expectations were fulfilled since the welfare rolls continued to increase despite ever-increasing expenditures for services. Conversely, it has been argued that the welfare increase during that period might actually have been greater had not a substantial amount of federal "social and rehabilitative" service dollars gone to support "administrative" services. The vague definition of services allowed states to use federal dollars for such administrative procedures as eligibility determination, thereby helping to keep the rolls down.[17] Nonetheless, that is small consolation for those who expected a dramatic decline rather than merely a slowed rate of increase in the number of welfare dependents.

Certainly, you may argue, the service strategy at least produced the results expected by those desiring to provide greater benefits to the poor. Not necessarily so, for it has also been argued that the policies merely shifted the funding base for services the states would probably have provided anyway, not to mention that much of the funding was used in support of administration.[18]

One can "blame" the states for being unaccountable to congressional statutory provisions especially as they became more clearly specified toward the end of the period. Yet the new regulations and implementing guidelines were often garbled, the states receiving one interpretation from one of ten HEW regional offices and quite another from its Washington, D.C., headquarters. Moreover, just as a state agency was getting settled into its new routine, a new set of guidelines [emanated] from Washington.

Additionally, there are a variety of more general reasons why the implementation of a national social services program through the states failed to achieve national purposes. Alterations in federal funding practices that require a state match, like those of the social service program, frequently require legislative as well as administrative actions at the state level; thus program implementation must be accountable to state as well as national interests. Yet the lines of authority and responsibility between the federal and state governments have never clearly been drawn; only the courts have had consistent success in achieving state compliance with federal policy. In addition, HEW's enforcement powers and methods are often ineffective. Their power is often diluted by political pressures from state officials and congressional representatives (meaning that the sanction of withholding federal funds, even if state practices deviate substantially from established federal guidelines, is often politically untenable); their methods for achieving conformity are cumbersome and ineffective; and their enforcement staff is in short supply.[19]

Accountability and Citizen Participation

In 1963 planning was begun on another set of programs, which [was] to become a second major element of welfare strategy for the ensuing decade; the result was the Economic Opportunity Act of 1964 (EOA). Together with the 1960s' Model Cities legislation—which established programs aimed at curbing physical deterioration in declining neighborhoods—the EOA was to become the major strategy in America's war on poverty. The war on poverty was government's official attempt to make its welfare efforts *accountable to the poor* through a strategy of citizen participation. And in apparent response to the tenet that policy makers can overcome resistance to change by constructing alternative parallel institutions that can do the job better, the philosophy, the principal actors, the structure, and the vast majority of programs that comprised the EOA differed substantially from those of the Public Welfare Amendments. Yet, the EOA retained one characteristic that was identical: the policy was extraordinarily and intentionally vague.

The Public Welfare Amendments were based on a loosely specified theory, which stated that the welfare rolls and dependency could be reduced through a strategy of social and rehabilitative services. The EOA planners were less concerned with the reduction of the welfare rolls, per se, than with the social, human, and family conditions that accompanied poverty, especially poverty in urban settings. Although widely accused of lacking a causal theory, EOA planning was dominated by the "opportunity theory" of sociologists Richard Cloward and Lloyd Ohlin.[20] Developed after exhaustive research on the problem of juvenile delinquency, Cloward and Ohlin's theory concluded that much deviant social behavior could be explained by a lack of opportunity to conform in socially acceptable ways to a variety of materialistic social norms. The result was alienation and deviant behavior; the cure was to create the opportunity to share in the fruits of mainstream American life. . . .

In addition to authorizing funding for services, requiring only a 10 percent local match, the EOA promoted a number of major structural changes as well. A new federal agency, the Office of Equal Oppor-

tunity, was created. Federal funds were to bypass the states completely (at the time there was widespread sentiment among urban officials that the rural dominated state legislatures didn't care about and state bureaucracies were incompetent to deal with pressing urban problems)[21] and go directly to the local community. Traditional categories of individuals were to be *neither* the target of different benefit packages *nor* a defining characteristic of programs, but rather *problem areas* and areas of opportunity were to serve as the object of funds.

If the statutory directives governing the nature of services were vague in the welfare amendments, those outlined in the EOA were no less so, stating only in the most ambiguous terms the desired ends of the various programs—to provide "education," "training," "useful work experience," and for VISTA volunteers to "combat poverty."[22] But this was not inconsistent with the major structural innovation of the act. Under Title II, the EOA provided funds for the establishment and operation of local Community Action Agencies (CAAs) which were to be responsible for all phases of program design, planning, and implementation embraced by the Act. Moreover, these were not to be agencies of local government, accountable to established local interests. Rather they were to be accountable to the poor through a *process* (not a set of rules or guidelines) emphasizing "maximum feasible participation" of the poor. . . .

Almost immediately two sources of tension emerged, because there was great uncertainty concerning to whose interests the local CAAs were to be held accountable. If the CAA boards adopted low-profile strategies closely aligned with established interests, they were often accused by the poor of "selling out." Other community action agencies—notably those in San Francisco and Syracuse—adopted the strategy of confronting the established interests, to the obvious disenchantment of those interests. Martin Rein has suggested that it was this variation in political styles and political allegiance that caused different CAAs to interpret the OEO implementing guidelines differently; as the political climate became more radical, the demand for political *involvement* by local CAAs quickly escalated to a demand for *control* of policy and program decisions.[23]

However, the major conflict was not between the various local interests but the accountability conflict created by local control of federal funds allocated in pursuit of national policy. In an attempt to reestablish accountability, the 1967 amendments to the EOA restricted local discretion by earmarking funds for some of the more popular, apparently successful, and least controversial programs like Head Start and Neighborhood Legal Services. Congress in the same year also adopted the Green Amendment, which gave local governments the option of bringing the CAAs under their control. Over the years, congressional and popular support for OEO declined, a war in Southeast Asia replaced the war on poverty on the list of top national priorities, and the activist Democratic philosophy of the Great Society was replaced by a more passive Republican policy of the New Federalism.

Many observers contend that the war on poverty failed because neither the federal policy makers nor local decision makers were able to resolve the inherent conflict between national priorities and local discretion.[24] When local priorities, even local political and administrative "styles," failed to match federal expectations—priorities and styles that might have existed in the minds of policy makers, but that were seldom articulated in the law or the guidelines—it was natural that such conflict would ensue. A national goal creates the expectation that a national problem will be solved, and indeed, as we have seen with both the EOA and the Public Welfare

Amendments, it is the creation of such expectations that allows the program to be sold to the Congress and to the American public.

Others claim that the program failed because of a more fundamental reason: simply, we knew very little about poverty or its causes, much less its cure. Daniel Moynihan, for one, has stated bluntly that "government did not know what it was doing."[25] Moreover, as Samuel Krislov has suggested, this lack of knowledge was, at least in part, reflected in the adoption of what he calls the "flexibility of ambiguity" inherent in the policy.[26] A principal source of this ambiguity lay within the rationale underlying the participatory strategy for achieving accountability. . . .

The reality, as the welfare amendments, the Economic Opportunity Act, and Title XX amply demonstrate, is indeed that participation is an integral part of the processes surrounding both policy making and implementation. But even if provided with a forum and substantial resources, it is not the ordinary folk, participating in structured "participatory processes," who will influence the key decisions. These decisions have already been influenced and made by "blue ribbon" committees of experts and interest group spokesmen in the upper echelons of the federal implementing organizations; in the budgetary recommendations submitted by the President, the governors, and the mayors; and by the congressmen, legislators, and council members who must authorize public expenditures. . . .

Accountability and the Courts

Among the most significant developments in social policy during the past two decades has been the increasing use of the courts as a vehicle for promoting social change and for shaping social policy. Normally, we think of only the U.S. Supreme Court as a powerful force of change through such decisions as that in *Brown* v.

Board of Education, which brought about major federal efforts to end racial segregation in the schools. Yet even the lower courts have become significant institutional settings for the creation of social policies and for ensuring that those policies are accountable to the public interest. . . .

One area in which the courts have been particularly active in enhancing predictability in reducing arbitrary discretion, concerns client eligibility and entitlement decisions; these are the judicial procedures commonly known as fair hearings. The established procedure in virtually all public welfare programs, fair hearings may be requested by persons who feel they have been unfairly denied benefits to which they are entitled. Once requested sparingly for fear of bureaucratic reprisal, the frequency of requests for fair hearings and other judicial proceedings has grown considerably in recent years largely because of the increased availability of legal services to the poor and the activist stance taken by advocate groups like the welfare rights organizations.

Normally, we think of a fair hearing or similar judicial appeal proceeding as a means of limiting arbitrary, discretionary behavior by administrative officials. But in recent years, the influence of the courts has moved beyond protecting the aggrieved party against the discretionary behavior of *individuals* to one of protecting against discretionary *agency* practices. . . .

If the court rules for a reversal of the administrative decision (as they have been known to do in a high proportion of disability appeals), they do not do so by appealing to their own set of rules; they have none. Rather they employ the technique of finding, in the particular instance, that there was insufficient evidence to support the administrative conclusion that the medical condition was not disabling.[27] The judicial process shifts the burden of proof from the individual claimant to the administrative agency. Liebman comments on the implications of this shift:

Attempting to implement Congress' clear purpose that benefits be provided to only those persons in fact medically disabled, the Secretary [of Health, Education and Welfare] establishes hurdles that make it difficult for someone to qualify solely on the basis of a persistent assertion that he is physically incapable of work or able to work only with great pain. Judges, on the other hand, need not consider the program as a whole or its annual budget. Their inquiry is normally focused upon an individual claimant, whose story is often sympathetic, whose perseverance in carrying the case so far is evidence of a sincere claim, and who will not be on Easy Street even if he wins the appeal.[28]

In essence, the judicial appeals process enhances accountability to the individual by its ability to identify legitimate *exceptions* to established administrative rules. . . .

The newfound activist role of the courts has created new standards for and new methods of achieving administrative accountability. But the use of judicial power for reconciling matters of policy implementation is not without its drawbacks. Although the judicial process is seen as the guardian of such important principles as "justice," "rights," "equity," and strict adherence to the facts, its use to achieve accountability to the public interest is often cumbersome, expensive, and time-consuming. More important, the judicial decision-making process often creates policy that is reactive and inflexible. The courts cannot propose policy but can only respond to a grievance, the particular facts of which may be atypical but the results all-encompassing, and neither judges nor the courts are well equipped to appreciate the nuances of program operation or the relationship of program to the total welfare structure.[29] And through the establishment of numerous precedents and ever-more complex sets of rules, the exercise of discretion—what James Thompson has called the essence of the administrative process[30]—is ultimately stifled. Unlike the judiciary, "the administrator is expected to treat experience not as a jailer but as a teacher."[31] Perhaps the significance of the courts' involvement in matters of policy is evidence that this expectation has not been fulfilled.

ACCOUNTABILITY AND THE SERVICE PROVIDER

While external sources of accountability impinge in various important ways on the social welfare enterprise, only indirectly do they influence the task related behavior of organizational participants. The constraints imposed must still be translated into some effective means for ensuring that the behavior of individual service providers is made predictable and accountable, for it is here—in the user-provider transaction—that social policy is truly implemented. It is here as well that provider norms and practices will come into conflict with other norms and other views regarding what constitutes accountable program behavior.

While the distinction is not always clear-cut, it is necessary to distinguish between professional and nonprofessional service providers because the principal norms and forces to which each will be held accountable are different. In view of their mastery of a body of specialized and often esoteric knowledge and the skills necessary to apply that knowledge in solving problems people cannot solve themselves, until recently at least service professionals have enjoyed a degree of autonomy and authority not normally shared by nonprofessionals. And although the degree of autonomy varies with the profession—clearly, physicians enjoy greater autonomy than schoolteachers or caseworkers—it traditionally has extended to embrace the two most fundamental decisions in the user-provider transaction: the authority to determine client needs and the authority to determine appropriate treatment.[32] This authority is controlled, moreover, by the dominant ethic of the social service professions: the

professional will be accountable to the client.

In the sixties, it was common for some professionals—planners, social workers, academics, and to some extent members of the legal profession and public administrators—to respond to the demands for greater accountability to the client by adopting an advocacy posture. In essence, and consistent with the rhetoric of the day that espoused, "If you're not part of the solution, you're part of the problem," client advocacy became one of only two possible modes of professional behavior. Richard Cloward and Frances Fox Piven, two of the foremost proponents of client advocacy in the social work profession, describe the mood of the time.

> The issue was whether we were going to take sides with the agencies and further our careers or with the victims of an aggressively cruel capitalist society. Were we in our daily work going to defend the practices and policies of the hospitals, courts, prisons, foster care agencies, welfare departments, and mental institutions for which we worked, or were we going to use our jobs to defend and protect the poor, the sick, the criminal, and the deviant against these agencies?[33]

But advocacy has its other side, especially if it is viewed as a *political* and not a professional response to unmet needs, a view which is likely if the legitimacy of the profession itself is in question. Even in the best of professional times, with the professional mandate on firm ground, Heinz Eulau has noted that the role of the advocate professional raises fundamental questions.

> What will happen if things go wrong? To whom will the advocate professional be accountable? His clients, his peers, his employers, or only his own conscience? What would accountability imply? Would it imply making restitution? Risking censure or suspension of license? Dismissal from the job? Most of these questions have yet to be answered.[34]

Lacking a client orientation that has been conditioned by professional affiliation, nonprofessional providers nonetheless do not behave as individuals but rather are accountable to service users, as Michael Lipsky puts it, "on behalf of their agencies and the public purposes they represent."[35] Despite the existence of controls to ensure that provider behavior is indeed representative of agency purposes, however, most social welfare agencies demonstrate, as James Q. Wilson has observed, the paradoxical quality that "discretion increases as one moves down the hierarchy"[36] to the level of the direct service provider. And indeed, some contend that a high degree of discretion at the level of the direct worker is *the* defining characteristic of social welfare organizations.[37] This is striking because it is increasingly the nonprofessional worker who shoulders most of the responsibility for direct contact with service users and frequently presides over a transaction—normally in one of a variety of intake processes—that has been characterized as follows:

> On the one side of the desk sits the applicant for service with all the needs, experiences, and idiosyncratic characteristics that combined to bring him or her there. On the other side of the desk sits a person whose function it is to determine the validity and appropriateness of the presenting request, the goodness of fit between it and the franchise, policies, and resources of the organization, and thus the entitlement of the applicant to service. The conversation may be brief, although the preliminaries are often lengthy. It ends with a decision, or a referral, which may satisfy or deny the presenting request. Any sympathy or antipathy that the agency representative may feel for the applicant is supposed to have no effect on the outcome of the episode. The resources of the agency and its formal policies regarding their use are expected to define the eligibility of the client for service.[38]

Oftentimes provider behavior in this transaction is guided less by formal agency policy and procedure than by the simple necessity of coping with a stressful situation. Placed in the situation of dealing with numerous people with countless problems that have little probability of solution— where they are continuously exposed to physical and psychological threat, where working conditions are poor, and where there are neither the organizational nor the human resources to perform the job adequately—service workers are forced to invent what Richard Elmore has called, "routines for mass processing," including the use of "formal procedures of the organization to strike an impersonal balance between oneself, as an individual, and the client."[39]

But how might administrators help ensure that providers are accountable to users on behalf of the agency? First, agency decision makers must know how they want providers to behave; they must be able to identify a preferred provider response for each identifiable contingency, and if the agency or program is the instrument of multiple objectives, they must be able to rank-order preferred provider responses. Second, administrators must be able to document provider behavior and to compare this with established agency preferences. . . . [T]hird, administrators must be in possession of various incentives and sanctions that can be applied to induce desirable patterns of provider behavior.[40]

If the needs and problems of service users were not unique, not idiosyncratic, there would be a finite number of user types, and it would be theoretically possible for administrators to create a set of preferred responses for each presenting situation. But the needs of individuals are unique and idiosyncratic and not readily susceptible to preprogrammed and rigid decision criteria; thus substantial discretion in matching services to needs is required. The problem here is one of striking a balance between discretionary and controlled behavior, to know when the clarification of program goals and preferred provider response "is desirable because continued ambivalence and contradiction is unproductive, and when it will result in a reduction in the scope and mission of public services."[41]

When this dilemma has been resolved, administrative attention turns to the methods by which provider behavior is controlled, a task based on a very simple principle: Administrators can exert control only over those aspects of behavior they know something about. In general, knowledge about provider behavior may be obtained in three principal ways: through analysis of written records compiled by the provider, by direct observation, or by inferring what that behavior was from an analysis of numerical performance measures.

Of the methods of knowing about provider behavior, probably the most important derives from written records maintained by the individual provider. In general, [they] will contain two types of information (1) information pertaining to the individual's presenting situation and (2) [about] the actions initiated or taken by the provider. Records are of extreme importance and value when the bounds of the user-provider transaction can be well specified, for example during the intake process when certain questions must be asked, verified, and recorded for all applicants. The answers are then matched with standardized criteria to determine eligibility and benefit levels. In addition, records may be useful for ensuring that process standards of service quality are adhered to, requiring that providers record whether or not specific tasks (for example, the provision of a referral or the administration of a test) were carried out. If records are maintained on standardized forms, moreover, [they] can help to ensure that provider decisions and actions have been uniform across the total range of service users.

Caution must be exercised in using standardized records to audit provider accountability, however, for it is all but impossible to create forms which can accommodate all of the intangibles and all of the contingencies that will influence the provider's response in a particular situation. Interpretation and recording especially of the presenting situation is highly discretionary, often dependent upon the provider's prevailing state of mind,[42] the written record guarantees neither an unbiased interpretation nor an appropriate response to the user's needs.[43]

Direct observation may be a way for administrators to evaluate the intangible factors that prevade the user-provider transaction, provided of course that the administrator knows what to look for and has some set of criteria for judging the transaction. (These attributes are among the major benefits derived from the common practice of drawing administrative personnel from the ranks of providers.) The administrator can, for example, observe whether a procedure is properly carried out, whether the provider behaves courteously, and whether the provider's interpretation of the presenting situation and action taken is consistent with his or her own judgment. Of course, the mere presence of an observer is likely to distort the transaction, since most seasoned providers already know what their supervisors want to see. Moreover, continuous observation is expensive and runs counter to the dominant expectation—held by both user and provider alike—that the transaction is to be conducted in private.

Quantitative measures of performance—the number of cases processed, accepted, rejected, or referred, the number of persons successfully completing a training program, and so on—may be useful for inferring whether provider behavior is accountable to the desired results of a transaction. But quantitative measures of performance are at best only crude indicators of actual behavior. The absence of statistical controls makes it difficult to establish relationships between results and the myriad factors—including provider behavior—that might have caused them. Moreover, the establishment and monitoring of numerical measures can create criterion behavior, behavior that may be accountable to the measure but not to the service user. Such behavior may inordinately highlight the importance of one dimension of the transaction at the expense of all others, particularly those that relate to service quality. Indeed, the greater the degree of provider discretion, "the less one can infer that quantitative indicators bear relationship to service quality."[44]

The best approach to achieving provider accountability to agency preferences is, for the most part, dependent on the model of organization one chooses to adopt for describing participant behavior. Research has shown, however, that the appropriateness of various methods for achieving control is largely dependent upon the nature of the provider task being performed. Where tasks can be well defined and where the preferred response is known—like that of eligibility determination—it is likely that centrally issued rules and guidelines, supplemented by standardized reporting requirements, will have substantial impact on provider behavior.[45] In essence, behaviors that are simple and come closest to being preprogrammable and readily evaluble, as one might suspect, are most easily controlled by rules.

Tasks that are not well defined or for which agency preferences are not well developed, but that are observable—for example, providing users with information about alternative courses of action—are less readily controllable through rules. Rather, close supervision is required. Supervisors should be recruited for their understanding of the transaction, trained in its intricacies, and sufficiently motivated to ensure that the agency provides the highest possible level of service to its users. Finally, for those apects of the user-provider transaction that are indefinable, not readily observable, and primarily evaluable only from a user standpoint—like the provider's apparent attitude, responsiveness, and "style"—some combination of supervision and provider training seems the most appropriate means of control.[46]

Like the various ways of generating the necessary *knowledge about* provider behavior, the quickest, cheapest, and apparently most easily implemented methods for generating *control over* provider behavior— centrally issued rules and procedures, for example—may only strike at the periphery of the transaction. What is seldom mentioned and never researched is the *residual* effect of these rules and procedures, not their effect on the benefits rendered or denied, but upon interpersonal dimensions of the encounter itself and upon the consequential behavior of the service user.

ACCOUNTABILITY AND SOCIAL PROGRAM ADMINISTRATION

Stated policy goals, as we have seen, may not prove to be the principal determinants of program decision and action, which arise instead in sequential response to various constraints imposed by external and internal forces. If a newspaper article appears proclaiming high levels of welfare fraud, administrators will probably respond by requiring that providers more closely scrutinize new applications and the family and income status of current recipients. If cumulative program expenditures are substantially higher than those of the budget time-line or if a budget reduction appears imminent, administrators may demand that eligibility procedures be tightened, caseloads increased, or that services previously provided individually now be performed in groups. Conversely, if it appears that a budgetary surplus will exist at the end of the fiscal year, the exact opposite—perhaps supplemented by a vigorous outreach campaign—may become the preferred program response. Or a federal judge may decide that state governments are no longer required under federal statutes to provide funding for abortions and, under strong pressure from a citizens' lobby, the state legislature restricts funding to only those cases where the mother's health is in question; administrators respond with revised program eligibility guidelines. . . .

As we have also seen, social program implementation requires a perspective that is inherently multi-organizational in nature, one in which different sources of authority exert varying degrees of control over different aspects of program operations. Some will control funds, others the qualitative characteristics of the service delivered, others the specific eligibility criteria in use, and still others the process of service delivery. Some forces may be governmental, but in a different level than that responsible for implementation, others may be nongovernmental and within the local community itself. Some will be highly organized and well financed; others, but loose, temporary coalitions of community interest groups. In this concluding section of this chapter, we shall investigate the impact of these separate forces on the integrity of the whole program and investigate the possible roles of the program administrator in guiding its implementation. . . .

Accountability and the Administrator: Roles and Options

If the programs of the social welfare enterprise are largely influenced by divergent and contradictory external forces, what are the possible roles and options available to persons in positions of administrative responsibility? It depends, say Jeffrey Pfeffer and Gerald Salancik, upon the perceived relationship among external constraints, administrative action, and or-

ganizational outcomes. In particular, they have identified three functional roles that might plausibly describe administrative behavior in organizations that are confronted by myriad external constraints: the symbolic role, the responsive role, and the discretionary role.[47] Each of these, in turn, promotes a distinct conception of administrative accountability.

Certainly the most iconoclastic of these roles, at least in terms of more traditional conceptions of administrative responsibility and behavior, derives from the view that administrative actions will have little or no effect on organizational outcomes. Since there is no relationship between administrative action and organizational outcomes, administrative behavior is largely *symbolic,* designed to promote only the *appearance* of maintaining accountability to external forces. The role is, they note, not lacking in importance, for it perpetuates the valuable illusion that causation exists, rational action is being taken, and that someone is in control.

> As a symbol of control and personal causation, managers and organizational leaders can be used as scapegoats, rewarded when things go well and fired when they go poorly. The knowledge that someone is in charge and that the fate of the organization depends on that person offers the promise of change in organizational activities and fortunes. When problems emerge, the solution is simple and easy—replace the manager.[48]

Closely related to this role is the symbolic conception of accountability itself—accountability that is "divorced from any systematic efforts to promote actual attainment of the desired values."[49] The promotion of symbolic reassurance through the use of verbal slogans, visible shifts in key administrative personnel, the establishment of blue ribbon investigation committees, the adoption of rules with no expectation nor any means of enforcing compliance, and other symbolic gestures, as Murray Edelman has noted, often enhance the short-run survivability of the organization by mollifying unorganized political groups, thereby making political self-mobilization more difficult. In the long run, however, simple symbolic reassurance may backfire, with the eventual realization that they have been manipulated, providing a rallying point around which groups may organize and become potent forces in extracting substantive organizational responses to their demands.[50]

The second or *responsive* role posits that the administrative function is one of processing, assimilating, and implementing appropriate responses to various external demands, usually by altering aspects of program operations that are not *currently* the subject of controversy. For example, to accommodate potentially greater program utilization in the face of an impending resource reduction, administrators may decide to provide a less expensive form of allocation by converting from professional to nonprofessional personnel or, alternatively, from individualized to group services. These "new" allocations, however, may prove less effective in alleviating the undesirable conditions that are the program's ultimate reason for being; thus a new set of logical disturbances may upset the program's integrity. Moreover, their implementation might be resisted by legislative, professional, or other forces having a stake in the nature of the allocation provided; what was originally a non-issue—the nature of the allocation—now becomes an issue of crucial importance.

The critical decision within the responsive role is, of course, to determine which of the often contradictory set of demands to heed and which to ignore.[51] The problem with this purely reactive posture, as Armitai Etzioni recognizes, is that "by and large, groups with more status, income, and education have more power and hence make the system relatively more 'accountable' to them."[52] An additional problem arises when the administrator uses the reactive posture as a means of abrogating his or her discretionary authority, as in, "But I was just following standard procedure."[53]

The third administrative role is consistent with the notion that the relationship between administrative actions and externally imposed constraints is reciprocal. This leads to the administrator's *discretionary* role, one in which the administrator actively seeks to shape the organization's external environment.[54] Considering the potential conflict between reduced resources and expanded utilization, for example, the program administrator might seek to open channels of communication and help to identify areas of possible compromise between the two opposing interests.

Central to an understanding of the discretionary administrative role is the view, first posited some time ago by Richard Cyert and James March,[55] that organizations are internally comprised of and are also more or less powerful participants in external bargaining coalitions. The most important aspect of the conflict-bargaining model—one that makes it especially attractive for use in the social welfare enterprise—is that organizational action need not be framed in terms of a clear, concise statement of organizational goals. Indeed, the organizations and organizational actors need share no commonality of purpose whatsoever, only the willingness to bargain and compromise; the result is a set of organizational outcomes that are temporarily bargained solutions implying no overall agreement on a single purpose. As in the responsive role, it is of utmost importance that the administrator be able to idenfity critical internal and external interdependencies; in addition, however, the administrator must seek to cultivate and preserve the bargaining arena within which differently valued ends will occur. This implies, as Thomas Schelling has noted, that "there is a powerful common interest in reaching an outcome that is not enormously destructive to both sides."[56] Schelling also notes that convergence upon a mutually acceptable outcome is largely dependent upon the ability of each actor in the conflict-bargaining process to discover the often implicit "rules of the game," or the expectations held by each party for the other.[57]

Significantly, these expectations may differ substantially from those implied in the law, written guidelines, labor agreements, or other formal demands made upon the program; what is important is whether administrators anticipate being forced to comply with those demands. In programs requiring substantial intergovernmental interaction, for example, an increasing body of research suggests that action in state and local agencies is largely dependent upon the expectation that federal officials will or will not enforce compliance with written policy.[58] If federal officials deem that state and local actions are not accountable to prevailing policy and initiate attempts to enforce compliance, state and local administrators will respond in part with greater compliance and in part with counterattempts to alter the policy; the process will continue until some temporary, but mutually acceptable compromise is achieved. And then it will start again. Thus, a system of centralized planning and decentralized implementation appears to work when administrators are able to negotiate a compromise between federal and local interests, creating as Martha Derthick has noted, "programs that are neither 'federal' nor 'local' but a blend of the two."[59]

An expansion of the discretionary administrative role creates what Etzioni has called the "guidance" approach to accountability, which he considers as having both a power and a moral base.[60] Within this view, the administrative role is neither one of symbol, of responsiveness, nor one

one of actively shaping the organization's external environment, but one of exercising what he calls "creative leadership." The principal difference between Etzioni's creative leadership role and the other possibilities discussed is that—while still maintaining accountability to the widest possible set of internal and external constraints on program operations—the administrator actively seeks to promote values *other* than simple organizational survival.

With respect to social programs in particular, Simon Slavin's observations regarding this often risky and difficult balancing act are of great value. He contends that the governing ethic of professional administrative behavior in the social welfare enterprise ultimately derives from a fundamental concern for clients and their needs. This ethical posture, however, requires political skills that transcend those associated with single-minded and heavy-handed advocacy, which may only weaken the administrator's professional credibility and may also heighten political conflict to a level at which no program change becomes possible. Rather, as Slavin notes, professional skills are concerned "precisely with the ways in which the administrator balances and orchestrates the interests of divergent constituencies, but from a client perspective as an organizing principle."[61] To do so requires first and foremost knowledge about clients, especially how the organizational and administrative technology of the enterprise both denies and fulfills their needs. . . .

NOTES

1. Richard B. Stewart, "The Reformation of American Administrative Law," *Harvard Law Review*, 88, no. 8 (June 1975), 1,077.

2. For an excellent summary of these differing views, see Thomas R. Dye, *Understanding Public Policy* (Englewood Cliffs, N.J.: Prentice-Hall, Inc., 1975), Ch. 2.

3. Graham T. Allison, "The Power of Bureaucratic Routines," in Francis E. Rourke, ed., *Bureaucratic Power in National Politics*, 2nd ed. (Boston: Little, Brown, 1972), p. 85, emphasis added.

4. Ibid.
5. Ibid., emphasis added.
6. Allice M. Rivlin, "Social Policy: Alternate Strategies for the Federal Government," in Randall B. Ripley and Grace A. Franklin, eds., *National Government and Policy in the United States* (Itasca, Ill.: F. E. Peacock, 1977), pp. 305–14.
7. Martha Derthick, *Uncontrollable Spending for Social Services Grants* (Washington, D.C.: Brookings Institution, 1975), p. 9.
8. Social Security Act, Sec. (403) (a) (3) (A) (iii) and Sec. 1603(a) (4) (A) (iii), *Compilation of the Social Security Laws*, pp. 135, 212.
9. Joel F. Handler, "Federal-State Interests in Welfare Administration," in Joint Economic Committee, Studies in Public Welfare, Paper 5, pt. 2, pp. 20–24.
10. Ibid., p. 75.
11. Monthly Status Reports for WIN (May 31, 1971), cited in Stephen F. Gold, "Comment: The Failure of the Work Incentive Program," *University of Pennsylvania Law Review*, 119 (1971), 495.
12. Joseph Heffernan, "Public Assistance and Social Services," in Joint Economic Committee, *Studies in Public Welfare*, Paper 5, pt. 2, p. 109.
13. Heffernan, "Public Assistance and Social Services," p. 114.
14. Frederick Doolittle, Frank Levy, and Michael Wiseman, "The Mirage of Welfare Reform," *The Public Interest*, no. 47 (Spring 1977), 65.
15. Heffernan, "Public Assistance and Social Services," p. 115.
16. Derthick, *Uncontrollable Spending*, p. 13.
17. Irene Lurie, "Legislative, Administrative, and Judicial Changes in the AFDC Program, 1967–71," in Joint Economic Committee, *Studies in Public Welfare*, Paper 5, pt. 2, p. 95.
18. Derthick, *Uncontrollable Spending*, p. 2.
19. Peter Sitkin, "Welfare Law: Narrowing the Gap between Congressional Policy and Local Practice," in Joint Economic Committee, *Studies in Public Welfare*, Paper 5, pt. 2, p. 52.
20. Richard A. Cloward and Lloyd E. Ohlin, *Delinquency and Opportunity: A Theory of Delinquent Gangs* (New York: Free Press, 1960).
21. See, for example, Frank P. Grad, "The State's Capacity to Respond to Urban Problems," in Alan K. Campbell, ed., *The States and the Urban Crisis* (Englewood Cliffs, N.J.: Prentice-Hall, 1970), pp. 27–58.
22. Theodore Lowi, *The End of Liberalism* (New York: W. W. Norton & Co., Inc., 1969), p. 235.
23. Martin Rein, *Social Policy* (New York: Random House, 1970), p. 366.
24. See, for example, Samuel Krislov, "The OEO Lawyers Fail to Constitutionalize a Right to Welfare: A Study in the Uses and Limits of the Judicial Process," *University of Minnesota Law Review*, 58 (1973), 213–14.
25. Daniel Moynihan, *Maximum Feasible Misunderstanding* (New York: Free Press, 1969), p. 170.
26. Krislov, "The OEO Lawyers," pp. 214–15.
27. Lance Liebman, "The Definition of Disability in Social Security and Supplemental Security Income: Drawing the Bounds of Welfare Estates," *Harvard Law Review*, 89, no. 5 (March 1976), 846.
28. Ibid.
29. Donald L. Horowitz, "The Courts as Guardians of the Public Interest," *Public Administration Review*, 37, no. 2. (March/April 1977), 150.
30. James D. Thompson, *Organizations in Action* (New York: McGraw-Hill, 1967), p. 54.
31. Opinion of Judge Wyzanski, *Shawmut Association v. SEC* (1st Cir. 1945), cited in Kenneth Culp Davis, *Administrative Law and Government* (St. Paul, Minn.: West Publishing Co., 1960), p. 323.
32. Heinz Eulau, "Skill Revolution and Consultative Commonwealth," *American Political Science Review*, 67, no. 1 (March 1973), 183.
33. Richard. A. Cloward and Frances Fox Piven, "Notes toward a Radical Social Work," in Roy Baily and Mike Brake, eds., *Radical Social Work* (New York: Pantheon, 1975), p. xii.
34. Eulau, "Skill Revolution," p. 188.
35. Michael Lipsky, "The Assault on Human Services: Street-Level Bureaucracy, Accountability and the Fiscal Crisis," a paper presented at the Conference on Public Agency Accountability in an Urban Society, Urban Research Center, University of Wisconsin-Milwaukee, Milwaukee, Wisconsin, April 3–5, 1977, p. 34 (emphasis deleted).
36. James Q. Wilson, *Varieties of Police Behavior* (New York: Atheneum, 1973), p. 7.
37. This is the position taken in Joel F. Handler, *Protecting the Social Service Client: Legal and Structural Controls on Official Discretion* (New York: Academic Press, 1979).
38. Robert L. Kahn, Daniel Katz, and Barbara Gutek, "Bureaucratic Encounters—An Evaluation of Government Services." *Journal of Applied Behavioral Science*, 12, no. 2 (May–June 1976), 181–82.
39. Richard F. Elmore, "Organizational Models of Social Program Implementation," *Public Policy*, 26, no. 2 (Spring 1978), 203.
40. Michael Lipsky, "The Assault on Human Services," p. 3.
41. Ibid., p. 16.
42. If you've not worked in a welfare office, Frederick Wiseman's film, *Welfare* provides a powerful portrait of the user-provider transaction.
43. Lipsky, "The Assault on Human Services," p. 12.

44. Ibid., p. 20.
45. Tana Pesso, "Local Welfare Offices: Managing the Intake Process," *Public Policy*, 26, no. 2 (Spring 1978), 326.
46. Ibid., 327.
47. See Jeffrey Pfeffer and Gerald R. Salancik, *The External Control of Organizations* (New York: Harper & Row, Publ, 1978), Ch. 4.
48. Ibid., 263.
49. Amitai Etzioni, "Alternative Conceptions of Accountability: The Example of Health Administration," *Public Administration Review*, 35, no. 3 (May–June 1975), 280.
50. Murray Edelman, *The Symbolic Uses of Politics* (Urbana, Ill.: University of Illinois Press, 1964). Ch. 2.
51. Pfeffer and Salancik, *The External Control of Organizations*, p. 266.
52. Etzioni, "Alternative Conceptions of Accountability," 281.
53. Thompson, *Organizations in Action*, p. 119.
54. Pfeffer and Salancik, *The External Control of Organizations*, p. 267.
55. Richard Cyert and James March, *A Behavioral Theory of the Firm* (Englewood Cliffs, N.J.: Prentice-Hall, 1963).
56. Thomas Schelling, *The Strategy of Conflict* (London: Oxford University Press, 1963), p. 219.
57. Ibid., p. 220.
58. See, for example, Helen Ingram, "Policy Implementation through Bargaining," *Public Policy*, 25, no. 4 (Fall 1977).
59. Martha Derthick, *New Towns in Town: Why a Federal Program Failed* (Washington, D.C.: Urban Institute, 1977), p. 98.
60. Etzioni, "Alternative Conceptions of Accountability," pp. 284–85.
61. Simon Slavin, "Editor's Introduction to Part II," in *Social Administration*, ed. Simon Slavin (New York: The Haworth Press, 1978), pp. 39–42.

Ralph M. Kramer

Contracting for Human Services: An Organizational Perspective

Although there is a long history of governmental contracting, the rapid spread of tax and expenditure limits has stimulated a renewed interest in reprivatization—the use of nongovernmental organizations as an alternative to governmental delivery of public services. The strong public dislike of bureaucracy, along with a belief in the overload of government, has led to paying greater attention to marketlike mechanisms such as user fees, vouchers, and, particularly, contracting to carry out public functions. Despite the enormous growth in purchase of service contracting (POSC), there is little available knowledge to guide policymaking and administration.

Contracting has been viewed from three perspectives, according to the kind of public service, the level of government, and the extent of reliance on profit making or nonprofit organizations: (1) one body of literature is focused on the use and the relative cost of profit making organizations providing upward of forty municipal services, such as refuse collection and disposal, street and traffic lighting, road maintenance, animal pounds, park and recreation services, as well as legal, engineering, and accounting services, and so on.[1] (2) A broader and a more political concern with the "contract state" is found at the national level, where there is extensive governmental use of both profit and nonprofit organizations, which results in a blurring of the boundaries between the three sectors. This "new political economy" is characterized by the proliferation of quangos (quasi-nongovernmental organizations), the widespread use of consultants and contractors by HEW and the Department of Defense, the reliance on universities and think tanks for research and evaluation.[2] (3) Less well-known to public administrators and policymakers is another body of information about POSC in the social services or, as they are increasingly called, the human services. This experience deserves analysis in its own right because of the growing involvement of local government in the field of human services[3] and because it can also contribute to a better understanding of the policy issues inherent in the use of nongovernmental providers in the production and delivery of public services.

BACKGROUND

Contracting with the nonprofit sector expanded greatly during the 1970s, paralleling the growth in state expenditures for the human services.[4] Earlier a precedent was established by the 1964 Economic Opportunity Act, but, more significantly, the 1967 Amendments to the Social Security Act and their three to one federal matching of local funds promoted the development of "private federalism."[5] The use of POSC has been encouraged by such legislation as Title XX, General Revenue Sharing, Community Development Block Grants, and programs authorized by the Older Americans Act, the Comprehensive Employment Training Act, community mental health centers, and alcohol and drug abuse legislation. Although the practice varies greatly among the states and local governments and from one kind of service program to another, POSC can have an extraordinary impact on voluntary agencies. For example, 40 percent of the voluntary agencies in metropolitan areas in California in 1979 derived almost half their income from governmental funds.[6] The relative decline in United Fund allocations to its member agencies and the increasing dependence on governmental funds

have resulted in a pluralistic, mixed, and more competitive economy in the human services, making the future of voluntary, nonprofit agencies quite uncertain.[7]

Some of the ideological support for contracting with the nonprofit sector stems from the perception that it is a bulwark against further governmental expansion or at least an alternative, if not a substitute, for it. For some, the private sector is seen as a means of recovering a diminishing, if not a lost, sense of community. In any case, the use of the voluntary sector in the years ahead is likely to be increasingly regarded as a solution to the dilemma posed by people who want more governmental services and less government.[8]

In this paper I examine the potential advantages and disadvantages of POSC in the human services from the perspective of not only government, which is the usual practice, but also from that of the voluntary, nonprofit agency as a provider. (Even though some profit making organizations provide certain human services under contract, the dominant suppliers are nonprofit organizations in this field of public service.) Although it would be useful to assess POSC from the standpoint of the consumer—whose interests have generally been considered synonymous with government—we have virtually no information on what difference it makes to the recipients if a service is directly provided or contracted.[9]

Despite the relative paucity of systematic data and the ubiquitous "softness" of the human services, there is still a sufficient basis for analyzing the relative organizational costs to and the benefits derived by both governmental and voluntary agencies. Drawing on this experience, a series of factors that should be taken into account in decisions regarding purchase or direct provision will be suggested, and based on the state of the art, some principles of contracting will be proposed.

Underlying many of the alleged benefits

and dangers of POSC are potential conflicts between the interests of government and its service providers, expressed in the strain between accountability and independence; the paper concludes with a reevaluation of these two key concepts.

POTENTIAL ADVANTAGES OF POSC FOR GOVERNMENT

1. For government, contracting has generally served as an expedient for extending limited resources because the *cost* of the human service is usually less than it would be if it had to be provided in accordance with civil service and other regulations.[10] In economic terms, the supply of the voluntary agency services and the demand of the governmental agency usually intersect at a price that is below the real cost for both parties. Usually it is easier for a governmental agency to obtain funds for the purchase of services than for additional provider staff. Apart from cost factors, government is often in a position of having authority and responsibility for a program, but it lacks appropriate and sufficient staff, facilities, expertise, and other resources. The utilization of voluntary agencies and institutions under these circumstances means that government can offer services, such as sheltered workshops or residential care, without high initial fixed costs as well as without undesired visibility.

2. Because human services can be initiated and terminated more rapidly and easily, contracting can give government considerable *flexibility*.[11] Contracting is also a means of bypassing rigid administrative and budgetary rules and regulations, such as a freeze on personnel hiring or salary standards. It is also a way of getting around political constraints. Unwanted, marginal, or highly specialized services can also be contracted out. More positively, the use of voluntary organizations can be an effective way of serving small numbers of hard-to-reach or controversial groups, cul-

tural or ethnic minorities, or widely dispersed populations whom government is obligated to serve but where fear or stigma inhibits utilization.[12] In addition to improving both the geographic and the psychological access for clients, voluntary agencies can be a source of volunteers for service programs and promote self-help.[13]

3. There may be some secondary gains in *external relations* for government because of the possibility of influencing the service standards of voluntary organizations, as well as potential leverage in integrating their programs in a more coordinated community pattern. There is also an opportunity to coopt and gain the political support of a community constituency dependent on government for a substantial part of their budgets.[14] Other external relations payoffs may be an improvement in the image of a "responsible and cooperating" governmental agency.

POTENTIAL DISADVANTAGES OF POSC FOR GOVERNMENT

1. There are inherent difficulties in maintaining standards and securing the adequate *accountability* of voluntary agencies.[15] Many are insufficiently bureaucratized and lack suitable information and cost-control systems. Smaller and newer agencies in particular have very limited managerial capabilities. These administrative deficiencies are aggravated by typically diffuse goals and methods and the inability of human service agencies, regardless of auspice, to produce evidence of effectiveness,[16] helping to explain the widespread substitution of such outputs as the number of interviews conducted for substantive outcomes in service reporting and program evaluations. The difficulty of specifying outcomes in the human services and the lack of uniform accounting and information systems augment the complaints of overregulation by government. Because certain processes and activities are easier to

count, these indicators become the focus of governmental involvement in the minutiae of agency management. Yet evidence suggests that underregulation and little monitoring are much more frequent because governmental agencies rarely have sufficient staff to oversee a contractor's performance.[17] This deficiency is aggravated by the fact that government is often highly dependent on voluntary organizations that may have monopolies over particular services. Equity suffers under these conditions because of a tendency for the voluntary agency to be highly selective in its intake policy, with the result that the more difficult and/or poorer clients end up as cases in governmental agencies, whereas the less troublesome and/or middle-class clients are served by voluntary agencies under contract.[18]

2. The policy of provider pluralism re-enforces *fragmentation;* the dispersed character of the service system lessens the prospects for a more coordinated and coherent pattern. So far, it has not been possible to use the fact that the government funds 80 percent of the human services to bring about a more efficient and rational system.[19] The increasing scope and decentralized complexity of the human services continue to defy a succession of legislative mandates requiring more planning, coordination, and service integration. Other major obstacles are the lack of communication, consistency, and coordination among governmental agencies in a three-tier system.[20]

POTENTIAL ADVANTAGES OF POSC FOR THE VOLUNTARY AGENCY

1. The main benefit of contracting for the voluntary agency is that it can continue to serve its particular clientele and also enlarge the scope of its services, sometimes as much as by a factor of ten. Governmental funds may even be regarded as a more se-

cure source of income than fund-raising events and public solicitations, although this perception is usually an illusion.[21]

2. The clientele of voluntary organizations may receive more individualized, less bureaucratized, and specialized services than those provided by a governmental agency. Funds from other sources, if available, could be used to pay for more sectarian, particularistic, or specialized purposes.[22]

3. Other advantages are enhanced community status—the prestige and visibility gained by the voluntary agency because of its function as a public service provider—together with some increase in its access to governmental decision making and the opportunity to influence public policy.[23]

POTENTIAL DISADVANTAGES OF POSC FOR THE VOLUNTARY AGENCY

1. There is usually a gap between the actual costs, assuming that they are known, and the rate of governmental reimbursement; consequently, the voluntary agency has to make up the deficit and, in a sense, ends up by "subsidizing" government. In New York City, where there is the most extensive use of the voluntary sector in the child welfare field, this fiscal gap was approximately 48 million dollars in 1976 and averaged about 16 percent of an agency's budget.[24]

The severity of the dilemma faced by voluntary agencies depends on the size of the gap between their actual costs and the prices paid by government. If they undercharge, they incur a deficit; if they overcharge, they can bring into the market competitive, profit making organizations, or they may price themselves out of the government's market.

Another hazard of being a nongovernmental provider of human services is the uncertainty of income, which is subject to legislative and bureaucratic delays, resulting in recurrent cash-flow problems, bargaining over reimbursement rates, and the diversion of organizational resources because of the continuing struggle for financing.[25]

2. The requirements for fiscal and program accountability for public funds are frequently regarded by voluntary agencies as excessive, onerous, and counterproductive, diverting resources from the goals of service provision. The demands associated with these organizational maintenance tasks are special burdens on small agencies because they force them to become more formalistic, thus vitiating the attributes desired.[26] Voluntary agencies that sell their services to more than one government agency find themselves confronted with multiple, inconsistent, and often conflictng requirements for accountability. Such voluntary agencies are caught in a dilemma because the diversity of income that lessens dependency on any single funding source engenders disparate demands for accountability. Such demands constitute major obstacles to the coordination of organizations dependent on numerous funding agencies at different levels of government.

3. The loss of organizational independence is widely believed to be another risk. In addition to being required to comply with demands for accountability, voluntary agencies receiving public funds are subject to various policy restrictions pertaining to who shall be served (client eligibility), by whom (staff restrictions), how (service delivery), and other kinds of interference in internal operations and management policies, including the imposition of requirements for consumer participation.[27] In addition to losing some degree of control over operations and program policy, voluntary agencies, in an era of cutbacks, face the erosion of their dependency on governmental funds. By becoming a private, public service provider, a voluntary agency functions as a substitute for rather than as an alternative to government or as a vehi-

cle offering choice. This leads to the last potential disadvantage.

4. Diminished advocacy, volunteerism, and particularism can be other consequences associated with serving as a contractor.[28] The distinctive advocacy function of a voluntary agency can be constrained through the fear of losing income or be restricted to the advocacy of self-interests through continuous lobbying for higher rates and fewer regulations. Direct service volunteerism can decline because of the possibilities of substituting paid staff for certain kinds of service volunteers. The active participation of board members can also decrease as the agency becomes more entrepreneurial and relies on government for most of its income. Voluntary agencies depend less on the fund-raising capabilities of board members and volunteers and more on the ability of professional staff to negotiate governmental contracts and on board members who have political contacts.[29] Finally, the distinctive particularism of the voluntary agency—its special religious, sectarian, ethnic, or other minority values—may be diluted or lost if it must make its services available to a broader range of clients as part of the price of receiving public funds.[30]

The preceding summary of the potential values and dangers of POSC to both government and voluntary agencies necessarily has a disconcerting, equivocal character not only because of insufficient data but also because of the inevitable influence of ideologies such as pluralism and the relative values ascribed to accountability, access, autonomy, choice, cost efficiency, equity, and effectiveness. Evidence that would help identify the conditions under which any one of the costs and benefits of POSC are likely to occur is scarce, and it is clear that we need much more research on such topics as the costs of POSC compared to the costs of direct provision; the impact on clientele of different modes of service delivery and auspices; and more objective ways of measuring service quality as distinct from various forms of professionalism.[31]

TO PURCHASE OR PROVIDE

Nevertheless, in considering whether to purchase or provide, both governmental and voluntary agencies may make better decisions if they carefully consider the preceding relative advantages and disadvantages and took them into account along with the following questions:

1. To what extent is there public acceptance of this service as a governmental or voluntary responsibility? How is the service viewed by legislators, public officials, clientele and others?
2. What is there in the nature of the service which seems to require governmental or voluntary auspices? Are there any sectarian or voluntaristic aspects of the service which are not within the province of/or which are appropriate for a governmental agency?
3. Where will the needed service best be integrated? What is the best way of avoiding fragmentation and encouraging coordination?
4. To what extent is the voluntary agency qualified and prepared to provide the service in accordance with the required conditions at least as economically, effectively, and efficiently as government? How would the acceptance of public funds affect or displace other aspects of the voluntary agency's program?
5. How ready is the governmental agency to delegate responsibility and provide the voluntary agency with the necessary standards and technical assistance? To what extent can government specify the service product and pay the full cost of service?[32]

Once the decision has been made to contract, there are six basic principles which have evolved in the field of the human services which may also be relevant for other kinds of public programs.

1. Provision should be made for full coverage of all persons for whom there is public responsibility, whether the service is provided directly by government or through a voluntary agency.
2. The service and its desired outcomes should be clearly defined; the specific clientele for whom there is public responsibility should be designated, together with the duration of the program.
3. Standards acceptable to both government and voluntary agencies should be made explicit regarding intake policy, personnel, and service delivery.
4. There should be adequate provision for joint planning on behalf of clients; for reporting, review, and audit; and for evaluation in order to ensure accountability for public funds.
5. Fair payment up to the full cost of the service, as determined by a cost analysis, should be made by government. Reimbursement rates should take qualitative factors into account and provide incentives for improvement.
6. A contract embodying these considerations should be developed jointly and should include procedures for conflict resolution.[33]

CONCLUSIONS: A REEVALUATION OF AUTONOMY AND ACCOUNTABILITY

In the human services, as in other public services, control by means of accountability is the most salient issue. Underlying much of the controversy and confusion regarding contracting are different, if not competing, organizational interests and values. For example, the much vaunted independence of a voluntary agency may be viewed by outsiders as arbitrary, idiosyncratic, or self-serving behavior, just as pluralism is frequently regarded by others as duplication, fragmentation, or even as "organizational anarchy." Autonomy is naturally prized by the supporters of a voluntary agency, but others, less partisan, may value equity more than provider autonomy and pluralism and be more concerned about the consequences of governmental domination by private interests. From the point of view of government or an underserved population at risk, a reduction in the autonomy of a voluntary agency would not be considered a calamity if it meant that the agency would function with a broader conception of the public interest, that is, its operations would accord with the wishes of certain groups of clientele rather than those of staff and board. Conversely, governmental demands for service and fiscal accountability may be perceived by voluntary agencies as unnecessary intrusions, resulting in administrative busywork and an illusion of "businesslike" accountability and illustrating the adage that one person's accountability is another's harassment. Voluntary organizations may also challenge the belief that there is more accountability in the public services on the grounds that governmental agencies are usually reluctant to disclose information regarding their operations, and they often fail to respect the client's entitlement to service and the redress of grievances.

On the other hand, the conventional dualism between autonomy and accountability may be more artificial than real: They may be much less opposed than many people believe.[34] For example, a strong independent voluntary agency can be more accountable because government can pinpoint responsibility. Furthermore, some accountability requirements can be beneficial to a voluntary agency as it seeks to improve the efficiency and the effectiveness of its performance. Contracts can be tools to structure and guide program operations. When a program description is broken down into mutually exclusive, sequential, and functionally interrelated components, it can be used as a monitoring guide, an administrative focus, a planning tool, and a basis for evaluation, as well as for contract renewal.[35]

In any case, it is evident that both terms are ambiguous, value laden, and require analysis. For example, how autonomous should or can a voluntary organization be and regarding what aspects of its functioning? To whom should a voluntary agency be accountable for what, when, and how? How much accountability should government require and in what forms?

To begin with autonomy, it is obvious that no organization can be completely independent because all policy decisions are subject to many external and internal constraints. Autonomy, being a matter of degree, is relative and conditional. Autonomy is not an end in itself but a necessary means for accomplishing the organization's task and maintenance goals, justified pragmatically by its contribution to more effective performance. The distinctive nature of organizations is that they are neither self-sufficient nor wholly self-determining but are, instead, inescapably dependent on their environment for their essential resources. The prevailing natural state of organizational life is one of interdependency in which organizations "use" each other via trade-offs in which resources are exchanged for a measure of control.[36] Furthermore, voluntary agencies are not private, freewheeling enterprises; instead, they are, strictly speaking, public agencies because they require sanction from the state in the form of a charter or legal recognition of their nonprofit, charitable, tax exempt, corporate status, and they must often be licensed. The community in which they function is the source of their legitimation, service mandate and domain, goodwill, and more tangible resources, such as funds, clientele, staff, and information.

What then is *autonomy?* The term seems to refer to the freedom of an organization to make decisions with an optimal degree of discretion, or, to put it in converse terms, free from the kinds of unwanted restrictions that circumscribe service delivery policy and practices (who may be served, by whom, and under what conditions); governance (the composition of the board and/or advisory committees); and administrative requirements pertaining to staffing, service standards, costs, reporting, and so on. Autonomy is diminished to the extent that an organization accepts a reduction in its preferred discretionary power; in so doing, it acknowledges the superior power of another group over a particular area of its jurisdiction.

There is, however, nothing unique in the concern with autonomy voiced by voluntary agencies because all kinds of organizations face challenges to their freedom to decide their own fate. Wealthy donors, third-party payments, United Way allocations, community clientele, and professional groups also put constraints on agencies' independence. In actual practice, the little evidence available suggests that there is much less encroachment on the independence of voluntary organizations than is commonly believed. In a study of voluntary agencies in the United States, England, the Netherlands, and Israel, it was found that dependency was significantly mitigated by the payment-for-service form of most government funding, the diversity of income sources, the countervailing power of a voluntary agency service monopoly, political influence, and the minimal accountability associated with the trade-offs flowing from a mutual dependency relationship.[37]

The concept of accountability is even harder to grapple with. We find that its popularity in the human services is exceeded only by the lack of agreement about its meaning. It has been viewed as both an end or a means; it has been defined in terms of procedures, results, disclosure of information, recourse, and compliance with regulations, and it is often indistinguishable from such concepts as evaluation, efficiency, effectiveness, control, and responsibility.[38] At a minimum, accountability involves the obligation to report in appropriate detail how the organization is discharging its service and fiscal respon-

sibilities so that evaluative and other decisions can be made. If this kind of reporting is essential to accountability, then it should be distinguished from restrictions on agency functioning that might limit its autonomy. Although the disclosure requirements of public accounting and red tape may be costly nuisances and even divert agency resources, they do not necessarily impair an agency's freedom.

Furthermore, a voluntary organization has multiple accountability; to its board of directors, to its bylaws, stated goals, and policies; to its various constituencies, including clientele, contributors, and other funding sources. But accountable for what? The simple answer that it is accountable for doing what it is supposed to do immediately raises another question: According to whom? Not only are there different conceptions of organizational purposes and expectations of performance held by various interest groups in the agency and the community, but, as noted earlier, the desired results of the work of human service agencies are notoriously difficult to demonstrate. This inherent weakness is sometimes masked by the overriding importance attached to independence and "innovation" by voluntary agencies.

Perhaps the issue can be rephrased not as the preservation of freedom, but how to make public service providers more accountable without restricting the qualities of flexibility and individualization that may make voluntary agencies desirable. At the same time, to prevent the regulated from regulating the regulators, we need to discover an appropriate organizational distance between government and voluntary agencies: a midpoint far away enough to preclude excessive restrictions, the overenforcement of rules, and cooptation but not so distant that it would not be possible to protect the public interest and ensure compliance with stated objectives. The search would be centered on finding that golden mean where government could hold its contractors accountable without unduly interfering with or constraining the distinctive features of voluntary agencies.[39]

In the process, each will have to acquire new or improved organizational competencies. Government will have to increase its capacity for more effective contract management and improve its bidding and review procedures, product specification, monitoring, and accountability requirements. It will have to learn how to cope more effectively with provider coalitions and how to use such structures to develop and enforce standards. Voluntary agencies, on the other hand, will have to strive for greater equity and efficiency in service delivery and improved managerial capability and accept a greater measure of paperwork, citizen participation, and some program restrictions when they become private, public service providers.[40]

The quest for formulating principles that would bring about a better balance between provider autonomy and accountability will be elusive and demanding, but it is essential to the preservation of pluralism and voluntarism in the local community.

NOTES

1. Typical examples of this perspective are R. S. Ahlbrandt, Jr., "Implications of Contracting for a Public Service," *Urban Affairs Quarterly* (March 1974) pp. 337–59; Lyle C. Fitch, "Increasing the Role of the Private Sector in Providing Public Services," in Willis D. Hawley and David Rogers, eds., *Improving the Quality of Urban Management* (Beverly Hills, Ca.: Sage Publications, 1974), pp. 501–59; Donald Fisk, Herbert Kiesling, and Thomas Muller, *Private Provision of Public Services: An Overview* (Washington, D.C.: The Urban Institute, 1978); E. S. Savas, "Municipal Monopolies vs. Competition in the Delivery of Urban Services," *Journal of Urban Analysis*, vol. 2, 1974, pp. 93–116; Lewis F. Weshsler, "Four Approaches to the Use of the Private Sector in the Production of Local Government Services," *Public–Private Collaboration in the Delivery of Local Pub-*

lic Services (Institute of Governmental Affairs, University of California, Davis, 1980), pp. 40–51; Rosaline Levenson, "Public Use of Private Service Contracts: A Plea for Caution," Ibid., pp. 12–27.

2. The following are representative of this broader perspective. Bruce L. R. Smith, ed., *The New Political Economy: The Public Use of the Private Sector* (New York: John Wiley & Sons, 1975); Ira Sharkansky, *Wither the State? Politics and Public Enterprise in Three Countries* (Chatham, N.J.: Chatham House Publishers, 1979); Daniel Guttman and Barry Willner, *The Shadow Government: The Government's Multi-Billion-Dollar Giveaway of Its Decision-Making Powers to Private Management Consultants, "Experts" and Think Tanks* (New York: Pantheon, 1976); John D. Hanrahan, *Government for Sale: Contracting-Out the New Patronage* (Washington, D.C.: American Federation of State, County and Municipal Employees, 1977); Lloyd V. Musolf, and Harold Seidman, "The Blurred Boundaries of Public Administration," *Public Administration Review*, vol. 40 (March/April 1980), pp. 124–30; Harold Orlans, ed., *Non-profit Organizations: A Government Management Tool* (New York: Praeger Publishers, 1980); U.S. House of Representatives, Committee on Post Office and Civil Service, *Contracting Out of Jobs and Services* (Washington, D.C.: USGPO, 1977); U.S. Senate, Committee on Governmental Affairs (1977) "Consultants and Contractors," a report of the Subcommittee on Reports, Accountants, and Management, 95th Congress, First Session.

3. The growing importance of this field is evident in the publication of a "green book," Wayne F. Anderson, Bernard J. Frieden, and Michael J. Murphy, eds., *Managing Human Services* (Washington, D.C.: International City Management Assn., 1977). See, particularly, Robert Morris, "The Human Service Function in Local Government," pp. 5–36, and *Opportunities for Municipal Participation in Human Services* (Durham, N.H.: New England Municipal Center, August 1975).

4. A definitive study of this period is Martha Derthick, *Uncontrollable Spending for Social Service Grants* (Washington, D.C.: Brookings Institution, 1975). See also Neil Gilbert, "The Transformation of Social Services," *Social Service Review* 51:4 (December 1977), pp. 624–41, and Elizabeth Wickenden, "A Perspective on Social Services: An Essay Review," *Social Service Review* 50:4 (December 1976), pp. 586–600.

5. Private federalism refers to direct national grants to voluntary, nonprofit institutions, as used in Charles Gilbert, "Welfare Policy," in Fred Greenstein and Nelson Polsby, eds., *Policies and Policy-making: Handbook of Political Science*, 6

(Reading, Mass.: Addison-Wesley Publishing Co., 1975), p. 167.

6. *Focus on California Legislation,* vol. VIII (February 1980), p. 3. National trends in the field of child welfare are reviewed in Ruth M. Werner, *Public Financing of Voluntary Agency Foster Care 1975 Compared with 1957* (New York: Child Welfare League of America, 1976). On the growth in the purchase of service under Title XX in which voluntary agencies account for about a third of all such expenditures, see Bill B. Benton, Jr., "Questions for Research and Development," in Kenneth R. Wedel, Arthur J. Katz, and Ann Weick, eds., *Social Services by Government Contract* (New York: Praeger Publishers, 1979), pp. 82–84.

7. Waldemar A. Nielsen, *The Endangered Sector* (New York: Columbia University Press, 1979); Gordon Manser and Rosemary Cass, *Voluntarism at the Crossroads* (New York: Family Service Association of America, 1975); and Ralph M. Kramer, *Voluntary Agencies in the Welfare State* (Berkeley: University of California Press, 1981).

8. This dilemma is discussed in Peter L. Berger and Richard John Neuhaus, *To Empower People: The Role of Mediating Structures in Public Policy* (Washington, D.C.: American Enterprise Institute for Public Policy Research, 1977); Morris B. Janowitz, *Social Control of the Welfare State* (New York: Elsevier Scientific Publishing Co., 1976); Theodore Levitt, *The Third Sector: New Tactics for a Responsive Society* (New York: Macon Press, 1973; and in *Giving in America: Toward a Stronger Voluntary Sector,* Report of the Commission on Private Philanthropy and Public Needs (Washington, D.C.: 1975), pp. 91–102.

9. Among the few attempts to measure services from the client's perspective are Michael A. Garrick and William L. Moore, "Uniform Assessments and Standards of Social and Health Care Services," *Social Service Review,* 53:3 (September 1979), pp. 343–57; and Leonard Miller and Robert Pruger, "Evaluation in Care Programs: With Illustrations in Homemaker-Chore in California," *Administration in Social Work,* vol. 2 (Winter 1978), pp. 469–78.

10. Cost comparisons are notoriously difficult in the human services not only because there may not be any public counterparts but because different methods of cost accounting result in different conclusions. For example, many comparable governmental costs of service provision do not include the overhead costs of contract management, whereas certain indirect costs are allowable in calculating the reimbursable expenses of provider agencies. Similar experiences have led some observers to conclude that "it's all an ac-

counting game." For one of the few attempts to compare governmental and nongovernmental costs, see Bill B. Benton, Tracey Feild, and Rhona Mallar, *Social Services: Federal Legislation vs. State Implementation* (Washington, D.C.: The Urban Institute, 1978), pp. 85–86. See also Fisk et al., p. 56, and "Title XX Purchase of Service: The Feasibility of Comparing Costs Between Direct Delivery and Purchased Services," (Berkeley, Calif.: Pacific Consultants, January 1979).

11. "Flexibility is the prime attraction of contracting," according to Ira Sharkansky, "Government Contracting," *State Government,* vol. 55 (Winter 1980), p. 22. Some of the alleged benefits of contracting in general are summarized by Fisk et al., pp. 6–7, 93–5, and by Fitch, pp. 505–10.

12. These particular advantages of voluntary agencies are regarded as their distinctive competence by Barbara Rodgers, country project director, *Cross National Studies of Social Service Systems: United Kingdom Reports, vol. 1* (New York: Columbia University School of Social Work, 1976), pp. 41–42.

13. Paul Terrell, *The Social Impact of Revenue Sharing* (New York: Praeger Publishers, 1976), p. 87.

14. In sharp contrast to a pre-1967 policy of opposition to governmental spending, the United Way of America subsequently gave strong support for governmental funding of the social services through their active promotion of a "partnership." To aid voluntary agencies secure three to one federal matching funds in which their allocation could be used as part of the local match, United Way published *Expanding Local Service Programs through Government Purchase of Services,* "Guide to Using Resources Made Available Through the 1967 Amendment to the Social Security Act," vol. 1 (Fairfax, Va.: United Way of America, August 1971).

15. Fisk et al., pp. 95–98, identifies nine other disadvantages of private contracting of public services. See also Kenneth R. Wedel, "Purchase of Service Contracting in Human Services," *Journal of Health and Human Resources Administration,* vol. 1 (February 1980), pp. 327–41.

16. On the distinctive nature of social service organizations, see Yeheskel Hasenfeld and Richard A. English, eds., *Human Service Organizations* (Ann Arbor: University of Michigan Press, 1974), pp. 8–22; Richard Steiner, *Managing the Human Service Organization* (Beverly Hills, Ca.: Sage Publications, 1977); and Hal G. Rainey, et al., "Comparing Public and Private Organizations," *Public Administration Review* 36 (March/April 1976), pp. 233–44.

17. On the problems of measuring outcome and

quality, see Dennis R. Young and Stephen J. Finch, *Foster Care and Non-Profit Agencies* (Lexington, Mass.: Lexington Books, 1977), pp. 232–33; and Arthur J. Katz, "Quality of Service, Professionalism, and the Purchase of Service Factor," in Wedel, Katz, and Weick, pp. 92–106. Criticism of governmental monitoring is found in *Grant Auditing: A Maze of Inconsistency, Gaps and Duplication That Needs Overhauling*, Report to the Congress by the Comptroller General of the United States (Washington, D.C.: GAO, June 15, 1979); *Purchase of Service: Can State Government Gain Control?* (Boston, Mass.: Massachusetts Taxpayers' Foundation, June 1980); Sharkansky, *Wither the State?*, pp. 9, 119–20, 132, 138; and Norman V. Lourie, "Purchase of Service Contracting: Issues Confronting the Government Sponsored Agency," in Wedel, Katz, and Weick, p. 20.

18. On client stratification as a result of the purchase of service, see Bertram M. Beck, "Governmental Contracts with Non-Profit Social Welfare Corporations," in B. L. R. Smith, B. C. Hague, eds., *The Dilemma of Accountability in Modern Government* (New York: St. Martin's Press, 1971), pp. 213–29.

19. Government is also frequently confronted by powerful provider associations and may not be able to influence standards and rate reimbursement policies that it deems in the public interest because of the pressures generated by such groups. Some of the more positive functions that such associations can perform in the development and maintenance of standards and setting reasonable costs are discussed in Candace T. Mueller, "Purchase of Service Contracting from the Viewpoint of the Provider," in Wedel, Katz, and Weick, pp. 52–53.

20. Internal governmental constraints on the development of a more rational pattern are discussed in Eleanor L. Brilliant, "Private or Public: A Model of Ambiguities," *Social Service Review*, vol. 47 (September 1973), pp. 384–96; Ann Weick, "Title XX as a New Context for Social Service Planning," in Wedel, Katz, and Weick, pp. 37–45; and Young and Finch, pp. 20–34.

21. See, for example, Bay Area Social Planning Council, *Sources of Government Funds Obtained by UWBA Agencies During Fy 1974–75* (Oakland, Ca., 1975). As a consequence of the decline in the high proportion of voluntary agency income derived from governmental funds, United Way allocations have even been described as "start-up funds" on which a base of governmental support can be built. Paul Akana, "The United Way System Needs No Defense," *Community Focus* 2 (September 1978), pp. 17–18. See also Herbert

S. Rabinowitz, Bruce R. Simmeth, and Jeannette R. Spero, "The Future of United Way," *Social Service Review* 53 (June 1979), pp. 275–84.

22. Gordon Manser, "Further Thoughts on Purchase of Service," *Social Casework* 55 (July 1974), pp. 421–34.

23. Ralph M. Kramer, "Public Fiscal Policies and Voluntary Agencies in Welfare States," *Social Service Review*, vol. 53 (March 1979), pp. 1–14.

24. Nellie Hartogs and Joseph Weber, *Impact of Government Funding on the Management of Voluntary Agencies* (New York: Greater New York Fund/United Way, 1978) p. 10. Voluntary agencies are advised to budget additional costs of 20 percent over and above funds for the additional cost of any governmental funds that must be raised from other sources. Nellie Hartogs and Joseph Weber, *Managing Government Funded Programs in Voluntary Agencies* (Greater New York Fund/United Way, 1979), p. 5. On some of the complexities involved in rate determination, the determination of allowable costs, the multiple modes of payment, and so on, see Mueller, op. cit., p. 320, and Lourie, op. cit., p. 22.

25. Robert M. Rice, "Impact of Government Contracts on Voluntary Social Agencies," *Social Casework*, vol. 56 (July 1975), pp. 387–95; William G. Hill, "Voluntary and Governmental Financial Transactions," *Social Casework*, vol. 52 (June 1971), pp. 356–61.

26. Hartogs and Weber, *Impact of Government Funding*, pp. 15–16.

27. Manser, p. 426; Rice, p. 388. The loss of organizational autonomy as a result of receiving governmental funds is a constant theme in the professional literature. For some empirical data contradicting this belief, see note 23.

28. For example, Lourie, op. cit., p. 23, states: "Advocacy, too often, becomes self-interest promotion." Also see references in notes 18, 25, and 27.

29. This is particularly evident in the Netherlands. See Ralph M. Kramer, "Governmental-Voluntary Relationships in the Netherlands," *The Netherlands Journal of Sociology*, vol. 25 (1979), pp. 155–73.

30. Church–state issues seem to have declined in importance in this field, particularly since the 1960s. For an analysis of the issue of separation as it was perceived at that time, see Ralph M. Kramer, "Voluntary Agencies and the Use of Public Funds: Some Policy Issues," *Social Service Review*, vol. 40 (March 1966), pp. 15–26. Some of the persistent concerns about the impact of public funds on sectarian social agencies are considered in Martha K. Selig, "New Dimensions in Government Funding of Voluntary Agencies:

Potentials and Risks," *Journal of Jewish Communal Service*, vol. 50 (Winter 1973), pp. 125–35.

31. For additional questions needing research, see Benton, pp. 88–90, and Katz, pp. 92–106, in Wedel, Katz, and Weick, op. cit.

32. In actual practice, the main determinants of contracting reported are community pressures and traditions, costs, and staff deficiencies: Benton et al., pp. 114–16; Fisk et al., pp. 3–6, 102.

33. Comparable principles for another public service are found in *Contracts Services Handbook: Issues and Impacts for the Park and Recreation Manager* (Washington, D.C.: U.S. Dept. of the Interior, Heritage Conservation and Recreation Service, October 1979). Other guidelines are offered in Gerald E. Caiden, *The Dynamics of Public Administration: Guidelines to Current Transformations in Theory and Practice* (New York: Holt, Rinehart and Winston, 1971), pp. 155–59.

34. Harvey C. Mansfield, "Independence and Accountability for Federal Contractors and Grantees," in B. L. R. Smith, ed., pp. 319–35.

35. John Gundersdorg, "Management and Financial Control," in Anderson et al., *Managing Human Services*, pp. 255–79.

36. This view of organizational behavior is articulated in David Jacobs, "Dependency and Vulnerability: An Exchange Approach to the Control of Organizations," *Administrative Science Quarterly*, vol. 19 (1974), pp. 45–59, and Sergio E. Mindlin and Howard Aldrich, "Interorganizational Dependence: A Review of the Concepts and a Reexamination of the Findings of the Ashton Group," *Administrative Science Quarterly*, vol. 20 (1975), pp. 382–92.

37. A summary of the experience in these four countries is presented in Ralph M. Kramer, "Public Fiscal Policy and Voluntary Agencies in Welfare States." Additional supporting evidence of provider domination of the system is found in Massachusetts Taxpayers' Association, op. cit.

See also Novia Carter, *Trends in Voluntary Support for Non-Governmental Social Service Agencies* (Ottawa, Ontario: Canadian Council on Social Development, 1979), pp. 53–55; Felice Perlmutter, "Public Funds and Private Agencies," *Child Welfare*, vol. 50 (May 1971), pp. 264–70, and William Burian, "Purchase of Service in Child Welfare: A Problem of Inter-organizational Exchange," Ph.D. dissertation, University of Chicago, 1970, pp. 173–94.

38. An overview of some of the different meanings of accountability can be found in Amitai Etzioni, "Alternative Conceptions of Accountability: The Example of Health Administration," *Public Administration Review*, vol. 35 (May/June 1975), pp. 279–86. See also Edward Newman and Jerry Turem, "The Crisis of Accountability," *Social Work*, vol. 19 (January 1974), pp. 5–17. Four components of accountability have been identified by the Child Welfare League of America and the American Public Welfare Association: the use of uniform cost accounting and reporting methods; the availability of complete fiscal records for review; the development of methods and criteria to evaluate effectiveness and efficiency; and the use of licensing standards in cooperation with government to strengthen them, *A National Program for Comprehensive Child Welfare Services* (Washington, D.C.: Child Welfare League of America, 1971).

39. A cogent case for "arm's length" governance instead of administration is made by Young and Fitch, op. cit., pp. 237–38. A related and more theoretical perspective is Eugene Litwak and Henry J. Meyer, "A Balance Theory of Coordination Between Bureaucratic Organizations and Community Primary Groups," *Administrative Science Quarterly*, vol. 11 (June 1966), pp. 33–58.

40. Paul Terrell, "Private Alternatives to Public Human Services Administration," *Social Service Review*, vol. 53 (March 1979), pp. 71–72.

Steven P. Segal

Community Care and Deinstitutionalization:
A Review

The policy of returning mental patients to their own communities assumes that the family will support individuals who can barely take care of their personal needs. However, few attempts have been made to specify the joint functions of the mental hospital and the family in providing care in the community for the mentally ill. Furthermore, little effort has been made to cite the responsibilities delegated to the family in the context of community care. Finally, there have been few attempts to elaborate on the social policies of community care and deinstitutionalization. This article addresses these issues, reviews the research related to the family as a helper in community care, and makes suggestions as to what the policies should be with respect to the family's role in this vital area.

GOALS AND FUNCTIONS

The concept of community care is an old one. It was reintroduced in the early 1930s as an adjunct of state hospital care. One of the goals of community care is to shift the responsibility for the care of patients from the institution to the community, with the institution acting in a supportive role to local mental health and social agencies, recreation and police departments, and the like. These community agencies coordinate their efforts to support the family in providing the care needed by the released patient. During the late 1950s and early

Reprinted with permission of the author and *Social Work* 24:6 (November 1979), pp. 521–27. Copyright 1979, National Association of Social Workers, Inc.

1960s, innovative state hospital programs, such as that implemented by the Dutchess County Unit of Hudson River State Hospital in Poughkeepsie, New York, maintained as many as two-thirds of their inpatients in the community. This unit instituted an easy-in and easy-out policy through which the hospital supported but not necessarily housed the patients. Its major goal was to help patients maintain their social role in the family.

Another goal of community care is to prevent chronic disabilities that are attributable to prolonged periods in locked wards of understaffed and poorly run mental institutions. In the 1960s and early 1970s, however, this goal became confused with the policy of deinstitutionalization, which involves the removal of the mentally ill from mental institutions. Although the goals of deinstitutionalization are to prevent chronic disability, protect patients' rights, and reduce the cost of care, hospitalized mental patients have been moved to communities without the provision of supportive networks in the community. For many of these released patients, the cost of leaving the mental hospital has not been as great as the negative impact of the institution itself; for others, costs have been considerable. The latter individuals have often been placed in communities in which they are unwanted and consequently become more isolated from social relationships than they had been in the hospital.

Gruenberg (1970) outlines the following functions of the mental hospital in providing short-term treatment of the mentally ill:

(1) to use treatment procedures that require continuous observation,
(2) to protect patients who endanger themselves or others,
(3) to remove persons temporarily from an environmental stress during a period when they cannot cope with the stress,
(4) to provide temporary relief for those who manage to live with patients, and
(5) to establish communication between patients and the hospital.

In addition to these functions, the mental hospital has served as a primary provider of long-term mental health care to the aged, as maintainer of the physical and mental health of the chronically mentally ill, and as a supportive social community (often with many negative factors associated with it) for the chronic population. These responsibilities, however, have been shifted back to the family, leaving primarily those functions outlined by Gruenberg (1970) to the mental hospital.

In considering the responsibilities delegated to the family in the care of the mentally ill, these questions must be raised: What is the readiness of the family to accept these responsibilities? What is the impact of these responsibilities on the ongoing relationships in the family and on the long-term adjustment of the patients to the community? In view of these questions, the supportive role of the family can be examined in terms of three levels of prevention: primary, secondary, and tertiary. The author discusses each level, starting with the third.

TERTIARY PREVENTION

Tertiary prevention includes community and family planning that leads to prevention of long-term chronic disability and "institutionalism," that is, dependence on and total orientation toward the mental institution. Research has shown that it is possible to achieve these two goals (Segal, 1978). However, is the family ready, able,

and willing to provide support for the chronic mental patient? To answer this question, the author will consider the following: (1) the current availability of family support for chronic mental patients, (2) the willingness of the family to assume the additional responsibility for the patient, (3) the impact of assuming these responsibilities on the family, and (4) the relationship between the placement of patients in a family context in the community and the prevention of chronic disability and institutionalism.

Availability of Family Support

Although only a small proportion of all admissions to mental hospitals in any given cohort of admissions is isolated or has little family support available to it, this proportion becomes the large residual population of chronic mental patients in the mental health system. Each progressive cohort of returns to a mental hospital has a larger percentage of people in the cohort who have no family support or who have a limited amount of interaction with family members (Miller, 1965; Pasamanick, Scarpitti, and Dinitz, 1967; and Davis, Dinitz, and Pasamanick, 1974).

In a study of former mental patients, aged 18–65, living in community-based, sheltered-care facilities in California, Segal and Aviram (1978) found that 52 percent of the patients rarely, if ever, had access to family members. In addition, 60 percent had never been married, 35 percent had dissolved their relationships, and only 5 percent were married. When examined by sex, these figures revealed that 73 percent of the men, as opposed to 44 percent of the women, had never been married, 22 percent of the men and 50 percent of the women were either separated or divorced, and only 4 and 5 percent of the men and women, respectively, were married.

These figures reflect a pattern that is characteristic of the population who require long-term institutional care. As any given cohort becomes increasingly involved with the mental health system, its marital status begins to approximate those described previously. Given these statistics, the question must be raised as to the extent to which the family is available to meet the needs of the truly chronic patient.

Willingness of the Family to Assume Additional Responsibility

To some extent the attitude of family members toward the ex-patient reflects their willingness to assume responsibility for a relative returning after a prolonged hospitalization or several short hospitalizations. Previous studies have shown that the attitudes of family members toward released patients seem to be significantly more positive and accepting than those expressed by members of society as a whole (Philips, 1963; Schwartz, Myers, and Astrachan, 1974; and Swanson and Spitzer, 1970).

Another indicator of a family's desire to assume such responsibility is its expressed willingness to accept the discharged relative back in the home. Research on this subject addresses three aspects. The first aspect relates to the family's attitude toward the return of the patient from the hospital; the second, to the family's attitude toward the former patient after he or she has been living in the home a while; and the third, to the psychological, financial, economic, and social burdens placed on the family by accepting the relative back in the home.

When looking at the first aspect, Rose (1959) observed an increasing reluctance on the part of families to accept discharged patients in the home as the number of years of hospitalization increased. In addition, Evans, Bullard, and Solomon (1961) reported that less than 50 percent of the families they interviewed favored the release of their relatives who had been hospitalized for five years or more. On the other hand, Freeman and Simmons (1963) re-

ported that 95 percent of their family members wanted the patients to live in their household. And Wing and his associates (1964) found that no family members refused to take back their discharged relatives, although 13 percent actively opposed their return and 21 percent were doubtful about it.

Three related factors influence the family's willingness to accept the former patient: the severity of the patient's symptoms, pessimism about the ability of the patient to recover, and stressful conditions in the environment that are related to lower social-class status. Findings reported by Doll (1976) revealed a relationship between the rate of rejection of discharged patients by family members and the onset of severe symptoms. For example, although 83 percent of all the families studied said they wanted the discharged patients to come home, 58 percent of those with severely disturbed relatives opposed their return. In addition, 71 percent who wanted to exclude discharged patients from their social lives were living with severely disturbed former patients. Moreover, Swingle (1965) indicated that half the families of a group of mental patients believed that the patients could not recover from their illness and thus were unable to return home. In addition, Hollingshead and Redlich (1958) found that members of the lowest social class were most unwilling to accept their discharged relatives in the home.

When faced with the actual responsibility of having a discharged relative in the home, however, families seem to respond better to the patient. Barrett, Kuriansky, and Gurland (1972) found that of 85 families whose relatives had returned home following a hospital strike in New York State, 60 percent expressed pleasure about their return. In addition, Brown and his associates (1966), in their study of 251 families, found that five years after the relatives' discharge, 75 percent of the families welcomed the patients in the household, 15 percent accepted them, and only 12 percent wanted them to live elsewhere.

Cost to the Family for Being a Caretaker

The key issue, as reported in several studies on this subject, is the extent to which the former patient actually places a burden on the family. For example, Grad and Sainsbury (1963a, 1963b, and 1968) noted that 81 percent of the families who rejected their discharged relatives had economic and social problems, whereas only 62 percent of those who accepted the former patients had such problems. Moreover, Barrett, Kuriansky, and Gurland (1972) reported that when patients placed no burden on the household, they were more likely to remain in the home and thus stay out of the hospital. However, in his study, Doll (1976) found that 67 percent of the family members interviewed were ashamed because they had a severely disturbed relative living at home.

In view of the cost to the family for housing a former patient, family members seem to tolerate a great deal of disruption. Hoenig and Hamilton (1969) reported on 179 families who lived continuously with a former patient for four years prior to the research interview. These researchers compared the "subjective" reports of burden made by families with the "objective" rating of burden made by a social worker. They concluded that there was a great deal of subjective tolerance in view of the objective rating of a heavy burden experienced by families. Although 90 percent of the families in the study were sympathetic toward the patient, 56 percent of them expressed relief when the relative was admitted to the mental hospital.

Prevention of Chronic Social Disability and Institutionalism

Research shows that the family plays a role in preventing as well as contributing to the development of long-term chronic social disability and institutionalism. For example, a study by Barrett, Kuriansky, and Gurland (1972) demonstrated a significant relationship between the attitude of family members toward discharged patients and the amount of time patients remained in the community. Results showed that 57 percent of the relatives of the patients who did not require rehospitalization were initially pleased with the patient's release and that only 7 percent of the relatives of those who were rehospitalized responded in this way.

In addition, a study by Greenley (1979) showed that discharged patients were more likely to be rehospitalized if their families expected them to have few friends outside the family, to create a childlike situation in the home, or to exhibit severe psychiatric symptoms. Greenley hypothesized that two types of dependent relationships existed between ex-patients and their families: the ambivalent and inconsistent and the ineffective and rejecting types, both of which involve a basic dislike and rejection of the patient. This hypothesis is consistent with the clinical observations of Stein and his associates (1975) who reported that repeated hospitalizations were a result of a pathological relationship between the patient and family. To deter such a relationship and prevent rehospitalization, these researchers are in favor of separating the patient from the family.

Other researchers also revealed that a relationship exists between the family's interactions with former patients and the readmission rate. For example, Brown and his colleagues (1958, 1962, and 1972) explored the emotional arousal hypothesis. This hypothesis suggests that some environments, which include the mother or wife, are too emotionally stimulating for ex-patients. Therefore, former patients living with their mothers or wives may have a higher readmission rate than those living with siblings, with distant kin, or in lodgings. Findings not only supported the hypothesis but also indicated that there was an optimal level of emotional arousal above which patients were more likely to return to the hospital.

Early studies by Freeman and Simmons (1958 and 1959) generated the tolerance-of-deviance hypothesis. This hypothesis assumes that families with a high tolerance will continue to accept former patients even when they fail to perform tasks related to work and housekeeping. These researchers found that fewer relapses occur among patients living with families that have low expectations regarding patients' performance. But later studies by Freeman and Simmons (1963), Angrist and her colleagues (1968), and Michaux and his associates (1969) failed to demonstrate a relationship between tolerance of deviance and the amount of time a patient spent in the community.

However, the results of a study by Greenley (1979) supported a hypothesis concerning families' tolerance of symptoms. It was found that former patients who were rehospitalized at a faster rate than others who lived with families that had a low tolerance for the expression of symptoms. Although further research is needed to replicate the findings of these various studies, there is reason to believe that a properly selected family environment can contribute to the length of time a patient spends in the community and thus to the prevention of long-term chronic social disability.

Factors that may contribute to the development of institutionalism are social isolation and the limited housing options available to a person. Institutionalism is not necessarily confined to the mental institution. Segal and Moyles (in press) reported that a significant proportion of the mentally ill residents in community care facilities developed a dependence on these facilities. In addition, Brown and his associates (1962) observed that discharged chronic patients who lived with their families were totally isolated in the home and evidenced behaviors associated with in-

stitutionalism. Thus internal aspects of the family as well as the institutional environment are crucial in preventing the development of institutionalism among ex-patients.

SECONDARY PREVENTION

Secondary prevention seeks to reduce the negative effects of mental illness by early diagnosis and treatment. The family can help patients by maintaining its role structure, thereby short-circuiting any attempts to exclude and thus deprive patients of performing normal family roles. As discussed previously, prolonged hospitalization is related to the increasing reluctance of a family to accept the patient in the home. In addition, researchers have offered other explanations for the reluctance of family members to accept patients. Pitt (1969), for example, argued that former patients exhaust a "reservoir of good will" toward themselves. And Dunigan (1969) concluded that there is a critical point at which the family's expectations of the patient's performance and the family's tolerance of deviant behavior change. Men coped well with one or two hospitalizations of their wife or mother. But with more than three hospitalizations, they tended to withdraw from their female relative, lower their expectations, and make more permanent changes in their households to allow for continued functioning without the presence of the female (Kreisman and Joy, 1974).

Mills (1962) pointed out that when the stress of having a mentally ill relative in the home became too great, families turned to the hospital for relief. Rehospitalization was often followed by a deterioration of the relationship between the patient and his or her family. Myers and Bean (1968) found similar results in their follow-up study, noting that the deterioration of relationships following rehospitalization was true in lower-class families.

Visiting is a crucial element to consider

when examining the involvement of the family with hospitalized patients. Rawnsley, Loudon, and Miles (1962) studied records of 230 private patients. They found that 20 percent of the patients had no contact with their families outside the hospital. In addition, the key factor in determining rates of visitation was the length of time patients spent in the hospital. The longer the patients spent in the hospital, the less they were visited. Sommer (1958 and 1959) also found that those patients who were hospitalized longer had fewer visitors and less correspondence with their family. Furthermore, Myers and his associates (1959 and 1968) reported less visiting and gift-giving among lower-class families.

It is unclear whether family members' failure to visit and their rejection of the mental patient are synonymous. In some studies they are (Alivisatos and Lykestos, 1964; and Myers and Bean, 1968). In others they seem to be independent (Gillas and Keet, 1965; and Rose, 1959). However, visiting and the family's involvement with the patient are related to negotiating the patient's release from the mental hospital, for it is the family who often negotiates the discharge.

An indicator of the restructuring of the family to exclude the ex-mental patient is the divorce rate of former mental patients. Adler (1955) found that divorce and separation rates among mental patients were three times higher than the national average. In addition, in a study of Puerto Rican couples, Rogler and Hollingshead (1965) noted that fewer spouses of schizophrenics said that they would remarry the same person to which they were currently married than did spouses of "normals."

These findings suggest that patients will have problems when trying to maintain their position in society and in the family. Thus the absence of patients over time is crucial in determining their slow exclusion from the ongoing family process in which they were previously involved.

PRIMARY PREVENTION

From the perspective of primary prevention, the family is delegated two roles: that of helping to define illness and that of providing the social supports necessary to protect individuals from stressful conditions in the environment that can contribute to the development of mental disorders. Often the family is reluctant to define the relative's problem as mental illness and consequently does not make the initial diagnosis. The crucial element here in relation to the family's functioning is the attempt of the family to explain the relative's behavior in a normal frame of reference. It is unclear, however, what the consequences of the normalization process are. Although this process may delay treatment for many serious cases, it may also serve as a supportive device for milder cases and as a preventive measure in the labeling of patients. Therefore, much more research is needed on the role of the family in the normalization and diagnostic processes.

"Social margin" refers to the set of skills, resources, and relationships one draws on to survive in society. It is one's "social bank account" that enables him or her to cope with stress. The family is one's major and enduring source of social margin. It is the source of one's biological inheritance, interactional skills, and significant others who function as a support system to help

> . . . the individual mobilize his psychological resources and master his emotional burdens, share his tasks, and provide him with extra supplies of money, materials, tools, skills, and cognitive guidance. . . . [Caplan, 1974, p. 6].

Loss of a family member through death or divorce, genetic predisposition, and intrafamilial patterns of interaction have all been implicated as factors affecting one's risk of developing a psychological disorder.

More specifically, with respect to the

role of the family in providing social support, the longitudinal study of Kellum, Ensminger, and Turner (1977) [is] more important. These researchers delineated as many as eighty-six family structures on the basis of different combinations of household members who lived in an urban area in Chicago. They pointed out that these different combinations were able to provide different levels of support for their children and therefore were differentially able to insulate them from the environmental stresses related to mental disorders. Furthermore, they noted that children in single-parent families faced greater threats to their psychological well-being than did those in other familial structures. The former encountered more threats because of the limited availability of social supports. However, in families in which the presence of a second relative served as an enabling or protective resource similar to that of the traditional nuclear family, the risks for mental illness were significantly reduced.

In addition, Robins found that

> children raised by both their own parents were more often well than other children, and children for whom responsibility was vested outside the parents were least often well [1966, p. 174].

Although this finding was attributed solely to the virtual nonexistence of an antisocial father in cases in which children were reared by both parents, it raises questions about the importance of support systems in the maintenance of psychological well-being. However, little is known about the role of the family as a support system in helping individuals to cope with the precipitators of mental disorders.

IMPLICATIONS

Policies That Support Tertiary Prevention

The original study of Pasamanick, Scarpitti, and Dinitz (1967) demonstrated that mental hospitalization could be prevented by administering antipsychotic medications to discharged patients. However, it was conducted with individuals who had intact families, not with long-term chronic patients who were often without family support. This suggests the need for the development of substitute family units, along with accompanying service supports, as an alternative for long-term chronic patients. Such substitute environments as small group homes and long-term care facilities that do not resemble institutions but are more family oriented should be organized and funded. To accomplish this, Section 8 of HUD (Housing and Urban Development) Subsidized Housing Programs could be expanded.

In addition, a true system of community care is needed rather than one that simply emphasizes the moving of people out of institutions into the community without proper social supports. The planning of activities for discharged patients should be an essential element in the system. Such planning could be conducted in coordination with a mental hospital or with a local community mental health center.

An implication of research on community care relates to the amount of burden absorbed by families who take on the responsibility of their chronically mentally ill relatives. For these families, options related to respite care must be considered. In the past, as previously noted, the hospital served as a temporary relief for patients who could not cope successfully with stressful conditions in their environment and for family members who lived with patients at significant cost to themselves. Either the hospital could again be used in this way, emphasizing an easy admission and easy discharge policy, or "crisis houses" in the community could be set up to fulfill this function. Crisis houses would probably be more desirable because of their location in the community and the nonmedical label attached to such facilities. The latter might be most helpful in preventing the occurrence of any iatrogenic effects associated with being in the hospital.

Another implication related to the reduction of burden on the family suggests the need for the development of a sound supportive social work program. Grad and Sainsbury (1963a, 1963b, and 1968) compared a traditional hospital program with a community care program. They observed that relatives of patients in the community care program experienced many more burdens than relatives of patients in the traditional hospital program. In addition, the major factor that influenced the amount of burden experienced by the family was the regular visits made to the home by the social work staff of the traditional program. It thus seems that a community care program that provides supportive social work services can be effective in reducing the amount of burden placed on the family.

In considering institutionalization, the problem of sheltered-care facilities or family housholds as community back wards should be addressed. To cope with this situation, policies are needed that aim at creating educational programs for community care workers and relatives of chronic mental patients. These programs should emphasize that social isolation in sheltered-care facilities or the family could lead to the development of the same type of dependencies experienced in the mental institution and could have negative effects on family life. They should further emphasize that the high expectations of workers and family members would enable former patients to fulfill their maximum potential.

In view of the emotional involvement of patients with other family members, someone should determine whether patients would function better in a sheltered-care facility than in the family unit. A social worker could make this determination and help the family work through its own needs and involvements with the former patient. This suggests, therefore, the need for a strong, locally based unit of social workers who would develop optimal placements and provide supportive services to chronic mental patients living in the home or in community care facilities.

Policies That Support Secondary Prevention

To prevent the exclusion of former patients from the family, the hospital and other supportive facilities such as crisis houses should function as short-term resources in providing community care. Patients who return to these facilities for brief periods of time should not be viewed as failures but as persons who want to cope with their illness in an institutional setting. Without doubt the easy-in and easy-out policy being advocated here places a burden on the family, especially in the area of work and social activities. Therefore, the family should receive supportive community services during the initial stressful periods of brief hospitalization.

Unfortunately, some patients may be unable to resume their previous level of work and social-role functioning. In this case, supports should be offered to other family members in meeting the demands of some of the roles previously performed by the patient. For example, work training programs could be offered to the wives of released patients who have experienced repeated hospitalizations and who seem to be suffering from a more or less permanent or total disability. This type of program might help the family maintain its commitment to the former patient and reduce the amount of pessimism and disillusionment often associated with helping the long-term chronic patient. Although a change in roles can create a significant amount of stress for individuals in the family, people often rise above stressful situations and maximize the potential of these situations for their own growth.

In addition, as part of the general orientation toward community care, social workers should help family members understand the fine line between maintaining realistic expectations and maintaining a "high expectation environment." The former prevents the disillusionment of family members; the latter prevents patients from drifting into chronic dependence and enables them to fulfill their potential. Although these may seem to be contradictory goals, the "fine tuning" of the balance between them is crucial to enhanced patient outcome.

Policies That Support Primary Prevention

Further research should examine the role of the family as a diagnoser of mental illness, especially the family's attempt to normalize all behavior before recognizing the presence of illness. In addition, education programs that promote a positive understanding of mental disorder should continue to be sponsored by federal agencies. These programs should include materials that illustrate the importance of the family in supporting the mentally ill. Finally, the social supports necessary to prevent the development of psychological problems should be provided. These supports should include child care and programs that enable single parents to exchange supportive activities and perhaps serve as an extended family.

After one hundred years the family is once again being asked to assume its major function as care giver for the long-term mentally ill patient. If it is to assume this role meaningfully, the community care movement must take the word *care* seriously. The community must provide professional manpower, professional expertise, and social activities. If such supports do not become available, the mentally ill will be rejected by the general community and their families and will live primarily isolated existences in isolated settings.

Their lives will perhaps not be too far removed from the lives of other mental patients who were found in the back wards of large mental hospitals or who were rescued from the jails by Dorothea Dix.

BIBLIOGRAPHY

Readers will note that bibliographical style has been used for references in this article. It is used only for reviews of the literature.

ADLER, LETA M. "Patients of a State Mental Hospital: The Outcome of their Hospitalization," in Arnold M. Rose, ed., *Mental Health and Mental Disorder*. New York: W. W. Norton & Co., 1955, pp. 501–523.

ALIVISATOS, GERASSIMOS, AND LYKESTOS, GEORGE. "A Preliminary Report of a Research Concerning the Attitude of the Families of Hospitalized Mental Patients," *International Journal of Social Psychiatry*, 10 (Winter 1964), pp. 37–44.

ANGRIST, SHIRLEY, ET AL., *Women After Treatment*. New York: Appleton-Century-Crofts, 1968.

BARRETT, JAMES E.; KURIANSKY, JUDITH; AND GURLAND, BARRY. "Community Tenure Following Emergency Discharge," *American Journal of Psychiatry*, 128 (February 1972), pp. 958–964.

BROWN, GEORGE; BIRLEY, J. L. T.; AND WING, JOHN. "Influence of Family Life in the Course of Schizophrenic Disorders: A Replication," *British Journal of Psychiatry*, 121 (September 1972). pp. 241–258.

BROWN, GEORGE; CARSTAIRS, G. M.; AND TOPPING, GILLIAN. "Post Hospital Adjustment of Chronic Mental Patients," *Lancet*, 7048, no. 2 (September 27, 1958), pp. 685–689.

BROWN, GEORGE, ET AL. "Influence of Family Life on the Course of Schizophrenic Illness," *British Journal of Prevention and Social Medicine*, 16 (April 1962).

BROWN, GEORGE, ET. AL. *Schizophrenia and Social Care*. New York: Oxford University Press, 1966.

CAPLAN, GERALD. *Support Systems and Community Mental Health*. New York: Behavioral Publications, 1974, p. 6.

DAVIS, ANN; DINITZ, SIMON; AND PASAMANICK, BENJAMIN. *Schizophrenics in the Custodial Community: Five Years After the Experiment*. Columbus, Ohio: Ohio State University Press, 1974.

DOLL, WILLIAM. "Family Coping with the Mentally Ill: An Unanticipated Problem of Deinstitutionalization," *Hospital and Community Psychiatry*, 27 (March 1976), pp. 183–185.

DUNIGAN, J. "Mental Hospital Career and Family Expectations." Manuscript, Laboratory of Psychosocial Research, Cleveland Psychiatric Institute, 1969.

EVANS, ANNE S.; BULLARD, DEXTER M.; AND SOLOMON, MAIDA H. "The Family as a Potential Resource in the Rehabilitation of the Chronic Schizophrenic Patient," *American Journal of Psychiatry*, 117 (June 1961), pp. 1075–1083.

FREEMAN, HOWARD, AND SIMMONS, OZZIE. "Mental Patients in the Community: Family Settings and Performance Levels," *American Sociological Review*, 23 (April 1958), pp. 147–154.

_____. "Social Class and Posthospital Performance Levels," *American Sociological Review*, 24 (June 1959), pp. 345–351.

_____. *The Mental Patient Comes Home*. New York: John Wiley & Sons, 1963.

GILLAS, L. S., AND KEET, M. "Factors Underlying the Retention in the Community of Chronic Rehospitalized Schizophrenics," *British Journal of Psychiatry*, 11 (November 1965), pp. 1057–1067.

GRAD, JACQUELINE, AND SAINSBURY, PETER. "Evaluating a Community Care Service," in Hugh L. Freeman and James Farndale, eds., *Trends in Mental Health Service*. Elmsford, N.Y.: Pergamon Press, 1963a, pp. 303–317.

_____. "Mental Illness and the Family." *Lancet*, 7280, no. 1 (March 9, 1963b), pp. 544–547.

_____. "Effects That Patients Have on Their Families in a Community Care and a Control Psychiatric Service—A Two-Year Following." *British Journal of Psychiatry*, 114 (March 1968), pp. 265–278.

GREENLEY, JAMES R. "Family Symptom Tolerance and Rehospitalization Experiences of Psychiatric Patients," in Roberta Simmons, ed., *Research in Community and Mental Health*, Greenwich, Conn.: Jai Press, 1979, pp. 357–386.

GRUENBERG, ERNEST. "Hospital Treatment in Schizophrenia," in Robert Cancro, ed., *The*

Schizophrenic Reactions: A Critique of the Concept, Hospital Treatment, and Current Research. New York: Brunner/Mazel, 1970.

HOENIG, JULIUS, AND HAMILTON, MARIAN W. *The Desegregation of the Mentally Ill*. London, England, Routledge & Kegan Paul, 1969.

HOLLINGSHEAD, AUGUST B., AND REDLICH, FREDERICK C. *Social Class and Mental Illness*. New York: John Wiley & Sons, 1958.

KELLUM, SHEPPARD G.; ENSMINGER, MARGARET E.; AND TURNER, JAY. "Family Structure and the Mental Health of Children," *Archives of General Psychiatry*, 34 (September 1977), pp. 1012–1022.

KREISMAN, DOLORES E., AND JOY, VIRGINIA D. "Family Response to the Mental Illness of a Relative: A Literature Review," *Schizophrenia Bulletin*, 10 (Fall 1974), pp. 35–55.

MICHAUX, WILLIAM W. ET AL. *The First Year Out*, Baltimore, Md.: Johns Hopkins University Press, 1969.

MILLER, DOROTHEA. *Worlds that Fail, Part 1: Retrospective Analysis of Mental Patients' Careers*. Sacramento, Calif.: California State Department of Mental Hygiene, 1965.

MILLS, E. *Living with Mental Illness: A Study of East London*. London, England: Routledge & Kegan Paul, 1962.

MYERS, JEROME K., AND BEAN, LEE L. *A Decade Later: A Follow-up of Social Class and Mental Illness*. New York: John Wiley & Sons, 1968.

MYERS, JEROME K., AND ROBERTS, BERTRAM H. *Family and Class Dynamics in Mental Illness*. New York: John Wiley & Sons, 1959.

PASAMANICK, BENJAMIN; SCARPITTI, FRANK R.; AND DINITZ, SIMON. *Schizophrenics in the Community*. New York: Appleton-Century-Crofts, 1967.

PHILLIPS, DEREK L. "Rejection: A Possible Consequence of Seeking Help for Mental Disorders," *American Sociological Review*, 28 (December 1963), pp. 962–963.

PITT, RAYMOND. "The Concept of Family Burden." Manuscript, Columbia University, 1960.

RAWNSLEY, K.; LONDON, J. B.; AND MILES, H. L. "Attitudes of Relatives to Patients in Mental Hospitals," *British Journal of Preventive and Social Medicine*, 16 (January 1962), pp. 1–15.

ROBINS, LEE N. *Deviant Children Grown Up: A Sociological and Psychiatric Study of Sociopathic*

Personality. Baltimore, Md.: Williams & Wilkins, 1966. P. 174.

ROGLER, LLOYD H., AND HOLLINGSHEAD, AUGUST. *Trapped: Families and Schizophrenia.* New York: John Wiley & Sons, 1965.

ROSE, CHARLES L. "Relatives' Attitudes and Mental Hospitalization." *Mental Hygiene,* 43 (April 1959), pp. 194–203.

SCHWARTZ, CAROL; MYERS, JEROME K.; AND ASTRACHAN, BORIS M. "Psychiatric Labeling and the Rehabilitation of the Mental Patient," *Archives of General Psychiatry,* 31 (September 1974), pp. 329–334.

SEGAL, STEVEN P. "Preventing Social Deterioration in Former Mental Patients." Paper presented at the National Conference on Social Welfare, Los Angeles, Calif., May 1978.

SEGAL, STEVEN P., AND AVIRAM, URI. "Community-Based Sheltered Care," in Paul I. Ahmed and Stanley C. Plog, eds., *State Mental Hospitals: What Happens When They Close?* New York: Plenum Publishing Corp., 1976, pp. 111–124.

————. *The Mentally Ill in Community-Based Sheltered Care.* New York: Wiley-Interscience, 1978.

SEGAL, STEVEN P., AND MOYLES, EDWIN W. "Management Style and Institutional Dependency in Sheltered Care." To be published in a forthcoming issue of *Social Psychiatry.*

SOMMER, ROBERT. "Letter-Writing in a Mental Hospital," *American Journal of Psychiatry,* 115 (December 1958), pp. 518–519.

————. "Visitors to Mental Hospitals: A Fertile Field for Research," *Mental Hygiene,* 43 (January 1959), pp. 8–15.

STEIN, LEONARD I.; TEST, MARY ANN; AND MARX, ARNOLD J. "Alternative to the Hospital: A controlled Study," *American Journal of Psychiatry,* 132 (May 1975), pp. 517–532.

SWANSON, ROBERT M., AND SPITZER, STEPHEN P. "Stigma and the Psychiatric Patient Career," *Journal of Health and Social Behavior,* 11 (March 1970), pp. 44–51.

SWINGLE, PAUL G. "Relatives' Concepts of Mental Patients," *Mental Hygiene,* 49 (July 1965), pp. 461–465.

WING, JOHN; MONCK, ELIZABETH; BROWN, GEORGE; AND CARSTAIRS, G. M. "Morbidity in the Community of Schizophrenic Patients Discharged from London Mental Hospitals in 1959," *British Journal of Psychiatry,* 110 (January 1964), pp. 10–21.

CONTRIBUTORS

ROBERT AGRANOFF   Professor, School of Public and Environmental Affairs, Indiana University, Bloomington, IN 47405.

RICHARD S. BOLAN   Professor, School of Social Work, Boston College, Chestnut Hill, MA 02167.

GEORGE BRAGER   Dean, School of Social Work, Columbia University, New York, NY 10025.

ANTHONY BROSKOWSKI   Director, Florida Mental Health Institute, Tampa, FL 33612.

EDMUND BURKE   Professor, School of Social Work, Boston College, Chestnut Hill, MA 02167.

BRUCE L. GATES   Professor, Atkinson Graduate School of Administration, Willamette University, Salem, OR 97301.

BURTON GUMMER   Associate Professor, School of Social Welfare, State University of New York, Albany, NY 12222.

STEPHEN HOLLOWAY   Associate Professor, School of Social Work, Columbia University, New York, NY 10025.

BARCLAY M. HUDSON   Executive Director, Barclay Hudson and Associates, Santa Monica, CA 90402.

WAYNE, KIMMEL   Human Resources Consultant, 10813 Rock Run Drive, Potomac, MD 20854.

RALPH M. KRAMER   Professor, School of Social Welfare, University of California, Berkeley, CA 94720.

CHARLES LEVINE   Director, Graduate Studies, Institute for Urban Studies, University of Maryland, Baltimore, MD 21201.

EUGENE LITWAK   Professor, Department of Sociology, Columbia University, New York, NY 10027.

DUNCAN MCRAE, JR.   William Rand Kenan, Jr. Professor of Political Science and Sociology; Chairman of the Curriculum in Public Policy Analysis, University of North Carolina, Chapel Hill, NC 27514.

THEODORE R. MARMOR   Chairman, Center for Health Studies; Professor of Political Science, Professor of Public Health, Yale University, New Haven, CT 06520.

DANIEL MAZMANIAN   Director, Program in Publc Policy Analysis; Associate Professor of Government, Department of Government, Pomona College, Claremont, CA 91711.

ARNOLD J. MELTSNER   Professor, School of Public Policy, University of California, Berkeley, CA 94720.

MARK H. MOORE   Guggenheim Professor of Criminal Justice, Policy, and Management, Kennedy School of Government, Harvard University, Cambridge, MA 02138.

JAMES MORONE   Assistant Professor, Department of Political Science, Brown University, Providence, RI 02912.

ROBERT MORRIS   Professor Emeritus, Florence Heller School for Advanced Studies in Social Welfare, Brandeis University, Waltham, MA 20173.

HARRIET H. NAYLOR   Director, Volunteer Development, Staatsburg, NY 12580.

JAMES C. NOAH   Chairman and Senior Consultant, Corporate and Organizational Behavior Analysis, Inc., Oakbrook, IL 60521.

ANTHONY F. PANZETTA   Professor, School of Medicine, Temple University, Philadelphia, PA 19140.

DENNIS N. T. PERKINS,   Assistant Professor, School of Organization and Management, Yale University, New Haven, CT 06520.

RICHARD C. RICH   Associate Professor, Department of Political Science, Virginia Polytechnic and State University, Blacksburg, WV 24061.

DENNIS A. RONDINELLI   Professor, Graduate School of Management, Vanderbilt University, Nashville, TN 37240.

PAUL A. SABATIER   Associate Professor, Division of Environmental Studies, University of California, Davis, CA 95616.

STEVEN P. SEGAL   Professor, School of Social Welfare, University of California, Berkeley, CA 94720.

HARRY SPECHT   Dean, School of Social Welfare, University of California, Berkeley, CA 94720.

JAMES TORCZYNER   Professor, School of Social Work, McGill University, Montreal, Canada H3A2A7.

MARYANNE VANDERVELDE   President, Pioneer Management, Inc., New York, NY 10021.

NANCY W. VEEDER   Associate Professor, School of Social Work, Boston College, Chestnut Hill, MA 02167.

ROLAND L. WARREN   Professor Emeritus, Florence Heller School for Advanced Studies in Social Welfare, Brandeis University, Waltham, MA 02154.

MARK R. YESSIAN   Assistant Director, Office of Service Delivery Assessment, U.S. Department of Health and Human Services, Boston, MA 02116.

FRANKLIN M. ZWIEG   Chairman, Doctoral Programs, University of Rhode Island, Transition Center, Kingston, RI 02881.